# Get a camera

# Get some stock

# Go shoot a MOVIE...

The Guerilla Film Makers Handbook
and Film Producers Toolkit

**Cassell**
Wellington House
125 Strand
London WC2R 0BB
http://www.cassell.co.uk

Distributed in USA by
Cassell & Continuum
370 Lexington Avenue
New York, NY 10017-6550



First published in 1996
Reprinted 1997 (twice)
Reprinted 1998 (twice)

**British Library Cataloguing-in Publication Data**
A catalogue record for this book is available from the British Library.

ISBN 0-304-33854-0

Layout and design by Chris Jones using his PC in true Guerilla fashion
Printed and bound in Great Britain by Redwood Books, Trowbridge, Wiltshire

Dedicated to the memory
and inspiration of John Holland

To Chris and Jo

# The Guerilla Film Makers Handbook

and

The Film Producers Toolkit

By
Chris Jones and
Genevieve Jolliffe

CASSELL

# The Guerilla Film Makers Handbook
# Legal Disclaimer

## Read This First!

The copyright in and to the sample contracts and documents in this book is owned and retained by the originator of the work ("the Owner"). These sample contracts and documents have been created for your general information only. The Owner, the authors of this book and the publishers cannot therefore be held responsible for any losses or claims howsoever arising from any use or reproduction. Nothing in this book should be construed as legal advice. The information provided and the sample contracts and documents are not a substitute for consulting with an experienced entertainment lawyer and receiving counsel based on the facts and circumstances of a particular transaction. Furthermore case law and statutes and European and International law and industry practise are subject to change, and differ from country to country.

# The Guerilla Film Makers Handbook

## Introduction

It's true that the road to becoming a successful film maker is a rocky, often bizarre and certainly unpredictable one. Neither of us expected to be writing the introduction to a book about film making on this hot July night, more likely our acceptance speech for the Oscar we would surely have been nominated for by now. That's the first lesson. Film making can take a very long time. There are exceptions the press love to quote, but on the whole, carving out a career in film making is not dissimilar to mounting an expedition to tackle the North face of the Eiger.

During our first expedition into film making, we made many mistakes. After regrouping we discovered a small group of persistent wanabe first time film makers pounding at our door, asking questions, the answer to which we had learned the hard way only weeks before. To keep these potential movie makers from consuming our every waking hour, we compiled some notes about how we made our first film and what pit falls could have been avoided. Soon after, due to great demand and overwork, our photocopier broke down. We realised then that there was a genuine need for a book about low-budget film making in the UK. Not some crusty manual written by a frustrated accountant, or an American guide that is so localised to Hollywood that it's all but useless, but a book that tells how it really is in the UK, how it's really done, what the penalties are, and what the rewards can be. And so, back in 1991, *The Guerrilla Film Makers Handbook and Film Producers Toolkit* was born.

If you have enough energy, half a brain and can convince enough people that you could be the next Orson Welles, you will become a film maker. Don't be put off by ridicule, poverty (although that can be very tough) or fear. You can do it. You will do it. Good luck.

Chris Jones & Genevieve Jolliffe
July 30th '96 (3.52 am)

Acknowledgements

We would like to thank all the contributors in this book for sharing with them their experience and expertise, helping to shed light on the way parts of the British film industry work. We would also like to thank everyone who has helped Living Spirit produce it's first two feature films *The Runner* and *White Angel,* especially those who have supported us, both financially and emotionally, whilst navigating the shark infested, ship wrecked waters that is low-budget film making. You were our life jackets - *literally.*

To all those people who said it can't be done, eat humble pie. To all those people who said it could be done, our sincere thanks for your encouragement.

Special thanks in particular for words of advice received on a running track all those years ago.

Thanks also for the phrase 'the surest way to succeed is to be determined not to fail'.

We would also like to express our gratitude to the following for their help in producing this book:- Helen Tulley, Cpt. CCR Jolliffe, Tina McFarling, Simon Perry, Stephen Cleary.

Thanks also to Mums, Dads and families.

# Contents

## Section 1 - Anatomy Of A Movie

# Section 2 - Case Studies

# Section 3 - The Toolkit



# Section 4 - The Directory

# Quick Guide To Low Budget Movie Making

Get a Great Idea

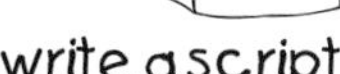

write a script

get a bit of cash

Determination

Make a Movie and...

it's a hit

it isn't a hit

Bankruptcy

the rest is history

Short holiday

Make enough to survive before back to square one

# Section 1
# Anatomy Of A Movie

## Solicitor Helen Tulley Of Hammond Suddards

***Q - Do you need a company to make a film?***

***Helen -*** You need a limited company which you can buy off the shelf for about £125 (inclusive of VAT). If you're going to be a producer then you must have a company, and it has to be a limited company. A limited company means limited liability so that, provided you have not acted unlawfully or wrongfully, if everything goes wrong, you can walk away without losing your personal property. Without a Limited company, your liabilities would then be *personal* and you could be made bankrupt - everything you own, home and belongings (except for the tools of your trade), will go to the Trustees in bankruptcy. If you don't have a company no-one will do business with you anyway. Some people will try and get round your limited liability status by asking you to give personal guarantees. If you were borrowing money from the bank, they may say *yes your company can borrow money but we want the directors to personally guarantee the loan.* You should try and avoid this where possible and just say that it's unreasonable. If you give a personal guarantee, that makes you personally liable and you can be made bankrupt which defeats the whole purpose of having a limited company. You can go two ways with a limited company - either set up a company and have an agreement as to how you want to treat individual projects brought in by the directors of the company. Alternatively, you can set up a separate company for each project.

***Q - We were advised initially to set up a limited company for each film, but never got around to it, now it's very complicated?***

***Helen -*** I think the reason why people are put off by setting another limited company is really because of the administration, it's another company you have to file accounts for, it's more money, just another thing to think about. People do make more than one film through a single company, but it does mean you have to be a little more careful when drafting documents. If the company is borrowing from a bank, you must make sure that the loan for one production doesn't jeopardise other projects by the fact that they also become security for the loan.

***Q - How important is a good solicitor to a film project?***

***Helen -*** I appreciate that legal costs can be high, but I think what people sometimes forget is that they could be entering into an agreement where the money involved may not be substantial but the

liabilities are huge. That's why it's important to have proper protection, to have somebody to say *this is what you've got to watch out for.* When it comes to the agreements, if you don't have very much money then you should concentrate on obtaining agreements to secure your rights in the underlying material or screenplay. Make sure that you own or have a licence to what it is that you are going to exploit. I have seen, for example, options from quite established agents which give you absolutely nothing, yet the paper says that it is an option. A proper option agreement will have the terms of the licence or assignment annexed. If you tried to get development money based on an imperfect option, a broadcaster or financier would not be interested. If you wrote a screenplay based on the underlying material you could be at risk and waste time and money if the owner then refused to grant a licence or assignment. Obviously you can go back to the person who owns the rights and say we didn't have a proper deal, but then you're in a difficult negotiating position and they can be awkward. They could refuse to give you the rights or they could turn round and say *Ok, we now want £10k for it.* That's why it's important to have a solicitor look at those agreements and say *it's ok, you can go ahead.* I appreciate that most new film makers will be making a film from their own screenplay or from something a friend wrote, but it's still essential to have those rights sewn up before you shoot.

***Q - How important are sales agents agreements?***

***Helen -*** Most have standard forms and you don't have much leeway. However, If you're not happy with the agreement for certain reasons, then generally, you can negotiate with them.

***Q - Can a conversation over lunch be interpreted as a binding contract?***

***Helen -*** It depends on the circumstances. For a contract to be legally binding (apart from there being an offer acceptance and consideration), what you have to look at is the intention of the parties. Did they intend, when having this conversation or even in letters or quite detailed memos, to create a legal relationship? If the parties did not intend that, at the time, there is no legally binding contract. It very much depends on what the practice is in the industry - a casual conversation over lunch with an actor saying *I'd like you to be in the film* is not going to be considered in the film industry as an offer which if accepted and consideration being agreed, is legally binding. If you're worried about your correspondence being misconstrued, you should always write at the head of any letter, *SUBJECT TO CONTRACT*, so it's clear.

***Q - So to be safe, you should get it all in writing - don't go with verbal agreements?***

***Helen -*** It's better to do so, but it's not always possible to get everything in writing. A contract can be made orally, but it is then difficult to prove the terms of any verbal agreement. Even if you are dealing with friends on a business level, confirm the arrange-

ment in writing as this will help avoid bad feeling over any dispute at a later stage.

***Q - If a solicitor felt that a project was good, would they introduce one client to other clients with a view to investment?***

***Helen -*** If I thought I knew somebody who would be interested in a project, I would introduce them. You can say informally to someone that you've *read something and think it's quite good, have a look and see what you think.* That's the level it works on, we're not acting as agents for people. It's in our interest to help clients, but we do not take commission. Conversely, if I you know that somebody has had a bad experience with a certain company or they're not reliable, a sales agent or distributor for instance, I would pass that information on too.

***Q - How is your time charged?***

***Helen -*** I think nearly all firms are on the same basis - you have an hourly rate. With smaller productions, where there is a fixed amount for legal fees, we can do an all in deal - you say, *ok we'll do a flat deal for £10k and that's it* - which is quite often the case. If things get more complicated then you might have to negotiate for a little more.

***Q - Would you read the script?***

***Helen -*** Yes, it helps to read the script because there could be areas that clients might not have thought about which could cause problems. I think it's quite good to pass it by a friendly insurance company and say what do you think - they will say to you *look you've got a lot of references here to contemporary names, it could be a problem, somebody might think it's defamatory.* Generally if you're doing anything about living people it is an area of difficulty.

***Q - How much would you recommend to be budgeted for a solicitor's time on a low-budget picture?***

***Helen -*** On a very rough estimation, depending on how much work you're doing, anywhere between £5k and £10k really. It does depend on what the project is and if you're going to be doing artists contracts, directors, producers etc. If you're doing all the finance agreements and negotiating deals then I think between £5k and £10k is realistic. It depends a lot on how much you have to negotiate on behalf of the producer, because it's the negotiating process that can take up a lot of your time, particularly if you're dealing with agents.

***Q - Could producers draw up their own contracts & bring them to you to be checked?***

***Helen -*** Yes, and obviously that would normally reduce the costs.

***Q - Most film makers would be put off from approaching a professional like yourself due to the fear of expensive charges?***

***Helen -*** There is a certain amount of leeway that we can give, for example, if a project is likely to get off the ground, what we sometimes do is run the clock whilst it is in development, and when it

## LEGAL HOTLIST

*Always set up a limited company to make a film. This will afford limited protection for you as the directors*

*Always have a contract between your company & the author, especially if a friend has written the screenplay as friendships do end. Also an assignment of rights must be in writing.*

*In all negotiation correspondence, write SUBJECT TO CONTRACT at the top. This way, no-one can misinterpret the document as a binding agreement.*

*Always send a copy of your screenplay to yourself (or your solicitor) in a sealed and postmarked envelope, don't open it, store it away for use should someone contest your original authorship.*

*Wherever Possible, get it in writing, signed and dated.*

goes into production and there is money available, then we'll recoup our fees.

***Q - In what areas do film makers have the most legal questions?***

***Helen -*** I would say, copyright and the payment or receipt of money, the financial side is of most interest to Producers.

***Q - Have you ever had any cases where producers have come along to you after they've signed a deal, and found themselves in a sticky situation?***

***Helen -*** It doesn't happen that often, but there are disputes and claims when people are owed money.

***Q - What should a film maker do to protect the copyright of a project?***

***Helen -*** If you're basing it on a work that's already in existence, like a book, then obviously you have to get the rights of the author of the book, or whoever owns the rights. They may have already assigned them to a publisher, or they might belong to the estate. You have to get the *right* to make the film. Most of the time, you'll either get an assignment just to make the film (i.e. the owner retains certain rights, like novelisation, theatrical, radio rights) or a license, and that'll be subject to negotiation. If you're getting somebody to write the screenplay, then you should commission them to write it and you will want them to assign all their rights in that screenplay to you. The most important thing is to own the rights. If you don't own them and you go ahead and then you try and sell it to, for instance, a small distributor who doesn't check the rights, who then shows the film - the person who owns the underlying work can go to court and get an injunction which will stop the film being shown.

As a basic form of protection, it's a good idea to post a copy of your work to yourself in a sealed envelope and not open it (then the postmark is evidence that you wrote it before a particular date).

If somebody comes along saying you stole the idea from them, and they say that your idea was created a year after theirs, then you have evidence that it was created earlier - it's just added security.

***Q - What happens when somebody puts an injunction on a film?***

**Helen -** They have to go to the court and prove to the court they've got reasonable grounds and sufficient evidence to warrant an injunction. An injunction may order the film to be withdrawn from distribution until the issues in dispute have been resolved. The party seeking the injunction, if successful will issue and serve a writ on the Defendant and the matter will be decided by the courts or otherwise settled.

***Q - Does it cost to get an injunction?***

**Helen -** Yes - in two ways. Firstly, if you're with a solicitor's firm you will be asked for money on account and it could cost £5-10k to obtain an injunction. Secondly, the person who applies for the injunction often has to make a payment in court so that if the injunction has been wrongly granted, due to evidence that later comes to light, for instance, there is money secured in court to pay the defendant, who might have suffered damages because of the injunction.

***Q - If you've written the script yourself, what's the procedure for copyright?***

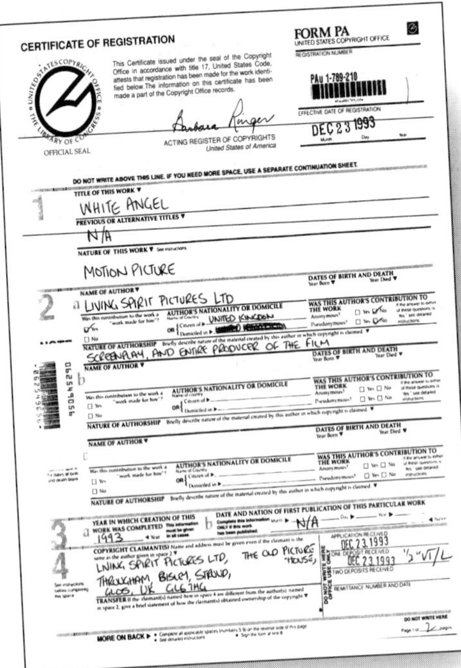

CERTIFICATE OF REGISTRATION

FORM PA
UNITED STATES COPYRIGHT OFFICE

REGISTRATION NUMBER
PAu 1-789-210

This Certificate issued under the seal of the Copyright Office in accordance with title 17, United States Code, attests that registration has been made for the work identified below. The information on this certificate has been made a part of the Copyright Office records.

UNITED STATES COPYRIGHT OFFICE • THE LIBRARY OF CONGRESS •
OFFICIAL SEAL

Barbara Ringer
ACTING REGISTER OF COPYRIGHTS
United States of America

EFFECTIVE DATE OF REGISTRATION
DEC 23 1993
Month Day Year

DO NOT WRITE ABOVE THIS LINE. IF YOU NEED MORE SPACE, USE A SEPARATE CONTINUATION SHEET.

1 TITLE OF THIS WORK ▼
WHITE ANGEL

PREVIOUS OR ALTERNATIVE TITLES ▼
N/A

NATURE OF THIS WORK ▼ See instructions
MOTION PICTURE

2 a NAME OF AUTHOR ▼
LIVING SPIRIT PICTURES LTD

DATES OF BIRTH AND DEATH Year Born ▼ Year Died ▼

Was this contribution to the work a "work made for hire"? ☑ Yes ☐ No

AUTHOR'S NATIONALITY OR DOMICILE Name of Country UNITED KINGDOM
OR { Citizen of ▶ / Domiciled in ▶

WAS THIS AUTHOR'S CONTRIBUTION TO THE WORK Anonymous? ☐ Yes ☑ No Pseudonymous? ☐ Yes ☑ No
If the answer to either of these questions is "Yes," see detailed instructions.

NATURE OF AUTHORSHIP Briefly describe nature of the material created by this author in which copyright is claimed. ▼
SCREENPLAY, AND ENTIRE PRODUCER OF THE FILM

b NAME OF AUTHOR ▼

DATES OF BIRTH AND DEATH Year Born ▼ Year Died ▼

Was this contribution to the work a "work made for hire"? ☐ Yes ☐ No

AUTHOR'S NATIONALITY OR DOMICILE Name of country
OR { Citizen of ▶ / Domiciled in ▶

WAS THIS AUTHOR'S CONTRIBUTION TO THE WORK Anonymous? ☐ Yes ☐ No Pseudonymous? ☐ Yes ☐ No
If the answer to either of these questions is "Yes," see detailed instructions.

NATURE OF AUTHORSHIP Briefly describe nature of the material created by this author in which copyright is claimed. ▼

c NAME OF AUTHOR ▼

DATES OF BIRTH AND DEATH Year Born ▼ Year Died ▼

Was this contribution to the work a "work made for hire"? ☐ Yes ☐ No

AUTHOR'S NATIONALITY OR DOMICILE Name of Country
OR { Citizen of ▶ / Domiciled in ▶

WAS THIS AUTHOR'S CONTRIBUTION TO THE WORK Anonymous? ☐ Yes ☐ No Pseudonymous? ☐ Yes ☐ No
If the answer to either of these questions is "Yes," see detailed instructions.

NATURE OF AUTHORSHIP Briefly describe nature of the material created by this author in which copyright is claimed. ▼

3 a YEAR IN WHICH CREATION OF THIS WORK WAS COMPLETED This information must be given in all cases.
1993 ◀ Year

b DATE AND NATION OF FIRST PUBLICATION OF THIS PARTICULAR WORK Complete this information ONLY if this work has been published.
Month ▶ N/A Day ▶ Year ▶ ◀ Nation

4 COPYRIGHT CLAIMANT(S) Name and address must be given even if the claimant is the same as the author given in space 2 ▼
LIVING SPIRIT PICTURES LTD, THE OLD PICTURE HOUSE, THROUGHAM, BISLEY, STROUD, GLOS, UK GL6 7HG

See instructions before completing this space

TRANSFER If the claimant(s) named here in space 4 are different from the author(s) named in space 2, give a brief statement of how the claimant(s) obtained ownership of the copyright. ▼

APPLICATION RECEIVED DEC 23.1993
ONE DEPOSIT RECEIVED DEC 23.1993 ½" VT/L
TWO DEPOSITS RECEIVED
REMITTANCE NUMBER AND DATE
DO NOT WRITE HERE OFFICE USE ONLY

MORE ON BACK ▶ • Complete all applicable spaces (numbers 5-9) on the reverse side of this page • See detailed instructions • Sign the form at line 8

DO NOT WRITE HERE
Page 1 of 2 pages

**Helen -** Generally speaking, if you create it, you own it (unless you are an employee and create work as part of your employment). In the UK there is no formality with which you must comply.

***Q - What about copyright in America - if you know your film is going to be released in the States, is it worth registering it?***

**Helen -** Since 1989 you don't have to register your work in the United states, but a lot of people still do because if you want to produce your film as evidence in a court in America, your film has to be registered.

*For extra protection, you may wish to register the copyright for your film in the USA. It will cost you $20. To get the forms, write to The Register Of Copyrights, Library Of Congress, Washington D.C. 20559 USA*

***Q - What is your job after the film is completed?***

***Helen -*** Most things should be in place by the time you've got to principle photography. Occasionally there are things to be done, but generally, that's it.

***Q - What happens if a production company can't pay off a debt?***

***Helen -*** You can do a deal with your creditor. Ultimately, if you can't do a deal or pay, your company could be wound up by the creditor, and the creditor could end up owning your film. Unless, as a director, you were found guilty of wrongful trading or unlawful trading, you won't have any personal liability - the company owes the money, not you - all the assets belonging to the company will go to pay off certain parties (Inland Revenue, Customs & Excise, secured creditors) including finally, the creditors.

***Q - How does a low-budget film maker go about independently raising investment from private sources?***

***Helen -*** There are a lot of problems with this area and I know that people do it, but they usually don't comply with the Financial Services Act of 1986. This Act was brought in to protect people from unscrupulous investment companies who went to unsuspecting people and said, *look at this wonderful proposal, you give me all your life savings and in ten years time I'm going to give you this huge return.* Since the Act, you can only seek private investment if you're an authorised person as set out in the Act. You also have to have the approval of an authorised person to give out an advertisement or prospectus that says *invest in this.* You must also give warnings, you have to say that this investment is not guaranteed, there are risks in doing it, and you're not necessarily going to get your money back. The people who authorised to do that include accountants or solicitors. I've had people who've said to me, I want to send out letters to investors, saying invest in my film, this film is going to be a great success and you're going to make a lot of money - they're infringing the Financial Services Act and it's a criminal offence. If you do not comply with the Act a further problem is that if someone says to you, we'll give you £100k and then when it comes to the crunch they don't, you wouldn't be able to legally enforce that promise because what you're doing is not itself authorised or legal.

***Q - What are the most common problems to resolve?***

***Helen -*** Ensuring that the Producer has sufficient rights in the work to go ahead and exploit a project with the maximum opportunity to make the film (and ancillary rights) a commercial success. This also means ensuring the stream of income from the film is properly and fairly distributed. If you think about the time you are going to invest in making your film, then it does make sense to have the correct basic structure.

PRE-PRODUCTION

# Accountant Simon Friend Of Coopers & Lybrand

***Q - When should an accountant be brought in on a film production?***

***Simon -*** Production accountants should be brought in immediately, in particular to help put together the budget and set up the systems for insuring the monthly tracking of costs.

***Q - Can an accountant be brought in during the stage of raising finance?***

***Simon -*** Yes, but there is the question of whether you want someone full time on your payroll at that time.

***Q - What is the job of the production accountant?***

***Simon -*** It would be the preparation of the budget, to go through every single item and analyse what is required. To produce a detailed budget, not only looking at the costs, but the timing as well because the other major concern is cashflow. The actual tracking of costs against the budget is important so that everyone can see just where the production stands, on a financial level, at any one time. Once he's got the budget up and running, his day to day job will be checking that all the information is coming in, processing the invoices and ensuring they are genuine costs that are allocated properly to the right cost code, then comparing that with the budget. It's then possible to re-forecast should he need to.

***Q - What kind of complications peculiar to film making should a film maker be aware of?***

***Simon -*** Dare I say, the emotions of the individuals he's dealing with. Generally those involved in film making are not financially aware and don't like constraints, they just hate the concept of budgets. With regard to preparing a budget, some of the costs are reasonably straight forward because you can get decent quotes when hiring out cameras, lights etc., where there are standard rates per week - it's just being aware of ALL the costs and not forgetting any of them. Other costs can be more complicated, like royalties, not only short term but long term - actually trying to come up with a number can be difficult.

Hands on film accountants are so important - if you have to reshoot a scene and it will cost £X,

which is a creative decision, your accountant can turn around to you the next day and say, *that's taken £X out of your entire budget and you'll have to replan.*

There is a problematic dynamic between the creative side and financial side of film production which does cause tension, but it's essential to monitor the cashflow and budget every day in order to avoid potential disaster. One of the keys to success is communication between the accountant and the production team - it's very easy for the creative talent to bury their heads in the sand and ignore the cash situation.

***Q - Are you involved in negotiating deals with the actors or crew members?***

***Simon -*** We tend to leave that with the producer. Generally, the people who get more involved are the lawyers because the legal terms, particularly if an actor takes a share of the profits, are important and complex.

***Q -Do you help put proposals together, for the Lottery fund for example?***

***Simon -*** One of the areas that we do deal with is applications for raising money through the National Lottery mechanism and putting through proposals as though it was a straight business plan. It's no different from going to the bank and providing them with a business proposal. However, for a lottery application to be successful, we must demonstrate how the film will benefit the wider community and the industry as a whole

***Q - Are there any tax incentives to invest in the UK?***

***Simon -*** The only thing I can think of is the various tax allowances that are available if you invest in a film. If you own the rights to a film, or create rights in a film, you can then get a significant write off for tax purposes. The only way that pays is where it enables you to defer paying tax for a period in the event of you going into profit. If you have a stream of films, then potentially, you can just keep on rolling the allowances and you never have to pay that much in the way of tax in the short term. Other incentives like the BES (Business Expansion Scheme) no longer exist.

***Q - What about the Irish Tax Incentive?***

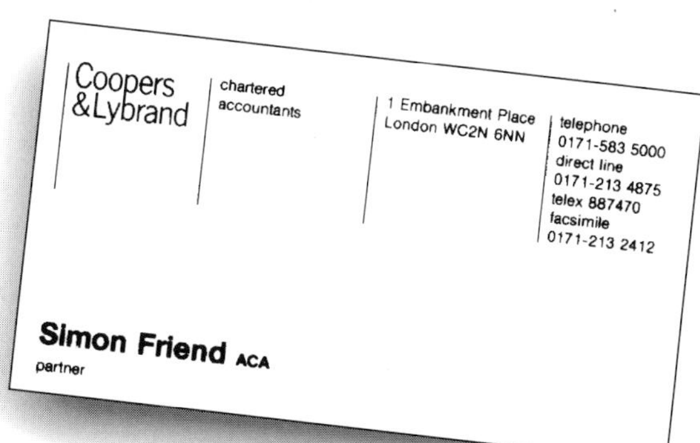


***Simon -*** It's a tax break to investors that gives them an additional deduction against their other income, so it's actually a break for the investors rather than for the industry. MEDIA II is a new body that's been set up to deal with European tax incentives - the DNH - Department of National Heritage - will have information on it. They have a unit that deals with films.

## Ireland's Section 35 Tax Incentive

*The Irish Government is committed to the development of an Irish film industry and supports the industry through tax incentives and the Irish Film Board. As a result Ireland is an attractive location and continues to be used by overseas producers.*

*Section 35*
*Film Finance Incentive is a tax break for both corporate and private investors. The films must be made in Ireland.*

*Amount*
*Individual investors can invest up to £25k per film per year. Companies can invest up to £2m per film per year.*

*Shares*
*The investor buys shares in a company that must be incorporated and based in Ireland. 60% of the budget for a low-budget film can be raised under Section 35.*

*Break*
*Private investors receive an 80% tax break on their investment. Corporate investors receive a 70% tax break.*

*Producer Benefit*
*On top of any other deals, producers get to keep 5-10% of any returns under Section 35.*

*TAX*
*Film makers and other artists who relocate in Ireland enjoy tax free earnings whilst companies enjoy a range of low taxes*

***Q - What happens about TAX, PAYE, NI on a film and will the producer deal with all of that?***

**Simon -** Yes, or the production accountant must notify the DHS office. The responsibility for the company is quite significant, to make sure that the books and records are kept up to date and that payments are made on time. The question is whether the people working on the production are going to be employees or self employed. If it's a long production, then those people who are claiming that they are self employed could actually be viewed as being employed and therefore responsibility would be with the employer to make the PAYE payments on time. In those situations, it is best to contact the offices of the DHS directly and explain the situation. If somebody says they are self employed, there are certain forms to fill in that will prove and demonstrate he is and take the responsibility off you, the employer. If you're talking about a one year production then there will be a number of people in your books who will be viewed as employees and not self employed.

PAYE can be a problem as the PAYE man, like the VAT man, is very serious. If payments are made incorrectly or not on time, then the PAYE man will come in and penalise. It doesn't matter whether you think you're right, if you haven't satisfied the rules, particularly where somebody has said that they are responsible for their own tax affairs and they are not, if the Inland Revenue deemed that he was an employee of yours, then the revenue would claim from you and you would have to pay all the taxes plus damages, and they can go back six years.

***Q - What happens with deferred fee films with regard to paying PAYE, TAX and NI contributions to the cast and crew members?***

## Money Matters

VAT
VALUE ADDED TAX

*If you make a film, you will almost certainly have to register for VAT. From that point on you will be able to reclaim the VAT on purchases, but must charge VAT on invoices to UK companies and individuals. Each quarter you balance the books and either reclaim VAT or pay VAT to Customs & Excise. Books MUST be done quarterly and VAT returns sent in on time or hefty penalties may be charged. NEVER cook the books for the VAT man or you could go to prison.*

PAYE
PAY AS YOU EARN

*Pay As You Earn. As a director of a Limited company, you are technically an "employee" and must therefore calculate your wages on a PAYE system. This will calculate the amount of income tax and national insurance to be deducted each month and to be forwarded to the Inland Revenue (Tax and NI tables are provided by your tax office). You MUST fill in PAYE returns each month, or fill in a declaration if you have received no salary. If you earn less than £52 per week per individual then you will not have to operate this system. At the end of each tax year (5th April) you will have to fill in a return (P60) for each employee. Most crew on a film will be self employed and there are certain categories where PAYE need not be applied (see Schedule D). However it is important to check their positions with the Inland Revenue otherwise the IR might declare them as 'employees' and therefore you may be liable to pay their PAYE plus severe penalties.*

***Schedule D:*** *There is a list of crew members who are entitled to be taxed under Schedule D where the employer pays them gross without deducting NI contributions or tax. It is then the employee's responsibility to pay their own NI and tax.*

*Notify the Film Industry Unit of the IR for more information:* ***Film Industry Unit, Inland Revenue, Tyne Bridge Tower, Gateshead, Tyne & Wear, NE8 2DT. Tel: 0191 477 0207 Fax: 0191 477 3064***

TAX

***Income Tax:*** *Any and all income is liable to tax. If you operate PAYE then the tax for your employees will be calculated under that system. If you are self employed, your tax bill will usually arrive twice throughout the year. If you pay taxes at 40%, in 1997 you may receive a tax return requiring you to calculate the tax due. Failure to complete this return on time will result in penalties.*

***Corporation Tax****: Tax on profits. Where a company makes a taxable profit, corporation tax must be paid within nine months of the year end. Where a company makes a loss, these losses can be set off against future profits of the same company in the same trade or may be carried back and set off against profits which have been taxed in prior years. A Corporation tax return must be filed within 12 months of the year end.*

***Capital Gains Tax:*** *A company will pay corporation tax on chargeable gains accruing during an accountancy period. An individual will be chargeable to capital gains tax in respect of chargeable gains accruing to him in a year of assessment after an annual exempt amount for individuals of £6300 in '96.*

***The Accounting Year:*** *This is generally set when you set up a company, but can be changed on application to the Registrar of Companies. For tax purposes, an accountancy period generally ends 12 months after the beginning of the accounting period. Individuals are taxed in the year to 5 April.*

***Relief for Raising Finance:*** *A company will generally obtain relief for interest payments on loans taken out for trading purposes, but the recent new rules on Corporate and Government debt should be carefully considered. Relief is also available to individuals who take out relevant loans.*

PRE-PRODUCTION

## MONEY MATTERS (CONT..)

NI
NATIONAL INSURANCE

*There are five categories of National Insurance contributions:*

*Class 1 - Primary: paid by employees*
*Secondary: paid for employees by employers (10%)*
*Class 1A - paid by employers who provide employees with cars/fuel for private use.*
*Class 2 - paid by people who are self employed*
*Class 3 - voluntary contributions*
*Class 4 - paid by those whose profits and gains are chargeable to income tax under Schedule D. These are normally paid by self employed people in addition to Class 2.*

*If you operate PAYE then the national insurance contributions for your employees will be calculated under that system. As an "employee" you will also have to deduct class 1 national insurance contributions from your income. However if you are self employed (run a partnership not a limited company, or provide your services as freelance), then you will be liable to pay Class 2 National Insurance and Class 4 if your profits and gains are over a certain limit. You may be entitled to 'small earnings exception' if your net earnings from self employment are under a certain limit.*

***Schedule D Earnings:*** *Most film crew members pay Class 1 Primary contributions as employees, on earnings included in the assessment of Class 4 contributions. Those earnings are assessed under Schedule D for income tax. Deferment and refund for Class 4 can be applied for. It is important to contact your local Social Security office for advice and information. Remember severe penalties can be imposed if contributions are late, or unpaid.*

***Freeline Social Security Telephone No: 0800 666555***

ACCOUNTS
COMPANIES HOUSE

***AUDITED ACCOUNTS -*** *As a Limited Company, it is a requirement to submit audited accounts to Companies House and to fill in an annual return, giving details about the company's directors, secretary, registered office address, shareholders and share capital. There is a filing fee payable of £18.*

*If your company has an annual turnover less than £90,000 your company is exempt from any requirements to have it's annual accounts audited. However, your investors or shareholders may request and insist on audited accounts.*

INVESTORS

*There are few specific tax incentives in the UK for investors in films and those which do exist favour investment by individuals rather than companies.*

***Individuals:*** *The "Enterprise Investment Scheme" (EIS) replaced the BES with similar rules. The capital cost of shares in certain circumstances may be treated as reduction against an individual's taxable income. Where such shares are held for at least five years, any capital gain arising is exempt but where a loss arises this is not a capital loss. The "Venture Capital Trust" (VCT) is a variation on this theme, and provides similar tax breaks for investors.*

***Businesses:*** *Interest payable on loans or other forms of business indebtedness can be deducted for tax purposes. The loan principal however cannot be deducted and is generally considered to be capital in nature. Other general tax incentives for investment give beneficial rates of tax depreciation for expenditure qualifying for capital allowances.*

***Simon*** - The fee you pay to cast & crew, if deferred, will be tax deductible as and when you pay it.

***Q - Do you deal with revenues from sales agents?***

***Simon*** - No, generally the producer will be dealing directly with the distributor although, initially, we might advise on the financial terms of the contract

***Q - What's the easiest type of investment structure to manage?***

***Simon*** - The investor is going to pick the route that they think will protect them the most, and also be the most attractive in terms of tax, be it a company offshore or onshore, or they might want to take shares in the company that's set up to make the film. However, if you're a film producer, the best scenario is somebody who sticks a lump sum into the business without taking a share but has an agreement about a share of the revenues. Generally though, the backers have complex tax arrangements to start with, so it's never straightforward.

***Q - How can a film maker keep costs down?***

***Simon*** - It comes back down to day to day monitoring and knowing what is going on and having the commitment and enthusiasm to keep costs down. If someone knows that there is a specific amount of money and no more, it's in their interest to keep the costs down, but if you've got somebody who thinks that the backers will continually fork out, then there is no incentive to keep costs down.

***Q - What does a filmmaker need to do with regard to keeping books?***

***Simon*** - VAT returns are the ongoing obligations, a large amount of it being VAT recovery on a film. This is because there's a lot of money going out with VAT you can reclaim on invoices. Aside from that, it's just going to be maintaining the books and tracking the costs. The important thing is making sure that there is a separate identifiable bank account which is reconciled with the books. Normally, a bank account is set up specifically for a film.

***Q - Is it true you don't need an audit if your turnover is under £90,000?***

***Simon*** - True for small limited companies. Your backers may want an audit though.

***Q - What is an audit?***

***Simon*** - An external, independent, advisor (usually an accountant) will look through the books and double check that it all stacks up. It is a health check but from a financial perspective.

***Q - Would a high street accountant do as good a job as a media accountant?***

***Simon*** - Coming in cold, probably not. It comes back down to the same principles of understanding how a production works - I don't think we're talking rocket science, but a lot of the *production accountant* side is simply managing cash whereas the *media accountant* may have more insight into the media tax side of it than a high street accountant. If a producer was looking for somebody to do the Books, look after the payroll and the VAT returns then a high street accountant should be able to do that.

***Q - So once the film is made and you have a distribution or sales agent, then it's worth going to your accountant to check over the royalty agreements before you sign?***

***Simon -*** It's probably the most boring thing in the world for a creative team to do, to sit down with an accountant and a lawyer and go through all the agreements and documentation, however it can make the difference between getting money and getting no money. For instance, if you signed a deal with a distributor who is shrewd, they might slip in a clause where you pay for all the P&A (prints and advertising) costs. A good accountant or solicitor would pick up on that.

***Q - How is your time charged?***

***Simon -*** By the hour. Tax specialists are more expensive but a high street accountant will be a lot cheaper than a city accountant. One thing film producers should always get before engaging anyone's service is an estimate.

***Q - For a film that was budgeted at around £250k, how much should be set aside for accounting?***

***Simon -*** For advisors in general, including legal, I would suggest 15%. It may seem like a huge chunk, but it is very well spent.

***Q - What are the most common mistakes that you have encountered?***

***Simon -*** Not properly estimating the budget. You need a large contingency for unexpected costs as there are lots of unexpected problems like bad weather that need to be accounted for. Tax, PAYE and VAT are all relatively easy to deal with, but they are an ongoing nuisance for producers, and if left alone, could cause very serious problems. If a producer doesn't wish to deal with these

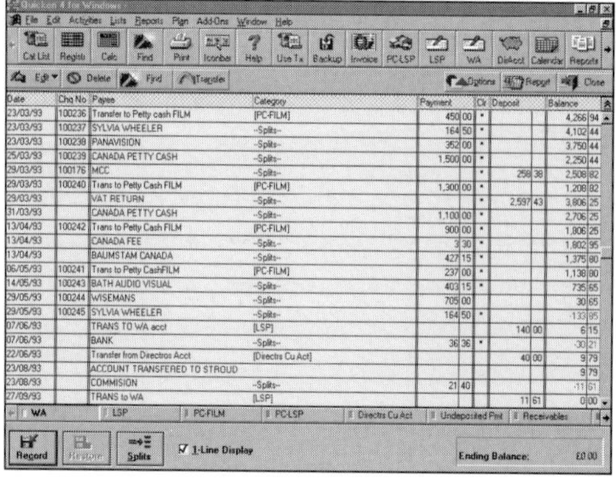

| Date | Chq No | Payee | Category | Payment | Clr | Deposit | Balance |
|---|---|---|---|---|---|---|---|
| 23/03/93 | 100236 | Transfer to Petty cash FILM | [PC-FILM] | 450 00 | • | | 4,266 94 |
| 23/03/93 | 100237 | SYLVIA WHEELER | --Splits-- | 164 50 | • | | 4,102 44 |
| 23/03/93 | 100238 | PANAVISION | --Splits-- | 352 00 | • | | 3,750 44 |
| 25/03/93 | 100239 | CANADA PETTY CASH | --Splits-- | 1,500 00 | • | | 2,250 44 |
| 29/03/93 | 100176 | MCC | --Splits-- | | • | 258 38 | 2,508 82 |
| 29/03/93 | 100240 | Trans to Petty Cash FILM | [PC-FILM] | 1,300 00 | • | | 1,208 82 |
| 29/03/93 | | VAT RETURN | --Splits-- | | • | 2,597 43 | 3,806 25 |
| 31/03/93 | | CANADA PETTY CASH | --Splits-- | 1,100 00 | • | | 2,706 25 |
| 13/04/93 | 100242 | Trans to Petty Cash FILM | [PC-FILM] | 900 00 | • | | 1,806 25 |
| 13/04/93 | | CANADA FEE | --Splits-- | 3 30 | • | | 1,802 95 |
| 13/04/93 | | BAUMSTAM CANADA | --Splits-- | 427 15 | • | | 1,375 80 |
| 06/05/93 | 100241 | Trans to Petty CashFILM | [PC-FILM] | 237 00 | • | | 1,138 80 |
| 14/05/93 | 100243 | BATH AUDIO VISUAL | --Splits-- | 403 15 | • | | 735 65 |
| 29/05/93 | 100244 | WISEMANS | --Splits-- | 705 00 | | | 30 65 |
| 29/05/93 | 100245 | SYLVIA WHEELER | --Splits-- | 164 50 | • | | -133 85 |
| 07/06/93 | | TRANS TO WA acct | [LSP] | | | 140 00 | 6 15 |
| 07/06/93 | | BANK | --Splits-- | 36 36 | • | | -30 21 |
| 22/06/93 | | Transfer from Directros Acct | [Directrs Cu Act] | | | 40 00 | 9 79 |
| 23/08/93 | | ACCOUNT TRANSFERED TO STROUD | | | | | 9 79 |
| 23/08/93 | | COMMISION | --Splits-- | 21 40 | | | -11 61 |
| 27/09/93 | | TRANS to WA | [LSP] | | | 11 61 | 0 00 |



*Low Budget films that cannot afford a Production Accountant can rely on dedicated accounts software to keep track of the budget, expenditure and cashflow. It's probably a good idea to still hire a book keeper to enter all the details as there will undoubtedly be more pressing problems for the production team to deal with.*

things, get someone in who can, even if it's a book keeper or accountant for a few hours a week. Another common mistake is not securing your royalty agreements correctly, you must make sure that it is sewn up and is crystal clear, it's very easy for distributors to blind producers with science if you don't really control that process.

***Q - What basic advice can you offer to new film makers?***

***Simon -*** Be realistic. That's not meant to be patronising, but set realistic goals and be prudent, particularly in managing the funds. Know who you're dealing with, particularly for new up and coming bright eyed film makers as they could come across somebody who would take them to the cleaners. Although costs will be a problem, make sure you can check over every agreement before you sign. Lastly, film-making is a business and will need to be run professionally. There is much more to running a company than initially meets the eye and it's easy for very low-budget film makers to get embroiled in red tape. It's important to learn and understand just how a small business runs - there are plenty of good books out there that will answer most questions, plus your business account bank manger should be able to provide help, as can your solicitor and accountant.

PRE-PRODUCTION

# Bank Manager Peter Hitchen Of Barclays, Soho Square.

*Barclays in Soho Square have for many years been a source of specialised film banking offering a service backed up by expertise in both the film making and financial areas.*

***Q - What kind of a service can a film company expect from a specialised bank manager, as opposed to a local bank?***

**Peter -** Within this unique centre we do business with a broad base of *entertainment and media* businesses, into which film falls. I and most of my colleagues understand the issues, working practices, peculiar cashflowing and dynamics of the film industry. At the very least, our experience saves time - if someone comes along and says, *I have a script in development or we have just been greenlighted*, I don't have to say - *What does that mean?*

Banking isn't simply about lending money - we do three things to earn a living. Firstly, we lend money, be it an overdraft or a full blown corporate loan. Second is to borrow money - for example, during a production, cash may sit in an account for a period. We would give advice on where and for how long to deposit those monies in order to get the maximum possible return of interest. Thirdly, the biggest service we provide is that we run bank accounts for the industry. At any one time we probably have 2-300 production accounts running here as well as the underlying business accounts for a whole range of film related companies. The production account is the vehicle through which a film project is run and once again, there's a whole series of ways we can help, not necessarily cut corners, but save time, money, and get the job done. The average high street branch, even a large bank in the centre of a city, won't have that specialist knowledge, and an independent producer will have to invest time in the banking relationship to get that idea across.

***Q - I assume the charges are in line with the other banks?***

**Peter -** Yes, small businesses would go on small business tariffs - free banking for first 12 months. For large businesses with large volumes we'd make a deal.

***Q - Do you ever advise clients about the integrity of other companies if you have had prior experience?***

**Peter -** It depends if the producer is a customer as I have duties to my customers which I don't have to non customers. If I could see a problem I might offer advice like, *who's advising you on this contract? Have you got the contract tied up tightly? Have you ever met Joe Bloggs? What kind of references have you got about this company?* Conversely, I might know a company very well and could say *'you are in safe hands there, a good choice'.* It depends on the situation - certainly if I saw somebody go in the wrong direction, I would say something. Just recently we became aware of three different production companies all of whom believed they had the rights to the same property and we advised all three companies to 'check' with their solicitors as to whether or not they actually held all the necessary rights.

***Q - Most companies are Limited, does their limited liability alter the way you treat them?***

**Peter -** No. Sole traders tend to be very small businesses, partnerships tend to be professional businesses and limited companies are the majority. If it comes to borrowing money, we would normally look for the personal guarantees of the owner/managers of a limited company. This would mean that the liability that's been limited by being a limited company is not limited as far as the bank is concerned. They would therefore be in exactly the same position as they would be with a partnership or sole trader.

***Q - Do you ever offer a loan or large overdraft facility for a film production?***

**Peter -** Yes, but we need to be clear on how we lend money - *we don't* provide money to develop a film project, or provide money as equity into a film project, or take points or shares in the company. What we are is a commercial, secured, lender. The problem with most production companies is that they are very small, they have no balance sheet, no assets; they don't have the size or track record to borrow the kinds of money that is nearly always needed to make a film. We don't make profits if the money we lend doesn't get repaid, so let's say we're a secured lender. If we have the budget covered by pre-sales, or other collateral such as corporate guarantors, then I can lend - as long as I have one or two other risks also covered.

Firstly the Producer must have the ability to deliver what is required, they must be professional in the process of film production. Secondly, we need to make sure that the documentation that underlies those contracts has no weasel words in it, that's for the benefit of the producers as well. Hopefully the producer is taking good legal advice from a firm of specialist lawyers. You could use your local law firm or family lawyer, but the chances of them knowing what they're doing in this very specialist area are slim. A good firm of lawyers to advise is critical. The final risk is that if we only get repaid by the project being satisfactorily completed on time and in accordance with the contracts which the distributors

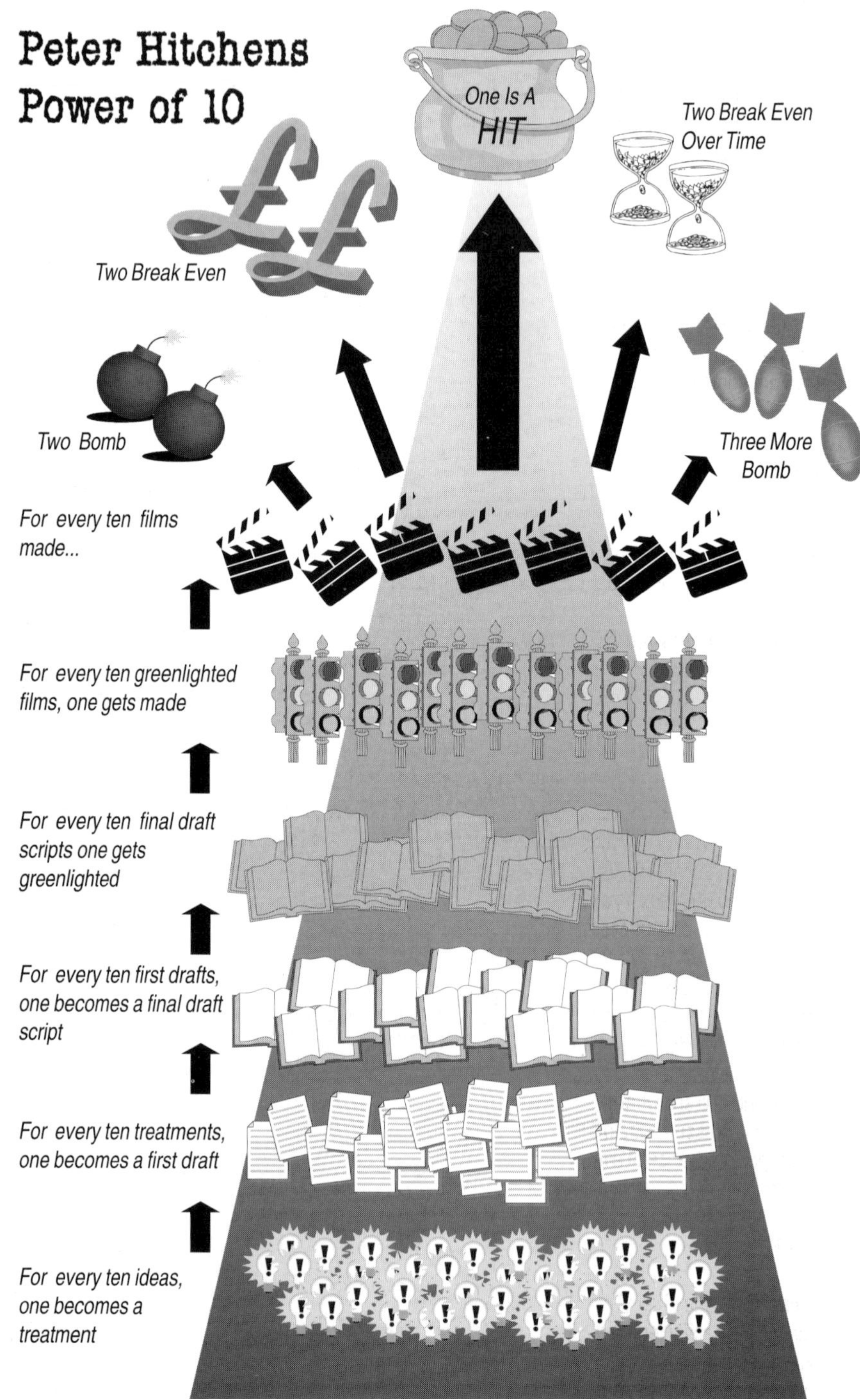
Peter Hitchens
Power of 10
One Is A
HIT
Two Break Even
Over Time
Two Break Even
Two Bomb
Three More
Bomb
For every ten films
made...
For every ten greenlighted
films, one gets made
For every ten final draft
scripts one gets
greenlighted
For every ten first drafts,
one becomes a final draft
script
For every ten treatments,
one becomes a first draft
For every ten ideas,
one becomes a
treatment

have signed, then we need to know that that's going to happen. If the fall back position is to a production company with no assets and no balance sheet then that leaves me somewhere out on a limb with not a lot to hang on to. Therefore we use the services of a completion bonder so that the bank or any other financiers are guaranteed that the film will be made, on time and to budget and in accordance with the contracts. That way we can be sure that all the deals are fulfilled.

***Q - What about small loans or overdraft facilities?***

**Peter -** What we can do, as can any other branch, is have a corporate lending relationship with a business. We have a large number of independent production companies banking here who have overdraft facilities and loan facilities, to buy equipment, premises etc - the criteria used is no different from the commercial criteria that's used for any other kind of business that borrows from us.

***Q - What would happen if a new film maker came to you with a great project, but very little experience or cash, no completion bond and everything on a wing and a prayer?***

**Peter** - If they were asking for borrowing it would be a very short conversation. If they were asking simply for an account I would consider it in order to nurture a possible future relationship.

***Q - All companies run into hitches - What is your advice on that score?***

**Peter -** The most useful bank manager is the best informed bank manager. Just as the Mark Twain expression says, '*bank managers are people who give you an umbrella and then ask for it back when it's raining*'. It's a lot better to be telling the bank manager about the potential rain when the sun is shinning, than waiting until the thunderclouds come along. There must be some method of communication that keeps the manager informed, maybe just a letter once a month, saying I'm doing this and that. Anything which pre warns of problems is always useful. There are two expressions in banking, *'If you're borrowing £100 from the bank and you can't pay them back, you've got a problem. If you're borrowing £1 million from the bank and you can't pay it back, they've got a problem'*. But the flip side of that is, *'If a customer issues a cheque which overdraws the account without arrangements and you pay it - you've got the problem. If you bounce it, the customer has got the problem.*' If an account becomes overdrawn without prior discussion, the manager has two choices, to pay the cheque or bounce the cheque. In the absence of any information and for the sake of risk management the chances are that the cheque will be bounced. The cheque will be represented three days later which gives the manager time to write or pick up the phone and say what on earth is going on. If the customer contacts the manager before the cheque is presented the odds are better. The odds are even better if the customer advises the manager in advance of even issuing the cheque - it gives everyone an opportunity to discuss alternatives.

***Q - What are the most common mistakes made by producers?***

**Peter -** There are many, ranging from overdeveloping a project that will never be made, underestimating the capital required to get a project off the ground, even getting stuck in development hell! However, unless I know the problem exists, I cannot help - information is vital. As I said, the best bank manager is the informed manager.

# Finance Angela Topping of BFI Productions

*The British Film Institute has been the catalyst for many successful British film makers and has an annual budget to spend on innovative film making.*

***Q - What type of projects can you help fund?***

***Angela -*** Our basic remit is that we fund innovative film makers with a cinematic vision. Leading on from that, we have script development funds, a couple of feature films production at any one time, and a new directors scheme which funds five or six short films a year. All of these schemes are supported by Channel 4. In addition, we have a project scheme which does small co-productions within the UK which are usually short films. It encourages regional film-making and partnerships that wouldn't otherwise happen, introducing filmmakers to talent and perhaps encouraging broadcasters to put money into various projects.

***Q - What kind of films are you looking for?***

***Angela -*** We don't go by the kind of film, we look to see if the project is innovative or not. Innovation is the word and also voices new to the screen.

***Q - So essentially somebody who comes to you with DIE HARD 4 hasn't got much hope?***

***Angela -*** Another decision our Production Board has made is that we're looking to make feature films in the half million pound arena, so DIE HARD 4 would be unlikely to be funded.

***Q - How does a filmmaker submit a project to you?***

***Angela -*** Usually in the form of a script. We have a script reading group and we get about 300-400 feature scripts a year. If a script obviously looks as though it's going to be a high budget film then we probably wouldn't read it but if it falls within our set limits, then it goes through the script reading process.

***Q - How long does it take for the wheels to grind into motion on a project?***

**Angela -** We aim to make a decision on a script within 6 to 8 weeks. Sometimes if there is a holiday period there will be some leeway on that.

***Q - With all the financing schemes, how much is available in each area per project?***

**Angela -** For the new directors short films, they're made for budgets of a maximum of £35,000. For the projects scheme we have small amounts of £1,000 for development, and for a production it's a maximum of £30,000. Sometimes we put small amounts into completion for films. With feature films, it's changed slightly because of the lottery coming on board and additional budgetary requirements, but we're still looking at the region of half a million pounds.

***Q - And you finance the entire production?***

**Angela -** Yes, we raise the finance. For one of the films we're trying to finance at the moment, we're looking for Scottish lottery money, English lottery money and the BFI-Channel 4 joint production fund. So we executive produce in terms of getting the finance package together.

***Q - If a new film maker came to you with a one page synopsis, or seven page treatment, would you look at it?***

**Angela -** It depends if they have a track record. We do have a small amount of money where we commission filmmakers to write the scripts but it's usually for a film maker or writer who has a track record and we probably wouldn't commission anybody to write a feature script who hadn't made a short film. That's one of the policy decisions we've made in terms of these half a million pound feature films. The film maker has got to have made something before.

***Q - Who and what would you consider to be your greatest success, or your greatest achievement?***

**Angela -** I think of the history of BFI production since the 50's and we've made short films with most famous British directors, Stephen Frears, Sally Potter, Ken Russell, Peter Greenaway, Terence Davies, Ridley Scott, Derek Jarman...

***Q - Have you ever done anything that you've thought was a big mistake and why?***

**Angela -** We had a difficult situation once with a filmmaker who was also a writer. He had directed a couple of commercials but he'd never directed a feature film and it quickly became difficult. I don't

ANGELA TOPPING
Deputy Head of Production
BRITISH FILM INSTITUTE
bfi
CELEBRATING THE MOVING IMAGE
BFI PRODUCTION
British Film Institute
29 Rathbone Street London W1P 1AG
Telephone 0171-636 5587
Facsimile 0171-580 9456

think we would repeat that experience without first going through some form of assessing whether the filmmaker was capable of making a feature film. But I think under our new policy of making half a million pound feature films, that film wouldn't have slipped through the net and we'd have had tighter control.

***Q - What basic advice would you offer to a young film-maker who's starting out?***

*Angela* - Have a good showreel and get as much knowledge and experience as you can in terms of short films. Also, with low-budget feature films, the more you know about production, the better the film you will make.

BRITISH FILM INSTITUTE

bfi

CELEBRATING THE MOVING IMAGE

**APPLICATION FORM FOR FEATURE DEVELOPMENT/PRODUCTION**

**PLEASE CONSULT THE GUIDELINES BEFORE COMPLETING . PLEASE TYPE OR WRITE IN BLACK INK USING BLOCK CAPITALS.**

1. NAME OF APPLICANT:
   RELATIONSHIP TO PROJECT:
2. TEL NO.:
3. ADDRESS:
4. PROJECT TITLE:
5. CIRCLE CATEGORY (IES) OF APPLICATION DEVELOPMENT • PRODUCTION •
   PROBABLE LENGTH:
6. GAUGE / FORMAT:
7. ESTIMATE OF FILM BUDGET:
8. SYNOPSIS:
9. PERSONNEL (if known) DIRECTOR: WRITER: PRODUCER:
   (Please submit CVs)
10. PLEASE LIST ANY ENCLOSURES AND SUPPORTING MATERIAL (e.g. Director's Showreel):

DATE:

SIGNED:

**BRITISH FILM INSTITUTE 29 Rathbone St, London, W1P 1AG (071) 636 5587**

## *APPLICATION GUIDELINES*

- *Script development and production money is allocated to British based writers and filmmakers with innovative treatments or ideas. This fund is limited and goes to filmmakers with a proven cinematic style.*
- *Development and Production funds are only available for proposals which take into account the BFI's film budget ceiling of £450,000 including parameters such as length, location and cast. Creative ways of achieving innovative production values are encouraged.*
- *BFI Production presents final scripts to the Production Board for allocation of monies. The Board considers both the creative and the practical elements of each script. They view showreels and evaluate the filmmakers' contribution to UK cinema.*
- *BFI Production currently receives around 300 feature scripts per year. Approximately eight will be developed further and two of these projects will go through to the production stage each year.*
- *If a script is not accepted by the Board the BFI will advise the filmmaker of other sources of possible funding.*
- *The BFI provides successful projects with professional production and distribution support. Included in this are substantially reduced office overheads, editing rooms and a preview theatre on the Rathbone Street premises.*

## *APPLICATION PROCEDURE*

- *BFI Features application forms are available for submission throughout the year from the address below.*
- *All applications should be made with the 'BFI Features' cover form and must be accompanied by a treatment or script, the proposed director's showreel (if any) and CVs of other key personnel.*
- *Scripts should be between 70-90 pages long and have potential for cinema exhibition.*
- *Film treatments should include a story outline and an indication of visual style.*
- *Feature length documentaries for the cinema are welcomed.*
- *60 minute documentaries and television drama scripts are not considered.*
- *All applications are received and logged by the Script Co-ordinator and acknowledged by post. They are read and discussed by a readers meeting. This procedure takes 6-11 weeks at which time you will be notified of the decision on your script.*
- *Applicants are not expected to submit a detailed budget but should be aware of the budget constraints.*
- *Applications should be sent to: BFI Productions, 29 Rathbone Street, London, W1P 1AG*
- *Faxed applications will not be accepted.*

PRE-PRODUCTION

# Finance
## Stephen Cleary of
## British Screen

*British Screen is a source of development and production finance for the film industry. British Screen develops 50 to 60 projects a year and invests in the production of between fifteen to twenty films. It is one source of cash in the country where producers can apply and be judged solely on the merits of the project, both culturally and commercially.*

***Q - What is British Screen?***

***Stephen*** - British Screen is a private company, funded in part by an annual grant from the British Government through the department of National Heritage. We are a kind of mechanism for state intervention in the film industry and we have an agenda which is a mix of business and culture. We're asked to get involved in the development and production funding of films that wouldn't get made without our support, that promote new talent, that are in some sense definably British and which also answer a marketplace demand. Technically, projects for production need to qualify as British films under the Films Act of 1985.

***Q - What kind of funding is available in terms of categories?***

***Stephen*** - We do two main sorts of funding. Development funding and Production funding. You don't have to have Development Funding from British Screen before you apply for Production Funding, but the projects that go into development here are intended to leave the development part of the building and go into the production part.

***Q- What kind of monies are available?***

***Stephen -*** For development there are two main streams of finance. Screenplay Loans are a low level loan of £5,000 to a writer only in order to enable them to get to first draft. This is intended for young or first time writers and payment is fairly straightforward - 50% on signature of contract, and 50% on delivery. The writer retains the copyright in the script that they have written. The loan is repayable in the event of the film going into production, so it's a very soft loan. There is a premium of 50% repayment so when you borrow £5,000 from us, you pay us back £7,500. The Development Loan is a loan to production companies. It is designed to enable the script to get written and

cover all the other costs of getting a film through development. We lend to the production company, and the producer uses the money to, for example, pay the writer, prepare the budget, recce locations etc. Everything that is needed to get the film into 'official' pre production. Again, there is a premium of 50% on those loans, and all of it is payable on the first day of principle photography. We also take 5% of a film's net profit. If the film doesn't go into production we do not get our money back.

***Q - How does the production side work?***

***Stephen -*** We have two main funds from which we loan money for production. They are The British Screen Main Fund and the European Co-production Fund. In essence, the British Screen Fund is there to promote films made by British directors, British writers etc. The European Co-production Fund is there to support films which are, as the name suggests, European co-productions. So in order to qualify for a British Screen Main Fund loan for production, the film must be British under the Film's Act, in most cases have a British director and in many cases a British writer. In order to qualify for the European Co-production Fund a film must be a genuine European co-production with a co-producing partner in another EC country. If it all works out then our money is loaned to a British production company. Also, for the European Co-production Fund, there must be some interest in the UK from a distributor. You don't necessarily have to have a signed distribution deal but when you come here you must be able to show evidence that there is someone else apart from the European Co-production fund that is interested in this movie in the UK.

We would not be disposed to get involved in a film which is entirely supported by subsidy money from around Europe for example, because we want evidence that there is demand for the film in the market place. If that evidence is incredibly strong then that's another reason for us not to invest. If we thought the film would get financed without us, because the casting is so attractive for example, then we wouldn't get involved. And there have been very successful British Films which we have declined because we knew that they would be financed without our help.

***Q - How does somebody approach British Screen?***

***Stephen -*** Applicants - either producers for Development Loans or writers for Screenplay Loans - submit whatever they have, be it a script, a treatment, or even in some cases a brief outline or a book that is the originating material. Once we've read and assessed the project we decide whether or not we want to take it further for development finance. If we do, then I prepare the project in conjunction with the producer and writer and present it on their behalf to a panel of industry consultants who meet

every ten weeks or so to review the development projects here at British Screen.

If a Development Loan project is passed by the panel then the producer comes to a meeting with myself and Simon Perry here at British Screen where we determine the exact amount of money that we are going to invest. We then start the legal process of contracting the loan and any paperwork that goes into an application is usually decided between ourselves and the applicants. Anything that helps the application look stronger is acceptable. That includes things like statements of intent from directors, writers and producers. Supporting material which has helped give a flavour of some of the previous projects we have been involved with have included books of poetry, writing samples, art work and even in one case, a prosthetic latex head.

Screenplay loans are much the same except simpler, because there is only a writer involved.

***Q - If someone has very limited experience, is that a problem?***

***Stephen -*** Not at all. We are driven by enthusiasm for a project. If a project comes in and there are things that we might be worried about, for instance, the lack of experience of various people, then we would do our best to alleviate those problems. Not by taking people off the project but by introducing them to more experienced people - that more experienced person may take on the role of the executive producer or simply act as an advisor or even a 'god parent' to the project.

***Q - Is a producer more likely to get production investment if they have already received the development loan?***

***Stephen*** - Yes. 20-30% of projects that we put money into come out of the development department here. Last year, we put production investment into 21 features of which I think seven came through development. It helps if you can get a project through development here, because you have an inside track, if you like, but as you can see from the statistics, it's not a decisive inside track.

***Q - What is the deal British Screen has with BskyB?***

***Stephen -*** Essentially, it's a straightforward output deal, which is to say that every film that British Screen and The European Co-production Fund (excluding films not in the English language or productions budgeted at under £1m) is automatically acquired by BSkyB for pay television broadcast in the UK and Ireland. The deal is currently worth approximately 8% of the total budget of the film at budgets of £2.5m or lower.

***Q - So if you make a film that's budgeted at £1.5m, BSkyB will agree to buy the UK Pay TV rights for £120k? Is this fee additional to any British Screen investment?***

***Stephen -*** Yes. They are two separate things

***Q - Are those funds available for production or is that something they will get three years down the line?***

***Stephen* -** Those funds are available for production.

***Q - What is the Greenlight Fund ?***

***Stephen* -** On behalf of the Arts Council Lottery Fund, we manage a certain amount of money. At the moment it's a trial first year. The Greenlight Fund is there to keep certain sorts of Directors working in the UK. It's for Directors who have established an international reputation and could be regarded as a national asset to the Film Industry, directors who now have to go to America to make expensive films in British terms. With a Greenlight Fund investment we wouldn't put in more than 30% of the budget and we can invest up to £1.5m per film. So the budgets of the films we're expecting are to be somewhere between £5-8m.

***Q - With technology advancing and multimedia, does British Screen have any future plans?***

***Stephen* -** Yes. We're looking at establishing some sort of multimedia development fund, but there are no firm guidelines as yet.

***Q - What does a Producer need to supply to make an application for the full production loan?***

***Stephen* -** You're required to have a script and a fairly rigorous idea of the personnel involved. You don't have to have all your cast, you don't necessarily have to have a director. But if you don't then it becomes a lower priority for us - projects that have a director attached are dealt with more quickly. Simply send to 'admissions for production' a copy of the script and a letter detailing whatever you think we ought to know about the project, that is, the history of it up to date, the ideas you have for the financing, the interest with third parties, the cast, the crew, and various other interested financiers to give an idea of how the producer thinks the finance will be brought in. Once you have the script and the letter, we then read the script, and if the script interests us, there will then be a meeting.

***Q - What kind of films are British Screen looking to become involved in?***

***Stephen*** - We're not looking for specific genres, however, there is a bias towards contemporary projects. We get involved in projects that would not get made without our help, but at the same time we also have to try to make a sound commercial investment. Films, that once they're made, the commercial marketplace thinks, God, we should have funded that film, we should have seen that it would work. So it's not completely off the wall films, but it is not completely mainstream films either. Exactly what those are, and how you identify them is a very interesting question because it changes all the time and it's very difficult to actually make the correct choice.

***Q - How many applications do you get, and what is the turnaround?***

***Stephen* -** For production investment, we get something in the region of 400-500 a year. Of those probably 250 are serious, in the sense that they are a complete package that could go if the production money came together. In the development department we get double to triple that. But

PRE-PRODUCTION

## British Screen Finance Schemes

All productions must be *'intrinsically'* British and demonstrate that the project has a place in the commercial marketplace.

### Screenplay Loan

*For Who* - Writers
*To* - Get to first draft
*Amount Available* - £5k
*Turnaround* - Up to 8 weeks
*Terms* - Paid 50% upfront and 50% on delivery. Repay in full plus 50% if screenplay is made into film

### Development Loan

*For Who* - Producers
*To* - Support producers through development
*Amount Available* -Typically up to £15k (first stage), £35-50k in total.
*Turnaround* - Up to 10 weeks
*Terms* - Paid in instalments throughout development. Repay in full plus 50% on first day of principal photography. Plus British Screen receives 5% of profits.

### Preparation Loan

*For Who* - Producers
*To* - Finance final development of a project where British Screen intend to provide Production Finance
*Amount Available* -Typically up to £50k (very negotiable)
*Turnaround* - Up to 8 weeks
*Terms* - Repay in full plus 50% on first day of principal photography. Plus British Screen receives 2.5% of net profits additional to 5% if Development Loan was secured.

### Production Loan From The British Screen Main Fund

*For Who* - Production Companies
*To* - Be used as part of the production budget.
*Amount Available* - Up to £400k
*Turnaround* - Up to 10 weeks
*Terms* - Repay in full plus 50% from receipts of film. Plus British Screen receives a share of net profits.

### Production Loan From European Co-production Fund

*For Who* - Production Companies with European partners
*To* - Be used as part of the production budget
*Amount Available* - Up to £400k
*Turnaround* - Up to 10 weeks
*Terms* -Repay in full plus 50% from receipts of film. Plus British Screen receives a share of net profits.

### Greenlight Fund

*For Who* - Established director driven productions
*To* - Be used as part of the production budget
*Amount Available* - Up to £1.5m

### BSkyB Output Deal

*For Who* - British Screen productions
*To* - Provide production finance secured against a Pay TV deal with BSkyB.
*Amount Available* - Typically 8% of total budget.

in development, conversely, we have at any one time, around 50 to 60 active projects as opposed to the 20 or so in production. The turnaround for production should be around 6 to 7 weeks before you get a detailed response. For development, I'm afraid, it's slightly longer. In fact sometimes, it can take up to 10 weeks or more. We try and keep it down to 6-8 weeks. It really depends on what time of year you apply. Also we don't farm out to outside readers - we read and asses everything internally with nearly all things read more than once and by more than one person.

***Q - Are there any other requirements for British Screen's involvement?***

***Stephen*** - In both development and production there are certain credit requirements. At the end of the film there is a *developed by British Screen* credit and there is a particular front board credit for British Screen Production investment. There are also the standard terms that any other production investor will have, such as access to financial records etc.

***Q - Does British Screen bring anything else to a production?***

***Stephen*** - Half of what we do is to work as an information exchange. For instance, a producer could come here and say, *I have an option for a book - I don't know who could write it - do you know of a writer who is interested in this subject?* Similarly a producer with a project can come in here and just talk off the record about how they might finance a particular film. Once we're on board, we're not like a conventional financier in the marketplace as we can offer guidance, advice and introduce people. It is also important for us to remember that we must allow the Producer to produce the film and we're careful not to become too involved in the way the film works.

***Q - What can a producer do to make your life easier?***

***Stephen -*** Make sure you send in the right material. In order to make a decision about something, we need to see a serious amount of work put into an application. We expect a treatment of a minimum of 7 or 8 pages and a maximum of twenty. Always if you have the script, send the script. Don't try to write a treatment from a script in retrospect and send that in. Also write a clear and concise letter detailing everything we need to know.

PRE-PRODUCTION

# Finance & Support
## Allon Reich
### Assistant Editor, Channel Four

*In recent years, Channel 4 have been responsible for the production of several extremely succesful British Films including Britains most succesful film ever, 'Four Weddings and a Funneral'*

***Q - What kind of material is Film on Four looking for?***

***Allon -*** We put money into about twenty films a year - all films for the cinema, which is crucial. What we tend to look for are individual voices, films with an edge or perspective, that in some way reflect the film maker and/or film writer.

***Q - What kind of budgets do you work with on average?***

***Allon -*** Our average input last year, was in the region of £900,000. That went from license fees, to slightly bigger films up to fully funding certain films with budgets of £1m or £1.5m.

***Q - How should a film maker submit a project to you?***

***Allon*** - If there's a screenplay that's most helpful. We read everything that comes in, even if it's a first draft. If you say it's a first draft, it gives a good indication of what the film will be and we can give a fairly considered response. We do look at treatments but we find they usually don't do justice to the material.

***Q - How long does it take Film on Four's wheels to grind into motion?***

***Allon -*** If we like it, then we'll meet. That's the first thing. Beyond that it really depends on whether it's one rewrite or twenty five rewrites. SHALLOW GRAVE, for example, happened very quickly. David liked the draft, he didn't know the film makers but within a year they had in fact shot the film. Our attitude to development is that we won't put 10p into a project unless we think we want to make it - that's always consistent. Sometimes things fall by the wayside for one reason or another, but we don't have a kind of quota that we develop 10 to one or anything like that. We only develop things we want to make. That process is impossible to put a time scale on.

***Q - So is it fair to say that if someone submitted a screenplay to you and you liked it, it's unlikely even in the best case, that they're going to be on set shooting within a month or two?***

***Allon*** - Its never happened that I am aware of. I've never yet read a submitted screenplay that is perfect and believed that we should move directly into production.

***Q - If somebody comes to you with a project you like but the screenplay isn't in place, do you ever put money into developing the project?***

***Allon -*** Yes, but it depends on the idea, the concept. We like to back the passion of film makers who say 'I've always wanted to do this story, it's about...' Then we might well give some money to take it to the next stage.

***Q - Would you ever consider offering an advance to a first time film maker in order to develop a project - or some money to help get the script in place?***

***Allon -*** Yes. Only recently in the development department we gave money to a film maker who had never made anything before, nor written a feature. They pitched an idea that we liked a lot and we gave them the money to go and write a screenplay. So track record is not essential - it depends more on your passion, if your idea is good and you can convince us that you are a film maker who will be good to work with.

***Q - If Channel Four is not interested, how long does it take for you to say no, we're not interested?***

***Allon*** - We try very hard to give 'No's' as quickly as possible. Because we read everything, we do have a huge submission pile every week, however, you should get a reply within four to six weeks.

***Q - In your experience, what are the most common mistakes made by somebody submitting a project. What slows down the process or makes projects less appealing to Film Four?***

***Allon*** - Firstly, the submission should look clean and be well typed. This makes you look professional, as if you know what you're doing. The screenplay should be properly paginated and have a covering letter that is literate, you'd be amazed at how many people write letters that are so grammatically inept, you cannot read them. Gimmicks are probably not a good idea. It's the obvious things, it should be clean, thought out and looking like a real screenplay.

***Q - What information should a covering letter contain?***

***Allon -*** I think it's useful to briefly explain what you think the script is. If it has interest from any people then fine, but I don't think there's any point in saying, I'd like to have Daniel Day Lewis in this film, or Speilberg to direct. Again, if it's a first draft, tell us that you know it needs more work, particularly if you know certain parts are weak, for instance if you know the end is not right but you just needed something to give the desired effect. That will help us asses where the project is at.

***Q - What advice would you give to a film maker or a scriptwriter when submitting a project?***

***Allon -*** There's no real point sending me a Sci Fi horror because we just don't do them. We are interested in 'who' and 'how' rather than just 'what'. Again, it's worth pressing the point - it's not just a concept, it's the actual passion of the writer, the feeling that you actually want to tell this story.

***Q - Do you have any good examples of that?***

***Allon*** - If you take SHALLOW GRAVE, and this is going back to the treatment versus screenplay idea, John Hodge was a writer we didn't know at all. Had we got a treatment for SHALLOW GRAVE, it night have felt too mainstream and formulaic for us and we may have passed.

We saw a first draft of the script which had that very individual angle on the genre - that dry Scottish humour etc. What Film Four responded to was the voice behind it, not the idea of 'lets do a thriller'.

***Q - SHALLOW GRAVE in some respects is a fairly low budget picture, but it's performed amazingly well. Are you surprised by that, did you expect it?***

*Bhaji On The Beach' - An example of the passion and 'lone voice of a film maker' that is an important part of the Channel 4 film making process*

*'Four Weddings...' & 'Shallow Grave' - Two recent Channel Four productions that exceeded all expectations at the box office*

***Allon*** - No, we never expected it. We completely believed in the film but would never try to predict box office success. It was fantastic to have a film that is contemporary, British yet cinematic, made for just over a million pounds, with no stars, no named director and that recoups it's money just in the UK cinema.

***Q - Do Film Four have a specific International Sales Agent?***

***Allon*** - Channel Four have a sales agent in house, Film Four International, which tend to deal with most of our films in one way or another, in conjunction with other distributors and sales companies. They are mainly the first port.

***Q - Any final hints or tips?***

***Allon*** - I think producers, sometimes more than writers or directors, have a feeling that mainstream equals commercial. In the British Film Industry there is very little evidence that that is in fact true. I think you have to do more than cobble together a mainstream formula, shove in a screenplay and say, this is bound to make money. In the UK we don't have the packaging with stars etc. that America has. In fact British telly does it rather well - I'm thinking of PRIME SUSPECT, CRACKER - brilliant mainstream formula if you like, with a twist and good writing, but also a type of genre film that traditionally, hasn't worked in terms of commercial British Cinema.

# Completion Bonds James Shirras of Film Finances

*Film Finances Inc. is the only UK Completion Bond company in the UK. It was established in the 1950's to help producers assure banks that productions would be completed. To date, they have guaranteed over 2000 productions.*

***Q - What is a completion guarantee?***

***James -*** A completion guarantee or bond as it is sometime called, is an instrument whereby a completion guarantor promises to the providers of the finance for a film that the film will be completed in accordance with the budget, the timescale and the script which they have approved. It is not a guarantee to the producers of the film that those things will happen, it's a guarantee to the providers of the finance, and it's quite an important feature of the completion guarantee that the producers are not able to invoke it or call upon it.

***Q - What does a Producer need to furnish you with to provide the guarantee that you can then present to the financiers?***

***James -*** In the first instance, the producer will approach us with the script, budget and production schedule. We don't encourage producers to send in their material before they are confident they have finance for their films because reviewing the script, budget and schedule is quite a time consuming business. Once we've reviewed the material we ask the producers to come in for a meeting where we will ask them to explain particular things in the script that have struck us as being perhaps slightly difficult or unusual. We'll ask them many things such as which locations they're planning to use for the film and who their heads of department would be so we can see whether they are people we know and feel comfortable with. It's at that meeting the producers would be able to give an account of themselves. We will also need to see, not necessarily at the same meeting, but at some stage, the director, to satisfy ourselves that he or she is a responsible individual who knows what they are going to do and they are indeed going to do what they say they are going to do. We believe that if the director has been in to explain to us what they're going to do, it's more likely they'll stick to it than they might otherwise do.

***Q - What kind of things are you looking for in the script?***

***James -*** Large crowd scenes, special effects, action sequences which might be logistically difficult. Those kinds of elements.

***Q - Are there any things you would advise to avoid in order to minimise the guarantee cost on a low-budget film?***

***James -*** The cost of the guarantee is a separate thing. Generally I think the script should be written clearly so it is apparent on the face of the document how every effect that is described is going to be realised. So flowery language and vague generalities of what the producers hope to see on screen should be avoided.

***Q - What is the lowest budget you would expect to issue a guarantee for?***

***James -*** About a million pounds at present. We have done films below that level fairly recently - we did a film for about £750,000 but that is fairly unusual, I think a million pounds is probably the general minimum. We impose a minimum fee which to some extent, determines the level to which it's not really cost effective for a producer to come in and see us about a guarantee, and that minimum will obviously vary from time to time, but on the basis of a million pound budget it would work out at about 5%.

***Q - What happens if a calamity occurs in production - the lead actor dies, the director is arrested and put in prison, or the production goes way over schedule for example?***

***James -*** We need to distinguish eventualities which are covered by the other insurance's. Producers will take out insurance on the cast and the negative and various other things. So if the lead actor dies, that should be covered by the cast insurance and the cast insurance should bear the cost of either replacing the lead actor or if that's not a practical possibility, then paying back the financiers what they have spent up to that point.

The other eventualities that you alluded to would probably be our responsibility. If the director is arrested and put in prison, that is something that you wouldn't have insured against, then that would be our problem and we would take the view that either we would wait for him to come out of prison and reschedule the whole thing, which would clearly involve some additional cost or we would get another director in to finish what the original director had started.

If you had a director who was very slow, or way behind schedule, you might have to apply some pressure on him and tell him to get on with it, otherwise you're going to replace him. Sometimes this has an effect, but some directors are completely incapable of working more quickly than the speed at which they are working. Remember, the director has assured us beforehand that he can do it within the allocated schedule so he's going to be aware that he's not keeping to what he originally said he was going to do.

***Q - At what point do you decide to step in and take action in a situation like that?***

***James -*** I don't think you would usually take action right at the beginning because it wouldn't usually be apparent that there was a terrible problem. Supposing the projections were showing that the film was going to go over schedule by 50% then that would be a serious thing which would have major cost implications.

It would almost certainly follow that the director was shooting far too much material - it's possible that he's taking too many takes for each scene or that he's shooting so much material that if it was up on screen, the film would be 50% longer than it's supposed to be. You might at that stage consider cutting certain things out of the script for which you would probably need the consent of the financiers depending on the deal.

You would also be concerned about expenditure - if you were looking at a 50% over-run on the schedule then you would probably decide that you wanted to exert slightly more direct control over expenditure. We would probably have decided that we wanted to become counter signatories on all cheques so payments could be directly controlled but we probably wouldn't consider replacing anybody on the production team at that stage. We might, depending on where they were, think it appropriate to send a full time representative to keep an eye on them, to make sure the director didn't slip behind any further.

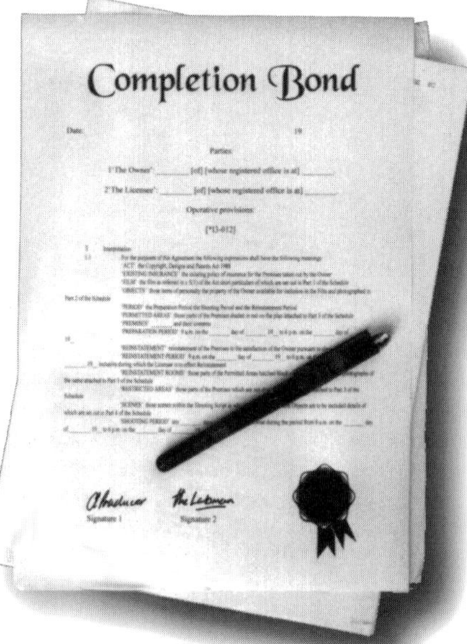


***Q - When you're looking at the budget, do you look at having a minimum contingency and what is it?***

***James -*** There's a requirement that we have a contingency of 10% of the direct and above and below the line costs.

***Q - What is the mechanism for calling in the guarantee, do you monitor the production?***

***James -*** We monitor the production very closely, so we get daily progress reports from the production while they're shooting which tells us exactly how much they've shot on a particular day, how much footage they've used for film stock, how many people were

there for lunch etc. On a weekly basis we also get costings to show how much money they've spent and how much they are projecting to spend. If the reports are accurate, which we hope they are, then we know where the production is at and can take the view as to whether we need to do anything or not.

***Q - Are you perceived as ogres that everyone fears and dislikes, or knights in white shining armour who come in when something has gone wrong?***

***James -*** Well I think it's probably somewhere between the two. I don't think we should be regarded as ogres because that's not really how we go about our job. We're usually quite humane about anything that has to be done, even if it's fairly draconian. The producers who work best with us really regard us as some sort of consultancy, able to provide advice whenever it's required. Ultimately, we can be relied upon to be there and see the production gets completed.

***Q - So once you're in place you are actually a voice on the end of the telephone that can help?***

***James -*** Yes.

***Q - Do you have any basic advice for filmmakers about how to deal with a company such as your own and has anything in the past proved to be problematic?***

***James -*** I think the main thing is that they should be absolutely open with us. If they are making a film and perceive anything to be a potential problem they should let us know straight away because we can give our advice to avoid them getting into difficulties.

I think it's important to realise that when we give a completion guarantee to financiers we also take fairly direct contractual controls over the production company and we do have very sweeping powers to step in to dismiss people, replace producers, or move in and complete the film ourselves if we think that is what is needed. It's extremely unusual for us to take that step because the producers are usually the best people to get the film finished - so even if they need to be put under a great deal of pressure in one way or another, it is usually better to leave them in charge.

PRE-PRODUCTION

# Insurance Gerry Peake of Aegis Insurance

***Q - Why should a producer talk to a film insurer rather than a high street insurance broker?***

***Gerry -*** In any class of insurance, not just entertainment, you need to speak to those who are intimate with the specialised business - they know the pitfalls, where you should buy insurance and where you needn't buy insurance. Deal with a specialist because that is exactly what he is, and he knows the most economic and best policy for the job. Film or entertainment specialist brokers will want you to treat them like partners. Tell them everything you do - we're not being nosey - we need to know. There might be something there that you think is immaterial but we'll be able to tell you that if you don't do X, Y and Z, then you won't be covered and so on.

***Q - So absolute honesty is essential?***

***Gerry -*** Yes it's imperative to be straightforward and you must be frank about your budget because if there's a problem, anything we didn't know could complicate and even negate any claims. If a claim comes along and we suddenly find out that we've been given duff information, that could jeopardise the claim in total, it can certainly throw spanners in the works.

We've been involved with people in the past and it's been half way through the shoot when they say *Did you know about the helicopter? - No, I didn't know you were using a helicopter*, and there's nothing in the script that portrays the use of a helicopter. That lack of information can cost dearly and can really put you in serious trouble, because you'll find when you need it, the policy is void. The broker will ask to see the script, the cast list and crew, because some people involved may have a 'record' and sometimes an underwriter will say 'no thanks'. The broker will then sit down and have a pre production insurance meeting and talk about how you're intending to make this project. And for that I always like to sit in with the director as well as the producers so that the director can explain how he's going to approach various problem areas.

***Q - What is the main insurance, or are there several insurances that a producer should secure?***

***Gerry -*** In a sense there used to be - years ago, all of the insurances were split up. There was something called a Film Producers Indemnity policy that dealt mainly with the cast, then you'd

have equipment policies, negative policies, everything. Nowadays we're lucky. Most insurers directly involved in film and television production have what we call the production package which includes cast, negative, faulty equipment, extra expense, cash, even, office. About eight or nine different headings that used to be fragmented are now under one package.

***Q - What are the most common problems causing a claim?***

***Gerry -*** There are more negative losses, more problems with the actual film material itself in processing or in the camera, than there are any other type of losses. Cast losses, can be crucial and very expensive, but are not nearly so numerous. If you're looking at heavy losses then the cast insurance is the one that's going to give you the problem or the extra expense.

***Q - What would have happened in the event of a lead actor dying?***

***Gerry -*** If it's truly impossible to finish the film, and you'll be surprised how you can salvage a film even if this disaster happens, then you'll go through abandonment. The insurers will agree, providing they know that all possibilities have been exhausted, to go to an abandonment in which case you'll get paid back all of that money you've expended in producing that negative. It won't pay for the rights in the story, or the music rights or royalties, for example, because they are still there. The project is then owned by the insurance company that pays for the abandonment - you can at a later date redeem it, and make an offer to buy it back.

***Q - If a producer came to you with a small British picture that was budgeted at half a million pounds - no helicopters, no car crashes, nothing particularly dangerous, as a percentage how much do you think it would cost to insure?***

***Gerry -*** I would suggest around 1 -1.5% of the budget. If it's got anything out of the ordinary, if you're using elderly actors, doing hazardous stunts or using volatile material, think in terms of the higher level, it may even go above 1.5%. In addition you'll need to buy public and employers liability, errors and omissions policy, motor insurance and any union insurance. If you're going on a foreign location, under union agreements in this country you have to cover them under certain travel and PA policies. Overall, if you include all that extra cover, you're going to come out with something like 2%, which in my view is a very small price tag for peace of mind.

***Q - What about Employers Liability and a Limited Company?***

***Gerry -*** Employers liability is a legal requirement for limited companies and covers yourself and the crew. A lot of the people you employ and use on a film are self employed people, operating either as partnerships, companies or individuals. If they are paid by cheque to a company as opposed to being on your payroll, they do not have to be

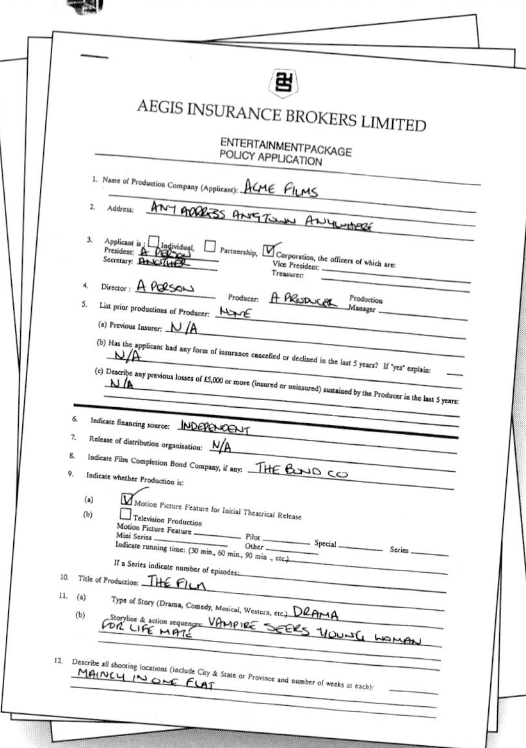

AEGIS INSURANCE BROKERS LIMITED

ENTERTAINMENTPACKAGE
POLICY APPLICATION

1. Name of Production Company (Applicant): ACME FILMS
2. Address: ANY ADDRESS ANYTOWN ANYWHERE
3. Applicant is: ☐ Individual, ☐ Partnership, ☑ Corporation, the officers of which are:
President: A PERSON
Secretary: ANOTHER
Vice President:
Treasurer:
4. Director: A PERSON Producer: A PRODUCER Production Manager
5. List prior productions of Producer: NONE
(a) Previous Insurer: N/A
(b) Has the applicant had any form of insurance cancelled or declined in the last 5 years? If "yes" explain: N/A
(c) Describe any previous losses of £5,000 or more (insured or uninsured) sustained by the Producer in the last 5 years: N/A
6. Indicate financing source: INDEPENDENT
7. Release of distribution organisation: N/A
8. Indicate Film Completion Bond Company, if any: THE BOND CO
9. Indicate whether Production is:
(a) ☑ Motion Picture Feature for Initial Theatrical Release
(b) ☐ Television Production
Motion Picture Feature
Mini Series
Pilot
Other
Special
Series
Indicate running time: (30 min., 60 min., 90 min ., etc.)
If a Series indicate number of episodes:
10. Title of Production: THE FILM
11. (a) Type of Story (Drama, Comedy, Musical, Western, etc.) DRAMA
(b) Storyline & action sequences: VAMPIRE SEEKS YOUNG WOMAN FOR LIFE MATE
12. Describe all shooting locations (include City & State or Province and number of weeks at each): MAINLY IN ONE FLAT

insured under the employers liability. Only people who are on the company's payroll need to be covered by the employers liability. Again, it's a comparatively cheap policy.

***Q - What happens about stunt men?***

***Gerry -*** They have to be insured for injury under their own stuntmans association scheme. If it's a liability accident where a stuntman is walking down a corridor in the studio office and he falls over a broomstick and breaks his leg, then the employers liability may pick it up, but not whilst performing as a stuntman.

***Q - Will the stuntman arrange his own policy?***

***Gerry -*** Usually they do their own and have their own special insurance policy.

***Q - Should the producer request to see that policy?***

***Gerry -*** I think you'll find that stuntmen have to sign a disclaimer. When they're employed, the stuntmans agreement actually gives a *hold harmless* clause for the producer. The cost of that insurance is obviously built in for the cost of the stuntman and the Producers pay for it in the long run, but not as a separate entity.

***Q - Do you act as Completion Guarantors?***

***Gerry -*** No we don't.

***Q - At what point should you start cover and what time should you stop cover?***

***Gerry -*** Once the master negative has produced an original release print and that print has been delivered to the people who have bought the film for distribution or transmission, that is the day that the cover will cease. To all intents and purposes, the product has been made and it's been handed over. There are storage facilities around this country, Pinewood, Shepperton and Elstree studios all have vaults where numerous original negatives and second generation negatives are stored and insured, but under totally different policies that are nothing to do with film production.

***Q - What would happen if during the shoot a re-write included a helicopter that previously wasn't there?***

***Gerry*** - You immediately notify your broker of any changes - it doesn't matter how trivial it may appear at the time, let your broker know, that is very important - he will then go back to the company and get a quotation for you to cover the changes you're talking about - the use of the helicopter or something like that, and he will buy the insurance for you. If it's only a minor thing, he will get it notified and hopefully there won't be an additional premium. But at least it's noted by the underwriter.

***Q - Producers tell a lot of white lies to get the best deal, but Insurance is one of those areas where you should not use those white lies?***

***Gerry*** - Don't lie to the insurers or you could end up paying for it in the long run.

***Q - If a deal has been put together correctly and a claim is made, how long does it take to be turned around assuming there is no complication?***

***Gerry*** - There is no real answer to that - it could be days if it's a straightforward claim. Like someone on set drops a bit of pottery and we have the suppliers invoice - it's simple documentation. If it's required that witness statements be collected, lab reports checked, how it happened, where it happened, then it takes a bit longer.

***Q - What are the most common mistakes that lead to problems in your experience?***

***Gerry*** - People trying to save money. Producers not buying the right insurance from the right people because they're trying to cut their insurance costs. They'll have fifty people in a crowd sequence, where they could easily have got away with forty, and yet they still won't buy the right insurances.

***Q - What basic advice would you offer a new film maker and new producer?***

***Gerry*** - Go to a specialist broker - there are many in London and they're all good. Have a meeting with the broker and give him the paper work that he will need, script, shooting schedule, budget, cast list and so on - all of the information that will tell him a great deal about the project you're making. Explain to him how you're setting about making the film - are you going on overseas locations are you doing it all in the UK - if you're going to studios, which studio, what lab are you going to use and what stock, all of these things are relevant. Don't try to penny pinch when it comes to insurance. Either you're going to insure properly or not, and my advise is always, if you're going to bother to make a movie, get it insured. It's got to be one of the top priorities in the expenditure, not one of the tack-ons like a lot of Producers think. It is crucial to have the right insurances and it's not exorbitant. When you look at the risks involved, the premium charge on motion pictures is extremely reasonable.

# The British Film Commission
## Sir Sydney Samuelson

*The British Film Commission was established in 1991 and is headed by Sir Sydney Samuelson, an industry figure with decades of experience.*

***Q - What is the BRITISH FILM COMMISSION?***

***Sir Sydney*** - It's a government funded body. We report to the Department of the National Heritage and our job is to promote the British film and television production infrastructure, primarily abroad. To sum up in a cliché, we open doors, sometimes get doors opened that have been jammed shut or are halfway open. We also cut the tape. We work with a network of commissions located throughout the UK and they handle production enquiries on a local level. We see it as part of our job to target international productions and bring them to the UK.

***Q - What are the problems the BFC faces from producers?***

***Sir Sydney*** - We are a permanent centre of responsibility - we are always here - if a film company doesn't behave itself, they can disappear overnight, but the British Film Commission has to take the telephone call the next day. We've been let down on some occasions by misbehaviour and it's extremely depressing when it happens. We work hard to avoid such situations.

***Q - How can the BFC help a British film production, especially one that is on a lower budget?***

***Sir Sydney*** - The BFC is always pleased to assist producers from the UK although, as I said before, our government remit is to make international productions top priority. We do have difficulties and we have had to say we cannot cope with, for example student films. I wish we had money to run the BFC as we would like to run it, in which case the staff would be three times what it is - we are nine people and we have a relatively small budget. However, we are always happy to offer advice - if someone calls and asks 'Who is the right person to talk to in the Metropolitan Police?' we will deliver that information. Regrettably for micro budgets, we're not always able to deliver as much service as we would like. The reason for that is that the government considers that the money that they put in, which is £800k a year, is to create inward investment from abroad.

***Q - What are the problems BFC faces in finding locations?***

***Sir Sydney -*** Firstly, I think it is important to say that we don't act as a substitute location manager or locations agency. The UK commissions, however, do maintain information - both in image and text form - on locations in their areas. We are here to promote the variety of locations that are available in the UK and when required by a production company we can assist with location problems or trouble-shoot. That might entail, for instance, liaising at high level with a location owner or manager who might not be keen initially to hire out their property for filming purposes.

***Q - Could you offer alternatives to locations that are out of the question?***

***Sir Sydney -*** Yes. It's usually the job of the local area commissions to offer alternatives as we don't have the local expertise. If you wanted those white stucco Georgian buildings in Belgravia for your background you have a problem - Belgravia is full of embassies, which means it is full of security problems, but Liverpool and Bath have wonderful lookalikes for Belgravia. We would circulate the requirements to all the area film commissions in the UK, and say this is what they are looking for, this is the producer, address, phone number, name, fax number, etc. The area film commissions that could help would then contact the producer directly.

A good example of finding a believable substitute location was achieved for the producers of 'Patriot Games'. Harrison Ford plays an American diplomat who in one scene is leaving a British ministry building in Whitehall just as there is an assassination attempt where a car is blown up. The Metropolitan Police were not about to allow anything to be blown up in Whitehall, let alone have parking for six unit vehicles and so on. We suggested shooting the sequence in a particular part of Greenwich that looked very much like Whitehall - it had better access and no security problems. It worked out very well.

***Q - What can a producer do to make your life easier?***

***Sir Sydney -*** The most important requirement is to give everybody time to actually come up with what is being asked of them. Our industry leaves everything to the last moment. We get phone calls saying "We need parking spaces for six trucks and we're shooting there tomorrow and we haven't got permission..." We do our best in that sort of situation but it is best to remember that we cannot work miracles on a daily basis.

However, a producer may have asked permission four weeks earlier, got it, and then the director checks the location the day before and says, "I didn't realise you can see that modern building at the end of the street on the skyline - this is supposed to be 1923 when they didn't have buildings like that concrete tower block". So we understand the reasons for these problems, but it doesn't change the fact that not having enough time to deliver is the biggest problem we face.

***Q - How do the local commissions link up with the BFC?***

***Sir Sydney -*** We do not handle the detail here. We're a conduit - we provide one stop shopping for producers. For example, you're looking for a fairy-tale castle that must have four turrets and a moat which still has water in it, and a drawbridge that still goes up and down, that's not too far from main road links, or too close to an airport. You can make one phone call or send one fax here to the BFC, we will contact the area and city commissions, who in turn will contact you, that is if they have the fairy-tale castle - you can then discuss the detail with the local experts. Our watchwords are Instant Response - we like to make sure you get a response within 24 hours.

***Q - I believe the BFC has a computerised national database of locations?***

***Sir Sydney -*** Yes we do, it's called FIND - Film Information National Database - but it does not hold information purely on locations. Essentially FIND is a film commission management system which is used by the BFC and area commissions to answer production enquiries regarding locations, production personnel, facilities and general issues such as the guidelines for filming with children or filming on railway property, etc. Image and text information on locations is held on the satellite FIND system which is based at the UK commission in which area the location is actually based. Aside from descriptions of the location, there is information on road access, car parking facilities, filming history and all essential contact details. Information on facilities is also held by the local commissions. Information on heads of departments such as cinematographers, line producers, location managers, etc, is held centrally at the BFC although the UK commissions may, in some instances, hold duplicate information. Generally, the BFC also acts as the prime source on information relating to general production enquiries.

***Q - What's the best job the BFC has done?***

*The Producers of 'Patriot Games' needed to film in Whitehall which would have created a serious security problem - an alternate location in Greewich, which looked enough like Whitehall, was chosen and used as a stand in for the production team.*

Area Commission holds location information on imaged based database.....

Example location profile

Location name: Manderston

Address details: Duns
(of the location) Berwickshire
TD11 3PP

Tel: 0361 83450
Fax:

Owners name: The Lord Palmer
Address: Duns
Berwickshire
TD11 3PP

Tel: 0361 83450
Fax:

Agents name: None

Area Commission holds location information on imaged based database.....

Location contact name: The Lord Palmer

Brief description of the location:
( inc. details of period /style / condition )

Building commenced in 1864, continuing on through the early years of this century. Manderston is possibly the finest Edwardian mansion in Britain. Designed in the classical style it is a superb country house; the swansong of its era. Sumptuous state rooms, bedrooms, bathrooms and original domestic offices can be found plus a unique and recently restored silver staircase.

Magnificent stables, a stunning marble dairy and 56 acres of immaculate garden complete this location.

Previous filming history:
(inc. dates, titles, prod company, production co.contact )

1989 'Changing Step' BBC
1990 Various commercials and fashion shoots
1992 'Diana - Her True Story' Sky Television Mini-series

***Sir Sydney -*** Our problem is quantifying our achievements - it's almost impossible to put our hand on our hearts and say *Judge Dredd* came to the UK because of the 18 months work we did before it came here. We solved a lot of problems, we answered a lot of questions, we provided a lot of contacts - if we didn't exist the film *may* still have come here. One particular job that we can absolutely quantify was a film called *The Cement Garden.* I got a phone call from the producer who said he was extremely disappointed as he had just been refused admission from the disused Beckton Gas Works (Where *Full Metal Jacket* was shot). He had taken the precaution of finding a second location which was in Germany and it looked like he was going to have to relocate there.

I got through to British Gas (the owners of Beckton) at a very high level and to cut a long story short, we were able to persuade the British Gas top brass to allow the film to shoot at Beckton using, of course, all British crew. It seemed to me during my exchanges with the senior British Gas management that the film being turned down in the first instance was owing to someone weighing up the work that saying "yes" to the film would have entailed difficulties for them and deciding to say "no" was an easier option. Since then, we have solved a great number of location problems for a number of major features, television programmes and commercials.

*The British Film Commission is a very approachable organisation that delivers at lightning speed.. The service the BFC offers is free.*

# Public Relations
## Ginger Corbett of Corbett & Keene

***Q - What is your job?***

***Ginger -*** Our job is to bring the film to the attention to distributors, other film makers and to the public via the press. The earlier we can be involved in the film-making process the better. To alert everyone that the film is being made, we send out start of picture releases as well as listings of cast and crew to the trade press worldwide. We also place pictures in the trade press and general media, plan interesting feature articles and ideas for location stories etc. The earlier we are involved, the better.

***Q - Photographs are vital for international sales agents, but they only want shots of the actors in scenes - do you need shots of directors etc?***

***Ginger -*** Yes we do, but not too many of them. What we REALLY need is the story in photographs. There is on every film, a still that every publication will use, so we have to decide, with the photographer, what those key scenes are and make sure they are photographed. For feature articles, covers etc. a far greater selection is required. We also keep an eye on the quantity and quality of the stills during the production, making sure that the photographer is taking the stills that reflect the mood of the film.

***Q - There are different areas of publicity - trade press, national press, magazines, television, radio and the international variations, do you take care of the whole lot?***

***Ginger -*** Yes, everything

***Q - So why should a low-budget film maker who's confident of getting on the phone themselves not do it, and you do it instead?***

***Ginger -*** A low-budget film maker has enough on his plate just making the film, without concerning himself with the press. First timers in general also try to get articles published at every opportunity. If they do manage to get something published in a major magazine during production they should try to limit this to one or maybe two articles. Too much and you destroy your chances of coverage when the film is being released - as the press rarely give you a second spread. By all means try to get a journalist or two on set, but get an agreement that they will hold the pieces until distribution.

Another thing that happens with low-budget films is that friends/or relations are invited to be the publicist or stills photographer. A recent case where we worked on the distribution campaign for a film, the actor's wife was the only person allowed on set as a journalist/stills photographer. Everyone was thrilled that she had a commission from a leading publication, but the ensuing piece made the production look tacky and very amateurish - not at all good for the film.

***Q - So when people hire you, they're hiring you for experience and contacts?***

***Ginger -*** Yes.

***Q - What materials do you need from the production?***

***Ginger -*** When we start at the beginning of the production process, we have scripts, cast and crew lists, schedules, locations, the biographies from the actors agents, we also research the projects to find out anything exciting about the locations etc., Then we put a writer on the job, to compile production notes - they will interview all the artists and principals and put together a press kit.

***Q - If money is tight, what are the barest minimum requirements from a publicity point of view that you would need?***

***Ginger -*** Stills are very important. I can't ever place too much emphasis on good quality stills, even if you only have a photographer on for a few key days.

***Q - Would you suggest it's a good idea, if the budget can afford it, to set up the lead actors in a studio with a professional photographer to take shots which are ideal for, say the cover of Premiere?***

***Ginger -*** It is more important for the production to spend money on good unit photography, if time and budget allow, then either the unit (if they are experienced) or a 'specials' photographer should take some special set ups and portraits of the principals in costume against a plain background.

The Production will need to supply to the distributor a quantity of good quality materials which will normally include approximately 200 pieces of colour and 100 black and white photographs.

Ginger Corbett
Corbett & Keene
122 Wardour Street, London, W1V 3TD
England
Tel 0171 494 3478 Fax 0171 734 2024

***Q - If the budget could stretch to it can a production take high quality images to offer to the glossy magazines with a story. Not a photograph on set but in a studio?***

## PUBLIC RELATIONS HOTLIST

*The Phone - get on it and make contacts, stir up controversy, pitch ideas to magazines.*

*Stills - The absolute cornerstone of good publicity is the image. Make sure you have plenty of good shots, and try to isolate a single image that will become synonymous with the project.*

*The Press Kit - Typed interviews with key cast and crew members, biographies, interesting facts, synopsis and treatment of the film. Also include stills.*

*The EPK - Electronic Press Kit is a Beta SP tape that has interviews with key cast and crew members, plus clips from the film and a trailer. All loosely edited. Never give away your master!*

*Radio Interviews - Supply notes to radio progs., plus taped interviews with key cast and crew on either 1/4" or DAT tape.*

***Ginger -*** This need not be a budgetary item. There are plenty of photographic agencies who will, if the actors are interesting enough and the film has potential, take them into a studio for a session with a top photographer and stylist. And they'll pay for it. They will retain the rights to exploit these pictures, normally in conjunction with the publicist at the time of release. The costs of the photographer, studio etc. will be recouped from picture sales.

***Q - Are Electronic Press Kits and video taped interviews with cast and crew important?***

***Ginger -*** Yes, because there are now many outlets on satellite TV stations around the world. Often, you believe that your cast will be available for the distribution campaign, but the young actress gets snapped up to star with Robert Redford, an elderly lead has died etc. Despite promises and good intentions you could be left with nothing, so it's a good idea to shoot interviews during or just after production ceases.

***Q - What should the tape contain?***

***Ginger -*** It should be a Betacam SP tape with 20 minutes of edited interviews with the principal cast and director (plus costume/art director and cinematographer - but only if their work is particularly unusual or interesting). There should also be some B-roll (behind the scenes footage of the crew at work) and some clips.

***Q - Is there a low-budget film you've done where you've got a bit more mileage than you perhaps thought possible?***

***Ginger -*** *Orlando* is a movie that went very well - a lot of it's success was down to the brilliant stills

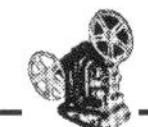



which were simply fantastic. Publications are using the stills well after writing about that movie and they're constantly used when talking about British Films. The stills were so beautiful and so rich.

***Q - So the Orlando team was smart enough to make sure they got good pictures, which gave you the correct tools to do the job?***

***Ginger*** - Yes. We were sending out pictures during production and publications were calling saying *'these are wonderful pictures', 'have you got any more', 'we'll do a spread'.* So it's worth while having good pictures.

***Q - Assuming somebody's making a low-budget picture and they have no money for PR and they have to do their own, what tips would you give them to maximise the impact and minimise the damage during production, to set it up for somebody like yourself when it comes to the distributor coming on board?***

***Ginger -*** To try and get as much information together - anything that's written about the film or the subject of the film, all your research material, notes on anything, such as shooting in an interesting location - keep a copy of every useful brochure and telephone number.

***Q - Do you have any basic advice?***

***Ginger -*** Let the publicist know as much as possible, even things that you don't want the rest of the world to know. Tell us so that we know not to mention or do it. Get a publicity plan worked out. Even if sometimes you can't afford a publicist, it doesn't hurt to have a chat, and get some advice.

*Orlando - A film where the photographic images were so strong, they're still in use today with reference to British films.*

PRE-PRODUCTION

# The National Lottery Fund

## The Arts Council Of England

***Q - How much money is available from the National Lottery for film makers?***

***Arts Council -*** Impossible to say because the Arts Council is not allowed to ear-mark specific amounts of money for film or anything else. So far, the most that has been awarded is £1.5m for a film based on *Hardy's* novel *The Woodlanders,* down to £12k for a short film. Around thirty productions have received funding. The total amount awarded is £15.7m.

***Q - What's the criteria for your involvement?***

***Arts Council -*** There are a number of government directives - three of the policy directives apply to film - the first one relates to public good. The Arts Council cannot give money that is exclusively for private gain, it must take the public good into account. Second is financial viability - the applicant must demonstrate that the project is financially viable. The third is partnership funding, there must be at least 50% funding from some other source. There is another criteria that isn't in the directives but is a policy of the Arts Council - the film must qualify under the Films Act of 1985 as a British Film. The money is only available to films that are intended for cinema release, not just for television and video and the applicants must explain how the project will be of benefit to the public.

***Q - So there has to be some intrinsic public value to the film, how can that be interpreted - could it just be that it will be a good film and lots of people will enjoy it?***

***Arts Council -*** Yes, and other people have interpreted it as meaning that it should be a film with some sort of intelligence, something to say for itself, some integrity.

***Q - So to get your involvement a Producer must have at least 50% partnership funding upfront and you would supply the other 50%?***

***Arts Council -*** Could, there's nothing automatic about it.

***Q - Is it more likely that if they come to you with 70% in place, the 30% is going to be more available?***

***Arts Council -*** No, not really. It depends where the money is coming from - in reaching its decision, the Arts Council takes advice from a number of sources. If the advice is that the film doesn't need

Lottery money because the partners in the project could wholly fund the film. For example, if it's clearly a commercial project with big names attached to it, then the likelihood is that they wouldn't get the Lottery money. If the partnership money is from industry sources, but are the sort of partners who wouldn't really be able to fund the whole project, that's a plus for the film because it's got market money in it. If all the money in place came from non industry sources, then there might be a question mark against the project.

***Q - How does a film maker make an application?***

***Arts Council -*** They fill in a form that we send them. The turn around for a decision is generally three to four months.

***Q - What are the terms of the investment?***

***Arts Council -*** In principle it is a grant - but the directives also say that in certain circumstances the money should be repaid, generally, if the film generates money - then the Arts Council expects to get a share in the proceeds. Normal industry rules will apply, so if there's a bank loan, the bank almost always gets paid first. The Arts Council would also expect to have a share in the profits (if there are any), alongside other funders.

***Q - Do you support very low-budget films?***

***Arts Council -*** Yes, the Arts Council has a film budgeted at £118,000 that's been offered money.

***Q - What can an applicant do to improve their chances?***

***Arts Council -*** Taking the questions on the application form seriously is important. Some forms have been filled in a very cavalier manner, where people seem to think they merely have to sign their names to get the money. That is not a prudent approach, so presentation will help, and I don't mean that in a superficial sense of a typed application scoring more points than a hand-written one, but take it seriously and give the information that's asked for.

***Q - So to recap, the money that you're talking about, is not development money, or speculative investment, but top up money, somebody who needs that extra push to get into production?***

***Arts Council -*** I think if we're contributing 1/3 of the budget, or even 1/2, I wouldn't say it was top up money, but yes, there must be some partnership money in place when the application comes in, or a very firm indication that money is going to be forthcoming.

***Q - What basic advice would you offer a film maker for him to be successful?***

***Arts Council -*** I would say timing, when to send in the application form, is important. They've got to bear in mind that there is going to be a delay until they get a yes or a no.

FOOTNOTE - As this book goes to press, the Lottery Fund for feature films is still in its pilot year and there may be changes to the scheme. Please check with the Arts Council. (Winter '96)

# First Film Foundation
## Ivan Mactaggart

***Q - What is the First Film Foundation?***

***Ivan -*** The First Film Foundation is a registered educational charity that was set up in 1987 to provide training and guidance to new film makers trying to get into the Film and TV industry. It works primarily with first time writers, producers and directors, working mainly on feature film and TV drama projects. We help those people get their first films made. Unfortunately, we can't invest any cash whatsoever into productions, however, we can offer help in other important areas.

***Q - What services do you offer?***

***Ivan -*** We've been through a lot of changes recently and not all our services are up to speed. The first one is our New Directions programme - we select half a dozen new film makers who have made outstanding short films in the last couple of years, and take them to the States (two weeks in New York and LA) to show their films and introduce them to the industry with the aim of moving their first feature projects closer to production. We introduce them to a variety of people; producers, distributors, studios, managers, but it's the agents who are the most important as they provide a longer term connection to the industry over there. Last year we took eight people in total; five directors, two producers and one cameraman - the mix of the group depends on the people who come to us.

***Q - How does a new film maker apply for this 'course'?***

***Ivan -*** They fill in our application form, outlining what they have done and the feature film project they have in development, and they return that form with a copy of their short film and send their feature script if they are shortlisted. If you've got a great short but no features in development, we wouldn't take you, likewise, if you had a great feature in development but no short to demonstrate what you can do, we wouldn't take you. There is also a £1,000 fee to help cover flights and accommodation etc. The whole trip costs us about £5000 per person to run - it's heavily subsidised by Panavision. Selection takes place at the end of September.

***Q - And have you had any success stories?***

***Ivan -*** Yes, among others we took Andrzej Sekula over to the States on the New Directions course, he got representation and subsequently shot *Reservoir Dogs* and *Pulp Fiction.*

***Q - What other services do you offer?***

***Ivan -*** We have other services including the Script Feedback Service - you submit a feature length script and within four weeks you will get a fully detailed readers report. We'll break down what's good, what's bad, how to improve it and give an assessment of whether the script is ready to find support elsewhere, and if it is, what avenues might be taken. There is a £25 fee to help cover costs for this service. Also, we occasionally run short or one day courses on various aspects of film production, from writing to using film software like Movie Magic.

***Q - What films have you been involved in?***

***Ivan -*** We were involved in *Leon The Pig Farmer,* where Gary Sinyor was working out of First Film Foundation as a producer for some time, Richard Holmes and Stefan Schwartz, who did *Soft Top Hard Shoulder* had an office at the First Film Foundation. First Film Foundation is generally involved more with film makers than specific productions.

***Q - So the people you are able to assist are people who've produced a short film?***

***Ivan -*** These days I'd say probably yes. Writers we can work with from scratch, if somebody writes a brilliant script it doesn't matter what they've done before. Producers will have to have produced something, directors will have to have directed something. Otherwise there are just too many people out there and we just can't tell who is talented and would benefit from our support. It may be that they've done work through workshops, a lot of people come to us through film school, some people come to us straight from the street and they've just got together and made a short independently, there are all kinds of different routes. All we need is that somebody brings us some kind of experience that shows us that they can benefit from our support.

***Q - What advice would you offer first filmmakers?***

***Ivan -*** There's no universal bit of advice, there's no universal answer and there's no easy way. Do your research, know who does what, find out how everything works, spend time in a library reading the trade publications, just so that you know how things operate. Be prepared to work extremely hard. The thing that everybody's looking for is something that's new and exciting, something they haven't thought of before. Remember, nobody really knows what they want or what they're looking for so it's important you cling to whatever unique vision you have and stand behind it with confidence (as it could take years to get to the screen). Perseverance & self belief ultimately get you through.

*Footnote: The FFF is in a transitional period. Please contact the office for up to date information on any of these schemes, and for information of any new schemes.*

# Actors Agent Jeremy Conway
## Of Conway, van Gelder & Robinson Ltd

***Q - What is an agents job?***

***Jeremy -*** An agents job is to get actors work, to create a career, to try and get the actors to work with the best directors and do the best projects.

***Q - Does an agent act as a buffer between the production company and the performer?***

***Jeremy -*** To some degree, but if an actor behaves badly on set, you're the one who has to sort it out. If an actor has a serious problem, they can tell us and we can do our best to sort it out. We also take care of all the negotiating and contracts which could be both embarrassing and problematic if an actor were to do that themselves.

***Q - With what would you supply an interested producer?***

***Jeremy -*** Initially a CV and photo, and if they have one, a showreel.

***Q - How soon before principal photography would you expect to be approached?***

***Jeremy -*** To do a deal on the actor? I think one gets less time these days but one can get everything done and sorted out with a months notice - more than that I think is a mistake.

***Q - What's your usual response if you find out the film is low-budget?***

***Jeremy -*** If it's a good script it doesn't matter. There's an awful lot of low-budget films with poor scripts in which I'm not interested, but if there is a wonderful script with absolutely no money, I would much rather an actor did that, than a major movie that's not very good for a lot of money. Certainly, I think English actors appreciate that, and would rather do a quality film than rubbish for bucks. A lot of new film makers believe their scripts are wonderful, but often I don't share their enthusiasm, so it is important for them to remember that if I say I don't think it's suitable, it's not because I don't want an actor to do a low-budget film, it's because I believe the script is below par. Everything stems from the screenplay - if it is good, everyone believes in it and most of your problems are over.

***Q - There is a myth in film making that the agent is simply an obstacle to get around. How would you feel about film makers who contact an actor directly, either by phoning them or sending a screenplay?***

**Jeremy -** If an actor meets film makers socially and they chat and it all works out then fine, but I know actors do not appreciate getting phone calls from desperate film makers. Nor do they like getting their post box filled with wannabe scripts.

***Q - If the budget is very low, what can a producer do to make you more interested in a project?***

**Jeremy** - All sorts of things, they can offer percentages of the gross afterwards, although they are not often in a position to do that. They can give really good billing or they can defer payments.

***Q - What are the main problems dealing with a low-budget production?***

**Jeremy -** There are basic things like transport, expecting an actor to get up at four o'clock in the morning and catch a tube to Neasden to start filming. I just say that is not on, it is the producers job to provide transport. An awful lot of low-budget films are being made by first time film makers who have no real background you can check up on so I just have to go with my gut feeling. They've just got to be honest to make you trust them.

***Q - If producers do not come to you directly, where should they advertise the jobs that are available?***

**Jeremy -** We keep an eye on most industry journals and will always investigate a new production. I look at both *Screen International* and *Variety*. You could also put information in newsletters like PCR or SBS and whilst I do not usually look at them, many other agents do.

***Q - Would it be a good idea for them to come and meet you?***

**Jeremy -** Absolutely. I'd be very wary of sending an actor off to a very low-budget film with people I've never heard of and never met.

***Q - What are the main concerns of an actor, especially if the budget is low?***

**Jeremy -** They're not being paid a lot of money so what they do want is comfort. I think pushing them all into the same car to take them to the location is not what you want to do because they need that time to be quiet, to think about what they are doing. Nor do you want to put them up in crummy hotels. I know it's difficult because the money should be on the screen, but I think the actors comfort is something that is often forgotten. Basic things like no chairs to sit on, no umbrellas if its pouring with rain, no tents - the sort of things which often don't cost very much. Everyone else on the set is busy most of the time, rushing around doing things, but often, the actor isn't doing much and is waiting for the next scene to happen. A green room is ideal, a place where they can sit and

**Conway, van Gelder, Robinson Ltd**

Jeremy Conway

18-21 Jermyn Street
London SW1Y 6HP
Tel 0171 287 0077
Fax 0171 287 1940

PRODUCTION

concentrate on what they are doing without being distracted by the crew. Somewhere warm, dry and quiet, even a kettle with tea and coffee can be so easily forgotten.

***Q - What is your worst experience of a low-budget film?***

***Jeremy -*** A client of mine made a film in Scotland that has never seen the light of day - it was an absolute nightmare. They hadn't scheduled anything, so he never knew if they wanted him the next day or not, that is until 10 o'clock at night - even then, they might not use him the next day as arranged. I think the most important thing is the pre planning, making sure everything is worked out well in advance and they know what they are shooting each day. Obviously things can go wrong and no-one expects any less, but one has to know what one is doing, when and where. Actors get cross if they don't know what's happening and they feel they've been mucked around, especially if they turn up and then they're not used.

***Q - How is payment usually made on a film?***

***Jeremy -*** Usually it's weekly cheques, one week in arrears. Sometimes, especially on the continent, they like to do a sum up front, then one in the middle and one after the shooting is over. I would prefer to get a regular weekly cheque. Of course other agents may well prefer a whole chunk up front, it's up to the individual deal. Also, there is the per diem - It's a sum of money that is agreed between the agent and producer for living expenses. Normally, on location the hotel is paid and some sort of per diem for the actors to buy food, lunch and dinner. Obviously it varies between £10 per day, to stars who get hundreds and thousands of dollars per diem. It's above and beyond the salary, and is agreed at the time of the contract.



***Q - What are the main areas in the contract that you would be looking to nail down?***

***Jeremy -*** Definitive dates. On a low-budget production, if an actor is doing just a couple of days, I would really like the days to be nominated rather than on or about. Billing is very difficult to negotiate and terribly important for the actor. On low-budget films, when actors aren't being paid very much, I try and make sure that everyone's on favoured nations (which is when the actors get the same, nobody is going to get more). If an actor is taking a big cut in salary and suddenly discovers that one of his contemporaries is getting a lot more, it can become very difficult, but if it's favoured nations there is no argument.

***Q - What is The Spotlight?***

***Jeremy -*** It's a directory of professional

## Never Work With Children Or Animals

*Anyone under 16 (who has not completed the school term following their 16th birthday) requires a licence to act. Licences are NOT required for children who work less than 3 days within a 6 month period.*

*Licences are obtained from the child's local education authority. These licenses list numerous requirements with regard to child employment, including hours of work, education, rest periods, meals, accommodation & matrons.*

*The use of animals on a production is governed by the Protection of Animals Act 1911, the Cinematograph Films (Animals) Act 1937, The Dangerous Wild Animals Act 1976, The Wildlife & Countryside Act 1981, relevant quarantine laws & The Royal Society for the Prevention of Cruelty to Animals (RSPCA).*



actors and actresses, stuntmen, young actors and the like. It is the main point of reference for agents and producers as I can say, turn to page one thousand and twenty to see a photo. I believe it is being released on CD Rom for computers too.

***Q - What can a Producer do to make your life easier?***

***Jeremy -*** I think being honest and absolutely straightforward. You know when people aren't telling the truth - when I ask, *'is so and so's client getting more than our client?'* and the reply is, *'well no, not exactly'* - *'well, what do you mean?'* - the answer - *'well, I can't say.'* You just want them to be straightforward and honest and say, *'well yes they are getting more money, because they're doing 6 weeks more work on it'.* I just think that good honesty in this business pays off in the long run. Agents all talk to one another and confer on deals. An awful lot of producers, especially young producers who are starting out, have very little respect for rather senior, well known actors, and expect to meet them without even giving them a script. The actor thinks *'why should I, I've never heard of this person'.* Producers should be careful not to sound too arrogant - if they are trying to get a star to work for them, they should be extremely respectful.

## The Spotlight

*Spotlight produce several directories including actors, actresses, stuntmen, North American actors (In the UK), ethnic background actors, actors with disabilities, children, new actors...Traditionally, these publications were only available as a set of books that when stacked measure more than two feet! However, most of their information is now available of a couple of wafer thin CDROMs for computer systems. Contact the Spotlight for pricing information.*

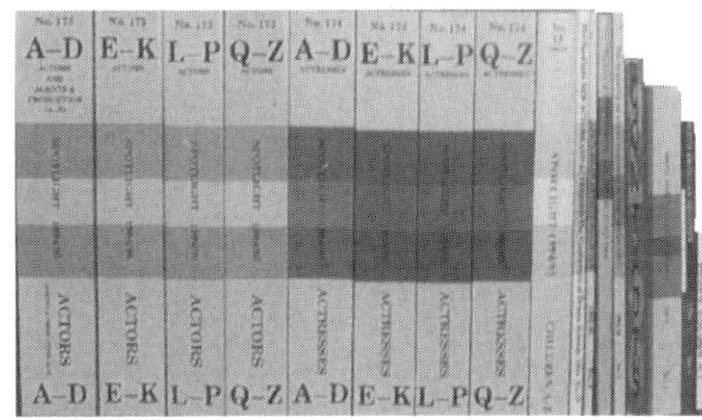

# Film Stock
# Roger Sapsford
## Of Fuji Film

***Q - What different gauges are available for film makers to make a feature film?***

***Roger*** - 16mm, Super 16mm and 35mm. 16mm is not really used for features now, but that is not to say that it cannot be used, it is just that Super 16mm is much better at the job. However, 35mm is the international feature film standard format.

***Q - What's the difference between 16mm and Super 16mm?***

***Roger*** - The only difference between 16mm and Super 16mm is that Super 16mm is perforated on one side only - Standard 16mm is perforated on both sides. The Super 16mm format allows for the picture area to be exposed to the absolute edge of the non perforated side which when blown up to 35mm (aspect ratio of 1:185) gives 40% more visual screening area than standard 16mm. So you could say the negative yields 40% more usable picture area whilst staying on a 16mm compatible gauge.

***Q - What length is 16mm delivered in?***

***Roger*** - The standard lengths are 400 foot and 100 foot rolls. For special purposes, we can supply it in 1000 foot rolls, but this is very unusual. 400 foot lasts about 11 minutes at 25fps.

***Q - What is film speed?***

***Roger*** - The film speed or ASA relates to the latitude against failing light. To put it simply, the higher the ASA, the less light is needed to properly expose the negative. Daylight photography with harsh sunshine would cope admirably with the slower speeds of stock, for instance the 64 or 125 ASA. Other speeds like 250 ASA can also be used for daylight exterior photography but can also be used for twilight or dusk. There are higher speeds such as 500 ASA stock which is mainly used for night photography where there are very low light levels.

***Q - Am I correct in saying, the slower the speed of the film, i.e. the lower the ASA, the less grainy the film looks?***

***Roger*** - Yes, to some degree. As little as five years ago a cameramen would select lower speeds

to keep the grain finer, as opposed to choosing higher speed with increased grain. However in the last five years, things have changed and high speed stocks have improved dramatically. Several factors have brought that about, one of which is demand from productions with restricted budgets and low light levels.

***Q - What is the best average all round stock for shooting in Britain?***

***Roger -*** From a personal point of view, I would go for the mid range 200 to 250 ASA but other cameramen may select another speed like the 125 ASA. That is true for both 16mm formats and 35mm.

***Q - What does the colour balance of film mean?***

***Roger -*** All light has a colour, interior light bulbs are 'orangey' whereas natural daylight is 'blueish'. Your brain can make adjustments for your eyes, but a camera can't adjust the film stock. There are two kinds of film stock, *Tungsten* which is generally used for shooting indoors with lights, and *Daylight* which is generally used outdoors for shooting in natural light. Different lights also have different colour temperatures or colour balance. *Tungsten* balanced stock is designed for use with tungsten lights - If you have selected HMI lights then it would generally be accepted that you use a *Daylight* base stock because of the colour temperature of these lights. HMI lights colour temperature is a lot higher than the tungsten and they yield a very daylight looking light.

***Q - If you find yourself having to shoot with tungsten stock whilst filming outside, or daylight stock whilst shooting inside (with tungsten lights), what can be done?***

***Roger*** - With tungsten stock outside one should always use a WRATTEN 85 filter on the camera (which should be supplied with every camera kit), otherwise known as a Daylight filter. This filter changes the 'colour' of the light entering the lens and exposing the negative. It isn't the end of the world if the filter is not used - indeed there are some leading photographers who do not use that filter and still get a lovely result. The negative is technically exposed incorrectly, but once it is graded at the labs, it falls within the realms of acceptability. You can also change the colour temperature of the lights by using specially coloured gels on the front of the lights, but this limits your latitude.

***Q - What are the advantages of shooting 35mm over Super 16mm?***

***Roger -*** 35mm is a global standard gauge that's recognised instantly. Super 16mm isn't (unless it is subsequently blown up to 35mm). Plus the negative is two and a half times bigger, sharper and also has two and a half times less grain on screen.

PRODUCTION

# Film Stock Formats

(Actual Size)

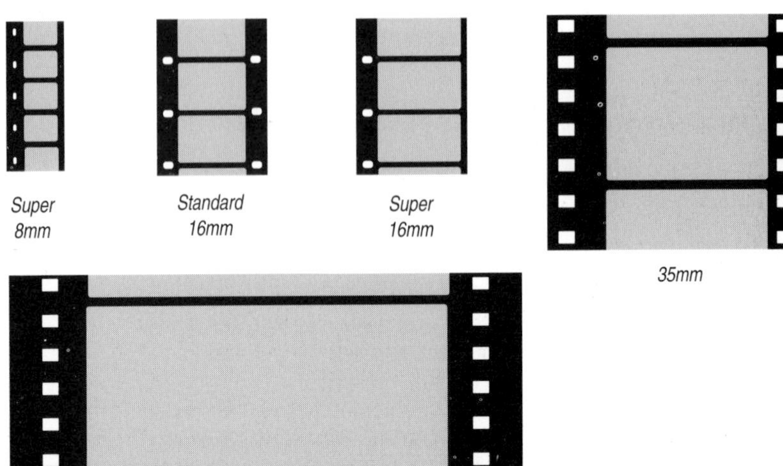

## Film Stock Weight Including Cans

| | 100 foot | 400 foot | 1000 foot |
|---|---|---|---|
| 16mm | 200grms | 500 grms | N/A |
| 35mm | N/A | 1kg | 2.5kg |

## Film Stock Storage Temperature

| | Up to 52 weeks |
|---|---|
| Colour negative | 10°C / 50°F |
| Black & White | 13°C / 53°F |

## Film Acclimatisation Times (Approx)

| From Fridge | Warm Up Time | |
|---|---|---|
| | 16mm | 35mm |
| 10°C /50°F | 120+ mins | 6 hours + |

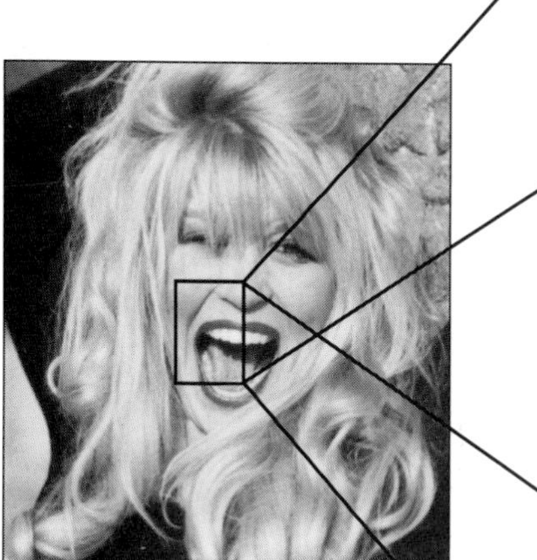

*Lower ASA speed with decreased granular structure.*

*Graininess is in essence an aesthetic quality. There is no practical point where an image becomes too grainy, however, many people do find increased grain unacceptable. Grain structure also takes on different qualities depending upon lighting and incorrect exposure (which has been subsequently corrected)*

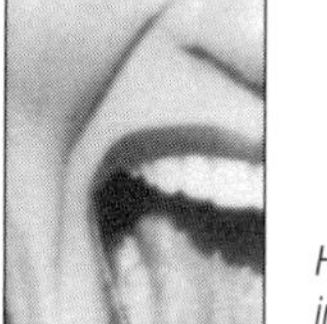

*Higher ASA speed with increased granular structure.*



***Q - What are the main problems shooting Super 16mm and blowing up to 35mm?***

**Roger -** When blown up, Super 16mm is very good. It's economic to shoot Super 16mm, but as step printing is so expensive, it's possible you could have shot on 35mm for the same price, if not cheaper. It could be a false economy.

***Q - In what length is 35mm delivered?***

**Roger** - 35mm comes in 100 foot, 200 foot, 400 foot and 1000 foot lengths. 1000 foot lasts about 11 minutes at 25fps. The ASA speeds are also the same as 16mm and Super 16mm.

***Q - What are the commonest problems with stocks?***

**Roger** - Long term storage outside the manufacturers warehouse. The life of the base negative can be affected by long exposure to heat whilst still in its tin. In places of high temperature like the desert, faults with the negative could occur because of the extreme heat. Always store the negative in the way the manufacturer recommends on the tin i.e. In a fridge.

***Q - Once film is exposed, must it be processed as quickly as possible?***

**Roger** - No, it can stay as long as a year without any problem as long as its kept at room temperature and doesn't go over 60° Fahrenheit. However, it is advisable to process exposed footage as soon as possible.

## 16MM & SUPER 16MM BLOW UP TO 35MM

(NOT ACTUAL SIZE)

*Standard 16mm - Only the middle part of the negative can be blown up to 35mm losing some 20% at the top and bottom of the frame.*

*Super 16mm occupies a wider negative which can be completely blown up to 35mm without loss. The combination of a larger negative and NO part of the image being cropped away yields 40% more negative to blow up to 35mm*

*35mm theatrical print with 1:185 aspect ration. The Super 16mm aspect ratio fits comfortably whereas the standard 16mm has to be cropped at the top and bottom which limits further the amount of negative that can be blown up to 35mm.*



***Q - Is the X ray machine at airports a film makers myth?***

***Roger -*** In places like Heathrow and New York you are fine, you can go back and forth through the X ray machine eight or nine times without any problem, but the machines that are based in third world countries may not be so safe. It's most dangerous in places that are far flung outposts with equipment we used to have 30 years ago. The problem is that they can adjust the level of X-rays emitted - if they come across a can they may just whack it up to full power - if you were using 100 ASA stock, that still isn't too much of a problem, but with the faster stocks, like 500 ASA, the possibility of damage is much more significant. The higher the ASA, the more susceptible the stock is to X rays. Even if a customs official is still unconvinced and opens the can you should be alright because inside is a non reflective black bag wrapping the stock in such a fashion that daylight cannot penetrate it. But if he insists on opening the bag, then you've got a problem.

***Q - On a low-budget film people are tempted to use outdated stock - is there any way a producer can be confident that this stock is fine?***

***Roger*** - If you are in doubt about the stock, you could send it in for a clip test. The laboratory would cut off 15 feet from the end of a roll and produce a gamma test which would determine whether the stock was still within the realms of commercial acceptability.

***Q - If one roll was all OK, would be safe to assume that the whole batch would be OK, as long as they were all stored together?***

***Roger*** - If they were all stored together with the manufacturer, then yes. If not with the manufacturer, then not necessarily - it would be wrong to assume that all the cans were OK, but it would be a fair bet.

***Q - At the beginning of rushes, I see a colour chart - what is that?***

***Roger*** - The colour chart is put on the front of each camera negative roll to assist in rushes grading at the labs - it ensures that the labs are printing the way the cameraman had intended. We can supply those charts to a production, as well as the labs.

***Q - What are edge numbers?***

***Roger*** - The edge numbers are a series of numbers generated at the time of manufacturing the stock. These numbers are unique to any particular roll and are used when negative cutting. All stocks now carry digital bar codes which are an electronic edge number. These are used to speed up post production and are mainly used with non linear editing systems.

***Q - Does Fuji do deals for bulk purchase?***

***Roger*** - Every single purchase is different - it depends whether you're a long standing customer, a new customer, a low-budget, medium budget or even God forbid a higher budget film. Everyone is different. The trend has been to help the low-budget film makers with cash deals, obviously that would affect the discount a great deal.

***Q - What common mistakes have you experienced with regard to selection of stock?***

***Roger*** - The main problem I have encountered is that of pressure when a new cameraman is given his first bite of the cherry. He's under enormous pressure to make the right decisions and choose the right stock - half way through that decision may have been proven to be the wrong stock but it's too late then.



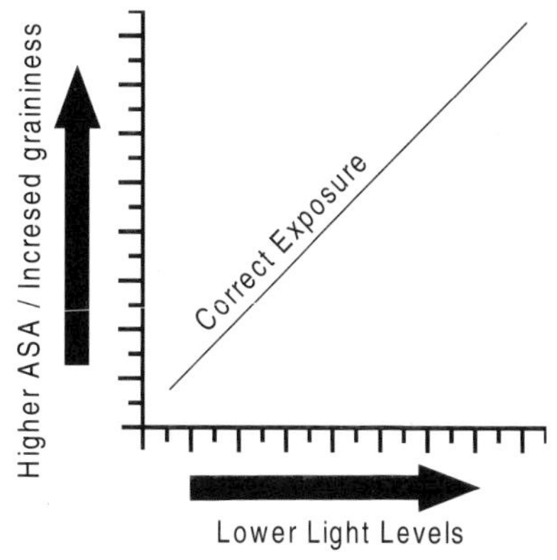


THE RELATIONSHIP BETWEEN ASA AND LIGHT LEVELS REQUIRED FOR CORRECT EXPOSURE

# Camera Hire Simon Broad of ARRI Media

***Q - When a producer comes to you to hire a basic kit, what does it contain?***

***Simon -*** For Drama, it doesn't really vary between 35mm and Super 16mm, it's always going to be a sync sound camera, possibly a second body for insurance, a set of prime lenses and nearly always a zoom, the filters are going to be reasonably standard; head, tripods and by and large a video assist.

***Q - From a hire point of view, what is the difference between Super 16mm and 35mm?***

***Simon -*** The cost of hiring Super 16mm is going to be around two thirds the price of 35mm kit. There's a lot of commonality between Super 16mm and 35mm so Super 16mm isn't always as cheap as people think.

***Q - When you say sometimes you hire two bodies for insurance purposes, would that mean that essentially that production had access to two camera bodies?***

***Simon -*** The Camera crew are looking at the second camera body and thinking second camera - we're looking at it thinking that it's supposed to be there for insurance, the production are taking it because they can't answer to the insurance company for a failure in Outer Mongolia. But it's inevitable that the director is going to ask for it to cover something. Also, if the production is using Steadicam (which can take a long time to setup) they can setup with the second camera body, then there isn't a major down time.

***Q - Is Steadicam usually something you hire with an operator?***

***Simon -*** We don't hire Steadicam - they're usually owned by the operators. I think its much better when it's user is the owner operator. Yes, Steadicam could be a great idea but it's going to cost time in getting it ready. If you have a guy who knows absolutely everything, it's not such a concern. We hold lists of people who hire Steadicam and other specialised kit.

***Q - Is there a limit to how much you can use a steadicam operator in a day?***

***Simon -*** I think it depends on the individual. Some of them are up and running for the whole day and they're fine about it - others aren't going to make it. I think a lot of inexperienced film makers would love to think about shooting an entire feature film on Steadicam, but from a lighting point of view that would be a nightmare, so they'll probably be talked out of it.

***Q - What's the best, most versatile, yet cost effective camera?***

***Simon -*** An SR2 which is converted to Super 16mm - it can take all the lenses any other camera can and they're very quiet. I think it's harder to go cheaper than that and get away with it. Additionally, you'd be looking at four prime lenses, zoom, head, legs and then you're wrestling about how many filters, because filters can cost - so you battle about how many filters are really needed.

***Q - In terms of lenses, what are the extremes?***

***Simon -*** Thanks to stills work, we can plunder stills photography lenses. For 16mm or 35mm you can now go from the most extreme fisheye - if you've got big ears as the operator then they're in shot - all the way to something that allows you to photograph someone on the next hill.

***Q - How well does an Arri SR2 handle slow motion?***

***Simon -*** A regular SR2 will go to 75 fps (frames per second), so you're effectively going three times the normal speed. A high speed SR2 will go to 150 fps. Beyond 150 fps, you're in to specialised high speed cameras and photosonics. As a general rule, 35mm sync cameras don't like going more than 50fps. You can also do stop motion with an SR2, if you have an extra bit of kit.

***Q - How quiet are cameras now?***

***Simon -*** They are very acceptable now. Whenever there is a real problem, they can be muffled with the supplied soft blimp. The new SR3 doesn't seem to need anything - it may need a soft blimp every so often but nothing serious. 35mm is just as quiet.

***Q - How are cameras hired - by the week, the day or by the deal with overages?***

***Simon -*** I think it's easier for the production manager if they have a figure and need the package to fit into that - at the end of the day we meet somewhere that works for us all.

***Q - Is it possible for the DP to come in and shoot tests with that camera?***

***Simon -*** Every company should encourage the DP to familiarise themselves with a camera or lens they've not used before. They should also encourage the camera technicians to do the same, so that on the day there are fewer phonecalls when the buttons are confusing, or the lacing has gone wrong.

***Q - What is video assist?***

***Simon -*** It's an adapter on the film camera that has a video camera in it, allowing the director to see what is being shot on a video monitor. We

have a real pain in this country with the broadcasting laws which mean that we're legally bound to drag a cable around (between camera and video monitor). Some people will use wireless systems, but in theory it's illegal because there's a broadcasting block - if it's happening one has to turn a blind eye.

***Q - So it is technically possible to connect a £25 video sender to the camera, run down to Tandys and buy a 4" Casio portable TV with a 3' aerial and the director can sit there with it in his pocket?***

***Simon -*** Yes, I'm sure it can be done. To be honest with you, dragging that cable about is ridiculous - it's the only thing that makes a film camera land locked. The great thing about a film camera, especially an SR2 with a battery hooked on the back, is that it's totally user friendly. You can pick it up and run around with it, you're not connected to anything. There's no umbilical cord - the only one is that damn video cable and it needs a runner to make sure it's out of the dolly tracks etc.



***Q - Should you not have the confidence in the team around you to get it right without a video assist to slow you down?***

***Simon -*** A lot of people have come from commercials, music videos or television and know no other way - they haven't got the confidence yet, to work with the actor and watch the performance because they are used to seeing it on a small screen, that's their term of reference.

***Q - What's your policy for insurance?***

***Simon -*** We encourage the production company to insure and would always ask to see an insurance certificate that covers loss or damage, plus 13 weeks loss of hire. Filters are always a problem as some inevitably get damaged - it's so easy. They cost around £120 each, so that's a major issue. There's always going to be something that's damaged and it would be a good idea for the producer to ear-mark some money (say £500) to pay for them when the production is over. Hopefully, it won't be needed, but it probably will. If the damage is serious, the insurance will then cover it.

***Q - What are your thoughts about just nipping down to the local Camera shop and buying a £6 gelatine filter?***

*The camera team is encouraged to go to the hire facility to shoot tests and familiarise themselves with the kit before finding out the hard way in the field.*

**Simon -** It's whatever works for the DP - people are still trying to find those DL stockings that are no longer made, but produced wonderful images years ago. If it works, why not?

***Q - On a low-budget picture, the use of stock is going to come down to who is the cheapest. Do stocks vary in quality?***

**Simon -** From a mechanical point of view, we feel Kodak is the most reliable because of their resources. It doesn't mean to say it helps the DP who may have the 'look' he wants from other emulsions.

***Q - What are your terms for payment?***

**Simon -** When it comes to a drama, there's usually very little trading history, so we have to take that into consideration. If you're able to work your cash flow (so you're offering a lump of money), I've got to be honest, it sounds very attractive.

***Q - What can a producer do to make your life easier?***

**Simon -** Be completely straight about what money they've got and cut to the chase. It's also important to be clear and organised about additional rentals - it's easy to agree a package and put it on paper so everyone knows what the main unit contains. But there's always going to be a second camera, the wild camera, the long lens etc. We had an incident with a film recently - the director always got what he wanted. Only now do they realise that they can't afford it - they've had so much second camera hire that they've blown it.

***Q - So it's a good idea to have an agreement with a member of production, not the director or the DP, that they'll have a definitive list and no more?***

**Simon -** Absolutely. We'll never take an order from crew - we always go back to production for them to sanction the hire.

***Q - Any final comments?***

**Simon -** On a low-budget, always seriously consider shooting 35mm before deciding on Super 16mm, as the hire costs aren't much more, but the advantages are enormous.

# Lighting Hire Eddie Dias of Michael Samuelson Lighting

PRODUCTION

***Q - What would be a good, basic lighting kit?***

***Eddie -*** The BBC used to have the best idea, they used to give a fixed package to the cameraman and send him off to shoot on location - *six weeks and there's your lights.* It really shouldn't be any different with feature films. The lighting cameraman had a 60Kw package including a large source, either a 12k or 6k, a couple of 4ks, four 1.2ks, a couple of 5.75ks, that's the HMI package - and the tungsten package may be two baby 5ks, four baby 2ks, four to six pups, some small lights, mizars, blondes, redheads - and that would cover them for all eventualities. They would also take a 60kw generator.

***Q - With that lighting set up, what kind of personnel do you need to service it?***

***Eddie -*** You could have a two person camera crew, camera operator (lighting cameraman) and camera assistant, who would pull focus and clapperload. You're going to have the gaffer, chief electrician and the best boy. The gaffer usually sits on the cameraman's shoulder, the cameraman explains what he actually wants and the gaffer will relay that to his electricians and tell them what they need. The best boy's job is to liaise between the lighting office and the production office, making sure he's got adequate crew, cranes are going to be there in place etc. - making sure that they're covered for all eventualities. If extra equipment needs to be ordered, the gaffer doesn't need to be tied up ordering it, that's the best boy's job.

***Q - So in terms of servicing the lighting you're going to have a Gaffer, Best Boy, plus two or three sparks?***

***Eddie -*** Yes, one of those sparks will be driving the lighting vehicle and one driving and operating the generator.

***Q - Would you normally have a generator with that kind of kit?***

***Eddie -*** Yes. You're not always going to be able to plug into the mains. Plus, many lights just can't be plugged into a socket on the wall. If you want to use all your lights at one time, you can do that

with a generator without having to worry about a good solid electric source.

***Q - And you supply the sparks as part of your package?***

***Eddie -*** Yes, we have to by law. Once you get to a vehicle that's over 3.5 tonnes, which is basically a transit van, you then have to have a license to operate heavy goods vehicles - so every 7.5 or 16 tonne vehicle is on our operator's licence. The people driving the vehicles are paid by us, the onus has to be shown to be on us from a safety point of view.

***Q - What's the situation if a producer hires out your people and they overrun?***

***Eddie -*** They carry on into overtime which would be paid at an agreed rate. The average daily rate is £141 - £185. If they're doing an extended day they have a set fee, if they're doing a night shoot, they have a set fee on top. It's always good to set up those parameters beforehand. We understand that films will sometimes overrun slightly, and if there's a bit of give and take, for instance if they finish early another time, we can be accommodating. As long as people are clear on that beforehand. People have lives outside the film industry. It may be very important to the producer and director, but an electrician, rigger, painter or a carpenter, isn't going to be taken on for their artistic abilities - to them it's just a job, at the end of the day they've got to bring the bacon home and put it on the table.

***Q - If we scale it down a bit, if we think small, what kind of lighting kit would you suggest to keep the costs down?***

***Eddie -*** We have made feature films on very tight budgets, but it's like going into a rent-a-car company and asking for a JAG with only £30 a day to spend. They'll turn round and give a bargain basement car, you've got to expect the same in equipment hire. We had a production come to us and said *we know we haven't got a lot but this is what we need.* I welcomed them to my bargain basement and told them that they could have anything they wanted from there. So they took it and four weeks later, the equipment came back and the film was made. They didn't do any special effects or high speed shots so they didn't have to worry about flicker free lighting or strobing.

***Q - What is flicker free lighting?***

***Eddie -*** If you're taking daylight lights - HMI's - you're susceptible, if you're changing camera speeds, to flicker. If you're shooting at 25fps there's no need to worry. Most productions now hire flicker free lighting which is obviously more expensive. For the lower budget films you can take non-flicker-free lights, they'll be cheaper to rent. If you do use more expensive flicker free lights, there is a ballast unit which gives you a high frequency hum. If your sound man says *we're getting a hum on the sound*, then we can supply special ballasts that don't hum.

***Q - With non-flicker-free lighting, can you run slow motion at all?***

***Eddie -*** Yes you can - what you do is adjust the shutter angle in the camera. A lot of cameraman are scared of doing this but there's a simple calculation you can do, and every cameraman should know this - after all, you're paying the cameraman for their expertise. For example, if you're shooting at 52.778 fps, then adjust the shutter angle to 190º, if you shoot at 40 fps, put your shutter angle at 144º.

***Q - Would you advise an inexperienced producer who has an inexperienced, artistic, cameraman to sit on him like a ton of bricks?***

***Eddie -*** Yes, or it will cost you. A lot of inexperienced cameramen want to be creative - but if you're on a low budget, you can't necessarily afford that. You need someone who is going to deliver the goods, to the technical standard needed, on time.

***Q - How does the process of booking and paying for lights work?***

***Eddie -*** Anybody who's waving money around, instead of asking for credit or thirty days, is going to get a good deal. The scary thing for us is somebody saying w*e're doing a low budget film* - immediately you tense up! (laughs). As soon as someone says low budget, it scares people - don't say low budget, say *we haven't got a big budget.*

***Q - What do you do about insurance?***

***Eddie -*** We ask the client to insure everything (plus 13 weeks loss of hire). Things do get broken

and lost, we're usually quite lenient on the odd bolt and screw and there are some things we can equate to wear and tear. But if something is blown over in the wind, then the production company has got to accept that damage. We also ask to see a certificate of insurance. We can insure the equipment, but we're not insurance specialists and we have to charge a premium rate. You'd probably be better off taking out your own insurance.

***Q - Does insurance cover bulbs?***

***Eddie -*** Yes, unless of course, the damage is through misuse. A 12k HMI bulb costs £2,000 and if they're misused or burnt incorrectly, it affects the bulbs life considerably.

***Q - And what are the most common mistakes that could be avoided?***

***Eddie -*** There are weekly consumables that the crew will go through. If the cameraman wants to adjust the colour (and colour temperature) of the lighting, he'll do that with CTB, blue transfer gels, orange transfer gels, neutral density gels, frosts and diffusers. When you're given a quote, 90% of the time, it's plus consumables. Always bear in mind that there are consumable costs on top of that - If you've got a generator and a truck and another truck, you've also got fuel to think of, which can be quite considerable. Even when crews are shooting in a studio, they often draw power from a generator as studio power is very expensive, sometimes five or six times more expensive than what comes out of the wall. We can give advice about how much should be budgeted for this kind of consumables. Don't be afraid to ask if you don't know something - if you ask a company for their advice they will give it to you open heartedly.

# Grips Mark Furssedonn

## Of The Grip House

*Grip House Limited are one of the biggest suppliers of Grip Equipment in the UK and they also have 5 studios on site. They have often designed new equipment for demanding shots and manufacture equipment on site. They have supplied equipment to both the biggest Hollywood features and the lowest budget UK 'wing and a prayer' movies.*



***Q - What is grip equipment?***

***Mark -*** It's all about camera support and movement. We can supply anything from a top hat so that you can get low shots, up to camera cranes which give you aerial shots looking down on the action. Essentially, we supply the equipment that allows the camera to move in a controlled manner.

***Q - What is the most versatile piece of grip equipment?***

***Mark -*** The camera dolly is the bread and butter of grips every day hire. It's basically a support which can run on track, or alternatively on rubber tyres, depending on the model. They are quite heavy and therefore very stable, producing smooth moving shots. Some models have hydraulic arms enabling the camera to be moved up and down in shot.

***Q - What is the most common piece of kit that is usually hired out for a low-budget film?***

***Mark -*** Most producers normally hire track and dolly.

***Q - Are there any particular extras that would be very useful?***

***Mark -*** There are many accessories, track being the most common. There are tongues which can

offset the camera, a snake arm which drops the camera down lower, small jib arms to give a crane effects etc. Most of the more technically advanced dollies come with a full set of accessories.

***Q - What size of van should be used to transport track and dolly?***

***Mark -*** A transit van.

***Q - What are your main considerations when hiring kit out from the Grips point of view?***

***Mark -*** I suppose the main one is who's using it - who the grip is. We generally know how good the grips are and you know that if you've got a good grip, you'll probably never hear from him from the first to the last day of the shoot - if he gets a problem, he solves it. Whereas the opposite applies to the less experienced grip - he'll be ringing every day asking questions. All our kit is in good condition when we send it out and it should return in that condition - unfortunately, it doesn't always return in good condition and sometimes we may have to make a charge if serious maintenance work is needed. The grip must maintain and service the kit to ensure that it stays in good working order.

***Q - What's your policy for insurance on the equipment?***

***Mark -*** The client has the option - they can take out our insurance which is charged on a percentage of the hire fee, or they can supply their own cover. In that case we will need to see documentary evidence as proof of cover. No equipment ever goes out without full cover. Generally, production companies supply their own cover. It is easier for them if they take our cover but I don't know how cost effective it would be. If it was a one off production then yes, probably more cost effective and easier for us to do the insurance.

***Q - What are the most common problems you have to sort out?***

***Mark -*** It depends who you get on the phone. With the producer, the most common problem is that they don't have enough money in their budget. The crew come to us with technical problems - something is not working - maybe they are not doing something correctly. We try to help wherever we can.

***Q - Does grip equipment differ between 16mm and 35mm?***

***Mark -*** No, that is the advantage of our equipment. We can put anything on it, any camera - 35mm, 16mm, video, all can be mounted. You would probably hire a slightly more lightweight dolly for 16mm than 35mm.

PRODUCTION

***Q - What other types of equipment can you supply?***

**Mark -** It's never ending really. We actually design equipment for specific shots so you could put a camera on the front of a roller coaster or on a camel's back for example. We have cranes, we put cameras on helicopters, we have put a crane on the back of a tracking car and driven down the motorway at high speed. The list is endless.

***Q - What kind of cranes are there?***

**Mark -** We have everything from a 9' to a 50' crane. Cost wise, the smaller the crane, the cheaper it is to hire. We also have electronic telescopic cranes which can telescope in and out during a shot. Nowadays, cranes tend to be used with a remote head instead of a camera man sitting on the end. The head is remote controlled and we can supply it as part of the package as well as the remote lens control. All our cranes have a dolly base which would run on track.

***Q - Cranes can be dangerous if abused, what is your policy?***

**Mark -** Our policy is that we would never send a crane out without one of our technicians. I would always advise that in addition to our technician the production company should supply two experienced grips but we can't stipulate that, only advise. At the end of the day, they are dangerous and we have people's lives in our hands. Because we have to pay the technician, it can make the hire of cranes more expensive than say dollies.

***Q - Give me a short run down of the different bits of kit***

**Mark -** The Fraser Camera Dolly is a Grip House design. It was designed by Dennis Fraser in order to compete with the American market which, until now, all hire companies have used. It is very different from the American counterparts and because we don't have to pay ongoing lease costs, we don't have to pass that cost onto the customer, so it's competitive to hire. It covers all cameras, 35mm, 16mm and video. As with all

PRODUCTION

dollies, track is extra and is hired in sections. The dolly comes as a package which includes comprehensive accessories.

The Super PeeWee is American and probably the most popular dolly at the moment. It is good for 35mm, 16mm and video shoots on both location and in the studio. It may be slightly lightweight for some 35mm cameras though.

The Panther is a German made dolly which is operated electrically and has a centre column that moves up and down so you can actually get up and down movement in shot (as you can with a Fraser and PeeWee). With the Panther, you can put a small crane on to get high shots at 12-14 feet which is quite an advantage.

***Q - An example of a small but useful piece of kit?***

***Mark -*** A turntable can be used to put a camera in the centre of a table for 360° pans.

***Q - What about vehicles?***

***Mark -*** We have car rigs and accessories and we can supply various types of rigs to mount the camera anywhere on a car, the bonnet, roof, looking at the wheel, looking at the bumper, the driver. Boats, trains, helicopters - we've done it all over the years. If we haven't got a rig to suit, then we'll build one for a specific shot.

There is also a range of tracking vehicles that are fully equipped with various mounts and platforms for the camera, and wherever needed, the crew. These are used for high speed car shoots, chasing horses down a race track etc. Some vehicles can also be mounted with cranes, again using the remote head, others just for a camera crew to sit on with the camera mounted on the tripod to shoot off the back of the vehicle. We supply a trained driver as it's very dangerous at high speeds.

***Q - What can a producer do to make your life easier?***

***Mark -*** A producer could have greater knowledge of the equipment available. In general they do not know enough about the current equipment and this has an affect when they're budgeting. Most

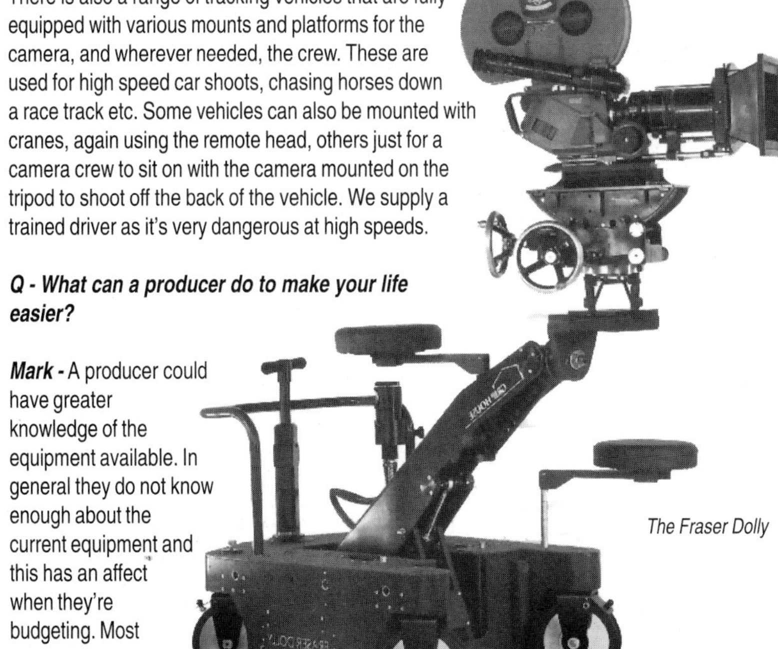

*The Fraser Dolly*

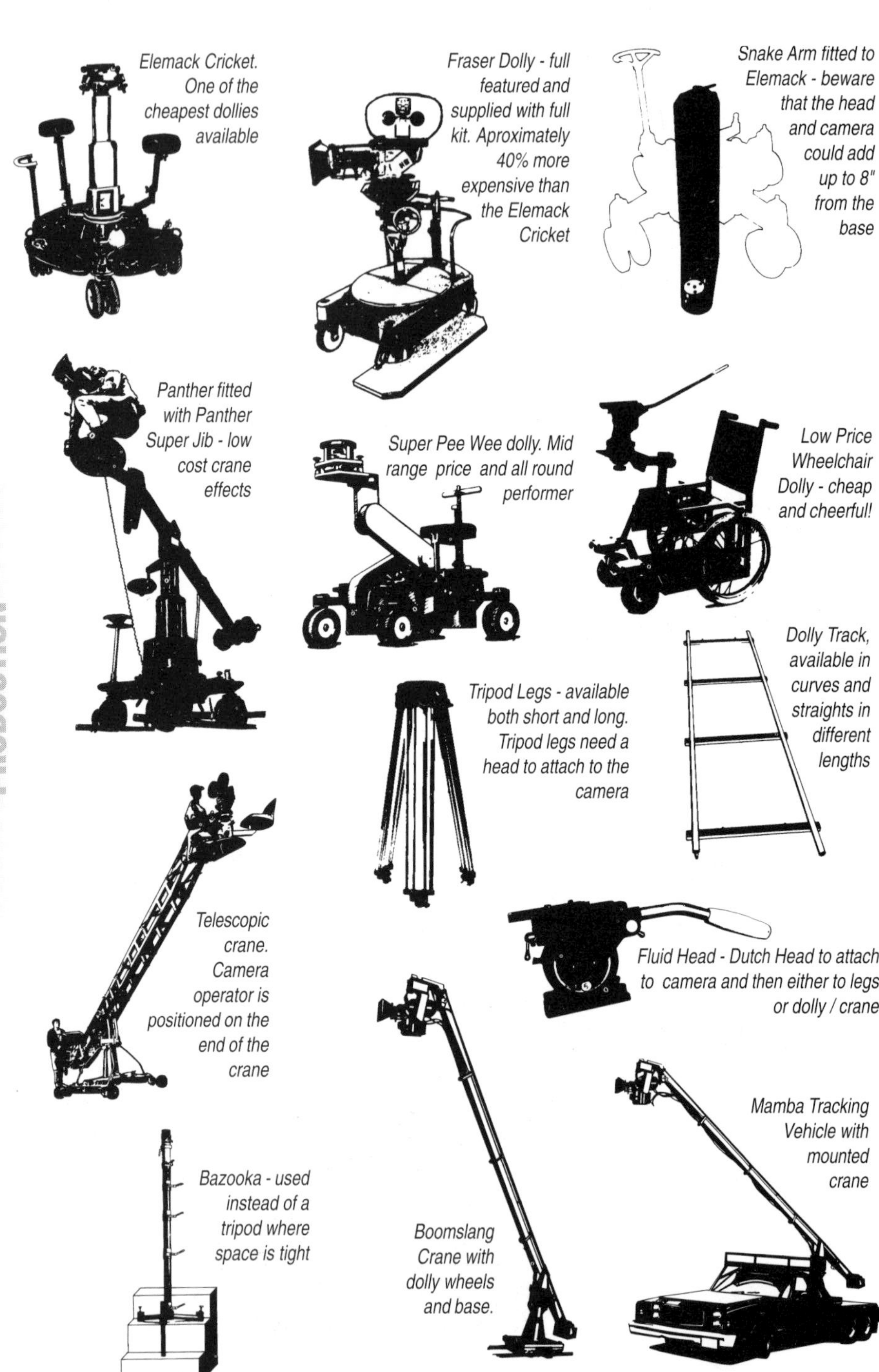

Elemack Cricket. One of the cheapest dollies available

Fraser Dolly - full featured and supplied with full kit. Aproximately 40% more expensive than the Elemack Cricket

Snake Arm fitted to Elemack - beware that the head and camera could add up to 8" from the base

Panther fitted with Panther Super Jib - low cost crane effects

Super Pee Wee dolly. Mid range price and all round performer

Low Price Wheelchair Dolly - cheap and cheerful!

Dolly Track, available in curves and straights in different lengths

Tripod Legs - available both short and long. Tripod legs need a head to attach to the camera

Telescopic crane. Camera operator is positioned on the end of the crane

Fluid Head - Dutch Head to attach to camera and then either to legs or dolly / crane

Mamba Tracking Vehicle with mounted crane

Bazooka - used instead of a tripod where space is tight

Boomslang Crane with dolly wheels and base.

professional Grips are excellent but there are occasions when production companies employ grips who don't know enough about the equipment. We often get calls from guys on location actually asking us how to operate the equipment. Obviously we tell them, but this should not be the case.

***Q - What are the most common mistakes made by a producer?***

***Mark -*** I guess the budgeting. I understand that there is never enough money and I know that it is not always their fault but a problem that they inherit. However, in general they do not seem to have a basic understanding of what the equipment does. To the producer, Grips often appear to be little more than manual labour therefore, the level of professional hired for a production can often be poor. Gripping is a highly skilled profession.

*The Super Pee Wee Dolly*

*Above - Cranes were used in CLIFFHANGER to get the camera into places that would normally be dangerous for an operator. The camera would be controlled remotely & viewed on a video assist.*

# Production Sound
## Richard Flynn

***Q - What exactly is the sound recordist's job?***

***Richard -*** The production recordist's first concern is to record as much useable production dialogue as possible, dialogue that will end up in the finished film. Because of the on-set technology available today, there's no reason why dialogue has to be post synchronised in the studio, unless you are shooting action or effects for instance. Your second concern is to try and record any sound effect that is unique to a production or location, a sound that would be difficult to recreate later. Things like water and crowds have very specific sounds that are very hard to find in audio libraries or to recreate in a studio.

***Q - Why not post sync the entire film?***

***Richard -*** The whole issue of post synching is down to the director. There are some directors like Robert Altman and Woody Allen who absolutely insist on using the original performance, and there are others, like John Boorman, who are very happy to post sync almost everything. Your job as a sound recordist really depends on what the director wants and what their attitude is. Having said that, I always try and make a scene work no matter what. If you need wild tracks to make a scene cut together and want to avoid expensive post synching sessions in the studio later, it's vital to get them on set.

***Q - So when a director is looking for locations, it's not only important to consider it's appearance, but also to stand and listen to see if you're right next to something like the M4?***

***Richard -*** Exactly. However, if there is a location that has a unique look to it, a big building or stunning exterior for instance, then obviously compromises may have to be made in order to capture that visual element. But when it comes down to a living room interior, quite honestly there is no excuse for shooting in a location where noise is a problem. If you can't afford a set, at least try and find a quiet street, a cul-de-sac.

***Q - What is the most basic kit?***

***Richard -*** The most basic requirement is that whatever audio recorder is used, the sound is going

to stay in sync with the picture. For that reason you can't use an ordinary domestic tape recorder, you must either use an analogue recorder like a Nagra with a sync pulse on it, or a digital recorder which is very stable. Either recorder will suffice. I would say use the best microphone you can afford as you really do need directional microphones. The Sennheiser 416 mike type is probably the most commonly used, although a lot of people use the 816, which is much longer and more directional. The point of using very directional mics is that they cut down on unwanted background noise, but the down side is that you will need a very good boom operator because the 816 is precise and unforgiving if it's not pointing in the right direction. As I said earlier, the idea is to get the dialogue as clean as possible and that's the reason we use that sort of mic.

***Q - What about radio mics?***

***Richard -*** I wouldn't attempt a drama production without radio mics, mainly because the way things are shot these days. The camera is a lot more portable than it used to be, the use steadicam and long tracking shots are very common, and that complicates matters from a sound point of view. The major advantage of a small radio mic is that you can get it very close to the actors mouth without having to connect the actor via a long cable. You don't necessarily need radio mics in the studio, but anywhere else they are pretty much essential. I'd advise hiring the most expensive ones you can afford, because the cheap ones are prone to interference.

***Q - When a producer hires the sound recordist, does he usually come with his own kit or does that have to be hired as well?***

***Richard -*** Most sound recordists who are freelancers, own all their own equipment and will generally hire it out as a package, which for most film productions is actually pretty fixed. It doesn't make any difference if your film costs £100k or £50m, the basic sound kit would be the same for all films, it's not like lighting and special effects.

***Q - So when a producer comes to you, they have to write out one cheque that covers the whole production sound department?***

***Richard -*** No, you would hire a recordist at a particular fee and then the kit for a particular fee. On top you would employ a boom operator and a sound maintenance person, but on low-budget productions the sound crew is usually two plus a trainee - if it's really low, there's no trainee.

***Q - How much of a problem can camera noise present?***

*Ultra low-budget feature productions can buy a cheap DAT recorder onto which they can record their sound in the knowledge that they should get excellent quality and rock solid sync.*

## Sound Advice

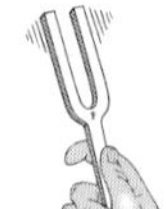

*KIT*
*Always hire or buy, the best kit you can afford, both recorder and mics. If you can afford it, hire radio mics.*

*LOCATION*
*Always recce a location for sound aswell as visual splendour*

*BLIMP*
*Always make sure you can blimp the camera, especially if it is old.*

*CLEAN*
*Always get dialogue as clean as possible. Always shoot guide tracks, even if the sound would be unusable*

*WILDTRACK*
*Always shoot a wildtrack of any problematic dialogue or effect. Always run off 30 secs of Atmos after each scene.*

***Richard -*** Not much of a problem with modern cameras, even with 16mm cameras. 35mm cameras are very quiet. If you're using older equipment, it's essential to have a blimp for the camera. It's mainly a problem in small hard surfaced areas as the sound bounces around.

***Q - How much is the production sound recordist involved in post sound?***

***Richard -*** The best way to educate yourself about production sound is to actually start the other end. Sit through a final mix of a film as it's only at that point the problems show up. Post production sound is usually a separate part of the film making process in this country, although there are a few exceptions. Before I start a film, I always phone up the people who are going to mix it and the people who are going to be doing the sound editing and have a good chat with them. For example, with stereo recording, some sound editors prefer things to be recorded in MS Stereo, I won't get into the details but there are different ways of recording stereo and different post production sound people prefer different ways of recording it, so I always check with them what they prefer. Similarly if recording digitally. It's important to sort out any technical problems with sync and timecode with the post production people before you start.

***Q - What are atmos and wild tracks?***

***Richard -*** Atmos tracks tend to be used to fix something in the sound editing, to smooth out any problems you have in a scene. For example, perhaps you've got a dialogue shot with tracking and there's tracking noise which doesn't actually cross the dialogue. If you have some atmos recorded from the same set up then you can use that atmos to fill in the gaps where the tracking noise was, which means that the sound editor can usually smooth out everything. There may also be other sounds like the directors cue's going along as the dialogue is being spoken. If you get through a whole scene and you're pretty sure that there aren't any major holes, then it's good to get a good thirty seconds of wildtrack 'ambience' and that's usually enough. It does depend on the scene that you're shooting as to what you need to get. For example, if you were shooting a dialogue scene in a real pub, then you'd shoot it without any actual background sounds and record the main actor's dialogue as cleanly as possible. The idea is to lay a crowd track, preferably with the real crowd from the real pub (who are actually there when you're shooting) over the whole scene later. If there are a few extraneous noises, they should be covered by the wild track. If there's an intimate scene between two people in a room, then any background noise is distracting and you have to really

## MICROPHONE DYNAMICS

*Whilst a directional microphone clearly gives better sound due to it's ability to 'focus' on a smaller area, it would be a mistake to draw the zoom lens analogy. Unlike a camera which has absolute crop off area's, a microphone, no matter how directional, is still subject to extraneous sound from all around. If you hear it, there's a good bet the microphone did too.*

insist that there aren't any unnecessary compromises made.

It's very important if you're recording wildtracks of actors, that you do them immediately, straight after a scene has been shot, as the actors still have it fresh in their mind - there's little point doing it an hour later because the actors won't remember how they performed in the shot. If you can't get good dialogue, still take sound because when it comes to post synching, the actors will need to hear the original performance in order for them replicate it in the studio.

***Q - What are the most common mistakes you come across?***

***Richard -*** The most common problems are things like roads, flightpaths, building works in close proximity, the list is almost endless. If the lighting unit has a generator, try to pick a sensible location, it doesn't have to be a hundred miles away but insist that it's far enough not to cause a problem for dialogue. Most modern generators are quite good, you only have to get a hundred yards away and they're effectively quite dead. On an interior, if it's near a busy road, pick a building with double glazed windows which can be closed - what you need to do is to communicate with the gaffer and arrange for cables to come round the back of a building, not the front where you're shooting, so you don't have to have the windows open to run the cables through. That is all part of the sound recordists job, to try and get the cleanest possible sound, because you want control when you come to final mix.

***Q - What basic advice would you give to a film maker considering the sound?***

***Richard -*** Always consider the implications of poor on-set sound due to location noise etc. Think carefully about whether actors are going to be capable of reproducing their performance in the studio, and consider cost implications (studio and actors fees), plus you'll probably never get it as good as the original. Think carefully about any locations that aren't that specific to the visual look of the film and always pick the quietest possible. Never try to save money by getting someone who can't boom operate - the boom is the key to getting good sound. By far the most important thing is to have someone who knows where to put the microphone.

# Costume Hire
# Tim Angel
## of Angels & Bermans

*Angels & Bermans are one of the leading UK suppliers of costumes to the film and TV industry, with decades of experience and a warehouse crammed with stock.*



***Q - What kind of costumes do you hire out?***

***Tim -*** We hire out any costume and any uniform from the beginning of time through to contemporary.

***Q - What if you don't have a specific type of costume?***

***Tim -*** We have production facilities within the company so we can make up any outfits - whatever needs making, we can get made.

***Q - Is that just the gowns themselves or do you take care of shoes, hats?***

***Tim -*** We don't actually make shoes in-house, but we can get those done. Hats we do make inside. We've got full millinery, dressmaking and tailoring facilities.

***Q - How many different styles of gowns do you have in stock?***

***Tim -*** Millions

***Q - In terms of budgeting, is there a great price difference between a very basic costume and something that is extremely elaborate and extravagant?***

***Tim -*** No, with films you tend to have a set price per costume that's dependent on the number of weeks and number of costumes hired. We'll always start with a book price, and then we'll discuss it with the producer or the accountant. When we're making up a costume, the prices can vary - if it's a simple outfit it will be a lower price and if it's a complex outfit it will be a much higher price. It depends on how much handwork, what sort of fabric and how much time is involved.

***Q - How do you usually hire out, is it a daily rate, a monthly rate, a weekly rate or by the production?***

***Time -*** For a film, it basically works out by the number of weeks and the daily rate wouldn't apply. Unless of course, a costume is only needed for a day or two.

***Q - Is it usual for a Producer to come to you and say, we want all the costumes for our production from you and for you to do a deal based on that?***

***Tim -*** It's better I think for the producer to do that, some producers do that, others don't and split it up between lots of different places. The advantage for a producer doing an overall package is that we can offer a much better deal.

***Q - Who usually comes to you first?***

***Tim -*** Initially, a designer will come with a production, sometimes the producer but at the end of the day we always deal with the producer when it comes down to the money as they are paying the designer.

***Q - Do you have your own in-house designers?***

***Tim -*** No.

***Q - If a producer comes to you with a low-budget period drama and assuming nothing needs making up, would you be able to offer a good deal?***

***Tim -*** Yes, we'll always do a deal. We're in a business where sometimes there are productions that have good budgets but the majority of the time, productions don't have good budgets and we just view each project as it comes along. One does negotiate prices and there are times when one does low-budget films.

***Q - How much should a basic costume budget be?***

***Tim -*** It depends on the production. Even if the costumes are from stock I couldn't give you an estimate - it's a bit different from cameras and sound equipment as everything is so variable.

***Q - But it's not going to be £500?***

***Tim -*** No, but if a producer rang us up, we would discuss the particular project with them - there is no magic figure. What a producer should do is ring up when they are budgeting, ask us for an estimate and work backwards from there.

**Q - What does the producer get for his money?**

***Tim -*** Angels is the only costume house in the world that is fully serviced. We have 200 staff and a costume designer would have backup from each of the departments, whether it be mens, ladies or military. Therefore, in preparation time, the producer doesn't need a great deal of backup staff for the costume designer. They are going to end up with one bill from one company and they are going to end up with a much more competitive package than they would if they went to three or four different houses. They get a fully serviced, one stop costume house.

**Q - What are your terms for hire?**

***Tim -*** Normally we like to get 100% before the production shoots, in other cases, it might be staggered payments that tie in with deliveries we've got. It really depends, but there is always an upfront payment.



**Q - What's your policy for insurance?**

***Tim -*** That's the responsibility of the production company and they have to insure the goods to the value that we specify.

**Q - Do you require to see that certificate of insurance?**

***Tim -*** Most of the companies would show us that they have a policy.

**Q - Do you ever get involved in Science fiction films where you have a bizarre production design?**

***Tim -*** Sometimes, but when we do, most of the costumes tend to be made. We'll get involved in anything that requires costumes, but low-budget science fiction films tend to be very difficult.

**Q - What are the greatest mistakes made by new film makers, first time film producers and first time costume designers?**

***Tim -*** I think the first thing they do is think that a place like this is too expensive for them to afford, so they try and find all different ways of doing it. The easiest way to deal with that is to ask the question at the beginning, come and

see us. We might say no, but we might say yes. Even if you've got no money you should at least try and follow the path that the people with money have rather than try and cut the corners.

For a low-budget contemporary film, they'll probably employ somebody who'll think 'Oh, I can't afford to hire anything' and they end up in Oxfam, charging around everywhere - and if they're first time people, that takes away a lot of their creativity. As a producer you're getting bills from Oxfam, Marks & Sparks, wherever, whereas if somebody actually asked the question the worst thing that could happen is we say 'No, you can't have all that', or 'we'll cut some of the crowd number'. There's usually a way.

***Q - So your advice would be, regardless of the budget, come in here with a wish list if only to have 'no' said to you?***

***Tim -*** Yes, if you can get the best, why go for second best. There are problems for us though as we don't have unlimited resources. If we are inundated with requests for Victorian gowns and a low-budget producer comes to us wanting Victorian gowns, we're less likely to do a competitive, low-budget deal. Also, there is a cost to simply organise and put clothes together and therefore there is a point when it just becomes uneconomical for us to do a production.

***Q - Do you have any tips for low-budget producers?***

***Tim -*** Come and discuss things at the beginning as it makes everything much easier. Some low-budget films don't necessarily need a costume designer, they might just need a very good wardrobe person.

# Director Of Photography
## Jon Walker

***Q - How do you approach the look of a film?***

***Jon -*** The *look* is more than just the photography, it's a joint effort between the set design, costume, make-up and other creative departments, they can all enhance the final look of the film. As well as being a 'science' combined with an 'art', lighting has an element of 'philosophy' in it, *What do I show?, What do I hide?, Should the scene be bright and happy* or *Dull and sad?.* The Director of Photography (DOP) can literally change the tone of a scene by the quality and style of the lighting used.

When a person watches a film they should be oblivious to the technical processes involved in making the film. If they are distracted by the editing, the sound effects or the lighting then something has probably gone wrong. The job of the technicians on a film is to re-create reality, or the illusion of reality. Both film and video are now very good at copying reality, however, they are not as accurate as the human eye and by understanding this, a good DOP can manipulate the medium to create a natural look. A DOP needs to understand four very important things. First, film stock is far less sensitive to light than the human eye. Second, film produces an image about 1.5 times more contrasty than the original scene. Third, our eyes and our brain, adjust for different light temperatures and situations; the amount of light striking the eye can vary greatly and yet the eye and the brain can even it all out. You can read a book with a torch or on a blazing summer day where the quantity of light coming from the sun is hundreds of times greater than with the torch. Lastly, we don't just see with our eyes we interpret what we see with our brains.

***Q - How important is the lab?***

***Jon -*** The best place to start when your are just about to shoot a film is to go where the film is going to end up, the Laboratory. An understanding of what the lab can and can not do is crucial - you need to know what grading can do for you and the technicians may be able to tell you something about the film stock you are using that isn't immediately obvious in any tests you might shoot.

The most important principle when dealing with the labs is communication. They will only do what you want if you tell them what you want and you can't assume anything. The lab is a very powerful tool if you bother to find out how it operates.

For example, the grader can change the look of the film in a way that could completely destroy the effect you had intended. On the other hand, if you help them they can make your film look fantastic - it's vital that you sit down with the grader and watch the film, discussing exactly what you intended when you lit the film. The grader hasn't read the script and may never hear the sound track - how are they supposed to know what you intended if you don't tell them?

***Q - What is the most important technical aspect of photography?***

***Jon -*** A properly exposed Negative - it sounds obvious, but because modern negative emulsions are so flexible there can be a temptation to over rely on their latitude. I shot a film on Super 16mm which was subsequently blown up to 35mm. To get the best result I slightly over exposed the negative - this resulted in a dense negative, producing a final print where the low key and night scenes have good solid blacks. If I had not done this the blacks might well have looked milky (where the blacks look grey and the grain of the film becomes so obvious it can be distracting).

***Q - What is the difference between 35 and 16mm?***

***Jon -*** The 35mm frame area is 4 x bigger so you're spreading your image over more grain to get a sharper, richer image which means you need a bigger lens to get more light in. The problem is that to get a decent depth of field you need a small aperture. For instance, on 16mm you could probably shoot at f2.8 but to get the equivalent depth of field on 35mm you'd need at least f4-5.6. This means that for 35mm you need up to four times as much light and a bigger, heavier camera, all of which will add to your budget.

***Q - How noisy are cameras?***

***Jon -*** 35mm cameras are extremely quiet. 16mm can be noisier, but modern cameras are still very quiet. If there's a real problem, you can resort to covering the camera and blimp with coats, but that's a real operators nightmare. Film stock varies. Most noise comes from the misalignment of the sprocket holes. You should always take some of the stock you intend to use to your Camera Hire company and run some tests so that if any adjustments need to be made, they can be done then and not on set.

***Q - How long does it take to change a roll of film?***

***Jon -*** A couple of minutes, but if you've just got one cameraman who's doing the lighting, operating and loading, it's going to take much longer.

***Q - What are gels and filters used for?***

***Jon -*** There's two basic areas. One is to correct light so it looks natural. For example, if you're filming inside and you've only got redheads and you've got daylight coming in through the windows, then you'll need to put a blue filter (gel) over the redhead to make the redheads orange light look blue to match the

PRODUCTION

daylight. Daylight is 'blue', and tungsten lights (anything that has a filament) is generally 'yellow'. Tungsten balanced stock (the most commonly used) produces accurate colours in tungsten light. Daylight balanced stock produces accurate colours in daylight. The other use of filters is to create an effect. You might want blue moonlight so you put blue gel on your redhead, or you want to have warm skin tones, filming with a candle for example, you'll put half an orange on the front of an already warm light.

***Q - What about Day for Night?***

***Jon -*** Essentially you under expose. On a film I did recently we shot some sequences in a house during the day, but it needed to be night. I simply added a bit of extra back light and under exposed by about 4 stops. I also put lots of neutral density grey filters over the windows so they wouldn't be too bright - sky is always the problem. Onscreen, the normal background light was basically black and the bits I added were highlights and it looked as though it was shot at night. If you're filming outside, as long as you don't have sky in the shot you can do day for night but as soon as you get the sky in shot it's no good. The best time to film day for night is the magic hour - which is just before it goes dark and you've got that blue light in the sky where you can see car headlights but still see detail - if you film that properly it looks wonderful.

***Q - What is trace and spun?***

***Jon -*** The smaller the source of light, the harder the shadows produced. Most film lights have 'small' filaments and therefore produce hard shadows, which isn't very flattering on people's faces. If you put spun or trace, which is actually like tracing paper but fireproof, over the light, it 'widens' the source of light and produces 'softer' shadows.



***Q - What are practical lights?***

***Jon -*** Practicals are lights that actually exist in the scene. For example an angle poise light is a practical. You can use the bulbs that are provided, 60-100watt which might be enough, but you can also buy 250watt bulbs (photofloods) that screw into the same socket. They give much more punch and are a good way to light moody interior scenes very quickly and cheaply - but be on the lookout for smoke rising because they do get hot and can cause a fire!

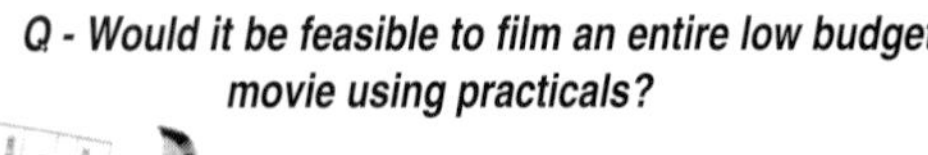

***Q - Would it be feasible to film an entire low budget movie using practicals?***

***Jon -*** Yes - if you were really low budget, I would suggest shooting on slightly faster stock because you need less light, something like 250ASA, and add a couple of red heads to the list.

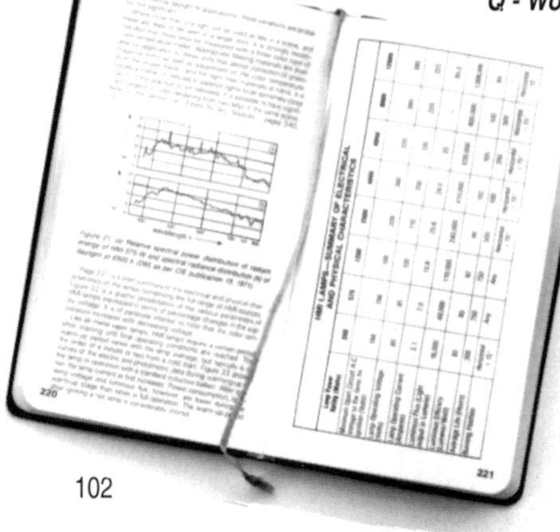

*The American Cinematographers Manual is the bible for cameramen. It's crammed with every piece of technical information you could ever want.*

## GET IT RIGHT FIRST TIME

*Make sure each shot has a board on it - either a sound clapper or a mute board.*

*Put a colour test chart at the beginning of each roll or when the scene changes.*

*Keep accurate lab report sheets - which shot is on which roll, etc.*

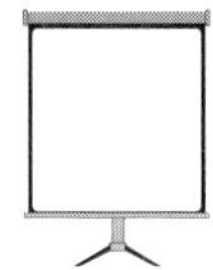

*When you watch the rushes make sure the projector is set up properly - some are not bright enough and are the wrong colour temperature.*

***Q - What is the basic lighting kit you can get away with to make an ultra low budget movie?***

***Jon -*** If look isn't your primary concern and you just want to get something exposed then you could go for a kit that an average ENG crew would use - a battery powered light that's used in the field (a PAG light or  SUNGUN) to fill up shadows. A couple of redheads for indoors and plenty of practical bulbs. But if you want to start lighting rooms from outside then you're going to have to get in to bigger lights - the minimum light you need there is a 2.5 HMI - you need something of that power to duplicate daylight. It's worth having one really good light, you'll be amazed how much you use it.

***Q - What about stock mixing?***

***Jon -*** Some stocks you can mix and some you can't but I would try to avoid it. Mixing speeds (ASA) is the same, it can be done, but it's best avoided.

***Q - Shooting outside usually means you don't need lights, although you may need a little fill light - what are the basic elements of actually lighting a shot?***

***Jon -*** The three most important lights are the Key Light, the Fill Light and the High Light.

The Key Light is the most important - it's the 'modelling light' and it's usually the main source of light, and sets the mood and texture in the scene. The positioning of the key light is dictated by the requirements of the scene - for example, the sun is the key light in a room where the only source of light is the sunlight coming through the window. Outside, on a clear day, the sun is the key light producing bright highlights and strong dark shadows. On an overcast day with heavy cloud cover, the sun is still the key light, but it is completely diffused by the clouds producing a very flat look, soft shadows and not much contrast between highlights and shadows.

When you light a scene the first question to ask is "What is the most important source of light in this scene?" It may not be obvious; you might be in a tunnel or in a sitting room at night with various light sources (lamps, candles, etc.). Often the job of the DOP is to enhance an existing 'key light'. The scene might be set in a room where the only light is coming from a candle set between two actors facing each other at a table. Without extra lighting the film will come back from the lab with a candle flame surrounded by complete darkness - remember film is not as sensitive as the human eye. So what do we do? We want to create the subtle look of a candle lit atmosphere without killing it by using too much extra light. By adding a slightly diffused key light that just adds to the candle light we can achieve a look on film that matches what the eye sees. The key light should be placed at the same height as the candle and on an axis that means that when you look through the camera the light from the key light looks as if it is coming from the candle. When you view the film you now see the flame and the actor.

Sun lit interiors can also be tricky. Overcast days can mean that without added light the windows are bright but the interiors are very dull (overcast light tending to come from above). The difference in contrast between the exposure needed inside the room and the exposure outside (through the window) is too great to be accommodated by the limited latitude of the film stock. The easiest solution, in order to simulate the look of a day lit room, is to place a very powerful and diffused key light outside the window. The further away from the window this light can go the more even the light in the room (the exposure drop is proportional to the distance from the light source - the further away the less difference it makes). The key light's colour temperature is the same as the daylight, but the key light only adds to the amount of light coming into the room; it does not add to the outside light so the contrast between inside and outside has been reduced and can now be captured on film, (important if the scene requires that both inside and outside the room be seen). The more diffused the key light can be the less harsh the shadows inside the room should be.



***Q - What if there isn't a single main source of light?***

***Jon -*** Sometimes you may have to deal with multiple key lights - a simple case would be a tunnel with overhead lighting at regular intervals. The scene requires the camera to follow the actors as they walk down the tunnel. The overhead lights may only be domestic 100 watt bulbs and provide very little light for the scene. By replacing the 100w bulbs with 275w or 500w photoflood bulbs (which look the same), you don't change the look of the scene, but it is now bright enough to expose film.

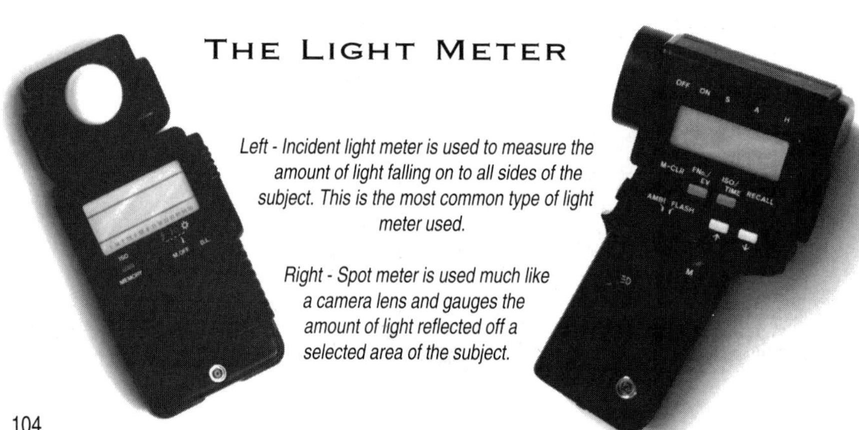

## The Light Meter

*Left - Incident light meter is used to measure the amount of light falling on to all sides of the subject. This is the most common type of light meter used.*

*Right - Spot meter is used much like a camera lens and gauges the amount of light reflected off a selected area of the subject.*

# Lighting Masterclass

1. The candle is the only light in the scene. The actors face and surroundings are too dark.

2. The candle light is enhanced with a light directly above, creating a pool of light around the candle on the table, but still the actors face is dark.

3. The key light is the primary source of light in the scene, sometimes called the modelling light. In this case, the light is placed to look as though the illumination is coming from the candle.

4. A Fill Light lifts the 'ambient' light of the scene (reducing contrast), adding detail to the dark areas of the frame.

5. A backlight increases depth and enhances the visual impact of the final picture.

# Creative Filters

*If you cannot afford to hire expensive special effects filters, gelatin filters can be used to great effect. Stills photographers use them with a special plastic holder which snaps on the front of the lens.*

*Split diopters, graduated, star, close up, diffusion - all can add to the image if used in a subtle manner. Best of all, they're very cheap.*

## Split Diopter

*The narrow depth of field means that the extreme foreground is out of focus.*

*The split diopter, half of a close up lens for want of a better description, allows both extreme foreground and background to be simultaneously in focus.*

## Graduated

*The sky is bright and bleached out.*

*The graduated filter darkens the sky slightly, creating a more broody look. Use graduated filters with extreme caution as it's easy to go over the top.*

## Mask

*Mask - Binoculars and a keyhole are perhaps the most common type of mask. They work best on the longer end of the lens and can be done in the lab instead (although that will cost significantly more)*

***Q - How does the fill light help?***

***Jon -*** If the key light 'creates' reality by enhancing the natural light sources, the fill light is the tool a DOP can use to give film the 'latitude' that the eye has.

Take the candle on the table again. Turn off the key light and look at what you've got. The candle light decreases rapidly the further from the flame you get. There's a ring of light around the candle on the table, the actor's faces are darker but still clearly visible and the walls, maybe 10 feet away, are just visible - not totally black. Now turn on the key light(s); you might have set a key light for each actor and put a light over the table shining down to simulate the ring of light produced on the table by the candle. Now film the scene. You should expose for the light on the table so that this is correctly or just under exposed and the actors (whose key light is slightly dimmer) look correctly and proportionally darker. However, the scene looks too contrasty and the background walls are completely black, this is not what we saw with our eyes. The solution to this problem is the fill light.

If you were sitting in a room with light coming through the windows, but the room was painted black, all the objects in the room would be side lit from the window, and the other side would be dark. The walls reflect none of the sunlight back onto the objects. If, however, the room is painted white the objects in the room would be lit by the light reflecting off the walls, as well as from the window. The objects would appear to be lit from all around. The white walls are acting as a fill light. The fill light must supply an equal amount of light to the whole scene without adding shadows to it. In the case of the candle scene, the easiest way to do this would be to bounce light from a powerful light off a white reflector placed just behind the camera. Reflected light is the softest light you can achieve and the position behind the camera means that any shadows created appear directly behind the subject and therefore are invisible to the camera. Experience is the best guide as to how much fill light to use. If there's too much the scene will lose all the texture provided by the key light and the scene will look over lit and flat. To the naked eye the addition of fill light will make the scene look slightly overlit and flat, however, remember that film is more contrasty and less sensitive than the eye. The use of the fill light reproduces the sensitivity of the eye on film. By using fill light the candle scene now looks on film as it did to the naked eye.

Outside on an overcast day the need for fill light may not be immediately obvious. However, overcast days, where the light is essentially overhead, can produce dark eye sockets on your actor. A simple piece of white polystyrene or a photographic reflector placed below the actor's face just lifts the details in their face, removes the harsh shadows and creates a softer more attractive look.

Sometimes providing a bounced fill light behind the camera is not possible. In a tunnel for example, the overhead lights provide the necessary quantity of key light, but also produce harsh and ugly shadows. There might also be pools of darkness between the lights. A light mounted on the camera might be the solution. The light is close to the camera so that shadows are kept to a minimum and by diffusing and dimming it the dark areas and shadows on the actor's faces are reduced without becoming obvious to the viewer. As long as the distance between the camera and the actors doesn't vary too much, the quantity of fill light will remain constant producing a natural look. If this distance is difficult to maintain then a hand held light (on the same axis as the camera) might overcome this problem. Discussing the positions of the actors should also ensure optimum lighting - if they stop and talk in a dark patch the scene might not work.

***Q - What is the back light?***

***Jon*** **-** The back light makes actresses look beautiful, bad guys look mean and can get around the problem of providing a light source where, in reality, none would exist; a forest at night for example. Subtlety is the key in most cases. Like the fill light, overdoing the high light can destroy the 'real' look of the shot.

In the candle scene we've created a realistic look on film, however, the actor's close-ups look a little dull. A light placed behind and slightly above the actor produces a highlight on the head. As long as it's not too bright the 'real' look will not be spoilt, however, the depth and texture of the shot has be enhanced - the high light separates the subject from the dark background and a sense of 'space' has been created.

Key lights and high lights can sometimes be the same. In a room lit by various lights - angle poise on the table, standard light by the sofa - one actor's key light might be the other actors highlight.

A real problem for a DOP is where in reality there would be no light at all. For example, a narrow unlit street at night or the woods at night have no natural sources of light for the DOP to enhance. Front lighting the subject with a key light would destroy the 'night time' look. A well placed back light is the solution to this problem. The intensity of this back lighting can help set the mood, harsh strong back light can create a powerful look suitable for action and a more gentle diffused back light might create the illusion of moonlight. Back lit smoke and shiny wet surfaces can be very effective in creating mood.

PRODUCTION

***Q - Why do lights have coloured gels, or filters on the front of the camera?***

***Jon*** **-** Light is essentially radiation produced as a result of heat (red hot and white hot). A domestic light bulb produces light when its filament is super heated, as the light source gets hotter the spectrum of light goes from red to blue. Candles burn at a 'low' temperature and are orange, the sun is very hot and produces white/blue light, (sunsets and dawn are coloured by aberrations in the atmosphere; a bit like putting a coloured gel over a light).

The human eye and brain balances these different colour 'temperatures'. Within a range 3200 Kelvin (about 3273°C) which is yellowish and 6000 Kelvin (6273°C) which is bluish to the eye, a piece of white paper is seen as white! However, film doesn't correct itself. Given that you film within these two light temperatures the lab can probably grade the colours correctly. Most film stock is balanced to produce accurate colours in TUNGSTEN light, which is 3200 Kelvin and is produced by heating a filament (Incandescent). If this film is used in daylight everything looks blue. Although the grader at the lab can correct this, a filter put on the lens to correct the colours at the time of filming provides a more evenly exposed negative and therefore a better looking picture.

Mixing light sources with different colour temperatures unintentionally could cause considerable problems. You might use tungsten light inside, but the windows and outside are daylight. The result would be either correct colours inside but a blue exterior or a yellow interior and a correct

## Depth Of Field

*Stopped Down*

*There's plenty of light here, so the aperture is closed down. This creates a greater depth of field. Notice how sharp the foreground post to the left and background tree to the right are.*

*Wide Open*

*There's much less light now and the aperture is opened up. This reduces the depth of field. Notice how soft the foreground post to the left and background tree to the right is.*

*Depth of field can be controlled for effect using Neutral Density filters and extra lighting.*

PRODUCTION

## Lens & Focal Length

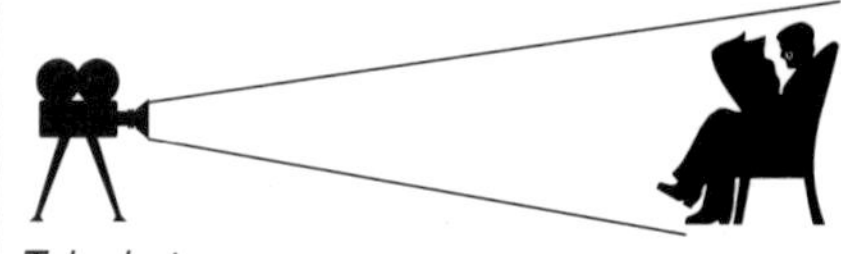

*Telephoto*

*The background is crushed and the figure appears more normal. There is less spillage of 'set and props' to the left and right.*

*Wide*

*The background is more distant and the figure appears more distorted - depth is enhanced with objects closer to the camera appearing much larger than those slightly further away.*

exterior. You can deal with these differences by using coloured gels on the lights to produce a constant even light temperature for the scene.

If in doubt, light your scene with one type of light source. Overhead striplights come in all sorts of different colour temperatures, the commonest are 'tungsten' sometimes called 'white' and 'daylight'. Because the spectrum of the light they produce is uneven - 'tungsten' is not true tungsten and 'daylight' not true daylight - when filming, make sure that all the striplights are the same type and you might rig up a 'light box' using the same type of lights for use as a fill light or key light. The lab can then make the small changes necessary to correct the colours.

***Q - You mention grading, what can the lab do to correct problems?***

***Jon -*** Grading shouldn't really be to correct your mistakes, it is to even out the small difference in exposure and colour that occurs when scenes are shot in different places and at different times. For example, you might film in a field all day, but in the final edit a shot from the beginning of the day is cut next to a shot from the middle of the day. Nature cannot be controlled and the colour temperature of the light might change, clouds form and you might even have to shoot some close-ups in the studio later. The grader can even out the colour differences so that from shot to shot, the flesh tones and the colour of the grass stays the same - the scene has continuity. The grader has a 50 point scale for the three colours - red, green and blue - with which to grade the film. The closer to the middle of the scale the negative is, the more variations the grader can make; this is why properly exposed negative is so important. If you shoot tungsten film in daylight without a correction filter (Wratten 85), the negative will have too much in the blue layer and not enough in the red. The grader will have to compensate by putting in less blue and more red light at the printing stage; if the negative is under or over exposed the grader's chance of correcting the problem completely will be seriously reduced.

***Q - What should you do in advance to ensure problems are ironed out?***

*Steadicam was invented to allow the camera to be moved with fluidity without the need of heavy, time consuming and BIG equipment.*

***Jon -*** Shoot tests. Film stock is a tool; it is the mechanism whereby the image is captured, copied and then transmitted. Film is made of several layers of light sensitive material - when light strikes it there is a chemical reaction, the more light the more reaction. Not enough light - no reaction and you get nothing on the negative (black), too much light and there's a complete chemical reaction and nothing on the negative (white). Most scenes you shoot will have varying degrees of light and dark; it is important to understand the sensitivity of the film. Your eye may be able to see into the shadowy areas, but will the film negative pick up that detail? All film stocks - Kodak, Fuji and Agfa, are slightly different; their grain structure may not be exactly the same and their sensitivity to different colours may vary. Contact the manufacturers who are usually more than happy to supply a free roll of any stock for tests. Design a series of tests that help you to access the characteristics of the film. A test scene should have a selection of different light and dark areas; you should know what the reflective quality of each area is (a spot meter may help), and by shooting a range of exposures you can see what they look like and how they relate to each other. Talking to the lab is crucial and shooting tests are a great way to gain experience in a short period of time. I have always tried to shoot tests in advanced of tackling tricky situations. For example, filming a TV screen and incorporating it into a scene so that it looks as it would in real life is very tricky. Shooting tests enabled me to experiment and therefore get the best results.

***Q - How much input should a director have with the look of the film?***

***Jon -*** It's vital to read and discuss the script with the director. It sounds obvious, but it's so often overlooked. A film should have a style and the photographic look should not radically change during the film unless the story requires it.

***Q - What are the most common mistakes made by the production?***

***Jon -*** Expecting stunning images with very basic lighting and crew. Getting a good image takes time and resources, and that means money. Outdoor locations at night take a long time to light, it's really hard work especially when you don't have enough lights. You're adding time, tiredness, and don't forget it's colder, long cable runs, all sorts of problems

Possibly the quickest way to shoot a low budget film would be entirely outdoors during the day - with a few good poly boards and reflectors you can be shooting shot after shot after shot.

# Special Effects Mike Kelt of Artem Visual Effects

***Q - What is the job of the Special Effects man?***

**Mike -** In very simple terms, to make the various things that are in a script that are difficult or impossible to achieve through normal channels, achievable. That could be anything from building a miniature of a medieval landscape to setting fire to a stately home which you can't actually damage.



***Q - There's a vague line between make-up and special make-up. Where does it cease to become the job of the set make-up artist and become the job of the effects team?***

**Mike -** The cross over is in the area of prosthetics. Make-up artists have facilities to make small prosthetic pieces but anything larger than say a false nose or a scar will usually be an effect and could entail making a full body prosthetic such as turning someone into a stone sculpture or an alien creature. Obviously we would work closely with the make-up department where such cross over occurs.

***Q - How easy and safe are bullet hits?***

**Mike -** They are perfectly safe providing you know what you are doing. On films they tend to want bullet hits that are theatrical. They are easy enough to do but can be costly because the pyrotechnics that you use tend to be expensive.

***Q - Is there a special way to shoot models or miniatures?***

**Mike -** Yes. We would liaise with the DOP as to how they are going to fit into the other shots and what lighting is going to be used or perhaps even duplicated to match other live footage, find out what lenses are to be used etc. It's easy to ignore all those things and just assume you can turn up with a model, plonk it down and hope that someone can light it and film it. It just doesn't work that way. We would be involved all the way through, in supervising the model, setting it up, helping to rig it and shoot it, and putting it in the skip afterwards.

***Q - For ultra low-budget pictures, can you do it yourself with an Airfix kit for spaceships and Dick Smith's £9.99 make up kit from Woolies?***

***Mike*** - You can certainly try, yes. There are big areas in special effects where there's no reason why you can't do it yourself, providing you have the basic knowledge and know what you are doing. The only areas where I'd say you couldn't do it yourself is where safety is involved, or where pyrotechnics are involved - that would be a legal minefield too. Anybody trying to do the special effects on their own films has got to draw the line at the point where safety starts to become an issue, but if you're doing a model, an Airfix spaceship say, then there's obviously no reason why somebody can't do it themselves, providing they've read enough books.

***Q - What effects are more costly - a car explosion or blue screen model shot for instance?***

***Mike*** - Blowing up a car would be much cheaper than doing a blue screen model. Generally, the more things you can do for real the cheaper it is. Man hours are the expensive thing - if you can do something quickly with the minimum preparation then that is the route to go down.

***Q - At what stage should a producer come to you and get you involved?***

***Mike*** - The earlier the better. Ideally when costing out a film, the producer should call us, then we can look at the script and actually make suggestions on how something could be achieved, rather than coping with problems which have been created after being brought in at the last minute. Often, there are things which can be done for a fraction of the price if we had only just been brought in at the start. It also means that the people involved have a more realistic idea of what the effects budget is going to be instead of just picking a figure out of the air. To keep costs to a minimum, there are always compromises of one sort or another that can be made and providing people are prepared to listen, substantial savings can be made with minimal loss of impact. I think the only area where that doesn't apply is safety where compromises can't be made.

***Q - Are there any spectacular cheat effects where you can avoid expense but still achieve something special?***

***Mike*** - One of the things which tends to be forgotten about these days which works very well is a hanging miniature - you're filming a scene with people in it, but you want to show say, people coming out of a spaceship, or walking up to a castle. If you make a miniature and hang it infront of the camera between the live action and the lens, you can get a very realistic feel, because the lighting is correct, it's out in daylight, and providing you dress the edge between the model and whatever the background is that it's sitting against, it can be totally convincing. It's exactly the same effect as a matte painting but it has the advantage of being three dimensional so you don't have to worry about the light - as the light changes in the background so it changes on the model, but

PRODUCTION

## Special Effects - Rough Guide

*Atmospheric*
*smoke, rain, snow etc..*

*Fire*
*ranging from making something look like it's on fire to a campfire that will always burn at exactly the same rate for continuity. Safety is always an issue with fire effects.*

*Pyrotechnics*
*blowing things up, ranging from huge fire balls to bullet hits on bodies.*

*Models & Miniatures*
*miniatures are a small version of a real object, a boat for instance. Models are things that are there to represent objects that are difficult to film or control, like an AIDS virus or an atom.*

*Mechanics*
*anything from a rig to control milk pouring out of a jug on cue and at just the right rate to a massive rig to knock down a wall (if it needs to be done mechanically rather than pyrotechnically).*

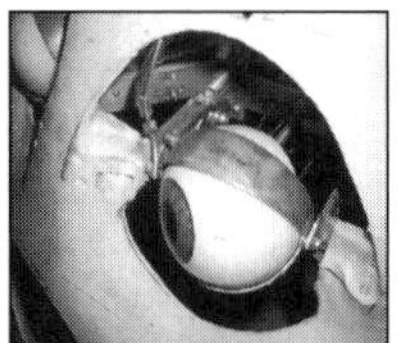

*Animatronics*
*making creatures up which have realistic movement, operated by radio control servos, cables, or computer operated these days.*

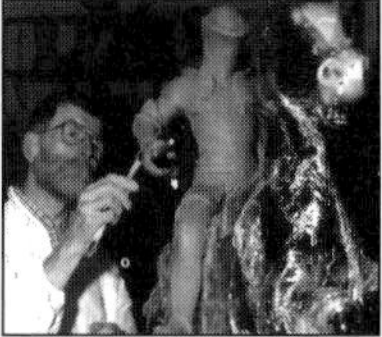

*Sculpture*
*covers a huge area; it could be a sculpture of an animal that's going to be used in animatronics, or an inanimate object that's going to be standing in the shot somewhere, a chocolate bar for instance.*

*Prosthetics*
*a latex piece that is attached to an actor that sometimes requires body and face casting enabling artists to sculpt 'onto' actors faces and bodies.*



with a matte painting you're stuck with it. So if it's painted on a sunny day and on the day you shoot it it's overcast, you have problems.

***Q - Rain, wind, mist and snow - people write those things into scripts without thinking - does that fall under the production design department or is that special effects?***

**Mike -** It comes under special effects and can be costly because, more than anything, man power is required. Plus, if you're not in a place where there's a ready water supply, it can be very costly because you have to tanker the water. 2000 gallons of effects rain doesn't go that far. If it's written willy nilly into the script for a low-budget film, the producer should weed it out very early on to avoid

unnecessary expense. Smoke machines, on the other hand, are very cheap and don't have to be used by special effects people.

***Q - What about computers and special effects?***

***Mike -*** I think as the years go by, the computer side of the business, actually generating images that go directly to the screen, is going to play a bigger part. What is starting to happen is no longer just a question of post production tinkering, it's the actual replacement of images with CGI. Replacing actors or animals with a computer generated image is now common, usually because it's cheaper to do that than try to get an animal to perform, or even because the actor died halfway through filming.

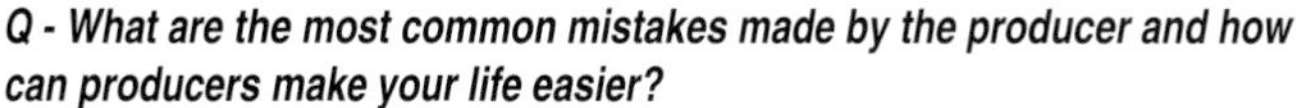

***Q - What are the most common mistakes made by the producer and how can producers make your life easier?***

***Mike -*** By giving us more time, telling us about their requirements as soon as possible, then we can get our heads around what needs to be achieved, and what the best and most cost effective way of doing that actually is. I've even come across people who've said, *we don't want to give you too much time because we don't want it to cost much* - I haven't quite got my head round that.

***Q - What basic advice would you offer a new filmmaker when it comes to special effects?***

***Mike -*** Don't be afraid to talk to people who are in the business. If you are going to use special effects, make sure you use people who are recognised and who have a track record because this industry is littered with instances of people being used who are not competent and in the worst instances, it's been very dangerous. Using inexperienced people can also end up costing more money than it otherwise would have done because something didn't work and it has to be done again. It's certainly worth talking to people who have a track record and even if at the end of the day you can't afford them and you use somebody else, at least you might learn something.

Photo - Graham Aikman

# Stunt Co-ordinator
## Stuart St Paul

***Q - What are the most common stunts that you are asked to perform?***

***Stuart*** - Fights that don't have people hitting each other. Here in Britain, producers are afraid that they won't get their film or TV programme shown before the watershed, so they develop fights that don't actually go anywhere, which is a bit like having a love scene where nobody gets to kiss or take their clothes off.

***Q - What are the most deceptively dangerous things to perform?***

***Stuart*** - The simple stunts are the most difficult ones. A trip fall is very hard to do, most people put their hands out and could easily break their wrist. People always seem to think that because they're using sugar glass, there's no problem, but sugar glass cuts very badly. I remember when Sting did *Brimstone & Treacle*, he went through a sugar glass window and ended up with over thirty stitches in his arm and had to get someone else to play bass on tour. There is no such thing as a simple stunt. Often money dictates what is and what is not a stunt, and that is the wrong way of doing it.

***Q - What are the best value for money stunts or action sequences?***

***Stuart*** - Using actors in a fight scene instead of stuntmen is obviously cheaper as you only need to hire the co-ordinator. And you can get some very good sequences like that too. However, once you start talking about falling off buildings or down stairs, you need to bring in a stunt performer who is going to cost more.

***Q - What makes a stunt work well?***

***Stuart*** - The most important thing in any script are the characters and the plot, and the best stunts will always come from those two things. If there's no character in a fight, if there's no point to a car crash, then there's nothing I can do that will make the audience have sympathy for what's going on. Most British writers don't know how to write action, they've probably never had a fight in their lives, they've probably never been involved in the kind of action that they're writing about and

PRODUCTION

therefore it doesn't ring true. When you ask a stuntman to perform a stunt, if he doesn't ask to read the whole script, you're not getting a good stunt co-ordinator. If he doesn't know the characters in your film, he cannot suggest how they will act or react in situations that require stunt work - he's not inside their heads.

***Q - So you would recommend speaking to a stunt co-ordinator, even at the script development stage?***

***Stuart -*** I think it's the only way to get a great picture. I don't think there is another way. I think you've just got to treat all your heads of department with the same respect. You talk to your costume designer, you don't bring them in at the last minute, and say *I've bought this mini skirt and blouse, do you mind putting it on the actress?* So why do it to a stuntman - *I bought this gun, and I'd like that guy to shoot him with it.* I just think that all too often, action is not done very well in this country because of this approach.

***Q - What happens about weapons? Guns are just written into the script without any thought from a production point of view?***

***Stuart -*** Certainly with guns, if there is going to any discharging of a weapon, you will need a specialist armourer. Beyond that, if money is tight, you can use replica guns in wide shots and some are good enough to be shown quite close up. The advantage with using non firing replicas is that you won't need an armourer present which will save you money. However, you must be careful not to abuse the presence of the dummy weapons as it could lead to a visit from the police. Also, does the actor know how to handle the gun without expert advice?

***Q - Will a second unit director work with the stuntman?***

***Stuart -*** The second unit director often is the stuntman or stunt co-ordinator. If you watch an American TV show or film, an episode of *The A Team* for instance, the second unit is always directed by the stunt co-ordinator. If you ring a stunt co-ordinator and ask them if they want to direct the second unit, but you don't have any money, they'd probably do it just for the credit, especially if you pick a young one. There are a lot of guys out there who are extremely helpful - if somebody rang me and said, *I've got a no-budget film, I'm shooting in Scotland, can you come and do a week for me?* - the chances are that I'd probably say I can't, but I would give you details of somebody who would do it. Remember, if you're inexperienced, to make a good film you must surround yourself with the most experienced people you can

STUART ST. PAUL

Stunt Co-ordinator

Tel 01923 820 330
Fax 01923 820 518

***Q - What actually happens about insurance for a film?***

***Stuart -*** If you've got an actor who's doing his own stunts, you're

probably in breach of your policy. Generally, although you should always check, if you bring a stuntman in, then he has his own insurance policy for his own accident liability. If the stunt goes wrong through a fault of his own or the stunt itself, then he can't claim against the production company. He can only claim against the production company if he was injured through the fault of the production company or one of it's employees.

***Q - How do you know if a stuntman is qualified?***

***Stuart -*** The best way is to look at their credits and check them. There is also an official register of stuntmen held by Equity. If the stuntman is not in that register, they aren't working full time within the industry. Equity will send producers a free copy of the register, it's a book where each stuntman or woman has a page with 3 pictures, measurements, credits, capabilities and the equipment he or she owns.



Every single stuntman is trained on very high budget, very professional films, even somebody who's only being doing stunts for three years or so is going to have twenty major feature film credits. Unfortunately, in this country, most stuntmen are treated like a piece of meat to do some action, or a bullet in a special effects gun. In fact, they are probably better directors and have worked on better material than the new directors and production companies for whom they sometimes work.

***Q - In terms of a stunt co-ordinator coming in and directing second unit, are there any requirements that you'd like to see the producer make available?***

***Stuart -*** I would imagine most low-budget films are a case of the stunt co-ordinator taking charge of the main unit (as there isn't a second unit), with the director sitting back watching - if he doesn't like something he can step in and say something. Obviously, if it's a true second unit, then you're going to need a camera and a small team. I was out in the desert last year, directing second unit for Boston Pictures. It was a huge shoot, with multiple cameras, hundreds of extras, horses, trucks etc., and I was left to do as I wished. The director wasn't interested in doing it, and being that she was American and not English, she said *just get on with it.* An English director would probably have said, *no I'm doing it, nobody else touches*

*it.* From a technical point of view, many stunts look better if shot in slow motion, so it's worth checking with the camera department that they can over-crank the camera and that they wont have any problems with HMI lighting strobe etc.

***Q - What are the most common mistakes that you come across when dealing with producers, experienced or not?***

***Stuart -*** Writing in a stunt which doesn't give them value for money. For instance, a car crash - where 2 cars speed around a corner and one hits the other - you write off two cars, it costs you two stuntmen, you close off the road - but at the end of the day, it usually looks fairly limp and audiences are so used to seeing this kind of action that it really has to be spectacular to be successful - and that means more money. There's a lot more to action than actually performing a stunt. Much of it is down to body language, it's about smelling pheromones coming off the screen, it's seeing the eyes focus on their target, as a cat does before it pounces on its prey. If you've never been in a fight or that kind of situation, then it's very difficult to imagine it and it's difficult to tell people how to do it. I just did a scene in a movie where an actor had to fend off five attackers who circled him - he had a knife and was supposed to go round the circle, but the actor couldn't do it because he was trying to twist round with the knife before he moved his legs and your body can't do that. All I did was to tell him how to move his body, and the scene looked great. All that it took was knowing what was wrong with his body movement.



We all like to work, but there does come a point, especially on low-budget films, when you just don't want to get involved because of the people. If the producer asks and is polite, it's human nature to want to help. If they don't like what a stuntman is doing, they can suggest trying something new - it's all about teamwork and co-operation - if the production understands that and operates accordingly, then I have no problem with them and they'll get the best work out of me.

*Real or fake? Even when examined close up, replica guns can be totally convincing, and don't require a costly armourer or stunt co-ordinators presence. However, if blank firing weapons are to be used, an expert must be present.*

PRODUCTION

# Studios
## Steve Jaggs of Pinewood Studios

*Pinewood is the home of the famous 007 stage, perhaps the most famous studio in the world. Yet, it's surprisingly inexpensive in which to shoot.*

***Q - Do low-budget films tend to shoot in studios or on location?***

***Steve -*** Generally, they tend to shoot on location due to budgetary restraints and the fact that it may be easier to pull favours in from locals. Plus, hiring of stages may appear to be expensive. But in the long run it may work out cheaper - you have total control in a studio - guaranteed weather coverage, sets can be built, you can get the right camera angles (which you can't necessarily do if you've rented a house for a couple of days).

Also, if you have a situation where there is an effect, like somebody charging through a glass door, I don't think anybody would be too happy about you doing that in their home.

***Q - From a production point of view, what other things can benefit a production?***

***Steve -*** There are lots of things in the studio that have to be arranged for on location - you don't have to get involved in catering, it exists, they can just break for lunch and go to the cafeteria or restaurant. There's all the other ancillaries like toilet blocks around the studio and dressing rooms in situ. We have a medical block with a nurse and a doctor, you're close to companies on the lot like accountants, special effects, preview theatres, and there's ample car parking, security, etc. There are so many extra costs whilst shooting on location that you don't have in a studio - transport, hotel bills, and the inconvenience of being far from the labs (if you're shooting in Yorkshire for instance).

***Q - What does the film maker get for their money when they hire a studio?***

***Steve -*** They get a sound stage, plus all the facilities that are on site that you need. On top of that there is an extra cost for production offices if required. They may wish to have make up and dressing rooms for the period of the picture or they may want them just on Tuesdays and

Thursdays depending on when their artists are in. Certainly with new or inexperienced film makers, we like to be involved as early on as possible so that we can advise them as to exactly what they will need and then there are no nasty shocks when the bill comes. Often, new film makers don't realise that they do need production offices, make-up and hair, a wardrobe area, a props area, a work shop - if there's plaster work involved they need a plaster shop, do they require an area where they need special effects work, and so on. Another thing that often gets forgotten is a build and strike period for sets - remember, sets and rubbish have to be cleared away by the production, and that takes time.

***Q - So whilst the studio is a hire thing, it's more of a service?***

***Steve -*** Yes. We're effectively supplying them with property for a limited amount of time, and a specific property for a specific purpose. Things like make up or hair, they are fully fitted, you don't have to hire a chair or hot and cold running water, we have proper barbers chairs to sit in, the same with art departments, with drawing boards, rooms for model making, set building etc.

***Q - Are studios as expensive as they sound?***

***Steve -*** No they're not - the perception is that they are. We always ask film makers to come to us and discuss the situation, lets see what your requirements are and let us give you a quote - maybe you'll be surprised. On the surface, it may look more expensive to shoot in a studio rather than on location, but there are so many inherent advantages to shooting in a studio, it will save you time and therefore money. Even your cast and crew don't need to be accommodated, you just say, we're in the studio, make your own way there.

***Q - What other companies are available on the studio lot?***

***Steve -*** That's one of the other advantages of coming here, we have about sixty tenants - we have several special effects companies, lighting hire companies, even a travel company that handles the film industry, accountants, insurance etc. There's too many to list here, but we have almost everything you could need, right here. If a bulb blows in a light, you only have a five minute walk to replace it, not an overnight delivery.

PRODUCTION

***Q - When productions are shooting at Pinewood, do they take production offices?***

***Steve -*** Normally they base themselves at the studio and they can come in and out as they wish, depending on their schedule.

***Q - What is the procedure for booking?***

***Steve -*** This is difficult because films tend

to change dramatically over time - we just ask for the film makers best guess, and ask them to keep us informed of any changes so we can alter any pencil bookings accordingly. However, there comes a point where we have to say pay up or shut up as we cannot indefinitely hold a stage on a pencil. If you have agreed the hire and the film is all set to go, then something halts it, we will still have to charge. We will do our best to sell that time and space to another production and if we do, we'd give you the money back.

***Q - Are there any rules or etiquette for working in a studio that cannot be broken?***

***Steve -*** Obviously there are certain restrictions, for instance if there's going to be a night shoot we like to be notified because out of courtesy we'd like to let the local residents know. There are certain things that you can't do - there are yellow lines on the stage where we request nothing is to be built over it because that's the fire escape. Also, we ask photographers not to wander around taking pictures as that can cause problems for other productions.

***Q - What are the most common mistakes you have experienced?***

***Steve -*** Under-budgeting, mainly because new film makers lack the experience - things like running over costs.

***Q - What is the procedure if the production runs over - do you throw them out as another production is booked in?***

***Steve -*** It could happen, but I don't think we've ever thrown anyone off a stage. We always try to juggle the elements so everyone is happy. Also, we don't book studios back to back as we know from experience that we will need some manoeuvrability.

***Q - What basic advice would you offer to film makers?***

***Steve -*** Don't dismiss studios, always discuss with the studio management what's happening. Also, for financial restraints, don't spoil your script to suit your location.

The Water Tank With Backdrop

Stage N 8

The Main Entrance

*Shooting in a studio can offer enormous advantages at a surprisingly inexpensive price. Make a call before deciding on shooting your entire picture on location.*

*The world famous 007 stage where many of the epic Bond movies were shot is yours for a mere £13,500 per week - and that's without a deal!*

For instance, you're using your mother's house, it's a lovely house but actually I really need to knock that wall out because I can't get my camera back far enough so therefore your script changes. Talk to studios as early as you possibly can because they may be able to advise about budgeting so that you can make a decision as to whether to shoot on location or in a studio.

The age old problem to avoid is when you have run out of money and still have two weeks to shoot. There are a lot of people in this industry, us included, who want to encourage young film makers because they're the film makers of the future, a lot of people are quite prepared to give up their time and talk - utilise it, don't think you know everything about this industry because, believe me you don't.

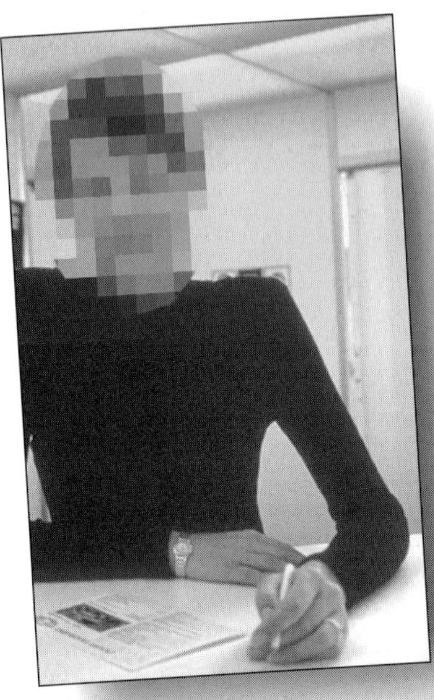

PRODUCTION

# Product Placement
## Identity Withheld

*Product placement and sponsorship is always a favourite prospective source of finance for low-budget film makers. Because this side of the industry is often frowned upon by advertising regulatory bodies, the interviewee requested anonymity.*

***Q - What is product placement with regard to feature films?***

***Anonymous -*** A producer will come to someone like myself, or approach a manufacturer direct, and offer to 'place' a specific brand product in a shot or sequence, in return for payment. Many Hollywood feature films do this and sometimes it's a little too obvious where a deal has been struck. We are concerned with getting our clients brand name promoted in a way that we feel is appropriate. So we may impose certain restrictions.

***Q - What kind of restrictions?***

***Anonymous -*** For instance, we might insist that if an alcoholic beverage was featured in the film, it was only consumed by the 'good guys' and not the villains and that the bottle was never used as a weapon etc.

***Q - How much money is available?***

***Anonymous -*** For a low-budget film, very little, as the film maker probably wont have the calibre of cast that we need, or a distributor who is going to really push the film out. It is a film myth that new film-makers will be able to finance their film from the product placement of huge brand names like Coca Cola or Panasonic. I am sure that both these companies will have large advertising budgets, but they are looking for the calibre of Mel Gibson or Julia Roberts, not some unknown actor in a film that might never see the light of day.

***Q - What about simply supplying the products for use in a film?***

***Anonymous*** **-** Very often we can help there as the cost of simply supplying a product is minimal to the manufacturer. We often supply anything from beer and chocolate bars to cars. Obviously, we expect the crew to drink the beer and eat the chocolate after all the shots have been covered, but we will want the car back! Also, with regard to cars, the producer will almost certainly have to cover the insurance for the driver. We may also ask for some photos of the cast with the product.

***Q - What do you need from the producer for you to make a decision?***

***Anonymous*** **-** In the first instance, if the producer was looking for some kind of payment, we would need to know about the film, the subject matter and theme, who is in it, who is making it etc. If we represent a client whom we think would be interested, we would ask to see the screenplay and if we decided to proceed, we would stipulate where and how we wished the products to be featured in a contract.

If you are simply looking for products to feature and no money, more than likely we would just send them to you, especially food and drinks. Often we will supply some hardware products, but then we do look for more assurances from the producer about the type of coverage in the film, plus an assurance that the various products are insured whilst being used by the film unit.

***Q - How much coverage of a product are you looking for?***

***Anonymous*** **-** We don't want to bombard the audience with product names to the point where they feel they are watching a commercial, so we aren't looking for excessive or unnecessary coverage. It's just that if there is a camcorder in a scene for example, we want it to be one that comes from one of our clients.

***Q - What are the most common mistakes you come across?***

***Anonymous*** **-** Many films are simply not suited to placement of products, a period drama and some science fiction for example. So in those instances, it's just not worth making the call. Producers often bend the truth too and I know that things can and do fall through. It's just frustrating for us when we are told that the lead is going to be a big Hollywood star, and that person simply doesn't materialise. Often, we will only pay a deposit and hold on to the balance until the film is completed and we have viewed it to agree the level of product coverage.

PRODUCTION

# The Laboratory Brian Dale of Technicolor

***Q - What is the job of the laboratory?***

***Brian -*** To take the exposed raw camera stock, process it, probably print it, but nowadays possibly not as it could be going to telecine (transfer to video), and then deal with the post production of that material in terms of producing the necessary facilities up to and including bulk release prints.

***Q - How important is it for the production team to meet the laboratory contact person?***

***Brian -*** The contact technician becomes the 'technical eyes' of the production and it's vital the producer and director meet him, to understand who they are and what they will be doing. Also, the cameraman and editor should meet the lab contact - he is a named individual who will be completely responsible for looking after the production, right the way through to the answer print and maybe beyond. If you've got a problem, a good contact man will be able, subtly of course, to suggest the changes that may be necessary to improve the look of the picture. After meeting the cameraman and discussing the 'look' he is trying to achieve and after the first one or two days rushes, the contact man will be able to advise what changes, if any, should be made - indeed it's his job to report on technical problems like hairs in the gate or a boom in shot for example.

***Q - What is the lab report sheet?***

***Brian*** - The report sheet is a list of scenes and takes which contains key numbers as well as the printing lights (a laboratory measure of the exposure of the red, green and blue emulsion layers). It's a listing of all the material that's shot, roll by roll, scene by scene, key number at the start of the scene, key number at the end of the scene, colour grading and any comments - it may be instructions from the camera man to say there is a flicker effect, fire or day for night.

***Q - What is the camera report sheet?***

***Brian -*** The camera report sheet comes from the production and is usually produced by the camera assistant on the job. It lists the material in use, by stock type, batch, roll everything down to the strip number. If there is a problem, and with the best will in the world, Agfa, Kodak and Fuji, all have their problems from time to time, they need to be able to trace back. It's an advice document for us to tell us whether there is any special effect, whether there's been any problems or if there's

been a jam in camera, so that we can deal with it accordingly. It will also give us information on scenes and takes, preferred takes, those takes that are to be printed and those takes that aren't.

***Q - How should they supply the exposed negative to you?***

***Brian -*** Have the film gaffer taped together, with the camera report sheets (or better still, box everything up), and drop it off at film reception at the lab.

***Q - What happens about sound?***

***Brian -*** Sound is an entirely separate channel as far as we're concerned. The only time that we would see sound at this stage of the operation is if all the materials from the shoot were coming in to us and we'd simply been asked to pass the sound on to an audio facility where the sound tapes are transferred to 35mm magnetic stock. In the case of film rushes, it is normal for the assistant editor to sync up the sound with the rushes and to project the picture - mute picture with the separate mag soundtrack. In the case of video rushes transfer, if sync sound is required, then the master audio tapes will need to be delivered along with the negative to the telecine facility, be it in the lab or another company.

***Q - What are the differences in the way 16mm & 35mm is handled?***

***Brian -*** Fundamentally there's no difference in that both are received the same way, but separated into Super 16mm or 35mm channels. They are processed in the same way, different machines, but the design of the machines is identical. Generally, 16mm is graded roll by roll, so you come up with a grading light for a complete camera roll which is an average of all the scenes on that roll. With 35mm, selected takes will be circled on the camera report sheet which will be extracted from the negative roll and printed, so you end up with 2 rolls of 35mm negative - one which is selected takes and the other, B Roll, (unused takes) which is stored away, to be called up if alternate takes are needed, but in general, it will probably never see the light of day again. With regard to 16mm and Super 16mm - most labs have a mixture of Super 16 and Standard 16 equipment, and the Standard 16 equipment doesn't have the relieved edges that are necessary for Super 16 film. To ensure that your Super 16 film doesn't get tangled up in a Standard 16 winder or something like that, then it is vital to identify it as Super 16 on the can and on the camera report sheet.

***Q - Can rushes be viewed at the labs?***

***Brian -*** Yes, rushes can be viewed at the labs. We would need prior advice to make sure we have enough theatre space available and that your contact man was here in the lab - subject to that, it's no problem at all.

***Q - If a film is cut using traditional techniques, what happens after the fine cut is completed by the editor?***

POST-PRODUCTION

***Brian*** **-** Obviously, the first stage would have been to process the negative as it comes from the production and supply a rush print which the editor cuts. Once the film is cut, we would then hold a cutting copy screening with the grader - the guy who's ultimately going to balance the colour and density of the image - plus the cameraman, director, producer and usually the editor, all of whom can have creative input. Comments will be made by all present and the grader will take notes, saying *we need more density, we need this colour* - whatever the changes are that are requested from the existing cutting copy. The negative will then be neg-cut, either in house or with a neg-cutting company. The big consideration here is that it is in the production's interest to talk to the laboratory about what they believe the schedule to be. The laboratory will be perfectly honest about it, they won't try and grab themselves more time than they actually need, but this particular stage is very important. It's where the original negative is reached with a pair of scissors and if there is too much pressure in terms of schedules, needing to see answer prints and check prints... lets say its probably not desirable to put pressure on at that stage.

We would then print it, taking into account the comments that were made at the actual cutting copy show. We would look at it internally - the grader would assess it, to see if he had the result on screen which he anticipated getting - the result of the colour changes, modifications he'd made. He would probably put it back in for a reprint, once or maybe twice, in order to make sure he was confident with what he had, and then he would be in a position to show that to the production. We would then screen that first answer print for the production. If there are any problems, we'll do a reprint, fixing the grading that the production isn't happy with - the production doesn't pay for this extra printing. The problem for us here is when you have four people all saying different things - *I want more blue - No more red - I want lighter - I want darker* - you end up getting into a loop that you can never get out of. Everyone should be present and the decision should be agreed by those people - it's important to avoid both Chinese parliament, repeat screenings or discussions, simply because one key person couldn't make it. That can cost time and is frustrating.

***Q - Leaders can be a problem, i.e. they can be BBC or ACADEMY - can Technicolor supply the leaders that you prefer to be used?***

***Brian -*** Yes, we would normally supply leaders on negatives and duplicates. The academy count down leader is standard for independent productions. We could also supply the BBC leader, but it's important to nail down exactly which type of leader is going to be used throughout the production. For the matching sound leaders, simply use the Academy leader which can be bought on Wardour street or wherever.

***Q - If the master sound mix has been done, is it possible for that mag to be sunk up and the film screened with sound?***

***Brian -*** Absolutely. It can be run with separate magnetic sound (sep mag), or alternatively, if the optical sound transfers have taken place, we could produce a married print for the first screening. Remember though, on first answer prints, both Super 35mm and Super 16mm cannot have a married optical sound track, but you can run with separate magnetic sound.

***Q - What is the optical sound?***

***Brian -*** The master sound can come to us in a variety of formats, optical disk, DAT, and of course 16mm or 35mm Mag (although this is now declining). That master will be transferred onto film, with a special lab camera, as an optical representation of the sound. That optical sound can then be printed alongside the picture for a married print. When that print is screened, the projector can read the optical sound and the audience hears it. New Digital formats are appearing such as DTS, Dolby Digital or SDDS, but the old style analogue optical sound always runs alongside it, just in case there's a problem with projection.

***Q - How does blowing Super 16mm up to 35mm work?***

***Brian -*** Firstly, an Interpositive would be made from the Super 16mm A&B roll cut negative, at the same grading lights as the answer print that has been approved - so all the grading would then be locked in. Then we make a 35mm blow up Internegative from that Super 16mm Interpositive, and from that, 35mm prints. That means we have a 35mm printing master from which we can make as many prints as you want, perfectly graded, without touching the original negative. Alternatively, if you're not looking for many prints, maybe only one, you can make a direct blow-up from the Super 16mm negative. However, producing prints from an original cut negative is a process with which you must take a great deal of care as you don't have any protection should damage occur. Again you're talking about the material where all your hopes and aspirations are lodged. Also, because special care must be taken when printing from an original negative, the costs are much greater.

***Q - What happens to the master neg once its been printed?***

***Brian -*** It will be vaulted. Most labs will store material, or you can take it out and vault it somewhere of your own choice. However, in the lab, it's secure and the conditions of storage (temperature & humidity) are maintained. It's not a good idea to keep it in your garage or under your bed.

# The Traditional Laboratory Process

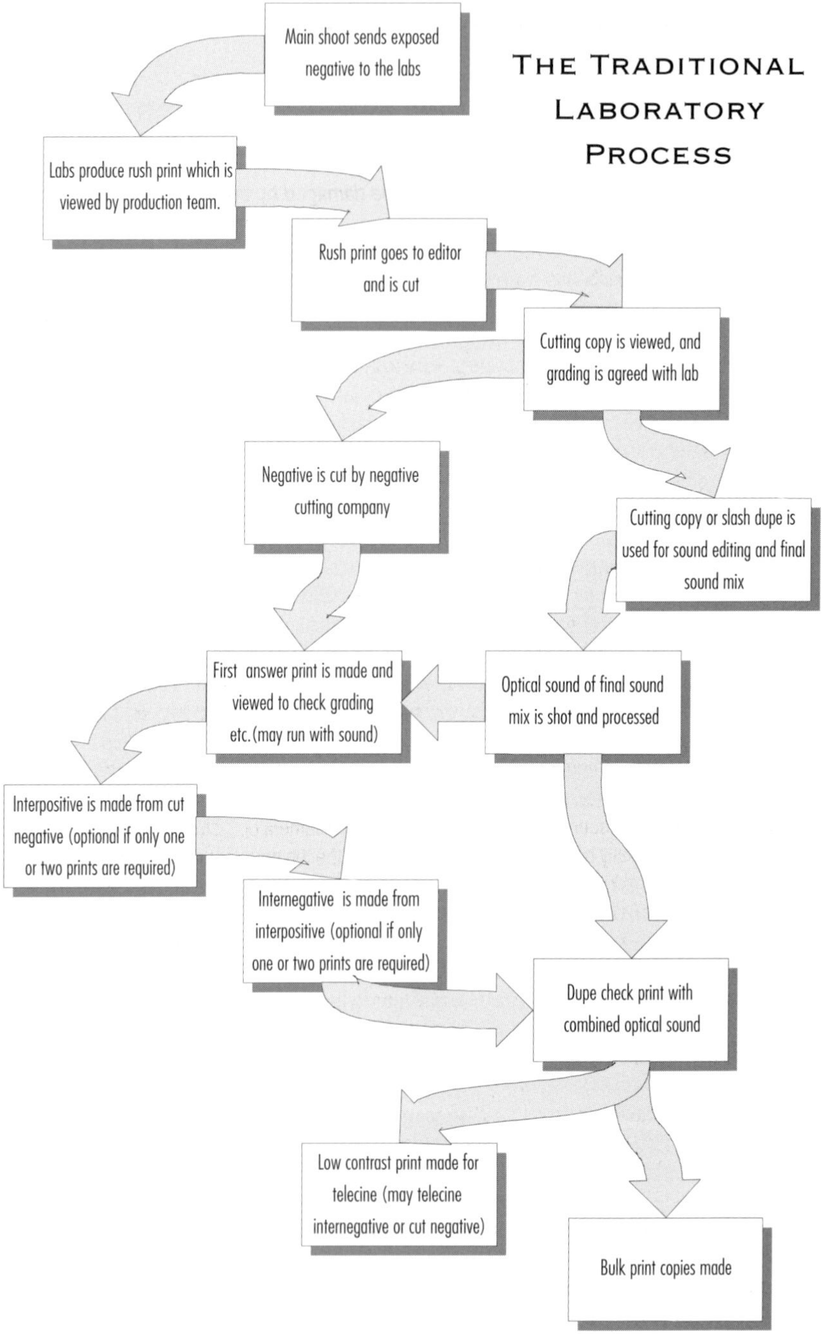

Main shoot sends exposed negative to the labs

Labs produce rush print which is viewed by production team.

Rush print goes to editor and is cut

Cutting copy is viewed, and grading is agreed with lab

Negative is cut by negative cutting company

Cutting copy or slash dupe is used for sound editing and final sound mix

First answer print is made and viewed to check grading etc. (may run with sound)

Optical sound of final sound mix is shot and processed

Interpositive is made from cut negative (optional if only one or two prints are required)

Internegative is made from interpositive (optional if only one or two prints are required)

Dupe check print with combined optical sound

Low contrast print made for telecine (may telecine internegative or cut negative)

Bulk print copies made

***Q - After the first answer print, are subsequent prints cheaper?***

***Brian*** - Yes they are. Any print from the original neg is going to be expensive by comparison with a print from a dupe (internegative). Most labs have a sliding scale of discount, depending on how many prints you are ordering on that dupe.

***Q - What is the procedure should the master neg be damaged by the lab?***

***Brian*** - If the damage is on the Internegative, we would go back to the Interpositive and make a new Internegative for which the producer wouldn't be charged. If it's the master negative, then things become a little more problematic. I can only speak for this laboratory, but our procedure is to be totally honest with the production company, apologise and accept the ear bashing you're quite rightly going to get. All labs have commercial protection in their terms and conditions which effectively protects them from expensive claims due to accidental damage. A good lab wouldn't hide behind that and would be prepared to talk to you about what can be done to alleviate the problem. The neg should always be covered by other insurance anyway. That insurance would be provided by the producer and not the lab though. It's therefore vital for the producer to insure the negative, right up to the time that you get your Interpositive made.

***Q - What is super 35mm and how does it work?***

***Brian*** - Very wide images, commonly referred to as Cinemascope, are usually produced using a special anamorphic lens that squeezes the image when shooting, and unsqueezes the image when projected. One problem with this is that the extra lens means you need more light to expose the negative properly and the lens hire itself adds expense. Super 35mm is an alternative to anamorphic photography. The image ratio is 2.35-1 and it's shot on normal 35mm film. You simply shoot the 35mm negative as normal, but with the viewfinder marked up for Super 35mm (so the camera operator knows where the edge of frame will be). As with Super 16mm, more of the film area is exposed (where the soundtrack traditionally lives). The camera operator must keep in mind that the image will eventually be widescreen (2.35-1) and so the top and bottom of the image won't be used - there will be markings in the camera eyepiece so everyone knows what the frame is. You then produce your rush print, grade it, neg cut it, all in the same way as normal 35mm. At the Internegative stage, on an optical printer, you put the anamorphic squeeze in. Then when you make the final projection print, it has the anamorphic squeeze, and when it goes to theatre, they unsqueeze it on projection and put it back to wide screen format.

***Q - So in the middle there is an optical process which is going to be slow and expensive?***

***Brian*** - Yes, but the extra lab costs may well be outweighed by the savings of not having to shoot with an anamorphic lens. It's simply a matter of paying your money and making a choice.

***Q - Like the dubbing theatre the labs are expected to perform miracles in terms of grading - you're not able to turn blazing sunshine into the dead of night are you?***

***Brian*** - We'd have a pretty good go, but no you're right. There are limitations. However, effects like day for night are achievable, though less necessary with modern, high speed film stocks.

# Super 16mm to 35mm Blow Up

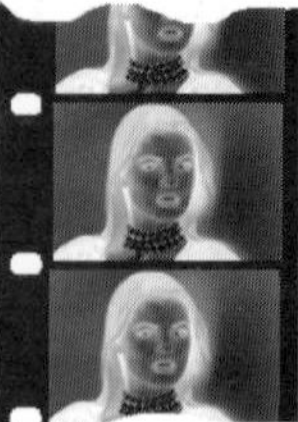

Stage 1 - Super 16mm Cut Negative - Once an answer print of this cut negative is agreed from a grading point of view, it moves on to Stage 2

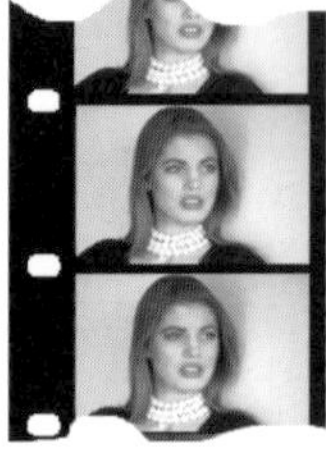

Stage 2 - Super 16mm Interpositive is made from the Cut Negative - This Interneg is low contrast and contains ALL the gradings agreed by the production company.

Stage 3 - Super 16mm Interpositive is blown up to 35mm Internegative. Notice The Super 16mm aspect ratio (1.66-1) has been cropped down with a mask to 1.85-1 for cinema release (optional).

Stage 4 - Check Print is made and agreed by the production.

Stage 5 - Optical Sound negative is made from master sound mix. This will be combined with Stage 4 to produce a combined, optical and picture Check Print. Note the digital sound encoded between sprockets on the left of the negative.

Stage 6 - 35mm release print, with combined optical sound.

# Super 35mm - Widescreen without anamorphics

*Stage 1 - Super 35mm negative is cut - notice the aspect ratio (not on negative but in camera viewfinder). Notice also that more negative is exposed than on flat 35mm.*

*Stage 2 - Answer print is made to check and confirm grading.*

*Stage 3 - Super 35mm interpositive is made from Super 35mm cut negative.*

*Stage 4 - 35mm internegative is made up - The image is now optically squeezed, freeing up the area on the left of the frame for the optical sound track. This internegative now conforms to standard 35mm formats and includes the anamorphic squeeze.*

*Stage 5 - Optical Sound negative is made from master sound mix. It can be combined with Stage 6 to produce a combined, optical and picture, print. (Com Opt). Note the digital sound encoded between sprockets on the left of the negative.*

*Stage 6 - Combined Optical and Picture print (a check print will be produced before show prints). Note how the image is squeezed, and the optical sound on the left.*

*Stage 7 - Theatrical Projection - when the print is projected in the cinema, the projectionist uses an anamorphic lens to 'unsqueeze' the image, giving a very wide image.*

ACME MOVIES

Acme Films, 123 Any Road, Anytown, Somewhere, London

To - The Chosen Labs
Somewhere
London W11 5NP
21/4/96

Dear Sirs,

We have granted to **ANY DISTRIBUTOR**, hereinafter called "The Distributor" the rights of Film Distribution, video, and television in **TERRITORY** on the following Film:-

**YOUR MOVIE**

This communication is your authority to allow the Distributor access to the following materials in your possession, for the purpose of manufacturing the Film and Trailer requirements:

**LIST MATERIALS (NEGATIVE & SOUND FOR EXAMPLE)**

It is to be understood that all costs in connection with the manufacture of their requirements are at the sole cost of the Distributor.

Also you will not impose any lien upon or against the materials by reason of any charge or obligations incurred by the Distributor. Three copies of this letter are enclosed for signature and return two copies to this office.

| *A Producer* | *The Labman* | *A distributor* |
|---|---|---|
| Signed<br>Acme Film | Countersigned<br>Laboratories | Countersigned<br>Distributor |

***Q - What is the laboratory access letter?***

***Brian -*** It's a letter that specifies who has access to the negative. It could be for different people in different companies, or it could limit the number of prints. It's simply a means of controlling who has access to the material, usually the negative, internegative and optical sound. Typically, sales agents and distributors will need a lab access letter.

***Q - Can you achieve artistic effects in the lab, like make Super 16 colour neg B&W?***

***Brian -*** Yes. If you want to end up with a B&W movie, then there's a strong argument for shooting in B&W in the first place. However, if it's a decision that has been made after shooting, the lab can produce a new B&W negative through various intermediate stages although, it tends to look softer on screen than B&W original negative. I once talked to a producer about a particular cameraman who was very artistic, where artistic is 1 stop underexposed, very artistic is 2 stops underexposed, and very very artistic is three stops underexposed. Seriously, it depends on the look you want. People do deliberately underexpose by a couple of stops in order to get a harsh, grainy, appearance and overexpose for the opposite reasons. The earlier you talk to the labs the better. You should be shooting tests and viewing them with a grader.

***Q - Is the Super 16 frame the same aspect ratio as the 35mm?***

***Brian -*** It depends. If you're going to shoot Super 16 on 1.66-1, you haven't got a concern. If it's to be blown up to 35mm for theatrical release, you should be aware that cinemas usually project at 1.85-1, so you would need to accommodate extra headroom at top and room at the bottom of the picture. The viewfinder in the camera should be set up this way by the camera hire company.

***Q - What are the most common mistakes made by the production team?***

***Brian -*** Communication is obviously an essential factor. Not completing the information on the camera report sheets, making sure messages and comments are received, particularly with regard to cutting negative or moving negative about (which is always confirmed in writing). Also, always shoot tests with the camera and stock you have chosen before shooting a film.

# GLOSSARY OF LABORATORY TERMS

**A & B CUTTING** - *A method of assembling original material in two separate rolls, allowing optical effects to be made by double printing.*

**A OR B WIND** - *The two forms of winding used for rolls of film perforated on one edge only.*

**ANAMORPHIC** - *An optical system having different magnifications in the horizontal and vertical dimensions of the image. (Used for cinemascope style effect)*

**ANSWER PRINT** - *The first Answer print is the first combined (action and sound) print produced by the laboratory from a cut negative for further customer grading comments. The final Answer Print is a print which has been fully graded and accepted by the customer.*

**ASA** - *Exposure Index or Speed Rating to denote film sensitivity.*

**ASPECT RATIO (AR)** - *The proportion of picture width to height.*

**CHECKER BOARD CUTTING** - *A method of assembling alternate scenes of negative in A&B rolls, used for 16mm which allows prints to be made without visible splices.*

**CINEMASCOPE** - *A system of anamorphic widescreen presentation. (Trade name).*

**CLONE** - *An identical copy, usually referring to a digital tape.*

**COMBINED PRINT** - *A motion picture print with both picture and sound on the same strip of film. Also referred to as COMPOSITE PRINT/MARRIED PRINT.*

**DAILIES** - *Daily Rush Prints. The first positive prints made by the laboratory overnight from the negative photographed on the previous day.*

**DENSITY** - *A factor which indicates the light stopping power of a photographic image.*

**DEVELOPING** - *The chemical process which converts a photographic exposure into a visible image.*

**DISSOLVE** - *A transition between two scenes where the first merges imperceptibly into the second.*

**DUPE** - *A copy negative, short for duplicate negative.*

**EDGE NUMBERS** - *Coded numbers printed along the edge of a strip of film for identification.*

**FADE** - *An optical effect in which the image of a scene is gradually replaced by uniform dark area, or vice versa.*

**FLOP-OVER** - *An optical effect in which the picture is shown reversed from right to left.*

**GRADING** - *The process of selecting the printing values for colour and density of successive scenes in a complete film in order to produce the desired visual effects.*

**INTERMEDIATES** - *General term for colour masters and dupes.*

**INTERPOSITIVE** - *A colour master positive print.*

**LIQUID GATE** - *A printing system in which the original is immersed in a suitable liquid at the moment of exposure in order to reduce the effect of surface scratches and abrasions.*

**MAG-OPT** - *A motion picture print with both magnetic and optical (photographic) sound track records.*

**OPTICAL SOUND** - *A sound track in which the record takes the form of variations of a photographic image.*

**PITCH** - *The distance between two successive perforations along a strip of film.*

**REVERSAL** - *The processing of film to give a positive image on film exposed in the camera or to obtain a copy negative by direct printing from a negative image.*

**UNSQUEEZED PRINT** - *A print in which the distorted image of an anamorphic negative has been corrected for normal projection.*

**WET PRINTING** - *A system of printing in which the original is temporarily coated with a layer of liquid at the moment of exposure to reduce the effect of surface faults.*

**WIDESCREEN** - *General term for form of film presentation in which the picture has an aspect ratio greater than 1.33:1. i.e. 1:66, 1:75, 1:85, the latter being generally used for cinema presentation.*

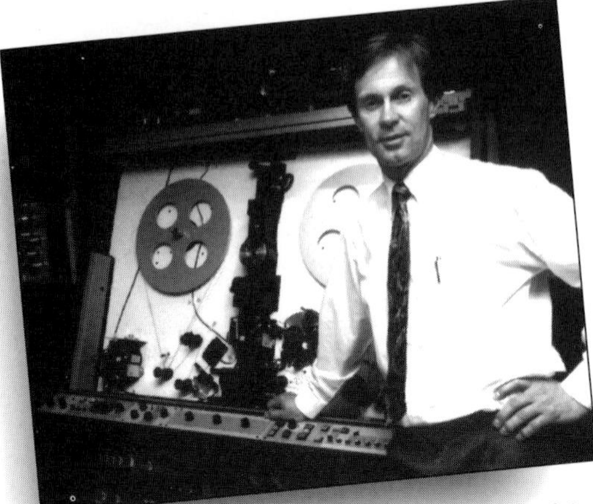

# The Laboratory - New Technology Paul Collard of Soho Images

***Q - Scenario - I'm a film producer about to make a picture, I have no preconceptions about what post production route I should take, but I'm working on a low-budget and a tight timescale, and I want to cut non linear because I believe that is the way to go. What are the options I have - I need to end up on a 35mm print and I'm either going to originate on 35mm or Super 16mm and do a blow up?***

***Paul -*** You're going to develop your negative, that's absolutely definite. You're then going to want some means of viewing that picture and to quality control check what you've shot and also something you can have to edit with. If it's a feature film, it's going to end up on the big screen, so you're going to need, at some point, to check that the images you're getting are going to look good on the big screen. Therefore, it makes a lot of sense to put in your budget, an amount of money for your first day's rushes or first three days rushes to be printed up onto film so they can be projected.

Putting that aside, you then have your rushes transferred on telecine direct to Betacam SP, which is the most common format for feeding into a non linear editing system. You can then view and edit all your material on the non linear computer. By choosing this route, you save the cost of rush printing all your material, your sound synching can be done at telecine, so therefore you don't have the added cost of audio mag transfers and synching - it's all done to the tape. At the same time as you sync your location DAT to the Beta SP tape, a copy DAT of all the used audio, with the same time code as the picture, is run off. You can then take those DATs with the EDL (Edit Decision List) you generate once you have edited your picture non linear and do an Audio Auto Conform prior to the final mix. The Audio Autoconform transfers all the different sound takes used in the film, in sync with the final edit, to either disk or tape. You end up with a digital version of what used to be multiple mag tracks.

As you can see, the process has a clear time scale and financial benefits.

***Q - And that's all done in house by your personnel?***

***Paul -*** Yes, we can deliver to you the next day, sync rushes with a copy DAT which has the same timecode on it as the BETA SP and that copy DAT is produced digitally from the DAT master - there

is no generation loss whatsoever.

***Q - What about the 24 - 25 fps issue?***

***Paul -*** Most features are shot at 24 fps (frames per second) but PAL telecine works at 25fps. There are a variety of ways of dealing with 24 to 25 frame conversions, but the one we use successfully is the method of simply telecineing at 24 frames per second, so we actually play out 24 frames of telecine picture in one second, but we record it onto Betacam SP which is PAL at 25 frames. The telecine sorts that out by putting in two extra fields per frame, so you end up with 25 frames of video in a normal PAL domain. A second of what you've shot is still a second of what you are working with. Alternatively, Lightworks and Avid both have systems for 'slowing down' a telecine from 25fps to 24fps.

***Q - Would you advise to shoot at 25?***

***Paul -*** Yes, it's simpler and there is less opportunity for error. Things like TV monitors in shot and some HMI lighting also cease to be a problem.

***Q - Are there any specific problems with the telecine that somebody should be aware of in advance?***

***Paul -*** I think the need for the cameraman to maintain a record of his exposures is important so that we can put the negative onto an analyser and give him a printer light report. Framing is also important and I think it's important to shoot a framing reference test before you start the film. The actual aspect ratio that you shoot super 16 is not quite the same as the theatrical release print, therefore when framing up you must consider you are going to lose a bit of top and bottom. 1:66 (Super 16mm) to 1:85 (theatrical) is a 5% crop at the top and bottom for which you have to allow .

***Q - If you are on location, how do you view your rushes?***

***Paul -*** There is controversy about what format you view the rushes in. One of the problems with viewing rushes for a feature off a VHS copy of the Beta in a hotel room with a hired TV and video is that you can't see that much. The focus puller is probably tearing his hair out trying to work out if he did get the focus he wanted. One of the better ways to do that is to view in a slightly higher format - I personally recommend S-VHS because it's a step up from VHS and it's not that much more expensive. We supply to all productions a VHS tape with a gray scale, framing reference and colour bars, so that the Director of Photography can line up the monitor (some monitors are dark or contain too much contrast for instance).

POST-PRODUCTION

## NEW TECHNOLOGY TIPS

*PLANNING*
*Always plan out every aspect of your post production route, well in advance. Especially with regard to film speed and time codes.*

*RUN UP*
*Always allow five seconds where both sound and camera are rolling before marking and calling action.*

*VIEWING*
*Watch your rushes on as high a quality format as possible, at least Super VHS.*

*NEGATIVE*
*Never touch or cut the negative, especially before it has been logged and telecinied.*

*STORAGE*
*Keep you BETA telecine tapes and DAT copies safe. Never work from a dupe copy of your telecine.*

***Q - So for a low-budget film, after supplying a line up tape, you would recommend that they go out and spend £1000 on a S-VHS deck and a good monitor and just put it in the boot of their car?***

**Paul -** Absolutely.

***Q - What if there appears to be a problem?***

**Paul -** If we or the production team see a problem on the rushes tape, we would produce a print straight away, screen it and supply the producer with a screening report.

***Q - What are the advantages of this particular method over traditional film cutting?***

**Paul -** In a nutshell, the real advantage is that you can dramatically cut down your post production timescale - time is money. If you have a non linear editing device on location or close by, and you shoot days one and two, by day four, the editor should have a rough cut of days one and two. When the director has spare time, he can have a look - by the time you've wrapped, three quarters of the film is already rough cut.

***Q - If you were on the ball, within a week of wrapping, you could have your first rough cut?***

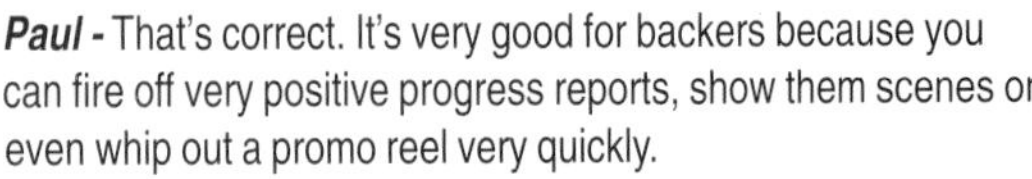

**Paul -** That's correct. It's very good for backers because you can fire off very positive progress reports, show them scenes or even whip out a promo reel very quickly.

***Q - And cutting non linear, it's easy to mock the whole film up in VHS quality, and say this is 80% of what it's going to be, or even test it with a small audience to get a feel for it?***

# Non Linear Laboratory Route For Film Production

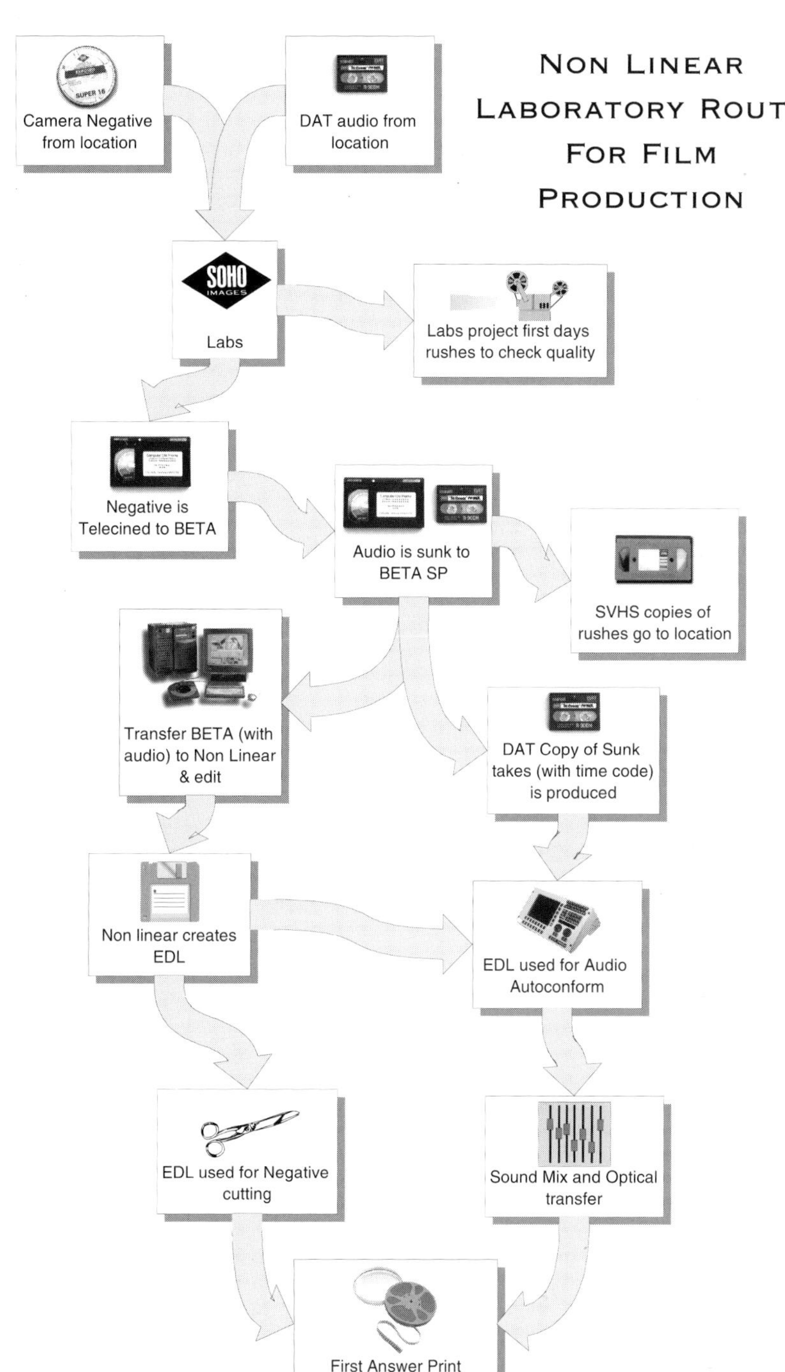


POST-PRODUCTION

***Paul* -** Absolutely. That is a huge advantage which I see as an enormous step forward in production.

***Q - What are the most common mistakes you come across?***

***Paul* -** Not allowing enough time for run up on the sound. If they're shooting timecode then they need to allow 5 -7 seconds of the camera running and the sound running before the clapperboard in order to get sync. Another mistake is not testing the kit beforehand. You need to allow yourself a day or two testing, DATS in particular are notorious for creating problems. A lot of people start shooting on DAT and then go over to Nagra as DAT's are not that secure when it comes to time code - if time code jumps all over the place, you can go into post production with all kinds of sync offsets and that costs a lot of money to put right.

A word of caution - when you are non linear editing, those original Beta tapes are your one and only link between your original film and your non linear pictures. The time code on those tapes is THE link to the edge numbers on the negative. If somebody messes with the time codes, for instance somebody else needs that Beta, *I'll go and make a copy of it,* and on the copy you use timecode that doesn't mean anything, then you start editing with it, the link between the time code and edge numbers is broken. You then provide an EDL to the neg cutter and nothing works.

***Q - But it is possible to dupe that tape and ensure that the timecode is copied?***

***Paul* -** Yes, it's possible to clone it.

## Time / Footage Chart

| Time/Minutes | 35mm @ 24 fps | 16mm @ 24 fps | 16mm @ 25 fps |
|---|---|---|---|
| 1 mins | 90ft | 36ft | 37.5ft |
| 5 mins | 450ft | 80ft | 187.5ft |
| 10 mins | 900ft | 360ft | 375ft |
| 15 mins | 1350ft | 540ft | 562.50ft |
| 25 mins | 2250ft | 900ft | 937ft |
| 30 mins | 2700ft | 1080ft | 1125ft |
| 60 mins | 5400ft | 2160ft | 2250ft |
| 90 mins | 8100ft | 3240ft | 3375ft |
| 120 mins | 10800ft | 4320ft | 4500ft |

**16 frames 35mm = 1ft**
**40 frames 16mm = 1ft**

***Q - Clone is the word, so what you're asking for is a clone tape, not a copy?***

***Paul -*** Yes. The important thing to understand about non linear editing is that there has to be an unbroken link between the timecode that the rushes were transferred with and the key edge numbers on the film. That is reliant upon that film roll not being cut or broken down in any shape or form, until it is logged against the timecode of the video tape. It can be broken down after that because it is all now on a computer, it is stored and any timecode we can get to on the edge number. But for arguments sake, if there was a bit of damage to the neg, or somebody went and cut a shot out *BEFORE* it had been logged, the whole relationship just fails. It's very important to appreciate that the non linear edit is not your film, you do not have a product until you've gone back and cut the negative. It is that chain between the key numbers and timecode that is vital.

***Q - What basic advice would you offer?***

***Paul -*** Always involve your production house and laboratory service from the outset. You will get good advice which is based on the experience of many productions and you will be able to agree a method of attack. If you don't tell them what you're going to do, and you reveal the parameters to them either after you've started or at the last minute, it could mean that you've taken the wrong route. Try and think of everything you want to do, and ask all the questions you can think of. Bare your soul and you'll get good advice.

***Q - Essentially put everyone in one room, and nobody leaves until everybody understands the process and knows the route that has been chosen.***

***Paul -*** Yes, we've had projects where we've called a pre-production meeting with the camera crew, the sound recordist, the editor, the director, producer and, sound post production company and other representatives of post production. And we say *right, we're going to start this on such and such a date, we're going to do this and this is the way we want to do it.* That couple of hours is worth it's weight in gold.

# Non Linear Editing
## Brian Hardman of Lightworks Editing Systems Ltd.

*In the past few years, Computerised non linear editing has made traditional cutting room techniques obsolete. The Lightworks Turbo is one of the preferred machines for feature film editors.*

***Q - What is 'non linear' editing?***

***Brian -*** Film editing is non linear, but most people mean computers when they say non linear - it's the ability to give video editors the flexibility that film editors always had, and to give film editors the advantage of removing the mechanical restrictions of working with film in the cutting room.

***Q - What are the major advantages over traditional film editing?***

***Brian -*** The major advantages are that you can edit and re-edit to your heart's content - as many different versions or combinations of footage with NO detriment to the quality of the final product. By removing the mechanical restrictions of the traditional film editing process, you are free to be more creative. For instance, scenes and their running order can be changed without having to strike another cutting copy.

***Q - Is it quicker to edit with non linear?***

***Brian -*** In general, the whole process isn't much quicker. However, if I can give you a quote from a film editing friend of mine, who is a traditional film editor - he says he used to be doing 12 to 14 hour days, 6 days a week on a very tight schedule, and never see his family - now "even my wife likes your bloody machine and she's never even seen it" because he's now doing the same work in a five day week and going home at six o'clock every night with a big smile on his face. It's a very sweeping statement to say it will save time, because you've got to look at the whole post production process, but it does save time in terms of decision making, and gives you the option to do far more in the time available.

***Q - How easy is it to learn to cut with a computer?***

***Brian -*** We love people who are mortified by computers, they are the people who are the biggest

converts to Lightworks products. Traditional film editors, who have never sat in front of a keyboard in their lives do a two day training course, a day on their own, and then are straight into cutting a feature film. That is how quick it can be.

***Q - Is that training course something that is provided free by Lightworks, or is there a fee?***

**Brian -** It depends. If you buy a Lightworks system, then you get free training. Outside of that, we have a number of arrangements with a number of the training organisations such as Skillset and the National Film School. In addition we hold technical and operational courses at our London offices. If people ring us up we provide a training course at a cost per day - we have cheaper rates for freelancers etc.

***Q - What materials are needed to edit on a Lightworks system?***

**Brian -** Basically what is presented to Lightworks is a tape of the telecine transfer of either the neg or the print. We try to get involved at the pre-production stage and point out the route that is required but there is no hard and fast route because there are a lot of external factors. These being whether you need to screen rushes on a daily basis, whether you are happy to do direct neg transfers, what your audio route is going to be, whether you are in PAL or NTSC land. These are all major questions that need to be asked, and when they are answered, we can recommend facilities and put people in touch with people to facilitate the various elements that are required.

***Q - And would that have synchronised sound?***

**Brian -** Not necessarily, again, this is part of the external factors. However, most productions will have synchronised sound on the rushes tape.

***Q - Should I use Betacam SP?***

**Brian -** Any tape format will work, but Beta SP is the most common in Europe. In the States, U-Matic still seems to be very common although they are moving over to Betacam.

***Q - How do I get my tape onto a Lightworks system, what is the process?***

**Brian -** It's a process that we call digitisation which is a real time process - if you've got 30 minutes of rushes that you need to get into the Lightworks system per day, it will take you at least 30 minutes to get those in. You play back the tape and 'copy' (digitise) it onto Lightworks hard disk.

***Q - How good is the image quality of the Lightworks Turbo system?***

**Brian -** We are now at a level where we can satisfy the most exacting profession-

## Compression - Putting On The Squeeze

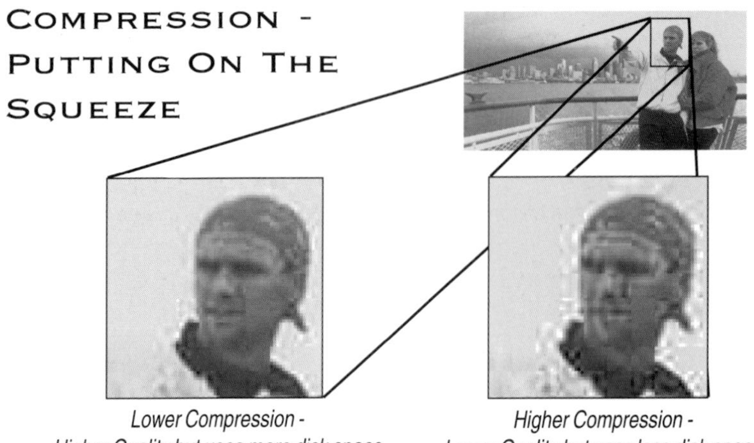

Lower Compression - Higher Quality but uses more disk space

Higher Compression - Lower Quality but uses less disk space

als - the Hollywood film market. It's all about the balance between cost and storage. The better quality picture you work with, the more storage you need to have on your system. Each frame of the film is digitised and then compressed to save space. The compression can be set at different levels so that the less compression used, the better the picture quality and the more hard disk storage you will need. The higher the compression, the lower the picture quality and less hard disk space is needed. I'm very wary of people trying to equate the digitised images to their analogue equivalents. People say it's better than VHS - It's not, it's different. You can have a picture that looks fantastic on a VHS but looks really poor in a non linear system, and vice versa.

***Q - How much material can I store on a Lightworks system?***

***Brian -*** However much you want to pay for - we recently installed a system to do *Mission Impossible* which has got 216 gigabytes of storage on it - about 170 hours of storage. Of course, if you are prepared to drop the image quality, you can store more. The way we measure picture quality is in minutes per gigabyte (1000 megabytes). Currently, on the Lightworks Turbo, we can store 30 minutes per gigabyte at the highest picture quality, down to about 90 minutes per gigabyte which is at the lowest picture quality. A good compromise is sixty minutes per gigabyte.

***Q - My editor has produced a rough cut of the movie, and we have put in some music from other movies. Is it possible to dump the whole movie in one big chunk down onto one VHS tape, take it home with me over the weekend and let the wife watch it and see what it's like as a movie?***

***Brian -*** Yes. No problem.

***Q - Is it possible to produce different edits without destroying any of the other edits?***

***Brian -*** This is one of the big advantages of non linear - some would also say a disadvantage, because you can potentially end up with, and there is no penalty in doing this, 50 versions of a

movie. You can have the producers cut, directors cut, cleaners cut if you want. And they are all instantly available and you don't need any more hard disk space. The material (picture and sound) only ever exists once - there is no copying involved.

***Q - Can you project a Lightworks Turbo edit?***

***Brian -*** Yes. It can be done and it has been done. It's obviously not 35mm quality, it's Lightworks picture quality. The image quality is probably somewhere between VHS and U-Matic at the higher picture quality.

***Q - What would be the best route for a low-budget film maker to take?***

***Brian -*** If it's low-budget, then there are certain compromises to make. The first thing I would suggest is that the actual transfer to tape would be a negative transfer cutting out the need for rush prints. The compromise means that the traditional relationship between the lighting cameraman and the Lab contact man, now comes down to a relationship between the Lighting cameraman and the telecine operator, because the telecine operator is the first guy who is going to see the negative. What often happens in this scenario is that the lighting cameraman may have, say four or five selected slates a day pulled out and printed up and he will have a projector set up somewhere, often on location. He can then compare the selected projected shots with what he's seeing on tape from the telecine. Often, that situation will settle down and for the first week he'll look at selected projected rushes, and thereafter, possibly only once a week if at all.

***Q - If there is a choice for the production to shoot at 24 or 25 fps, what would you recommend?***

***Brian -*** Our job should be to not restrict a production as far as possible and it is undoubtedly the case at the moment, that 24 frame production does need a bit more careful planning than 25 frame production, purely because of this thing called the PAL video signal. The NTSC situation is very different, and is no problem at all.

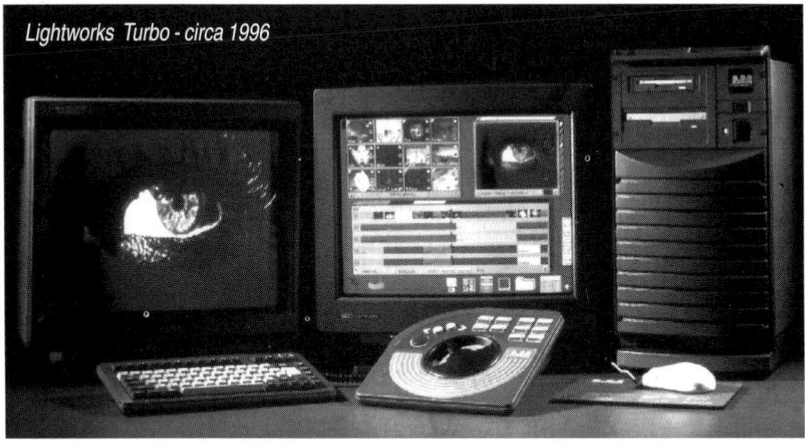

*Lightworks Turbo - circa 1996*

# Suggested Lightworks Non Linear Post Production Route

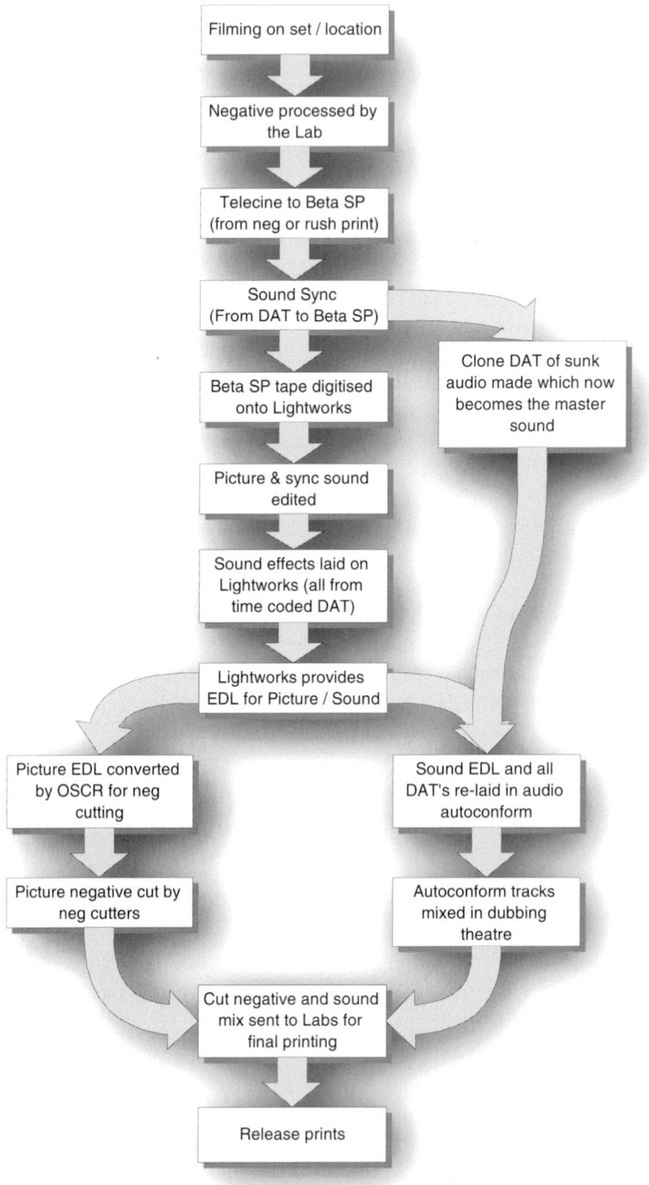

- Filming on set / location
- Negative processed by the Lab
- Telecine to Beta SP (from neg or rush print)
- Sound Sync (From DAT to Beta SP)
  - Clone DAT of sunk audio made which now becomes the master sound
- Beta SP tape digitised onto Lightworks
- Picture & sync sound edited
- Sound effects laid on Lightworks (all from time coded DAT)
- Lightworks provides EDL for Picture / Sound
  - Picture EDL converted by OSCR for neg cutting
  - Picture negative cut by neg cutters
  - Sound EDL and all DAT's re-laid in audio autoconform
  - Autoconform tracks mixed in dubbing theatre
- Cut negative and sound mix sent to Labs for final printing
- Release prints

POST-PRODUCTION

*Film editors like the Lightworks Turbo system because it mimics the cutting room environment, even down to dedicated controllers that look much more like a Steenbeck than any mouse and keyboard combination.*

***Q - Am I correct in saying that if an inexperienced, low-budget producer has the option, they should shoot at 25fps and not 24fps just to avoid potential headaches?***

***Brian -*** I hate to say it but yes.

***Q - When and how is the sound synchronised with the picture?***

***Brian*** - There are two options with slight variations. People generally sync you up at telecine and that covers a myriad of sins. Most facilities will offer you a sync rushes service, but what they actually do is sync up in a sync suite after the telecine transfer. They will take the mute video tape and your source audio and synchronise the sound with every take. If the sound was originated on DAT, the whole process will stay 100% digital. Once each shot has been sunk, the sound is transferred to the video tape. At the same time, a clone DAT that is an audio mirror of the beta tape is made. That clone DAT becomes your audio master for the whole of the rest of your production. It's all digital and it's not a copy it's a clone.

***Q - And the other method being that we come to Lightworks with just our picture, digitise it and sync the DAT up on a Lightworks system?***

***Brian -*** Yes, but there are two major disadvantages. Firstly, the first time you see sync rushes is on the Lightworks system. The second is that you have twice the digitising time, thirty minutes becomes sixty minutes for example. Having said all that, the big advantage, certainly for low-budget production, is that your telecine transfer cost is significantly reduced because you're asking a telecine house to provide you with a mute transfer with corresponding time code and nothing else.

***Q - Is the Lightworks Turbo sound broadcast quality?***

***Brian -*** It's your option. If your source is on DAT, we can take it digitally into Lightworks and you can work with it in Pro Sound, broadcast quality. But the disadvantage of that way of working is the storage cost. There is approximately 12% storage penalty if you were working in Pro sound as opposed to working in what we call Edit Quality audio, which is actually half sample rate audio, so instead of 48 Khz audio it's 24 Khz. Which is perfectly useable for editing and is actually used in Hollywood for screening in theatres and nobody gets too upset.

***Q - Can you then track lay your sound effects on a Lightworks system?***

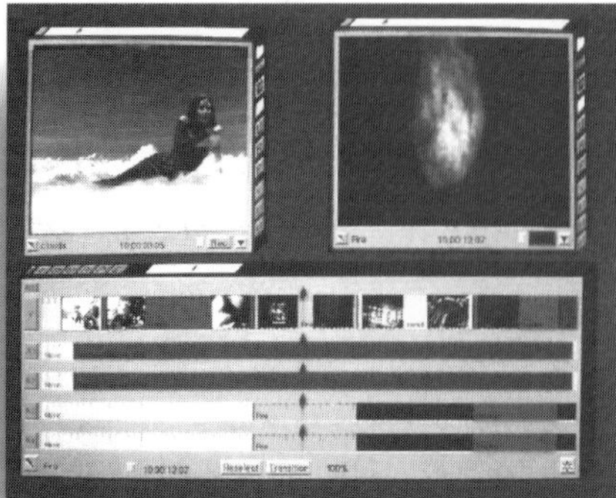

**Brian -** Again, the Lightworks system, from a sound point of view, is a mimic of the film cutting room and a bit more. We can track lay up to 16 tracks currently on a Lightworks, and again that can be at Pro quality or Edit Quality depending on your route. If you are working at Pro Quality, it means you can bring in CD effects, material that is non time coded, lay it in, leave it, and it exists as part of the track lay. If you're working on Edit Quality and you're going for an auto conform, then any sound you lay on the Lightworks must be time coded or re-laid later - if you have CD effects that you want to lay in and they are going to be part of the final track then put them onto a time-coded DAT so you've got a reference for the auto conform. Certainly, for lower budget features, you can do a reasonable track lay with the Lightworks system. You've got 16 tracks available - it's extremely quick to track lay because you've got a non linear picture locked to your non linear sound at every stage. Controlling levels is quite crude but it's possible to produce basic test mixes or premixes.

***Q - So it is conceivable for you to do a rough premix of your entire movie just to see if it all hangs together?***

**Brian -** Very much so. You could easily get your film to a position where it looks and sounds pretty much complete to the untrained eye and ear which is ideal for copying to VHS for test screenings.

***Q - If we've gone for a Pro Sound edit and we've track laid our effects at maximum quality, how do we get those tracks to the final mix?***

**Brian -** There are several ways you can go - the most common is to use an eight track Hi DAT tape format which uses Hi8 tape for eight tracks of digital audio. The most common machine is the Tascam DA88. The other option is to take the tracks in their digital form on disk to the sound autoconform. The advantage here is that it is fast to transfer and you can take out as many tracks as you want, straight onto disk.

***Q - What is the capacity of the optical disks that currently come as standard?***

**Brian -** 1.5 gigabyte - it's probably around 3 or 4 hours of audio and 1 to 2 hours of video.

***Q - How is the negative cut from the Lightworks edit?***

**Brian -** This depends on what facilities you've got available, who your neg cutter is, what facilities they have available and how much you want to do on the Lightworks system. We are fortunate in Britain because most of the negative houses, are geared up with systems like OSC/R or Excalibur. Now the beauty of these systems is that all the headaches, in terms of tracking film numbers, are taken away from you. They take total responsibility for the film side of things. All you have to do, as

far as the Lightworks side of things is concerned, is to produce a video EDL (Edit Decision List). A Video Edit List in terms of time code. That's like falling off a log for Lightworks, it's most basic function which it does very well. So most, I'll say almost all feature film production that happens in the UK has utilised OSC/R or Excalibur as the negative handling management system.

***Q - So you take the EDL that Lightworks produces, and OSC/R translates that into a format that the negative cutter likes - then they go and cut the neg?***

***Brian -*** Yes

***Q - What about short shots that don't have an edge number?***

***Brian -*** That's not a problem for us. That's a problem for the neg cutters. OSC/R is a logging system in its base form. It logs every film frame against a timecode frame. We give them a list of the time code and they know where the film frame is. Instead of having a reference every 40 frames, with OSC/R you get a reference every frame.

***Q - Does the Lightworks system stop you from reusing the same shot?***

***Brian -*** Yes, we have a system of flagging frame reuse. You can predetermine what your boundaries are for that, whether it's 1,2,3 or 4 frames (with a 2 frame overlap) for example.

***Q - Can the Lightworks system produce a VHS with SMPTE time code for the musician?***

***Brian -*** Yes, and we can also produce burnt in time code.

***Q - How transportable is a Lightworks system for location work?***

***Brian -*** It fits in the back of my car although it can depend on how much peripheral equipment you have. When we transported a Lightworks system to North Wales on a production last year, it went in a van because we took a very large desk and some very large PAL monitors with us. The largest part of the system is the monitor, but it will all fit in an Escort estate.

***Q - Is it possible to lose data if the computer crashes?***

***Brian -*** The Lightworks system has it's own back up routine which is operating all the time in the background which means that as you are editing away, it backs up your movements once every minute. On one particular project, Lightworks was on location in a Portacabin in North Wales. For the first week we had a dodgy power supply and we were losing power once an hour for the first couple of days. But we never lost an edit because the of the Lightworks backup routine.

***Q - What are the most common mistakes editors make?***

***Brian -*** Picking the wrong post production route and not pre-planning - which is why we encourage people to ring us and talk to us before they go into production.

# Music Law
# Ian Hierons
## of Music In Motion

*Ian Hierons has worked as an independent music supervisor and also for a specialist sound track record company. He currently runs a music production and publishing company servicing the international film industry.*

***Q - Film music is a complex business, what rights need to be cleared to use music for a film?***

***Ian -*** If you want to obtain permission to use a song by a well known band or artist, there are two types of rights you have to obtain. The first are the rights to the composition or song, which you obtain from the music publisher. There are several multi-national publishing companies like EMI Music Publishing or Warner Chappell Music, as well as thousands of smaller independent ones, they grant you the right to synchronise a composition to the film, hence the name 'synchronisation rights'. Secondly you then have to licence a recording of that composition or song, from the record company that owns the recording.

For example "Yesterday" was written by one person, but has been recorded by numerous recording artists. Therefore several record companies may own recordings which you can choose from, but there may be just one publisher. The producer will then pay a fee to both the record company and the music publisher for the use of one recorded song. If however you choose to re-record the song then you would only pay the publisher and you the producer would own the rights to that recording.

If however the song has been co-written by two, three or four writers there may be separate music publishers for each writer. Although usually the larger publishers control the world-wide rights to a song. Smaller publishers may only own the song for specific territory and you will have to talk to other publishers own rights in other countries. The same can be true of record companies who only own a recording for a specific territory, although they may have the right to licence for the world on behalf of other companies.

Obtaining synchronisation rights to one song can sometimes involve building a complex web of contracts from several record companies and music publishers, but thankfully not always. Also don't fall into the trap of only clearing a song for limited territories and then find yourself repeating the exercise months later if the release of your film has grown internationally.

***Q - How do you find out who owns which particular rights?***

***Ian*** - Either look on the back of a CD or telephone the Performing Rights Society (PRS) in London or the Mechanical Copyright Protection Society (MCPS). The PRS collects performance royalties on behalf of music publishers and can tell you who publishes which song (if you know the names of the writers) and the MCPS can tell you which record company owns which song if you know the performer.

***Q - How much does it cost to use a song in a film?***

***Ian*** - This is really down to the process of negotiation. The factors that will determine the price are; your film project, how the song is being used and the playing time, who the artist or group is and how famous they are and also how contemporary or popular the song is. As a very rough guide some publishers start at around £1,500 per 30 seconds of use. So if you have two minutes, that's 4 x £1,500 which is £6,000 for the publishing rights only. Then you have to add on top of that the record or 'master' rights from the record company. Some publishers are cheaper than others, however sometimes the larger ones are more expensive. Often if they know you really want a specific song then that may inflate the price. You may also be able to negotiate concessions if you buy a bundle of rights that includes several compositions from one publisher. The rights you usually buy are the rights to put the composition in the film, i.e. to use it theatrically, on cable TV, pay TV, satellite, free TV - in a specific territory or world-wide and also on a set number of videos.

***Q - You said you can get deals by saying I'll use five of your copyrights. Is it possible to get a better deal in return for the rights to release a sound track record?***

***Ian*** - Some record companies many be happy to release an album and perhaps include some songs in a package for you to use on the film. Some may pay you an advance and still ask for payment for using their records in the film, others may not. Some may waive their fee in return for the rights to the album. It all comes down to trading the value of each set of rights, and sound track album rights can be sometimes hard to value. Record companies are now much more cautious than five or ten years ago, simply because they paid huge advances to film companies for albums that then did not sell. The model works better in America where you have the corporate synergy between record companies and film companies like Sony, Time Warner and Polygram.

A note of caution! - Merely licensing the right to use a record and a song on the sound track of your film does not give you the right to use that song on a 'sound track' album. These are separate rights and are negotiated separately. You can negotiate both sets of rights at the same time but a major record company will not grant rights to you to pass on freely to another record company without prior approval over their identity and without knowledge of their royalty accounting procedures.

***Q - You mention royalties, where do they come in?***

***Ian -*** Royalties are generated from music performance on radio, television, cinema as well as live performance and also from the duplication of tapes records and compact discs. These are collected and distributed by the PRS and MCPS and their sister societies world-wide. For a sound track album you will get a percentage of the retail selling price from the record company that releases the album and they will pay a royalty to other record companies who own tracks compiled onto that album. There is also a percentage of the retail selling price paid to the music publishers of the songs on the album on behalf of the writers of those songs. Royalty accounting can be very complex and it is often advisable to place the onus on the company releasing the sound track to pay any third part royalties directly. You do not want to be obliged to prepare royalty statements every three or six months for a sound track album.

***Q - If you want an original score, how do you go about getting a composer?***

***Ian -*** Have a look in the sound track section of a record store and talk to agents and managers. The large talent agencies represent composers as do smaller specialist composer agencies. They will send tapes for you to consider.

***Q - When is the composer brought in?***

***Ian -*** Usually towards the start of post production. Although I would advise talking to a composer as early as possible as it is a common problem that they don't have enough time. Also another problem is that the music budget is often eaten into if the film has gone over budget. I always talk to them very early, and try to work to a fixed budget as this can lead to better results.

***Q - How do deals with composers work?***

***Ian -*** They work for a fee, paid in instalments, usually half on signature of a contract and half on delivery of the score or recorded music. The producer then pays additional sums for the recording sessions in a studio and for the orchestra or musicians. Some composers will work for a fee that is inclusive of their salary, recording and orchestral costs. Depending on the fee a composer may also retain music publishing rights to the music ('the copyright') created as these rights have a value that can be realised at a later date, by selling them a music publisher. Or the producer may negotiate to keep them as he/she is commissioning the work.

***Q - Do they organise the orchestra?***

***Ian -*** Orchestral Fixers are used to employ the orchestra and musicians. In the UK they work to very strict union rules with regards to payment and hours worked.

***Q - If the composer retains the publishing rights, and we sell the film in Taiwan, do we then have to pay the composer a slice of that payment?***

## KNOW YOUR RIGHTS

*PUBLISHING RIGHTS*
*Copyright owned by the author or composer of the work, literally the notes on the page. These become public domain 50-75 years after the death of the composer dependent on the country. These rights are controlled by a music publisher on behalf of the composer or author. Where there is more than one writer, then two or more publishing companies may own a share of the work.*

*RECORD / MASTER RIGHTS*
*Copyright in the recording of a song or composition owned by either a record company or the entity that has paid for the recording and thus owns the master tape. Different record companies may hold the copyright to a recording in each separate country.*

*SYNCHRONISATION RIGHTS*
*Rights granted to a film maker to 'synchronise' the copyrighted music in conjunction with the film. Publishing rights granted for the composition or song by a music publisher on behalf of the composer or author. Record / Master rights granted by record company to use a recording of that song or composition.*

***Ian -*** No - you are buying the composers performance and the right to exploit that copyright with your film. You would pay no more for showing the film in Taiwan unless you did not have the right to do so. The performance of the music in the film would however generate performance revenue that we discussed earlier.

***Q - How does a director work with the composer?***

***Ian -*** You hire a composer, talk to them, let them read the script, show them a rough cut of the film and then go through a process of spotting where the music is needed Often in the States, there is also a music editor and a music supervisor who would work out where the music was going to start and end, and what the dynamics and the function of the music is. Sometimes editors will use a 'temp' score (pre-existing music) on a film to give an indication of the style required. Also, by this stage you will have worked out where the songs are going to go and know how much music there is going to be. Composers like as much time as possible, but are usually given 3 - 5 weeks. A lot of composers will do mock up scores, using synthesisers, enabling you to hear what they have done, and discuss changes before you go into a studio and hear it with a full orchestra.

***Q - Can you use synthesisers if the music budget is prohibitively tight?***

***Ian -*** Synthesisers are as much a creative consideration as a financial one. For example listen to Eric Serra's score for 'The Big Blue' (Luc Besson), which is a brilliant mix of electronic score and real instruments. If the music budget is tight then I would tend to suggest that a composer does something more interesting than just trying to recreate an orchestral score with keyboards.

***Q - If for instance, you want to release the music on disc a year later, and you have that separate fee to pay to the performers, is that fixed in advance or is that something that is renegotiated later?***

***Ian -*** When you record music with an orchestra you can choose just to pay for the work of the musicians on the film or you can pay a 'Combined Use Fee' which also covers sound track albums. You would also have to pay an album royalty to the composer, generated from the sales of the album. This percentage would have been fixed in their contract.

***Q - How much does it cost to hire an orchestra?***

***Ian -*** Musicians are paid for each session which lasts 3 hours and are also paid for any overtime. PACT has a very useful booklet on the subject. Although I would suggest employing an Orchestral Fixer to organise it for you. Many scores are now recorded in mainland Europe as this can save orchestral costs, but then you will have to pay for travel and accommodation.

***Q - Who could release the sound track album ?***

***Ian -*** Major record companies like Warner Brothers and EMI own sound track labels. There are also several independently owned specialist sound track companies. They would want to know, who is releasing the film in each territory, and how wide, what the P&A spend is, and how can they tie in the sound track in the publicity.

***Q - Is it usual for a low-budget film to get a sound track album deal?***

***Ian -*** If the film becomes a hit and is seen by many people and the music is good then the album could have a shelf life of many years, think of 'The Postman' or 'Diva'. There are no rules, but generally if the film is going to have a very limited theatrical release, a sound track album deal is very unlikely.

***Q - Something like the Young Americans had a lot of contemporary hit songs in it, how much would the production company get for that album if they sold it to EMI or whoever?***

***Ian -*** I don't know the details of that deal. However as we discussed earlier, a record company may pay an advance to the production company, or may agree to provide a certain number of tracks for the film and album in return for the right to release the album. You can negotiate a trade off on a compilation type album. However a lot of score only

*Composers and their agents will gladly send you copies of their work on CD or cassette if they believe there is a feature film available for scoring*

*Copyright problems can occur in different countries. Under UK legislation, Rachmaninoff who died over fifty years ago (1943) would now be public domain and out of copyright. Other countries, including the USA have a time limit of 75 years which would mean Rachmaninoff is still in copyright there.*

sound tracks don't even get advances from record companies. Score albums have to be re-mixed and edited (the 'conversion cost') and although that money will be paid by the record company it will be recouped out of your royalty, so in a way they are paying an advance.

***Q - When is the best time to talk to record companies?***

***Ian -*** Once you are in production. They are not really going to be interested in talking to people when they are in development because there are thousands of scripts in development that never get made. It's just a waste of time for them.

***Q - Where can I get a list of record companies?***

***Ian -*** There is a trade publication called Music Week that publishes the Music Week Directory which lists all the record companies and artist's managers.

***Q - Am I correct in saying that if a new band is 100% behind the project, they will do it for free in return for the exposure, and percentages down the other end?***

***Ian -*** The record company and the management company must be 100% committed as well. The agenda of the record company is to market a band and sell records and to recoup the massive cost of recording. If your plans for the film fit their agenda and schedule then there is a basis for a deal. A band providing services for free is another matter and depends on how a deal is structured and who stands to gain the most from the situation, the artist or the film.

***Q - What is library music and how does that work?***

***Ian -*** Library music, which also known as 'Production Music', came into existence for companies that wanted pre-recorded off the shelf music, it now covers the whole gamut - rock, jazz, funk, and everything else. The clearances are obtained through the MCPS and costs £280 per 30 seconds for a world-wide licence for cinema, television and video use. You simply register with the MCPS and they send you an information pack.

***Q - Can you release a sound track album built from library music or does it just cover synchronisation rights?***

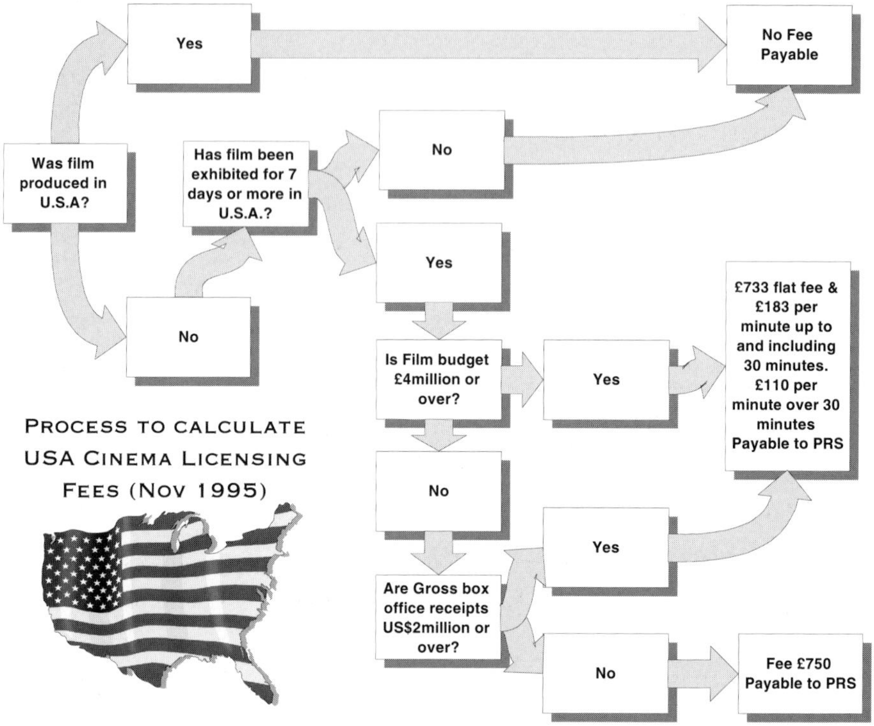

**Process to calculate USA Cinema Licensing Fees (Nov 1995)**

- Was film produced in U.S.A?
  - Yes → No Fee Payable
  - No → Has film been exhibited for 7 days or more in U.S.A.?
    - No → No Fee Payable
    - Yes → Is Film budget £4million or over?
      - Yes → £733 flat fee & £183 per minute up to and including 30 minutes. £110 per minute over 30 minutes Payable to PRS
      - No → Are Gross box office receipts US$2million or over?
        - Yes → £733 flat fee & £183 per minute up to and including 30 minutes. £110 per minute over 30 minutes Payable to PRS
        - No → Fee £750 Payable to PRS

***Ian -*** The initial fee only covers synchronisation to the film, you then pay additionally for sound track album use.

***Q - For instance, we thought of using some Holst as we believed he was out of copyright, having died over 50 years ago. However, we found that if we wanted to release our film in either America or Japan, he also had to be out of copyright there, and therefore dead for 75 years***

***Ian -*** Yes. Up until recently music fell out of copyright (and became 'public domain') 50 years after the death of the composer or writer, in some countries it is now 75 years, and some music has therefore come back into copyright. The EC are trying to ratify it at the moment.

***Q - When a composer is out of copyright can you do whatever you want with the music?***

***Ian -*** You can do whatever you want with the composition, but not with a specific recording of that composition, because that recording is still owned by a record company.

***Q - When we made WHITE ANGEL, we discovered there was an extra fee we had to pay in America, why was that?***

***Ian -*** Performance royalties are generated when film music is played in a cinema. In the US there is no performance income from the cinema so the producer has to pay a fee, by law, to the PRS in the UK for using a UK recorded score in America. (See diagram).

***Q - Is that something the sales agent would take care of?***

***Ian -*** No, it is usually a delivery requirement from the production company.

***Q - What is a music cue sheet?***

***Ian -*** A music cue sheet is basically a chronology of all the music that is used in the film. It details how it is used, (foreground or background/front title etc), who the songwriter/composer is, and names the publisher and record company. A cue sheet is then sent to the PRS and one is given to each publisher whose music you have used.

***Q - What is the differentiation between background and featured music?***

***Ian -*** Background is music heard by the actors, for example, it's coming out of a radio, from a juke box or played in a nightclub. Featured music is music that is not heard by the actors, for example, an opening title song is featured.

***Q - On the first film that we did, we got a friend to write the music with a synthesizer, are there any problems doing that?***

***Ian -*** There are no problems, but I would ask you two questions. Did you like it? And did it work for the film? Beware of people who haven't scored films before, beware of using songwriters who think they can score a film because it is a different discipline. Always look at the composers credentials and the training they have had, and beware of inexperience. If you have a very tight budget talk to composers studying at the NFTS or other film schools. They will understand the discipline better than a friend with a synth. Although there are more composers than work for them to do, so talk to everyone you can.

***Q - Do you have any final advice?***

***Ian -*** Producing music takes a lot of time and effort to get it right. People always have problems with music either because of inexperience, lack of money or both. Seek advice from someone who has experience and can advise you on the best approach, either a fellow producer, a solicitor or a music supervisor. Also talk to music publishers who may offer a range of services for the film maker.

## Music Composer Simon Boswell

***Q - When does a composer first get involved in a film production?***

***Simon*** - There's no normal scheme of things, I've been involved from script stage and at the very last minute. Having said that, the most common thing is that the production will concentrate on finishing the picture and it will be very close to a finished edit before they start thinking about music.

***Q - Do you ever get a phone-call from a producer, saying 'what are you doing tomorrow and for the next three weeks?'***

***Simon*** - That's kind of rare, but it has happened. I actually prefer to be involved at the last minute because the nightmare for a composer is things changing all the time, not only from a technical point of view, it becomes a real pain to rewrite for different lengths or for scenes that disappear altogether, but because creatively, it does my head in to have the ambience of the film changing all the time. I'd prefer to be watching it as a punter, if you like, to get a very instinctive response to an almost finished film.

***Q - How does a film producer get to a composer?***

***Simon*** - Usually they've seen something that I've done that they like, or they've heard from friends or people in the business and I think then quite often they'll call me direct and we'll just talk about it. Then if I'm interested, the next thing is to talk to my agent about the business side of things.

***Q - As a composer, what do you need to actually produce the score?***

***Simon*** - I need as near to a locked picture as I can get. A final edit on Umatic videotape with visual SMPTE timecode on it, which also refers to the audio timecode on one of the channels of the audio. I can then synchronise and lock all my equipment to it. Like the majority of composers now, I'm very much computer based so that I actually write locked to picture. My keyboards will record every move I make, every note I play.

***Q - If the decision was made to stay with the digital soundtrack as opposed to a traditional orchestra, do you have all the equipment on site, and would that be part of the package or would you need to hire more equipment in?***

***Simon -*** I have my own studio, and if I'm doing it all myself, I can finish it here.

***Q - How good are synthesisers and samplers now, compared with ones that we all heard in the eighties?***

***Simon -*** It's a very personal thing what you actually do with the technology. Whether you're trying to emulate an orchestra, or you're trying to do something original with the technology in a different way. Everyone handles it differently. I've done scores where they simply couldn't afford an orchestra and would say, *please can you make it sound like an orchestra.* Yes, I'll do that. And then there are others like *Hackers* where we don't think a real orchestra is going to work with the film, let's make it as synthetic or as artificial as the environment, which is obviously computers.

***Q - How large a band do you need to get a real big orchestral sound?***

***Simon -*** A good example would be *Jack & Sarah.* I had done an earlier synthesised version and the production now wanted it with real instruments and a full orchestrated score. We recorded that with 65 players which is an average sized orchestra. The cost of doing that I would estimate at $175k, but that's with a top orchestra and a top studio.

***Q - But you could do it for considerably less?***

***Simon -*** Yes you could do it for less if you're prepared to juggle around the components. What you could do is use a much smaller group of musicians and add samples to it. A lot of people do it because you can get a more interesting sound. Or, you can go abroad, which is the other scenario that is always coming up. There are certain orchestras in Eastern Europe where they are much cheaper and you can get a *buy out* deal as opposed to a *residuals* deal.

***Q - What you're saying is that you can lay down the basics of the music with samplers and synthesisers and then you can bring in your violin soloist?***

***Simon -*** Yes, to give a human aspect to what you are doing. And vice versa, you can use a small orchestra, and then use synth pads to thicken the sound without really being aware of it, just to make it sound bigger. And of course you can use sounds that an orchestra can't do.

***Q - How do you deliver the final music mix?***

***Simon -*** If they want a lot of control over the music during the mix, then you break the component parts of the music down into separate stereo tracks, for example, if there's a lot of percussion drowning out dialogue, they could be taken down whilst leaving the other elements, such as strings, mixed up. I've done a lot of films where I've just delivered a stereo mix and that's it. Without doubt, that's the cheapest and easiest way to do it. In that case, the final music is usually supplied on DAT.

*Using synthesisers, composers can now 'mock up' the final score. If push comes to absolute shove, then this type of score can be used in place of an orchestra. It doesn't necessarily sound like an orchestra, but as long as it supplies the correct emotive qualities, it can work just as well.*

***Q - What are music cues?***

**Simon -** Strictly speaking, my job starts when the picture is locked and you have spotted the picture. Spotting the picture means going through the film and saying *we want music from here to here* and so on. 1M3 for instance would be the third piece of music on reel one. Very often they've done temporary music that has been pulled from other films or albums, usually the director or music editor has dug around and found stuff that's pointing the composer in the right direction. Having listened to the temp music, you would then sit with the director and discuss with him what you think is required. How much you're left to do yourself is variable and depends on the director.

***Q - When it comes to the soundtrack album, do you have any control over that?***

**Simon -** Yes. I always redo everything for the soundtrack album, not only remix, but rewrite, use bits of dialogue and special effects to make it interesting, because a lot of scores are just lifted from the final mix of the film and I think they're really dull. I try and spice it up a bit as a listening experience and I've been very involved with the albums that I've made.

***Q - Do you find that directors or producers have a tendency to want to over score or underscore a movie?***

**Simon -** Usually they want you to do wall to wall music and then cut out what they don't want.

***Q - Are you involved with the songs that are used in films?***

**Simon -** I'm involved in discussions with the director on a creative level, not on a budgetary level. Very often they hire music supervisors who's job it is to make legal clearances of tracks and get them as cheaply as possible. It's a very highly developed department in America and becoming more so over here.

***Q - What are the most common mistakes that producers make when it comes to the music?***

**Simon -** Producers always under-budget and as a result they ask the impossible. They're incredibly unrealistic. The thing about getting bands and good songs is that it's expensive. Record

A videotape of the final, locked edit of the film with SMPTE time code is all most composers require for them to produce an original score.

companies know what they're going to charge these days and it all adds up. I had a phone call today from a production manager who's putting a new film together asking me what I'd advise them to put in the budget. That's quite an intelligent call to make but very rare. The commonest mistake that I've encountered are to do with the songs aspect, leaving it too late to license the ones you need. That happened with *Shallow Grave*, it's happened with *Jack & Sarah*, and it's happened with *Hackers*.

***Q - What can a production do to make your life easier?***

***Simon -*** The big thing is not to keep editing the film whilst I'm working on it. I guess having a director who knows what he wants and is very polite and straightforward about it is also good. Aside from that, having a sensible budget. The other thing to remember is that whilst you're watching the film over and over, everyone else is going to see it just once, and very simple things are often the most effective.

Music is often thought of as a means of fixing things in a film. There's no question that music transforms a film, but above and beyond that? I think people will say, *this scene really doesn't work - fix it.* And that's very often why scores get thrown out, because music is the very last stage in the production before people have to admit that their film is crap. So if they score it, and the film still doesn't work they blame the music. What can they do? They can't reshoot it, so music has a terrific weight of responsibility.

# Sound Mixing Mike Anscombe

## of Cinelingual

***Q - What is the dub or final mix?***

***Mike -*** It's where the final soundtrack is made - dialogue, sound effects, music, atmospheres are all put together.

***Q - What is the producers job at the dub?***

***Mike -*** In order for us to have a successful relationship with any production, the producer needs to keep a tight reign on things. He has to marry the constraints of the production and it's budget with the artistic wishes of the director and editor who would probably take a year to dub it. If we have quoted a production certain amount of days or hours, the Producer must take that onboard and make sure that we get it done in that timescale, or be prepared to budget for an over-run. So from our point of view we like to see a producer who is in control of the situation. It's also vital to work out a schedule in advance. What we often do when we've established a figure with the production company is to break it down into so many days of foley, ADR, and final mixing. At the end of each day there's a ball park guide of where you need to be, you need to be at the end of reel one, or having premixed reel one - it's very important to stick to your schedule otherwise you can bet your life things are going to run over, and that's when there are tears. We always try to get the director and editor to preview the movie with us, we'd just get a free afternoon in the theatre and say, come along in a dead slot and let the dubbing mixer sit down with the director and editor - run the cutting copy with sync sound and a bit of music and effects spun in here and there to get a feel for the film and the director to say, *OK, this is a problem scene but here's what I want to achieve* - if we can get an advance preview then it does help us to get a feel of what the production wants.

***Q - What materials do you need to do the final mix, like stock?***

***Mike -*** Now that things are moving away from magnetic, stock is less of an issue. In the old days stock could account for thousands of pounds on a feature film. Now it's a fraction of that. In situations where a non linear cut has been done we would work to a Beta SP picture and the tracks would be inputted and formatted digitally, probably on DAT. Mag stock in those instances is a thing of the past.

***Q - What are the premixes?***

***Mike -*** Premixing is the prepping of the individual elements of dialogue, effects, and foley etc., prior to the final mix. Premixing the dialogues for instance, where you smooth out the rough edges.

Dialogue premixes are the most important part of any premixing process, if you can't hear what's going on in the dialogue, if they're at different levels and not properly balanced against the other, you've got a problem. We usually premix the foley, effects and atmospheres then mix them all down into a handful of tracks so it's easier in the final mix.

***Q - Is that the time when camera noise is taken out?***

***Mike -*** Yes, things such as when cameras haven't been sufficiently blimped, you've got a problem with air conditioning noise, fridges, anything that has been overlooked, that kind of thing can often, not always, be taken out with a little dipper which hones in and targets certain frequencies. It's very good for getting rid of camera noise, but please try to get it right on set.

***Q - How many tracks could there be on average?***

***Mike -*** On a final mix, you might be dealing with a couple of dialogue tracks, four or five effects tracks, two or three atmosphere track - it depends, six to eight tracks, maybe less. If you've got something like *DIE HARD 3*, wall to wall pyrotechnics and explosions, then you have to do premixes of premixes, it just depends on the complexities of the operation.

***Q - What are the charts and how important are they?***

***Mike -*** The charts are our roadmap - they need to be clear and concise. They tell us what's happening, when it's happening, when music is coming in and going out, what effects are to be faded out, or cut off totally, they give us dialogue cues so that we know what's happening before it happens. It really is like a map in sound terms. It's a simple to learn layout but absolutely vital. If you are unsure of what your charts should contain, drop in with the mixer and ask what he prefers.

***Q - If you were in the mix and you've got real problems because somebody forgot to put a sound effect in, can that be dropped in there and then?***

***Mike -*** Nine times out of ten, yes. If the sound effect that has been forgotten is very obscure, then we might not have it. But if somebody had forgotten to lay a doorbell, a door shutting, a cow mooing - yes, we'll just bring it up on CD out of the effects library. We and other dubbing theatres have massive effects libraries which the client can utilise.

***Q - What is Foley or Footsteps?***

***Mike -*** Mr Foley was an American guy who had the idea of post synchronising footsteps and effects to pictures. Foley recording is the post synchronisation of footsteps, moves, glasses being placed on tables, keys jingling, every thing and anything that is synchronised to picture. A good foley artist can be an absolute life saver, and relative to their cost, are fantastically good value.

POST-PRODUCTION

## DOLBY - ROUGH GUIDE

*DOLBY*
*Formerly known as Dolby Stereo is a four channel "surround" system for cinemas (Left, Centre, Right, Surround). Can use Dolby A or SR noise reduction.*

*DOLBY SR*
*High quality noise reduction system used whilst mixing analogue audio for feature films and on release prints.*

*DOLBY DIGITAL*
*Six channel digital sound system for feature films (Left, Centre, Right, Left Surround, Right Surround and Sub Woofer.)*

*DOLBY SURROUND*
*Four channel system used for mixing television and video programmes and found in domestic equipment. Not used for mixing theatrical feature films.*

*Dolby and the double-D symbol are trademarks of Dolby Laboratories.*

***Q - What is the M&E mix?***

***Mike -*** The M&E mix is the Music and effects track, that is everything minus dialogue and your sales agent needs that for overseas sales. If you think you have the slightest chance of an overseas sale, in God's name budget for the making of an M&E. It would be either a mono M&E, where you have the Music and Effects combined, or a twin track M&E, where you have the music on one track and the effects on the other. It's horses for courses, but it is effectively the final mix minus the sync dialogue. Check with your sales agent what format they want (split or mixed M&E).

***Q - What is the optical sound?***

***Mike -*** Optical sound is a universal medium for reproducing sound in cinemas. Optical sound is used for married prints in a theatrical release where, literally, a photograph is made of the sound modulations from the magnetic or digital master mix. That photographic version of the sound is put onto a print of the film. When it goes through a projector in the cinema, the optical sound track is read by a photo cell which then reproduces the sound. The optical sound is produced from the master sound mix at the lab, not at the dubbing theatre.

***Q - What is Dolby A and Dolby SR, Surround etc.?***

***Mike -*** Dolby A and Dolby SR are both proprietary forms of noise reduction and belong to Dolby Laboratories. Dolby A has been superseded by the technically superior Dolby SR. In the opinion of many, Dolby SR enables 35mm magnetic sound to approach digital sound in terms of its clarity and lack of noise. Either of these noise reduction systems may be used when mixing and releasing a Dolby (previously called Dolby Stereo) analogue soundtrack. This is where a lot of producers get confused. A Dolby soundtrack always includes a surround channel and uses either Dolby A or SR noise reduction. If you want a Dolby soundtrack you have to pay a service fee to Dolby Labs, which for features is around £3k. For that you get the necessary equipment, up to 16 hours of a fully qualified Dolby engineer's time and the right to use their logo in connection with your film.

***Q - What would happen if the producer took the decision to drop the Dolby fee and just mix in stereo?***

***Mike -*** You would mix in stereo and when it came to projection in the cinema, the sound would pass through the Dolby matrix and you could get some strange effects, but it can be done although it's not recommended.

***Q - If you have a digital master, can that be put on a print optically?***

***Mike -*** If you have a Dolby optical soundtrack, non digital, you have a photographic track down the side of the print, but if you go Dolby Digital, the digital information is contained in the space between the sprocket holes.

***Q - How much better is Digital over Analogue. Can it fix problems in the mix?***

***Mike -*** If you've got hiss at the beginning, digital will preserve that hiss faithfully. If you put shit in you will get perfectly formed shit out. If your sound going in is good it will be very good coming out. What digital will not do is make bad sound good, it will make good sound even better because it will not distort or degrade. If you have analogue sound going in that's under recorded and hissy, there's not a lot you can do with that, and digital won't cure it.

***Q - What is Audio File?***

***Mike -*** Audio File is a proprietary name for a digital hard disk editing and recording system, of which there are several, but it happens to be the one that our company uses.

***Q - If we cut on Lightworks, how do you get your sound from Lightworks into something like Audio file?***

***Mike -*** The sound is transferred in what is known as an Auto conform, where an events list will be

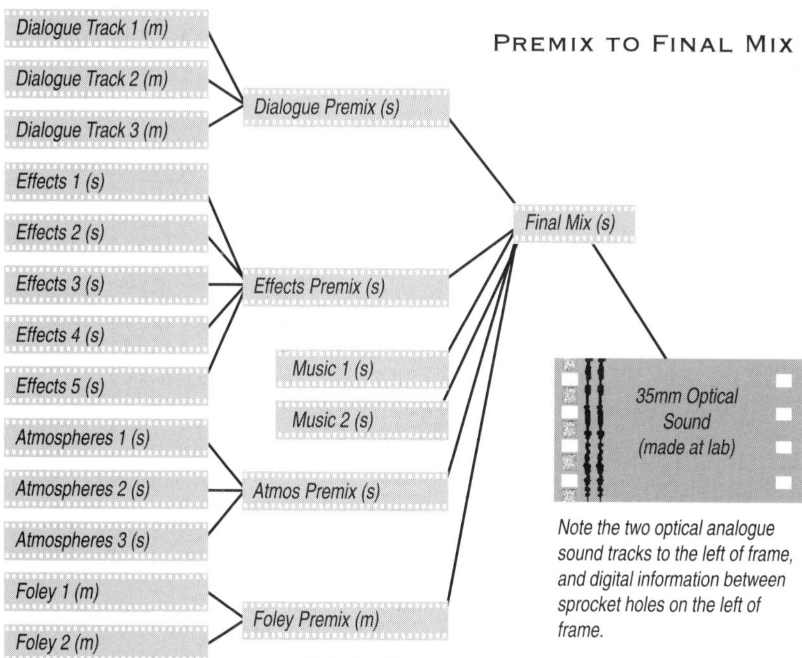


*Note the two optical analogue sound tracks to the left of frame, and digital information between sprocket holes on the left of frame.*

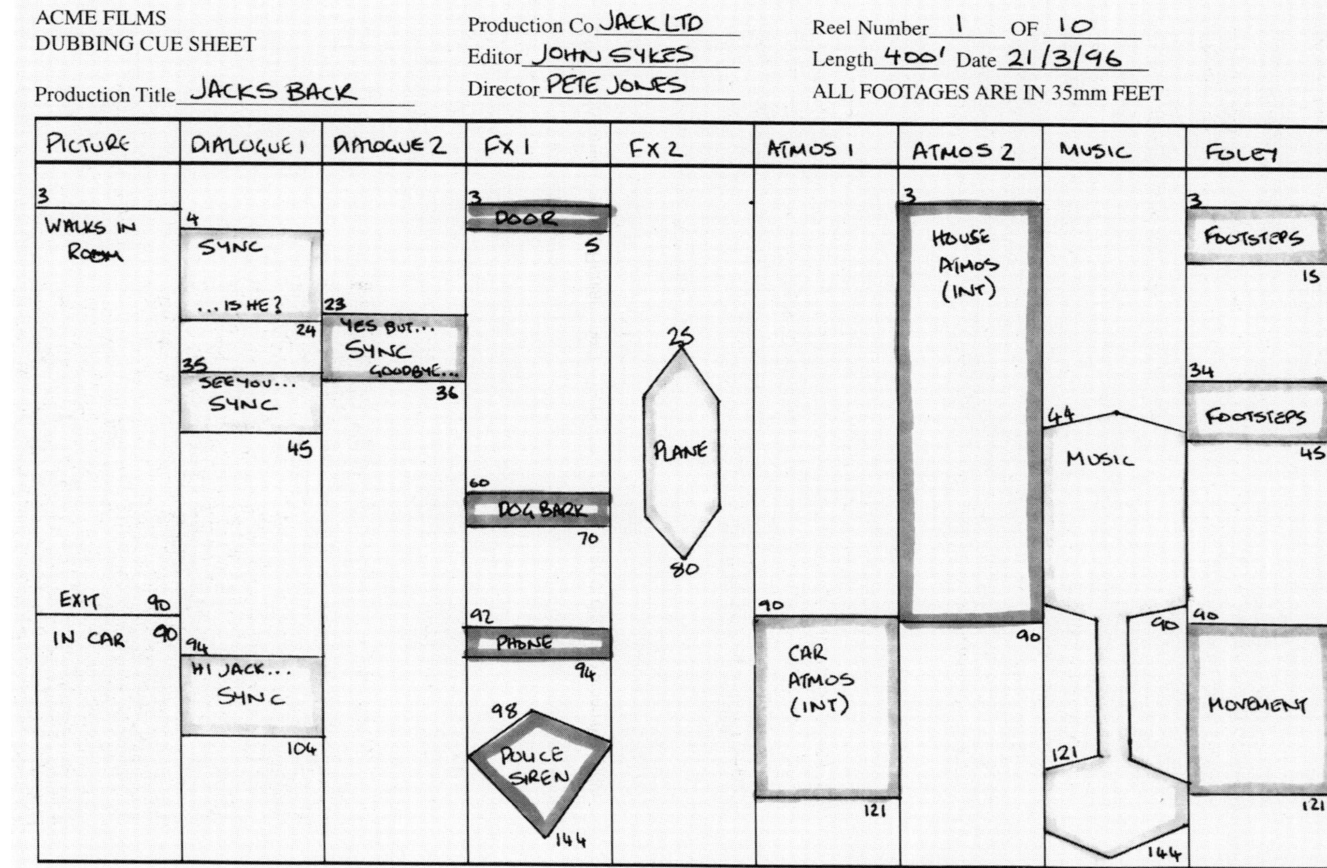


The Dubbing Chart

The Final Mix - a time and a place where all the elements of a film come together. Make sure all your creative decisions have been made in advance.

prepared. All the various bits of sound are transferred digitally to a new master, each effect or sunk sound in exactly the right place. That new master is used as an effects or atmosphere track for instance, in the final mix.

***Q - What is ADR?***

***Mike -*** Automated Dialogue Replacement - the post synchronisation of dialogue when the audio from the set is either too poor to use or has some kind of problem.

***Q - How can a producer get the best deal?***

***Mike -*** If you're on a low budget and you want to do a deal, some compromises have to be made. If you came to me and you pay up-front, my compromise is that I'm sacrificing my hourly rate, your compromise would be that you would be fitted in, as and when. It's the difference between private and national health. I would always look favourably on a pre payment and would sacrifice a margin to do so, but I would ask that the Dub is done in slightly unsociable hours.

***Q - What are the most common mistakes you come across?***

***Mike -*** Make the artistic decisions in the cutting room and not the dubbing theatre. At the best part of £3 per minute, it's an expensive place to start making creative decisions that could have been made in the cutting room. Also, If you're projecting film, make sure ALL the joins are double backed so they don't come apart in the projector. Make sure you put sync marks on the picture and all the audio tracks every 100' so that if there is a sync question, you don't have to go back to the head of the reel, which is time consuming.

***Q - What advice would you offer a film maker?***

***Mike -*** If in doubt, ask. Nobody's going to think you're a prat if you ask, in any area of the film making process. It's got to be a safer bet than cocking it up and risking disaster and damnation after. After all, everyone has to start somewhere.

*NB - Cine lingual has now changed name to dB Post*

# Titles & Opticals Alan Plant of Howell Opticals

***Q - What does a producer supply you with in order to make up their titles?***

***Alan -*** First of all, a typed script of all the titles, setting them out exactly how you require them in frame, what type faces and style of lettering you want. We would then produce a proof for you to look at and approve, making sure that everything's OK. Once that's done, we produce acetate cells from which we shoot the final titles. If it's simple white titles on a black background, then it's just a question of shooting them on a rostrum camera.

***Q - Everybody seems to have a computer now that is capable of printing titles, would it help if people set out their titles, with the correct font and positioning?***

***Alan -*** Yes, then we don't have to get involved in the headache of design (which a designer should do), we can just make up the acetate from the text you provide and shoot the titles.

***Q - Can you make titles from a piece of paper straight out of a desktop computer laser printer?***

***Alan -*** Yes, but it's not ideal and the results can be poor. The best way is to make up acetate cells.

***Q - So, for a low budget production, the cheapest, good looking titles are simply white titles on a black background?***

***Alan -*** Yes, that's the cheapest way of doing it.

***Q - What's the procedure if the titles are in colour on black?***

***Alan -*** If it's just one colour, then it's not too difficult, we just put a coloured cell underneath the title on the rostrum. If the title is multi-coloured, then you really need to have that made up by a designer as a piece of camera ready artwork, it's not something that you can produce by laying different cells on top of each other.

***Q - What about an animated logo?***

***Alan -*** To be honest, most of that side of things has moved into the computer world, we don't get calls about animation very much now.

***Q - And how is the end roller produced?***

***Alan -*** Pretty much the same way, if you want it just as white on black we would produce the artwork on one long black acetate cell with clear lettering. We would then lay it on the rostrum camera and the artwork is physically pulled across the lightbox.

***Q - Can you dictate the length of the roller?***

***Alan -*** Yes, generally it's dictated by the client. They will say the roller needs to run for 2 minutes. It's also dictated by the speed that an end roller can run, if it runs too quickly it will strobe.

***Q - What's the procedure if titles need to be put on top of picture, for instance, at the beginning of the movie?***

***Alan -*** It's exactly the same process as far as producing the artwork is concerned, so the artwork is presented to us in the same way as if the titles were going to be white on black. We film those titles on high contrast stock and, without getting too entangled in technical details, combine that with the original negative on the optical printer. At the end of that you'll have a new negative of the sequence with the titles in place. If you start to put titles over picture area or backgrounds, then you can probably multiply the cost of producing simple white on black titles by three. Remember, your sales agent will need the original negative of any sequences where we have combined it with titles - they need it for foreign countries who will put titles in their own language on it.

***Q - And what materials do you need, aside from the acetates of the titles to achieve that?***

***Alan -*** Once we have the titles shot on high contrast black and white stock and we have access to the lab materials, such as the negative / internegative, and a cutting copy or a workprint where the editor has marked up in chinagraph the points that he requires the titles to come in and go out. We take the timings from that and can then make up the titles.

***Q - Obviously, non linear editing has become popular, what happens when there isn't a cutting copy?***

**Alan -** This has caused us problems in the past. What has previously happened is that the Neg cutter will supply us with some frame counts for the titles. We can't work if someone sends us a VHS tape with timecode or a floppy disk, it doesn't mean anything and you can't relate those back into frame counts. I've done work with several editors where the production has cut non linear, but resorted to making rush print cutting copies for the title sequences so they can mark it up with chinagraph pencils. At this stage, there doesn't seem to be one method that's been devised for converting these video edits back into frame counts, but I'm sure it will soon be overcome.

***Q - How does it affect you if the film originates on super 16mm because the titles are almost always produced on 35mm?***

**Alan -** If the titles are going over a live action scene, we always shoot the title elements onto 35mm. We then make the title sequence and either leave it on 35mm or make a reduction back to Super 16mm.

***Q - How long does it take to produce titles, from the day I supply you with my artwork, and what do I get from you in the end?***

**Alan -** If you're talking about producing half a dozen titles over a couple of scenes at the front of the film, with perhaps a small end roller that was just white on black - if all went well, I would say five to seven days. If it's just straight black on white titles, it could be shorter. The producer would then walk out with the rush print that they have approved - the negative would be stored at the lab with all the other negative from the film.

***Q - What other kind of opticals are common?***

**Alan -** The most common opticals are the basic ones - slow up a scene, speed up a scene, freeze a frame on a scene, do an optical zoom in on a shot to lose something like some scenery that shouldn't be there, reposition frames, reversing the action, flopping (mirroring) the action over. Wipes are rare. Dissolves, which were common as opticals, don't tend to be done so much now, as they're done in the lab as part of their service.

***Q - But if you wanted a unique dissolve?***

**Alan -** Then it's got to be optical. The labs are governed to set frame lengths, they can do 8, 12, 16 frame dissolves, also 20, 24, 32, up to 96, which is the maximum they can do on their printers. On our optical printer we can do anything from 2 to 999 frames and any number in between.

***Q - And complex montage sequences? The lab can't do that can they?***

**Alan -** No, they can't do multiple exposures. Doing it as an optical, you can govern the exposures - sometimes it doesn't work by superimposing two scenes on top of each other at 50% exposure each - depending on the nature of the scene you've got to jiggle around with the exposures.

***Q - For Super 16mm films that are to be blown up to 35mm, the labs will usually try to get the job, but is that also a job an optical printers could do, perhaps more cheaply?***

*The optical printer - different film gauges and stocks are combined to create titles for films, as well as a host of other optical effects such as zooms, flopping, slowing down and speeding up.*

***Alan -*** 35mm blow ups have constituted most of the work that I've done over the past three years.

***Q - Is it fair to say that because titles are at the end of the production process, the money that's supposed to have been allocated has often been eaten up by earlier problems?***

***Alan -*** Yes, and not just that, the time factor is always a problem - somebody coming to us saying, *I've got to have this done, will you do it in the next three days?* - and it's something they've been working on for six months. We're at the end of the line, when both money and time have run out.

***Q - What can a producer do to make your life easier and what are the most common mistakes you've come across that cause problems?***

***Alan -*** The most common problems are spelling mistakes. The guy who does the graphics for me is excellent, he doesn't make mistakes, he produces the artwork in the form that the proof has been supplied and approved. We've just done a Scottish job where the main title is in Gaelic - and they have just found out after it's been screened at festivals, that they spelt the main title incorrectly. This kind of unforeseen cost is a problem for production companies. Also, inexperienced film makers often supply us with a scrap of paper with a list of titles and no idea of fonts, sizes or positioning. That can be very difficult.

# Negative Cutting
## Mike Fraser of Mike Fraser Ltd

***Q - What is the negative cutting?***

***Mike*** - Whenever you shoot a film, you always edit it on what is called secondary material, you never touch the master until the final conformation of your film, be it on video tape, be it on film, whatever - you only ever touch a copy. The negative cutting is the final conform of the master negative to match the final edit you have decided upon. The final edit usually comes to us either as a film cutting copy or some form of edit decision list (EDL).

***Q - Am I correct, in saying that once a film is neg cut you can never go back and rejoin a cut?***

***Mike*** - Certainly on 16mm there is no going back, but on 35mm we have a method whereby you can extend shots without loss.

***Q - How long does it take to neg cut an average feature film?***

***Mike*** - An average feature film, lets say 110 minutes long with say 800 cuts would take 2 weeks or so. It can be done quicker, and it depends on how many people you have working on it.

***Q - Are there any special requirements when cutting super 16mm?***

***Mike*** - Yes, stability is important because it's single perf only. Super 16mm is often blown up to 35mm so the joins have to be very smooth and seamless. It is vital to find out if the negative cutter has worked with super 16mm before and that he is set up for it, otherwise you could end up having to go to great expense and re-neg cut the whole picture. Super 16mm is cut A and B checkerboard. Every shot is on an alternate reel so that the joins don't show and you can have dissolves etc. With 16mm and Super 16mm you have to have an overlap which effectively destroys the frame before and after every shot. The important thing to remember about 16mm when in the cutting room or edit suite is that you must always lose one frame at the beginning and one frame at the end of every single shot of your film - that's the absolute minimum requirement. Also, laboratory printing machines can only do dissolves or at the rate of either 16, 24, 32, 48, 64, 96 frames. They can't do anything else - if you want it done at any other length you have to have it done optically which will produce an interneg. Also when you're doing A and B roll, you have to leave on 16mm at least 20 frames between a cut and the beginning of an optical or the end of an optical and a cut, and you must always leave a minimum of 4 frames between the end of one optical and the beginning of the next.

***Q - What do you need from the production team to enable you to cut the negative?***

***Mike -*** We need to have logged the negative in the first place, we need either a cutting copy if it's edited on film, or an edit decision list if it's been edited on non linear. We also need full instructions if there are requirements other than what is shown on the cutting copy or EDL.

***Q - What happens to the negative when it's cut?***

***Mike -*** The cut rolls are sent to the laboratories where they are graded, frame cue counted, cleaned and printed, and you get a first mute answer print. If you are going to blow up to 35mm it is important to check with the lab the maximum roll size they can handle on their optical printer. It's usually either 10 minutes or twenty minutes, including leaders.

***Q - What happens to all the unused negative?***

***Mike -*** It stays with the negative cutters, until such time the producer says "Junk it" or "store it" or "Can I have it back?"

***Q - How does non linear computer based editing affect negative cutting?***

***Mike -*** For feature films, regardless of how you edit it, you still need to neg cut. Non linear editing affects neg cutting in a very specific way in so much as you no longer have a cutting copy to check your neg against. As non linear is digital, we do not get any kind of cutting copy to physically check against the picture, shot by shot. All you have to work with are numbers. Therefore it is absolutely vital that those numbers are generated by something you have total confidence in. If the numbers are wrong and you cut the negative you're in a lot of trouble. There are various ways of doing it, but the way we've pioneered has always been the most frame accurate and in our view, the most comforting. We use software called *OSC/R* which in itself, has never let us down, it always produces the goods. There are other ways of doing it, other systems such as *Excalibur, Computer Match*, and also *Lightworks* and *Avid* have their own ability to produce key neg cutting lists - the only problem with that is that the negative cutting list produced out of a *Lightworks* or *Avid* is only as good as the information that the *Avid* and *Lightworks* received in the first place. If the telecine reader head has read the Key Kodes incorrectly or has been offset incorrectly it could be a disaster - and remember, there is no visual guide, no cutting copy to check it against.

***Q - What is the telecine head reading then?***

***Mike -*** The telecine machine must be fitted with a Key Kode reader which translates the Key Kode to numbers. On the edge of new negative stocks is a bar code - Kodak call it Key Kode, it's their trademark All manufacturers carry this type of 'bar code' now and they are all completely compatible. Everyone

Answer Print

## 16MM & SUPER 16MM A & B ROLL CHECKERBOARDING

The A & B roll cut negative rolls are printed to produce a single positive print. A & B rolls must be used in all 16mm formats as there is no room in between frames to make a clean join between two shots. By using two rolls with black spacer, a whole frame can be used for the join. The black spacer covers the join and creates a 'window' for the incoming shot on the alternate roll.

### 16MM NEGATIVE JOIN IN DETAIL

← ***Exposed negative frames*** - the frame directly before and after a shot is used to join the negative to the black spacer

← ***Overlap Frame*** - used to join onto black spacer and effectively destroys the frame

← ***Black Spacer*** - used to create unexposed windows for printing A & B roll checkerboard negative

# Cutting Copy Markings For The Negative Cutter (16mm & Super16mm)

All chinagraph instructions should be written on both the cell and the emulsion sides of the cutting copy. Markings for 35mm are the same.

## Dissolve

( Shown is a 24 frame disolve). Dissolves can be 16, 24, 32, 48, 64 and 96 frames in length. A minimum of 4 frames must be allowed between the end of the dissolve and the start of another. A minimum of 20 frames must be allowed between a cut and the start of a 16 frame dissolve and 20 frames between the end of a 16 frame dissolve and a cut.

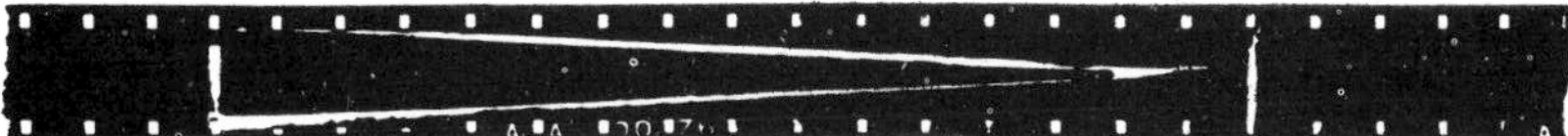

## Fade Out

(Shown is a 16 frame fade out) See fade notes below.

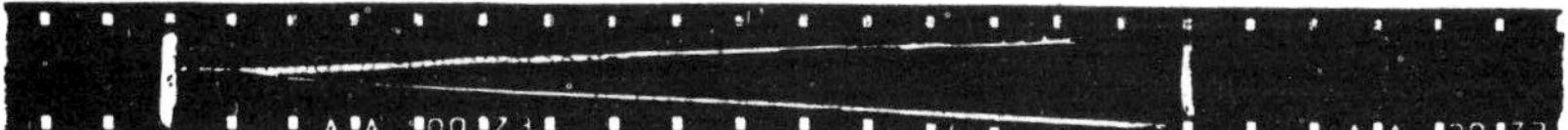

## Fade In

(Shown is a 16 frame fade in) Fades can be 16, 24, 32, 48, 64 and 96 frames in length. A minimum of 20 frames must be allowed between the start of a shot and the start of 16 frame fade out. A minimum of 20 frames must be allowed between the end of of a 16 frame fade in and the end of a shot.

## Jump Cut

Used when only a few frames are cut out. Marked to ensure the neg cutter doesn't mistake it for a rejoined cut.

## Unintentional Cuts

Used when only a cut has been rejoined. Marked to inform the neg cutter to ignore it.

# 35mm Negative Cutting

35mm is marked up for neg cutting in the same way as 16mm.

35mm is neg cut as a single A roll.

There is no B roll unless there are dissolves or fades in the film. If there are dissolves, then a B roll is made up which comprises mainly of black spacer. The only negative on this B roll is the second half of any dissolve, or the clear spacer for a fade.

To the right are rolls A and B with a 16 frame dissolve. Please note that a 16 frame dissolve needs 20 frames outgoing (not the 6 that are shown).

At the far right is a wider view of the 35mm negative. Roll A has several shots, roll B is black spacer except for the negative of the second half of the dissolve.

Note - some labs only use the B roll for the second part of a dissolve.

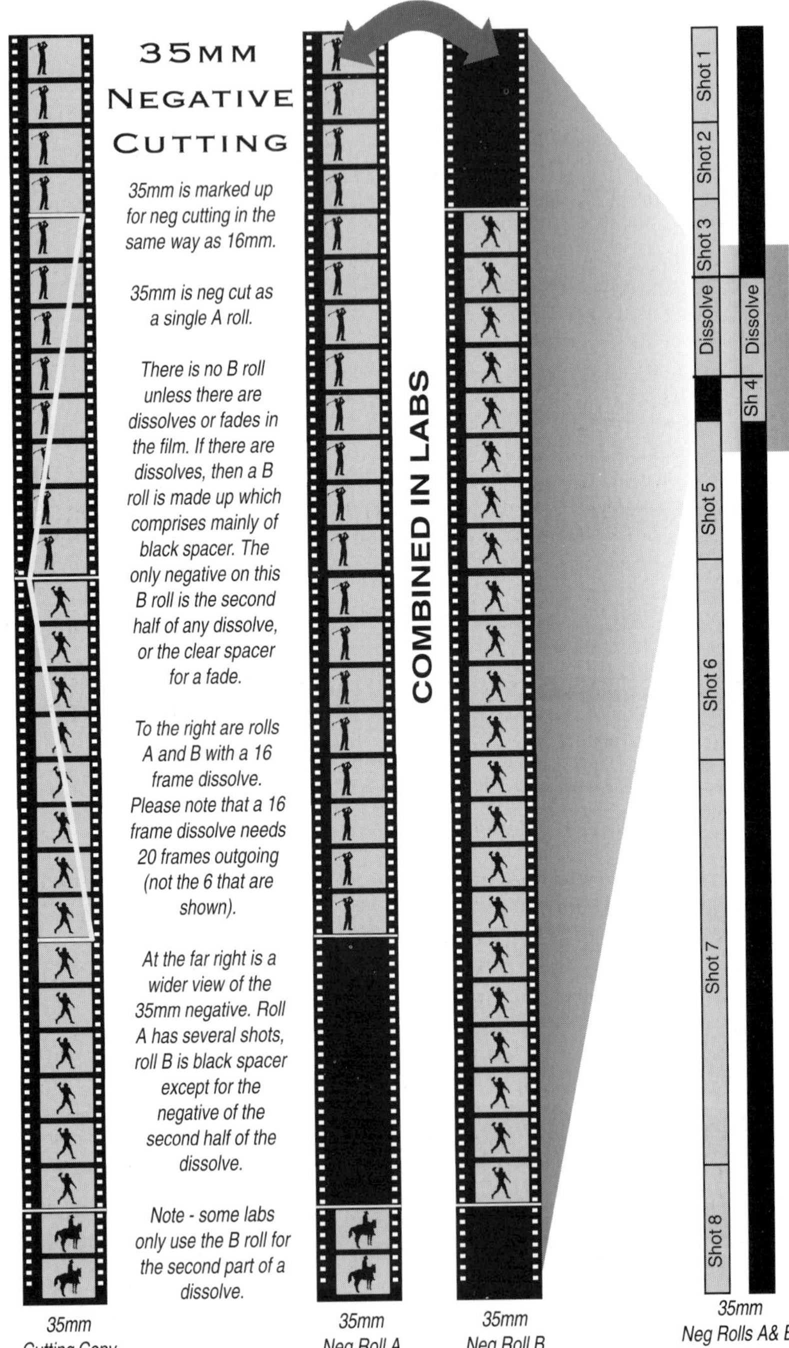


35mm Cutting Copy

35mm Neg Roll A

35mm Neg Roll B

35mm Neg Rolls A& B. Wider view

## NEGATIVE CUTTING 35MM / 16MM

*35mm contains enough space between frames for the negative cutter to actually cut the negative and join it up as one single roll.*

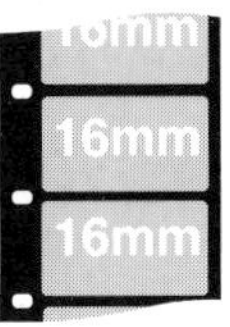


*16mm and Super 16mm is considerably smaller with virtually no space between frames. This forces the negative cutter to conform using A&B rolls*

refers to it as Key Kode but it is actually edge numbers in a bar code form.

It reads those bar codes and converts them to edge numbers. You're not always able to read the Key Kode because the negative may be fogged, certainly around ends, dissolves and splices etc. Problems can arise. For instance if a reader head goes through a splice and the next roll of material (with different Key Kodes) is fogged for the first 10, 20, 100 feet or whatever, the first thing that the telecine reader does is to stop reading. It merely accumulates the previous numbers which are incorrect because the neg has changed. It also flags the operator but if the operator doesn't notice, you're going to get 10,20 100 feet of negative where the edge numbers have been incorrectly read.

***Q - In the telecine, how do you check that the Key Kode that is being read is correct?***

***Mike*** - You can't. There is no practical way of checking that the Key Kode that is being read is correct. That is why we do not log it that way - we log it on a bench, with a Key Kode reader. These numbers are later fed into the computer and should match the telecine timecode numbers, that is unless there is a problem. Either way, you are aware of the problem before the damage is done.

***Q - What methods of post production are available to a producer?***

***Mike*** - Currently, there are several methods of producing an end result. Firstly is the traditional film edit where rush prints are sunk and cut by the editor. The final cutting copy is sent to us where we re-cut the neg to match the cutting copy. The cut neg goes off to the labs and is printed. This is the most tried and tested method that has worked for decades, but it is a little labour intensive on behalf of the editor. There is a general trend to non linear editing systems now and traditional film cutting may become a thing of the past. Method 2 - after the telecine of the rushes negative, you stay on tape, and you don't come back to film. During the telecine you do a 50-80% grade of all your rushes, transfer them onto whatever final conform tape you want, Beta, D2 etc. That footage is then digitised from tape onto hard disk in your AVID or LIGHTWORKS - you edit the movie. Then you conform the final picture purely on tape - the final grading is done in the edit suite and you never go back to cut the original negative. There's advantages there but obviously the completed production can only ever exist on tape and never be projected in a cinema.

Method 3 is pure non linear, where the rushes are telecinied and digitised into a system like Lightworks or Avid. The movie is edited and the computer produces an EDL. We use the EDL to cut the negative and the final neg is then printed at the labs. Both Avid and Lightworks have got ways of getting around the problems of productions shot at 24fps which can entail slowing down and speeding up - it's all tried and tested but it's something of which to be aware. There are other systems and without doubt new systems will have been developed by the time you read this. The system to opt for is the one your post production team has the most experience with, or with which they are happiest.

***Q - As traditional editing was mechanical, the speed at which film was shot was 'academic' with regard to the negative cutting. Is this the same for non linear?***

***Mike -*** No. It's important if you are shooting a theatrical release, i.e. if you are shooting at 24fps that you are aware of how you are going to post produce as your film is 24fps and will be using 25fps timecode. If you shoot at 24fps and telecine transfer at 25fps, your picture is going to be shorter than your sound. The only way to get them in sync is to do something to either the picture or the sound, and you don't want to do that. You want to keep the sound at the proper speed the whole time - AND the picture at the proper speed the whole time. One of the ways of doing it is with *Avid* - you shoot at 24fps, transfer at 25fps and take it into *Avid*. *Avid* can then slow down the picture to 24fps so that it will match your sound. Now you edit and send the final EDL to us and we do the neg cut. Lightworks has a similar method to combat this problem too.

***Q - WHITE ANGEL was shot at 25fps to avoid technical headaches so it is possible to shoot a feature at 25fps and not 24fps.***

***Mike -*** Every feature film that's been shown on television here for years was shot at 24fps and transferred at 25fps yet few know the difference. Nobody watching television knows that the *Guns Of Navarone* or *The Magnificent Seven* has been speeded up by 4% to be transferred at 25fps instead

*The huge negative storage warehouse at Mike Fraser Ltd.*

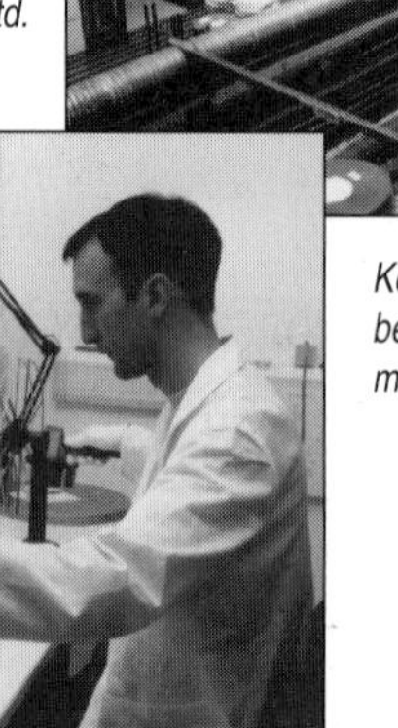

*Key Kodes are checked on the bench before the actual negative cutting, just to make sure there are no mistakes*

of 24fps. However, it's not recommended to shoot at 25fps if you intend to finish up screening at 24fps.

***Q - What are the most common mistakes made by a film maker that you encounter?***

***Mike*** - Not preparing the post production route in the early stages. Producers tend to think, *Oh well, we'll get that done later when we go into editing* and they simply don't give it enough thought. Planning and preparation.

***Q - What extra things can a production team do to make your life easier?***

***Mike*** - The most important thing is for the neg cutter and the editor to sit down and talk about how he's going to do it. We're talking film editing now, the way the cutting copy is marked up is vital, so it must be marked up in either a standard way or a way the neg cutter understands the editors wishes. With non-linear editing you do not have a film cutting copy to check against. Therefore you are cutting to a neg cutting list, which has been generated by the translation of timecodes from an EDL (edit decision list). Therefore the translation has to be absolutely frame accurate. It's very important that an editor on a non linear system understands the logging in of his material so that he gets the right tape numbers and so forth. If you're using something like OSC/R it doesn't matter, because OSC/R will sort it all out. On a more basic and cautionary level, always put plenty of leader at the head and tail of any reels, if you are going to blow up Super 16mm to 35mm, check with the labs that you have made the rolls up to the right length, label all your cans with as much information as possible - it's amazing how quickly material accumulates and people forget what's in a can. That often leads them to the last point, NEVER handle your negative - get it sent straight from the labs to the neg cutters and have your problems checked out by professionals in the right environment. Remember absolutely everything you have worked for is contained in that negative.

*Neg can be telecinied directly to tape with 'Key Kodes' linked to timecode. The picture can then be edited non-linear or on tape before being conformed, either as a film neg cut or purely on tape for TV broadcast - & all under one roof!*

POST-PRODUCTION

# Digital Effects Dennis Michelson of The Computer Film Co.

***Q - What is the basic concept when it comes to computer / film, and manipulating a 2D image?***

***Dennis -*** The broad concept is that you have this moving image, a series of 24fps, each one a single image on film - with computers you can control the colour, the saturation, the contrast, insert objects, remove objects, distort the image - the possibilities are limitless (aside from budget and time). Only recently have computers got to the level where they can handle the volume of information that film contains within it. The smallest unit of data that film contains is a grain - a pixel on a computer is now of that scale, and even smaller, so computer manipulation enables us to do work with film, down to the most minute detail. In theory, given time and money, you can do anything - colours, shapes, people's exploding eyes, turning sunset to day, morphing, also repairs - we've had shots where we've fixed blemishes on actor's faces for instance, that can never really be foreseen.

***Q - How does it work?***

***Dennis -*** You send us the negative of what you've shot. We scan that in - by scanning I mean, we put it on a machine that rolls the film through a frame at a time, and as each frame is held in the gate, it is literally scanned and turned into digital bits, millions of bits - once you've entered that domain, the manipulation begins, be it effects, removing wires, darkening skies etc. The work is then approved by the producer and the image is then put back on 35mm film using a Film Recorder Output Device (where an extremely high resolution electronic image is rephotographed) - again a frame at a time. We then give you the negative to cut into the final picture.

***Q - What are the most important issues to be considered in advance when you know something is going to involve some kind of digital manipulation?***

***Dennis -*** The most critical thing is for the people on set to be completely aware of what the effect they want actually is, because any given visual element interferes with other visual elements. If you do a shot of a table and want us to add an angle-poise light to it, not only will we have to put the light in, but also the light it casts, the reflections and the shadows - all elements affect all other elements - if this isn't done properly, the unschooled eye knows something is wrong, it may not be able to say what it is, but it can tell - then you have a bad effect. Recreating those lighting effects in a computer can be costly and time consuming. If on the day, the lighting cameraman had lit the area of table that was to be illuminated by the lamp (that would be inserted later on computer), everything would become so much easier, the effect would be better and cheaper. Always

consider the lighting implications of any elements to be inserted, be it props, casting shadows, even lightning.

***Q - If you're not going to storyboard the whole film, it's essential to storyboard the sequences with the effects?***

***Dennis -*** Yes, it's essential. That way we'd know what the angle of the house that is being lit by the lightning is, if the camera is moving or not, what elements cross in front of others, what has to happen etc.

***Q - Currently, can Super 16mm be used with computer technology and what type of stock can be used?***

***Dennis -*** Yes. A rule of thumb regarding film stock is not to shoot grainy, fast, film-stocks for effects elements. We have some issues with DOP's who say *we're shooting the rest of the film on it...* it makes sense from the point of view of the DOP that you would maintain continuity that way, but that betrays a complete misunderstanding of what this process is all about, because we can make the end result look like the film stock they shot the rest of the movie on. We need to start off with the highest resolution image we can get.

***Q - Say we have a shot of a landscape and a horseman rides past - we need to replace the sky as we want a sunset - what things make this easier or harder to achieve?***

***Dennis -*** If it's a clear, constant, sky, we can do that in an instant with the software tools we have. If, for whatever reason, the sky is cloudier, or the horseman goes infront of the sky, then it becomes more difficult and therefore more time consuming. People have to be aware of this so that they can make creative choices on set - so it's a question of educating people, to know that these are the factors involved, this is what will impact your budget - it may be acceptable to have the horseman pass by a rock instead of across the skyline for instance.

***Q - If the budget was low you would be able to advise the producer of certain elements to avoid with sequences that involved any form of digital manipulation?***

***Dennis -*** Exactly. A more economical way to achieve an effective result.

***Q - You also spend time fixing problems - what kind of things can you fix?***

***Dennis -*** It ranges from things like a camera scratch, which is often an insurance claim - previously the only option had been a re-shoot, now you can simply fix it, even if a line crosses an actor's face, we can paint it out. A blemish on an actors face, a microphone boom can be taken out, depending on what it crosses, we can darken

POST-PRODUCTION

## Do It On Your Desktop
### Using a domestic PC or MAC to emulate Hollywood effects

(Note - the images below did NOT originate from the Computer Film Company)

*Desktop effects (left and below) - Relatively inexpensive software & hardware can now create images & animations that are technically good enough to be used in low-budget feature films. Autodesk 3D studio was used for certain effects in T2 & Lightwave created almost all the effects for Babylon 5.*

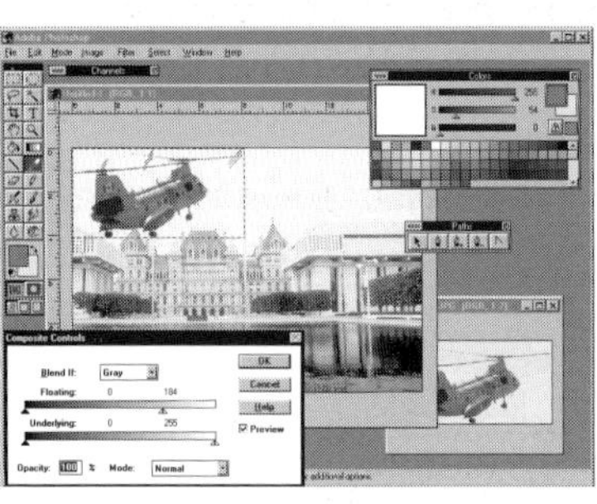

*(left) An appreciation of the way certain software tools work in programs like Adobe Photoshop strengthens the understanding of what is actually possible using computers and film - without breaking the bank.*

bleached out skies, stabilise camera shake, smooth out pans and tilts. This is where I see the greatest potential in the future for digital technology, actually changing the quality of the film in term of its overall colour balance, the level of blacks, the contrast throughout etc.

***Q - How much does it cost?***

**Dennis -** I can't give you a formula, but generally, a stationary shot will be cheaper than a moving shot. Well shot blue screen will be cheaper than poorly shot bluescreen. The fixed costs are scanning and recording, plus the laboratory costs. It works out at about £6 per frame or £144 per second. That gets you into the digital world, the big variable then is how much time needs to be spent making the effect work. These variables are the number of elements and complexity, the larger one clearly being complexity. It's practically impossible to define complexity in financial terms. The bottom line is that digital compositing and effects aren't as expensive as people think.

***Q - Who are the most important crew members aside from the producer?***

**Dennis -** If there's an effects supervisor they're our liaison with production. If not, the cinematographer, editor and director.

***Q - CGI (Computer Generated Images) - Going back to the shot we discussed earlier, the valley and the sunset, the director decides he wants a UFO going across the sky, how would you go about doing that?***

***Dennis -*** Currently, I would still go for a miniature or model shot against a blue or green screen. However, the advantage with CGI is that once you have created the *model* of the space ship in the computer, you can do anything with it, and you don't have to set it up and shoot it on a stage.

***Q - Correct me if I'm wrong, that kind of CGI effect could be done on a very low budget?***

***Dennis -*** I'd say it can be done quite economically if you choose the right people. If it was very low budget, you could approach people with PCs with software like Autodesk *3D studio* or *Electric Image* on the Mac. It's quite possible to produce high quality, high resolution images and animation using this lower end technology, although the processing time is greatly increased.

***Q - You mention 3D studio - this is a £2k program that you can buy and run on a fast PC on your desktop. With it, you can create anything from a whizzy logo to a number nine bus, at the pixel resolution required for 35mm film, dump it onto DAT or CD, bring it to you and you can then comp it into the final shot?***

***Dennis -*** Yes, it's certainly do-able. A friend of mine is part of a CGI team, he does all the effects

DIGITAL COMPOSITING

(THE NUTTY PROFESSOR)

*Shots 1 and 2 - Eddie Murphy is shot against Blue Screen. Shot 3 - the two shots are composited on computer, along with a separate background shot. The final sequence would then be output back to 35mm negative to be cut into the film.*

## Digital Compositing Basics Techniques

(These images were produced using Adobe Photoshop on a desktop PC)

1. Original stock has unwanted elements removed

2. The sky is keyed out and a new cloudy sky, shot separately, is comped in.

3. Visual effects elements are added. This time, a shot of a plane, again, filmed separately. This could easily be a CGI plane against a blue screen.

2. The final composite with added CG (computer generated) sun and a little lens flare.

## DAVID LEAN CROWD SHOT - NINETIES STYLE

*1. A group of extras are photographed several times (2) and eventually, all the separate shots are composited to turn a small group into a vast crowd (3)*

animation on his MAC at home, so this is already being done. I like the idea of putting something together for a release print in your bedroom (laugh).

***Q - What about camera movement, if you have a sequence with an actor who is playing twins and we need to move the camera?***

***Dennis -*** That would have to be motion control. Motion control is basically a camera on a motorised head/dolly that is computer controlled. It enables you to perform a camera move, the computer records the move, then the same move can be automatically replayed, but with the actor in a different place for instance - then we can combine the two shots and you've got twins.

***Q - Do you have any basic advice to offer inexperienced film makers?***

***Dennis -*** Visual effects occur in two stages - it's both an *Art* and a *Craft* - the first one being in the concept stage, in the story-boards, what does the story need, what propels the narrative at this point - there we can be part of the creative team. Once that's nailed down, we put on the problem solving hat. I also think that the mystique and propaganda about digital has been too effective, people think anything can be done with digital effects - that's why people feel confident of coming in after the effect saying *wave your hands over this and make magic.* Then questions of time and expense come in and they may have problems. Involve the digital effects facility or the supervisor as early as you would your production designer and cinematographer to avoid costly mistakes.

***Q - Any final words?***

***Dennis -*** I'd reduce it to a single word - *preparation.*

# Telecine
# Paul Grace
## of Rushes

***Q - What is the Telecine?***

***Paul -*** Telecine is a machine where you put film in one end and get a video signal out of the other. - it's a film to video transfer machine.

***Q - What does the producer need to supply you with for you to make the telecine?***

***Paul -*** Firstly, we ascertain what gauge the film was shot on, the aspect ratio - was it academy, open aperture Super 35mm etc? Then we discuss the sound, what format would that would be coming on - DAT, NAGRA ¼", 35mm magnetic etc? Always give us as much information as you can as it can save so much time and money.

***Q - If a film has been shot on super 16mm, are there any special requirements for telecine?***

***Paul -*** No. If it's come in as 35mm that's been blown up from Super 16mm, it's nice to know the history of the process. Historically, new telecine film gates had to be produced for Super 16mm to accommodate the full Super 16mm image, plus many machines had to be adapted to avoid scratching the film. It's not such an issue now as most good telecine houses can handle Super 16mm, but it's still important to appreciate just how delicate and vulnerable the film actually is.

***Q - Can you telecine from negative as well as a print?***

***Paul -*** Most of our work is now direct telecine from the negative. Most high end telecine facilities have equipment that can do a really good job from negative, but if you go down the scale to certain film labs that do rushes, their machines aren't particularly suited to negative. They are usually vintage machines there to do a cut price Avid type transfer.

***Q - Going back to the low-budget film maker, more than likely money is a serious issue to them, what is the most cost effective way to get the final film onto video tape?***

***Paul -*** I personally wouldn't scrimp on the telecine stage. If I was a low-budget film maker I would choose one of the premier places because the rate actually isn't a lot more. Plus, you can get a good deal if you are prepared to work out of hours, late at night for instance.

***Q - Technically, what would you expect the film maker to supply?***

**Paul -** It depends on the nature of the job and the budget available. Most of our work is with high end commercials, so the material is originated on 35mm. We also work with Super 16mm, usually for music videos or short films. If you come to us with a completed, cut project, a feature film for instance, we would prefer a low contrast 35mm print or an internegative. It's no use using a standard cinema projection print as this will give very poor results.

***Q - If a producer wants to get a telecine done quickly, but properly, he should strike a low contrast 35mm print?***

**Paul -** Yes.

***Q - Assuming there are no problems or grading, how long would it take to transfer a 90 minute feature film?***

**Paul -** It depends. We'd advise about three times the overall running time because there's invariably some grading that needs to be done, there are a lot of reels to load up and the machines need to be calibrated inbetween. Three times is a good yardstick.

***Q - Cinema sound mixes are very dynamic, whereas television is much more compressed, does that cause a problem and if so what can be done?***

**Paul -** Yes it does. The dynamic range in the cinema is much greater than domestic VHS and TV can handle - quiet parts get very quiet and loud parts can peak so much they run the risk of distortion. It's best to produce a copy of your final master sound mix that is compressed so the peaks and troughs are evened out. You could do that at the same place that you did your final master sound mix and bring it along to the final telecine.

***Q - What happens about noise reductions like Dolby SR?***

**Paul -** For a long time Dolby A was the standard. Dolby SR is now the favourite for the film market, and then there's all the digital formats that are popping up, like Dolby Digital. Just make sure your telecine facility knows what sound format you are going to be bringing in so that they can make arrangements. That goes back to what I was saying about making us aware of all technical aspects in the first place.

***Q - What is the best videotape format to master onto?***

**Paul -** Currently, I would say D1, but that's not a format you'd put a feature film on as the tape length is only 90 minutes. A lot of films get put on to D2 which is a horrible composite format, but the tapes are very long. Digibeta is brilliant, it's a very

POST-PRODUCTION

# Video Tapes - Common Formats

*1" - Analogue reel to reel format, industry standard of the 1980's. Called 1" because tape is 1" wide. Commonly used in foreign territories for delivery of masters. Not suitable for mastering.*

*Betacam SP- Cassette analogue component format. See Digital Betacam. Commonly used in foreign territories for delivery of masters. Not suitable for mastering. Maximum running time of approximately 110 mins.*

*D1 - Currently the ultimate digital videotape format with no generation loss. Digital component quality means it is ideal for mastering. High tape and running costs. Maximum running time of 90 mins.*

*D2 - Composite digital videotape format. High quality tape format, D2 is vastly superior to 1", but not superior to D1. Commonly used in foreign territories for delivery of masters.*

*Digital Betacam - A 'compressed' digital version of Betacam SP - made by Sony. Common format that is ideal for mastering as tapes can easily accommodate a feature film. Robust and has a relatively low tape and running cost.*

*Domestic Formats - Low Band Umatic, HiBand Umatic, VHS, SVHS, 8mm and Hi8mm can all be requested at various stages of production and are commonly used for preview tapes and sync tapes.*

## VIDEO FORMAT FACTS

*Analogue*

*Technically inferior to digital. Picture noise is introduced when tape copies are made. This 'generation loss' can lead to unacceptable quality.*

*Digital*

*Technically superior to analogue. Virtually eliminates generation loss as information is recorded as a series of numbers.*

*Composite*

*The 3 basic components of a TV signal (red, green & blue) form one combined signal. Good for transmission/ distribution as only one cable is needed.*

*Component*

*the 3 basic components of a TV signal (red, green & blue) are kept as separate signals. Vital to post production applications like D1 editing, chroma-keying, & computer graphics.*

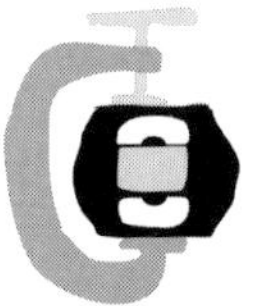

*Compression*

*A complex mathematical technique that condenses digital picture information to make it take up less space on a videotape. Compression gives longer playing times, similar to the Long Play function on VHS.*

good format, it's cheap and stunningly beautiful. I would advise Digibeta for low-budget feature films.

***Q - What are the different TV standards and how does that affect things?***

***Paul -*** All around the world there are different television standards, that's why you can't just pop a VHS from America into your VCR. There are two major formats, PAL (UK) and America (NTSC) with lots of variations in between, like SECAM, PAL-M etc. Because we work on digital formats, the most important thing to us is whether the final telecine is going to be 625 or 525 lines. Where the actual television standard is an issue, is when you do copies that are analogue, such as Betacam, 1" or U-matic.

***Q - If I master to Digibeta in PAL, can I use that tape for both America and Britain, PAL and NTSC?***

***Paul -*** No. Digibeta is either PAL or NTSC.

Ultimately, you'll have to supply at least two masters, one 625 and one 525. For a very low-budget film I would suggest mastering to Digibeta in 625, and if the budget can stretch to it, make a second telecine to Digibeta in 525. Otherwise, make a 625 to 525 standards conversion onto Digibeta. Some of the new standards converters are pretty good, but if I was making art I wouldn't want my piece of art to go through one, but that's just me.

***Q - What happens about Cinemascope or widescreen images?***

***Paul -*** There are two ways you can do it, the most common way is a black band at the top and bottom. If you do what is called a *pan and scan* version, you zoom into the image and have to start

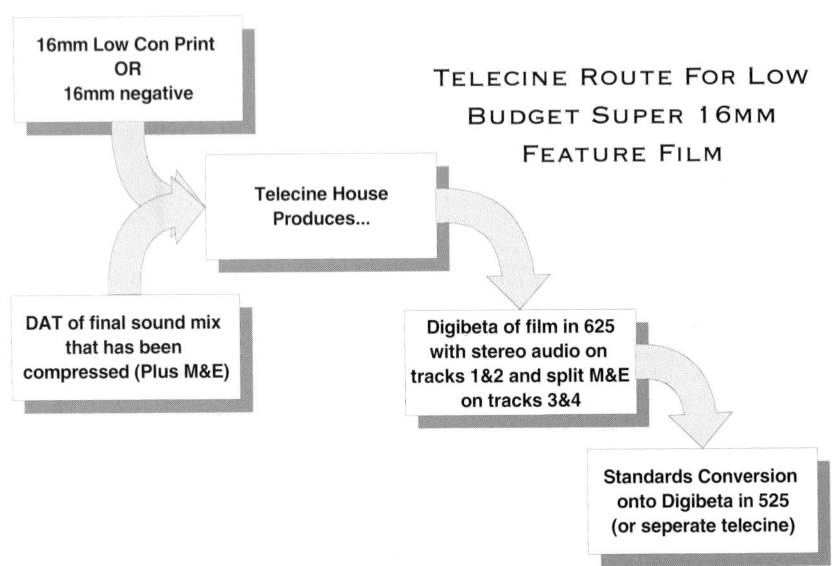


making editorial decisions about what section of the image to show at any one time. You can make or break a movie at that stage. Unfortunately, most overseas buyers, outside some European territories, will undoubtedly ask for a *pan and scan* master and will not accept a widescreen tape.

***Q - Is it expensive to do a full pan and scan?***

***Paul -*** Yes, because you're analysing each and every shot, going back, moving it around etc. - it all amounts to a long and tedious session.

***Q - If a film shoots super 16mm and they want to cut non linear, what's the process to get that super 16mm on to Lightworks or Avid?***

***Paul -*** Telecine to Betacam as you need a useable image to work with. That Betacam is then digitised onto the hard disk of the Lightworks or Avid.

***Q - Can special effects be produced on video tape and transferred to film?***

***Paul -*** Yes - a title, wire removal or even a wonderful morph. We normally work at resolutions much higher than video, typically 2000 lines or even 4000 lines, but it can be possible at video resolution and much cheaper. It depends on the budget, where the effect is going to be used, and in what context and the results can be quite good. There's more than one Hollywood blockbuster that's used effects at this resolution.

***BITC*** *- Burnt-in-time-code. Time code numbers recorded from camera tapes and visually displayed on screen giving a frame-by-frame picture reference. BITC is used on reference copies of rushes, which in turn will be used for the off-line edit.*

***BLUE SCREEN*** *- Foreground subject is shot against a plain blue screen, on film or video, so that background images can be added electronically in post production. Blue is chosen as it is the least naturally occurring colour in flesh tones. (see Chromakey)*

***CHROMAKEY*** *- Technique which allows a vision mixer to substitute a saturated colour (usually blue or green) in a picture for another picture source. (see Blue Screen)*

***DVE*** *- Digital Video Effects. Devices such as ADO, A53, Encore and Kaleidoscope, for picture manipulation.*

***DVTR*** *- Digital Video Tape Recorder. Multiple generations or passes on DVTR's (see D1/D2) do not suffer from tape noise degradation associated with analogue tape formats.*

***DROP OUT*** *- Momentary loss of signal on a video tape, showing up as randomly occurring white spots on the picture, present in worn or poor quality tape.*

***525*** *- This is the standard, specifying the number of horizontal lines that makes up the TV picture. 625 being the U.K standard and 525 being the American.*

***FIELD*** *- Area of a TV screen covered by alternative lines. 2 fields are equal to 1 frame i.e. picture (see Frame)*

***FRAME*** *- Single television frame or film image. In European television 25 frames per second are scanned to give an illusion of continuous movement. Each frame is composed of 2 fields.*

***HUE*** *- Colour tone of a picture.*

***KEY*** *- Effect that allows a picture to be superimposed over a background.*

***LUMINANCE*** *- The black and white information of a video signal.*

***MATTE*** *- An area blanked off within a frame in order to include additional material, or remove unwanted material.*

***MOTION CONTROL*** *- A computer assisted camera and rig with multiple moving axes, enabling high precision, repeatable camera moves.*

***N.T.S.C*** *- National Television Standards Committee. Colour standard used in USA, Canada and Japan.*

***OFF-LINE*** *- A pre-edit used to establish edit points for the on-line edit, usually on non-broadcast standard equipment.*

***ON-LINE*** *- The main edit during which mixes, effects and audio are brought together using broadcast standard equipment in order to create a 'master' edit.*

***PAL*** *- Phase Alternate Line. Colour system used in Europe (not France), Scandinavia, China, India, Australia, South Africa etc.*

***PAL M*** *- A version of PAL standard, but using a 525 line 60 field structure. Used only in South America.*

***PIXEL*** *- Smallest picture element on a television display.*

***Q-LOCK*** *- Device for synchronising audio with video machines.*

***R.G.B*** *- Red, Green, Blue. Primary television colours before encoding to a composite signal if required.*

***RESOLUTION*** *- The definition of a television picture, and the ability to determine small objects.*

***625*** *- This is the standard, specifying the number of horizontal lines that make up the TV picture. 625 being the U.K standard and 525 being the American.*

***SECAM*** *- French and East Europe, USSR colour television standard. Stands for Sequential Colour with Memory.*

***STANDARDS CONVERSION*** *- The process of converting between different TV transmission signals. Usually refers to conversion from and to PAL and NTSC.*

***T.B.C*** *- Time Base Corrector - device required to correct time base errors of a VTR which build up during operation. Needed in dubbing, particularly for poor quality material.*

***TELECINE*** *- Device for transferring film to video tape. Film can be colour graded during this process.*

***TIME CODE*** *- Binary Code recorded on video and audio tape recorders which uniquely identifies frames. Used for synchronising recorders and editing.*

World Distribution Of The Three Major TV Standards

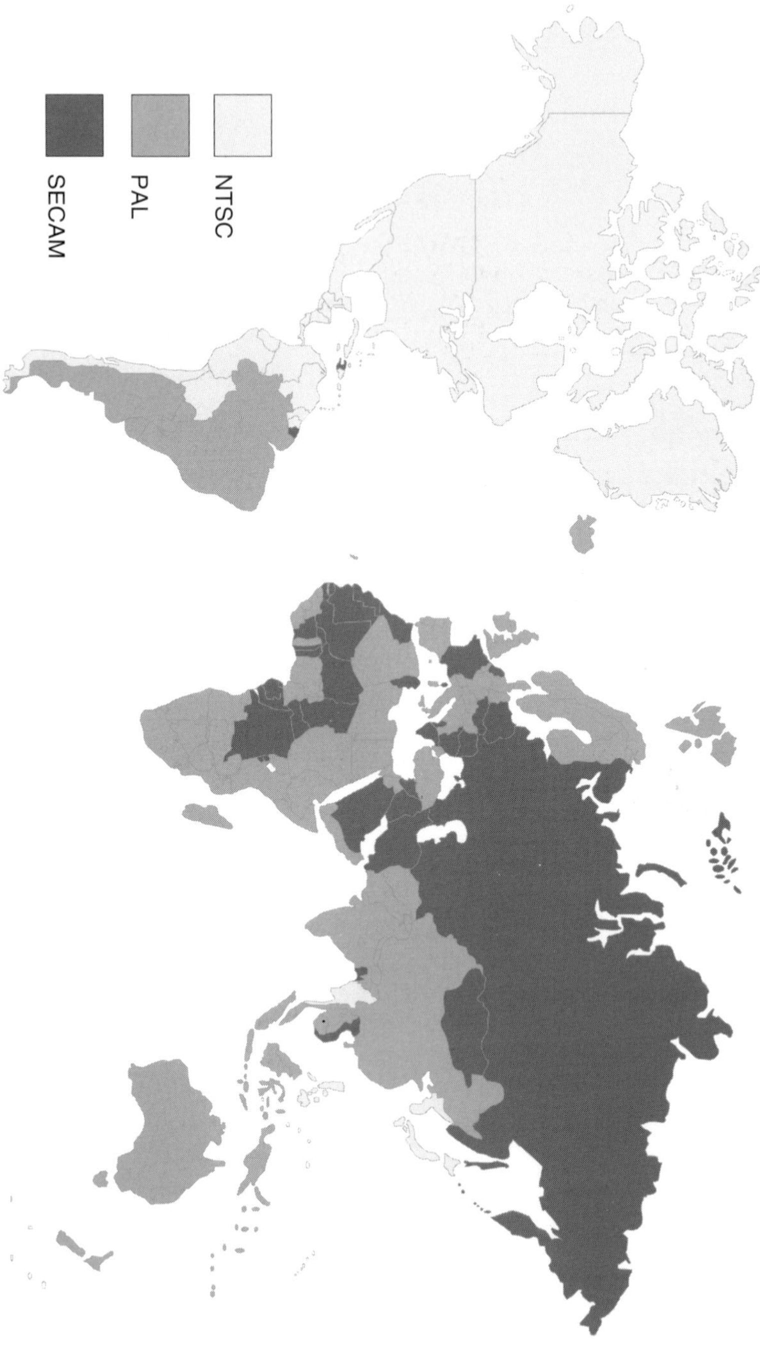

NTSC

PAL

SECAM

POST-PRODUCTION

## TELEVISION STANDARDS - BY COUNTRY

Abu Dhabi - 625 PAL
Afghanistan - 625 PAL/ SECAM
Albania - 625 SECAM
Algeria - 625 PAL
Andorra - 625 PAL
Angola - 625 PAL
Antigua - 525 NTSC
Argentina - 625 PAL N
Australia - 625 PAL
Austria - 625 PAL
The Azores - 625 PAL
Bahamas - 525 NTSC
Bahrain - 625 PAL
Bangladesh - 625 PAL
Barbados - 525 NTSC
Belgium - 625 PAL
Belize - 525 NTSC
Benin - 625 SECAM
Bermuda - 525 NTSC
Bolivia - 525 NTSC
Bophuthatswana - 625 PAL
Bosnia/ Hercegovina - 625 PAL
Botswana - 625 PAL
Brazil - 525 PAL M
British Virgin Isles - 525 NTSC
Brunei - 625 PAL
Bulgaria - 625 SECAM
Bukina Faso - 625 SECAM
Burma - 525 NTSC
Burundi - 625 SECAM
Cameroon - 625 PAL
Canada - 525 NTSC
Canary Islands - 625 PAL
Central African Republic - 625 SECAM
Chad - 625 SECAM
Chile - 525 NTSC
China - 625 PAL
Colombia - 525 NTSC
Congo - 625 SECAM
Cook Islands - 625 PAL
Croatia - 625 PAL
Cuba - 525 NTSC
Curacao - 525 NTSC
Cyprus - 625 PAL/ SECAM
Czechoslovakia - 625 SECAM
Denmark - 625 PAL
Djibouti - 625 SECAM
Dominican Republic - 525 NTSC
Dubai - 625 PAL
Ecuador - 525 NTSC
Eire - 625 PAL
Eqypt - 625 PAL/ SECAM
El Salvador - 525 NTSC
Equatorial Guinea - 625 SECAM
Ethiopia - 625 PAL
Faroe Islands - 625 PAL
Fiji - 625 PAL
Finland - 625 PAL
France - 625 SECAM
French Polynesia - 625 SECAM
Gabon - 625 SECAM
Galapagos Isles - 525 NTSC
Germany - 625 PAL
Ghana - 625 PAL
Gibraltar - 625 PAL
Greece - 625 SECAM
Greenland - 625 PAL
Grenada - 525 NTSC
Guadalope - 625 SECAM
Guam - 525 NTSC
Guatemala - 525 NTSC
Guinea (French) - 625 SECAM
Guinea - 625 SECAM
Guyana Republic - 625 SECAM
Haiti - 625 SECAM
Honduras - 525 NTSC
Hong Kong - 625 PAL
Hungary - 625 SECAM/ PAL
Iceland - 625 PAL
India - 625 PAL
Indonesia - 625 PAL
Iran - 625 SECAM/ PAL
Iraq - 625 SECAM
Israel - 625 PAL
Italy - 625 PAL
Ivory Coast - 625 SECAM
Jamaica - 525 NTSC
Japan - 525 NTSC
Jordan - 625 PAL
Kampuchea - 525 NTSC
Kenya - 625 PAL
Korea (North) - 625 SECAM/ 525 NTSC
Korea (South) - 525 NTSC
Kuwait - 625 PAL
Laos - 625 SECAM/ PAL
Lebanon - 625 SECAM
Leeward Isles - 525 NTSC
Lesotho - 625 PAL
Liberia - 625 PAL
Libya - 625 SECAM
Luxembourg - 625 SECAM/ PAL
Macedonia - 625 PAL
Madagascar - 625 SECAM
Madeira - 625 PAL
Malawi - 625 PAL
Malaysia - 625 PAL
Maldives - 625 PAL
Mali - 625 SECAM
Malta - 625 PAL
Martinique - 625 SECAM
Mauritius - 625 SECAM
Mexico - 525 NTSC
Monaco - 625 PAL/SECAM
Mongolia - 625 SECAM
Morocco - 625 SECAM
Mozambique - 625 PAL
Namibia - 625 PAL
Nepal - 625 PAL
Netherlands - 625 PAL
Netherlands Antilles - 525 NTSC
New Caledonia - 625 SECAM
New Zealand - 625 PAL
Nicaragua - 525 NTSC
Niger - 625 SECAM
Nigeria - 625 PAL
Norway - 625 PAL
Oman - 625 PAL
Pakistan - 625 PAL
Panama - 525 NTSC
Papua New Guinea - 625 PAL
Paraguay - 625 PAL M
Peru - 525 NTSC
Philippines - 525 NTSC
Poland - 625 SECAM
Polynesia - 625 SECAM
Portugual - 625 PAL
Puerto Rico - 525 NTSC
Qatar - 625 PAL
Reunion - 625 SECAM
Romania - 625 SECAM
Rwanda - 625 SECAM
Sarawak - 625 PAL
Samoa (Eastern) - 525 NTSC
San Marino - 625 PAL
Saudi Arabia - 625 SECAM
Senegal - 625 SECAM
Seychelles - 625 PAL
Sierra Leone - 625 PAL
Singapore - 625 PAL
South Africa - 625 PAL
South West Africa - 625 PAL
Spain - 625 PAL
Sri Lanka - 625 PAL
St. Kitts & Nevis - 525 NTSC
Sudan - 625 PAL
Surinam - 525 NTSC
Swaziland - 625 PAL
Sweden - 625 PAL
Switzerland - 625 PAL
Syria - 625 SECAM
Tahiti - 625 SECAM
Taiwan - 525 NTSC
Thailand - 625 PAL
Togo - 625 SECAM
Trinidad & Tobago - 525 NTSC
Tunisia - 625 SECAM
Turkey - 625 PAL
Uganda - 625 PAL
United Arab Emirates - 625 PAL
United Kingdom - 625 PAL
Uruguay - 625 PAL M
USA - 525 NTSC
Former USSR - 625 SECAM
Vatican City - 625 PAL
Venezuala - 525 NTSC
Vietnam - 625 SECAM/ NTSC
Virgin Isles - 525 NTSC
Yemen - 625 PAL/ SECAM
Former Yugoslavia - 625 PAL
Zaire - 625 SECAM
Zambia - 625 PAL
Zanzibar (Tanzania) - 625 PAL
Zimbabwe - 625 PAL

# International Sales Agent Victoria Singleton & Grace Carley of Stranger Than Fiction

***Q - Is there a kind of film that sells most? Should a new film maker ask a sales agent what the trends are?***

***Grace -*** It's rare that they would come and ask such an open ended question. Usually people have a script or project that is very dear to them that they want to make. But what we're finding is that an awful lot of films are getting made which don't seem to tap into any particular genre, and they are really difficult because only one out of a hundred of those is going to be special enough to actually break through. I've recently seen a couple which were kind of twee, feel good, set somewhere in England with very soft stories. It's fine if you're coming from the British sitcom tradition, but they really don't work in the world film sales market. The films that I have seen that have been made on a low-budget and have actually have done some deals, are ones that fit into a genre, generally a video genre. So something like *Funny Man* has a horror angle *White Angel* has the serial killer type market - and those are the ones that if they don't have the big breakthrough potential, can still make some money. If you want to make any money back at all, you should be aware of the commercial viability of your film in advance and not just assume that it's going to be bought. I think British low-budget film makers have to get away from the TV traditions that seem to underlie a lot of what comes out of this country.

***Q - Would you say that one problem of low-budget British films have is that they don't quite seem to have the same kind of edge as American independents?***

***Grace -*** Yes, and I would also say that there is a big difference between the mentalities of the film makers here, and the film makers in the States. The young film makers that we have dealt with in the States are cineliterate, tuned in and completely obsessed by the cinema, whereas you actually don't seem to find that here. There are a lot of film makers here who don't have a great deal of film background and don't even go to the cinema.

***Q - If you were to be brutal about White Angel for instance, what could we have done, if we had come to you with the script, to improve the commercial viability of the film?***

***Victoria -*** The female lead - I think you could have possibly brought someone in, a video name as *White Angel* is a very video driven movie - that would be the first thing I would do. I think it was

very well structured and it unfolded very well. To be perfectly honest, it's rare for a film to be submitted to us that we sit and watch from beginning to end. And we did with this one because it does hold you and keep you involved. The other thing I would add, but again this is a budgetary matter, is that I found the sound very empty and that design wise, it was lacking. But from the point of view of getting the story across, I thought it was fine.

***Q - What do you need from a producer to sell the film?***

***Victoria -*** We have a full delivery list of all the items, but firstly, it would depend on whether there was going to be theatrical potential. If there is, then we would need the theatrical elements - an interpositive and an internegative. In an ideal world, you need a second internegative that could possibly travel because there are certain territories that will actually print their own release prints.

***Grace -*** One thing we find always lacking are good visual elements like slides. The *White Angel* stills were very good compared with some $3-4 million films that we've worked on where you just get crap. Basically it seems to me that there is no regard for the skills of a stills photographer - it's actually a very definite skill, you can't just bring your pal, the photographer, on the set every so often, you need someone who is there and who has the kind of personality that would force the actors to do something that they really don't want to do to get good images.

***Q - Is it fair to say that stills are a vital element that should in no way be overlooked?***

***Grace -*** Absolutely. We couldn't emphasise that strongly enough. It's a selling tool, it's for the brochure that we use to sell the film and the video covers that every distributor uses - it is crucial.

***Victoria -*** Which is why you need a really good stills photographer who knows what you need to sell a film. Ideally, we like to work with filmmakers on generating a piece of key artwork because we feel that's our area of expertise, its' better to be involved so we can have something that's going to be acceptable, not just in Britain but throughout the world. The more you can make your basic materials exportable, then ultimately, the less the distributors are going to have to spend and the more you are going to get back. So get it right in the first place. But it's not just how exportable the elements are to save money down the line, but it's so that when they walk into your office at Cannes, Milan or the AFM they go - *'Woa - I can see us automatically taking x amount of units on this, or I can see x amount of prints being released because that looks fantastic'.* That really does make a big difference. A lot of distributors that you get coming to the markets buying films have marketing managers and they don't automatically come along with them, so you've got to show them how they can sell the film.

***Q - What kind of deal would a producer get with a sales agent?***

POST-PRODUCTION

FOUR MEDIA COMPANY

2820 W. OLIVE AVENUE, BURBANK CA 91505-4455 818.840.7100

QUALITY CONTROL REPORT

Part 1 of 1

Title: White Angel

Series: Eps. # : 4MC ID. # : LS700724

Client: Colimar Ent. W.O. # : 134615 P.O. # : 370 TRT: : 95 : 26

☐ PASS ☒ Fail ☐ Hold Comment: AUDIO TICKS ON CH 3&4

| | | | |
|---|---|---|---|
| QC Date: 6/18/96 | Record Date: | ☒ Full QC | ☐ Spot Check |
| QC Vtr # 22 | Record VTR # : | ☒ Video | ☐ Film |
| Stock Mfg: Fuji | Vendor: Soho601 | ☒ 2 ch. Audio | ☐ 4 ch. Audio |

| | | | | |
|---|---|---|---|---|
| ☐ D-1 | ☐ D-Betacam | ☐ Transfer Master | ☐ Letterbox | ☐ DFTC |
| ☐ D-2 | ☐ NTSC | ☐ Protection Master | ☐ Pan/Scan | ☐ NDFTC |
| ☐ 1" C | ☒ PAL | ☐ Edit Master | ☒ Flat | ☒ EBUTC |
| ☒ Betacam | ☐ Conversion | ☐ Clone | ☐ Scope | ☐ ASTC |
| ☐ DCT | ☐ DEFT | ☐ Dub | ☐ 16 x 9 | |

| | | | | | |
|---|---|---|---|---|---|
| 11.4 | Horizontal Blanking | 1.4 | Front Porch | ☒ RF Envelope | ☒ Format |
| 0 | Setup | 19:21 | VITC | ☒ Control Track | ☒ Slate |
| 300/300 | Sync/Burst | | CC | ☐ Channel Cond | ☒ Labels |
| 26 | Vertical Blanking | | VITS | ☒ Tension | ☒ Tape Wrap |
| | Serrations | | VIRS | ☒ Tracking | ☒ Shipper |

PROGRAM VIDEO LEVELS Luminance Avg 500 Luminance Peak 700 Chroma Peak (Flat) 700

Audio Specifications

| Channel | Track Content | Levels Avg | Levels Peak | NR Dolby | Tones 100 | Tones 1K | Tones 10K |
|---|---|---|---|---|---|---|---|
| 1 | English Stereo Comp | 0 | +13 | | | 0 | |
| 2 | English Stereo Comp | 0 | +13 | | | 0 | |
| 3 | Music Mono | -9 | +12 | | | 0 | |
| 4 | Effects Mono | -12 | +16 | | | 0 | |
| cue | | | | | | | |

General Comments

Line up tone under bars are down 5DB when left in unity.

Time code not set at regular format picture starts at 00:03:00:00

Copyright 1993 Living Spirit Pictures Ltd. Failed because audio ticks are only on ch 3&4.

At childrens party scene the back ground music is on both ch 3 & 4 should only be on ch 4 as an effect

Inspected By: Valerie Moore-Porter

4MCWANGEL DOC REV07/9/95 FM

*The Quality Control (Q/C) on delivery items can be stringent. Dust particles, scratches, bumps - anything technically imperfect could stall a deal. This company actual found a negative scratch on White Angel that Living Spirit had never seen in 62 screenings!*

***Victoria -*** Most sales agents would look to secure, exclusively, all media throughout the world. Sometimes they will take the world excluding North America. Time scales - they would look for five to seven years minimum. The agent would get 20 - 25% commission off the top of any deal. If you're in a situation where a sales agent has given you an advance, then you can expect a much higher percentage - 30 to 35%.

***Q - How long does it take to see returns on a film and how many territories or countries will you sell to?***

***Grace -*** From the time we get the film (plus support materials) and can go to market with it in a deliverable state, you could see the first trickle, assuming it's us, within six months. But the lions share comes in over a year later - it's because release patterns are very long, particularly at the low-budget end where there's no great urgency to get the film out. On average, we sell 10-15 territories - that might include South America as one sale and Scandinavia as one. There are some films we have that sell around the world and there are some that do only three deals.

***Q - Is it fair to assume that for a low-budget film, it's going to recoup, or at least see returns, somewhere between one and five years, if at all?***

***Victoria -*** Absolutely.

***Q - Is an advance likely for a low-budget film?***

***Grace -*** One hears of very small advances for low-budget films, usually completion money. Also, the sales agent may step in with say $30,000, if there's no way the film maker can meet the delivery list. Generally, that would be a bigger sales agent who is confident that they can get that kind of money back on the output deals that they have with certain companies around the world.

***Q - How much can get eaten up by expenses?***

***Victoria -*** That's a real big warning to smaller film makers - we've seen sales agents take on films

and just prorate expenses across the board. You could have a bigger company selling both a $30 million film and a $500k film - then they just split the expenses equally. I can't really emphasise enough how smaller film makers have got to go out there and make sure they see a budget from their sales agent before they sign - make sure that there is a cap and that anything above and beyond that is approved by them. Otherwise they will be screwed.

***Q - What are pre-sales and how does one get them if you're a first time film maker?***

***Grace -*** (laugh) Forget about it! First time film directors are difficult to get money on. Even more established film makers are tough to secure pre sales. It really depends on your entire package - if you've got Tom Cruise attached, then pre-sales aren't going to be a problem. The component parts can be broken down and a if distributor sees there's a casting element that works well in their territory, then you'll get that deal.

***Q - If you are fortunate and do get a pre-sale, how does it work?***

***Grace -*** If you're clever and lucky, you can get a certain amount to help cash flow the production, a certain amount on the first day of principle photography, some more on the last day, more on delivery, but generally you will find you will get most of it on delivery. If it's from a good company you may be able to find a bank that will lend against it, up to 70 maybe 80 percent of the deal, not the whole thing. Even gilt edged companies still find it tough to get money from banks against pre-sales because film companies do go under. Instead of pure pre-sales and from the UK features point of view, we're seeing a lot of co-productions with distributors, like German or Italian distributors who are putting up say $400k per territory. Only part of that money is the 'pre-sale', the rest is an investment - usually, they can justify that investment through various subsidies in their own country - it's just another angle.

***Q - Given that a low-budget film is low-budget, how important is casting?***

***Grace -*** Terribly important - if you don't have names that are recognisable (which can really help sell a film), you've got to have at least good actors. So many British films are ruined by no 'stars' and no good actors.

***Q - How does a first time film maker go about getting a sales agent?***

***Victoria -*** Screen the film, don't send out cassettes as it's not taking the business seriously. Go through a copy of *Screen International* or *Moving Pictures* bumper edition from one of the big markets, look at all the sales agents, see what they're selling, see what type of sales agent has got the type of product you'd like to be associated with and get those people excited enough to come to a screening at a well known venue. Then field the offers, or chase them for a deal if no-one is too interested.

***Q - How important is it to launch the film at a festival?***

***Grace -*** It depends on the film itself - if it has potential to go to one of the really prestigious festivals then it would be a shame not to do that. We find that films have come to us when they have sort of done the rounds at unimportant festivals because the film makers didn't know any better. The trouble with those festivals is that once a film has been premiered in a particular territory, the big festivals in that territory won't even take a look.

***Q - What's your advice for a first time film maker with a personal project and low-budget?***

***Victoria -*** They should make a film like that for as little money as possible, turn it over and use is as a calling card so people can see the talent, so you are no longer a first time film maker. If you go out and make a three million pound film as a first time film maker and you've screwed it up, then getting the money back will be your biggest nightmare. And if you haven't recouped that investment the first time, then nobody's going to want to give you the money the second time.

***Q - How important is the technical quality of the delivery items ie. tapes, trannies?***

***Grace -*** Critical, because if you can't deliver, you don't get paid, and if you're delivering sub standard items that we have to spend a lot of money to make better, then it's going to be a long time until you see any money back from us. After all, we're spending your money. Don't ever cut corners over the technical quality of your delivery items.

***Q - What are the biggest technical problems you come across, aside from stills?***

***Victoria -*** We wish everybody would cut a trailer as we end up having to do this by ourselves all the time. A trailer is such an important element, you're probably going to have to deliver one at some point down the line anyway and there's no reason why you can't use a trailer as a promo reel to go to a market. As people walk in and see it, so their interest is peaked and they end up going to see the entire film. This is the first thing that somebody can see from the film, apart from the key art, and it should be good. The M&E (music and effects) track is something that also keeps popping up, because it's something that producers don't really think about at the time, but six months down the line it's much harder to do than when you're doing your final mix. Book an extra day in the dub for your M&E and an M&E for the trailer and you'll be grateful in the long run. From a creative point of view, I think one of the things lacking a lot in films is a good editor who is prepared to be a bit ruthless.

***Q - What are the most common problems you encounter?***

***Grace -*** The expectations of film makers can be a big problem. Young film makers often make films with, say, family investment, everyone is telling them how wonderful they are, everybody expects that their film is going to be the next big thing. And if they get into a few festivals, the festivals will do even more ego massaging, everyone's wonderful, the film is a work of art , blah, blah, blah. And the reality of it is that it may be terrific for the constraints under which you made it, but it still has to compete out in the open market place. You don't want to deflate any expectations but at the same time you have to be realistic. We have found that hard to get across, because everyone thinks their film is the next *Four Weddings*. You have to understand that only one out of every 100 low-budget films is going to be a must have and will sell like hot cakes.

# Delivery List

1. Release Print - 35mm com/opt print (Combined optical print)
2. 35mm Interpositive - made from the original negative
3. 53mm Internegative - made from the 35mm Interpositive
4. 35mm Optical Sound Negative - made from master sound mix
5. 35mm Magnetic Sound Master - master sound mix, may be supplied on digital formats too
6. 35mm Music & Effect Mix (M&E) - may be supplied on digital formats too
7. Textless Title Background - 35mm Interneg / Interpos / print of sequences without title elements
8. 35mm Trailer - Including access to interneg, interpos, optical sound, magnetic sound master and M&E mix.
9. Video Tape - Full screen (not widescreen) perfect quality video cassette of film, including stereo sound (on tracks 1&2) and M&E (on tracks 3&4). Digital Betacam is currently the preffered format.
10. VHS Copies - two viewing cassettes
11. Video Tape Textless Backgrounds - Full screen (not widescreen) perfect quality video cassette of textless background sequences, including stereo sound (on tracks 1&2) and M&E (on tracks 3&4). Digital Betacam is currently the preferred format.
12. Video Tape Trailer - Full screen (not widescreen) perfect quality video cassette of the trailer, including stereo sound (on tracks 1&2) and M&E (on tracks 3&4). Digital Betacam is currently the preferred format.
13. Stills set - 100 full colour transparencies
14. Screenplay Transcript of final cut including all music cues
15. Music Cue Sheet
16. Continuities - a full, professional continuities action and dialogues continuity (not to be confused with continuity report sheets).
17. Chain of title - information and copy contracts with all parties involved with production and distribution of the film
18. Distribution restrictions - statement of any restrictions or obligations (such as cast billing etc.)
19. US Copyright Notice - Available from The Registrar of Copyright, Library of Congress, Washington DC, 20559, USA.
20. Certificate of Origin - Available from solicitor
21. Certificate of Nationality -
22. Certificate of Authorship -
23. Credit List - A complete cast and crew list, plus any other credits
24. Errors and Omissions Insurance Policy (E&O) - Available from specialised Insurers (approx. cost £7-10k)
25. Lab Access Letter - A letter giving access to materials held at lab to the sales agent
26. Press and reviews - copies of all press and reviews
27. Alternate TV takes - sound and picture of sequences to create an edited version of film
28. EPK, Electronic Press Kit - Betacam of interviews with actors and principle crew. Shots of crew at work, plus clips from film and trailer.

*Not all of these items will be needed by a sales agent, but most will. Some items, like the E&O policy can be negotiated around as it is usually only needed for the USA. The cost of making up this extensive list of items could feasibly cost more than the production costs of an ultra low budget film. Speak to your sales agent and negotiate an exact list, with a budget for making up that list, BEFORE you sign any sales agreement.*

# Domestic Distribution Mick Southworth Of The Feature Film Company

## Now Managing Director of Film Four Distributors

***Q - When a producer has an idea for a project, or wants to make a film, when should they come to someone like yourself to talk about the domestic market?***

***Mick*** - At the earliest possible time, even at the script stage or when they're thinking of the basic plot and packaging elements like cast and heads of department.

***Q - Does it matter if they have little or no experience of feature production beforehand?***

***Mick*** - It's probably even more important they come to speak to us if they haven't made a film before.

***Q- What are the areas that FEATURE FILM handle in terms of distribution?***

***Mick*** - Firstly we are a UK distribution company. We do everything from designing concepts, marketing, publicity - all the way to the actual physical distribution, providing the administration to sell and distribute to cinemas, on video and through TV media. For all rights, generally we'd offer an advance set against a percentage of the theatrical take. Generally speaking, with all the costs, prints and advertising and distribution fee 'off the top'.

***Q - Say for instance, if someone brought a picture like WHITE ANGEL to you for UK theatrical , video and TV?***

***Mick*** - Generally speaking on a relatively low budget movie an advance could be £50,000 - it could be £100,000, or £200,000 or then again it could be a straight distribution deal where no advance will be paid - it all depends on the film. If we are not very confident about the film it's fair to say you would be unlikely to get an advance. For a straight distribution deal you would probably be looking at some kind of penny one percentage - gross participation in every bean that comes back through the door - If you've got an advance, let's say £100,000, then you would probably be on a 50/50 split after recoupment of that advance plus all Prints and advertising (P&A), and then on a percentage of the video. Generally speaking you would get 25% of the net dealer price of video on rental, and 12.5% on net wholesale price. Usually the distributor will charge a distribution fee of 30% of penny one until recoupment of the prints and ads (P&A) and advance. However, this is not cast in stone and it's down to the best deal you can get.

***Q - What materials do you actually need for a UK video and theatrical release?***

***Mick*** - Access to the interneg, interpos, a master on any of the digital video tape systems, separate M&E (music and effects mix) if the producer can provide it, but we can get by without it. As much photographic material as you can possibly provide. It's vital the video tape we receive is full screen and not widescreen - widescreen may look good for the producer but the rental retailers won't touch it and a new (expensive) 'pan and scan' telecine will have to be made up.

***Q - Are things like Electronic press kits necessary?***

***Mick*** - They're nice if you've got them, and they are useful and very helpful for us to have, but you will be surprised the condition that some films get delivered in, and then you've got producers saying afterwards, why can't we have a fantastic theatrical poster and video sleeve? That is after all they provided were 3 trannies of them having their picture taken with the cameraman. Absolutely hopeless. It is essential for distribution that you have as much material to exploit and market the movie as you can possibly get your hands on. We also need access to the cast. Ian Hart of *Clockwork Mice* has just agreed to do a wide selection of media interviews - that can only help and support the movie because people are very keen to hear the views and stories the cast have to tell.

***Q - If a producer brought a low budget film to you for Feature Film to do the theatrical - how much might you spend on expenses and the P&A?***

***Mick*** - For *SOFT TOP HARD SHOULDER* we spent over £70k, for *THE HAWK* we spent £120,000. It all depends on how much you need to spend on the film - 40% of your budget can go on prints, but you have to advertise and make funds available. It's an expensive business buying advertising space, and it's getting worse daily.

feature film COMPANY
68-70 WARDOUR ST.
LONDON W1V 3HP
TEL: 071-734-2266
FAX: 071-494-0309
Mick Southworth

***Q - How are the UK theatrical receipts broken down - JOE BLOGGS spends his £5 at the cinema, how is that £5 broken down?***

***Mick*** - Cinemas have a break figure known as a nut figure. This is worked out with the value that they put on each seat in the cinema. Generally the distributor would get 25% of everything on the door up to a figure, lets say its £3k or 90% of everything - whichever is greater - that's how the nut figures work. Generally cinemas in the UK and America work off nut figures. If for instance, a film grosses £300k, and the average distribution share from the cinemas is 33.3%, you would make £100,000 back. If I've paid an advance, and I'm up on the P&A, that £100k would first go against paying that off. Lets say a joint P&A and a minimum guarantee of £70k was made - that leaves an overage of £30k to be

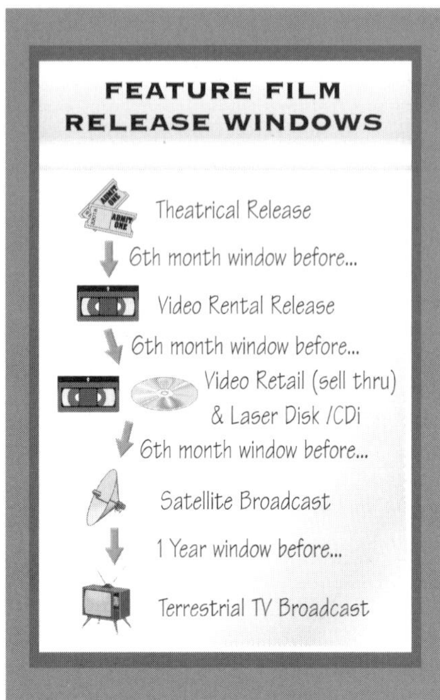


split whichever way your deal works with the producer. As I say, it varies.

***Q - Is it usual for a film to just about break even, or not make much on the theatrical in order to generate exposure for the video & TV sales?***

***Mick*** - The idea of minimal low end theatrical release is to build a profile or platform for the video release and also for the TV and satellite sales.

***Q - How are the receipts for the UK video broken down?***

***Mick*** - It is normally 25% of the net dealer price - you will be on 25% of every tape that goes through the machine - that is of course, after any outstanding recoupment for the theatrical P&A, should there be any.

***Q - And what's the average cost of a unit for the video dealer?***

***Mick*** - It can vary - they start at £45 but your average net could be somewhere in the region of £30. Plus your big clients out there can force a discount down to quite a low price

***Q - And how many tapes on average do you sell for an average low budget picture?***

***Mick*** - With *BEYOND BEDLAM* we did 8000 units, with *SOFT TOP HARD SHOULDER* we did 2500 units - it varies. There's a massive fragmentation - it all depends on how the market is at that particular time and how successful your film is perceived as a solid 'video'. Also the marketing and press are important.

***Q - What happens about television rights?***

***Mick*** - The price on satellite can vary when taking into account the video rental success - you can get a lot more money if the film is perceived as being a rental success - maybe it's something to do with the demography of the people who use satellite - and theatrical tends to have more of a bearing on free TV.

***Q - How long does it take for a film maker to see money from a release?***

***Mick*** - Generally, it's about three months after any release. Remember that some releases, like TV, can be three years down the line, especially if we have to hang on to a film for six months or more to get the right window for the theatrical release.

ANNUAL THEATRICAL ADMISSIONS 1994
TOTAL ADMISSIONS 123.53 MILLION
(Source Screen Finance)

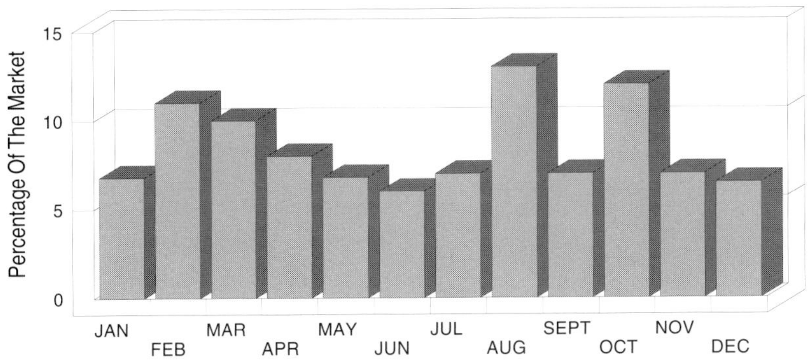


ANNUAL VIDEO RENTAL PERCENTAGES PER MONTH 1994
(BVA Yearbook)

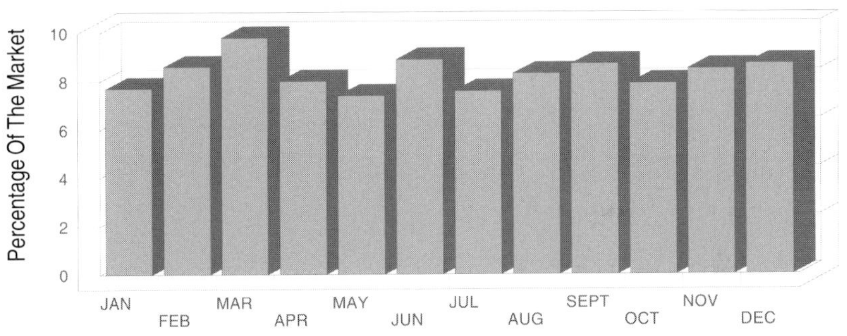


***Q - If a release is to be successful what are the most important aspects of a production, apart from being a good film?***

***Mick*** - I think look, listen and gauge the market place - if there would be a taste for - lets say *Four Weddings and a Funeral Part 2* was coming up, it would be a pretty fair assumption that if one made a film to be released around the same time, then the audience would have a taste for light romantic comedy... certainly if there was some epic Dracula movie coming up - then a vampire movie would be more saleable to video at that time. It's very hard to predict the market, we could all be very confident that a film is going to do well, and no-one goes to see it.

***Q - What is the best example of a release that you handled and why was it so successful?***

***Mick*** - I think it goes back to the Virgin days - *Sex lies and videotape* - it was successful because we managed to get two separate audiences to see the movie - those that were driven by the

## RENTALS BY REGION (JULY-DEC '94)
## CALCULATED USING ITV REGIONS

(BVA Yearbook)

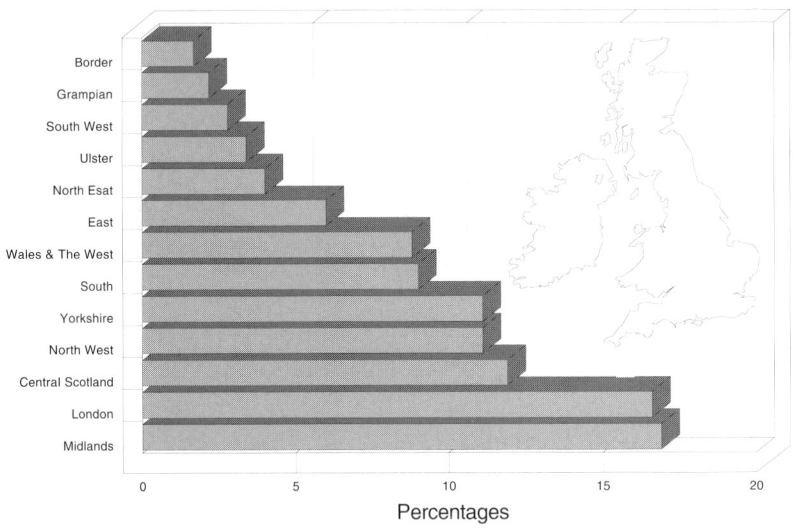

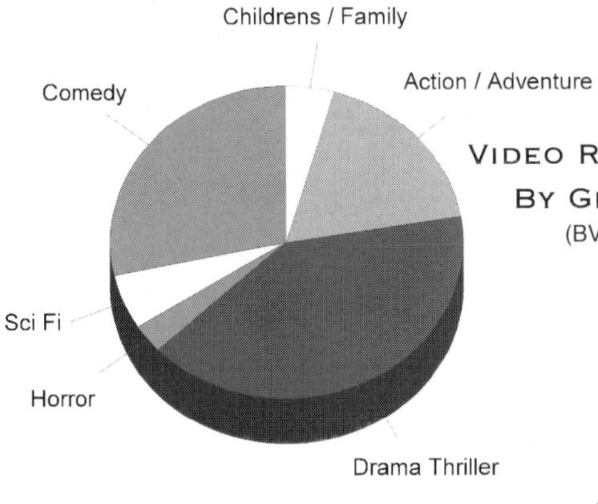

Childrens / Family
Action / Adventure
Comedy
Sci Fi
Horror
Drama Thriller

## VIDEO RENTAL SHARE BY GENRE 1994

(BVA Yearbook)

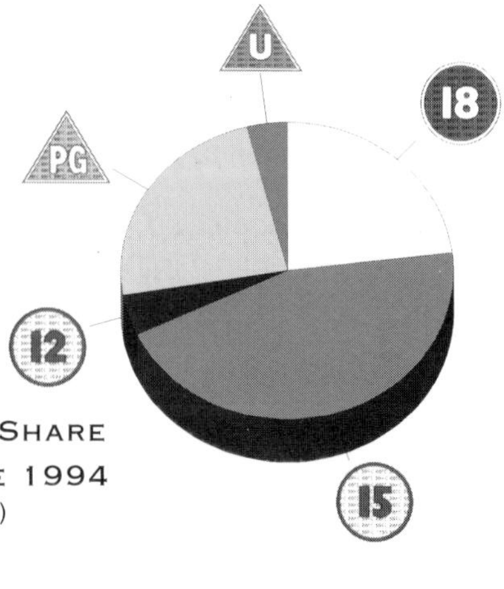

U
18
PG
12
15

## VIDEO RENTAL SHARE BY CERTIFICATE 1994

(BVA Yearbook)

POST-PRODUCTION

*Sex, Lies and Videotape managed to capture two audiences, the youth sex drive audience, and the more mature, Cannes Award Winners audience.*

Cannes Film Festival Award winner and there was another campaign that catered for a very sexy modern drama, so the two different campaigns did two particularly different things and managed to get 2 separate audiences in.

***Q - How does the theatrical release work?***

***Mick*** - There's no point taking delivery of a movie that the cinemas won't play, the cinemas have running costs and they are businesses, they have to be sure that those movies will generate enough revenue to cover their costs, that's why they have a nut figure on the house. So the first obstacle, is to get the cinemas to come to some business arrangement with you on that particular movie - each movie is a different deal - and then you've got to get the campaign together, you've got to get the PR plans sorted, you've got to get the image of the movie correct, and its positioning and profile - so there's a whole catalogue of things to be done.

***Q - What's the SFD?***

***Mick*** - Society of Film Distributors - its a society for the distributors to go and exchange information - its a monitoring service to ensure that we all tow the line - and the CEA - The Cinema Exhibition Association - does a similar thing for cinemas. Its a sort of governing body to harness the industry.

***Q - What are the most common mistakes made by a producer?***

***Mick -*** I would say that we never have enough support material, especially stills. It's impossible to market a film without stills, if we don't have any then we have to get some together, maybe even get the cast back and into a studio to take some new shots. Whatever happens, it will add costs to recoup from first sales. Most other things can be ironed out, but stills are always a headache. Be prepared.

# British Council
## Geraldine Higgins

*The British Council can help promote British films and culture abroad, often with the aid of grants. They are situated ten minutes walk from Wardour St.*

***Q - What is the British Council's job when it comes to feature films?***

***Geraldine*** - There are two sides to our feature film operation. One where we acquire feature films on 16mm for non-theatrical use overseas which means screening on British Council premises (we are based in 108 countries) and certain educational establishments. The second operation is where we support and organise film events around the world i.e. film festivals, film weeks, retrospectives, European Community film events etc. utilising 35mm prints borrowed from distributors and production companies. The organisers of these events approach either the local British Council office or Films, Television & Video department direct for help in selecting films. After the films have been selected we collect the prints and any publicity material and despatch them overseas. We will also arrange for a director or actor to go out in support of the event. Sometimes we are asked to arrange a viewing programme at our office for a festival director where we will screen on video as many recent films as distributors and production companies let us have. Therefore it can be in the interest of smaller production companies to let us know about their film so we can suggest it to a festival selector.

***Q - What kind of British Feature Films does the British Council help in general?***

***Geraldine*** - We try to highlight new British features - to get them seen around the world. However the final selection does depend entirely on the organiser of the event. If it is a week of British Film, we will try to include films from new directors.

***Q - How does a producer engage your services and what does that producer need to supply you with to do a good job?***

***Geraldine*** - We need to know about new films and have copies of the film on VHS together with a press kit, just a few typed sheets on the film, synopsis, cast and crew list and some photos. We need material that we can then send to a festival director, if they are not coming to the UK, so that they can look at the film and have some background information which will help them make their choice. Press packs are vital and very cheap and easy to put together.

***Q - Would it be advantageous for the producer to invite you to an early screening of the film?***

***Geraldine -*** The earlier we see the film the better. We are handling feature film events all the time and we may miss a film that might be ideal for an event simply because we do not know it exist. So yes, the earlier we know about a film, the more festivals/events we can submit it to.

***Q - If a film is selected to play in a festival abroad and the director or producer is invited, can the British council help with finances?***

***Geraldine -*** All our offices around the world have a small budget for travel grants. If a film was selected for a festival, we would contact the office in that country and ask if they would be prepared to offer a travel grant for the director to attend. It really depends on the budget of the local office and if they support films. But yes, you can theoretically get a travel grant.

***Q - And the shipping of prints etc?***

***Geraldine -*** Once we get involved in an event, we will take on all the administrative work i.e. sending out preview cassettes, publicity material, entry forms and ultimately the films selected. So we will do everything.

***Q - Will the festival ever help out?***

***Geraldine -*** If the British Council provides a travel grant we would expect the festival or event organisers to pay all onshore costs i.e. hotel and meal allowances. This is the normal practice.

***Q - Can the BC help with attending commercial markets like the AFM or the Cannes Film Festival?***

***Geraldine*** - The British Council is not a commercial organisation. Our purpose is to promote a wider knowledge of the UK and the English language. We encourage cultural, scientific, technological and educational co-operation between the UK and other countries. We do not give grants for people to attend film markets.

*The British Council can be enormously helpful. It's worth giving them a call in advance of the completion of a film just to let them know that it's going to be around soon. They can work wonders but do need plenty of time to be truly effective.*

POST-PRODUCTION

## Sundance Film Festival

Sundance Institute, 307 West 200 South, Ste. 5002 Salt Lake City, Utah 84101
Tel: (1 801) 328 3456
Fax: (1 801) 575 5175
E-mail: sundance@xmission.com
LA contact: Sundance Institute
225 Santa Monica Blrd, 8th Floor
Santa Monica, CA 90401
Tel: (1 301) 394 4662
Fax: (1 301) 394 8353
E-mail: sundance@deltanet.com
http://sundancefilm.com/festival/index.html
Deadline: 20 October

## Brussells Int. Film Festival

Christian Thomas, Ch. de Louvain
50 Levvensesteenweg, B-1210
Brussells, Belgium
Tel: (32) 2 218 53 33
Fax: (32) 2 218 18 60
E-mail: c.thomas@netcity.be
http://www.netcity.be/ffb/
Deadline: 31 October

## Miami Film Festival

Film Society of Miami,
Ste. 229, 444 Brickell Avenue
Miami, FL 33131
Tel: (1 305) 377 3456
Fax: (1 305) 577 9768
w.w.w.filmsocietyofmiami.com
Deadline: 1 Nov.

## Portland Int. Film Festival

N.W. Film & Video Center, Portland Art Museum, Berg-Swann Auditorium
1219 S.W. Park Avenue
Portland, OR 97205
Tel: (1 503) 221 1156
Fax: (1 503) 226 4842
http://www.film.com/industry/filmfests//portland.95.html
Deadline: contact Festival

## Berlin Film Festival

Internationale Filmfestspiele Berlin,
Budapester strasse 50,
D-10787, BERLIN
Tel: (49) 30 254 89225
Fax: (49) 30 253 89249
Deadline: December

## Goteborg Film Festival

Box 7079, S-402 32 Goteborg, Sweden
Tel: (46) 31 41 05 46
Fax: (46) 31 41 00 63
E-mail: goteborg.filmfestival@mailbox.swipmet.se
http://www/goteborg.se/kultur/film/festival
Deadline: 1 Nov

## New Directors/New Films

New York Film Society of Lincoln Center70 Lincoln Center Plaza
New York, NY 10023-6595, USA
Tel: (1 212) 875 5610
Fax: (1 212) 875 5636
E-mail: filmlinc@dti.net
http://www.filmlinc.com/hyff.htm
Deadline: 17 Jan

## Hong Kong Int. Film Festival

Festivals Office,
Urban Services Development
Level 7, Administration Building,
Hong Kong Cultural Centre,
10 Salisbury Road.
Tsim Sha Tsui, Kowloon, Hong Kong
Tel: (852) 2734 2903
Fax: (852) 2366 5206
http://www.asiaonline.net/hkiff/
Deadline: contact Festival

## Int. Festival of Fantasy and Science Fiction Films,

111 Ave de la Reine,
Koninginnelaan,
B-1210 Brussels, Belgium
Tel: (32) 2 201 17 13
Fax: (32) 2 210 1469
Deadline: contact Festival

## Cleveland Int. Film Festival

Suite 428, 1621 Euclid Avenue
Cleveland, Ohio 44115-2017, USA
Tel: (1 216) 623 0400
Fax: (1 216) 623 0103
www.clevefilmfest.org/
Deadline: November

## Cartagena Int. Film Festival

Calle San Juan de Dios
Baluarte San Francisco Javier
A.A. 1834 Cartagena
Colombia, South America
Tel: (57) 5 600 966
Fax: (57) 5 660 0970/1037
E-mail: spyder@escape.com
http://escape.com/~spyder/CART.HTML
Deadline: contact Festival

## Singapore Int. Film Festival

400 Orchard Road #24-09
Orchard Towers
Singapore 238875
Tel: (65) 7387567
Fax: (65) 7387578
E-mail: filmfest@pacific.net.sg
http://www.pacific.net.sg/siff/
Deadline: mid Dec.

## Houston Int. Film Festival and Market: Worldfest Houston

2700 Post Oak, Ste. 1798
Houston, TX 77056 USA
Tel: (1 713) 965-9955
Fax: (1 713) 965-9960
E-mail: Worldfest@aol.com
http://www.vannevar.com.worldfest/wfest.htm
Deadline: March

## Cape Town Int. Film Festival

Film Education Unit
University of Cape Town
Private Bag, Rondebosch 7700
Cape Town, South Africa
Tel: (27) 21 238257
Fax: (27) 21 242355
Deadline: contact Festival

### Istanbul Int. Film Festival
Istanbul Foundation for Culture &Arts
Istanbul Kultur ve Sanat Vakfi
Istiklal Cad. luvr Apt. no. 146
Beyoglu, 80070, Istanbul, Turkey
Tel: (90) 21 2 293 3133/34/35
Fax: (90) 21 2 249 7771
Deadline: January

### San Francisco Int. Film Festival
1521 Eddy Street, San Francisco,
CA 94115 - 4102, USA
Tel: (1 415) 929 5000
Fax: (1 415) 921 5032
E-mail: filmfest@sfiff.org
http://sfiff.org/
Deadline: Dec.

### Valenciennes Int. Action and Adventure Film Festival
Festival du Film D'Action et D'aventure
De Valenciennes, Bureau de Festival
6 Place Froissart, 59300 Valenciennes,
France
Tel:(33) 27 29 55 40
Fax: (33) 2741 67 49
Deadline: contact Festival

### Madrid Int. Film Festival (IMAGFIC)
Gran Via 62-8, 28013 Madrid, Spain
Tel: (34) 1 5413721/5415541
Fax: (34) 1 5425495
Deadline: mid Feb.

### Cannes Film Festival
99 Boulevard Malesherbes, 75008
Paris,France
Tel: (33) 1 45 61 66 00
Fax: (33) 1 45 61 97 60
Deadline: 1 March

### Auckland Film Festival
PO Box 9544, Te Aro
Wellington 6001, New Zealand
Tel: (64) 9 385 0162
Fax: (64) 9 801 7304
Deadline: 31 March

### Rivertown Int. Film Festival
Minneapolis and St. Paul
425 Ontario Street SE
Minneapolis, MN 55414, USA
Tel; (1 612) 627 4431/32
Fax: (1 612) 627 4111
Deadline: end Jan.

### Philadelphia Festival of World Cinema
Intl. House, 3701 Chestnut Street,
Philadelphia, Pennsylvannia. 19104, USA
Tel: (1 215) 895 6593
Fax: (1 215) 895 6562
E-mail: pfwc@libertynet.org
http://www.libertynet.org/~
Deadline: 27 January

### Melbourne Int. Film Festival
1st Floor, 201 Johnston Street, Fitzroy,
PO Box 296 Fitzroy Mail Centre, 3065
Melbourne, Victoria, Australia
Tel: (61) 3 9417 2011
Fax: (61) 3 9417 3804
E-mail: miff@netspace.net.au
http://www.cinemedia.net/MIFF
Deadline: April

### Seattle Int. Film Festival Cinema
Egyptian Theater, 801 East Pine Street,
Seattle, WA 98122, USA
Tel: (1 206) 324 9996
Fax: (1 206) 324 9998
http://www.seattlefilm.com
Deadline: mid March

### St Petersburg Festival of Festivals
190 Kamennoostrovsky Ave
St Petersburg 197101, Russia
Tel: (7 812) 2385811
Fax: (7 812) 2332174/
Deadline: 1 April

### Sydney Int. Film Festival
P.O.Box 950, Glebe,
NSW 2037 Australia
Tel: (61) 2 660 3844
Fax: (61) 2 692 8793
E-mail: sydfilm@ozonline.com.au
http://www.sydfilm-fest.com.au
Deadline: 8 March

### Southampton Film Festival
City Arts Civic Centre, Southampton,
S09 4XF
Tel: 01703 832457
Fax: 01703 832153
Deadline: mid Feb

### Munich Film Festival
Internationale Munchner, Filmwochen Gmbh
Kaiserstrasse 39, D-80801 Munich, Germany
Tel: (49) 89 38 19 04 0
Fax: (49) 89 38 19 04 26
Deadline: end May

### Midnight Sun Film Festival
Malminkatu 36, 00100, Helsinki, Finland.
Tel: (358) 0 685 2242
Fax: (358) 0 694 5560
Deadline: March

### Florida Film Festival
1300 South Orlando Avenue, Maitland,
FL 32751
Tel: (1 407) 629-1088
Fax: (1 407) 629-6870
Deadline: 1 April

### Wellington Film Festival
PO Box 9544, Te Aro, Wellington 6001,
New Zealand
Tel: (64) 4 385 0162
Fax: (64) 4 801 7304
Deadline: 15 April

### The World Film Festival
1432 de Bleury St., Montreal H3A 2J1
Quebec, CANADA
Tel: (1 514) 848 3883
Fax: (1 514) 848 3886
E-mail: ffm@Interlink.net
http://www.ffm-montreal.org
Deadline: 5 July

### Brisbane Int. Film Festival
Level 3, Hoyts Regent Building
167 Queen Street, Brisbane
Q. 4000, Australia
Tel: (61) 7 3220 0333
Fax: (61) 7 3220 0400
E-mail: brisfilm@thehub.com.au
Deadline: 26 May

### The Norwegian Int. Film Festival
PO Box 145, N-5501 Haugesund, Norway
Tel: (47) 52 73 44 30
Fax: (47) 52 73 44 20
Deadline: 7 May

### Drambuie Edinburgh Int. Film Festival
Filmhouse, 88 Lothian Road,
Edinburgh EH3 9BZ, Scotland
Tel: 0131 228 4051
Fax: 0131 229 5501
E-mail: info@edfilmfest.org.uk
http://www.edfilmfest.org.uk/
Deadline: Mid May

### Locarno Int. Film Festival
Casella postale, Via della Poste 6,
CH-6600 Locarno, Suisse
TEL: (41) 91 751 02 32
FAX: (41) 91 751 74 65
Deadline: 31 May

### Espoo Cine
PO Box 95, 02101 Espoo, Finland
Tel: (358) 0 466 599
Fax: (358) 0 466 458
Deadline: contact Festival

### Alexandria Int. Film Festival
Secretariat, 9 Oraby Street
11111 Cairo, Egypt
Tel: (20) 2 5741112
Fax: (20) 2 768727
Deadline: mid July

### Aspen Film Festival
110 E. Hallam, Suite 102, Aspen,
Colorado 81611
Tel: (1 970) 925 6882
Fax: (1 970) 925 1967
Deadline: 15 July

### Telluride Film Festival
National Film Preserve, 53 South Main
Street. Suite 212, Hanover,
NH 03755, USA
Tel :(1 603) 643-1255
Fax:(1 603) 643 5938
E-mail: Tellufilm@aol.com
http://telluridemm.com/filmfest.html
Deadline: 1 August

### Cinefest: The Sudbury Film Fest.
218-40 rue Elm Street
Sudbury, Ontario, P3C 1S8, CANADA
Tel: (1 705) 688 1234
Fax: (1 705) 688 1351
Deadline: contact Festival

### South Africa Int. Film Festival
Lyle Britton, 139 Smit Street
Braamfontein, Johannesburg
2000 South Africa
Tel: (27) 11 403 7111
Fax: (27) 11 403 1025
Deadline: contact Festival

### Tokyo Int. Film Festival
4F, Landic Ginza Bldg.11, 1-6-5 Ginza,
Chuo-ku,Tokyo 104 Japan.
Tel: (81) 3 3563 6305
Fax: (81) 3 3563 6310
Deadline: June

### New York Film Festival
New York Film Society of Lincoln Center
70 Lincoln Center Plaza
New York, NY 10023-6595, USA
Tel: (1 212) 875 5610
Fax: (1 212) 875 5636
E-mail: filmlinc@dti.net
http://www.filmlinc.com/hyff.htm
Deadline: 12 July

### San Sebastian Int. Film Festival
PO Box 397, Plaza de Okendo s/n.
Donostia-San sebastian, 20080 Spain
Tel: (34) 43 48 12 12
Fax: (34) 43 48 12 18
Deadline: contact Festival

### Annual Toronto Int. Film Festival - Festival of Festivals
16th Floor, 2 Carlton Street, Ontario,
M5B IJ3 CANADA
Tel: (1 416) 967 7371
Fax: (1 416) 967 9477
http://www.bell.ca/toronto/filmfest/review.html
Deadline: 28 June

### Shots In The Dark Film Festival
Broadway Media Centre, 14 Broad Street,
Nottingham.
Tel: 01159 526600
Fax: 01159 526622
Deadline:Aug/Sept.

### Venice Film Festival
Venice Film Festival, La Biennale di Venezia
Settore Cinema e Spettacolo Televisivo
Ca' Giustinian, 1364 San Marco,
Venice 30124, ITALY
Tel: (39) 41 521 8711
Fax: (39) 41 522 7539
Deadline: End of May by invitation

### The Copenhagen Film Festival
Vesterbrogade 35 A, 3. 1620 Copenhagen V
Denmark
Tel: (45) 33 25 25 01
Fax: (45) 33 25 57 56
Deadline: July

### AFI/Los Angeles Int. Film Festival
American Film Institute, P.O. Box 27999
2021 North Western Avenue
Los Angeles, CA 90027
Tel: (1 213) 856 7707
Fax: (1 213) 462 4049
www.afionline.org
Deadline: March

### The Hamptons Int. Film Festival
3 Newtown Mews, East Hampton, NY
11937, USA
Tel: (1 516) 324 4600
Fax: (1 516) 324 5116
http://www.peconic.net/arts/hampton/film-festival/
Deadline: August

### Chicago Int. Film Festival
415 North Dearborn Street
Chicago, IL 60610 - 9990
Tel: (1 312) 644 3400
Fax: (1 312) 644 0784
http://www.chicago.ddbn.com/filmfest
Deadline: 1 July

### Mill Valley Film Festival
38 Miller Avenue, Suite 6, Mill Valley,
CA 94941
Tel: (1 415) 383-5256
Fax: (1 415) 383-8606
E-mail: finc@well.com
http://www.well.com/user/mvff/
Deadline: 30 June

### Denver Int. Film Festival
1430 Larimer Sq., Ste. 201,
Denver, Colorado. 80202, USA
Tel :(1 303) 595 3459
Fax: (1 303) 595 0956
E-mail: DenverFilm@csn.net
http://www2.csn.net/DenverFilm/
Deadline: July

### Vancouver Int. Film Festival
Suite 410 - 1008 Homer Street,
Vancouver, V6B 2X1,
British Colombia, CANADA
Tel: (1 604) 685 0260
Fax: (1 604) 688 8221
E-mail: viff@viff.org
Deadline: mid July

### Vienna Film Festival
Viennale, Stiftgasse 6/7,
A - 1070 Vienna, Austria
Tel: (43) 1 526 59 47
Fax: (43) 1 93 41 72
E-mail: office@viennale.or.at
http://www.Viennale.or.at/
Deadline: 31 July

### Sao Paulo Int. Film Festival
Mostra Internacional De Cinema,
Alameda Lorena, 937
cj.303 01424-001 Sao Paulo, BRAZIL
Tel: (55) 11 883 5137
Fax: (55 ) 11 853 7936
E-mail: info@mostra.org
http://www.mostra.org/
Deadline: Sept.

### Valladolid Int. Film Festival
P.O. Box 646, 47080 Valladolid, Spain
Tel: (34) 83 30 57 00/77/88
Fax: (34) 83 30 98 35
Dealine: 30 June

### Flanders Int. Film Festival
1104 Kortrijksesteenweg, B - 9051,
Ghent, Belgium.
Tel: (32) 9 221 8946
Fax: (32) 9 221 9074
E-mail: filmfestival@infoboard.be
http://www.rug.ac.be/filmfestival/Welcome.html
Deadline: 10 August

### Raindance Independent Film Festival
Raindance Film Showcase, 81 Berwick Street
London. W1V 3PF
Tel: 0171 437 3991
Fax: 0171 439 2243
Deadline: mid Sept.

### Cork Film Festival
Hatfield House, Tobin Street, Cork, Ireland
Tel: (353) 21 271711
Fax: (353) 21 275945
E-mail: ciff@indigo.ie
http://www.eirenet.net/ciff/
Deadline: 15 July

### Mannheim-Heidelberg Int. Film Festival
Collini-Center-Galerie, D-68161 Mannheim, Germany
Tel: (49) 621 10 29 43
Fax: (49) 621 29 15 64
E-mail: post@mannheim-filmfestival.com
Deadline:1 August

### Kiev Int. Film Festival "Molodist"
Union of Filmmakers of Ukraine
vul. Saksaganskogo, 6, office 115
Kyiv 252033, Ukraine
Tel: (380) 44 227 4557
Fax: (380) 44 227 3130
Deadline: 15 July

### Thessaloniki Int. Film Festival
36, Sina Str., Athens 106 72 Greece
Tel: (30) 1 3610418
Fax: (30) 1 3621023
or: 154 Egnatia Str., Thessaloniki,
526 36 Greece
Tel: (30) 1 286678
Fax: (30) 1 285759
E-mail: filmfestival@compulink.gr
http://www.compulink.gr/filmfestival/
Deadline: contact Festival

### Fort Lauderale Int. Film Festival
2633 East Sunrise Boulevard
Fort Lauderale, FL 33304, USA
Tel: (1 305) 954 563 0500
Fax: (1 305) 954 564 1206
E-mail: brofilm@aol.com
http://vcn.net/filmfest/
Deadline: 1 September

### Puerto Rico Int. Film Festival
70 Mayaguez Street, Suite B-1,
Hato Rey, Puerto Rico, 00918
Tel: (1 809) 764-7044
Fax: (1 809) 753-5367
Deadline: contact Festival

### Oslo Int. Film Festival
Ebbelsgate 1, 0183 Oslo, Norway
Tel: (47) 22200766
Fax: (47) 22201807
E-mail: filmfestival@login.eunet.no
http://wit.no/filmfestival/
Deadline: August

### London Int. Film Festival
South Bank, London. SE1 8XT
Tel: 0171 8151323
Fax: 0171 6630786
http://www.ibmpcug.co.uk/lff.html
Deadline: August

### Stockholm Int. Film Festival
Box 3136, 103 62 Stockholm, Sweden
Tel: (46) 8 20 05 50
Fax: (46) 8 20 05 90
http://www.filmfestivalen.se
Deadline: 12 September

### Ankara Film Festival of European Films
Festival on Wheels: Ankara, Izmir,Bursa,
Eskisehir, Bulten Sokak No 13, Kavaklidere
06680 Ankara, Turkey
Tel: (90) 312 468 71 40
Fax: (90) 312 468 71 39
Deadline:January

### Hawaii Int. Film Festival
700 Bishop Street, Ste. 400,
Honolulu, Oahu, HI 96813 USA
Tel :(1 808) 528 3456
Fax: (1 808) 528 1410
E-mail: hiffinfo@hiff.org
http://www.hiff.org
Deadline: 1 July

### Fantasporto
### Oporto Int. Film Festival,
Cinema Novo, Multimedia Centre
Rua da Constitucao 311
4200 Porto, Portugal.
Tel: (351) 2 550 8990/1/2
Fax: (351) 2 5508210
E-mail: fantas@caleida.pt
http://www.caleida.pt/fantasporto
Deadline: 30 November

Notes - Fax or phone festivals for their details and entry forms. Remember, many festivals work well in advance so you should be thinking about applying several months before the festival happens.

If you have access to the Internet, check out the YAHOO database of film festivals at http://www.yahoo.com/Enteıtainment/Movies_and_Films/Film_Festivals/

# Image Chris Fowler of The Creative Partnership

***Q - What does a producer need to do in order to exploit their film?***

***Chris -*** The basic rule of thumb to getting a film out to the public and making them aware of it, is the earlier you start the better. It's common, particularly with first time filmmakers, that somewhere along the way they kind of forget the reason for making the film in the first place - they start with *"I know I want to make a film about a talking horse"* and by the time they've been through this incredible learning curve, they hate the film and say, *"well can we bury the talking horse"*. What we do is deconstruct the film and take it back to the pebble of why they wanted to make the film in the first place, back to what the public would be interested in seeing.

***Q - From a marketing point of view, you're saying it's important to latch onto a single concept in order to exploit the film?***

***Chris -*** Yes, people are not waiting to be told how wonderful your film is, they don't give a shit. If they see a trailer for it, it will be by complete accident - they will be more concerned with putting their coat somewhere safe and getting popcorn. If they get a handbill thrust into their hand for it, it's another piece of paper they don't want. It's common for new film makers to naively believe that the whole world is just dying to see their film, and the world really isn't that interested.

***Q - So does this go as far as suggesting new titles for a film? With our film White Angel, we felt, in retrospect that a title like Interview With a Serial Killer would be better?***

***Chris -*** I would be the first person to tell you to dump *White Angel* as it tells you nothing. Also the conjunction of the words *White* and *Angel* suggest a U certificate aimed at kids, they're very feminine words, it feels wussy - it's not the image you want to give. We retitled *The Crying Game* - originally it was called *The Soldier's Wife* which gives off two things - a happily married man - boring - and a soldier - which at that time was a massive turn off. We ended up going through the Book of British Singles - *The Crying Game* doesn't mean anything except there's some kind of tension about it - a Game - a bit of mischief, it feels like there's a bit more to it. So yes, it starts with the title and some kind of strap line. Even though you probably won't end up using the strap line, it's quite a good idea to establish it in the crew's mind.

***Q - How do you go about designing the poster?***

***Chris -*** The subject matter will suggest itself. For example, we're just starting on a film that Marc Samuelson's making, an entirely British financed production called Wilde, a biography of Oscar

Wilde. The first thing you think of is Oh! flowery lettering - Merchant Ivory, lovely and pretty. Then you hear that Stephen Fry and Jude Law are the leads and it's much more modern, so we scrap the idea of it being flowery and think, we'll go for a very modernistic approach. So your design is decided by the flavour of the script as much as the subject matter of the film. It's all about the subject matter and the approach of the director. Ben Ross, on the film *The Young Poisoner's Handbook,* had a very specific agenda on the film. The script read like True Crime and it had actually been filmed once before for the BBC or ITV as a one hour show. But he wanted to play it as a black comedy and this is the sort of stuff only the director could tell you - it's not always there in the script. We were then able to say let's not pull any punches and we did a series of very black posters - we did it like a kid's chemistry set with all those fifties happy families on the front and he's making poison to kill them all. So first the script, and then the director's view of the script.

***Q - How do you go about creating a good trailer?***

***Chris -*** Usually, there are two different trailers, one for here in the UK, and another for overseas (that's also used by the sales agent). We're doing Mike Leigh's *Secrets and Lies* for both the UK and International territories, and we're taking two completely different approaches. The UK one is dealing with people who know Mike Leigh, so it's very much on personalities. His films are entirely character driven studies, but the international trailer requires more of a story, more setting up. The first rule is that the trailer can't lie - you have to reflect the film directly and these days you have to do it harder and faster. Other things are cyclical, trailers are getting longer now, after several years of being shortened. We did the *Trainspotting* trailer and it was very much in your face but it also used techniques of the film, freeze framing, captions, talking to camera, things like that so the rule of thumb is a distillation of the film.

***Q - When do you normally get involved in a film?***

***Chris -*** We handle anything from very small films to blockbusters like *Goldeneye,* and a lot of films in between. We do an awful lot of nurturing of new talent, but we are happier working when the film has been sold to a UK territory, or it has a sales agent or something. Often, we are prepared to be the first show of faith, but there's only a certain amount we can do.

***Q - Am I correct in saying that the service you offer should be looked on as being as important as the solicitors or accountant's advice?***



***Chris -*** For most of it's 100 year life, advertising a film has been an after-thought. It's often that the gestation of a film is so long and so slow that by the time the film comes out, the subject matter is no longer appealing to the film makers or the public. But if we're there from the beginning and we can see it through, we can actually help to solve problems. In the last fifteen years people have sat up

(left) Pitch - Teen mag image designed to display the piece as a bright summer feel good movie. FFD (Film Four Distribution) Response - Liked very much, but it didn't quite take in the whole picture. Nice try though.

(below) Pitch - Teen nightmare image. We wanted a far more abstract and menacing visual and this was the outcome. FFD Response - The whole image smacked of druggy violence. Very clever though and not without merit.

(left) Pitch - Troubled people living in difficult life of urban decay. The in your face 'if you don't like it, tough' pitch. FFD Response - Oh dear! Not our film at all. Never really a contender.

(below) Pitch - The relationship feel. Something more intimate. Urban but openly hopeful and good natured. FFD Response - Really liked it, but just a little messy. Getting to the place we wanted to be though. Loved the rainbow.

(left) Pitch - The urban, joyous, funny, sunny happy ensemble campaign. FFD Response - Getting there but a tiny bit awkward.

## Poster Perfection

*Film Four movie, 'Beautiful Thing' had two campaigns. As the film had a gay theme, it was decided to target the gay media, but also push the mainstream media with a different campaign. Many poster images are mocked up for the distributors in order to find the image to sell the film to the right audience in the right way.*

*This was it. Bold, in your face and aggressive. This would lead the 'gay' media push.*

*The final agreed mainstream image. Much better organised than its predecessor. Really bright sunny and feelgood. Translated wonderfully to press ads too.*

*photo by Donald Milne*

and become aware that without advertising and publicity, a film is dead in the water. At the other end of the scale, you cannot keep chucking millions at a film - you get a good first weekend, then you get 30% drop off for the second week, and it spirals down from there. There is an argument that we're all firm believers of here, that is to keep one single idea in everybody's mind so that when you do come to the end of it, you have a very clean cut, clear, straightforward campaign that you can nail into somebody's head - go see this film.

***Q - Shallow Grave was enormously successful, considering it's humble beginnings. How much of the success of Shallow Grave was the result of your input rather than the film on it's own?***

***Chris -*** This is like one of those chicken and the egg things that we argue about in the pub all the time. The film is undeniably superb, I loved it. We came in very late, we weren't involved in *Shallow Grave* early at all - I believe that it was a really simple and strong idea to put the shovel on the poster. I can't remember who came up with the shovel idea, it was probably someone at Polygram video. There was a wonderful trailer for it which we cut - it reflected the film beautifully because it got the humour in there. If you take the title out of context - *Shallow Grave* - it sounds like a horror film. But it's a horror film with funny bits in it, it's shot very kinetically, it's been made by young people - wow! so it was a novelty. So you put all these things together and you get a very good trailer. We also had the age old problem of having no stars and a very good film, that without careful handling, could get lost between the cracks. It's true in this industry nobody knows anything as films do often die. *Reservoir Dogs* dropped dead in the States because they had a traditional campaign. We did a poster with the guys walking and lots of blood - very in your face - it really took off and the time was right for that. The American campaign for *Shallow Grave* is very different, it's got the three actors and a spiral staircase. The spiral staircase hints at mystery, three friends says warmth and friendship. It flopped in the States. I think the signals you give off with a poster are very limited, you can only really make it look one thing. We've just done the poster for *Things To Do In Denver When You're Dead* - it's a hip film, there's not much else to it other than it's hipness, so it's a very hip poster.

***Q - The Reservoir Dogs poster had some blood spattering on it, did that cause any problems?***

***Chris -*** There is a committee called the SFD who give a yes or no to posters.

***Q - They are the Mary Whitehouse of posters?***

***Chris -*** They are. One of the things they dreamt up was that you cannot have anything on a poster that a lonely woman on a deserted train platform at night might by upset by. Either this suggests that women are of a very hysterical nervous disposition which is offensive, or it's pandering to the feminist body. It's true a poster is in the public arena, but few people are disturbed by them, beyond the Benetton type of poster. There are very few images on a film poster that are very shocking, but it still causes us major problems. You can't have a gun facing out for instance, or blood. We certainly had a problem with a film called *Salvador* which had a silhouette of two people, one pointing the gun at the other. We said *they're silhouettes*, and they said, *well yes, but if they're silhouettes, what sex are they?* I *said they are no sex, they are silhouettes.* And they said, *so one*

*could be male and the other a female.* I said *yes.* They said, *then the victim could be the female and the other the male.* I said *yes.* They said, *it's banned.* That evening I spent the entire night with two helpers licking and sticking panels over the offending images, all 25,000 of them.

***Q - What does a Producer usually supply you with for you to do your job?***

***Chris -*** Ideally a set of stills. It's a good idea to allow one day for a special stills shoot. If you don't, then there's a good chance that most of your stills will be crap, through nobody's fault, just from the sheer messiness of the shooting process and actor availability. So a special shoot is a good idea. One day with the principles and if you can cover some kind of image that will help you sell the film at that point, it will save your film in the long run.

***Q - What should a producer do for a low budget campaign?***

***Chris -*** Firstly, stills are absolutely essential, and there's no use taking pictures of the crew at work, because no-one in the world wants to see the crew at work - they want the leads in action. Next is the mindset - if they have a clear, lucid way of explaining how and where and why they see this film being made then it's an enormous benefit. You should write, upfront, a one page synopsis of the film. It would be good to do a flyer, a colour image on one side, the synopsis on the other. The image can be built up from either a scene you've shot or a special shoot. It shouldn't be expensive because somebody on the crew will have access to a computer and if they've got somebody who knows Photoshop, they can put it together themselves and save the time and expense of someone like us doing it for them. If they're smart, they can do me out of a job and do their own trailer, which makes sense. However, it's true that film editors very rarely make good trailers because they are too close to the film - the director is standing there saying put the bit in where we blew the car up, it cost money to do that bit - it may have cost money, but it might not be the thing that appeals to the audience.

***Q - What are the most common mistakes you've experienced from producers?***

***Chris -*** From my point of view, it's a lack of clarity and vision, fuzziness of who they see the film aimed at. It's often the case they don't see the film aimed at anyone in particular. Communications are a massive problem. You can't believe we're in a communications industry from the way people fail to tell each other the most basic things.

***Q - What basic advice would you offer a low-budget film maker?***

***Chris -*** Don't do it! (laugh) I would say be aware that you're probably not going to make money. Don't do it because you think you're going to be rich, or become famous. Don't overestimate people's interest in you and your film. We won best British short film of the year in 1993, we got theatrical distribution, TV distribution in the UK and around the world, and we've yet to break even on it. Most people I know that keep going kind of have another job. Make sure you have time to do it. When I worked on a short film and I went to follow it up and do a feature, the three of us couldn't find time to do it - we couldn't even get meetings together because we have our day jobs. So if you're going to take it seriously, you have to allow for the fact that A, you're not going to make money from it and B, you're probably going to lose money from doing it by not doing other jobs.

# PACT
## John Woodward
## Chief Executive

***Q - What is PACT?***

***John -*** PACT is a non profit making trade association aimed at helping TV and Feature Film production companies. Most small companies don't have in-house services to handle business affairs, contracts, legal etc. PACT can help those producers go around the daily business of producing a film - for instance we have collective agreements with the Trade Unions, particularly Actors Equity, Musicians Union, Writers Guild etc., which produce standard industry rates of pay. So when you go into production, rather than going round and negotiating 300 separate deals you can use these agreements as a starting point. Our agreements operate as a fairly effective template around which people negotiate.

Also, each year we run six or so seminars for film & TV. Last years ranged from *How The National Lottery fund works* to a *Walk Through With The Makers Of Four Weddings.* Most are free but some are cost recovery, a nominal fee of £5 for instance. We also run a business affairs service, music consultancy, co-production and distribution surgery, legal service and various other things that production companies can access. We have business affairs advice which is run by a consultant who works for a large number of mainly TV and sometimes film companies - that's a free service to members, all you have to do is ring up and book an appointment.

***Q - If somebody has a legal problem, can they call someone in your legal department?***

***John -*** We tried that but unfortunately it didn't work. We now have a discounted legal service with a law firm called Marriot Harrison who provide professional legal consultation and help for £50 an hour - it's a proper legal service with lawyers acting for you rather than somebody doing you a favour and advising on minor problems.

***Q - If somebody comes to you looking for a partner, either financial or creative, can you put them in touch with the right people?***

***John -*** Yes, we do that informally and don't advertise it as a service, but it's one of the most important things we do. Members phone up regularly saying *we've got a script or an option, where should I go with it.* We can then advise them. We also produce directories of TV production and of Film production companies.

***Q - How much does membership cost?***

***John -*** If you're just starting out you would join us as an affiliate member which is £160 per year. Membership with PACT is open to a company, not to individuals, that's a fundamental point.

Affiliate membership entitles you to all the services, however, if you make a film which is not "low-budget", or your turnover exceeds £100k a year then you must become a full member. There is also a production levy on films made by PACT members, calculated at 0.5% of the budget up to a ceiling of £4,500. We class low budget as less than £1.5m. It's easy to make a low budget film and not to make any money out of it as a production company, so the intention of the affiliate section is to give members everything that PACT has to offer at a fairly low rate. As and when the production company can afford to, it will move into full membership. Full membership rates are banded by company turnover. Under £0.5m is £500 per annum. Between £0.5m and £2m, is £625 per annum, and over £2m is £745 per annum.

***Q - PACT has a lobbying remit?***

***John*** - Yes, PACT acts as a political lobby group for the film production sector. We spend an lot of our time hanging around the corridors of Parliament trying to persuade the government to create a proper Film policy. Some things have worked well, we've been quite efficient in helping to get things like the British Film Commission set up and lottery money set aside to go into film production, but what we haven't as yet managed to secure is a tax shelter for film investment. This is an ambition to encourage new investment in British movies.

***Q - With your government lobbies, do you have any say in what British Television picks up? There seem to be a lot of late night, poor American films whose slots could be filled by low budget British features.***

***John*** - BBC1, ITV and Channel 5 when it comes online next year, are targeting themselves very much as mass market channels. In terms of their own commercial imperative, I think it's unreasonable to expect them to screen low budget dramas because they don't really conform to the large numbers of the audiences they need. I think BBC 2 and Channel 4 can do that. The BBC picked up Richard Holmes *Soft Top Hard Shoulder* and it rated well. The sad truth is that those American films that you're talking about provide very good value for money for broadcasters because they can go out to the AFM and purchase them in very large packages, bringing the unit cost way down - they're actually very good "value for money" in terms of screen time. Whereas doing an individual deal with British Film makers can be more expensive.

***Q - What advice would you offer new film makers?***

***John*** - Don't develop unrealistic scripts, don't start optioning books or paying writers to put together a screenplay which requires a two week location shoot on Venus - it's staggering how many first time screenplays you receive, where you sit reading it and all your mind can focus on is the sheer cost. Develop projects covering something you know about or understand and work from your own experience.

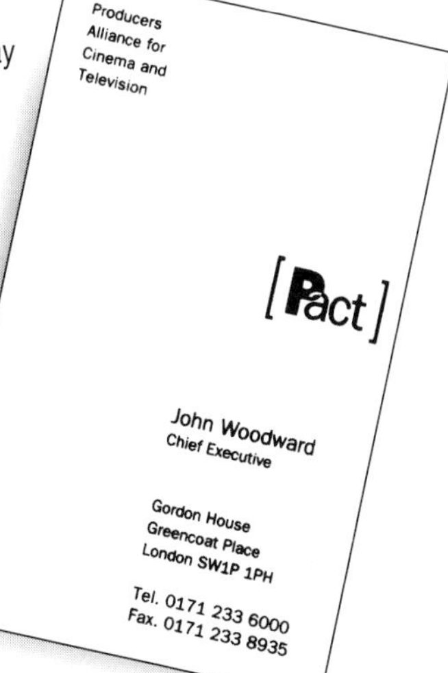

# New Producers Alliance

## Peter Bloore & Harriet Bass

*The NPA is a body of young film makers dedicated to help aspiring and low-budget producers in the UK.*

***Q - What is the New Producers Alliance?***

**Peter -** It's an organisation of producers founded four years ago out of a sense of frustration of what the existing organisations were providing, for new film makers in particular. There's a trade organisation called PACT which has represented film makers for a number of years, but it was seen, at the time, to be representing more television producers than film producers, as well as the more established producer. The NPA started as a number of producers coming together, setting up their own organisation in order to assist young film makers in their desire to get their films made. So it has an educational remit to encourage people to make their films more efficiently and to teach them how to fund their films. It also has a lobbying remit of some form where we also try and improve the lot of young film-makers.

***Q - What services can it offer to its members and what do you get for your membership?***

**Harriet -** When you join up, you get a monthly newsletter containing information about what we do. Each month, we hold at least one major seminar on a wide variety of topics and members receive free entry to all these seminars, plus additional workshops. You receive a directory which details all of our 900 plus members, contact numbers and their credits. I think most people join up for the networking facilities - after all our events, the producers meet up with each other and form alliances and friendships which will hopefully lead to more productions.

***Q - What kind of events do you have?***

**Harriet -** We have a variety from quite technical seminars - editing, sound, right through to script doctor sessions. One of our most successful seminars was on development and financing. We had people from Samuel Goldwyn and Lumiere, and people from funding bodies and companies coming in and telling us what they look for in a script.

**Peter -** Networking is vital to the success of the NPA, because it's all about getting people out of

their attic, out of their bedroom, where they've been slaving around their word-processors or fax machine for years, and putting them together with other people who are in exactly the same situation, enabling them to pool their information and resources and hopefully make them feel a little less lonely. We have a number of telephone hot-lines where members can contact, free of charge, solicitors, accountants and other professionals for advice. You also get access to the BFI Library and free associate membership of BAFTA and the Green Room Club on the Strand.

***Q - How do you become a member?***

***Harriet*** - Phone up the office and ask for a membership form, send it back with your cheque for £40 as a member, or £60 as an affiliate (which is anybody with an interest). There is also corporate membership at £175.

***Peter*** - We agreed at the outset that the producers subscription would be no more than a weeks dole money. So however bad your situation, you will be able to afford to be part of the organisation. That is why we allow the corporate members and the affiliate members to subsidise the producer members, so we can keep down the cost of the producer membership.

In four years, we've gone from no members at all to over 1000. 52% of the British Films that were shot in Britain in 1994 were made by members of the NPA. So that is an enormous growth. Also, many more people are starting to try and produce films off their own backs. It was round about the time that *Leon the Pig Farmer* and *Soft Top, Hard Shoulder* came out - they proved that you could just go out there and do it, you could raise money from the city, you could raise private investors and could just go out there and make a film. In the last four or five years there has been an explosion in deferred fee film making of this sort and the NPA seems to have reflected that sudden interest and passion in getting films made. If you can't get it funded through the usual sources, then lets find new ways of doing it. The NPA has been spreading information on how you can get it done, plus how to do it through the usual sources as well.

***Q - What basic advice would you offer a new and young film maker?***

***Peter*** - There are two things. To get a film made, you have to have a script into which people are willing to put money. And if it's a really good script, even if you're an unknown writer, then everyone will want it and it will eventually get made. To get a good script, doesn't mean you can write one draft and think it's a good script, you have to redraft it, and redraft it until you get it right. Point number two is to get the package of director and cast on board, because in the marketplace, a project is chiefly valued by the story and the cast. That means building up relationships with agents, casting directors and talent. Get networking.

# Section 2
# Five Case Studies

# The Ten Low-Budget Film Commandments

Thou shalt never shoot standard 16mm, thou shalt shoot Super 16mm or 35mm.

Thou shalt shoot hundreds of high quality stills of the actors and action.

Thou shalt get the best deal by paying cash upfront.

Thou shalt always shoot two takes of every shot possible.

Thou shalt disregard friends and colleagues ridicule of your ambition.

Thou shalt cast out of thine mind, the phrase 'it can't be done'.

Thou shalt shoot at 25fps, no matter what anyone tells you.

Thou shalt never work a crew more than 12 hours a day, 6 days a week.

Thou shalt ask if in doubt. If not in doubt, thou shalt ask anyway.

Thou shalt make a film through the legal mechanism of a limited company.

# The Living Spirit Story

case 1

## Prologue

Chris Jones and Genevieve Jolliffe met at Bournemouth Film School in 1989.

Chris, born and bred in the North of England, had started making amateur horror films on super 8mm many years earlier. His first triumph, an unashamed homage to the films of George Romero and the *Evil Dead*, was an immense success at his college. After 'bluffing' his way into film school, he began work on what he believed would be his greatest film yet, *Rundown,* a sci-fi thriller.

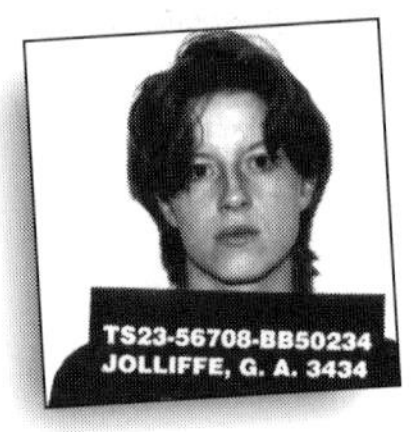


Genevieve was inspired and terrified at an early age, by the black & white classic, *Dracula. Star Wars* quickly followed and she knew that she wanted to make movies. She started out working in the industry, attending markets such as the Cannes Film Festival and dabbling in animation before travelling the world with her Nikon and Super 8mm camera. When she eventually attended film school, she quickly became frustrated by the lack of inspired leadership and was eager to make a movie.

After meeting, Chris and Gen decided to make *Rundown*, Chris' 'graduation' film, but too many obstacles were put in their way. They decided to leave the film school, Chris after two and an half years, Gen after only six months. Neither of them made a movie or shot a single frame of film whilst at Bournemouth film school.

*First Assistant Director, Lisa Harney on 'The Runner'. Photographed after five weeks shooting at 3 a.m. in a Manchester ghetto. It's all a bit much.*

***Q - How did Living Spirit Pictures Ltd. come about?***

***Gen -*** Film School, at the time, was about making depressing TV style drama, full of pessimism, about minority issues - anything that involved a social problem. They didn't want to do anything that strayed from that formula, there was no variety, just one particular kind of film and if you didn't fit into that, then you didn't get a film made. Therefore, when we came out of film school we just wanted to get into the real world and do something that was BIG. The frustration of Film School had built up in us to such a degree that when we considered what to make, there was one thing we really wanted to do - Blow everything up! We were both great fans of ALIENS and DIE HARD, so we knew that we wanted to make an action thriller.

***Chris -*** I was in my third year at Bournemouth Film School. Gen

Image Copyright Jon English

*Game Shows on which the contestants are killed - **Rundown** was at a very developed stage when Chris and Gen left the film school. However, due to problems with special effects, and the Schwarzenneger vehicle, The Running Man, the project was eventually binned in favour of **The Runner***

was in her first. We teamed up and decided to make a film school project together. I was taken onto the film school course as a director and I was supposed to be directing a film that year. I put forward a script that I had written in my first year and had been developing ever since. It was about a game show in which contestants were killed and after endless script development meetings with the staff, it became apparent that this was not going to happen in the form that I wanted. It wasn't going to be the sci-fi action-adventure that I wanted to make. Gen felt the same.

One night we sat down and thought - What would happen if we didn't actually make this movie at film school? We'd worked out a budget of around fourteen thousand pounds. We went down the list and calculated that the film school offered us a crew (which in any case we could persuade to work with us) and equipment (which would cost us four thousand pounds if we had to hire it). So, in reality, all the film school could offer was a few thousand pounds worth of equipment hire and some serious headaches (and they got to retain the copyright!)

We still had to raise fourteen thousand quid and if we could raise fourteen, we could raise eighteen and make the film outside the film school. It was ludicrous and we decided to leave film school, go on the enterprise allowance scheme (a

government small companies incentive scheme that existed at the time), set up our own company and make the film the way we wanted. We worked out which county would provide us with the most grants for setting up a business, and eventually settled on Cheshire. London was out of the question as it would just be too expensive to live in.

***Q - Is that when you approached the Princes' Trust?***

***Chris*** - We found that we were eligible for the PYBT ( The Princes' Youth Business Trust, an organisation headed by HRH Prince Charles which helps eighteen to twenty five year olds who have the ideas, guts and determination, but no seed money). We put our application through and got a soft loan of three thousand pounds and a further two thousand a year later. This enabled us to get all our business equipment, computer, fax, letterheads, all that kind of stuff. And so Living Spirit Pictures was born.

***Q - Why the name Living Spirit Pictures?***

***Gen*** - We wanted a name which expressed the way in which we were going to run our business and make movies. Everyone seemed to like it, even the strange people who still ring us and ask if they can join our religious cult! (no joke)

***Q - Did you start a formal company?***

***Gen*** - Yes, we were no longer in the playground. We took an accountant's advice and started a Limited Company. There is so much to running a company that you can never know until it goes wrong, and it's very expensive. You can waste a lot of money if you don't know what you are doing. Read some books on starting a company, they're a lot cheaper than advice from a solicitor or accountant.

***Q - After you began trading, what was at the top of the agenda?***

***Gen*** - The movie. We were at home, planning the film, looking at the reality of the project. We had a script for a forty-five minute film costing about £18k and had sent off details to potential investors informing them about the project. We weren't sure what to expect, maybe one or two replies. Every single one wrote back to us, offering finance, saying - if you make a feature, we will put in more money.

## Short V Feature

*The obvious starting point when making a low budget film is to make a short. Whilst your short may be a great movie, it isn't a feature and you will have terrible problems trying to sell it to get your money back.*

*1. A feature film is a saleable product which will generate interest from buyers. A short will generate virtually no interest.*

*2. A feature film is three or four times longer than a short - therefore three or four times more work (not exactly true, there is a sharp learning curve)*

*3. Don't expand a short screenplay into a feature. This almost always produces a very padded out, slow feature version of a short idea. Start from scratch.*

*4. If a feature film is a success, you could find yourself at the helm of a Hollywood feature. If a short is a success, you will collect an award from a bizarre film festival from a place no-one has ever heard of.*

*5. Shorts are good to make up a showreel of the work you have done.*

We started thinking, maybe they're right. Eighteen thousand is a lot of money for a short - why don't we double it to make a ninety minute film costing thirty six thousand quid. Naively we believed that to be the equation. We're not going to sell a forty five minute film. But we could sell a ninety minute film and suddenly, a much larger market was opened up to us. No longer would we be confined to television - but now the feature market, which included, the cinema, video, television and now the booming satellite market.

And so *The Runner* began to take shape. The only problem was that the initial interest in investment came at the height of the eighties boom. When we came to make the movie, the country was heading towards recession, and suddenly all this goodwill money disappeared.

**Q - Weren't you apprehensive about skipping that short film stage?**

**Chris -** Yes of course, but we were no longer in film school, we had to pay the rent and put food in our stomachs. We weren't going to get rich making a short film, that's for sure. I have spoken to so many film makers who say - *I'll make a feature film next but I've got to do another short and learn a bit more.* And I say - *What do you need to learn? - You'll learn three times more if you make a feature film and regardless of how much you mess up, you'll still be able to sell it. More than likely you'll make back your money. If you don't. So what! Make another one.* You've just got to go for it!

**Gen -** I think you've got to be prepared to take the risk - we were prepared to do that, to plunge in head first. We realised that if we wanted things to happen, we couldn't wait in the hope that Hollywood would give us a call and offer us *Jurassic Park 2*. Those who play safe, who want everything to be hunky dory, problem free, are going to be sitting on the sidelines for a long time.

**Q - Have you chosen the projects you have undertaken on commercial viability?**

**Chris -** It's strange, we've talked endlessly about how we chose the stories we make into a film. Anyone who has seen both *The Runner* and *White Angel* would agree that they are poles apart. We are aware of commerciality, we have to be. No matter how much we ever thought we were being hard

## Starting A Company

*1. There are several ways of operating, each with their own advantages and disadvantages - sole trader, partnership, co-operative, limited company etc. Take advice for what is best for your purposes.*

*2. Accountants and solicitors are very expensive. Buy a good 'business start-up' book, 95% of your questions will be answered in it.*

*3. If your turn over is high enough, you will become VAT registered and reclaim the VAT on your purchases (currently 17.5%)*

*4. Limited companies cost a lot to run. You need to supply information to companies house and if your turn over is high enough, you will also have to supply audited accounts (expensive). However, they do offer some 'limited' liability in case of problems.*

*5. Some film makers opt to start a limited company for each film. This protects all their projects should one turn into a disaster.*

# Raising Money

## *Ordinary Ways To Raise Money*

*1. Get a bank loan - (!?)*

*2. Get venture capital investment*

*3. Speak to the British film funding bodies such as British Screen.*

*4. Pre sell your film - almost impossible if you have no track record.*

*5. Approach other production companies, or TV companies for capital in return for shares or joint production status (Dodgy).*

*6. Product Placement. Get large companies to pay you for putting their products in your film. They won't be very interested unless the production is mainstream commercial, or you have a star. They will often give you the products, but no money, which could help out in the catering budget.*

*7. If your script is good, and a star is in place, a distribution company may put some money in. You will have no track record, so it is unlikely.*

*Give up on this lot and move onto Extraordinary Ways To raise Money*

## *Extraordinary Ways To Raise Money*

*(Some of these are not recommended)*

*1. Get accounts with all the facilities houses you need to hire or buy from and work on credit.*

*2. Get a credit card with a big limit. If you use it a lot and make regular repayments, the credit card company will ask you if you want an increased limit.*

*3. Get friends and family to invest a little seed cash and use it to shoot a two minute trailer. It will greatly increase your chances of getting investment as the film will no longer be words on a page, but a moving image with sound (and hopefully quite good too)*

*4. Get friends and family to invest a little more and get your movie in the can (and worry about the debts later). It's possible to shoot a feature film for £10,000.*

*5. Approach ANYONE with money and invite them to invest (you will need a good prospectus).*

*6. Approach ANYONE and ask them to invest, regardless of whether you think they have money or not. Many people have a little stashed away and may be prepared to gamble. If you get money off friends and relatives, make sure they understand they could loose it all (likely).*

*7. Turn to illegal acts (Not advisable at all).*

*8. Let a bored, rich person pay to play a small role in the film (and then cut them out if they are bad).*

nosed business people, it all boiled down to one thing - What did we want to make?

*"A verbal contract isn't worth the paper its written on"*
*Samuel Goldwyn*

When we made *The Runner* we were into movies with serious muzzle flash, semi automatic weapons and lots of explosions - and we did just that. It turned out to be a pretty dreadful movie but we blew a lot of things up. I guess in context, *The Runner* is a knee jerk reaction to the inhibitions of film school. It felt VERY decadent.

***Q - Did you have problems talking to people at the top?***

***Gen -*** To begin with we did - it depends on your approach. Many young film makers, particularly those fresh out of film school, are arrogant, they assume that they have an unwritten right to freebies, discounts and will get offered the best projects. We didn't feel that way and chose not to be arrogant. We reasoned that we were more likely to get help if we asked politely. And it worked, we haven't really made any enemies yet (either that, or I am still pretty naive).

***Q - In general, how did people in the Industry react to these two young upstarts?***

***Chris -*** At the time, the industry was depressed and didn't seem to understand what we were doing, we were so far removed, we were almost a cottage industry. It was obvious that if we wanted to make movies in the UK, then it was up to ourselves to generate our own projects. We've just had to do it with the limited means at our disposal, with whatever talent that we had, and on a micro budget. Risk it all and hopefully at the end of the day it will all come together, and no matter how bad the movie is, it will still sell. We were in a *need-to* situation.

*The Runner - a movie with lots of blue light and "serious muzzle flash"*

# 10 Low Budget movies to see... and Why

*THE EVIL DEAD - The grandfather of the modern low budget film which hit the horror movie market just at the right time. Made by teenagers with $50,000, guts and determination. The Director, Sam Raimi, is now a top Hollywood director.*

*LEON THE PIG FARMER - Not the lowest of budget films, but a good example of what can be done. Very successful in the UK but not as successful abroad due to the subject matter.*

*EL MARIACHI - The now legendary made for $7,000 movie. Shot entirely from the hip and a good example of what can be achieved if you ignore everything and just shoot film with a bunch of friends.*

*HALLOWEEN - One of the most successful movies ever. Produced for $100,000 (in the seventies). Mainly shot on steadicam (which undoubtedly saved on set up time). Lots of long shots and a lovely cinemascope presentation giving the illusion of budget.*

*HOLLYWOOD SHUFFLE - Notorious because it was allegedly financed entirely with on credit cards*

*DARK STAR - John Carpenters first feature film which was an expanded short (stars screenwriter Dan O'Bannon). Many of the sets were built in Carpenters kitchen and garage. Check out the plank Dan O'Bannon is lying on in the elevator scene. This has to be one of the best low budget films ever.*

*LETTER TO BREZHNEV - One of the first ultra low budget films to receive acclaim in the UK. Shot on super 16mm in Liverpool.*

*TEXAS CHAINSAW MASSACRE - Another legendary horror pic that promised so much blood and guts, no-one could stay away. Tobe Hooper went on to be shadow directed by Spielberg on Poltergeist.*

*CLERKS - Seriously off beat American story shot over weekends and in evenings at a convenience store. Picked up by Miramax, the rest is history.*

*THE BROTHERS McMULLEN - New York tale of three brothers, financed by directors family and shot over nine months. The film and director were discovered at Sundance Film Festival.*

*To prove to EGM that Living Spirit had what it takes, they produced a short two minute action packed trailer. This was a very successful course of action to take as it convinced everyone the picture was going to happen*

***Q - Are there any film makers who have been a source of inspiration?***

***Gen -*** We knew the story of Sam Raimi, the director of *The Evil Dead.* And when we saw *The Evil Dead* documentary on *The Incredibly Strange Picture Show* hosted by Jonathan Ross, we heard how he shot a promo on super 8. He then went round to the houses of doctors, dentists etc. He would get out his 8mm projector and pin a bedsheet to the wall, and show these potential investors what he wanted to make - and these people put money in. He was only eighteen. We thought - Wow! Maybe we could do this.

*Director Sam Raimi was the inspiration for both Chris' early horror movies, and Genevieve's business plans for Living Spirit. He produced The Evil Dead at the age of eighteen, with a budget of $50,000*

***Q - You tried getting investment for The Runner from several sources, but because you had no real track record, you didn't get very far. How did you eventually get things going?***

***Chris*** - We met a company called EGM Film International, a Cardiff based production company. We said - Hey! We're young film makers and we've got this idea for a film. We showed them a promo tape of films (made by other people) and they were very impressed. Now, we had a one page synopsis which we had written the night before because we thought that we should look like we knew what we were doing. And they said - We'll make this but we need to shoot in three weeks time. If you're not going to be ready then the whole show is off. And we said - Of course. - We're all poised. - And we walked out of the office thinking; - Great! We've got this chance to make a feature, but what are we

going to do? We're shooting in three weeks time *and we don't even have a script!*

Like most things on *The Runner*, the script was written on a need-to basis. We'd been floundering about, trying to make this great movie and just never got around to putting words on paper. Now we had a real big problem.

***Gen*** **-** We said we'd fax them the budget, so we had to go out to Dixons and buy a fax machine! EGM had said, *we don't want to spend over £40k*, but we knew it would cost more. We said, *we need £140k* and they said, *We'll give you forty.* We said *Okay, we'll send you the budget tomorrow.* We consulted our figures and saw that we really had to have at least £100k. They said - *No! No! No! We'll give you £60k.* We realized then that once they committed funds, they would have to finish the film. Beside, they were supposed to be executive producers and should have known that it costs a certain amount just to expose negative and feed a crew.

Now, we didn't really waste a lot but it actually cost a certain amount of money to blow up half of North Wales, so we spent a lot on pyrotechnics and bullets and all sorts of things - the budget escalated to £140k, exactly what we thought.

***Q - With only three weeks pre-production, no money, and no script, how did you manage to get everything going?***

***Chris*** - We rang a few friends and asked, - What are you doing for the next couple of months? Do you want to come and live at our house and make a movie? - Everybody said yes and moved in. About thirty people in all. It was great. There were very few problems. Lots of relationships sprung up between various crew members, perhaps because the work was so crisis ridden, everyone needed a shoulder to cry on and it all got rather steamy at various points.

I suppose there was a tremendous sense of camaraderie, that no matter what was asked of anyone, they would do it. It was very bizarre. I've often felt like I knew what kind of team spirit troops must feel before they go into battle for the first time (not that our job is anywhere near as demanding).

***Q - The screenplay usually takes months of development?***

## Making a Contract

*A contract is an agreement between two or more parties. It can be a verbal agreement, but a piece of paper which clarifies the terms of the contract, who will do what, when, how etc. is much better. The contract is really there so that each party knows what they have to do - it's written there in black and white. It also protects you if things go wrong. Unless you are prepared to be ripped off, consult a solicitor when it comes to making a deal (especially if large sums of money are involved).*

*1. Remember, a contract is just a piece of paper and if someone is intent on doing something which breaks the contract, there is nothing you can do short of legal action (which you may not be able to afford).*

*2. If money is involved, get it up front, preferably on signing. If not all up front, as much as possible.*

*Cont...*

Cont...

*3. ALWAYS make a contract for everything, even when friends do work for you. If your movie is ultra successful, all those freebies and favours will cost you.*

*4. When entering a deal with a company where they will supply you with goods or a service make sure they put the quote down on paper and fax you. We had one deal fall through because the chap we struck it with had died - his predecessor wasn't interested and we had no proof of the prior deal.*

*5. Follow your instincts - if something is too good to be true, it probably isn't true.*

*6. If in doubt consult your solicitor.*

*7. Always sign a contract before any work begins (especially actors).*

*8. It's obvious, but read and understand all the text of the agreement, including the infamous fine print.*

***Chris -*** Yes - We had to write a script, good, bad or indifferent. We had to have ninety pages of words to give the actors, to say on the day. Neither Gen nor myself could afford the time to divorce ourselves completely from the much needed three weeks of pre-production.

Mark Talbot-Butler, the editor of the film, seemed to be capable of writing a screenplay, so we commandeered him. He did a commendable job when you consider that this was his first screenplay, and the timescale involved. There was simply no development process. When it came to the point where we were shooting, I would walk on set, be given my pages of the script, hot from the photocopier, and read it for the first time. I'd think, - Oh!, so that's what we're doing! - and Gen would read it and see that there were three helicopters needed - she'd say to me - *Give me three hours* - and off she would go and come back with three helicopters. Really, she did get three helicopters. It was incredible.

There were so many cock-ups because we were totally unprepared. It was a serious crash course, and I emphasise the word crash, in how not to make films. We learnt so much. At the end of the day the film was pretty bad. It looked and sounded great, and consequently sold, but it's five years on we still haven't received a penny, and I don't think we ever will.

***Q - How did you get a cast crazy enough to involved in this movie?***

***Gen -*** We put an ad in the actors newspaper 'The Stage' and received sack loads of mail, CV's and photos. It really was sackfuls. The postman once brought three sacks up to the

*Three helicopters for free in as many hours...*

front door and then he informed us that he wouldn't deliver to the door but would leave it all at the back gate. We sifted through these replies and thought, there can't be this many actors in the world, let alone Britain - It was hopelessly overpowering - we just didn't have enough time to sift through all the details, so we sorted them into two piles, *looks OK, doesn't look OK*. Then sorted the *Looks OK* into two piles, *Done Film Work, Haven't Done Film Work*. It still took a few hours to short-list, and the list wasn't very short, but it did cut down our work load

LOW BUDGET BRITISH FEATURE FILM
Lead actor and actress required for low budget action thriller feature film to be shot in North Wales. Please send a recent photo and CV. Tel 0270 71411

*Advertising for cast is often a good idea, but prepare your postman, and NEVER EVER print your phone number - actors are persistent and will make your life hell.*

***Q - So what did you do about the lead actor?***

***Chris*** - Tough man Jack Slater had to be played by a star - but we couldn't afford a star - so we got the brother of a star.

***Gen*** - We rang up a few agents, told them who we were and that we were affiliated to The Prince's Trust (which made people see us in a different light).

One agent came back to us and said, - *I've got this guy called Terence Ford* - we'd not heard of him - *Well, he's been in Dynasty and Dallas and guest appearances in similar stuff* - still we weren't impressed. *Then she said - he's the brother of Harrison Ford.* We thought great! Apparently Terence had read the treatment and liked it, so he rang up. Chris would speak to him about the part over the phone because we couldn't afford to fly out to audition him - *He sounds OK said* Chris.

***Chris*** - They sent us his CV which was pretty unimpressive with regard to feature film work, but his photo was good. He looked like a younger, more rugged version of his brother. We felt we had found our lead actor. He was Harrison Ford on a budget. We offered Ford a fee of five grand. EGM took over at that point. We said Harrison Ford's brother's interested. Their ears pricked up and they gave him the job.

Gen picked him up from the airport and brought him to the studio (which was actually our garage). When we first met, I feared we might have problems as he had last a lot of weight and his hair had silvered. His photo had portrayed him as a much more rugged and tough looking actor. As he was Harrison Fords *younger* brother, we all imagined someone like Harrison Ford ten years ago. In fact, they were only

*"The hardest thing about directing a film, is managing to stay awake for nine weeks"*
*Micheal Winner*

*Screen hero Jack Slater as portrayed by Terence Ford... The Man, The Myth, The Legend, The Brother...*

separated by a few years so looked about the same age.

***Gen*** - We didn't have much choice. We'd spent loads of money on his flight over here and were about to start shooting. We'd have to change him a bit. Dye his hair for a start.

***Chris*** - We had cast another guy in the role of the villain, he was an American living in the UK. A week into shooting, he didn't turn up. We thought, where is our villain. Gen got on the phone to his agent and found out that he was on holiday in Turkey and didn't want to come back.

***Chris*** - So, here we were, I was on set and Genevieve came up to me and said - *We have a problem with shooting McBain tomorrow* (The lead villain), *well, he's on holiday in Turkey and he's not coming home.* - and I said, - *Fine, Okay.* - because I had become used to this kind of crisis every twenty minutes. I relied on the company slogan - *Gen'll fix it!* - Anyway, that night I returned to the production office and there were two photographs on the production office wall, one of this rather delicate looking actor from Amsterdam and the second, slightly less delicate, living in London.

*"Actors are Crap"*
*John Ford*

***Gen*** - They both looked like models.

***Chris*** - The one in London was an 'associate' of the lead actress and she suggested him as he could play American, so we decided to interview him. We asked him to take the train up to Cheshire and we gave him an interview. This is an interview that took place at two-thirty in the morning after a long day's shooting, with the whole crew asleep in this house. We had twenty bunk beds in our living room and there I was in one of the bedrooms with fourteen people farting and snoring giving an interview to this guy who must have thought - oh my god! What am I doing here?

*Paris Jefferson and Andrew Mitchell - Heroine and Villian. Andrew gave such a psychotic interview that Living Spirit nearly rejected him - as it happened, he turned out to be one of the best things about the film.*

***Gen*** - The other actor from Amsterdam actor had said - *Whatever happens, I will come over from Holland for an audition* - And I said, - *Well. Look, we can't afford to pay for you to come over. And if you don't get it, then I'm sorry, it's your tough luck!* - And he said - *That's fine. I'll get it! I'll get it!* - and I said - *Okay. Fine.* - And so I drove to pick him up from Manchester - he didn't have enough money to fly, so he had spent thirty hours on a ferry and train. It was about two thirty, maybe three o'clock in the morning when we get back and it's straight upstairs to do the audition.

***Chris*** - He was quite good looking and very pleasant. We took him into a room full of bunk beds and asked, *'what would you like to read for us?'* He replied in a strong Dutch American drawl. - *Okay man. I don't want to read no words. I've prepared my own interpretation of the part. Do you want to hear it?* We agreed and he exploded into this incredible, violent, one-man play about killing babies in Vietnam. I was sitting on the bed thinking - we cannot employ this guy, he will murder us in our beds. In fact. I'm going to double lock my bedroom door tonight. Mark, the editor and writer, was sat next to me and he was equally terrified whilst watching this performance with dinner plate eyes. We left the room.

*Keep the cast in their place with a firm hand, and automatic weapon*

## Casting

*1. No-one is out of reach. Make out a list of people who could play the parts in your picture and approach their agents. Actors can often have a bad year and be eager for feature work, or may have a soft spot for the decadence of low budget film making. If you don't ask, you'll never know - and they may say yes.*

*2. Agents are all difficult. Their sole job is to paranoidly protect their client, hustle as much money as they can, moan and groan about conditions. Agents often neglect to inform their clients of the potential job as the money is likely to be so bad. Agents are paid on commission, and if the percentage is poor, why spend time and energy on negotiations if there isn't a pot of money at the end?*

*3. If you have a way into an actor, bypass the agent and get the script to them. No agent will be able to stop an actor who is determined to be involved in a project.*

*4. Get a copy of THE SPOTLIGHT, a book with all the equity actors in Britain listed with pic). Spotlight 0171 437 7631. Fax 0171 437 5881.*

*Cont...*

I said to Mark - *Oh my God. What are we going to do? This guy's completely insane.* And Genevieve is hyper, saying - *He's great. He's so energetic* - So we had a real conference. What should we do? The actor from London was a little more bankable, a little more secure. We knew he would at least read the words on the page (when they were eventually written).

Then there was the method maniac who might have been a little more exciting on the screen, but I just couldn't get over the paranoid thought that he might actually kill us all.

We couldn't decide so we promised to tell them in the morning after sleeping on it. So, the Dutch actor had to sleep on the kitchen floor, since there was no space anywhere else.

In the morning, we decided not to give him the part. We said, '*We are really sorry. You can't have the part. We're going with the other actor*' - he was absolutely devastated. He was so shocked.

***Gen*** - You shouldn't admit this.

***Chris*** - It's fine now - but for some reason, something said - *this man's not as loony as I thought he was.* It was something he was projecting in the hope of getting the role and I had this gut feeling - *Hire him quick!* - So I dragged Gen out of the room and said - *I think we should take him* - she said - *You've spent all night saying we can't* - and so we had another debate and decided to go with the psycho dutchman.

I went out and told him - *Andrew, I'd just like to tell you that you've got the part. That was just a test to see how you would react* - and he bought it. He really believed me.

***Q - How did you go about crewing?***

***Gen*** - Most of the crew were very young, and everyone was inexperienced. I suppose we were all cheap labour. The crew got nothing but a five pound donation from EGM, halfway through the film. One day, Geoff came in with a brown envelope full of used fivers. He handed them out on set. Actually, he ran out, so a few crew members didn't even get a fiver.

*Windmill Cottage - Living Spirits' base in cheshire. Served as hotel, kitchens, locations, studios, indeed everything for the thirty strong crew and production of The Runner. "We were evicted three weeks after shooting, but at least we got the movie in the can."*

***Q - With thirty five people living in your house. What was it like?***

***Chris*** - Everyone was living in this one cottage. There were at least eight people to a room, mixed accommodation. We sectioned off half of the main room. That was the office. The other half was the bunking quarters. One bathroom, one loo, no shower, no washing machine and we shot like this for over one month. We ran out of locations, so we built a lot of them in the garage, in our back garden. And it was hell on earth. But it was great and everybody loved it. We could ring everyone of those crew members up tomorrow and say - There's a reunion - and everyone would be there. The only way I can explain it is like this.

Sometime during the shoot I remember being driven around North Wales, I'm not entirely sure where and I'm not entirely sure how many hours we'd been out there, I just sat in the van, looking across this dark landscape and tried to remember what it was like to sit down in front of the TV at night. I had completely lost contact with that side of my life. And it felt that we could do anything we wanted to. Really, seriously weird.

***Q - How did you deal with preparing locations with so little time?***

*Cont...*

*5. There are several casting services where ads can be placed very cheaply, or even free.*

*6. Videotape auditions, it will help you put a face to the hundreds of hopefuls you will doubtless see.*

*7. Be honest and up front about money and conditions - preferably on the phone when arranging an audition. It's better to know then rather than on set if there are going to be problems.*

*8. If you are paying below equity recommended levels, don't shout about it. Equity can be rather aggressive and tip the cart a little. Remember, that no matter how much equity scream and shout, we live in a free world where people can do as they like. Just lie low.*

*9. Where should you hold auditions? Many agents and casting facilities have rooms for this purpose, but you can hold them in your front room if you like - we did.*

*10. Once you have cast a part, sort out ALL financial arrangements in a contract, before you shoot.*

**Working From Home**

*1. Working from home can reduce your overheads and maximise your time. You won't have to rent offices and you can start work the moment you get out of bed (No tubes or traffic queues).*

*2. Working from home can decrease your time - it's all too easy to sleep in, or get distracted into fixing the kitchen sink etc. It is difficult to separate business and pleasure.*

*3. If you intend to shoot a movie from home, rent a very big house - I mean BIG! Preferably in the country where you cannot disturb the neighbours. A call to the police from an angry neighbour could shut down production and force you to relocate.*

*4. Inviting a client or investor into your living room can have two effects. It can either make you look very amateur, or it can make you look home grown and honest. People do like home grown talent and this is an angle which could be very effective. Just look as professional as possible and stress that working from home is a way of minimising overheads.*

*5. If you mess around too much, be prepared to be evicted - landlords DON'T like the self employed. Keep it quiet.*

***Gen*** - Because we were so eager to get going, we didn't have any pre-production time. The general method of business was - *What are we going to do today? We've got to do this or that scene and we'd better do this tomorrow* - And so we'd sort out the locations a day in advance, two days if we were lucky. The money situation just made things worse - on the first day of principal photography the backers didn't turn up. We had to carry on without them but we didn't have any money to get the food. We had no advance. A week later they turned up on set and said *-Do you want some money?* - And so we got our money, and quickly bought some food.

Occasionally, we ended up in deep trouble - I remember one time, we drove for hours, a whole crew and cast in convoy, to a mine in the middle of Wales. When we got there, they wouldn't let us in. And that was one of the times when we had actually *got* permission!

***Chris*** - That's right. We were about to do the final scene in the film - the climax of the movie. As usual we were trying to set up the shoot the day before and Gen was flying (she'd given up driving) across North Wales to find a mine in which to shoot. She found a brilliant one in Llan-something. We got to the mine/power station and took all the kit in.

It was like driving into a Bond set. The middle of this mountain had been quarried out. There were houses, office buildings, everything *inside* the mine. Roadways, traffic lights and cars parked inside the mountain. We shot for two days without any problems, and on the third day we had to film in another location. Come the morning of the fourth day, we returned to the mine and there was a new guard on the gate who said - You can't go in.- We protested. - We've clearance. But it was clear we weren't going to get in, no amount of bribery could budge this guy.

It transpired that the original guard had been sacked for letting us in as part of the mine was a top secret, ministry of defence, nuclear air raid shelter. It was so high level that even the guard who had let us in didn't know it was there!

Gen thinks - Okay we've been filming in a high security establishment and we're not getting back in. We've got to finish our movie. What are we going to do? - So, she gets back into the car and zooms off to find another mine - she did! However, it was in some horrendous place.

The next day, the convoy drove a hundred miles into what seems the heart of hell. It's raining like a waterfall - all we can see is wet black slate. It's so depressing. We arrive at the mine entrance and unload the gear. Everyone is soaking.

Quickly we check out where we can film - and it is a half mile walk underground with the equipment. We have twelve hours to shoot the last fifteen pages of the script of our action-packed adventure, the most action-packed sequence in the whole film. And I'm thinking - Let's go for it. Lets go for it! We're going to finish it.

*The mine in Wales - a great location, but unfortunately, it turned out to be a secret Ministry Of Defence Nuclear Air Raid Bunker.*

Five hours later, we're still lugging *IN* all the gear. Eventually it's all in. We're about to go for the first shot. It's taken five hours to set up. Terence is there. Lead actress, Paris is there. I rehearsed. I called for silence... Then we realised there were no guns. This was the big shoot out. The armourer says - I'll go and get them - Fifteen minutes later the guy comes back looking kind of sheepish and says - I don't know how to tell you this, but the guns are in the back of the prop girl's car. And I said - Fine, then get them. Then he says - But the prop girl has gone back to Cheshire twenty minutes ago. The props are four hundred miles away and we have got six hours to shoot the climax to our movie!

The next thing I can remember is being woken up by Jon Walker, the DOP. Apparently, I'd just fallen asleep on a large rock. Both body and mind had gone into retirement - for a short time I was in a vegetative state.

*Things got pretty nasty on set.... A good rule was, 'Never argue with the director when he has a gun...'*

## Shooting on Location

*If you have no budget, shooting on location is probably the only option for you*

*1. This can be a major advantage as you will have to do minimal set work, merely dressing if at all.*

*2. Space can be a major problem as even the biggest of rooms will become sardine like with a full crew.*

*3. Shooting outdoors can be a problem as there is no way to control the weather. Consider shooting in someplace like Spain where there are long days with great light. The locations will be cheap too.*

4. Always try and get permission to shoot wherever you intend to be. Sometimes, if you can foresee problems, it is best to simply dash in, shoot, and get out as quick as possible. If someone turns *up to find out what is happening, try to get them interested and involved, and claim complete ignorance.*

*5. Getting to and from difficult locations can be very costly in terms of time - one hour travelling is one hour less shooting.*

*Cont...*

***Gen -*** Then it got worse. We had a massive argument with the cast. It became apparent that we weren't going to finish the film that night. Also we had been rushing to finish the film because the lead actress, Paris Jefferson had said she had to fly off in the morning so that she could get to another shoot somewhere in Europe.

We knew this was the last day we had with her. We knew we were running out of time, and we'd lost the guns - it was absolute hell. Then Paris says - *Well, why don't we all come back tomorrow? -But you're not going to be here tomorrow!* - we reply - *Oh, no. I can be here if you want me to be* - Shocked, we blew up at her and had a massive argument with all the actors. Everyone took sides, mainly against us. It all got pretty heavy and many enemies were made. I think most of us made up later, but there are still a few grudges floating around.In retrospect, Paris was quite within her rights, it's just the insanity of low-budget film making creates a crazy atmosphere.

Our executive producers John and Geoff had gone off to America. We didn't know where they'd gone. We couldn't contact them. So, we decided to pack it all in for the night and come back in a month when we had the guns, the mine and the actors. Then we'd finish The Runner.

***Chris -*** It has to be said that a lot of the time the actors were quite right. There was such hell going on, they couldn't help but snap, because they spent ninety percent of the time just waiting for us to decide what to do. And everybody was ill. Everyone had flu. However, one day we had a real medical shock.

I was shooting on set and Gen comes up to me and says...

*- Have you heard?*
*- Heard what?*
*- Terence is dead.*
*- What!*
*- He's dead. He's just been air lifted to Bangor Hospital. He's dead. What are we going to do?*

We'd got so used to problems that the concept of our leading man being dead was simply another obstacle to be overcome. What had actually happened was that Terence was ill, the doctor had given him a sick note and sent him to

bed. By the time we heard about it, the Chinese whispers had changed it to - *Terence is dead* - It was something out of Fawlty Towers. The entire production was thinking - *What is going to happen?* whilst Terence is wrapped up in his bed with a hot water bottle and a Lemsip. That was a bad day.

***Gen*** - I remember my state of mind at that time. I had been told that Terence was in the morgue - it was some kind of Welsh joke by the hotel owner. So I was racing through the narrow winding roads at a hundred miles an hour, thinking of ways we could write him out of the story without it looking crazy. I wasn't bothered that he might be dead - all I wanted, was to make sure that the film didn't suffer! That is the degree to which we were all affected by the insanity of low-budget film making. It gets into your blood and takes over your soul, I guess that's why it feels a little like going to war.

We were staying in a tiny Welsh village, where the villagers thought that this kind of joke was really funny. The other joke they played on us was potentially more serious. Someone rang the hotel telling them that they had planted a bomb as they hated the Americans. So we had the police round searching everyone's room. I remember being in dreaded fear that the police were going to check my room, because that morning I had just taken delivery of a crateful of semi automatic weapons from our armourer, AND a fake bomb for the bomb scene. Luckily they didn't check my room.

***Q - The Runner has many action sequences with one breathtaking highfall. How did you get stuntmen involved?***

***Gen*** - The week before filming, we received lots of phone calls because we were trying to find actors and crew. I got a call from a guy called Terry Forrestal who said he was a stunt man and wanted to help. I said - Yeah, great, great. - thinking he was another karate expert from down the road who wanted to get into the business.

Terry said - "I've been working on Indiana Jones, this, that and the other and I used to do James Bond." He reeled off a list of a hundred A movies. So, I asked for his CV and said I'd get back to him. You have to understand that we had taken so many weird phonecalls from so many wacky people that we were very cautious. Then his CV arrived, and I looked at his list of movies - it looked like my video collection! I realized

*Cont...*

*6. Facilities for the crew on location can be a problem - a place to eat and sit will be needed, and a loo must be provided - you can't ask your star to squat in the bushes.*

*7. Closing down streets in the UK is difficult. The police will be as helpful as they can, but they have crimes to stop and don't relish the thought of holding the hand of a crawling producer.*

*8. When choosing a location, don't forget the sound. there isn't much use shooting a period drama next to an airport (unless you can post sync the dialogue).*

*9. Film crews trash locations. Try and clean up after yourself, leave muddy boots outside, ban smoking inside etc. Remember, you may need to return to the location if there is a problem with the negative - try not to burn your contacts.*

*10. Think creatively - many locations can double for several different parts of your story. This will minimise the time you waste moving between places.*

- this guys for real! Immediately, we rang him up and arranged to meet up. He was so keen and wanted to do everything he could to help us out. Everything was possible. In fact, he was so enthusiastic that he wanted to do more stunts than were in the script!

***Chris -*** Terry had read the script and saw the bit about the high fall. - How are you going to do this? - Well, we'll probably dress the actor up and jump off a low point onto some cardboard boxes. Ten feet or so. You know, we'll cheat it. It'll look alright. - And he said - No, no. You need a proper stunt. (These guys are perfectionists) I'll do a high fall for you. - And I said - How high is high? Fifteen or twenty feet ? - Oh no, - he said, - I'll do a ninety foot high fall for you. - And he pointed to this house in the distance which seemed pretty big and explained, - It's about that, and a half again.

I was stunned. So we went on this recce in North Wales to find a cliff from which he could jump without killing himself. Finally we found a cliff. On the day he just turned up with his airbag man, blew the bag up and jumped off the cliff. Well, in fact there were two high falls. We co-ordinated this with Terry. The first one was off the cliff into the airbag. The second, the more dangerous was off the cliff into the water. On each stunt attempt we had three cameras. Two would have done the job but we really wanted three. So we had three cameras set up and shot each stunt twice. We ended up with six separate shots, all in slow motion so that they would cut together to make it look like the fall lasted for ever. Well, the actual high fall lasts for nine seconds in the movie - a serious amount of screen time for somebody to be hurling towards earth at two hundred and thirty five feet per second. So it gave the impression of an immense fall which really did get gasps in the theatre.

To be honest, one of the best things about *The Runner* is that stunt and even Terry considers it one of the best falls he's

### Stunts and Pyrotechnics

*There is a certain gung ho approach when shooting stunts and effects. Everyone knows that what is happening is potentially dangerous and could result in tragedy.*

*. Stunts are dangerous. Don't push a stuntman to do his job quicker, or with less safety equipment. Remember, they are putting their life on the line for you, and the last thing anyone wants is a repeat of the Brandon Lee tragedy on the set of The Crow because the producer was hurrying everything along.*

*. Stunts aren't as expensive as you may think. A good stunt can make the film look like it cost much more than it actually did.*

*. If a stuntman or pyrotechnician is eager or very willing to reduce safety standards, be wary. They may not be fully qualified and therefore a liability. Don't mess, get a qualified person to do the job.*

*Cont...*

*Stuntman, Terry Forrestal considers the jump he is about to make*

ever done. I think he means in the way it comes across on screen. He's done other, more dangerous falls, much higher but somehow they do not look as dangerous. Perhaps the circumstances were never quite as wild as on one of our shoots. We were totally into Sam Peckinpah and action movies, so we wound the slow motion dial until it wouldn't go any further - no matter how fast the film was whizzing through the gate, Terry still went flying through frame.

***Gen*** **-** And there really was, as with all stunts, a real sense of danger. When Terry jumped into the lake he said - If I don't come up after five seconds, either I've hit my head on the bottom or I'm dead. It was a very long five seconds.

***Q - Once you had the film in the can, was it all down hill?***

***Chris*** - Not really, we had to fix all the problems we had given ourselves during the shoot. A good example is the firing range scene - there are shots in that sequence from five different locations, shot at seven different times, with up to seven months separation - piecing it together was a logistical nightmare.

Mark Talbot-Butler edited the film after we finished shooting. Unfortunately, we were evicted from our house for having thirty five people living there which broke the terms of our tenancy. This meant that we had to put most of the work in Mark's court - he had to go off and do a lot of the cutting on his own, locked in his attic. It was all very rushed.

*Cont...*

*4. Be careful with blank firing weapons. Although they fire blanks, there is still a possibility of injury and even death through misuse.*

*5. Try and organise all your stunts into one shooting block. This will minimise time wastage by dedicating the production to stunts and effects during this period.*

*6. There are many books on the subject of home made (safe) effects and cheats, some of which are excellent and safe. This approach could save you lots of money. For example, a helicopter flying over in the dusk can be achieved by panning a strong light over the set and mixing the chopper sound over it.*

*7. Sound is a major consideration with stunts and effects. A good 'Whack' sound in a fist fight can hide a dodgy stunt. Track lay these sequences with extra care and attention.*

*"Making a film is like going down a mine - once you've started you bid a metaphorical goodbye to the daylight and the outside world for the duration."*
*John Schlesinger*

EGM wanted the film ready for the MIFED film market in Milan which took place in October and we therefore made sure it was done. This really compromised the movie. We only had about seven weeks post-production. A great deal of energy was spent getting the picture to look good, the audio to be full and rich, and to make sure the cuts flowed. But at no point do I remember sitting down to ask whether the story was actually working. This neglect meant we had a good looking, great sounding, boring movie. And even then, the sound was rushed with effects still being edited whilst we began dubbing.

Mark didn't even have an assistant. He was in his Mum's attic with a Steenbeck (editing machine) working a good eighteen hours a day. No pay, no nothing. Each time I saw him, he began to look a little weirder - not surprising really.

Whilst Mark was cutting away, we were working on the score with an old school friend who had done the music for my amateur Super 8mm Zombie films. He had gone on to play in a local band and was excited by the prospects of being involved in a *real* film. He had to fake an illness and take time off work to spend seven days at his keyboard. There was no music budget, so we had to create that big orchestra sound with some synths and an Atari computer locking it all together. It worked out really well, the music was pacey and dynamic - and recorded in our front room.

When John Eyres came to view the final cut, he wasn't particularly happy. He wanted some stuff cut out. We agreed but never cut the scenes out. He wanted to remove the helicopter rescue at the end of the film, because it said RAF

*The score for The Runner was conceived, composed, performed and recorded by an old school friend, Gary Pinder, in the Living Spirit living room!*

*The Living Spirit team - Left to right, Chris Jones - Director, Genevieve Jolliffe - Producer, Mark Talbot Butler - Screenplay & Editor, Andrew Mitchell - Actor and Jon Walker - Cameraman.*

*Cast and Crew of The Runner at the London Premiere - A great night!*

on the choppers (giving away the fact that the film was shot in the UK and not in the USA as claimed).

***Q - How was the premiere?***

***Chris*** - Everyone clapped, but it was hollow polite clapping. I think people were amazed that we had managed to get it made, a film that looked and sounded good. But what a dreadful story.

***Gen*** - It was the achievement, rather than the actual film that was applauded. The audience were saying well done for getting this far. We were caught up with it all. We didn't get nervous. We just enjoyed it.

***Chris*** **-** In our opinion, it was the best movie ever made. We were like old time moguls. It was terrific. We were not aware that we had actually made a really crap film. But at the time, that didn't matter - it was OUR premiere!

***Gen*** - However, we do have people coming up to us who saw The Runner, saying how much they like the movie, how they've gone out and bought their own personal copy of the

*"Pictures are for entertainment, messages should be delivered by Western Union"*
*Samuel Goldwyn*

film. I think the film is an example of what low-budget film makers who want to make *Aliens* or *Die Hard* can look to. It's nothing like *Leon The Pig Farmer* or *Soft Top Hard Shoulder,* it's not the type of quirky movie that is so often labelled Low-budget British Film.

***Q - How much did The Runner make you?***

***Chris*** - To date, not a single penny. Living Spirit did not make the proverbial 'fortune' out of *The Runner.*

What happened to us, and what happens to most first time feature makers, is that we got caught with a standard distribution deal. Basically, EGM financed the film and acted as the sales agents. They received thirty-five percent commission plus all expenses before they started to recoup their investment. This meant that they got all their money back, plus thirty percent commission, plus expenses, before we would even see a penny. It means we will never get paid, never ever, which means that we'll never be able to pay our cast and crew which means it's a bit of a downer really. This is a very common story that many film makers tell.

*The International Sales booth for The Runner at the Milan Film Market 1991*

***Gen*** - You see, we were very naive when we took the film on. Our attitude was - Let's do the film, We've got three weeks. Let's just do it, get our foot in the door rather than just sit on our arses. So, when the contract came, we had a lawyer go through it, and he advised us not to sign it. But at the end of the day, we thought, well, we have a choice here. If we sign it, there is a possibility that we could get ripped off. If we don't, the film may never happen. So we went with it. I am very glad we did, it gave us a track record and a showreel. Most important was the experience, *that* was invaluable. If you have nothing to lose, just go for it. The younger the better.

***Q - How do you feel about it all now that it is ancient history?***

***Chris*** - We went with it and got the chance to make a film. We got to go mad in North Wales, with Hollywood stuntmen, bombs, guns and a bunch of actors - it was a fair trade off. My only regret is that nobody got paid - I guess and hope that

everyone was rather philosophical about it. For many of the crew the experience was worth more than the money.

***Gen*** - A lot of the crew members were either still at film school or had just left and had never worked professionally on any kind of film. I remember at the first production meeting, Chris asked who had worked on a film set before. It was quite a shock when only two people put their hands up. The average age was 19/20. There was even a fourteen year old - I felt old at 20.

*"Experience is the name every one gives to their mistakes"*
*Oscar Wilde*

***Q - Can you protect your rights as film makers on the first film?***

***Gen*** - The main problem you're facing is that it IS your first film. You are so desperate to make it that you will sign anything. If it comes to the crunch, I would advise anyone to sign because what is important is that you make the film. Just make sure you invest none of your own money or money that you are responsible for and therefore reduce your losses. If you can make your first movie without losing anything, then go for it because nobody is going to give you free money and nobody's going to invest in you because you've never made a film before. It is easy to be completely shafted, everyone from Tobe Hooper to Steven Spielberg has been ripped off, and not just on their first films. I think it is the nature of the business.

Once we had finished *The Runner*, we had a lot less trouble making *White Angel*. We had more control and simply refused to sign anything unless we had total control.

***Q - I believe you are in the Guinness Book of Records.***

***Gen*** - Yes, as Britain's youngest producer for *The Runner*. I was 20, not so young when compared to American film makers.

***Q - Because of your connections with the Princes Trust, Did you invite the Prince of Wales to the screening?***

***Chris*** - We actually won an award - the PYBT/Readers Digest Editors award for being a tenacious business. There was a special award ceremony with a screening of The Runner at the BAFTA theatre in Piccadilly. HRH came along and presented the award. We had a chat afterwards and I will

*Living Spirit are presented to HRH Prince Charles after receiving their award.*

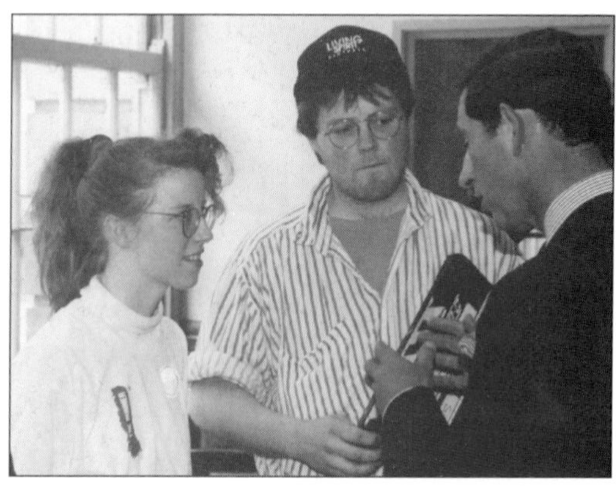

say that the Trust is terrific. I would recommend it to anyone but don't think that it is an easy ride. They are tough business people and though they're not in it to make money, they make sure that they don't lose it. You can't approach it feeling that they're a soft pushover and I'm going to walk out of here with three grand. You might as well forget it because it's a fight all the way. Bit like the real world.

***Q - Did HRH see the Film?***

***Chris*** - He saw some of it but he couldn't watch it all because he had other appointments on the schedule. He said it looked a little too violent for him.

*The Runner has been released across the globe. It is released in the UK under the alternative title, SURVIVAL ISLAND. If you rent it, fast forward through the first twenty minutes to the part where the helicopter lands on the beach - the first twenty minutes are simply glacial in pace!*

*Ellen Carter fights Steckler in the climactic scenes of White Angel.*

***Q - How did WHITE ANGEL come about?***

***Chris*** - Obviously, after *The Runner*, we wanted to make another film. *The Runner* had crippled us so much, that we didn't have any funds at our disposal. The only way we could possibly get out of the great financial hole we were in was to make a movie. We decided to make what we considered to be the most commercial film possible with the least amount of money.

*White Angel* was conceived the same day that we saw *Henry, Portrait of a Serial Killer,* in an extremely seedy cinema with an audience of seedy looking men. We thought it was a great movie but it was offensive, at least my mother would think so. However, we thought we could make something with the same feel, but not quite so graphic - turn it into a taut Hollywood thriller.

***Q - What research did you do for White Angel?***

***Gen*** -We also saw *Silence of the Lambs* and felt that we could do something similar, that was contained, but not awash with gore. Also we didn't think that Hannibal Lecter

*"Ninety five percent of films are born of frustration, of self despair, of ambition, for survival, for money, for fattening bank accounts. Five percent, maybe less, are made because a man has an idea which he must express"*
*Sam Fuller*

gave a true portrayal of a serial killer - sure, he was a terrific character which the audience had a love hate relationship with - he had been glamorised for Hollywood. We researched British serial killers, reading lots of books, for example Dennis Nielson's biography, *Killing For Company* by Brian Masters. We became fascinated by the British serial killer and his peculiarities.

Admittedly, most of our research was very lightweight, we didn't want to start making psychological assumptions, merely chart the actions of a killer. The closest that we came to real research was through my Uncle who worked at the top security Parkhurst Prison on the Isle of Wight. He would tell us of his encounters with the Yorkshire Ripper. We also saw some home movie footage of Dennis Nielson which gave us the idea of using video taped interviews.

***Chris*** - Everyone has a morbid fascination with death, and especially the serial killer. The motivation seems so meaningless, and it's now a bit of a cliché, but it could be the person next door. Audiences like to dip into horror, to experience the shocks and come out the other side unharmed and emotionally purged.

***Q - What are you looking for in a no-budget script?***

***Gen*** - We knew the limitations of our location, so we developed our story from that single point. We were looking for containment, to keep the majority of the story in one place. The production office would be there, all the facilities such as makeshift changing & make-up rooms, a kitchen and equipment store. The location chosen was inside the M25 around London, at the end of the tube line, we could see the tube station from the front door of the house. This meant that

*The house that was used for the primary loaction in WHITE ANGEL had to double up as both production office and set. Ruislip outside central London was the perfect location and was steeped in suburbia.*

the cast and crew could be given a monthly tube pass and therefore their travelling expenses were minimal. The location was also close to many shops, parks etc., all the other locations required in the screenplay were within five minutes walking distance. It worked quite well.

***Chris -*** Where we went wrong with *The Runner* is that the production was sprawling, shooting in locations that were hundreds of miles apart. That would eat up our shooting time. We had to put people up and pay for hotel rooms, catering, travelling etc. The number of principal cast was five, far too high. This in itself was very expensive which is why we limited the principle cast in *White Angel* to two, with Don Henderson bobbing in and out (we actually only shot for two days with Don).

***Q - So The Runner was a good exercise in how NOT to make a low-budget film?***

***Chris -*** Yes, after *The Runner* we sat and looked at the budget to see where the money went. A lot of money was wasted on American actors, flying them over, making them comfortable and getting them in front of the camera. So, we said, what has Britain got to offer? And we made a list. Now it is true that we have wonderful landscapes in Scotland but we couldn't use them. We didn't have the resources. But in Britain, we do have great actors and we knew that if we could find a really good actor who was willing to do it for virtually nothing on the assumption that they will get paid eventually (and also receive a percentage), then we were made. We made a conscious decision to try and get a really good, classical actor and Peter Firth filled that bill.

On the other hand we felt that we had to have a North American in the film, or we would be in the position where the Americans don't understand the film because it doesn't have the appropriate accent in it. And we've all heard the stories of *Gregory's Girl* and *Mad Max* being dubbed for the American market. We knew that *White Angel* had to sell in the states as in financial terms, the American market represented a huge slice of world sales. In retrospect, we were being over cautious. If we could have persuaded a great British actress like Helen Mirren (*The Hawk*) to play Carter, I think it may have improved sales and I think it would have been a better film. The American character of Ellen Carter (played by Harriet Robinson) felt inserted into the

## The Story So Far...

*Ideas are cheap and easy, it's implementing them that is difficult.*

*1. Decide what kind of film you will make - a comercial film, or a film for yourself (which could also be commercial). A commercial film is the kind of picture that sells, that the video shop rents. No matter how much you like your idea, it doesn't necessarily make it a commercial one. There is nothing wrong with being commercial or non commercial, each have their advantages, but it is essential that you know what it is.*

*2. Other movies are a good source of stock ideas. Get two successful pictures and mix the concepts. 'Outland' with Sean Connery is a good example, 'Alien' meets 'High Noon'.*

*3. If your artistic temperament is such that the idea of plagiarism disgusts you then I am afraid that you will have to come up with everything yourself. Can't help you here (but see the notes on writing a screenplay).*

*4. Anything written by an author who died over 75 years ago (50 years in some countries) is out of copyright and now Public Domain. For example, if you want to adapt a Dickens novel, you won't have to pay any royalties.*

*5. Speak to a sales agent, they will tell you if your idea is comercial or not, and give you an idea of what kind of cast will help.*

Peter Firth and Don Henderson - Great British actors are worth every penny or percentage you pay them. They will bring quality and experience to any production

story, which she was. Having said all that, Harriet does have a quality that people like - I don't think we could have made a better choice with a North American.

***Q - Why genre subjects?***

***Chris -*** Most low-budget film makers choose a genre, not because they've sat down and clinically thought, *'now if we make a sci-fi thriller the Japanese market is going to like it'*. I think most first time film makers make the kind of film that they really want to make. Either that works or it doesn't. With *The Runner* we wanted to blow as much up as we could - we wanted to throw as many people off cliffs as possible - we wanted to create mayhem because we loved *Die Hard* and similar Hollywood movies. Low-budget film makers seem to be products of their youth. In terms of myself, I was raised on John Carpenter, horror movies etc.

However, because of our dealings with EGM and visits to trade markets, we knew that certain genres at certain times were not saleable. Horror movies went through a rough patch in the late eighties. Some couldn't be sold at all. The market was so flooded with cut off the head and let the blood flow movies, or teenager lovers axed to death in the barn by deformed brother movies etc.

"If you want art, don't mess around with movies, buy a Picasso"
Micheal Winner

More than anything, on your first film you get the chance to do whatever you want. More than likely, the money will come from someone who knows nothing about film making. You've got so little money at risk that you can go out on a limb and in retrospect, we could have been more daring with some

aspects of *White Angel* - to arouse a little controversy.

***Q - The script idea is strongly rooted in the idea of a very British murder?***

**Chris -** We said let's make this film British. As British as *The Long Good Friday.* The intrinsic Britishness emerged during script development. We didn't start off saying, let's make a film about a VERY British serial killer. We said let's make a film about a serial killer in Britain and the true British angle came out when we started on the research and also with the involvement of Peter Firth. He manipulated the script in the way that we wanted him to. The scripts that we've produced are functional. They get from A to B without showing *too many of the footprints in the wet paint.*

"Insecurity, commonly regarded as a weakness in normal people, is the basic tool of the actor's trade"
Miranda Richardson

Peter Firth took the screenplay and changed Steckler from this mid Atlantic, non-existent, psychopath and brought the character into the English home. Many of the mannerisms in the film were invented by Peter. A number of people have been surprised by this. They think everything in the film comes from the director or writer, when in essence, the director, writer and producer are merely the people in control (hopefully) of the creative talent. Actors have the last say by virtue of their own performance.

We felt Peter's ideas were good. You know on set whether something is working or not and we agreed with Peter to use the cup of tea as a main prop in the film. It was there in the script but Peter made much more of it - each murder was followed a cup of tea. Even the way Steckler dresses, the top button being fastened was Peter's idea.

*Peter Firth as the mild mannered serial killer, Leslie Steckler. Peter's experience brought a new dimension to an otherwise run of the mill screen killer.*

There was a conscious decision to make Peter this *out of date character,* in so much as the film is set in the nineties but everything about him is stuck in the late sixties and early seventies. He wears those trousers and that tie that only weird people still wear. He was very much stuck in that vein and of course Oxfam was the best place for him to shop. This is what people of quality bring to a production. An experienced and talented actor, or star will bring so much to any production, it is worth moving heaven and earth to engage their services. From a marketing point, everyone always thinks that big actors cost big bucks. This isn't necessarily so, and their mere presence in a film will raise it's value.

*"I never had a goddam artistic problem in my life, never, and I've worked with the best of them. John Ford isn't exactly a bum, is he? Yet he never gave me any manure about art."*
*John Wayne*

***Gen*** - We had seen so many American movies about serial killers - but nothing that really explained why they do what they do - so we wanted a more realistic approach, looking into what urges these characters to do it - Hollywood had shown these killers in a kind of glamorous light - never exploring why. We thought that the British serial killers were more interesting. In the States, the serial killers use all methods of murder that are quite violent - for example with guns, axes, chain saws, etc. and they were into cannibalism. They also had that weird look about them - One eye, seven feet tall, a limp - strange characteristics that you expect from a James Bond movie. But in the UK, the frightening thing, was how these killers really blended into society - how normal they looked... what fascinated us most was - could it be the guy living next door to you?

***Q - The Killer next door seems to be a concept which keeps coming up?***

***Chris*** - Yes, we decided that the screenplay should take the serial killer living next door right to its logical conclusion, to create a killer who is actually very likeable as a human being. We never see him murder except in small details*, and when

*Polaroid photos are one of the only times we see Stecklers victims. It is amazing how multi talented your crew can be when pushed*

** In order to secure deals later, extra scenes of sex and violence were shot and added.*

it does happen, it has a kind of humour to it rather than horror. Therefore, apart from his memories of various crimes, we never experience Steckler, the serial killer. But we do see Carter kill and she is not the serial killer, which in turn is an interesting slant.

Several people have mentioned that Carter was a bit of a cold character and that they liked Steckler. Yes! This is exactly what we wanted. A lot of people seem to like this completely different slant on the killers. At the end of the day if you get two killers together in a house and get them to talk about killing it's going to be strange, it's going to be funny, it's going to be horrifying and it could get very nasty. We wanted to get that seething atmosphere into the house, lock the doors and see what happened.

Some of the elements from the screenplay we lost. For instance, the heating was supposed to have gone insane during the film so that it was always hot in the house. We wanted a pressure cooker. We wanted claustrophobia. That is something that harks back to the needs of a low-budget film. You need to look at what you've got and turn that into an advantage. We had a small location, so we thought, let's make it claustrophobic.

***Q - Had you seen 10 Rillington Place?***

***Chris -*** We saw *10 Rillington Place* a long time before we made *White Angel*. After *White Angel* was completed, we saw the film again and were pleased and to some extent shocked by the similarities. I don't think there were any major conscious similarities when we were making it. I don't know whether Peter had seen it but he had done research into serial killers and we watched some quite shocking home videos of Dennis Nielson

I remember Harriet asking Peter whether he had a defined idea of how he was going to play the character and he said no, *I don't have a clue, I'll tell you how I'm going to play it on the last day of photography*. And it is interesting as he didn't know, you could see it sometimes when he was unsure how Steckler was developing. He had in him that ability to say, *I'll try this out and if it doesn't work, then fine.* This was a very valuable asset to have.

***Q - A serial killer moves in with an undiscovered***

## Dressed To Kill - The Costume Budget

*Costumes can be an expensive part of your budget, but they need not sink the boat.*

*1. Keep a tight reign on your designer, don't let them go over budget.*

*2. Most actors can be persuaded to use their own clothes, but beware of damages.*

*3. Charity shops are a great source. Often, if you can return the items, you can negotiate a good deal if not for free.*

*4. Film & TV costume houses are not as expensive as you think. Give them a call and set up a meeting to view their warehouses, it's astounding what they have got. Remember, everything is negotiable.*

"If it aint on the page, It aint on the stage"
Anon

***murderer. Where did that idea come from?***

***Chris*** - I don't know really, I guess by a process of development from a single concept. What we do is play around with this single concept. For example, we want to make a film about a serial killer. We have to make it in one house. We can't have him just going out and killing people because that would be boring so we introduce a woman to get a male/female thing going. What could she be? Well, if she knows he's a serial killer, maybe his wife, but it's not original. Maybe she can be a crime writer, an expert on serial killers and he wants her to write his story. That's good. But why would she do it? Well, maybe she murdered her husband, bricked him up in the wall of the house and got away with it. Maybe the serial killer finds the body and blackmails her? Then, they're both murderers. Hey! That's a good idea. Before you know it you have a structure.

***Gen*** - Then you write the first one page synopsis, give it to your mates and ask what they think - *well, this is good, this is crap - OK.* Turn it into a two page synopsis. You keep building and building. What we like to do is to write it as a novella first or at least a thirty page short story. When that reads well, then you've got something. It is structured very heavily. We have two plot points which come thirty minutes from the beginning, thirty minutes from the end and we have a sixty minute centre section.

So, we have act one at thirty minutes, act two which is sixty minutes and act three at thirty minutes and in addition, in the middle of act two we have a mid point. If you watch any good Hollywood feature, you'll see that they stick to this. When

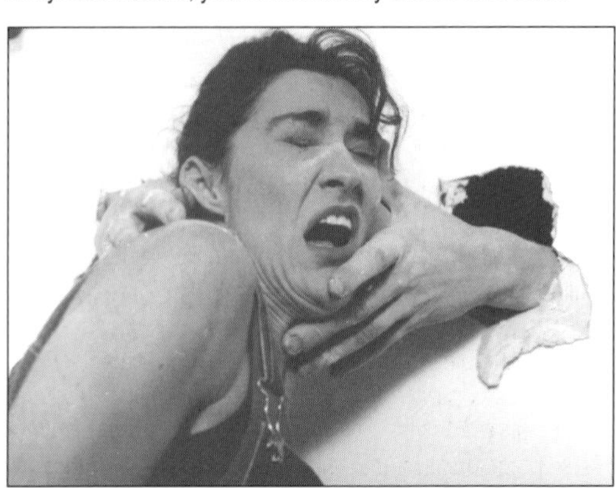

*In a scene cut from the final film, Ellen Carter has recurring nightmares about her husband's body trying to escape from it's living room wall tomb.*

*The fingerprint computer creates the timescale for the movie. It is a time bomb ticking down, and ready to go off. A little artistic license was used - a real fingerprint computer could produce results in minutes - but I guess that's the movies!*

editing, what usually happens is that you end up cutting some of the junk out of the middle where it gets too wordy and slow and it ends up around ninety minutes.

***Q - What are the plot points in White Angel?***

***Chris -*** We spend the first ten minutes setting up the various stories which combine to form the main plot and characters. Ellen Carter has killed her husband and hidden the body - she has 'got away with murder'. She is a crime writer who studies serial killers. There is a serial killer in London killing women who wear white, and the killer may also be a woman. Mild mannered Steckler is probably the serial killer, he cuts up newspapers and has dead bodies in his living room. He moves in with Carter as a tenant. The police are closing in as they have a fingerprint on a hammer.

The plot is completely set up, we had a framework in which to work, and the fingerprint is the time bomb waiting to go off. This gives the movie the sense of impending doom and momentum.

Plot point one is where Steckler says - *I am the White Angel and I Want you to write my story.* Up until that point he has been getting on with his life, Carter has been getting on with hers. We've been setting up various parts of the story. But at that point the film changes direction. It sheers off at ninety degrees. Carter's life is totally destroyed. Steckler's is totally fulfilled because he's got the writer he wanted to do his book.

We then spend the next forty minutes of the movie exploring this theme of writing the book and what Carter is interested in. The mid point of the film is where Carter interviews Steckler and he says about his wife - *She deserved to die,*

*"I know audiences feed on crap, but I can't believe we are so lacking that we cannot dish it up to them with some trace of originality"*
*Darryl F. Zannuck*

# How To Write An Ultra Low-budget Screenplay

*What makes a good screenplay? There are many things and it is impossible to go over such an important subject here, but some of the main areas to consider will be dictated by the budget of your film. We would recommend reading further on the subject and the "Screenplay..." books by Syd Field are about the best place to start.*

*1. A screenplay roughly translates as one page per minute. Therefore, the screenplay should be between 90 and 120 pages.*

*2. If the movie to be made is designed to make money, consider a strong genre film like a thriller or science fiction film.*

*3. The title of the film is very important - JAWS, FRIDAY 13th, STAR WARS tell the reader (and ultimately the viewer) what the movie is all about - it sets the tone.*

*4. A low-budget screenplay should try to minimise locations and cast. Quentin Tarrantino's 'Reservoir Dogs' is a fine example of minimalist location film making. Note that he didn't shoot the most expensive part of the film, the actual robbery. A disused warehouse costs very little and has enough space for the production to spread out.*

*5. Don't try and win an Oscar, write something solid with plot and defined characters. Oscars will come later.*

*6. Writing a screenplay on a computer is the easiest way to write now - use a screenplay formatter to take the headache out of script layout.*

*7. The author of a screenplay is automatically the copyright owner. As added, cheap protection, post a registered copy to yourself in a sealed envelope and don't open it.*

*8. All screenplays are different, and every film maker will tell you what makes a good movie. However, we subscribe to traditional Hollywood values. Tell the story through the eyes of a person who has the odds stacked against them, present problems that they must overcome throughout the film, and set an ultimate goal that they strive for, which they attain (or don't attain) at the end of the story. The problems are simply barriers that keep the audience guessing as to whether the hero or heroin will actually achieve their ultimate goal, be if find a missing wife (as in 'The Vanishing') or kill the shark (as in 'Jaws').*

*9. There is a very defined structure in a good Hollywood thriller - beginning, middle and end - Acts 1,2 and 3... These three sections are roughly thirty minutes, sixty minutes, thirty minutes. (thirty, sixty, thirty pages).*

*At the end of act1 there is a plot point which changes the direction of the story. In the 'Pelican Brief', plot point one is where Julia Roberts lecturer is blown up, she is approached by mystery cops and she realises that someone is trying to kill her.*

*The mid point is halfway through act 2 when something happens and the characters psychological goal clarifies, when they realise what has to be done and once more the movie shears off in a different direction. In 'Jaws' the midpoint is when Roy Scheider's son is nearly eaten in the pond by the shark and Brody realises that he is going to have to confront his fears of the water and go out on the ocean and hunt the shark down. This is a very defined midpoint which is brilliantly honed down to almost a single slow zoom of the ocean.*

Writers Block - Try and get past page 1

*Plot point 3 is an event that brings the story to a climax. In 'Aliens' it is where Ripley loses the little girl Newt. They then fly into the reactor to rescue her, once more a very visual cut to act 3. There is much more going on in a screenplay than these basic elements and further reading is essential.*

*10. Initially, forget rich and fleshed out character, work on a strong, solid plot - then work on the characters. No matter how thin the characters seem, they always flesh out on the screen. This tip is not intended to encourage bad writing, but to put paranoia to bed.*

*11. The first film that you make will probably be the only one that you will have complete control over. Don't be afraid of going over the top with elements like sex or violence. This will cause controversy and help get the film, and you, noticed.*

*12. As the scriptwriter, ensure that you get a full screen upfront credit.*

*13. Remember, everything on screen costs money - some things like good locations don't cost very much, but be aware that things like helicopters, explosions, crowded night-clubs etc. are all serious headaches for the production staff that will be expected to work miracles.*

*14. Keep the screenwriter around when shooting - because of time or lack of cash, quick rewrites will be needed. Better the screenwriter do it than an actor in a flash of (later to be regretted) inspiration. If someone comes up with a good idea on set, and it can be used, don't be precious about the script - use it. At the end of the day, the scriptwriter gets the credit for the script, no matter where the ideas come from.*

*15. No matter what - keep writing, regardless of whether you think it is good or bad. Writers block can be crippling. Just keep writing.*

*16. KISS - KEEP IT SIMPLE STUPID!*

Don't even think of an epic

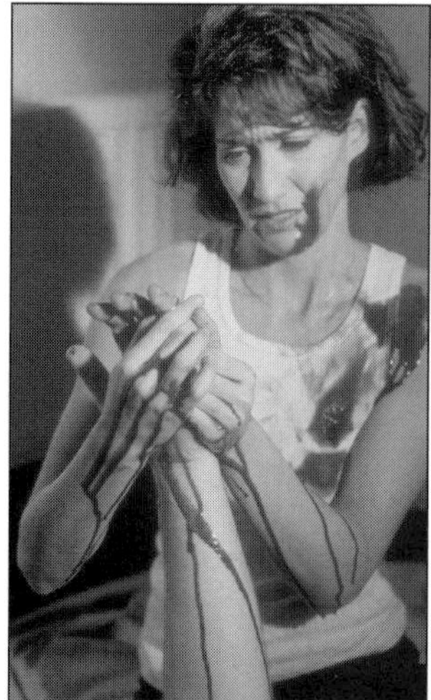

*The original premise for White Angel explored the differences between murder and manslaughter through the eyes of two killers*

*the world is a better place without her.* In the same scene, Steckler turns the interview around to Carter and she says of killing her husband, *He deserved to die. The world's a better place without him* - And she realises that she has said the same thing as Steckler, therefore it questions the differences between them.

It's a very subtle mid-point but it is a character point when Carter suddenly realises that she is essentially the same creature, a human being with the ability to kill.

Therefore, the rest of act two continues with the plot and develops this theme - her attempts to poison him etc. Plot point two is where Carter finds out (wrongly) that her friend, Mik, has been killed by Steckler. She finds the glasses covered in blood - that's a pinch point - just before plot point two.

The exact position of plot point two is where she sees the blood and the knife in Miks flat and comes home to find Steckler burying the body in the garden. Again, at this point, the film sheers off at ninety degrees. Carter is no longer interested in writing the book. She has one thing on her mind and one thing only. To kill Steckler. To get him off the face of the planet. She can't turn him in to the police because she'll go down for murder. So she makes an elaborate plan which the audience discovers as it happens. This leads us to the exciting climax and twist in the tail. Most people like a good twist, it lets them leave the theatre feeling fulfilled in a strange sort of way. However, it can often backfire and make the audience feel cheated.

We are not saying White Angel is the greatest screenplay

*The hammer in White Angel was the device which provided the plot and twists. This evidence would eventually lead the police back to the killer, and straight back to Ellen Carter for the final twist in the plot*

ever written, but it does work as a thriller. Most people say the story was 'gripping', which is a real compliment when considering the constraints under which the film was made.

***Q - So the treatment was extremely detailed before you wrote the script?***

***Gen -*** Absolutely. *White Angel* wasn't a short treatment. I think that the final version was twenty five pages. It is important that you can write a thirty page treatment and you know the structure (page eight is plot point one and on page 22 you have plot point two, with the mid point on page fifteen.) We structure everything, so when writing, you don't lose control of your characters nor will the story lose its direction. Every scene has got to move the story onward to its final conclusion - otherwise you will be boring your audience. You have around 2 hours to get everything across, and leave no loose ends.

***Chris -*** Screenplays and stories are all about mystery and exploration. Hollywood is obsessed by character - let's stop the movie and have a talky scene where the character confesses that he's shot a kid in a back alley ten years ago - this is often resolved later in the film, it's divisive and obvious.

What a movie is really about is getting on to the next scene. One of the interesting things that we did on *White Angel* was when we finished the first rough cut we went back and started to cut the end out of every single scene and some of the middle. So, what originally was a very well structured scene now felt unbalanced, not finished. The audience felt there was more, that they were not being told everything. This is not a hard and fast rule. But a good rule to stick to is not to tell your audience everything, it keeps them wanting more. This is something I learnt during *White Angel.*

***Q - There is a great deal of video footage used. Was this in the script?***

***Chris*** - Yes. There were two reasons for the inclusion of video tape footage in the film. I am from the amateur film making scene and whilst I started on Super-8, VHS soon became a medium that was very accessible.

I loved the way that in science fiction movies of the eighties, video footage was heavily used, eg. *Aliens.* It always looked

## Cutting Ratio

*The cutting ratio is the amount of film stock you shoot in relation to the final length of the movie. The less stock you shoot, the lower the ratio.*

*1. Save stock wherever possible. It is expensive to purchase, and expensive to process.*

*2. Work out a system between sound, camera and clapper loader so the camera starts turning over at the last possible moment. Just a couple of seconds wasted at the head of every shot will accumulate to possibly a full roll on a feature shoot.*

*3. Don't get too anxious to call cut - often in the cutting room, you will need that extra second on the end of a shot. When you feel the shot has ended, wait a beat before calling cut.*

*4. If you shoot on 24 frames per second (as opposed to 25 frames per second) you will save 4% of your overall stock and process budget (as the film is moving through the gate slower). Most features are shot at 24, most TV at 25. We would recommend shooting at 25 but your cameraman might feel different.*

*Cont...*

*Cont...*

*5. Know in your heart if you have got what you need in your first take. Takes that are not needed waste time as well as stock.*

*6. If you get a hair in the gate you should re-shoot. If stock is very short and you are having to get everything in one take, don't bother to reshoot, (unless the hair is massive - many major features go out with hairs in the gate.)*

*7. Rehearse as much as possible, block the scene for the cameraman so he knows what is going to happen and when. If the scene could be spontaneous in terms of performance from the actor, allow the cameraman to widen the lens so there is more space in frame to accommodate the unexpected. This will avoid losing the frame or focus forcing a retake (which will probably be wider anyway).*

*8. If you are shooting 35mm, you will only develop and print the shots you want. If you shoot 16mm or Super 16mm, you will print everything.*

*9. Storyboards will often help, but it is likely that too many shots will be boarded and that when it comes to shooting, the shots will not be possible due to the location being different, or a script re-write.*

grainy and really gaudy and I thought it was great. What an image. So, wouldn't it be great to get Steckler's monologues on video tape because that is a format that is much more 'real'. People believe what they see on TV. They understand that a film is drama but the news is 'real'. People believe video images.

In the film, Steckler gives interviews, and I thought, if we can do the interview on tape, then we have a five minute take in one. It would look really shocking and real, which is what everyone has come back and said. The other important reason is that five minutes of the film translates to about seven percent of the final product. We had fifty five rolls on which to shoot this film. I was fully aware that to get a five minute monologue in one film take, which is what I wanted, was going to be difficult. So we shot it several times on video tape which is reusable and then transferred the final result to film. So you have a chunk of your film finished with a cutting ratio of one to one which is pretty damn good. The cutting ratio is how much stock you shoot in comparison to how long your film is. If the film is to be one hundred minutes long and you shoot one thousand minutes of stock, then you would have a cutting ratio of ten to one. Most feature work is between eight and twelve to one. I think we shot *White Angel* on four and a half to one. It's all about preventing waste. Don't do endless takes. I learnt on *The Runner* that take one is often very similar to take fifty five.

Often in the editing room your can hear your voice calling "Take four. Loved it darlings!" and you wonder why you got that far - there was nothing wrong with takes one to three. If you've got the shot and your cameraman says that it's fine and the gate's clear. Go with it. It saves you time and it saves you stock and it saves you money.

***Gen*** - We had seen the effect of video images in films like *Henry - Portrait of a Serial Killer* - where it was pretty nasty (they watch a video of massacring a family) - and the reason it was more horrific than seeing the other killings on film, was simply because it was shot on video tape. It was real. Its like seeing the news nowadays - the images can be shocking. Also the video camera had been used in *Sex, Lies and Videotape* - as a tool to get into the minds of a group of people - and it worked. It was exactly what we wanted for *White Angel.*

***Q - Some writers chose an imaginary cast when working on a script, to give characters life. Did you do this?***

***Chris*** - Yes. This sounds really bizarre. When Steckler's character was formed, I had two people in mind. There is a guy in Romero's *Dawn of the Dead* who turns into a zombie at the end. I always thought of him. I don't know why. And I also thought of Jeremy Irons and for Carter, I only had one person in mind. No chance of getting her, of course. Jane Fonda.

***Q - When you started pre-production you had very little money, why didn't you wait until you had your full budget in place?***

***Chris*** - Mainly because we would have had to wait forever. We had worked out that it was possible to make a feature film for less than ten thousand pounds and we looked at how we made *The Runner* and where the money went. There were obvious things like film stock, processing, camera gear, things that you cannot avoid. You can get a good deal, you can get discounts, you can get some things for free but there is always going to be an expense. There are however, other expenses that you can avoid or minimise. The reason why *The Runner* went over budget was the fact that it was set in

*"Talk to them about things they don't know. Try to give them an inferiority complex. If the actress is beautiful, screw her. If she isn't, present her with a valuable painting she will not understand. If they insist on being boring, kick their asses or twist their noses. And that's about all there is to it"*
*John Huston*

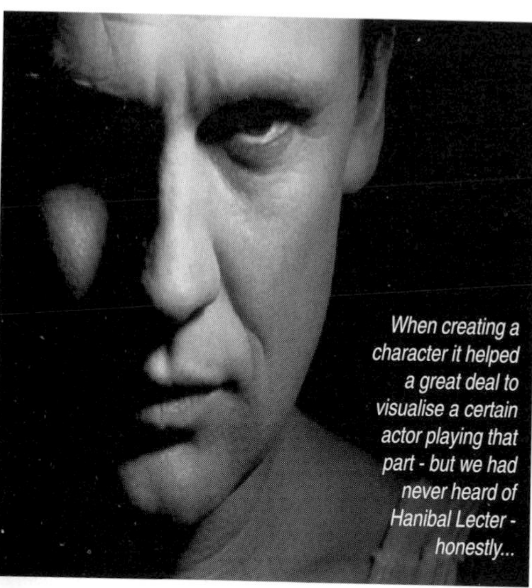

When creating a character it helped a great deal to visualise a certain actor playing that part - but we had never heard of Hanibal Lecter - honestly...

*"You spend all your life trying to do something they put people in asylums for"*
*Jane Fonda*

lots of locations, so out of a twelve hour shooting day, you'd spend a quarter of it, or thirty percent, driving between A and B, and then twenty percent getting the cameras out and the lighting set up. I guess we lost thirty to forty percent of our time through location changes. *The Runner* was filled with events that just wasted time through ignorance or lack of forward planning. *White Angel* was going to be different.

***Gen*** - The rules for low-budget scripts are all cost related. Money is the one thing you have little control of because on a no-budget film, you don't have it. The big expense we had on *The Runner* was crew and accommodation expenses. That took fifteen to twenty thousand quid out of our budget. On *White Angel* we decided to shoot in London and buy everyone a tube pass. It cost about twenty five quid a week to get cast and crew on location and often, on time.

*White Angel* was based in one house and there are very few scene changes - this minimised time wastage and allowed us to finish the film in eighteen shooting days as compared with nearly forty on *The Runner.* From *White Angel's* point of view the two golden rules we had were, minimise locations and get your cast and crew in a position where they can spend the night at home. This saves money in other ways. For example, if you wrapped early, you did not have to provide a meal in the evening. So, we'd not need catering that night. Catering is one of the areas where basic expense can't be avoided and it is actually a bad idea to skimp on it. If you feed your cast and crew well, you'll get twenty percent more out of them. You have to feed them something so why not make it good! Catering is another area that must be done correctly. It must be good. A low-budget shoot needs good food to look

*In a scene cut from the final version of the film, Police find one of Stecklers victims. Ultimately this shot was restored for an international 'uncut' version of WHITE ANGEL.*

*All the night-time sequences for WHITE ANGEL were shot during the day with the windows covered by black bin bags. A routine is very important if the cast and crew are going to perform to the best of their abilities with limited resources.*

forward to. Out in the rain, or the cold, good food keeps the spirits up.

***Q - What would be an average menu?***

***Gen -*** We didn't supply breakfast because everyone lived in London and we looked at it as coming to work. Lunchtime, we would provide sandwiches, rolls, very easy food that could be served from a cardboard box anywhere. For the evening meal, always something hot, baked potatoes, stews, shepherds pie. Warm, stodgy food with plenty of carbohydrate to keep people going. We'd also send out chocolate bars to break up the times between meals and persuaded a local bakery to give us all their cakes that were left unsold at the end of the day.

***Q - What happens on a late shoot?***

***Gen -*** Not often, maybe once a week, we provided beers afterwards. It is the same idea as getting chocolates etc. You give people beer and they think, *this isn't so bad* and it holds the team together.

***Q - Where were all the meals prepared?***

***Gen -*** There just wasn't room in the kitchen, so Mark Sutherland, the set constructor, found a skip outside a pub which was being refitted. He pinched the old bar and set up *'Stecklers Diner'* in the garage. Meals were prepared and consumed in the garage, it was pretty squalid - the caterer

## Catering

*A film crew looks forward to only one thing - lunch time. It is best not to engage their wrath by providing dodgy grub, or too little.*

*1. A film crew works better on a full stomach - especially if they are out in the cold. Tea and coffee should always be available, with someone making sure that the key personnel (who are working harder than others) have their drinks brought to them.*

*2. Feed a crew as much food as you can.*

*3. Film caterers are very expensive but they do provide a wonderful service. Try negotiating them down to a price per head that you can afford.*

*4. If you can't afford a film caterer, find someone who is used to catering for large groups and employ them full time for the duration of the shoot. They may bring their own equipment and will certainly have good ideas. Catering students can also be a good option but they*

*cont...*

*Cont...*

*will be inexperienced and unprepared for the barrage to which they will be subjected.*

*5. Large bread roll sandwiches are a good lunch time filler, easy to prepare and distribute. Beware of crew boredom with this simple culinary treat. Try and make up a simple menu (also catering for vegetarians) and give people an option. This will prevent arguments and give them something to look forward to.*

*6. Actors are more fussy than crew. Actors could be used to being treated well and your budget may not be able to cater for their tastes. Be aware of this very important factor.*

*7. Sweeties and beers after a hard weeks shoot can offer a good emotional bribe to get back in favour with a disgruntled cast and crew.*

*8. Concentrate on foods that are easy to prepare, cheap to produce, and fast to distribute and clear. Draw up a list of meals and outline them in the schedule. This will allow certain meals to be rotated.*

had a simple gas fired stove, but still managed to feed thirty mouths, twice a day. I guess the crew named it *'Steckler's Diner'* because sometimes we just didn't know what was in the stew!

***Q - From a production point, what advantages did White Angel present?***

**Gen -** We had a film set in suburbia, a location that would be cheap to shoot in, which would be near central London so that we could get the cast and crew to it easily. It was set in the present, so actors could wear their own clothes, or we could buy stuff from Oxfam, down the road. I'm not joking. We had a deal with Oxfam. It cost us fifty pounds for all our costumes in the film. And it worked. At the end of the day, when you have ten thousand pounds to make a film, two and a half goes on film stock, one and a half on cast and crew because you've got to give them something. Before you know it, the whole budget has gone on essentials. Therefore fifty quid for costumes.

At each production meeting, Mark Sutherland, our production designer, would proudly announce that out of his total budget of one hundred pounds, he was going to spend another forty pence on nails. He couldn't get them for free and was quite distressed about this.

***Chris*** - He became notorious for going around skips. The skip is a production designer's supply base on a low-budget shoot. Another man's junk is a production designer's dream.

***Q - How detailed was the budget?***

***Gen*** - Very, we had to know where every penny was going to go. We worked out what we thought the entire production was going to cost - everything down to petrol and telephone bills. Then we started to work out what things we actually needed to pay for to get the movie in the can - we just couldn't raise the entire budget before we shot, so we concentrated on getting the movie shot.

Eventually, we narrowed our list of essentials down to around £11,000. We knew we might need more than this, but once the snowball is rolling down the hill, it is difficult to stop it.

***Chris*** - That's right, it is weird but you spend months just

trying to get this thing going, and then a few days before the first day of principal photography, the production runs itself - it's like you have built a huge machine, and all you need to do now is maintain it to ensure it doesn't stop working. If you get to the first day of photography, you will probably make it all the way to the finish line.

*"We must choose material not only on the basis of whether we feel deeply, but on whether or not anyone's bloody well going to see it"*
*Richard Lester*

***Gen*** - First of all, we concentrated on getting the right house that was cheap. Then we could start sorting out everything else. We rented the house in Ruislip and based the production there. Most of the film would be shot there and the production office would also operate from one of the upstairs bedrooms. Then we visited all the hire companies and I spoke to them about the film and of course, getting free deals. I told them who we were and what we were trying to do - "...to make a career for ourselves - we are young film makers, the film is very low-budget, and we need the best deal ever - please, please, pretty please..."

Remember that any initial is the quote they give anyone. 30 percent off is just standard. No one pays full price. Tell them how little you have. Get a quote. Look at your budget and decide what you can afford. Then ring them back and try to make a deal. They can only say no. I used to ring up, say a lighting company and say - *Look, I've got five hundred pounds. Can you do it for that?* It is also important to pick a time to shoot your movie when you know that there is less

*If money is tight, the basic Super 16mm Camera, Tripod, Lens, Nagra, Mic and stock is all that is needed to make a cinematic quality feature film... Oh and a script and cast and... Pic - Jane Rousseau, camera operator for White Angel.*

## How to get deals

*1. Every quote is negotiable. Every list price you will ever be quoted will have another figure next to it which is what the person you are negotiating with is allowed to go down to. The trick is to find out what that figure is.*

*2. Find out from friends what kind of deals they got - it's a good yardstick.*

*3. Set up an account with the company and stretch the credit as far as you can. It is cheaper than a bank loan. Always keep in touch with the company you owe money to, never lie and never ever try and get away without paying. Good will can be stretched if you are civil, have a good reason for not paying, and can offer a schedule of payments within a set time frame.*

*4. When approaching people for deals or freebies, be polite and DON'T try and hustle. Most people who are in the Industry have been in it for many years and can spot ignorance and arrogance a mile away. Both these qualities are not desirable. Go to a person for help and advice - everyone likes to help someone out, it makes them feel good inside. Follow up thank you letters will often get a repeat performance if it is needed.*

*5. Many things can be begged, borrowed or stolen. If there is any opportunity for a companies logo to be*

*Cont...*

work around in the industry. Then you will receive good discounts. Usually December - January - Feb - March.

You must make sure that you tell them exactly what you want and for how much. *This is all I can afford, and I need an all in deal, all the kit, all the accessories, all the gel, all the spun* - ask if there are any hidden extras, or if you pay extra if you go overtime. And get a quote that lays everything out in detail. The best deal to get is always an 'all in' deal.

***Q - And what about cast and crew?***

***Gen*** - You've most probably started thinking about who would be an ideal cast for your film, and you may have been speaking to agents who have been asking the kind of money that is completely impossible - tell them that you need help and they will be helping the British film industry. Again, it is best to be straight with these people and not to attempt to deceive them. If an actor likes the script and wants to do it, their agent will probably be unable to stop them. Some actors will only work for money, so don't get disheartened if they tell you to stuff off.

***Q - How did you budget for crew wages?***

***Gen*** - We put the crew on deferred payments. We agreed to pay their expenses so that they wouldn't be out of pocket. The film was shooting in London so we concentrated on people who could get the tube rather than paying petrol expenses which are harder to estimate before shooting. Also, we always over budget for expenses because there are tiny elements that you just don't expect. Somebody can't get the tube. The shoot runs after tube hours or someone rings up and has to get a taxi for some reason. That money has to come from somewhere so it is best to over budget on transport.

***Q - Crew members need to eat and pay the rent, but low-budget films just can't afford to. How do you get around this?***

***Chris*** - What we did on *The Runner* was very different from *White Angel*. On *The Runner*, we couldn't pay anybody anything and we didn't want to do this again, because people have to live. So, what we did on *White Angel* was cover everyone's expenses, a tube ticket everyday and everyone

received £50 a week, to keep them in beer and fags. On top we offered a deferred payment so that when the film was sold, they would receive their wages. This would be more than they would have got since they have to wait two years or more for it - and don't kid yourself by promising money in two weeks. There is also a very good chance that they will never get paid. Selling a film is a long process. You've got to be straight with people. This is the money we've got - they can say yes or no. And make sure you pay it to them and reward them with good catering.

***Q - What's in it for them?***

**Chris -** There are very few films getting made in the UK, so there is an experience value. Most pro film-makers earn money through commercials, television etc. but they usually want to make movies. There are also a lot of new students being turned out from colleges - take advantage of their enthusiasm and give them responsibility. In my experience, most people will deliver if you give them the opportunity to do so. There is a great debate over deferred films - are they ethical? Well, almost all big budget features take advantage of free labour by taking on free runners - we are doing the same, but giving them more opportunity and experience, and a possible fee if it all works out. At the end of the day, everyone can say no. As a rule, if you can pay someone, do it, you will get a better worker, and no nasty phone calls two years down the line if you were not able to pay as promised.

***Q - What shooting elements proved a problem later?***

**Gen -** Something hit us when we were doing the effects on *The Runner.* The sheer quantity of stock needed to shoot action and effects. So on *White Angel*, we deliberately had very little stunt work or effects.

By remaining in London, there was another saving. Because we were near the facilities houses, anything could be dealt with by a phone call and a quick trip in the van. For example, if a camera went down - it was easy to get a replacement without costing much in time and therefore money. Also, we were close to the labs and could view rushes everyday and make sure there were no problems.

When we were shooting *The Runner* up in North Wales, the camera did go down and it was a serious problem. We had to

*Cont...*

*featured on screen, they will probably supply you with free samples of the product. Cars, costume, cigarettes etc. These can all reduce your budget. They may even pay (product placement).*

*6. Be thorough, ring around and get the best quotes. You will get a feel for who will be able to help you.*

*7. Many companies, not related to the film industry will often render their services for free just to be involved in the production (for the fun) or for a credit on the end titles. Tickets to the premiere can be a good bribe.*

*8. Go into negotiations with a maximum you will pay and don't go over it. If you are prepared to walk out without making a deal, you are in a very strong position.*

*9. If you can pay cash on delivery, you can push harder for a bigger discount. This is the best way to get the biggest discounts. Avoid doing non declared deals - it may be good at the time, but when Customs & Excise or the Inland Revenue ask you where the money went, you may have some problems.*

*10. If you can't get a discount, get something thrown in for free.*

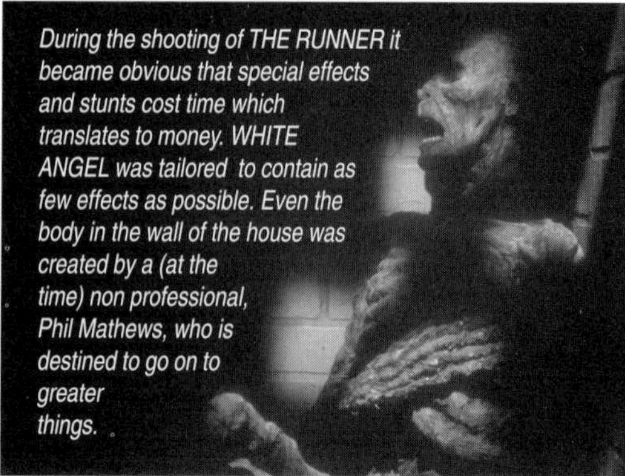

*During the shooting of THE RUNNER it became obvious that special effects and stunts cost time which translates to money. WHITE ANGEL was tailored to contain as few effects as possible. Even the body in the wall of the house was created by a (at the time) non professional, Phil Mathews, who is destined to go on to greater things.*

ring up London to get a new camera delivered - and then wait for them to Red Star it up by train. With transport on location, always expect your trucks to break down or worse. They always will. Either they'll get stuck in mud, stuck in snow, completely fail or crash. We had a few crashes - no-one was hurt, seriously at least. People get in too much of a hurry. This is one of the major problems of low-budget film-making. Safety.

Everybody knows there is a limited time scale. The production team is rushing to and from the set. Props must get to the set or the crew is sitting about waiting - so the foot goes on the accelerator and you speed along windy roads of North Wales. On *The Runner*, I remember nearly losing my life when I was driving at about 100 mph on a busy winding road on my way to the set. A truck pulled out in front of me at the last minute and the brakes made a horrific noise - luckily I am still around. It is incidents like this, when you realise that although it's important, is it really worth losing your life over?

***Q - What about insurance?***

***Gen*** - You always think - do we need insurance? Can we get away without it? But you can't. You certainly need car insurance and make sure that whoever is driving is definitely insured to drive that vehicle, because things will happen and they could be quite serious - and if you are not insured, you are liable because you are the employer. You must also insure the equipment from the hire companies - you have no choice since they will not let it leave their premises unless it is covered - they will ask for a copy of the policy. You can take

*"A producer shouldn't get ulcers, he should give them"*
*Samuel Goldwyn*

out a policy with the company, but this will cost far more than purchasing a separate insurance policy. A good broker can get a reasonable deal for you. We went to a local firm and it worked well.

"You don't need to pray to God any more when there are storms in the sky, but you do have to be insured"
Bertolt Brecht

Negative insurance is something that costs a fortune and that we have never done. It covers damage or some delays in shooting. Say for example your camera goes down or you are transporting your neg to one of the laboratories, the van blows up and you lose all that work, all those hours of shooting. Neg insurance will cover your re-shooting everything that you have lost. There is a lot of money involved and therefore it is not cheap.

The E&O policy is the Errors and Omissions Policy which is something that as a low-budget film, you will only come across at the distribution end and probably for America only. It will cover legal suits brought against the film for any reason from breach of copyright to contract errors. It is there to protect whoever buys the film but you will have to pay for it. This could set you back ten grand!

***Q - What was the total that you needed to raise to make White Angel?***

***Gen -*** The grand total was eighty five thousand pounds. We didn't raise all the money at once. Initially we could only raise eleven thousand pounds and we thought - either we hang around waiting for all the rest or we take a risk and shoot it with what we have. The cast and crew were working on deferments and we could just about do it if we shot for eighteen days.

Once we had the movie shot, we could show investors what they would be investing in, and it worked, it was much easier to get people to part with money when they could see where the other money had been spent. A lot of people think they need the full budget to make the movie but I would say, if you can't raise it all, and it's your first movie, just go for it. Once you've got something there, then people are more likely to put money behind you because they see you are not just talking about it but actually doing it. We both know a lot of people who have been waiting years to get their first movie off the ground because they haven't managed to get their two million budget yet - Dream on!

"Money is better than poverty, if only for financial reasons"
Woody Allen

***Q - How do you approach investors?***

**Gen -** We decided to go to private investors so we could maintain control - on our previous film, a distributor had come in at the beginning to provide the finance before we actually got round to fund-raising ourselves.

With *White Angel* we knew that we did not want a distributor to become involved right away because we would lose control. So, we approached people who we thought might have a bit of money stashed away, and asked if they were interested in investing it.

Also, people who might be specifically interested in investing in films. Lots of people want to be a part of the film business, it's something to talk about over drinks. Starting with the local area, we made a list of doctors, dentists, lawyers etc. and sent letters off to them, working our way from A-Z. Obviously this can cost a lot of money, sending out letters etc., so we decided to make a short-list of firm contacts, people who we'd met or people to whom we could get an introduction.

Also, news of *White Angel* travelled by word of mouth. We would meet a lawyer and he would be really keen so we'd send a full package of information. We'd have a second meeting and he'd say - I've got this friend and she's interested. Would you like the number? We had more success that way, rather than by cold calling.

*The original artwork on the cover of the WHITE ANGEL investment proposal. With virtually no material, we tried to make it look as much like a shocker of a movie as possible.*

***Q - What's in an investment proposal?***

**Gen -** We would put a package together that would include a synopsis of the film, a brief of the budget, a breakdown of their investment and the returns that they could expect. The returns were calculated on the *cost* budget rather than the *total* budget. For example, if we were making a movie for £200,000 but only needed £100,000 to cover all immediate cash costs on the film (the remaining £100,000 would be on deferred payments) the investment percentages would be calculated from £100,000. This meant the deal was even more interesting and showed we didn't want to waste a penny.

Once initial investment monies are recouped i.e. all investors get their money back, deferments are then paid (cast, crew, facility houses etc.) Once the film has broken even (paying

# WHITE ANGEL Schedule Breakdown

## 1991

**October**
*Commence writing screenplay. Begin to attract finance.*

**November**
*First Draft Complete*

## 1992

**January**
*Approx. £16,000 raised. Decision to shoot in February is made. Casting and pre production move into top gear.*

**February**
*Principle photography begins and lasts 21 days.*

**March**
*Begin editing, continue day jobs and continue raising production finance*

**May & June**
*Several small reshoots to patch some of the holes left in the main shoot. More investment comes in.*

**September**
*First fine cut complete.*

**December**
*Fine cut complete. Begin track laying sound and music*

## 1993

**February**
*Final mix at dubbing theatre. Negative is cut and labs begin very long process of printing*

**March**
*Labs damage the master negative. Living Spirit recall cast for reshoot of damaged stock. Re-mix quickly.*

**April**
*First Prints viewed. Publicity gearing up for Cannes. London based sales agents view the film. No-one bites.*

**May**
*Cannes - meet several companies who all express an interest*

**July**
*Re-edit film and remix as it needs tightening and there are some sound problems.*

**August**
*Pilgrim Entertainment signed as sales agents for one year.*

**September**
*Premiere at the Montreal Film Festival. Goes down well. German, Korean and US companies express interest and negotiations start.*

**October**
*UK premiere at London Film Festival. Plan for an April theatrical release using money expected from Germany, Korea and US to fund it.*

**December**
*Korean and German deposits paid.*

## 1994

**Jan - March**
*Publicity for theatrical release*

**April**
*Theatrical release. Film performs badly due to opening on bad weekend. Deals with US and Korea fall through. PANIC.*

**June - December**
*Pilgrim fail to deliver any deals. Publicity works a bit too well and Chris and Gen spend short time in Police cells. Chris and Gen lose home.*

## 1995

**January**
*Labs threaten court for monies owed. Living Spirit sack Pilgrim. Feature film comes on board to handle the video release.*

**Feb - March**
*Video release begins publicity. New version with more sex and violence is edited to help bolster sales*

**April**
*A song, performed by local band, is included in the new edit. It's later discovered to be owned by the Elvis Presley estate and carries a price tag of £1m. Re-edit - AGAIN!*

**May**
*Video release.... Film performs poorly*

**September**
*Living Spirit approach and secure new sales agent, Stranger Than Fiction. They are confident of making sales.*

## 1996

**February**
*White Angel is sold to Benelux, Italy and several far Eastern territories. Monies as yet have not been received.*

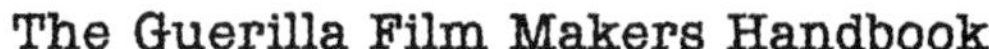

*The involvement of TV and Film faces such as Don Henderson help solidify the project in the eyes of potential investors.*

back the total budget of £200,000) then all monies received from that point are deemed to be profit. Monies are returned and are split 50/50 between the production house and the investors.

Therefore, the investors provide £100k and the deferred cast and crew provide the other £100k. The first sales would repay the investors back their £100k, then the deferred £100k would follow. The remainder would be split 50/50 between the production company and investors - an investor who put in £10k would receive 10% of the 50% split (5% of total profits).

***Q - How do you confirm an investment?***

***Gen -*** We would provide a very simple contract, two or three pages and as long as they were happy, they would sign it. We would have all the control. The only thing that they would be doing is putting their money in and receiving reports from us on the progress of the film. For them it was a risky investment but they knew it and wanted to do it. We will see if they are ultimately satisfied with the results.

There are many payments that must be met whilst in the sales process, all of which eat into any potential returns, such as making delivery and marketing. These figures need to be nailed down wherever possible. Obviously, they will be deducted from any sales and will push the investors profits further away, but there is nothing that can be done about this. Without your delivery items, you won't be able to *give* your film away - it's like a car without an engine.

***Q - Do investors give the money up-front?***

***Gen -*** We don't cashflow the payments because our budgets are so small, but if someone wished to invest a larger amount, say fifty thousand pounds, then we might link that in with a cash flow prediction. We didn't do this on *White Angel* because the money was raised in instalments anyway, so there was no need. We were almost doing a cashflow without knowing it.

*"I felt like an imposter, taking all that money for reciting ten or twelve lines of nonsense a day"*
*Errol Flynn*

As soon as we had shot something we invited the investors down to the set, showed them around to prove that we were filming something and they met the lead actors. It creates the buzz and raises more money in itself. Once the filming

finished we then concentrated on raising money to finish the film. We cut a trailer and showed that to investors - we kept the trailer short and punchy, left them wanting to see more - I think it only ran sixty seconds.

***Q - How long did it take to raise all the money?***

***Gen*** - One of the big problems with no-budget film-making is that if you raise money in instalments you often take time off from finishing the film, so the film takes a lot longer to produce. We were still raising money nearly a year after we shot it.

***Q - So, you must finish shooting?***

***Gen -*** Yes. It is vital to cover the screenplay as thoroughly as you can. You don't know if your lead actor could die, get awkward, move to the States. This could cause major problems. Even if you have to drop close up cut-aways during the shoot, do it in order to cover the main action and the screenplay. I know several other movies that were shot over, say ten consecutive weekends, but I guess the cast must have been made up from either friends or actors who lived locally. I wouldn't like to do it that way, but it is by all means, an option.

Once we had completed shooting *White Angel*, we had no problem raising money for post- production. People could see what was there on film. They could watch it to see how it was working, see it was working well and put more money in. Not rushing the film allowed us to have a few test screenings, reshoot the ending and polish the feature as a whole. To check that everything was in place and that the story was going as planned - and that people were going to be gripped. It's better to do this than rush the post-production, only to discover your problems when you are sat in a cinema with a crowd of a hundred on the day the movie opens.

***Q - Control is important. Why?***

***Gen -*** On *The Runner* we had given the final cut to the distribution company, they had a lot of say in the picture because they had put all the money in, in one lump sum. At the end of the day the film was not the film we wanted to make. The producers kept changing the film, trying to force the material to be more commercial, sacrificing the

### Keeping Investors Sweet

*1. Where possible, fulfil any promises made. It may not always be possible to fulfil a promise (one of the disadvantages of low budget film making), but make it a priority to do so at almost any cost.*

*2. Regular updates need only be a photocopied sheet of information which keeps the investor in touch with what is happening. If the line of communication goes cold, so will the investor.*

*3. Press - this is great for keeping people happy. Everyone associates press coverage with success, but beware, this may produce a false sense of financial returns on the part of the investors. If press coverage has used artistic license, let investors know.*

*4. Several low budget pictures have allowed investors to act in the film in return for cash. It works and everyone is happy. Beware of problems if their scene is cut - make this possibility known in advance.*

*5. Send them a VHS tape of the final film & invite them to the premiere.*

*6. If things are going badly, let them know. As long as there is trust and they can see that you have done everything possible, Investors have no real come back (check your agreements though). Investors would rather know things are going badly than hear nothing at all.*

*7. Give them a credit on the end of the film*

*"All you need for a movie is a gun and a girl"*
*Jean-luc Godard*

characters and the story - we ended up with a film that didn't make too much sense. With *White Angel* we didn't want a situation to arise where people whose opinions we didn't agree with had a creative say in the process - *"Wouldn't it be a good idea if her head exploded" etc.* - We wanted to keep full control so that it would end up the movie that we wanted to make. That's not being possessive. It comes back to the writing stage where we will involve quite a few people to discuss the project, and screenings where we ask the audience to criticise the final result.

From a financial point it is also important - any changes cost money. If an investor or executive producer wants to screen the movie with all the scenes that you have cut, put back in, it will cost money and time - and when you have neither, this becomes a serious problem.

*WHITE ANGEL publicity shot - Sexy girl, big gun, blue light - this kind of image is about as far removed as possible from the attitude of many (but not all) UK based production companies and institutions. This was a problem for Living Spirit as we couldn't afford to hire a model - so Louise Ryan, from set construction kicked off her overalls and dockers, then slipped into something slinky..*

***Q - Did you have any experience with British Film companies and institutions?***

***Gen -*** Yes, but limited. When we set up Living Spirit, we approached several companies and Institutions who were set up to help and aid British Film Makers. They would read our ideas and the first thing they asked was - *This film seems very much like a Hollywood project - do you see it as commercial?* - and we said - *of course - we hope it's going to be commercial, make money etc so that we can make another film.* They said - *I'm sorry. We can't support this kind of film because it's not alternative. We only support films that aren't commercial.* We were dumbfounded by this. Thankfully, things now seem to have changed dramatically, but there are still some frustrating problems for new film makers.

***Q - What were your main legal questions?***

***Gen -*** The main contracts are for your actors and your crew. Especially, with the actors, you have to make sure that everything is in there. You have to have total control, to make certain that you can do anything that you want with the picture, reshoots and with the publicity afterwards. You do not want an actor refusing to do something because it's not contractual and they request more money. The price that you have agreed to pay includes everything. The music contract is also very important to nail down. The composer composes the music. You have permission to use it in the film. You think

## Product Placement

*Product Placement is a relatively new opportunity available to film makers interested in making the most of the budget of their film. It is a form of advertising. To place one of their products in a film, large companies will provide certain items for the use of the film company. The companies who arrange this have several clients and can offer a variety of options.*

*1. What can you get? Cars, computers, office space, soft drinks, alcohol, cigarettes, courier services. In fact, anything that needs advertising and is useful to the production. For some items, you can even get hard cash!*

*2. What do they want? The companies are not doing this for free. They want advertising. First, they want a credit at the end of the film. But the real desire is for them to see their car, their cigarette, their toothbrush on the screen, preferably in very close proximity to the lead actor. You have to achieve this.*

*3. Time period. Is it set in the present day? This makes things easier. If your lead character does not drive a car in the script, add that scene to the script. A car manufacturer will want that space. Every room, every street, every prop offers the possibility of product placement.*

*If your film is a period piece, it is more difficult but use your imagination. Some companies did operate in the nineteenth century so with a bit of research, their product can appear in its original form and show the logo.*

*If your film is set in the future, there should be no problem. All props should carry logos of the relevant companies. Space shuttles with 'Ford' stamped on the side. etc.*

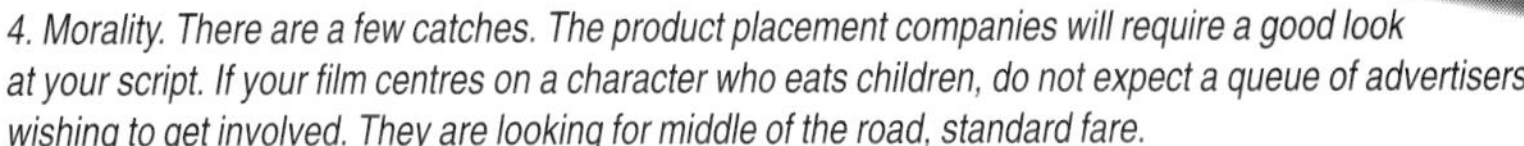

*4. Morality. There are a few catches. The product placement companies will require a good look at your script. If your film centres on a character who eats children, do not expect a queue of advertisers wishing to get involved. They are looking for middle of the road, standard fare.*

*5. Star. The better your star, the greater the desire for the product to be placed. A photograph of the established actor, driving, smoking, drinking the product is useful for in house publicity. It is evidence that the placement company is doing its job. Seldom do the clients see the film, but they might see the photo.*

*6. Costs. Product placement does cost money. It is possible to acquire a fleet of cars to shuttle actors and crew around but you will be responsible for insurance. This can cost a large amount and should be taken into account.*

*7. When you do a deal, make sure that you deliver on the film. Provide what you agreed to provide. If you say that there will be a close up of a cigarette packet, make sure it is there. You will have to make another film, one day.*

everything is fine, however, there are other *hidden* problems.

There are mechanical and synchronisation rights along with publishing/performing rights that all have to be cleared. Various societies may have the right to collect royalties on behalf of the composer if you do not obtain a complete buyout of all such rights. Mechanical reproduction is perhaps the most important for low-budget films since a good deal of money is recovered through video. If a buyout is not agreed, money is payable on every single copy of the video reproduced worldwide and it comes out of the producers pocket. On *White Angel* we covered all such rights and no further payments are to be made. Anyone buying this film will ask to see these contracts and not having them in place might prevent any sales occurring.

***Q - Did you use a lawyer?***

**Gen -** We used a lawyer on *The Runner*, but not an entertainment lawyer. This was a problem because the film industry is very specialised and needs a legal expert, which is expensive. But, again, you may be able to come to some kind of arrangement. If not and you shoot anyway, just read carefully through any contract before it is signed. With *White Angel,* we were in a more fortunate position since we had gone through the process once and had copies of all the contracts. Ultimately, we didn't use a lawyer and it hasn't caused us any problems yet, but it could well do. I would strongly advise consulting a lawyer at some stage, if only to put your mind at rest.

***Q - What did the schedule for White Angel look like?***

**Gen -** The schedule for White Angel was twenty days with a day off each week, so that gave us seventeen shooting days. We made sure we never had more than a twelve hour day. If you start running into long hours because you are trying to cover ground, you will pay for it further down the line. A crew can only work so long and we said, no more than twelve hours a day. Only the producer works longer. In fact, the producer never sleeps! When I schedule, I look at locations first, making sure I shoot all the scenes around a certain location at the same time. This saves time getting in and out of a location. Try to bunch an actor's scenes together so you use them for the least possible time. It's not possible to make everything work, but minimising waste will save money. It's

### When to shoot

*1. Traditionally, January and February are slow times for hire companies. It may be to your advantage to shoot during these months as you could get better discounts.*

*2. If your film is set entirely at night, it will take longer to shoot as every shot will need to be lit. If you shoot during the day, it is possible to get away with little or no lighting. Shooting from the hip during daylight is the best way to cover a lot of ground when you don't have much time to shoot and money is really tight. Consider the possibilities of moving the production outdoors as much as possible during the hours of daylight. It is easier to manage an outdoor location, and there is less to damage.*

*3. If you do shoot outdoors, remember British weather. Consider shooting abroad in southern Spain or Portugal - it isn't as expensive as you might think. Days are longer and brighter as well.*

*4. Crews and actors (especially), don't like being cold and wet. Try and work around bad weather, or if the script calls for it, control the weather by creating it with wind and rain machines.*

*After producing The Runner, the production of White Angel ran smoothly and without hiccup.*

like putting a massive jigsaw together when you don't have the cover of the box to tell you what the picture looks like.

If you have a star who is costing you real money, then there is no doubt that they should become the priority.

We also decided to shoot in February as this was a lean time for hire companies and we were able to get great deals.

***Q - What was the worst day?***

***Gen -*** I can't think of a 'worst day' on *White Angel*. I can think of several on *The Runner* but you see, *White Angel* profited by the disasters on the first film. We learnt from our considerable mistakes. On *White Angel*, we knew the ropes - we knew how to shoot a movie for little or no money. In a way it was quite boring because from a production point of view, we got it right.

We did lose one location and had to make a bank out of absolutely nothing. There is a scene in the film where Carter goes to a bank where all the evidence against her is locked in a safety deposit box. So Carter gets through the reception and into the bank vault. We had planned to use a real bank which was agreed but they pulled out at the last minute, the day before we were due to shoot. Someone found an empty gutted out bank that we could use. There was nothing in there and it was like a warehouse, but it did have the vault door intact. We decided to paint deposit boxes on the wall and we all worked on it, painting away through the night and half an hour before shooting in the morning it was finished.

*"It's true, hard work never killed anybody, but I figure, why take the chance?"*
*Ronald Reagan*

*The bank vault was nothing more than a metal door with cardboard security boxes painted grey. Little white stickers were added at the last moment to give the impression of key holes.*

The paint was still wet in the shot. To be honest, that was not a real disaster. Film-making breeds this kind of situation. If you can't handle that, you shouldn't be making films.

***Q - Were there any problems shooting on location?***

***Gen -*** Nothing above the run of the mill stuff like weird people hassling the cast and crew, or the weather. One thing to consider when looking for locations is the sound. Film making is always biased toward the image, but we had real problems with one or two scenes because we shot near an airport. We also had real problems in a flat where kids were running about upstairs - this really held us up.

***Q - How do you find working with actors?***

***Gen -*** Actors tend to flock together, as do the crew, and sometimes this can generate a *'them and us'* situation which is very unhealthy. There were a couple of incidents that proved a bit problematic for the production team. For example the lighting for the scene might take a little longer than expected and the actor might have gone for a walk or something. We did lose all our actors on one occasion. We had told them that the set up was going to take a little time so they decided to go off together. We had a room for them but they weren't there. The whole crew had to search Ruislip High Street, looking for them and they were finally found having an Indian in the local restaurant. They were just having coffee and wouldn't be long. It all got sorted but it was a bit of a heart stopper at the time.

"I've done the most awful rubbish in order to have somewhere to go in the morning"
Richard Burton

On *White Angel*, none of the actors really put pressure on us, they were all great. But on *The Runner*, we did have terrible problems with the cast, clashes of interest, egos, impatience,

frustration - all combined to create a volatile pot of angry energy.

***Q - How do you go about casting a movie?***

***Chris -*** We never finished the screenplay to our satisfaction and were still rewriting the script on the set, but when it was in a position where we felt - *this will work* - and we had our eleven thousand pounds in the bank we had to start casting.

First, we put an ad in *The Stage* and *PCR* (Professional Casting Report). As usual, we received sackfuls of mail. The ad said - *'Wanted. Sophisticated Psychopath'* - we got some very strange letters back. One from a guy who had pasted a reply from pieces of newspaper and enclosed a photograph of himself, hooded in black, holding a carving knife. It read - *Give me the role or I will kill you* - I looked quite hard for the sophisticated angle in this guy's approach but I couldn't quite see it. We also had photos of naked girls saying - *give me the role and I'll make your dreams come true* - It is very strange. People are desperate. I even had one woman come to the house and offer to take a shower with me in exchange for the lead role. Dead serious.

So, you have to be careful how you deal with actors and be as fair as possible. We broke the replies down into a short list of fifty, then to twenty five and initially interviewed them all. We found a church hall in Shepherds Bush, which cost ten quid for the day and was heated by a thermo - nuclear burner in the centre of the room. It had two settings. Off and meltdown. You couldn't hear yourself shout when it was on. So, we spent the day alternating between ice and fire. We ran through the actors and they were all slightly inexperienced, professionals but no weight. We realised that no-one had what it took to fill the role so we started thinking about classic, British actors.

We knew that we needed someone with quality and ability. So, we went to the top. We approached top British agents. We liked the idea of Michael Caine but he wasn't available or interested, and another famous actor we approached seemed to warm to the idea. We said that we were young film makers trying to make British movies, we needed support. He liked the idea so we sent him the script. Two days later we received a phonecall and he absolutely destroyed us. *The script is complete crap. What you are doing is immoral.*

## Getting Good Sound

*Sound is an area that is neglected by most inexperienced film makers "We'll fix it in the cutting room" usually means several thousand pounds of post production (opposed to three more minutes for another take on set).*

*1. The best way to get good sound is to hire the best sound recordist you can. Inexperienced sound recordists may be paranoid and request further takes when they are not needed.*

*2. Everyone is a perfectionist. Learn to recognise when the sound is good enough.*

*3. When looking for locations, bear the sound in mind. Traffic and planes are usually the worst culprits. Most natural sounds can be covered up and disguised in post production.*

*4. Don't believe anyone when they tell you that it is possible to filter out the camera noise. It is possible to filter most out, but never all. A heavy atmosphere track could cover this problem.*

*5. Post sync dialogue is a pain and expensive. Try and avoid it.*

*6. Good track laying in post production doesn't cost the earth and makes the film sound much more expensive.*

*7. Final mixing should be done at a features studio & not a TV theatre used to mixing local news. This is the stage which shapes your final sound and if you mess around, you will only have to spend more money fixing it at another studio.*

*Peter Firth liked the screenplay very much and had experience of low budget films - he accepted with little hesitation. Harriet Robinson was a little more unsure - she had no experience of low budget film making, but once she heard Peter was involved, it tipped her mental scales in our favour.*

*You're destroying the British film industry by making this sort of crap.* He just decimated us. We were shattered. This great British actor who I'm not going to name, poured cold water over our entire concept.

Eventually I said -*well, it's obvious that we're not going to be working together* - and he said - *why don't you make something beautiful and wonderful like Baghdad Cafe?* and I said *What's Baghdad Cafe*? I'd no idea what he was talking about. I wanted to make *The Fog* or *Halloween* or *Return of the Living Dead Part IV*. He asked -*Why are you making this kind of film? - Because I like it.* We went around in circles. - *Why can't you adapt a Shakespeare play - Because, I don't know anything about Shakespeare.* I still don't understand why you have to conform to succeed in Britain.

***Q - How do you approach an agent?***

***Chris -*** Agents exist to protect actors and to negotiate for them. The problem with agents is that they have opinions. In other words, if the agent doesn't like the script then it might not get to the actor. That is when you are in a problem area. It

Give Me The Job Or Die... Call Paul on 081 555 9999

Some actors can get a little too involved in the role when applying for the job

is not in the agents interest to have a client attached to a no-budget film and it is not worth their while to go through the contracts and take a client off their books for ten percent of nothing. Even the actors will be aware that another job might turn up and they don't want to commit to your film, especially if Spielberg is considering them for his new project. The trick is to get the script to the actor rather that going through the agent but not to intrude on the actors privacy. That is the easiest way to piss off both actor and agent.

***Q - Can an agent stop an actor from doing a low-budget film?***

***Chris -*** By virtue of not even telling an actor a film is being cast, an agent can stop an actor getting involved. However, the bottom line is that if the actor wishes to do a film, then they will do it regardless of anything else.

You have an advantage as a no-budget film-maker. Your screenplay should be different from typical British scripts popping up from British Screen, Channel 4, the BFI and other similar institutions - more than likely it will be rough around the edges, maybe contain some dire clichés but it will hopefully have a bit of energy about it. At the end of the day, actors want to work, to stretch themselves artistically, even experiment. They like to do things that are different, things that might win awards or get some attention and low-budget productions are famous for this.

***Q - What about approaching the top actors?***

***Chris -*** Actors are more available in the UK. In America we wouldn't get anywhere as near as we could here. Always start at the top. Do not start at the bottom because you will undersell yourself. We tried Michael Caine and got a

"They ruin your stories. They trample on your pride. They massacre your ideas. And what do you get for it? A fortune."
Anon

resounding *NO*, but at least we tried.

***Q - And how did Peter Firth get involved?***

"Acting: It's not a field, I think, for people who need to have success every day: if you can't live with a nightly sort of disaster, you should get out" John Malkovich

**Chris -** His agent was helpful although we never told anyone what the budget was. We always said that it was under a million. The fact that we had eleven thousand pounds in the bank was a closely guarded secret.

When ringing round agents, Peter's agent mentioned his name - I'd seen *Lifeforce*, possibly one of the worst movies ever made, where Peter Firth runs through the streets of London and saves the world from a plague of space vampires. I was aware of his Oscar nomination for *Equus* and his work on *Tess*. We also knew of the low-budget film *Letter to Brezhnev* that was a huge success. We were interested. His agent offered us the usual twenty five thousand pounds per week deal and I said - *would it be possible for Peter to just read the screenplay?* - He was sent the script and he called me - he liked it - he understood what low-budget meant, and after a discussion over the treatment of the violence in the film, he agreed that he would like to be involved.

I filled the agent in on the fact that we didn't have any money. A certain chill entered the negotiations. She said - I have to say that this is not what we are in to. Then I got this phone call from Peter who said - *whatever my agent says, I do want to do this movie. You guys just work it out with my agent and come to an agreement. I just want to do it.* That was great because we knew we had to pay him something but we had a very limited amount of money. We paid him what we could afford and gave him a deferred payment and a percentage so he will get more, once the movie was sold - his agent was fine.

*When trying to attract a star cast on a low budget film, the screenplay is without doubt the most valuable asset a production company can offer an actor*

WHITE ANGEL

Draft5

By Chris Jones
and Genevieve Jolliffe

Contact Living Spirit Pictures
Tel 01083 8558588

***Q - Don Henderson came in. How?***

**Chris -** All we did was try to fill all the big roles with as big 'names' as possible. There was another role we tried to get Barbara Windsor for, but we ran out of time. Don Henderson was originally thought of as the gangster, Alan Smith, from whom Carter gets the gun. The role of Inspector Taylor was available and one night I suggested to Gen that Don should be Inspector Taylor. Now, we paid Don more than we could really afford but his agent was being a real stick in the mud

and we ran out of time. But Don was a great chap. He's the best.

One of the great things about British actors is they just get on with the job. Harriet who is from the American school of acting needed a lot of direction - *Am I doing it right etc.* I guess this kind of acting can produce some dazzling results, but when time is running out, you often want *one take wonders* like Don and Peter.

I never really had to direct Peter, he just hit his mark and delivered the goods. Occasionally he would look to me to see if he was going down the right alley, or I would ask him to emphasise something, but that's about it. There was one scene with Peter and Don. What a dream it was. One take. Perfect. It was that simple.

*"You could heave a brick out of the window & hit 10 actors who could play my parts. I just happened to be on the right corner at the right time"*
*Boris Karloff*

***Q - So, it's a false economy to use method actors?***

***Chris -*** It can be. If time is very short and there just isn't money to get it right, it's better to get a scene covered badly than half the script covered well - half a script doesn't make a feature film. Peter didn't need to immerse himself in the character to play Steckler - he didn't need to keep a knife in his inside pocket, or follow women home from work, just to see how it felt.

*This isn't a desperate attempt to raise much needed funds, it's the multi talented crew helping out as the cast!*

*Not all performances require highly skilled thespian abilities...*

It's great if you're Daniel Day-Lewis in a multi million dollar movie. Time is a luxury we did not have. People who have lots of experience in front of the camera know what it takes to play the lead in a film, they know about pacing a character, knowing when to say - *no, we don't need another take.* I remember a scene with Don Henderson - I ummed after a shot and he said - *no, that was fine.* I'd never come across an actor who didn't want more screen time. Don knew that he couldn't give any more so why waste time and money doing another one.

***Q - Stars often won't sign until the last minute?***

***Chris -*** We were shooting before Peter actually signed. Principal photography had started. Peter only became involved two days before we began his scenes. It was very tight. That is a problem but it is one of the burdens of having no money. You have to keep a reserve in mind in case your star can't or won't do it.

***Q - Did you have to wait until the last minute?***

***Chris -*** If an actor says - I want to do this film - there are usually a couple of provisos. They might want the dialogue altered to suit them, or a say in the co-star. You have a choice then, to say yes or no. They will only sign at the last moment, just to make sure they don't get that call from Spielberg after they are signed to some low-budget thing. As you get close to shooting the chances become more remote of that call coming and your chances get better.

***Q - Main cast professionals. Minor cast are friends?***

***Chris -*** Absolutely. Every single crew member of *White Angel* appears in the film. Genevieve actually plays four different characters. A classic example - we were shooting a late night scene with an actress who was to play a prostitute, but she didn't turn up so Gen put on the wig etc and did the scene. I'm in it as a forensic expert. It's unavoidable, but it makes the film very personal and saves you a whole heap of money. Why employ the services of a professional 'extra' to stand around or to hold up a hammer and say - *I found it sir* - I'm not trying to knock actors but often, it's not demanding.

When you've got ten grand, you're not going to waste even ten quid when anyone can do it. Get friends and relatives.

"The principal benefit acting has afforded me is the money to pay for my psychoanalysis"
Marlon Brando

Get them to pay to be in it. Get them to invest money in the film and you'll give them a role. One guy paid a thousand pounds to play one part in *White Angel* (unfortunately, we had to cut him out).

***Q - Did you give him back his thousand pounds?***

***Chris*** - No

***Q - What about crew. How do you get the best people possible?***

***Chris -*** The initial crew was myself (the director), and Genevieve (the producer). Jon Walker, the DOP who shot *The Runner,* was also very involved with the script for *White Angel and* we have a very good working relationship with him. For the rest of the crew we sent the feelers out - people who knew people who knew people. We had some experienced professionals come in. They said how much they wanted. Then, we'd say - *I'm sorry - Can you do it for this?* Sometimes we got a yes, but mostly a no.

We had very few industry names involved. What we did get was intense dedication from a crew of relatively inexperienced people. Everyone who was there, wanted to be there, and that got us through the rough. Our experience in production pacing also saved the production from disaster.

On a film school project, the crew could work anywhere between three and ten days, and for 24 hours a day. That's fine for film school, but you can't work people like that for anywhere near as long as it takes to shoot a feature film. You can run a film crew into the ground in the first week but by the third week you will pay severely.

When we made *The Runner* the crew had even less experience and I had never made a feature. I didn't think - *let's run the crew into the ground* - but I did think - *Whatever it takes to get the shot* - On the first day we shot for twenty hours and everyone had two hours sleep. The next day another twenty hours - it was okay for the first few days because everyone was high on adrenaline and the buzz of making a movie.

Then, two weeks into the film everyone got the flu, and on virtually the same day. It closed the production. People could

## Using Friends as Actors

*Actors cost money. Even if they offer to work for free they will at some point probably ask for money for train fares etc. It is almost essential that your principal cast are pros, but if push comes to shove, friends and relatives are an option. If casting a friend or relative...*

*1. You will still need a contract. Always make a contract with everyone that appears in front of the camera - carry release forms that can be filled in on the spot. Not only will this protect you legally, but the sales agent will require these documents.*

*2. Unless you are sure of their skills, don't give them any important role. Be aware that they could be spectacularly awful. They may also be unprofessional.*

*3. It is more likely that they will endure hardship and abuse than an unpaid actor - so if you need 'a body in the lake', ask a relative (you will still get earache, but you will be able to persuade them.)*

*4. Equity, the actors union won't like it - so beware.*

*5. Friends and relatives are great if you need a crowd - they will even come in costume (but beware of damaged egos when a costume is terrible).*

## The Skip
### A Production Designers Dream

*One man's rubbish is another man's treasure. And a skip can be a treasure chest for the production designer who has to build the impossible with a budget that would barely buy lunch.*

*1. Skips are often filled with wood, the main material needed in construction. Don't be proud, scavenge.*

*2. Don't buy materials from a DIY shop, find a local timber merchant, or building supplier where you can buy at trade prices.*

*3. Everything is reusable. Don't be tempted to get a skip! Keep everything in storage until the shoot is over. It is guaranteed that if you junk something, the next day it will be needed.*

*4. Keep a close eye on tools, they are expensive & have a tendency to go walkies.*

*5. When it comes to the person who is going to oversee the construction of any sets, find someone who is ready to 'go for it'. The construction supervisor is like the caretaker - at the end of the day, whatever they say, goes.*

*6. Think about re-using sets & locations. Although White Angel is set in a large house, we only shot in one rooms. A few posters, different curtains, a false plywood wall & a lick of paint all created the illusion of different rooms.*

work four hours, maybe six, and only at half speed. Treat your crew professionally. Never work more than twelve hours. Never work more than six days a week. If you treat them professionally, they will act professionally. Actually, there's not a lot to film-making if you have the right team behind you. The heads of department should lead. If you have the right producer, DOP, Assistant Director etc the crew need not be as experienced. They will be told what to do.

A classic example is the production designer on *White Angel,* Mark Sutherland. He'd never been near a movie in his life but he became famous for getting the job done. Sometimes he'd have stupid deadlines. The house where we shot *White Angel* was a three up, two down semi-detached in Ruislip. Now we had three bedrooms upstairs, one of which was the production office, one of which was a bedroom for the production team and the other was make-up and wardrobe. So, no bedroom scenes could be shot upstairs. Downstairs there was a living room and a back room. The backroom became the storage room. So, apart from the halls and the kitchen, we had one room in which to shoot - this one room would have to change, when required, into the front room, backroom, all three bedrooms and anything else that needed a set.

Day one - it was dressed as Steckler's bedroom. Overnight, Mark tore that down and built Carter's bedroom. Day two - we shot Carter's bedroom. It was torn down overnight and replaced with the living room including one huge hole in the wall. Virtually, the entire film was shot in that one room and we never waited for the set to be finished. Mark always got the job done on time and under budget. Everybody would muck in and pick up a paintbrush. Once a film begins shooting, it's like a rolling ball - difficult to stop - It's just a matter of how quickly and how well it will be done.

Another example of Mark's flexibility came when we had finished the film and we had a test screening where the audience offered suggestions. The one thing that was clear is that the ending was wrong.

In the original ending, Steckler shuffles in after being stabbed, shot, bashed etc, straps Carter into a chair and starts drilling into her head with a dentist drill. It was a great bit of *Friday Thirteenth* style movie hokum, but everyone seemed to say that it felt like the end of a different movie - it

just didn't fit. So we decided to re-shoot the end. We returned to the house where we shot the original footage. Unfortunately, in the interim, American drug dealers had taken over this house and wouldn't let us within a thousand yards of it. So, Mark Sutherland came up with the idea of a set. But where could we build it? In our garage of course. So, we built the hallway and part of the living room in the garage at the front of our house

*"In my own mind, I'm not sure that acting is something for a grown man to be doing"*
*Steve McQueen*

We painted the walls, put wallpaper up, built false windows and re-shot the whole end section of the film. The actors were very good and never said anything, I guess they were used to our peculiar ways. I must admit that when I said to Peter - *let's go to the studio* - I think he was expecting something different from our garage. I remember him walking in - he was very impressed and said *this is fine*. But he did say it was one of the strangest places he'd ever had to shoot. No-one ever knew and we got away with the cheat.

***Q - Everyone does everything. No-one seems to do one thing.***

***Chris*** - People like to put film-makers in boxes. This person is an editor, that person is a designer. Most film-makers are just that. People who love making films. Everyone would like to direct but most don't expect to be doing that to start with. So, you get this crossover where everyone can do everyone else's job. One day the sound man was ill so Jon Walker took over and recorded sound as well as lighting the film. That's a tremendous asset. Whatever shit happens (and it always does) you can deal with it.

*Because the location where WHITE ANGEL was shot appeared to have been taken over by American drug dealers, the house had to be rebuilt in minute detail - in the garage! - Inset above, how the garage looked in the final film.*

## Employing Crew

*1. Wherever possible, hire the best person you can get.*

*2. Ask around your industry friends & crew (who are in place) if they know anyone who would work on the film.*

*3. Crew up in advance, especially the main departments like sound, camera, design. If you don't, you may find yourself on set wthout a sound recordist. Don't put an amateur at the head of a department like photography or sound.*

*4. Film schools are a good source of cheap & cheerful labour. A dedicated student will work wonders.*

*5. Try & pay everyone, if only a little. People work better with cash in their pockets.*

*6. Try & avoid deferred payments and offer everyone a buy out deal for a lesser amount.*

*7. Get production staff in as early as possible. They can start solving simple but time consuming problems. Again, a dedicated film student would excel in this area.*

*8. Always cover travel expenses & feed the crew. This will avoid rebellion when you least need it.*

*9. Treat everyone with fairness & honesty. Never lie about the money or the conditions. That way, no-one will ever have cause for complaint.*

*10. Avoid working more than twelve hours a day & six days a week. An exhausted crew becomes demoralised & ineffective.*

***Q - Did you ever overcrew?***

**Chris -** We just made sure there was enough crew to do the job. For instance, we had two make-up artists which was a conscious decision. The film is about two characters who were needed for shooting almost every day - with two make-up artists we were ready to shoot half an hour earlier every day. That was worth it.

***Q - You say it was a small crew, but the credits do seem to be quite extensive?***

**Gen -** Yes, if you have a low-budget picture it's a good idea to make up about fifty fictitious names in your titles especially if you only have 15 or maybe 20 people working on the team - it makes your movie look more expensive. A few extra credits can also stretch the length of your film if it is a little on the short side. Chris edited the film and I edited the sound. We chose to use pseudonyms to make it look as if we could afford an editor and sound editor.

***Q - Was the main reason for editing the film yourselves financial?***

**Gen** - Yes, it was mainly because we couldn't afford to get anyone to cut it for us, so we thought why not do it ourselves. Plus the fact, we wanted to learn the process of editing.

***Q - And are you pleased that you did it in the end?***

**Gen** - Yes, because we saved ourselves money and learnt a lot in the process.

***Q - What were the main difficulties in editing?***

**Chris** - Objectivity. Staying objective on something that firstly, you wrote, then directed, saw the rushes, sunk up, rough cut, fine cut - It's like the third part of a triathlon. Just being objective about material, *'should that scene have gone or should it have stayed?'* - and keeping the energy up whilst being wracked by paranoia. Technically, we didn't know what we were doing, we'd never cut anything before, so we just had to start on day one, with oops how do we edit film, and learn by our errors.

***Q - Did you find there was trouble keeping the story-line***

***running through it?***

***Gen*** - No, it was obvious when things either weren't working or when the pace was slower than a glacier. We actually didn't shoot too much, our cutting ratio was 4 or 5 to 1 so we didn't have too much material with which to go crazy.

*"The relationship between the make-up artist and the film actor is that of accomplices in crime"*
*Marlene Dietrich*

***Q - Did you storyboard?***

***Gen*** - No, we thought it to be a waste of resources for a low-budget picture. If you have a good storyboard artist and you can afford the time, then great, but otherwise you don't need it - WHITE ANGEL was also restricted by the locations and many times, the rough shooting script that Chris had worked out had to be scrapped because it just couldn't be done in the location we found, or because we just ran out of time and money and ended up shooting the scene in a single wide shot just to cover the action and plot.

***Q - Why Super 16mm?***

***Chris*** - Super 16mm is different from standard16mm in so much as the negative houses a larger picture area. It's pretty much standard 16mm stock with the right hand redundant sprocket hole dropped. This allows the picture area to expand giving a larger negative AND it maintains roughly the same aspect ratio as 35mm. This means that when blown up it creates an image that is roughly 40% better than if it were blown up from normal 16mm. It costs just as much to blow up

*The crew for WHITE ANGEL looks large when everyone is standing together, but every department was honed down to the absolute minimum required to get the job done quickly and efficiently.*

normal 16mm as it does Super 16mm, and it's expensive, but there is no denying, it is cheaper to get a movie in the can on Super 16 than 35mm.

*"Editing is crucial. Imagine James Stewart looking at a mother nursing her child. You see the child, then cut back to him. He smiles. Now Mr Stewart is a benign old gentleman. Take away the middle piece of film and substitute a girl in a bikini. Now he's a dirty old man"*
*Hitchcock*

***Q - How does it technically work?***

***Chris*** - Firstly you shoot super 16, that is expose super 16 neg. That neg is then rush printed, the rush print is cut by the editor, the final edit is agreed and the original Super 16mm negative is cut. That cut is then printed onto Super 16mm stock and when everyone is happy with the way it all looks (the grading), it gets blown up to 35mm interpositive then from that 35mm interpos to a 35mm interneg. That interneg is now the final master 35mm negative from which all the prints are made. (Both the 35mm interneg and Interpos need to be present for delivery to the sales agent). It is possible to do a direct blow up from the Super 16mm to 35mm print, but it is hellishly expensive and kind of pointless. If money is tight, you could produce a Super 16mm interpos and blow up at the interneg point - I've never done it but I have heard of other films doing it.

***Q - How did you decide the final cut for WHITE ANGEL?***

***Chris*** - We had about 95 million different final cuts - this is going back to being objective, because you're so damn close

*The Arriflex BL (right) is perhaps the cheapest camera that can be considered. Solid, robust and often somewhat noisy - and hey, it looks like a real movie camera*

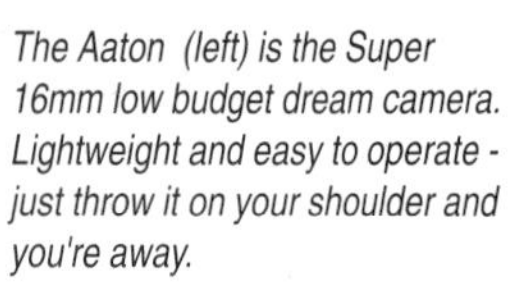

*The Aaton (left) is the Super 16mm low budget dream camera. Lightweight and easy to operate - just throw it on your shoulder and you're away.*

to the thing. We were really happy with our first final cut and had begun track laying and getting ready for the dub when our cameraman, Jon Walker came round and took a look at it. We were saying 'Isn't it brilliant...' but he reckoned we could loose some stuff. We went through the film slowly and Jon's point of view made us sit and think about it differently. We ended up cutting about 12 minutes out of what we thought was our final cut - we neg cut, printed it at a running time of 99/100 minutes and we went to the Montreal Film Festival and watched it with a full audience - they enjoyed it but it was quite obvious more needed to come out.

When we returned to the UK, we thought lets have another fine cut - we went back and cut another 6 minutes out, called that the final movie - re-premiered it at the London Film Festival and everything was going swimmingly. Then only 5 to 6 months later, we decided that we had to do yet another re-cut for the international market, to make the film more sexy and violent. We cut out 10 minutes, put some other stuff back in - all this is about 3 years after the film was shot in the first place! We needed more 'oomph' so we re-shot stuff, got Harriet back, with a completely different hair cut and reconstructed the film yet again. All the new stuff was shot on Hi8 video and helped give it a much more seedy and voyeuristic look - we are kind of pleased with it now.

***Gen -*** We also had an audience test with our first rough cut. We arranged a screening at some offices where the staff agreed to stop behind to watch the film - they were all complete strangers and we wanted to see what effect it had. They came back with - *well we thought it was great in this part, but maybe too slow in the middle* - so we decided we could chop out more in the middle. That was also the dreaded point when we discovered that the ending of the film was wrong and we had to go back and reshoot that.

***Q - The music is a strong part of WHITE ANGEL. How did you decide on a theme?***

***Gen*** - There were certain composers whose music we liked a lot, for instance Bernard Hermann who did most of Hitchcocks' movies, and we felt that WHITE ANGEL needed a Bernard Herman type score, with mystery, intrigue, suspense and a big orchestra feel. When we initially started out, we were going to have computer synthesised sounding music - then we found Harry Gregson-Williams who could

*"The length of a film should be directly related to the endurance of the human bladder"*
*Hitchcock*

## Choosing a lab

*The lab is where all your film is processed & in some respects it's the most important link in your chain. If something goes wrong at the lab, the consequences could be disastrous.*

*1. Lab contacts are usually very friendly. It's a good idea to go and look round a lab just so that you know roughly how everything is done.*

*2. Keep in contact with the labs & try not to run up a serious debt without funds to pay. When the film is ready for delivery, the lab could withhold the neg until payment is made. This is a big problem & should be avoided. Find out who the accounts person is & keep them sweet.*

*3. Find out which labs are used to feature film work and avoid the other labs.*

*4. Don't always believe what a lab tells you. Their staff can be ignorant and stubborn. Your cameraman can be a useful source of information here.*

*5. Get some figures from other production companies to see if the quotes you are being given could be bettered.*

*6. Labs are often a source of a good free lunch!*

## Choosing a film stock

*1. Choose the cheapest stock you can get. Ring round and get the best deal possible. Purists will tell you that X stock is better than Y, but at the end of the day, it's all graded and intercut and in our experience, mixing different film speeds (ASA) is much worse than mixing stocks.*

*2. Keep tabs on how much stock is being shot - if you are running low, make sure you can always get your hands on some quickly or simply buy more than you need.*

*3. Old stock is usually OK, but get it clip tested. Remember that everything you are doing is encapsulated in that negative.*

## Choosing a Film Format - 16mm V 35mm

*1. If you are seriously strapped for dosh, shoot super 16mm, it gives you a format which can later be blown up to 35mm, yet retains the price advantage.*

*2. Super 16mm is smaller, so the cameras are more lightweight, allowing shooting in smaller spaces. It requires less light to be correctly exposed, so it will save on lighting too. The down side is that when it comes to blowing up to 35mm it can get expensive and a little complicated - mistakes can be made costing the production money.*

*3. 35mm really has that feature look. Sure, it's expensive & bulky, but it is the industry standard.*

*4. If you are undecided, try for 35mm, you can always fall back on the saviour of the No Budget film maker, super 16mm.*

*5. For the whole lab process, from rushes to print, 35mm is about 3-4 times more expensive than super 16mm*

*6. If your film is never going to be projected, shoot Super 16mm and telecine the negative.*

## *Choosing Your FPS (frames per second)*

*The frames per second (fps) relates to how many still images are shot in any one second. The speed at which film is shot has several far reaching consequences. Traditionally feature films have been shot at 24fps and television films at 25fps.*

*1. Shooting at 24fps will mean when you project in the cinema the sound will stay the same as when you shot it. If you shoot at 25fps, the sound will be 4% slower. This can often be a desirable effect as it slightly lowers the tones of your cast.*

*2. Shooting at 24fps increases the possibilities of flicker whilst lighting with certain lights such as non flicker free HMI's (often hired on low-budget productions). We produced some tests and found there was no noticeable difference, but we would recommend you shoot your own tests.*

*3. Shooting at 24fps means you will shoot 4% less stock and 4% less processing. This can be a considerable saving.*

*4. Ensure that your soundman knows the speed at which the film is shot as he will need to include it in his sound report sheets. It is a good idea to get all sound and camera people together on day 1 and confirm the film speed. This will avoid possible disasters.*

*5. We would always recommend shooting at 25fps.*

## *Choosing your film speed (ASA)*

*1. The speed of a film is determined by its ASA. The lower the ASA the finer the grain and sharper the picture. However the lower the ASA, the more light is needed to expose the negative which has a direct effect on your budget. There is no real answer to this except try and shoot on as slow a stock as possible (The lower the ASA, the slower the stock - this does not relate to frames per second). White Angel was shot on Fuji 125 ASA Super 16mm stock.*

*2. It's always worth keeping a few cans of really fast stock in the boot of your car in case of disaster.*

*3. Film is balanced to the colour of the light in which it is exposed - that's why when you take snapshots indoors without a flash they come out orangey - tungsten light bulbs produce a warm coloured light which your brain automatically corrects for daylight. Check which kind of stock, tungsten or daylight, you will need before dashing out and buying 100 rolls. However, most low-budget films are shot entirely on tungsten stock (which is corrected with a filter if shooting outdoors).*

## *Looking after your negative*

*All your efforts as a film maker are sealed up in the negative which is exposed on set. It is therefore quite a good idea to treat your neg as though it were gold dust.*

*1. Make sure it is processed as soon as possible, but don't panic if you can't. Film is very tough stuff, it's just best not to try and temp fate.*

*2. On the whole, unless your ASA is very high, X Ray machines don't present too much of a threat to exposed negative, so don't attempt to bribe any official in a weird banana republic when entering customs - just let it pass through the machine and stay out of jail!*

*3. For a small fee the lab will store your neg in a vault at the correct temperature and humidity.*

## Final Cut

*It's likely that at some point, you may need to get involved with another company. If this happens they will more than likely demand 'final cut'.*

*1. Try not to give up the final cut. However, listen to what people tell you. If they say they are bored, it is likely something needs to be done, cutting scenes down for instance.*

*2. If you do have to give up the final cut, fight for your version in a diplomatic way. If you don't & things get nasty, you'll be sure your opinion will never be heard.*

*3. If you hate the final cut, don't worry. Five years down the line you'll never think about it, & if you see the picture, you may well agree with the re-edit!*

*4. Often, Directors will cling to scenes when they need to go. The final cut isn't an attempt to ruin the film, merely make it more palatable to the audience. In general, everyone has the film's best interest at heart. Remember this & don't let things get out of hand.*

*5. If the worst comes to the worst, then take action if you have to. James Cameron allegedly crept into the neg cutting rooms on 'Piranha 2 the Flying Killers' & re-cut the movie AFTER the executives had agreed on the final cut.*

*6. As a director or producer it is likely that you have less objectivity & more emotional investment in the film than anyone. Listen to other people's comments.*

pull off a brilliant 'orchestral sounding' theme and we jumped on him. He could take a few musicians and turn them into what sounded like the London Symphony Orchestra.

***Chris*** - At various stages during the editing, we cut a lot of music from other films into WHITE ANGEL in order to make it feel more like a finished movie. We used a lot of *Basic Instinct* - that had the right feel and pace. When it came to the music being composed by Harry, we said, listen to this, this is kind of what we want - and then he took all of what that music was 'saying' and regenerated it in his own original way and worked in his own theme and composition. At the end of the day the music doesn't sound anything like what we originally wanted, it sounds better as it is a completely original interpretation of the film. Dubbing on other music just helped everyone focus on what we were aiming at.

We also considered using out of copyright music because it's free. You don't pay copyright on the music, only on the performance. There were loads of music libraries and we could have used anything, from Brahms to Beethoven with a full orchestra for about £250 per thirty seconds. That's world-wide rights. The problem was finding the right music to fit the scenes. If you're doing Amadeus Part 2, then you're fine, but not a UK based serial killer thriller.

***Q - Sound mixing is where it all comes together, how did that go?***

***Chris*** - Most of the sound in WHITE ANGEL, apart from the dialogue, has been recreated in the studio, and by the studio, I mean our front room, not a several thousand pounds a minute studio. Most low-budget films suffer from poor sound and we were determined that WHITE ANGEL was at least going to sound good.

***Q - How does the dubbing process work?***

***Chris*** - We ran through the whole movie and we added an effect for every single little thing that happened, be it somebody putting a cup down, somebody scratching their face, whatever it was, we add an effect - all those sound effects were then track laid onto different pieces of magnetic film (which is the same size as picture film, but instead of pictures it's got a magnetic coat) - you can cut and chop it about any way you like.

We ended up with I guess about 12 - 15 tracks of sound - 2 music tracks 2 dialogue tracks, 3 or 4 effects tracks which would be stereo as would be the music, 2 Foley tracks, 2 or 3 atmosphere tracks - which would be background sound, and then on occasion 1 or 2 extra tracks for when we had problems or when there was a heavy sequence. All those tracks are then premixed, we mixed the 2 dialogues into one, the 2 music into one, the effects into 1, the atmos into 1 - we end up with 4 or 5 different pre-mixed tracks being atmos, music, dialogue, effects whatever, and those were finally mixed into one Dolby (surround) master, which is when it sounds great.

***Q - What is Dolby stereo?***

***Chris -*** There is a lot of confusion about this, Dolby produce several noise reduction systems which are free to use, but Dolby Stereo, often referred to as surround sound, carries a hefty license fee. To a low-budget film, Dolby Stereo isn't important at all, you can still mix in stereo, stereo doesn't cost a penny. *Dolby A* and *Dolby SR* are just noise reduction systems and they don't cost a penny to use either. Dolby Stereo (now called simply Dolby - helpful terminology huh?) is a type of encoding that creates a four track mix - left, centre, right and surround speakers. It's clever because it encodes those four tracks into two to make it backwards compatible with pretty much all the sound equipment in the world - that's why it carries the hefty license fee. When we made WHITE ANGEL, I think there was a licensing fee of about £3k, which was a lot of money, and they won't budge on it. But it adds that extra bit and you can stick their logo on the end - Dubbed In Dolby Stereo - it adds a little value to the film. If it doesn't have that at the end, then it's a sure sign that the film was ultra low-budget - really cheap. So it's worth considering but in terms of technical quality it's not absolutely necessary. THE RUNNER was not dubbed in Dolby Stereo and it can be argued that THE RUNNER has a better soundtrack than WHITE ANGEL. This may all be academic soon as digital sound is coming in and that doesn't need noise reduction and has it's own surround systems.

***Q - How did you prepare for the dub?***

***Chris -*** We had a hell of a time as we weren't ready for our dub. We had a new computer system on which the sound was laid and three days before the mix we found out that it

## The Final Mix

*This is when all your sound effects, music & dialogue are mixed into one. It's the most exciting moment of the whole process as your movie seems to leap into life.*

*1. Sound studios are expensive. Make sure you are prepared, your charts are clear & any creative decisions have been made.*

*2. You will more than certainly mix in stereo. You can opt for Dolby which is a four channel system, but a license fee will have to be paid. It isn't necessary to mix in Dolby, and don't let anyone bully you into it.*

*3. Dolby 'A' and Dolby 'SR' are noise reduction systems. It is advisable to make all your premixes with some kind of noise reduction. Dolby 'A' is more older and 'SR' is superior.*

*4. Get to know your dubbing mixer, and push them to be satisfied with 90% and don't waste time trying to get that last little effect absolutely perfect. A lot of the time, a film will mix itself so avoid trying to get that last 10% out of the mix, it will cost you 90% of your time!*

*Cont...*

*Cont ...*

*5. It is possible to mix a feature film in four to five days (with M&E - see point 8). Don't let the mixers persuade you into three weeks.*

*6. If you have a camera noise problem, it is possible much of it can be filtered out, but not all. Either post sync the dialogue or lay a heavy atmos track over it, eg. a plane flying over, or a printing press.*

*7. A good foley artist (or footstep artist) can work wonders. A foley artist is the person who adds all the rustles, footsteps etc. Spend a good two day session here and you will have a much livelier soundtrack.*

*8. Produce a Music and Effects mix (M&E) at the same time as your master mix. The M&E is a mix of the film without any dialogue, to be used for dubbing in foreign territories. This is essential and you will be unable to sell your film without it.*

was all out of sync. We had to start from scratch and re sync every effect. We worked solidly for three days and nights, I had never done that before, and I hope never to do so again. We were still cutting hours before the mix but we got there. Fortunately we had been good about track laying and everything was pretty much covered so there weren't any panicked cover up jobs.

***Q - What was it like in the dubbing theatre?***

***Chris -*** Great, it's where everything comes together. It's dark, it's loud and there are lots of plush sofas and free coffee. The only down side is that it's so expensive and there is always this urgency to get to the end of the picture. There is absolutely NO room for perfection in a low-budget dub. We paid about £200 per hour and mixed for two days, the second day we went late into the night. Big overtime, so I guess we needed three days. I would recommend a minimum of three days and five is better, that would give you time to cover the M&E mix as well. If you're not prepared, you're going to have a terrible time so have everything track laid, know your movie inside out, and just go for it. Good charts are also vital.

We had some pretty bad camera noise which the mixer managed to filter out - not all of it though, so we added a printing press over the top. Don't ever believe that you can get rid of 100% of a noise, unless you're prepared to cut it out completely (dialogue and all). There are amazing things possible at the dub but it all takes time, if you have a 2 hour movie, it takes you 2 hours just to go through it, and you have to go through it at least twice, once for pre-mixes and then your final mix, so you've lost 4 hours just in screen time, never mind changing reels. All this and there's still only 8 hours in the working day.

We did all our pre-mixes on 35mm mag as opposed to 16mm mag as the sound was better. Sure the stock was more expensive but you could get more on each roll. 35mm can handle up to six tracks where 16mm can only handle two. It also gets you up onto that 35mm industry standard format sooner.

***Q - What is the M&E mix?***

***Gen -*** The M&E is the Music and Effects Mix. When you're selling overseas, the buyer will want a copy of the soundtrack

without the dialogue so that they can dub over in their own language.

*"In a good movie, the sound could go off and the audience would still have a perfectly good idea of what is going on."*
*Hitchcock*

***Chris -*** To actually do the mix is easy, all the mixer has to do is to pull the dialogue tracks out - if you've properly track-laid it and there's good foley, there shouldn't be any problems. The problems with the M&E mix come when you're deciding on what format to mix. Full M&E in stereo or split Music and Effects? We did both in the end but the one we use most, if not all the time is the traditional split Music and Effects, music on track one, everything else on track two.

We also ran headlong into a problem at the telecine. Whilst the video format we chose could take four tracks of sound, (The full stereo mix on tracks 1 & 2, the M&E mix on tracks 3 & 4), we couldn't lay it all down at the same time as the telecine machine could only handle one set of 16mm magnetic sound at a time - we had two separate mixes, two separate sets of mag. We ended up having to telecine it once and then re-run the whole lot for the M&E mix - that doubled our telecine budget straight away, and like the dub, it's damn expensive to start with.

The way around this problem is to do a sub master of your final dub which would have a twin track stereo mix on tracks 1 and 2 and the M&E on 3 and 4. This would also act as your backup copy of the final dub should anything bad happen to it. When you get to the telecine you can then dump all four tracks down at the same time. The operator may give you crap about not being able to monitor it, but if it was alright in

*The dub can be a harrowing event and there is no space for perfection. Make all creative decisions in advance as a five minute discussion about a bird sound effect could cost you £30!*

the dub it should be alright in the telecine. The other problem we had is that the cinema mix is very dynamic and occasionally it would go too loud for the telecine. The only way around this is to compress the sound when doing the sub master of the final dub and M&E. That smoothes out all the spikes.

Again, check with your sales agent as to exactly what they require as it does differ.

***Q - By the time you go to the DUB do you always have a sales agent?***

***Gen*** - We didn't, but we did speak to a sales agent to see what they would want. By that time you should have sales agents interested enough for them to explain to you what they would require.

***Q - What happened about foley?***

***Gen -*** We had an amazing woman called Diane Greaves do the foley - the foley, or footsteps as it is sometimes called in the UK, is where someone adds all the sounds that an actor makes just moving around. She would add the leather creak in a jacket, the footsteps on gravel, the sitting on sofas. Diane would make a sound for pretty much everything that happened on screen. She would watch the film through and then do all the foley in one pass! She truly was amazing. We foleyed the whole picture in one very long day and it made all the difference in both the full dub and especially the M&E mix.

***Q - What was the first print like?***

***Chris -*** The first 35mm print we saw wasn't great - the sound disappeared half way through, it was really dirty and it was a bit of a nightmare as some cast members were present.

At the very last stage there was an accident in the lab and our neg was ripped. We didn't have any insurance so had to go back and reshoot! Thank goodness there were no actors in any of the shots that were damaged or that could have turned into a complete nightmare.

***Q - What was it like seeing the print for the first time?***

## Television Standards

*If you buy a videotape in the USA, it won't play back in the UK. This is because they have a different Television standard - NTSC. We operate on PAL. When you look at the world it becomes apparent that there are many different TV standards for which to cater.*

*1. When sending out a VHS copy for viewing, it is acceptable to send a PAL copy. Most companies now have multi standard VHS players.*

*2. PAL is a superior system to NTSC. If you intend to master a video tape, but also have to supply the tape in NTSC or SECAM, produce in PAL & make digital systems transfers to NTSC or SECAM. It is possible to do a separate NTSC telecine but this may well cost far too much.*

*3. SECAM & PAL tapes are partly compatible. If one is played back on the other system, the picture will go black & white, but it is still viewable.*

*4. Some domestic video recorders can play back NTSC & SECAM. There are some pro VHS decks which can playback & record PAL, NTSC & SECAM, the Panasonic WV1 for instance.*

***Chris*** - It was fine, we just knew it was going to be another uphill battle to get it all fixed.

***Q - Did you have any problems with the telecine?***

***Gen*** **-** Yes, firstly we produced a widescreen telecine which no distributor could use, so we had to do another. We mastered to D1 and the film was supposed to fit, but the tape ended fifteen seconds before the final end credit, so we had to recompile on another D1 tape.

*"The movies today are too rich to have any room for genuine artists. They produce a few passable craftsmen, but no artists. Can you imagine a Beethoven making $100,000 a year?"*
*H. L. Mencken*

The sound was not compressed in advance so we had to do another sound dub and lay the M&E down at the same time. The first print we got out of the lab was too dark so we had a battle with the lab to make up a new Super 16mm print with the printer lights increased to give a brighter image. So yes, we had some problems, it all got fixed eventually but it cost an arm and a leg in both time and money.

*The final telecine is an invigorating yet terrifying experience. It is the very last stage of production and once traversed, the film is technically completed. However, it is hellishly expensive and fraught with potential technical errors.*

"The Future. That period of time in which our affairs prosper, our friends are true and our happiness is assured" Ambrose Bierce

***Q - What was the first thing you did once you completed the film?***

***Gen*** - Slept for a week.

***Chris*** - Yeah but when we got our own VHS of the film we literally drove home at 100mph ran into the living room, put it on the telly and watched it. We'd spent the past two years seeing this film in bits and we didn't know what it looked like all strung together.

***Gen -*** We didn't know whether the film worked as a thriller or not. We never saw it in one continuous stream and this was the first time we could watch it from beginning to end.

***Q - What was it like?***

***Gen -*** Quick, it seemed to fly through. It was brilliant

***Q - What was next?***

***Gen -*** We then had to decide what on earth we were going to do with it. We started to contact sales agents...

*After completing the White Angel, Living Spirit began the lengthy and often painful process of trying to sell the film and make some money back.*

***Chris*** - We didn't have a sales agent or a UK Distributor on board. Miramax had made a few phone calls to ask what this strange film called *White Angel* was about, and a few of the big American players like Paramount and 20th Century Fox faxed us at three in the morning, which was quite fun, but essentially we had to start from scratch. Firstly, we set up meetings with five UK based sales agents and sat them down to watch *White Angel* - the idea was that we would then field the offers from those meetings.

***Gen*** - We couldn't afford screenings at a theatre where everyone would sit down and watch together, so we decided it would be better to give everyone their own individual screening in a small studio - we set up a really good sound system and monitor, dimmed the lights and let the film do the job. We sat outside, between the door and the lift so there

ORION PICTURES CORPORATION

VIA FAX: #011-44-

September 13,

SENT BY: JOHN FERRARO ; 6- 7-93 ; 2:17PM ; PARAMOUNT PICTURES→ 0285 82 843 ;# 1/ 1

Paramount Pictures

John E. Ferraro
Vice President
Acquisitions

MOTION PICTURE GROUP

June 7, 1993

Ms. Genevieve Jolliffe
Living Spirit Pictures
FAX: (44-285) 821-843

Dear Ms. Jolliffe:

I recently read about your film WHITE ANGEL and would like to discuss it with you at your earliest convenience.

Would you have a print of the film available for me to screen here at Paramount in Los Angeles?

I look forward to hearing from you soon.

Kind regards,

JF/dm

5555 Melrose Avenue, Hollywood, CA 90038-3197 (213) 956-5942 FAX: (213) 956-0240

A Paramount Communications Company

was no chance of them making a swift exit.

**Chris -** The reactions we got were mixed. First of all, Manifesto didn't turn up and we had to drop a tape off with them, Majestic watched it and left 5 minutes before the end saying it was too long and didn't have enough scope for them, Mayfair saw it and would get back to us, The Feature Film Company saw it and liked it but ummed and aahed. Finally, Miramax saw it and visibly liked it a lot - obviously Miramax is THE biggest distributor and sales agent of low-budget independent features in the world, and the fact they were interested was very exciting.

**Gen -** Their UK acquisitions rep sat and watched the movie and thoroughly enjoyed it. She told us that she believed White Angel could be a hit at the up-coming Cannes Film Festival - Peter could win awards and we would win Best First Film. She was sure Miramax could do a great deal with it. We talked about advances etc.

*Midnight faxes from Hollywood did prove to be a tremendous giggle and ego boost, but ultimately bore no sales. However, it was good to establish contacts and worth noting that even small obscure British productions do get noticed by the major players of LA.*

**Chris -** Yes, we were very specific about what we wanted - a big cash advance to cover the budget and pay the cast and crew, and that was all we wanted. We said we needed an advance of £450,000 against all rights, which was double what we needed, and that we wanted an answer quickly. She said, *No problem, I think we can probably do that and I can give you an answer in 48 hours.*

**Gen -** She told us that she was flying to New York for the weekend to see Bob and Harvey, and that she would like to take a copy of the film, and get back to us on Monday. She did get back to us, telling us that they had seen it but they hadn't got an exact answer yet - '*but we're all really positive*

*about it'*. She was very hyper about it, and again, we thought it was great.

However, as we ran up to Cannes the channels of communication dried up, even after this amazing amount of interest and promises. When we tried to contact her, our calls would either be directed somewhere or she was 'out of the office'. This was a little weird after she had been so positive. Then we got a letter in the post, saying *Thanks very much, we're not interested. Goodbye*; pp'd by somebody else.

*"It's much easier to do a £2m deal in Hollywood than to get a film on the BBC for £5,000"*
*Nick Marston*

Remember, this was after the intimation that we were going to get a very large cash advance with world-wide distribution, and we would pretty much win the Palm D'Or.

***Chris -*** The basic message is to take everything you hear with a pinch of salt, keep your options open, hassle for the money, and don't let the situation rest, pursue it. If you can't speak to the person, and they say they are still thinking about it, then you are in an awkward situation - they may still be thinking about it, or they may be giving you the run-around. However, if they really are interested they will come up with an offer within 7 days, and anything over 7 days, then I think you have to say, well thank you for the interest but really we want to show it to somebody else now.

***Q -Six weeks later you went to Cannes - did you take a print with you?***

***Chris*** - No, we didn't have a print then, remember we had shot on Super 16mm and making the 35mm blow up was going to be costly and we didn't want to incur any extra costs yet. We took about 40 tapes of the film (telecinied from the Super 16mm answer print) and 40 tapes of the trailer that we had cut the night before. We also put together some sales literature that was literally cut and pasted together and printed on a colour laser photocopier before being laminated - it cost us about £100 to do 50 of these brochures, but they looked really good. When we got to Cannes, people were very impressed and thought we had spent thousands on the marketing!

***Q - How do you gain entrance to the festival?***

***Gen -*** You are supposed to apply in advance, but most people end up leaving it to the last minute. The easiest way

"...It's Genteel English Dementia is Quite Unlike Anything Else"
David McGilvary
Film Review

WHITE ANGEL

The streets of London are once more in the grips of a serial killer - THE WHITE ANGEL, preying upon innocent, young women.

Ellen Carter, an award winning crime writer, once had everything going for her - an exciting career and a wonderful house.. However, with the investigation into the disappearance of her husband she became a suspect in a possible murder hunt - but without a body and no evidence, she was acquitted. Carters writing suffered and soon her financial situation forced her to rent rooms.

When Carter receives a reply to her ad in the paper for a 'Third Woman to share house', she & Mik, her friend and tenant, eagerly await the arrival of Leslie Steckler. Leslie, however, turns out to be a male - 'I'm sorry - I must have misread the ad.' Steckler turns out to be harmless, and quite charming. Mik enjoys his presence & soon Steckler has managed to worm his way into Carters confidence..

Steckler is in.

Soon, a darker side of Steckler begins to show.. He installs heavy locks, disappears late at night.. And seems to have a strange fixation with the young and pretty Mik. And all the time, Inspector Taylor, an old adversary of Carters is asking questions.

Steckler rifles through Carters cupboards and drawers - & with pleasure he makes a discovery - the plans of the house showing that a new wall has been erected.

Steckler smashes down the wall to discover what he suspected all along - the dry and decayed corpse of Stephen Carter - Ellens dead husband. As Carter returns from work she is confronted by Steckler - he explains who he really is - and what he really wants.. "You're a writer - I want you to write the life story of Leslie Raymond Steckler - the WHITE ANGEL - so that when I am gone, people will know the truth of my actions."

Carter has no choice - she is trapped - she cannot go to the police.. "You see, I have all the evidence against you in my safety deposit box, and should anything happen to me, it will go straight to the police.."

Carter reluctantly agrees and begins work on the book - Steckler is almost jubilant, he has found what he considers a kindred spirit..

Carter delves deeper with terrifying interviews. A bond of disgust and pity begins to develop - Carter is amazed and horrified at Stecklers evil deeds which go back years, even the murder of his wife.

Mik, Carters pretty friend mysteriously disappears and Carter returns home to find Steckler burying a body in the back garden. Carter is left with no option - she MUST stop Steckler - at any cost..

Posing as Stecklers dead wife, Carter manages to get into Stecklers safety deposit box and remove the evidence against her. Now Steckler has no bartering tool - no blackmail device. He has turned from the hunter into the hunted.."

(C) 1993 Living Spirit Pictures Ltd

*Glossy sales brochures were out of the question so a full colour A3 sheet was pasted up with photos and a synopsis of the film - the torn paper effect was in keeping with the serial killer theme. The results were colour laser copied and laminated. They turned out to be both cheap and effective.*

to gain access to the market is to turn up with a business card and two passport photos (just in case). Go to the festival accreditation, stand in a hot sweaty line, call yourself a producer when it's your turn and after a bit of pushing, you'll get a pass which will get you into everywhere you need to go.

***Q - So if you had to sum up Cannes in one sentence what would it be?***

**Gen -** Hot, blisters, hard work, expensive, bullshit, pornography, free drinks, little pieces of strange food on plates which you eat lots of because you can't afford the food.

***Q - Did anyone show an active interest in the film?***

**Chris -** Yes, we rented an apartment outside Cannes and drove in every day which worked out quite well as it was quite cheap to do that. We targeted every single world sales agent, visited all the hotels and every stand and told them that we had made this feature film called *White Angel* which was terribly good, *and* would they want to see the trailer, *and*

would they like to keep a copy, *and* would they like a copy of the sales literature, *here you are and thank you very much,* gave them a business card and took one of theirs.

*'All television ever did was shrink the demand for ordinary movies. The demand for extraordinary movies increased.'*
*Clive James*

***Gen -*** We felt we had to see exactly who was who, and what kind of films they did, so we knew precisely who to target. Obviously it was difficult to see the top people like Fox, Paramount or Universal etc., but everybody else who would have been impossible to see if you walked into their offices in LA, would be willing to see you in Cannes, especially if you have a film.

***Q - So Cannes is a great place if you have a film to sell?***

***Chris -*** Cannes is an experience which brings the film sales business into sharp focus.

***Gen -*** It is also about finding out which companies do what, learning the marketplace, meeting people either in their sales suites or at parties.

***Q - What happened when they saw your trailer?***

***Gen -*** We would walk in to their suites, chat to them about the film, show them the trailer and get some feedback - yes, no or maybe. Those who were interested asked to know if we were going to have a screening back in LA after Cannes. No company made an offer there and then.

*The British Pavilion at the Cannes Film Market - a hotbed of moaning film makers basking like beached lobsters in the sun.*

***Chris -*** The main problem is that sales agents are not at the market to acquire product but to sell their product so it's actually one of the worst places to go to get a sales agent. Cannes is about the only place a film maker can go to and know that anyone who is anyone in the film industry is within one mile from where they are standing. That in itself can make getting a meeting doubly difficult and you do have to be very persistent - most people are booked up before they even leave for the airport to go to Cannes!

***Gen -*** Out of the 100 people we saw, 80 of them were not the type of people who would pick up *White Angel* - they would go for schlock horror, movie rip offs, ninjas or porno - it's pretty sleazy. Films of quality seem to be sold independently and not at the market.

We saw a bunch of Iranian guys who saw the film and were interested, but we suspected they could be terrorists and decided not to do a deal with them. There was also an American company who thought it was wonderful and were very interested, but the thought that we would sign our film to a sales agent who was on another continent was quite terrifying in terms of keeping tabs on them and how much they were spending.

The only company who showed a real interest, was Beyond Films. Being an Australian company they felt more in tune with our way of thinking, and because we knew that they had picked up *Leon the Pig Farmer*, we felt there was more of a connection. Also at the time, they were doing incredibly well with sales for *Strictly Ballroom*. A week after Cannes we set up a screening for them in London - we felt everything was riding on this so we hired a screening room in Soho and sat their rep down to watch it in a theatre. He liked it.

Beyond made an initial offer of something like £8k and then upped it to £25k and finally up to £75k, which was structured over a period of three years. The delivery requirements were quite horrendous and they wanted the film for a term of fifteen years.

We were concerned because of our experience on *The Runner* and the idea of handing the film over to Beyond for fifteen years with a staggered (over years) advance that wouldn't cover our minimal budget didn't sit too well. We had immediate debts that needed to be met so we offered them a £300,000 buy out for all rights but they didn't go for it.

***Q - In retrospect, would it have been a good idea to take the deal?***

***Chris -*** Now that we know what we know and don't forget they were leaving the UK to us, perhaps it would have been a good idea - just to get rid of the film. The thing to remember is that we were acting in the best interests of the investors and the company, we felt we couldn't accept what we considered a low offer when the film had only just been completed.

The other thing is that we did believe in the film, we were confident we had a very high quality low-budget film. It is a

## *Cannes - A Survival Guide*

*1. The Cannes film market can be daunting. It brings the business of film sales sharply into focus and for that alone, it is a valuable experience.*

*2. If you are of a sensitive artistic nature - Don't go!*

*3. To gain entrance to sections of the market you need a pass. The pass is free but you need to get to the registration area at the Palais during office hours with a business card and two passport photos. Get your photos at home or get ripped off in town.*

*4. All the companies have suites in the hotels along La Croisette (the front). It's a hot, long and hard trudge to do them all.*

*5. Book your meetings before you go and be prepared to be shuffled around without notice.*

*6. When you arrive at the airport, get a train or the bus into Cannes as a taxi will cost you £50.*

*7. Arrange your accommodation in advance. There are villas and small holiday flats which are quite cheap but are a good drive out of town. Staying in town is very expensive. Sleeping on the floor and sharing with twenty other film makers is also an option worth considering.*

very hard decision to make and I guess one gets more experienced - what do you do if you believe your product is worth much more than your initial offers? How long can you wait before you have to take one?

***Q - When you were faced with delivery requirements, was there anything that you didn't know about?***

***Chris -*** We knew about basic delivery requirements because we had done *The Runner,* so we knew about the immediate things like the Music and Effects mix or colour slides and that kind of thing. What we weren't prepared for from Beyond was the 25 page fax of the most unbelievable requirements, even down to things like alternative out takes on original master negative. Half of these we just didn't have and couldn't get - I'm sure they thought it was necessary but for a low-budget picture, some of the requirements were totally out of the question. Most companies had this kind of list, some differing slightly - but when it comes down to it, if they wanted the film, they would compromise as long as the main elements are in place, and that's no mean feat!

***Gen -*** The one thing that we didn't know about at the time which came as a big shock was the Errors and Omissions Policy - an insurance policy which insures the producer and distributor against all sorts of weird legal actions, such as a person in America saying that the film is based on their brother - the only thing was that this would cost around £7k!

***Q - So the best thing to do, is to have a good idea of what you need to deliver and say there it is, take it or leave it?***

***Chris -*** If you can't afford to make *full* delivery, then essentially yes, but you do have to be sure of what the sales agent really does need to sell the film. There are a lot of things that don't actually cost a lot that are on the delivery list, like having the proper contracts with every one involved, waiver forms, release forms, chain of title, legal documents proving country of origin. All of these are cheap to get together, but they do take time.

A delivery list will usually say 75 high quality B&W photographs and 75 high quality colour photographs. With the best will in the world you're not going to have that many good quality pictures on a low-budget film, It's just not going

*8. Eating out is very expensive. There are lots of cheap food joints if you are prepared to search in the backstreets.*

*9. Parties are the lifeblood of Cannes - try and get as many tickets as possible. They are also a good source of free food and drinks. Whenever there is free food, eat it as you never know where your next meal is coming from.*

*10. The European pavilion offers a free message service for producers if you do not have a base. If you do have a base, take your answer phone.*

*11. Cannes isn't a place where deals are signed, it is a place where contacts are made and negotiations are opened. Almost all your business will be completed when you return, so don't expect to return with a napkin contract.*

*12. Remember why you are there and don't get too side-tracked by the glitz or the nightlife. Sure, enjoy yourself, but remember, EVERYTHING is business.*

The Hotel corridors at Cannes are packed sales booths all adorned with hard sell posters for a dizzying array of low brow B movies.

to happen - some lists require as many as 500 high quality photographs.

***Q - Apart from Beyond, was there any other interest at the film?***

***Gen*** - At Cannes we went to a solicitor's party and started chatting to two brothers, Simon and Andrew Johnson (Pilgrim Entertainment), who had made a film called *Tale Of A Vampire.* They told us how they had sold the film themselves to a US company, turned a healthy profit and managed to hold onto the UK rights. We felt they were on our wavelength. It appeared they had gone through the same process we were going through but had frustratedly decided to do it all themselves, and they had come out on top. They were very interested in teaming up with us, because we all shared the same goals.

***Chris -*** At the point of us turning down Beyond, Simon and Andrew of Pilgrim told us that they could guarantee deals with America and Japan through their contacts. They only wanted a three month window and ten percent so we decided to let them have a crack of the whip, after all they had been very successful with their film. Sure enough, within months we did have several deals on the table including a deal memo from Trimark who wanted the US rights plus Canada for US$120k advance plus extras which would top it up to roughly $250k.

***Q - How did the American deal come about?***

***Chris*** - Michael Cole from Trimark acquisitions had seen the film at the Montreal Film Festival in September where we had four totally packed screenings. Michael Cole sat in on our last and best screening with an amazing audience who loved it, and negotiations began.

"Shooting a film is like taking a stagecoach ride in the old West. At first you look forward to a nice trip. Later you just hope to reach your desination"
Francois Truffaut

Because of their previous relationship with Trimark we allowed Pilgrim to take over negotiations and they came up with the deal memo. Because of the Montreal screenings we started to get a lot of offers, Germany came in as we stepped off the plane from our return. We had to decide what to do, whether to extend our agreement with Pilgrim as sales agents or to carry on the negotiations ourselves. Because of the Trimark deal, we decided to extend the agreement and to leave all the negotiating to Pilgrim. The German deal

happened and we actually got some money.

***Q - How much was Germany?***

***Gen*** - Roughly £62,000 which was paid in three lump sums. Pilgrim took a slice off the top, about half was used to pay off some immediate debts and running costs which had piled up and the remainder was used to finance our UK theatrical release. Korea also came in at this point with an offer of $35,000 which we took. So at that point, we had nearly $350,000 signed, sealed but not delivered.

***Q - How quickly did things happen?***

***Chris*** - Firstly it would take weeks and weeks to negotiate a deal. The one thing that was really infuriating was that somebody would make an offer, and then you wouldn't be able to contact them until they came back from their 3 week holiday or whatever - time just goes by. And because you can't sit across a table from these people, you had to call and get through their secretaries who weren't speaking the same language - certainly, in Korea, I know that became a real nightmare. Whatever we did, we just couldn't get an answer quickly.

***Q - Were you ready to deliver once a deal was signed?***

***Chris*** - Aside from making up the 1" dupe tape, and patching up a few problems with the M&E, yes we could have delivered. The problem we had with the states is that Pilgrim negotiated what they called minimum delivery i.e all you need to sell and exploit the film. Trimark agreed and signed in a deal memo, and then changed the goal posts in the long form agreement. They asked for additional items that we didn't have, so we then had to go back to them saying we don't have these, and we've already agreed that you don't need these. Because we only had a one page deal memo that was not specific, they simply stood firm and stated that the detailed delivery list must be completed if they are going to take delivery. One major problem is that in the delivery list they mentioned the master 35mm negative - of course, we had shot on Super 16mm. Whilst this obviously made no difference to Trimark in terms of quality, they could use it to completely stall the deal.

***Q - Did Trimark have a copy of the film?***

*Delivery List*

*This list is by no means comprehensive, it is what we believe is the absolute minimum needed to deliver a film. Sales agents may add to this, or cover the cost of producing some items (deducting from any advance).*

*1. 35mm theatrical print with optical sound.*

*2. 35mm Internegative.*

*3. Master sound mix on magnetic film.*

*4. Music and Effects mix on magnetic or DAT.*

*5. Broadcast telecine (Digital video formats are now preferred). M&E mix should be split off onto separate channels.*

*6. Stills - at least thirty good shots, you can never have enough stills.*

*7. All contracts with ALL artists both in front and behind the camera. This is to prove that the producer actually owns the copyright of all aspects of the film.*

*8. Certificate of origin (proving where the film was made and by whom).*

*9. Full transcript of all the dialogue and action.*

*10. Errors and omissions policy (may only be needed for a US deal - will cost around £7-10k).*

*11. Lab access letter (From your labs).*

*12. Textless backgrounds (for shots where you have laid titles over images ).*

*13. Trailer on both 35mm and tape (plus internegs and sound mixes and trailer M&E).*

*14. Music cue sheets.*

*15. Continuity Report - like the transcript but in much greater detail writing down every single word, lyric, action, cut and shot.*

*16. Copyright notice for the USA.*

*17. Title research report (full US title search report).*

*18. Full cast and crew list.*

*19. Press pack with biographies and synopsis.*

*20. Billing requirements and restrictions (actors billing for instance).*

***Gen -*** They had a copy for about five months - it's a tricky situation because they said that everyone in the company needed to see it for them to finalise. They could have used that time to show the film to their prospective buyers and field the responses - basically get a commercial assessment of that product. Ultimately we couldn't agree on the delivery items and they refused to take the film.

***Q - What happened with your Korean deal?***

***Chris*** - After paying the £6k deposit the company who acquired the rights just disappeared off the face of the earth for six months - Pilgrim just couldn't get hold of them. After the American Film Market in February '94 they got back to us and explained that the film had been banned as it had 'immoral social values' - they faxed through the certificate of 'banning' (which for all we know could have been an insurance form) and asked for their deposit back. We told them that we had spent it and it was their problem if the film had been banned. So now, not only had we gone stale on the US deal but we had also lost the very considerable balance of the Korean deal.

***Q - If you made another film, what could you do differently, how would you overcome this problem?***

***Chris -*** You can't. The only thing you can do is make a film that will make the buyers go mad i.e. make a good film, give it to the sales agents and let them go for it. Hopefully you can trust the sales agent, but at the end of the day you can never really be sure - if a sales agent screws up, there's very little you can do as you have assigned the rights to them. I've never heard of any film maker being really happy with their sales agent on their first film.

***Gen -*** I suppose try and get a reputable sales agent and build up a relationship to make them want your next film.

***Q - So you make a loss on your first film in order to make your second film and get it right then?***

***Gen -*** I think our problem was that because we didn't get any money back from *The Runner*, we just didn't trust any other international sales agent with *White Angel* - that was the main reason why we went with Pilgrim. In retrospect, it was a mistake.

***Chris -*** The basic problem is that selling a British film is very difficult. There is a lot of 'quality commercial' product out there, satellite and cable are making prices drop with only the real hit films getting the premium sales. A good example is *Death Machine* which was handled by *Victor Films* - it was a sci-fi thriller, very unoriginal, but very slick - it was also relatively cheap, certainly no \$25m budget - yet the buyers went ballistic for the picture. That was a good position to be in - Vic Bateman could hold out and get the best deal and everyone's happy. But when you're making deals to territories for a few thousand dollars, those few thousand dollars are instantly eaten up on expenses.

외국영화심의확인서

1. 수입심의영화명(원명): 백색의 공포 (WHITE ANGEL)
2. 수입영화내역
가. 수입영화사 및 대표자: (주)유성필림, 대표: 김 용 동
나. 제작국 및 제작자: 제니에브조플린 (영국)
다. 색채 및 종류: 천연색, 극영화
라. 규격: 35미리
마. 감독: 크리스존스 (영국)
바. 주연: 피터퍼스 (영국)
3. 심의확인 내용(영화법시행령 제11조 수입추천기준에 의한 적합성여부)
가. 반국가적인 내용이 있다고 인정되는 영화
나. 사회질서를 문란하게 하거나 미풍양속을 해할 우려가 있다고 인정되는 영화
다. 외국과의 국교관계를 해할 우려가 있다고 인정되는 영화
4. 심의결과: 수입불가 (근친살해 및 잔혹살상 등 범죄수법 세부묘사)

영화법시행령 제10조 및 전문심의위원회규정 제4조에 의하여 상기와 같이 수입심의하였음을 확인합니다.

1994. 2. 21.

공연윤리위원회 위원장

as the Original

*Is this the Korean equivalent of the BBFC's certificate banning White Angel from public viewing, or is it an insurance form, or even the back of a Korean cornflakes box?*

What could end up happening is that the basic sales merely cover the cost of attending markets in the first place - it's a vicious circle. There really is very little you can do except make as good a film as possible and maybe speak to an agent before setting out - find out what they think they will be able to do with the project before it is committed to film.

***Gen -*** You can either make a movie like *Death Machine*, or go completely the other way and make an offbeat picture like *Clerks,* which Miramax picked up at Cannes when we were there. However, I guarantee the guys who made *Clerks* haven't seen anywhere near the money Miramax will have made. I guess the fact that they are now working for major studios is payment enough.

***Q - How do you get a film into a festival?***

***Chris*** - First of all you need to find out which are the best festivals, and where they are, when they are and apply at least 3 months in advance.

***Gen -*** For Cannes, which is really more of a market, there is a guy who comes over from Paris and watches all the British

## Selling - A film is worth what it cost (or it's perceived value)

*Without doubt, this is the area most neglected by first time film makers. Most films are produced in the blind belief that the movie will sell, often based on the film makers love of the project, and not on any form of market research. One of the main advantages with a low budget picture is that so little cash is spent in it's production, that very few sales need to be secured to recoup the cost. The disadvantage is that the film makers ignorance of how 'the business' works will probably result in them being ripped off.*

*1. Consider the viability of your film as a salesman. If I were a hard nosed buyer, would I want this film, and if not, why not?*

*2. First films are usually the fruit of a long held dream. From that perspective, if you feel the desire, don't worry about the commercial viability of the production. As long as the film isn't totally awful, and as long as you don't spend too much money, you should come out ahead.*

*3. Whatever format you shoot the film on, pretend it was 35mm. You don't have to lie, just don't tell anyone it was Super 16mm (Unless they ask, when you take a deep breath and tell a white lie, or cough up the truth). This is because buyers think 16mm is poor quality and cheap. It doesn't matter if they have seen the film and like it, they will still think it is a poor man's format, and the value of your film will plummet.*

*4. During marketing, think about whether you want to shout about how little you shoot the film for. Other films have used this tactic successfully in the UK, Leon The Pig Farmer for one, but abroad it can damage sales. In the eyes of a buyer, a film is worth what it cost.*

*5. Sales agents are tough to deal with, especially on a first film. If they sign your film, they will more than likely want a period of 15 years, 25% of sales, plus expenses. If the film is low budget, they will look at you as inexperienced and refuse to offer any cash advance. The upshot is that you will probably never get paid. You MUST try to get a cash advance, and one large enough to cover your costs. You will have to assume that you will never get any more money from the agents. It is sad but a fact that most first time film makers get seriously stung by unscrupulous sales agents / distributors.*

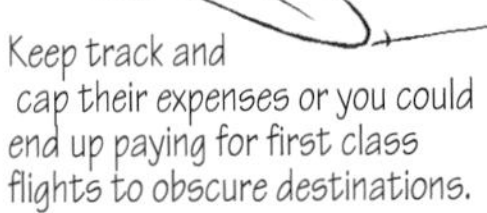

Keep track and cap their expenses or you could end up paying for first class flights to obscure destinations.

*6. Keep some territories for yourself. If your sales agent messes you around, this will mean you can approach distributors in a different country and make a direct sale. You will get a lesser fee because you are not a sales agent, but it's better to get 100% of a $50k than 100% of nothing.*

*7. Alongside your film, you will have to supply a huge amount of delivery items ranging from stills, NTSC versions, Errors and Omissions Policy, Chain of title - the list goes on (See Delivery list Sales Agent section in Anatomy of a movie). These are very important and often overlooked by first time film makers. Without these items, no sales agent will touch the film, or they will fulfil the delivery list and charge you. The cheapest and best way is to take care of it yourself. Study this list and make sure you know what each thing is, how much it will cost, and where you will get it.*

If a deal sounds too good to be true, it probably is....Get it in writing.

*8. In the UK you will have to consider certification from the British Board of Film Classification (BBFC) . Remember they will produce a certificate card which you will have to shoot and edit onto the front of every print.*

*9. Attending one of the big film markets like Cannes, MIFED or the AFM will broaden your outlook of sales agents, and of how films are marketed and sold.*

*10. In general, work on the assumption that if you are lucky enough to get an advance, that will be all you are going to get. £50k on the table can be worth more than a promise of £250k in twelve months.*

*11. Work out your budget, multiply by five, and use that figure as the official cost of production. This will raise the value of the film.*

*12. When negotiating, know your bottom line, and don't accept anything below it. If an offer is made, double it at least and more than likely a new offer will be made.*

*13. Get a sales agent involved early. They will be able to tell you how viable your project is. Listen to their advice on casting and script changes.*

*14. Remember, at the end of the day, the film must stand up for itself. Does it deliver all it promised? If it does not, don't hold on to dreams of millions - get out of the deal as fast as you can - take any sensible offer. The most important thing is to get your money back, make some profit for yourself and your investors, and move on to the next film.*

Demand regular updates and let them know you expect results. Don't be passive or they may be too.

submissions one after the other and then decides which will be put in for competition. You can contact him either in Paris before he leaves or in the UK when he comes over. Obviously he will be booking the films into his schedule so it is important to contact him as early as possible. He turned down *White Angel*, but a few months later faxed us and offered us another place at another festival in France. You can also hire a theatre in Cannes when you get there - many low-budget films do this to generate a buzz about the movie.

For a festival like Sundance (held in Jan) you have to make sure that they have seen the film by the end of July and obviously the earlier the better. So really you're looking at nine months in advance before applying. You should be scheduling your film festivals before you start principle photography.

The film only ever has one world premiere so it's important to use that on the best festival you can get - pass it around and field the offers - a good sales agent will advise you which are the best festivals to go for. In some respects we blew the premiere of *White Angel* at the Montreal Film Festival. If we knew more about it, we would have premiered at the Toronto Festival (which followed on from Montreal) as it has a reputation for being a buyers festival whereas Montreal is a bit more arty.

***Q - Do they pay for you to attend the Festival, how does it operate?***

***Chris -*** Send a VHS tape with the application form to the festival co-ordinator, they will then come back to you with *no we don't want it thank you very much,* or *yes, we would like to invite you to attend the Festival.* They will then invite the film and at least one member of the film making body which is usually the director, and may possibly invite an actor or the producer as well. Normally the Festival will cover the hotel bills of anybody who can get to the screenings (who is directly related to the film). They should also cover the flights for one person, sometimes they will do it for two, but not too often - it depends on how high

Fantastic Burgos 1994
WHITE ANGEL
Premio Feliciano Vitores
Mejor Opera Prima

*With the aid of the British Council, White Angel attended many film festivals & won 2 awards, Best First Film at the Burgos Fantastic Film Festival in Spain & Best Actor at the Valenciennes Festival of Action & Adventure in France. Below - a publicity shot taken in a back garden to publicise the awards, later printed in several magazines*

profile the film is at the festival (The festival will also pay for all shipping of the prints). Essentially the film maker should not spend a single penny to attend a festival.

***Gen -*** Watch out for small print - sometimes a festival will say that the producer must take care of the return shipment of the print, which can prove to be expensive.

***Chris -*** We got inundated with requests to attend festivals and it became impractical to attend them all. At a festival in Puerto Rico we met a top UK sales agent who charges $300 on top of ALL expenses. If a festival comes to us now and we don't want to go, they can have the film for $300 plus all expenses.

***Gen -*** I wouldn't recommend adding a fee if it's a festival you

*White Angel premiered at the Montreal Film Festival where it was very well received. The festival paid for the shipping of the print, one flight and accommodation for four in a five star hotel.*

## *International Film Festivals*

*1. There are hundreds of film festivals around the world - be selective.*

*2. Use your World premiere wisely - you only get one.*

*3. Choose the festivals with competitions, you may walk away with a prize.*

*4. The festival will cover ALL costs like flights, accommodation and shipping of the prints. Do not pay for any of these yourself.*

*5. Contact the British Council Films Department as they will offer assistance.*

*6. Make your application as early as possible, and if you can, send a press pack with stills (including a shot of the director).*

*7. Send a pile of press packs to the festival in advance, they will then set up interviews with their press. Take a BETA SP tape with clips (in both PAL and NTSC). Never leave that tape at the festival or you will never see it again!*

*8. Remember, it's a free trip, so go for a festival where you actually want a holiday - we spent a week in the Caribbean, all expenses!*

want to attend, particularly if they've agreed to pay for your flight, accommodation and a weeks stay in their country. But if they are asking to screen your film, and they're not going to accommodate you, or you don't really feel as though their festival is going to do so much good for the film - it's a small festival in the middle of nowhere - then, if the Festival wants your film, they will have to pay for it.

***Q - Did you find Film Festivals to be useful in the process of selling films?***

**Gen -** Yes, it's a FREE showcase for your product and it can create a profile for your film. If you enter a film and win Best Film or Best Actor, it creates a bit of a buzz about the movie, you get publicity and it becomes an '*award winning film*'.

***Q - Which Film Festivals has White Angel attended and has it won any awards?***

**Gen -** *White Angel* has attended 13 Film Festivals around the world - Montreal, London, Ankara, Sao Paulo, Puerto Rico, two in Rome, Mannaheim, Emden, Valenciennes, Burgos... and we won two awards - Best First Film at Burgos Fantastic Film and Best Actor for Peter, at Valenciennes.

**Chris -** The people that you need to speak to are the guys at the British Council Films Unit - get them involved as soon as possible, as they can help pay for you to go to Festivals. The other major thing to consider is that Festivals are a very good source of free holidays. I did more travelling last year than I had done in the rest of my life combined, and it was all expenses paid. Make a film just for the holiday.

***Q - What was the weirdest festival you went to?***

**Chris -** I remember I got a phone call from the British Council about a terrific film Festival that I should attend, give some lecture, go on telly and generally be a high profile British film maker. I said fine, where is it - 'Oh, it's the Gaza Strip Film Festival' - there was a very long pause. Eventually I was persuaded to go - I was even going to be sneaked across borders with guards being bribed! The whole trip got called off a few days before because some tourists were murdered and the Gaza strip was closed down. That was pretty weird.

***Q - Do the festivals expect you to promote the film?***

**Chris -** Yes, usually local press and radio, sometimes TV. The worst TV interview I had to do was in Turkey where I had been lined up for an interview at the local station. When I got there I was more than a little concerned as it was surrounded by razor wire and I had to pass through metal detectors and sniffer dogs to get in - I realised they were looking for bombs and weapons! Suddenly, it dawned on me, I was going on state TV - exactly the kind that was hated by extremist terrorists. I was then informed that my interview was going to be live, and it was the equivalent of the Turkish Wogan show going out to 47 million homes!

'To refuse awards is another way of accepting them with more noise than is normal.'
Peter Ustinov

The interview was nerve racking as it descended from chit chat about movies to hard hitting political rhetoric - I kept saying, *'I'm sorry but I don't know anything about the political situation in your country'* - which was then translated into a three minute speech! The last thing I wanted to be was a Westerner telling the natives what to do in their own seemingly fundamentalist religious country.

After it was over, both Gen and myself were thanked, passed back out, through the metal detectors, past the sniffer dogs and razor wire before being dumped on a dark and cold Turkish roadside.

**Gen -** Did you ever see *Midnight Express?* That sums it up.

***Q - When and how did the London Film Festival come about?***

**Gen** - The London Film Festival is the major UK festival. There is also Edinburgh, but London occurs in November and it's more of a showcase for British Films over a period of 2 weeks. *White Angel* was selected to play as the 'centre-piece' of the festival and was up there with *Remains of the Day* and *Farewell my Concubine.* We sent them a print of *White Angel* and they were very enthusiastic about it and wanted to push it. Eventually it was screened at the Odeon Leicester Square and it was great.

***Q - Was this good for the film?***

**Chris -** Yes, it was fabulous for the film. At the time it seemed to crystallise what we thought - firstly, we've got a fabulous film, and secondly, it was very commercial. This small film was suddenly put right up there, right next to 'Remains of the

15 MON 16.00 & 21.00 ODEON WEST END 1

**White Angel**

***Dir: Chris Jones***

UK 1993
Scr: Chris Jones, Genevieve Jolliffe
Leading players: Peter Firth, Harriet Robinson, Don Henderson, Anne Catherine Arton
Rt: 92 mins
UK Dist: Living Spirit Pictures

*White Angel* heralds the arrival of two young, talented filmmakers: producer Genevieve Jolliffe and director Chris Jones. More a film about serial killing than about a serial killer, *White Angel* offers a novel and very British view, whilst dealing with the complex (subtle?) differences between manslaughter and murder. Leslie Steckler (Peter Firth) is a soft-spoken dentist who rents a room in Ellen Carter's (Harriet Robinson) house. She is a successful writer on criminal psychology who is being hounded by the police in connection with her husband's disappearance. Meanwhile, London is in the grips of a serial killer, 'the White Angel', and the dentist and the writer become entangled in a dangerous game of blackmail. The plot is full of surprises, twists and turns (all best left untold) that keep you on the edge of your seat, relying on powerful psychological devices and avoiding unnecessary gore. In many ways it's a first in its chilling (fictional) portrait of a very British way of serial killing. Mesmerizingly good, and a triumph of British independent production. *Rosa Bosch*

*Great reviews a plenty at the London Film Festival, helping create a false sense of security*

Day' in Leicester Square. We got a lot of press and a very high profile. Suddenly we felt that it was all going to happen right here and right now. We felt very confident that the film was going to be a hit.

***Gen -*** And remember, at this time we were negotiating with America, Korea, and Germany - signed deals were on the table, it's just the money still hadn't come through.

***Q - What about the UK theatrical release?***

***Gen -*** The theatre manager of the Odeon Cinema at Leicester Square told us that he liked *White Angel* - *'it had an amazing effect on the audience'* - and that he would like the film to be screened at his theatre. He told us that if Rank Film Distributors picked it up then he would get it - he had a few colleagues at Rank that he would put us in touch with and put a good word in for the picture.

We decided to get in contact with Rank Film Distribution who requested a private screening there at their offices. They laid on sandwiches and wine, all the razzmatazz, and had four or five of their people viewing the film. They told us they loved it, thought it could work very well and they wanted it.

***Chris -*** After we screened the film, we sat down and they made an offer of something like £25k advance against a UK theatrical plus half of the UK video. After several discussions

and haggling we got that up to I think £65k. In reality we believed that if we took that deal we would never see more than the £65k offered, and I still believe that, although it was still a very good deal.

Rank guaranteed to do a P&A spend of around £70k which again sounds a lot but it's not huge. It would have ended up going out in five theatres with a lot of advertising. We did the maths and felt we could make more if we did the release ourselves, so we turned down the deal which I think was a shock for them. In hindsight we should have taken the deal, we still wouldn't have broken even but we would have been a hell of a lot closer. Out of everything we ever did, I feel that turning down that deal was the only real and stupid mistake we made.

***Gen -*** That said, the money Rank were offering would mean that we still would be unable to pay the cast and crew. As the German, Korean and US deal which totalled $350k were about to come in, we thought that we could afford to take a risk to make more by self distributing. Pilgrim did their own release with *Tale of A Vampire* and did extremely well, certainly better than Rank's advance. We watched *Tale of A Vampire* and in comparison, we felt *White Angel* was a superior film and would therefore do better. It doesn't actually work like that as we later found out. It's more to do with marketing, the type of film and timing - but at the time, we didn't know that.

***Q - So you decided to release your film theatrically, so what is involved in doing that?***

***Gen -*** Firstly we had to decide how wide we were going to release, on how many screens and work a budget out accordingly. Because of Pilgrims experience with 'Tale Of A Vampire' we took a lot of their thoughts on board and they wanted to open quite wide. Initially we were going to open in three theatres only, but they had a screening with the exhibitors who offered them more screens - everybody liked it which meant that it would be picked up by the multiplexes. So our three screens then developed into fifteen scattered around the country in the major cities which increased our advertising budget. The other thing we had to do, was to get hold of a theatrical booker to actually get the film in the theatres, someone who knew how the system worked.

'When producers want to know what the public wants, they graph it as curves. When they want to tell the public what to get, they say it in curves'
Marshall McLuhan

***Q - Who is the Booker?***

***Chris -*** The booker is the person who engineers and schedules the booking of screens and the moving of the prints. For instance, they will tell you the dates where your film will be screened, and the dates that the film is moved from one theatre to another. So with 15 prints we would move from 15 theatres to another 15 theatres, moving around the country until, hopefully, we had covered every major city and town.

***Q - What happened about publicity?***

***Chris -*** We had to hire a publicist, but a lot of the publicity we did ourselves, and eventually became quite good at getting newspaper interviews, radio and TV. We discovered that telling the occasional white lie or even complete outright lie would always be good for publicity - always managing to get a good column in a newspaper. That was a good way of generating interest around the film.

***Q - Did you arrange a press screening before the theatrical release?***

***Chris -*** Yes, there's a thing called the SFD (Society of Film Distributors) which sets up special screenings for journalists. We set up several in the 'local' towns and cities as well as the major screening in London. We went to the one in London and introduced the film to a bunch of famous journalists who were shocked and seemed offended that I actually turned up to introduce the film. One guy actually wrote that I came out begging for a good review. We seemed to get universally bad reviews from that screening which,

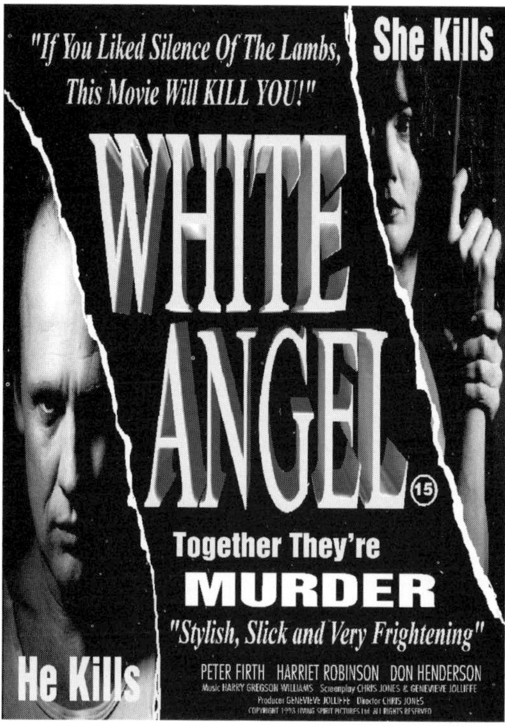


*There was so little money for the release that the film's poster had to be put together on a PC*

sour grapes aside, I think was rather unfair. Surely it's not THAT bad a film?

***Q- Do you think the London Film Festival's good press had an effect?***

***Chris -*** Obviously they all had their own opinions about the film, but I think it's fair to say that having the London Film Festival putting us on a plinth and actively using the phrase "Mesmerisingly good and a triumph of British Independent Production" perhaps nurtured a false sense of quality in our film that actually may not have been there. It certainly raised the expectations of the critics as what they actually got was a standard, commercial, ultra low-budget thriller. One interesting thing is that almost ALL the magazines gave us fair to good reviews whilst the 'dailies' unanimously slaughtered us. Maybe that has something to do with youth culture, I don't know.

'Asking a working writer what he thinks about critics is like asking a lamp-post what it feels about dogs'
Christopher Hampton

***Q - In retrospect, would it have been a good idea to take***

***some of these people out to dinner and tell them how you made the film, win them over so to speak, instead of hyping the film out of proportion?***

***Gen -*** Yes, because the journalists who we did sit down with and have long chats with were the people who gave us favourable reviews and all of them were loyal enough not to mention the budget. The problem here was that we were in essence sitting between two goal posts and we were stretched to the limits. We didn't have the financial resources to schmooze people, nor did we have the contacts in the first place. We didn't have the power to demand a favourable or non committal review (or we'll pull £10k worth of advertising from your mag for instance), and you read a lot of non committal reviews. Quite simply, we didn't have the resources to do the job properly within the set time frame. That's the job of a distributor.

***Chris -*** I think the problem with the WHITE ANGEL release was the film itself. I think we aspired to a big budget style film with very little money. When you see a thriller up there on the screen, people expect Bruce Willis, blue light and a lot of gloss. We didn't have all that. What we had, was a TV style film that was a competent thriller and we were actively marketing it as an 'A' movie super duper thriller.

***Chris -*** To some degree, a film appears to be valued at it's perceived cost. If you go down to a used car salesman and say how much is this car, '£1,000' he says. Then you ask how much is this other one? and he says '£10' - they may both look the same but you'll think there is something wrong with the £10 one. And it's the same with films. Why go and see a film if it only cost £50,000 to make when you can go and watch Bruce Willis in a film that cost $40m, or another film that has been critically acclaimed. Why bother going to see this small British thriller? That was the double edged sword we were on. So on the one side of the coin you want to get on top of the building and shout *"you won't believe what we made this film for"* but at the same time you know when you do that you devalue the film, which is exactly what Barry Norman did on Film '94.

"White Angel is stylish, slick and often very frightening - everything you don't expect from British movies"
SELECT MAGAZINE

"Unpretentiously gripping and solidly commercial, White Angel deserves more than a little glorification"
Mark Wyman
FILM REVIEW

"A chillingly impressive film... White Angel is so scarily sinister, it makes Psycho look like an old Ealing comedy."
Sam Steele
NME

"A cracking thriller with plenty of edge-of-the-seat tension... and more twists and turns than a Dune sandworm"
VIDEO WORLD

*'In the arts, the critic is the only independent source of information. The rest is advertising'*
*Pauline Kael*

He criticised the film, which is fair enough, he's a critic and it's his job. But one particular comment absolutely destroyed us. And that comment was "This is no more than a 90 minute student film" - Why bother going to see a 90 minute student film, when you can go and see a 90 minute "real" film. If he had panned the film it would have been alright as people do have opinions, however he put a value on the film and consigned it to the bargain basement. That's the problem you're up against with a low-budget film.

"This occasionally laughable and often inept British thriller from young hopefuls... hard to take seriously"
Wally Hammond
TIME OUT

Also, low-budget films were fairly passé when we released 'White Angel' - 'Leon The Pig Farmer' had done it very well and there were a couple of other films that had done it, and nobody seemed interested in yet another low-budget British film.

"It's crass and amateurish, and looks as if it was shot for about threepence-ha'penny...
DAILY MAIL

***Q - So you claimed not low-budget, but fairly low, you claimed to have made the film for just under a million?***

***Chris -*** The phrase we used, was that the film cost less than a million.

"I had a bad feeling about this one even before the opening credits had rolled because its young director, Chris Jones, gave a grovelling speech at the premiere begging us to like his movie"
Julian Brouwer
HARINGAY INDEPENDENT

***Q - In retrospect, do you think you should have been straight?***

***Chris -*** I don't know. I think a lot of critics may have thought where did all the money go, but then again, we never said it cost a million, just under a million. It is impossible to gauge how much of an effect the bad reviews had, they sure didn't help, but I'm not so sure they damaged us terribly. Most people seem to ignore critics. There were probably other factors other than the reviews that helped the film fail at the UK box office.

"aaaaargh!"
Alexander Walker
THE TIMES

***Gen -*** There were other things, like when we booked our opening weekend, we didn't have six months leeway to book in reviews with the big glossy magazines, so we lost a lot of publicity there. The youth magazines could fit us in as they had a much quicker turnaround, and luckily we got in there with some great reviews. And we just couldn't afford TV advertising.

*'Take heed of critics even when they are not fair; resist them even when they are'*
*Jean Rostand*

*The old 'director pointing' press shot - it was actually taken a week before the London Film Festival in a front garden.*

***Q - Would it have been a good idea at the time of production to have got more journalists involved?***

***Gen -*** We did attempt to do that. 'Empire' were interested, they came on set for a day, took another day taking photos - it seemed to go well. But nothing came of it. They never used it in the magazine. Unless you have Liz Hurley and she's wearing 'that dress', most journalists aren't interested. You need a good sensational angle.

***Q - In terms of the prints & advertising, how important do you think the poster is?***

***Chris -*** The poster is the only point of sale that the film actually has. Posters are expensive, they're a couple of grand, but that's for as many as you could ever really want. I believe they are absolutely vital. It's the only point of sale where you can make your movie look like all the other Hollywood major movies - we made the name as big as we could on the poster so that people remember it.

Two small ads were placed in the Evening Standard, probably two inches by 3 inches over the weekend of the release, which cost us around £5,000 (and the Evening Standard isn't even national). 5000 A1 full colour posters cost us £2,000. You can see how cost effective posters are.

***Q - You had a fairly wide UK release with the film but it didn't go very well, what happened?***

***Gen -*** The big thing that went wrong, was that we released on a dreadful weekend, one of the worst weekends in the year. We had no control with the theatrical booker and were naive about the distribution side of the industry. We only found out afterwards by actually visiting the theatres, usually to help promote the film, and talking to the managers. They all said, 'why did you pick this weekend? This is traditionally one of the worse weekends in the year'. Oops.

***Q - What weekend was it?***

***Gen -*** It was the weekend immediately after the Easter Break. Everybody had gone to the cinema the week before and there were box office records, but the following weekend, our weekend, they were all going back to school, back to

college, back to work after their Easter break. Unfortunately nobody wants to open on that weekend, but because we didn't know, there we were in that slot.

**Chris -** Again, if we had gone with a reputable distributor, that distributor would have said, we're not having that weekend, forget it. So again we learnt. But in retrospect we now know all these things, which we wouldn't have found out if we had gone the other way.

***Q - It occurs to me that Films have a very short shelf life?***

**Chris -** The film only gets one premiere, people can only hear about it for the first time once - that's the point to hit. If the American deal had been made through a reputable sales agent, the sales agent would, firstly, have a relationship or, secondly, the clout to say 'put up or shut up'. If that deal hadn't happened, something else would have come into place. But because it hung about on the shelf, nothing happened and *White Angel* was old news.

***Q - So the belief you had in the film from the London Film Festival was one of the downfalls?***

**Gen -** It inflated our perception of the value of the film. In our own minds we believed it was worth much more.

***Q - Do you feel that sales agents, international buyers etc, are out there to rip you off?***

**Chris -** It's not that they're out to rip you off, but again, it's the inherent problem of having a low-budget film. It's not worth very much, and it's not worth anybody's trouble to sell it. And even if they do sell it, they'll never make enough money to make any real profits, and at probably just cover their own expenses.

The advice I would extend to a new film maker is to get to the best sales agent you can, get to the best UK distributor you can, get as much money up-front as you can, and write the rest off.

Do not assume you'll ever get anything else back. Try and get an advance that covers your debts because your investors may never get paid anything else. The rest is really

## *The Press*

*1. Try and get a PR agent on board. If you cannot afford one, go ask for advice and do it yourself.*

*2. Doing press for a film is pretty much a full time job, especially in the run up to a release - don't try to take on too much.*

*3. A press pack is vital. It should contain a synopsis, cast and crew biogs, production notes and four or five good stills, including one of the director.*

*4. Work out the unique selling angle of your film and play on that. If the film is controversial, stir it up even more.*

*5. An electronic press kit is also helpful - a copy of video taped and loosely edited interviews with cast and crew with long clips from the film and shots during production. Usually supplied on Beta SP.*

*6. Journalists will almost always hunt out the story - if you don't want it to be printed, don't tell them - EVER.*

*7. Magazines work with long deadlines, contact them as early as possible.*

*8. Your story will probably only break once, so try and time it for maximum effect i.e., the weeks leading up to your release.*

*9. Local press, TV, newspapers and radio are easy to get and can help solve pre production problems.*

*10. Avoid talking about the budget and focus on the film and it's unique selling point.*

*EPK - The electronic press kit contains shots taken during filming, very roughly edited interviews with key cast and crew plus several clips from the completed movie. It should be delivered on Beta SP and is vital if any TV coverage is to be expected.*

up to the performance of the film and whether the sales agent is honest. If you cling on to it you're dead in the water anyway. Psychologically, write it completely off the moment you have completed the film, don't hang around, get going on your next picture or your first film will become a millstone around your neck. That's what happened with *White Angel.*

***Q - What other problems did you encounter?***

***Gen -*** We had unexpected events that occurred after our theatrical release which delayed our entire process.

***Chris -*** Basically the film was released and the press were saying how amazingly well we were doing and that we were making loads of money. In real terms we were doing terribly badly. At that point we also lost the US deal and the Korean deal. Suddenly, from having around $350k coming in to us we found ourselves high and dry owing £30,000 from the losses on the UK theatrical release, which was pretty much paid for by the German deal. Not only had we lost all our deals but we had also lost all the money that we had made.

At this very point (long pause) - we had a bit of bad luck. We had just got back from the Cannes Film Festival and at seven o'clock in the morning the doorbell rang. Three of us were living in this house. Myself, Gen and another friend. I went downstairs and eight policemen barged in, and arrested all of us, searched the entire house, drawers, shelves, floorboards - you name it, they searched it - and impounded all our Living Spirit files, floppy disks and equipment.

'All publicity is good, except an obituary'
Brendan Behan

***Gen -*** This also included sifting through my underwear, reading my diaries, looking through photo albums... They

discovered the fake gun that we used for the film and there was a flurry of excitement... "Weapons possession..." I entered the office to see three policemen holding the gun on the end of a pencil, examining it in every detail. I pointed out that it was a replica used for the film - "oh yes, of course, we knew that"...

'I'm not against the police; I'm just afraid of them'
Hitchcock

***Chris* -** Basically, they believed we had been making lots of money without declaring it. At that point we had applied for housing benefit as we had absolutely no money, especially with everything falling through. They had read all the press and seen the publicity and believed that we were not entitled to that benefit, firstly because the newspapers said we were doing well, and secondly, they couldn't believe that a film company could make and release a film and be broke. Obviously if they read this book they may see things differently. Anyhow, we were taken down to the police station, shoved in a cell, belts and shoelaces taken off to make sure that we couldn't hang ourselves, read our rights - the works.

***Gen* -** That was if you were wearing a belt and shoelaces, and not still in your nightshirt like myself.

***Chris* -** They closed the cell door and it felt like they were throwing the key away. That was it, Kaput. We asked them to call a duty solicitor which they finally did, and a few hours later, which felt like days, the solicitor turned up. He asked what was going on as he was used to representing murderers and rapists - and we certainly didn't look like the murderers or rapists he usually dealt with. It was really bloody horrible at the time. We didn't know what the hell was going on. He told us he would sort it out and we would be out immediately. It didn't quite work that way.

***Gen* -** Eventually we were given our interrogation where all our positive attributes as film makers, bullshit, bending the truth, running through the wet paint etc, became indicators of criminal intent. They were quite sure that we had committed serious criminal fraud and continued what we felt were ludicrous lines

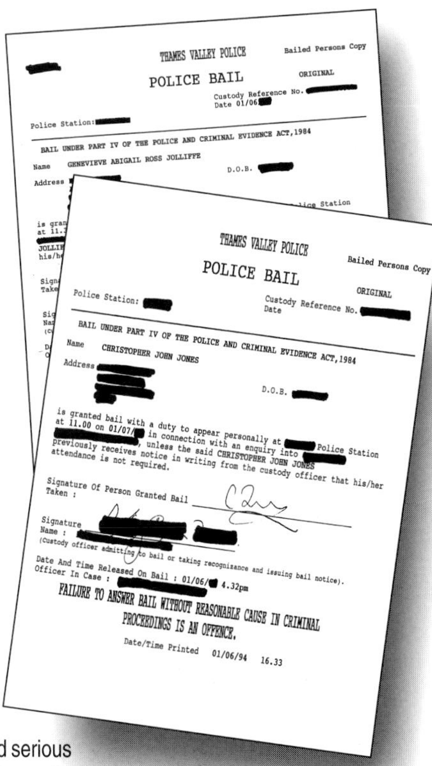

THAMES VALLEY POLICE
Bailed Persons Copy
POLICE BAIL
ORIGINAL
Custody Reference No.
Date 01/06
Police Station:
BAIL UNDER PART IV OF THE POLICE AND CRIMINAL EVIDENCE ACT,1984
Name GENEVIEVE ABIGAIL ROSS JOLLIFFE
D.O.B.
Address

THAMES VALLEY POLICE
Bailed Persons Copy
POLICE BAIL
ORIGINAL
Police Station:
Custody Reference No.
Date
BAIL UNDER PART IV OF THE POLICE AND CRIMINAL EVIDENCE ACT,1984
Name CHRISTOPHER JOHN JONES
Address
D.O.B.
is granted bail with a duty to appear personally at Police Station at 11.00 on 01/07/ in connection with an enquiry into , unless the said CHRISTOPHER JOHN JONES previously receives notice in writing from the custody officer that his/her attendance is not required.
Signature Of Person Granted Bail
Taken :
Signature
Name :
(Custody officer admitting to bail or taking recognizance and issuing bail notice).
Date And Time Released On Bail : 01/06/ 4.32pm
Officer In Case :
FAILURE TO ANSWER BAIL WITHOUT REASONABLE CAUSE IN CRIMINAL PROCEEDINGS IS AN OFFENCE.
Date/Time Printed 01/06/94 16.33

## Long Arm Of The Law

*Lets hope you never have to spend an evening in a cell - but if you do...*

*1. When you are arrested & taken down to the station you are offered a phone call & a solicitor. Use them. The solicitor is independent - you do NOT have to pay him as he's supplied free, by the state.*

*2. If things look difficult, refuse to answer any questions until you have spoken to your solicitor. You don't know what angle the police are looking for so keep stum.*

*3. You can have your solicitor present during interviews and can stop the interview to talk to your solicitor.*

*4. Assuming you are innocent, or at least relatively, co-operate as much as you can, but always with the solicitors 'say so'. Remember, the Police are very powerful - don't antagonise them.*

*5. Unless you are charged, they cannot take your photo or prints.*

*6. Stay calm & listen very carefully to all the things they say to you - this isn't the movies, you have rights & they have rights.*

*7. Remember, you are innocent until proven guilty in a criminal court. You have to be proven guilty beyond all reasonable doubt (unlike civil).*

*8. Don't panic, unless you have committed a serious offence you will be out in under 24 hours.*

*9 . Remember, a civil offence is NOT a criminal offence - there is a world of difference between the two.*

of questioning. And remember, at this time we are surrounded by a bunch of pretty hefty police officers in a room with a tape recorder and pretty much being shouted at. When you hear about it, you always think I would do this or that, but until you have been put in a cell and had your entire life and home opened up in minute detail, you just can't appreciate what it's like.

Anyhow, we were released on bail to appear in one months time for an interrogation, sorry, interview. We couldn't leave the country, so it was a damn good thing we had no festivals to attend and in fact, as everything to do with the film or Living Spirit was in the Police station, we couldn't actually do very much apart from watch our future go down the tubes. Our bank managers and investors got letters from Thames Valley Police, asking for information relating to Living Spirit, ourselves and fraud. Our poor friend who lived with us, and who has nothing to do with making films, was considered to be an accomplice in our big operation. They went and interrogated our landlord, not surprisingly we ended up leaving a few weeks later. We were all in this together according to the police. It was astounding.

***Q - So how did this all happen?***

***Chris*** - Quite simply, they had seen some of our press, wondered what on earth a big film company's directors were doing claiming housing benefit, put two and two together, got three million and decided to jump on us. They even had press clippings we didn't have, so they must have done a lot of research. They confused off shore bank accounts belonging to my brother, who at that time lived in Germany, with me - they also confused Gen's father's credit card with me - they thought I had about six different identities! Slowly, it became apparent that what they thought was a big fraud operation was actually a couple of people who were completely broke trying very hard to make the best of a very bad situation - and they had just made it infinitely worse.

***Q - How long did it take them to solve this case?***

***Chris*** - About four months to assess everything and to say *'No, we're not going to press any charges'.* Two months after that we got all our information back. So all in all, 6 months, during which we got heavily fined by the VAT office for not having completed our return in time.

***Gen -*** And that was the end of it - but it had created a ripple effect that, combined with the failure of the film at the Box Office and the falling through of all the international sales, crippled us for 12 months or so. During that twelve months, Pilgrim Entertainment did zero business - we couldn't chase them because our plate was more than full just picking up the pieces. One month after we were in the clear, Rank to whom we still owed £30k, sent us a letter saying pay us within 48 hours or we will force you into liquidation. We then had to start negotiating how we were going to get out of this hole. At that point, we decided the best thing to do was to terminate the agreement with Pilgrim Entertainment and take the film ourselves to find new UK distributor and international sales agent. Within days we had The Feature Film company on board to handle the UK video, satellite and TV through Polygram. We had some interest from some international sales agents but couldn't nail anything down. But the UK video was a new source of real cash that could come in for us.

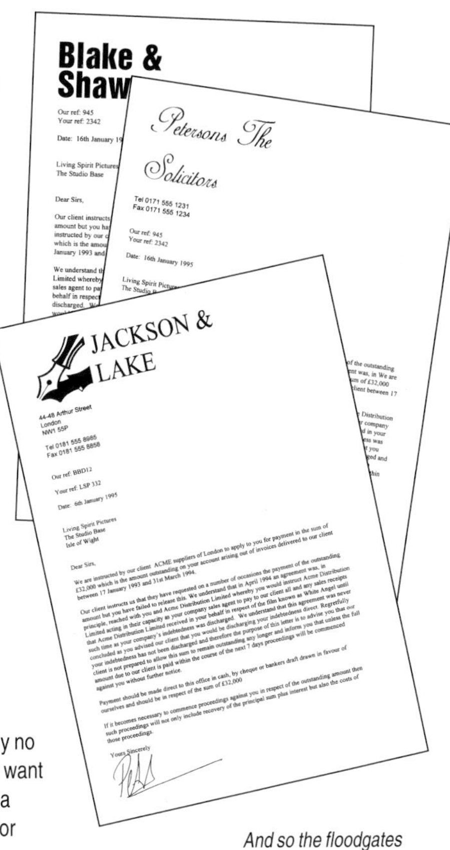

Blake & Shaw

Our ref: 945
Your ref: 2342

Petersons The Solicitors

Tel 0171 555 1231
Fax 0171 555 1234

Our ref: 945
Your ref: 2342

Date: 16th January 1995

Living Spirit Pictures

JACKSON & LAKE

44-48 Arthur Street
London
NW1 55P

Tel 0181 555 8985
Fax 0181 555 8858

Our ref: BBD12

Your ref: LSP 332

Date: 6th January 1995

Living Spirit Pictures
The Studio Base
Isle of Wight

Dear Sirs,

We are instructed by our client ACME suppliers of London to apply to you for payment in the sum of £32,000 which is the amount outstanding on your account arising out of invoices delivered to our client between 17 January 1993 and 31st March 1994.

Our client instructs us that they have requested on a number of occasions the payment of the outstanding amount but you have failed to release this. We understand that in April 1994 an agreement was, in principle, reached with you and Acme Distribution Limited whereby you would instruct Acme Distribution Limited acting in their capacity as your company sales agent to pay to our client all and any sales receipts that Acme Distribution Limited received in your behalf in respect of the film known as White Angel until such time as your company's indebtedness was discharged. We understand that this agreement was never concluded as you advised our client that you would be discharging your indebtedness direct. Regretfully your indebtedness has not been discharged and therefore the purpose of this letter is to advise you that our client is not prepared to allow this sum to remain outstanding any longer and inform you that unless the full amount due to our client is paid within the course of the next 7 days proceedings will be commenced against you without further notice.

Payment should be made direct to this office in cash, by cheque or bankers draft drawn in favour of ourselves and should be in respect of the sum of £32,000

If it becomes necessary to commence proceedings against you in respect of the outstanding amount then such proceedings will not only include recovery of the principal sum plus interest but also the costs of those proceedings.

Yours Sincerely

*And so the floodgates opened as solicitors, undersheriffs and bailiffs made Living Spirit their business...*

We had been made homeless and had absolutely no money. We were entitled to benefit but just didn't want to take it as the last time we did, we ended up in a Police cell. We ended up living with my parents for nearly a year.

***Q - When was your video release and how did it go?***

***Chris -*** We had to do yet another re-edit of the film to put more sex and violence in which would make the film a lot more commercial and had even thought of re-titling the film for the international sales market as *"Interview with a Serial Killer"*. With a new edit and a new title, we could in some respects re-invent the film for international sales. But with regard to the UK video, it didn't perform particularly well, I don't think that's a reflection on anything apart from the fact that the market is particularly depressed. We did business, I think we sold somewhere between 2,500 to 3,000 units but at the end of the day we will only get around £7k which doesn't do much more than put a dent in Living Spirit's debts.

*'The toughest thing about success is that you've got to keep on being a success'*
*Irving Berlin*

**Gen -** The only thing we hope for now is for the video release to raise the profile of the film to get a better satellite and terrestrial TV deal. The UK satellite, television and sell through video may just about bring the film back to zero, that is if some people will accept deals. If we can then do something internationally we could start to pay back the investors - but it doesn't look good.

When Rank sent us the solicitor's letter giving us 48 hours we decided to fight, to work as hard as we could to make good the debts. Pilgrim also owed Rank from the UK release but they decided to simply go bankrupt.

***Q - In all of this you could have opted for bankruptcy, why didn't you do that?***

**Gen -** We felt a moral responsibility to everybody involved, particularly the investors. When this whole thing happened with Rank, our first reaction was fair enough we'll go minus £27k to zero overnight. What a really good way to clear your debt. But it was also a big slap in the face, a big failure and failure doesn't make you sleep well at nights. Not that we've had a great deal of success either but we didn't want to accept failure and lie down and die, they would have to kill us off with extreme prejudice. We were legally advised to fight it and let them force us into liquidation, but the real reason was that we didn't want to write that letter to our investors and have to say Dear investor, thanks for your money, by the way, we've given up on it, and we've gone into liquidation. That would have been too difficult a letter to write. That may not be good business sense - maybe a good businessman would say, Oh well, it's a bad deal, get rid of it and move on.

***Q - In either of your past lives do you think you did something that meant that White Angel went through what you could say is the most unlucky curve of all - not only were you practically made bankrupt, your release went totally wrong, you spent time in prison - but then a real life situation was discovered within 20 miles of where you made the film?***

**Chris -** The first we heard of Fred West was when we were on the plane coming back from the Ankara Film Festival, just a few weeks before the film's theatrical release. We heard rumours of a serial killer in Gloucester and my first thought

was 'Great PR, the film must be really getting out there' - I thought it was people talking about the film and didn't realise that it was a real serial killer. When we found out that it was reality, it was a huge shock.

Initially, Fred West was only accused of two murders, but then the body count started growing and we began to worry that the press would jump on us. The story did break on Easter day '94 - a lot of the big newspapers carried a small column about it, but we played it down. It was a very bizarre occurrence. I think what is most bizarre, and this book will reflect this, is that many of the interviews in this book have been conducted over a period of years (before Fred West was caught). When you refer back to when we talk about the screenplay and what we say about why people find serial killers fascinating, that *it's the man next door...* well for us, it pretty much was - we used to park our car outside his front door when we went into town! That was very chilling and brought everything into sharp focus - as we were making a piece of fiction, only a mile or two away it was happening in reality.

What was frustrating is that we were being accused of being sick 'cash in' film makers by the people who were printing the story saying Sick West Film made in Front Garden. Actually, the only people making any money out of this story were the people selling the newspapers. We pointed out that the film had been completed and premiered at the London Film Festival before Fred West was known to anyone other than his milk man and neighbours.

We had to defend the film and say *'well it's not that sick and nasty'*, which diluted the impact for the theatrical release of the film. I couldn't say, *'it's a real shocking, real blood and gutsy thriller'*, because the press would say, *'isn't it a bit sick releasing the film the same time as all these revelations about Fred West?'*. What could we do? We couldn't afford to put off the release, we were 4 weeks away and it was all moving - we were in a no win situation.

***Q - Why did you decide to write this book?***

**Gen -** First of all, we wanted this kind of book when we started up, a book that gave other people's experiences - showing where they got it right, and where they didn't. Obviously there's nothing better than your own experience,

### *Going under*

*When that letter from the solicitor comes & you can't pay, there are several things you can do*

*1. Make a deal - if your creditor thinks they won't get paid, offer them half or even less & they may take it, but you will have to pay there & then.*

*2. Offer to pay it off at a small amount of money per month. If it is vaguely reasonable, they will accept.*

*3. No-one wants to force you to go bust, it costs a lot, takes a long time & often, no-one wins out.*

*4. If you do want to go into insolvency, let them push you into it. They will then have to pay the liquidator or receiver rather than you.*

*5. If you do go into liquidation, you will have to supply all your books & records which will be scrutinised. Make sure you didn't do anything illegal or undeclared.*

*6. If serious negligence or fraud is discovered, you will be barred from being a Ltd company director again.*

*7. Hopefully you will have made your film under a Ltd company as if you didn't, you can be made bankrupt and everything you own can be taken, bar the tools of your trade.*

*8. If things get bad, let it go & move on. Liquidation may not be avoidable & is a good way of washing your hands of a serious problem.*

*9. Keep talking to your creditors & it may not even get that far.*

*10. Seek legal advice immediately - let's hope the company forcing you into liquidation isn't your solicitors.*

It could be the man next door - in Living Spirit's case, it literally was, in the form of serial killer Fred West

but hearing somebody else's experiences really helps and I'm sure we've had a few bad experiences that can be avoided by other film makers.

***Chris -*** I think the other reason why we wrote the book is that it's about the only way we can make money out of our experiences now. That's the tragic reality of the whole situation.

***Q - What basic advice would you give to somebody about the attitude it takes to make low-budget films?***

***Chris -*** There are two kinds of new film makers who will go out and attempt to make a film. One is somebody who thinks they want to do it but will cop out, the other is the kind of person who actually believes, quite literally, that they are a genius and that they have no possible way of failing.

Quite honestly when we started out we believed ourselves to be mini geniuses, it was absolutely impossible to fail - that is intrinsic to a low-budget film makers psyche, it's the only thing that will get you to do these ridiculous things that will destroy your life and financial standing.

***Gen -*** Most new film makers, ourselves included, are never prepared for the chaos that will happen after having made the film - making the film is actually the easy thing, dealing with it afterwards is the difficult thing. My basic advice would be, if you can pay yourself, pay yourself and don't put your own money in. Not because you don't believe in the project, but because if it all goes wrong you won't be left so high and dry that you cannot function for several years. I'm not saying abandon the project at all, I'm just saying don't be so financially screwed that you cannot operate if it all goes wrong.

***Chris -*** The other thing is to get out as quickly as possible and start on the next project - don't be too concerned about quality, turnover is much more important. Quality will come later, with experience and serious development budgets.

***Gen -*** For a first film, you should make the kind of film you want to make as later you will not have that luxury - many other fingers will be in your pie, each with an opinion.

***Q - So to make a film you need to be an optimist, but also a realist?***

***Gen*** - Not to make it but to deal with it after it is completed. You need a vast quantity of optimism, dedication, self will, self motivation, and I believe, honesty and integrity. Those are the things that allow you to get it done properly. The moment you finish the film and take off your director's or producer's cap, and put on your sales agent cap, or 'now I have to go and make this business work' cap, then you need to dash your optimism and replace it with pessimism and realism - put on your accountancy cap, look at all the figures and take as much money as you can, as and when you can, and as quickly as you can. Treat it as a hundred yard sprint. After a hundred yards, kick it into touch and move on, because after a hundred yards you're not going to get any more.

***Q - What would be your advice about the balance between the budget for the actual film production and film sales?***

***Chris*** - It's inevitable that new film makers are focused on getting to day one of principle photography and aren't too concerned about things like screenplays or casting - it's just get the movie shot. It's an insane desire to shoot vast quantities of 35mm negative and then deal with the chaos that you have created for yourself. With the best will in the world, I don't think that a new film maker is going to say, well I've got my £100,000 to make the film, but I'm not going to make it now, because I need another £100,000 to sell the film afterwards.

All I can suggest is be aware of it, know that you are going to have problems and say *I know that I can make the film for £100,000, but the real budget is going to be £200,000 after I have fixed all the problems, paid my rent, been to a few festivals and made delivery to a sales agent.*

If at the end of the day the film doesn't sell you'll never make any money, you'll never pay your investors back and you'll have this millstone around your neck for several years. At which point either everyone will get bored and go away or they'll sue you and you'll be made bankrupt.

***Gen*** - Get your screenplay to a sales agent and say 'I have this screenplay, this is the cast I'm thinking about, this is the

*Your Credit Rating...*
*As we move into a more computerised age, every detail of your financial history can be bought and sold by money lenders. The upshot is that if you have abused money, you may find it tough to get a mobile phone, credit card or even a mortgage.*

*1. Always make good your debts and always get a letter to prove that you have made good your debt.*

*2. Credit agencies hold details of your credit status and rating. Their details are available from Citizens Advice and if you write to them, they have to supply you with your details.*

*3. When researching your credit status, remember to check all your previous addresses over the last six years.*

*4. CCJ - County Court Judgements are a pain. If you get one, it's a big problem. However, if you pay up immediately or can settle out of court, no CCJ should be lodged against your name on your records.*

*5. If you started a limited company and the company goes into liquidation - it's not you that has been made bankrupt and you shouldn't be affected. But...*

*6. If you ran the company from home and you get a CCJ, it's almost as big a problem as CCJs are held against an address too (even though it may have nothing to do with you).*

*'The surest way to succeed is to be determined not to fail'*
*Anon*

budget I'm thinking about, what are your ideas and they'll give you a fair appraisal of the films commercial value

***Q - So test your idea out first and be aware that if you are going to make any money you've got to sell it afterwards?***

***Gen -*** When we talk about making money out of it, it's nothing to do with profit. We would all love to have our own yacht in the Caribbean - what we're talking about is making enough money to pay people back what they have put in and to pay for your rent and food. Any film is going to take 12 to 18 months of your life. Who is going to pay for those 18 months?

***Chris -*** Nobody would buy a house for £200k if they didn't know they could pay the mortgage - making a film for £200k is like buying a house and you've got to know that you can pay that mortgage, or you'll loose that money and get repossessed. It's a hard reality. It's naive to blindly assume you're going to make a lot of money. However, if you are prepared to enter the arena and say, 'well I'm going to loose it all, and if I do, I don't care', then great go for it. 'And if I loose it all, I can still survive and start again'. I guess that low-budget film making is designed to launch careers, it isn't about getting rich quick.

***Gen -*** However, I think we've been spectacularly unlucky.

***Q - Maybe you are just talentless?***

***Chris -*** I think we had better end the interview here.

# Epilogue

Chris and Gen have continued to work in the film industry, but have taken a back seat for the two years since White Angel was produced, working mainly in journalism.

*The Runner* has yet to make any money for Living Spirit. Chris and Gen believe it never will. *The Runner* has been released across the world under various titles including *Survival Island and Escape from... Survival Zone.*

After an eighteen month sabbatical, *White Angel* has re-emerged on the international market with a new sales agent, *Stranger Than Fiction.* New promotional material, a trailer and even an Internet web site have all been prepared in order to secure deals. Initial signs are hopeful with several territories already signed up, although as yet, nothing has actually landed in the Living Spirit bank account.

Chris and Gen intend to start a new company called Living Spirit 96 to produce their new feature film (upon the advice of their accountant and solicitor). The plot is still under wraps, but there is interest from the UK film industry, and all indicators point to a sensible budget. Phew!

To be continued...

25/7/96

# Case 2
# Ultra Low Budget
## 'Boy Meets Girl'
### Chris Read & Jim Crosbie

***Q - Why did you decide to make Boy Meets Girl? How did it come about?***

***Jim -*** Chris, Ray Brady (the director) and myself were all at LCP (London College of Printing) Film School and we wanted to make a film. We needed an idea that we could make cheaply and that would be very easy to market - so we decided to keep the story in one location, and to be about something that would attract a lot of attention - a female serial killer - the rest was built around those two elements. We originally thought of making it as a short, but why make a short when you can make a feature?

***Q - Why the subject of a serial killer?***

***Chris -*** We knew that it was a popular theme. Instead of a male serial killer we decided to be slightly different and look at a female serial killer.

***Q - Were you still at Film School?***

***Chris -*** Yes, we were in our first year at Film School, we only graduated in June '95.

***Q - How much did the film actually cost to make?***

***Chris -*** It's difficult to say how much it actually cost. We combined our student loans which gave us about £7k, enabling us to shoot for a week. We then had to raise the rest, so we went to Cannes and tried to get some kind of interest going there. That's where we met Metro Tartan and they were very interested. We then set a production date and two weeks to raise more money so we could shoot the rest of it. On the Friday night before we started shooting (everything was booked and the cast & crew were coming on the Monday morning) we were sitting around thinking we haven't got any money have we? So on that Friday night, we started ringing round everybody we knew, asking them if they wanted to put £50 into this film. We raised another £1500 which was enough to make sure that the film stock and camera were there. We continued calling up everyone we could and borrowing money, that was how we got the film completed.

***Q - How long did you shoot for in total and on what format?***

***Jim -*** Three weeks and we shot on standard 16mm

***Q - How big was the crew?***

***Chris -*** Small - a sound recordist, cinematographer, focus puller, clapper , hair & make-up, special effects. Along with Ray, I was the producer, the grip, the gaffer, stills photographer etc.

***Q - So it was the core group of the three of you (Ray, Chris and Jim) that made this film?***

***Chris -*** Yes

***Q - How long was it between you sitting down and saying 'Lets make this movie' and actually exposing raw neg?***

***Jim -*** We started writing the script in December and then in February we started filming.

***Q - So you really only had 8-10 weeks to write the 90 page screenplay?***

***Jim -*** Yes, but I don't think that's to be recommended. It wasn't even completed when we started shooting. We knew what was going to happen in the story, but didn't have it committed to paper.

***Q - How did you get the cast involved? Were they serious amateurs or professionals?***

***Chris -*** Professionals. We advertised in PCR and got hundreds of CV's. We then held auditions over a month or so.

***Q - So people weren't paid - did you have any union problems?***

***Chris -*** No they didn't know it was even happening. Everyone in the cast and crew was contracted and working for minimum wages which were then deferred until we sold the film. The actors were also given a percentage of the profits along with the deferment. It's unlikely that anyone will get anything though.

***Q - Did you have proper legal contracts from a solicitor or did you put them together yourselves?***

***Chris*** **-** We couldn't afford solicitors, but I had a solicitor friend who went through the contracts, helping us with wording etc. Thankfully, we didn't have any problems with the agreements.

***Q - Did you shoot on location or in a studio?***

***Chris*** **-** We shot in a two room council flat with a kitchen and a bathroom. We used one room as a set, the kitchen as a production office and the other room as a hanging out room, cum make-up, cum wardrobe, cum chill out room.

***Q - In terms of production, what gave you the most headaches?***

***Chris*** **-** The second shoot had the biggest problems - making sure there was enough money for filmstock and to feed people. There were times when there was £20 in the kitty and no food in the fridge - it was that bad. There were a few headaches regarding equipment, the camera equipment wasn't up to scratch for instance.

***Q - Did anybody let you down?***

***Chris*** **-** Two people dropped out half way through as they weren't happy with the subject matter. That was the point I actually became the producer, it had started off more of a joint *let's just make the movie thing.* But we had to consolidate some things if we were going to finish it. So I had to make the decision to either forego my student loan or try and make something out of it. I decided to make it happen.

***Q - How did you approach post production?***

***Jim*** **-** We telecinied our stock straight onto video and then persuaded a video facility house to give us lots of free 'down' time. We then edited a version on video which we could show to people. That's when Metro Tartan became interested in distributing *Boy Meets Girl.* So far we had spent £13k getting it in the can, but had no money for post production.

***Q - How did you survive from the time that you shot Boy Meets Girl to the time you got any money back, if any?***

***Chris*** **-** It seemed as though we managed to survive on absolutely nothing. That was a real low point. We were students who had invested all our student loan into making this film. Because we were students, we couldn't sign on. I remember going through our kitchen cupboards trying to find something to eat. Our only entertainment was watching videos that we'd taped a while back - at least we still had a TV and Video.

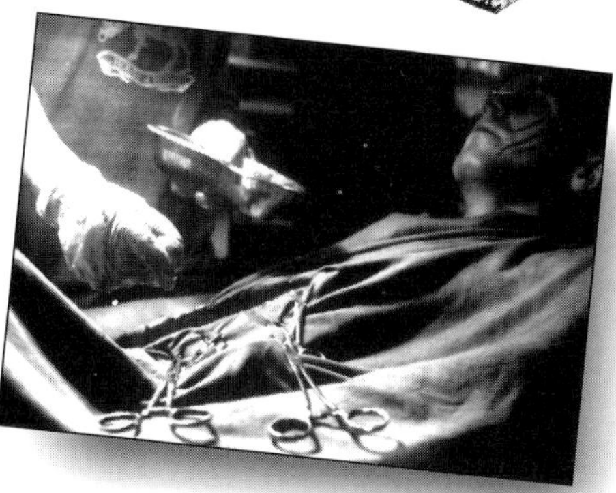

***Q - At any point, did you waste cash?***

***Jim -*** Yes. We got some money from Metro Tartan for post production and we hired an experienced editor who we paid a considerable amount. We hoped he could work miracles with the edit we had done, but it turned out to be a waste of time and money.

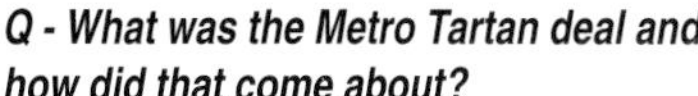

***Q - What was the Metro Tartan deal and how did that come about?***

***Chris -*** We started talking to them because they showed interest. We set up a meeting which was around ten months after shooting. They wanted it so we started sorting out the contracts. We told them that we needed an advance to cover the post production so we could deliver the film to them. So whilst the contracts were being drawn up, they started paying for things directly. We continued post production and they were invoiced directly. Thankfully, we managed to complete the film.

It was then that Metro Tartan approached James Ferman of the BBFC (British Board of Film Classification). We were still in post production and they were funding us as we went along, whilst the contract was still being drawn up. Then Ferman told Metro Tartan that he thought it was unlikely that the film would get a video certificate and that he couldn't guarantee anything. From that point, Metro Tartan locked up.

***Q - So how much did you get out of Metro Tartan?***

***Chris -*** £13k, but then there were companies who had previously billed Metro Tartan for work and whose invoices we were then sent, and we had no way of paying them. Metro Tartan stopped answering our calls, and stopped speaking to us. We even ended up in court with one of the bills, even though we had always explained to every company that we went to, that we didn't have the money, Metro Tartan were paying the invoices. But ultimately, we didn't have the contract with Metro Tartan to back up our argument. This was the first time that we had dealt with a distributor. We didn't know how things were done, we were learning as we did it. All of us were walking around with our eyes shut, including Metro Tartan. They had put all this money in and then were faced with the fact that if the film wasn't going to get a video release, they probably wouldn't be able to get their money back. The theatrical release wouldn't have made them any money, they'd have done one or two prints if we were lucky, so video would be where they'd get their money.

***Jim -*** At one point, Metro Tartan even gave us a grand over Christmas because we didn't have any money. It was strange.

***Q - So it became apparent that you were never going to receive a UK video certificate?***

***Chris -*** It wasn't clear at that point as James Ferman had just said unlikely, and the killing of Jamie Bulger occurred which then re-opened up the video violence debate. Ferman told us that the film was un-editable, the only way to get a certificate was to re-shoot it, which for us, was impossible. The BBFC gave us a theatrical release, cert 18, because they argued that in cinemas the only people to see it would be ones of the right age and mind set, whereas with videos, youngsters could see it and sections could replayed and replayed.

***Jim -*** It dawned on us that what we had unwittingly done, was to make a film that we couldn't sell.

***Q - Did you just give up then?***

***Chris -*** No, we then got the 16mm neg cut and a 16mm print made. We went to Cannes that year and took a 16mm with us and ended up screening it in a cafe on the Rue d'Antibes, just round the corner from the Petit Carlton - we got a crowd of twenty or thirty people, some of whom were from film festivals, and got some hype going. We managed to get the Guardian and Screen International to do short pieces on it and then an Italian sales agent started to show interest, enough so that they paid for a proper market screening, which isn't cheap. From that screening we were invited to lots of Film festivals across the world, but the Italian company refused to answer any of our faxes when we got back to England. Obviously it didn't go down too well. Getting the print done and doing the Festival run boosted our belief in the Film again. That's what helped us hold up against all these people who were chasing us for money. The Film started to get a lot of publicity and we had quite a nice time attending festivals in Spain, Rome, Vienna, Fantasporto, Edinburgh.

***Q - You've not been able to sell Boy Meets Girl in Britain, and don't have an International Sales Agent - have you managed to get any sales yourself?***

***Jim -*** Yes we're just finishing a deal with somebody in Japan who wants to distribute it theatrically, and we're doing a deal with Troma for the rest of the world excluding the UK and Japan.

***Q - Combined, will those deals pay off your debts or repay your investors?***

***Jim -*** No, it won't pay off all the debts. It'll never break even, except in the unlikely event that it gets a UK video certificate. Then there is a possibility.

***Q - There are two sides to this film. There is the creative side and the commercial side. It is clearly a commercial disaster. To what do you attribute that disaster?***

***Jim -*** It's not a classic thing of making a series of bad financial decisions as we had no money to spend badly. We were unlucky, particularly with the BBFC. If we had the deal with Metro Tartan which would have been for £25k, we would have broken even and be in profit. Channel 4 also expressed an interest in showing the film and if it wasn't for the certification problem, they probably would have taken it on board.

***Q - If, from the onset your object was to make money out of this film, what would you have done differently?***

***Chris -*** If we wanted to make money, we'd have stuck on a happy ending.

***Q - Is it fair to say that because you had non existent production values, and a story that a lot of people in high places found unpalatable, the film was forced into commercial failure?***

***Chris -*** Yes. But on the other side of the coin, we learnt a lot and received some good reviews at festivals. You can't expect to make any money out of films at this level. It's possible but British independents have a lot more going against them than American independents. Did some of those American independents make any money? Probably not, but it doesn't matter as they went on to sign deals with Miramax or whoever. They've broken into the industry and that's what this is all about, learning about the industry. Making a film is both the quickest and hardest way to learn.

***Q - Were you all happy with the film when it was finished?***

***Jim -*** I was happy that it was what it was, understanding from where we came from and how we made it. We had only made short films before, and a feature film turned out to be a completely different animal.

***Q - If you were to remake it again, would you make it less offensive?***

***Chris -*** We'd have to, so we could justify people's investment, we'd have to guarantee that it would get a release. We'd also open up the locations more, take it out of one room, which isn't particularly cinematic in itself. We never considered the film to be offensive and didn't set out to make an offensive film - quite frankly, we were shocked by the BBFCs denial of certification, and still are today. We are appealing the decision as we and our lawyers feel we have a strong case.

***Q - What basic advice would you offer to film makers who are thinking about embarking on their first feature?***

***Chris -*** Get a rich father.

***Jim -*** You have to be incredibly bold, independent and have enough courage to go for it. Don't be afraid of stepping out and just doing it. If you've got nothing to lose when you start, then even if someone sues you, you just can't lose anything, but you will have a film to your credit.

***Chris -*** Have a script in which you really have faith or you'll find it difficult to keep going. I've got debts that most people would be tearing their hair out over, so you just deal with what is physically possible.

# Case 3 Low Budget 'Staggered' by Philippa Braithwaite

*'Staggered' was produced by Philippa Braithwaite, written by Paul Alexander and her brother Simon Brathwaite, and was directed by and stars TV actor Martin Clunes. It's a light-hearted British romp whose UK success has to be partly attributable to phenomenal timing with 'Four Weddings and a Funeral'.*

***Q - Why did you decide to become a film maker?***

***Philippa -*** Like most people who want to make films, it was when I was really young - it was something I always wanted to do, I just loved films. I started off working on commercials and promos before moving into TV. I knew that I wanted to make films but didn't really know how to do it. The last ten years have been difficult for anyone who wants to make films anyway, and I was always wondering if I'd ever really get there. I was always reading scripts, trying to find something to do, and then I thought, even if I find it, I've got to be in with the only funding sources around at that time - British Screen and Channel Four really - and I thought I'd never get it funded. As soon as I had read the script for *Staggered*, I thought I should do it. I'd read how Gary Sinyor had done *Leon the Pig Farmer* and decided I'd do just that.

***Q - What attracted you to Staggered?***

***Philippa -*** It was a combination of things. It was the fact that it was easier, because my brother's a writer and he came to me with the idea, so the project sort of landed on my desk. I didn't have to search or do contracts with writers I didn't know. He had this idea for a film which he was going to do with another writer Paul Alexander who writes for TV, and I thought it sounded like a great idea - they pitched it and I said Yeah, lets go off and make it. I liked it because it was light-hearted. At that time, all the British films that were coming out were so boring and worthy and I just thought, rightly or wrongly, that those weren't the kind of films I wanted to make, nor did I believe those were the kind of films people wanted to go and see, which was why the Industry was in a rut. *Staggered* sounded like a great idea and I thought we could get a good British cast together and just do something that somebody would want to go out and see on a Friday night, no more, no less. I also felt that it would work well outside London in the multiplexes.

***Q - Did any UK companies put any cash up front to develop the film?***

***Philippa -*** In December 1992 I had a well paid job and quite a secure position, but I just didn't want to do it anymore. The only way I was going to make a film was to just do it, no one was going to give me development money for the script, no one knew who I was, or who the writers were, so I just took a decision to save some money and leave the job in January. I knew the only way to get it made was to give up and commit 24 hours a day to it. Take the risk

***Q - What other people were involved in the project who were central to getting it made?***

***Philippa -*** My brother Simon was the associate producer on the film, and his enthusiasm was brilliant and it helped to work with him - also, he was somebody I really trusted and we had the same vision. The lawyers, Gouldens, who put together the Business Expansion Scheme package were great. We couldn't have done it without them and they deferred all their fees.

***Q - What format did you shoot the film on?***

***Philippa -*** 35mm. I just thought that was the only way of getting a good chance of a theatrical release.

***Q - How long did it take from sitting down saying, 'Yes, lets do this', to the first day of principle photography?***

***Philippa*** - It was the middle of December when we had a two line idea, and we started shooting on August 24th 1993, so it was just over eight months. We then shot for six weeks.

***Q - Did you shoot six or seven days a week?***

***Philippa*** - We shot six days a week, but quite long days and another thing that was really hard, was that everyone was working on deferred payment. We couldn't afford to go into a studio nor could we afford to pay for locations, so we were all over the place. You just lose so much time running around and also trying to keep up the morale of people who aren't being paid.

***Q - Were you entirely deferred?***

***Philippa -*** Yes, we were entirely deferred but I made sure that nobody was out of pocket. We paid their petrol expenses and fed them, but they weren't paid anything. Although actually having said that, we did pay the actors a bit up front probably 80 % of their fee was deferred but I thought there was a better chance of getting actors involved if you can say there's something here.

***Q - Did you have any union problems?***

***Philippa*** - Yes, I had Equity slamming the phone down on me. I got a couple of calls saying they didn't agree with what we were doing - it's like well, who cares.

***Q - How long did it take for you to cut the film?***

***Philippa*** - We didn't have the money to cut non linear and our editor had a steenbeck anyway, so we cut it on film. It took longer than I thought to edit - as with all low-budget films, our editor didn't have an assistant, so he was doing everything and Martin was also cutting it, so it just seemed to take forever. We finished shooting the end of October and we had a finished print by the end of February, which actually isn't that long, it just felt like it was.

***Q - Did you have all the money in place before you shot?***

***Philippa -*** We had the money to shoot it but not complete it. We raised private finance, and it was only by the skin of our teeth that we had it in place in time. I had to set a date for filming and get everything lined up because otherwise, it was all going to fall through and we wouldn't be able to get the cast we wanted. The extra money to complete the film came in three days before the shoot, so it was a bit hairy and I couldn't tell anybody. The usual producer problems.

***Q - And did all your initial finance come from a private source?***

***Philippa -*** Lots and Lots of private sources. I just rang up everybody I knew and everybody I didn't know. The minimum investment was £500 and I received one lot of £10,000, but a few £5000 and a lot of £500. When I was raising the money for the film, I was doing lots of interviews on the radio, we got a good publicist to help place us on the radio and to print interviews. I was doing a live interview on Kaleidoscope on Radio Four and this guy kept pushing me saying well what else can you offer? And my mind was just going blank - I had this idea and said anyone who puts in over £500 can be an extra in the film... and the phone didn't stop ringing. We got so many people writing cheques for £501 - it was great because we got all the extras we wanted, all turning up in their best clothes and all excited. We had a big wedding scene and all the investors were there. It was funny.

***Q - Did you go over budget or over schedule?***

***Philippa*** - We didn't go over schedule as we had a brilliant 1st Assistant and Line Producer. They were just so good. They managed to keep things literally on time. Over budget? No we didn't, but

that's a slightly difficult one. We had the cash to make the film, which was £180,000, but when we came to do the post production, I suddenly realised that with all the delivery requirements, we needed a lot more to complete. Somehow we would have done it but because we were paid an advance we spent more.

***Q - So in essence you didn't have an accurate budget at the outset of the project, because the budget didn't reflect the delivery requirements?***

***Philippa*** - Yes, I suppose so. I still think I would have made sure we could have done it, by getting Technicolor to defer a bit more or just to do something so we could have done it within that budget. But it's the age old story, everybody says you get into trouble in post production and I think everybody does.

***Q - In terms of production, what were the biggest headaches?***

***Philippa*** - Scheduling around actors was a real headache, who could do what dates, but we got round that. We shot in the Outer Hebrides for a week and getting the crew there and back was a real nightmare as we couldn't afford to fly everybody up and the only way over is by ferry. When you realise that you're going to lose three days out of your six weeks just travelling you start thinking, 'well lets just go and shoot it in Cornwall'. One of the biggest problems was simply trying to find a toy shop for three days.

***Q - Did you have any problems with actors?***

***Philippa*** - They were all brilliant (hearty laugh!). They really were actually.

***Q - Did you have any major technical problems?***

***Philippa*** - No we were really lucky. I knew it would be a problem if it was out of focus, or if the assistant didn't know how to load the camera - so obviously, we got the best people we could.

***Q - So did you manage to get the crew for nothing up front and were they all willing?***

***Philippa*** - Yes, I did. The hardest people are always the grips and the sparks. It was much easier getting heads of Department because they obviously wanted to work on features and it's much more valuable for them than for a spark.

***Q - Did you manage to pay yourself?***

***Philippa*** - It was really difficult, even though I had saved up some money from my job. Actually what I did, and I'm dealing with it now, I put some money aside for tax from my job and used that - I'm now trying to negotiate with the tax man about it to keep me out of jail. How else? I borrowed a bit. You just do somehow, God knows how.

***Q - What were the most expensive things in the budget?***

***Philippa*** - The professional catering. Film processing and reprints cost quite a bit too.

***Q - How did you get the cast and director involved?***

***Philippa*** - It was much easier than I thought it would be. I had a lot of people involved before I raised the money so that I could use their names and that was a good lesson in marketing. I rang the agents and sent the scripts and all but one said yes, which just amazed me, I couldn't believe it. And that was through the agents, and still saying things like very low-budget, and deferral. I was very honest as I knew there would not be any real money up front. Some agents were tough, and I did have a problem with a few of them, but ICM for instance were really helpful. In the last two years since I made *Staggered* it seems like there are so many more low-budget films being made.

***Q - What was the actual budget of the film?***

***Philippa*** - The up front budget was £180k, and it cost us another £100k in post production. That wasn't just a sort of screw up in post production, it was just things like the interpos, interneg, answer print and the trailer, which I hadn't even thought about. The budget ended up at £280k - then with all the deferrals and everybody to be paid, it would total £700k.

***Q - Who cut your trailer?***

***Philippa*** - The Creative Partnership cut it, but because we couldn't afford to get them to do the whole thing I got them to do an off-line and we then had to match it with the film print and film cut it all ourselves.

***Q - Where did the money come from and how did it break down?***

***Philippa*** - The initial budget came from the Business Expansion Scheme which is made up of private investors. The top up budget for post production was an advance we got from a UK sale and that was it. *(the business expansion scheme no longer exists).

***Q - You had a UK distributor but not an international Sales Agent on board?***

***Philippa*** - We had an international sales agent on board before we started shooting but we got the distributor half way through shooting.

***Q - How long was it between final print and UK theatrical release?***

**Philippa** - Four months. We were planning the release before we even completed the film, although I didn't know the exact release until three months before.

***Q - Who handled your theatrical release?***

**Philippa** - Entertainment Films.

***Q - Did you find the Summer a good time to release as you were up against the block-busters?***

**Philippa** -Yes, I don't think there's really a good time to ever release a British film as there's always something big up against it. We had the *Flintstones* and *Maverick* opening a week after us, but those were the only two big films. I think it would have been worse if it was this year because there are loads of big films.

***Q - Was your release successful?***

**Philippa** - Very. In it's opening weekend it took a quarter of a million which was so exciting. We opened in 108 theatres, it was a nation-wide release and it did very well at the multiplexes. It took a lot more than some of the American films that were playing.

***Q - It came out around the same time as 'Four Weddings and A Funeral', how much did Entertainment spend on your P&A roughly?***

**Philippa** - I can't say, but it was a lot for a low-budget film. However, it was a good decision to make. If they get behind a film, they really get behind it.

***Q - Did you have any problems making delivery?***

**Philippa** - Time wise we were up against it a bit, because I really thought we'd allowed enough time to deliver, I added on another month and thought we were fine. But we really weren't. I think the morning I was at Technicolor doing a final grade was the day we were supposed to deliver.

***Q - In terms of international delivery requirements, did you deliver everything that the sales agent wanted?***

**Philippa** - Yes, but it wasn't exactly on the nose with the contract. Some things came in afterwards which I'd agreed with them. There was one thing that I really argued about. In the contract it was written that they wanted a mono optical sound track and I said, this is ridiculous no one is going to want this, and it was going to cost us £5k to do. Anyway they agreed to delete that. They cover themselves so much though.

***Q - Did you cover yourselves with Errors and Omissions in advance to shooting and how much did that cost you?***

**Philippa** - No, I did that afterwards and it cost £7,000. It was a stipulation on the UK distributors part, they needed an E&O.

***Q - Did you take it around the festivals?***

**Philippa** - Yes. It was in Venice in the audience participation side, and it went down really well. And there was a Charlie Chaplin comedy festival in Switzerland where it won four awards. It's been entered into a few festivals around the world but nothing major happened.

***Q - Has the film performed well around the world in terms of sales?***

**Philippa -** It's made sales. People say to me, *'You know it's really British and it won't travel, especially the humour"*, but I don't know about that as I've seen it with French and Italian audiences and they've all loved it. Its sold in most territories but it hasn't sold in France, Italy or America. I think those are the only three territories outstanding. Australia picked it up but they released it in New Zealand first. It was a bit odd because they did a huge 15 print release but they didn't do any real publicity, even though Martin is well known because of his TV stuff. I would have thought it was quite short sighted and again, quite frustrating because you can't tell them how to do their job. We haven't sold it to Japan and I don't think we will. They don't get it, they just don't get it. It baffles them. Germany gave us our biggest deal. UK comedies have always done well in Germany for some reason.

***Q - Are you unhappy with the way the UK distributors and the international sales worked?***

**Philippa** - Not as far as the UK release is concerned, I think that was handled brilliantly. The international was something else - it's a hard question - yes, I'd like to have seen more sales, I'd liked to have seen more money, I'd liked to have seen it handled differently when it opened in different countries but unless you've got a big distributor like Polygram managing the world sales, I think it's hard.

***Q - What were your reviews like?***

**Philippa** - They were very mixed but I always knew the high brow critics would hate it and most of them did, although Alexander Walker really liked it. The tabloids loved it and Time Out was incredibly weird.

***Q - Are you pleased with the film?***

***Philippa*** - Yes, really pleased with it because it's done really well, and people like it. It seemed to tap into a young audience which is great, and some of them just love it. I'm pleased with the fact that we created this thing out of nothing and we showed everyone we could do it when everyone was saying we couldn't.

***Q - Have you made any money, either your company or you personally?***

***Philippa*** - No.

***Q - Has the film helped your career?***

***Philippa*** - Yes. I've now got two films that I'm trying to get off the ground, both of which look like they will happen. I didn't do it because I wanted to become a big movie mogul and be very rich, but because I want to make films. I knew making *Staggered* in the way that I did was the only way I'd be able to get to make films - going out on a limb and taking the risk. I can ring up people I want to talk to and now they talk back to me.

***Q - In retrospect now, what do you think are the strengths and weaknesses of the final film?***

***Philippa*** - It's very hard as I am so close to it. I'd say the strengths are the acting, Martin is brilliant, and I think the pace works, I've seen it with lots of different audiences and it's interesting that people laugh all over the world at the same things so it obviously works on one level. Not everyone likes it, some people hate it. I think the weaknesses are from the budget, where it does show it's low-budget. But I think it looks more than it costs. Its very hard to say. You always think you would go back and do things differently.

***Q - What are you doing next?***

***Philippa*** - We have one film that's exactly the same team which I've been working on for the last year. We've just got the script right and it's gone through various different drafts.

***Q - What advice would you offer a new film maker?***

***Philippa*** - I think they should think very carefully about how they are going to market and distribute the film because at the end of the day, film is a business - how many people will go to see that film - I think too many people don't think of that. They just think of their vision which doesn't necessarily extend to businessmen who are trying to turn that vision into dollars. Be aware of who you are making it for, the audience, be aware that there are people out there who are ready to rip you off every step of the way, it's been written a thousand times, but it's true. Get a really good production team around you so you don't go over budget or over schedule. Good luck.

# Case 4
# Medium Low Budget
## 'Clockwork Mice'
## by Paul Brooks

*Paul Brooks has produced more British features in the last four years than many established film makers have in their entire career.*

***Q - How and why did you become involved in films?***

***Paul -*** Because I always wanted to. Since I was six years old I've been obsessed with film. My other great love is architecture, for no other reason but that I love buildings. I read English and Philosophy at London, then had to decide whether I was going to go into property or films and decided to go into property. I made a lot of money, lost a lot of money, then got into films.

***Q - What is it specifically that attracts you to a project?***

***Paul -*** There are two things - in the first instance there is *Can I finance it?* and in the second instance there is *Can I finance it?* That's what attracts me to a project. Beyond that, there is - *is this a project that I actually love that I'm really into,* and *is this a project that can help me build my business.* If either of those things make sense then I'll do it, but what I won't do, is get involved in a film with a script that I love, if I don't think I can finance it. In other words, I don't have the time to devote myself passionately to a project when it's going to be very difficult to finance. I hope in two or three years time, when I've built the business sufficiently, I might be fortunate enough to make the films that I want to make on the basis that it is completely love driven.

***Q - What had you done prior to Clockwork Mice?***

***Paul -*** My first film was *Leon the Pig Farmer* and then I did *Bedlam*, then I commissioned *Solitaire for Two* and then I did *Clockwork Mice.*

***Q - How did your first film Leon come about?***

***Paul -*** I stuck the word out that I thought I could help people finance some films, I was actually on the dole at the time. Vadim, Gary and I put it together for £150k. The funny thing was that at that point, it was right in the belly of the recession and £150k was a lot of dough. We each raised £50k

- it was really hard and at one point we were the only film in production as I recall.

***Q - How did Leon make out in terms of recouping it's costs?***

**Paul -** The investors did fine.

***Q - Was that due to it doing particularly well in the UK theatres or was that down to International sales?***

**Paul -** *Leon* didn't sell well internationally, although it did very well in the UK. It was bought by Channel 4 for a reasonable figure, it did reasonable video and very good theatrical business - it worked well.

***Q - With regard to Clockwork Mice, how did you find the project, did it come to you?***

**Paul -** Yes, a friend with whom I was at college sent it in. That was THE script of the seven I've been involved with that I really fell in love with. It made me laugh and cry off the page and I leapt into a taxi and optioned it straight away. We then spent a year developing further with British Screen, who were terrific. They actually rejected the script first time round, so Vadim, Rod (the writer) and I spent two or three months just doing some work on the script, ripping thirty pages out of it, and then I re-submitted it and they picked it up second time round. Then we did another thirteen or fourteen drafts, I'd say it was probably in for a year or so before they committed production finance and off we went.

***Q - What was the production budget?***

**Paul -** The cash budget was £800k. Of that, British Screen put in £400k, we got £100k from BSkyB and I put in a private investment syndicate (including Winchester Multi-Media) of £300k.

***Q - British Screen have certain prerequisites - they take copyright and want their money out at the same time as everybody else. Those are presented as non negotiables, would it be fair to say that really there is no such thing as a non negotiable?***

**Paul -** Yes, I think if you're dealing with reasonable people, everything's negotiable.
British Screen money is much harder than people suppose and they do push for very hard deals,

but they are very supportive too. It just depends on how far you can push the envelope.

***Q - Have you ever gone over budget or over schedule?***

***Paul -*** No. One of the problems with *Clockwork Mice* was that the completion bond company didn't believe that we could deliver the film for the price, but we managed to persuade them and we didn't touch a penny of the contingency. Most people forget that you've not only got to make the film, but you've also got to manage the film, and then you've got to sell the film.

***Q - How do you avoid going over budget and over schedule?***

***Paul -*** You use a very big stick. It's just about managing, preparing it as well as one can, doing deals, being as professional as one can, but above all, manage the project properly.

***Q - What was your total budget for Clockwork Mice?***

***Paul -*** £1.3m.

***Q - I know that with completion bond companies they can be reticent to give bonds to films under a million?***

***Paul -*** I think now that as long as they are comfortable with the production team then they'll be persuaded, although they'll always look for deferrals of directors and producers fees, until the end of principle photography.

***Q - On a low-budget picture, what are the biggest headaches you have encountered?***

***Paul -*** The one thing that everyone underestimates is the delivery schedule for the sales agent. It's a serious headache in terms of the practicalities and is always more expensive than everybody supposes. But if you can do a creative deal with the sales agent then that shouldn't necessarily present a problem. We ended up spending an extra £50k on *Leon* mainly on Delivery. That was a huge schedule. Now, I won't necessarily do a huge delivery schedule, but rather do it on a piecemeal basis, as and when things are requested.

***Q - What would your advice be to new filmmakers as to how they should approach professionals such as financiers?***

***Paul*** - Anybody in film is fairly used to what people in film look like. But as far as getting hold of private investors, I think they have to look presentable. Unfortunately, if you want to get money out of a surgeon who lives in Regents park, you just can't turn up with tattoos and a ring through your nose. First impressions are crucial. People should stick their *right on, this is the way I am*, in the cupboard until they get the money. Then when they can pay back, they can turn up and give the fella his cheque back with the earring and scruffy T-shirt.

***Q - Who handled the international sales for Clockwork Mice, and how did it perform?***

***Paul*** - Victor Films handled the sales and it performed reasonably internationally, although it was difficult. In Germany I had three distributors chasing it, but in the end, the film didn't work at all well there. I had the most fantastic screening in LA. I've never had anything like it, but I couldn't get anyone to pick it up. The US, as you know, is an incredibly difficult territory anyway. It was really a very frustrating scenario.

***Q - Who handled the UK?***

***Paul*** - The Feature Film Co. handled the UK distribution.

***Q - How did it perform at the Box Office?***

***Paul*** - Crap.

***Q - What do you attribute that poor performance to?***

***Paul*** - The film didn't work, as simple as that. One could say, *well, we opened it in the Summer, we went too wide, we should have platformed it, we should have played the festivals, it was the distributors fault* - bottom line, the film didn't work. Film business is the toughest business in the world bar none.

***Q - What about the video for Clockwork Mice, how did it do?***

***Paul*** - It sold about 4500 units which was OK and apparently it's renting very well. We also have the pre-sale for £100k with BSkyB which is part of the deal with British Screen.

***Q - What about the ancillary rights, soundtracks etc.?***

***Paul*** - Soundtracks don't really work unless you have a big film, and when I say big, I don't mean big in budget terms, I mean big like *Trainspotting*, otherwise the economics don't really add up. Novelisations are OK. *Solitaire for Two* carried one. As long as there's enough theatrical exposure they make some sense.

***Q - What would your advice be to new film makers?***

**Paul -** Just go and make the film. That's an awful thing to say, in the sense *of That's really helpful Paul, thanks very much.* If you've got a project you really believe in, do everything you can to try and finance it through conventional channels, but give yourself a time limit and as soon as you hit that time limit then go and make the film - if you have to rob your grandmother, if you have to sleep with your school mistress, if you have to shoot it over 50 weekends, just make the film.

***Q - So bottom line is, at all costs avoid perpetual development hell?***

**Paul -** Yes. You have to be prepared to jump out of your comfort zone. You have to be prepared to take off all your clothes and jump into that very cold water. You'll find it warms up OK once you're in there. The problem we have in this country is what I call the Cappuccino theory - we have loads of 'producers' who drink cappuccino all day and talk about another rewrite, flying to Cannes and going to this party or that party, and yet another rewrite - and they never make a film. Of course a script has to be as developed as much as it can, but I would also say, I've done this before and doubtless will do it again, even when things aren't quite right, you have to go. You have to get into the game. It's no good knocking on the door, nobody lets you in, you have to smash your way through the door. You're in the game if you've made a film and if you haven't, you're not. It's as simple as that.

***Q - How important is it that once you've made your film, you're poised, and have an idea of what you want to do next?***

**Paul -** Very important. I'm about to start my eighth film, which is two films a year for the last four years, and that's been very deliberate. You have to deliver product, because it's all a numbers game. You're only going to get one film in ten that works - you have to be aggressive. The other thing that so often happens is that the gap between first film and second film is two or three years. There's too much competition out there, people have to be prepared to bite the bullet, not just for the first film, nor the second film, but also with the third film. It's tough, there are a lot of talented people out there. The problem here in the UK is that we're just that tiny bit reticent, *I'll just wait until the crease of my trousers is exactly right.* Of course, one has to be completely professional

and do the best one can, but it's a luxury to expect that you're going to go into your first, your second and even your third film with everything right, it won't happen, or if it does, you'll make three films in nine years.

***Q - With regard to money, it's obvious that filmmakers will sacrifice their fees, but there does come a point where they have to make money to survive?***

***Paul -*** Hopefully they can raise enough money to get the film financed in a conventional way, with a standard fee and so forth, but on first films, that's not often possible - and that's part of the bitter pill that you have to swallow if you want to break into this game. In this country there are a lot of people playing the cappuccino game and love the notion of being producers, and they never make anything. Whereas in America, they get out of college and say they're going to make a film and just do it - *can I borrow your camera? can you lend us $20,000? Cool.* There's never been a better time for making films in this country than now, it's extraordinary, the Lottery, Channel 4, BBC, British Screen, the new ITV initiative, it's unbelievable, but still most people are going to miss the boat because they're not aggressive enough.

# Case 5 From 'Shopping' to Hollywood Jeremy Bolt

***Q - Why and how did you decide to make films?***

***Jeremy -*** When I was 12, I saw *The Elephant Man* and was overwhelmed by the experience. Whilst having a cigarette behind the bike shed after the film I discussed with my friend what we were going to do with our lives, I think he was talking about running ICI and I thought I'd quite like to make films and thought I'd be a director. When I was eighteen I made a film of the Salome story which was absolutely disastrous, a kind of sort porn epic in Southern Turkey. I realised then that my talents lay in the ability to persuade people to do things, and that my skills lay in production rather than direction. I'm grateful for that experience because I didn't waste any more time in trying to be Stanley Kubrick.

***Q - How did that film in Turkey lead on to Shopping?***

***Jeremy -*** I left University with a clear goal of becoming a producer and started to work for Ken Russell. On *The Lair of The White Worm* I was a runner and on *The Rainbow* and *Whore* I became the producer's assistant. Finally, I became associate producer on some of the films he made for the South Bank Show. That was an amazing apprenticeship in production. Whilst working for Ken Russell, I went to a party and met a beautiful girl - I was chatting her up, and this other guy was chatting her up. So we were both sort of competing for her interest, but she wasn't interested in either of us and we ended up chatting each other up. I said to him that I wanted to be a film producer, I was a great fan of Ridley Scott, *Lethal Weapon* and *Die Hard* and I really loved action movies. He said I should meet this young director/writer called Paul Anderson. He had just come down from Warwick University but already had a number of commissions for Television.

I met up with Paul and we just got on extremely well, we had exactly the same taste. He had a treatment called *Shopping* which was inspired by the joyriding that was taking place in Newcastle, Paul's home town. I said to him, *look I haven't got any money, but if you write the script then you can direct it and I'll produce it.* That's how it began. It took us four years but we managed to pull it together, with a lot of lying and a lot of luck.

***Q - What was the budget?***

***Jeremy -*** The budget was £2.3m which was quite a lot of money for a first time young director. It

couldn't be made for less because there's a lot of action in the film. We had tremendous support from Channel Four and David Aukin, without whom we couldn't have made the film.

***Q - Where did the finance come from?***

***Jeremy -*** It came from Channel Four, a German company called WMG, a Japanese company called Kazui and from Polygram. Channel Four were the first to be interested and then the others came on board.

***Q - And you put that deal together with your limited experience and limited track record?***

***Jeremy -*** Yes

***Q - What unique qualities would you say you had that enabled you to do that, because most new film makers might find it quite intimidating?***

***Jeremy -*** Just persistence, a desire to learn. I'm very suspicious of the mystique of the producer. There is nothing particularly difficult about doing these deals if you have a reasonable understanding of business. What is hard about this business is the energy level required, the persistence, the will to make the film. It's extremely difficult to pull everything together and you must have tremendous self belief to keep yourself going. The rest is your own creative judgement which you either have or you have not got.

***Q - There are a lot of new film makers thinking of making their first film for £25k for instance. From your experience with Shopping, would you say that it's a good idea to forget £25k and aim for £2m?***

***Jeremy -*** It's a good idea to do a low budget film and then work up. When I was 23, I line produced a film for £800k called *Turn Of The Screw* (which still hasn't been released due to legal complications). That was a very important part of my education as it gave me the confidence to negotiate deals and to operate in the film world. It also gave Channel Four and the Completion Bond company the confidence to let me produce *Shopping.*

***Q - Were there any problems in the making of Shopping that you didn't expect, anything that you could warn new film makers about?***

***Jeremy -*** Editing. First time directors and producers tend to leave too much in and kill the pace of the film. They should just let the film go and let the editor cut it because they'll probably do a better cut. The other problem is to give yourself enough time in post production.

***Q - How did Shopping perform, both in the UK and internationally?***

***Jeremy -*** Badly

***Q - Why do you think that is?***

***Jeremy* -** I think we made a film that was confused as to what it was. It didn't know whether it was a rather moralistic drama about the dangers of youth-crime and joy-riding or whether it was an out and out action movie. From the beginning, you have to be absolutely clear about who the market is. The other problem was that the final cut wasn't as good as it could have been. Since then, we've cut 15 minutes out and it's a much better picture

***Q - Do you think that young directors make their first film without realising that it fits between genres - for instance, Shopping and White Angel didn't really fit into one genre?***

***Jeremy* -** The classic American distributor comment is *"It's not New Line and it's not Fine Line - it's somewhere in the middle."* Well that's really helpful, thank you! I think that's something to do with a lack confidence to say - *"I am making a horror film"* for example. We had £2m to make something as entertaining as *Lethal Weapon,* and perhaps in retrospect, we didn't have enough confidence in ourselves to state that clearly.

***Q - You didn't have the balls to put on the screen what you really wanted to do?***

***Jeremy* -** Absolutely. I think now, we would say this is what we're making - we're very clear in our concepts now.

***Q - What happened when Shopping was finished and how did you move on to new deals and new things?***

***Jeremy* -** We had a truly remarkable experience. We made a film that didn't work but have done extremely well out of it. I think we sold ourselves very well, particularly Paul. We got two very important people, a manager and an agent into Paul's life in America. They watched *Shopping* and saw potential. At The Sundance Festival, Paul's manager, Phyllis Carlisle (also a producer) got him *Mortal Kombat,* a concept film in need of a director. Peculiarly, directors appear to be an amazing rarity in America.

***Q - It's advisable after a first film to get an agent and a manager?***

***Jeremy* -** Yes, you need a lawyer and an agent, or a agent and a manager, you don't need three.

***Q - So you're suggesting that it's a good idea for a first time film-maker to be thinking forward when they're making their first picture, and say "as soon as I finish shooting, I'm on that plane to LA, shouting about myself"?***

***Jeremy* -** Absolutely. Think about who you want to represent you and why you want them to represent you. The relationship I have with Phyllis has ultimately benefited Impact Pictures, even though I had nothing to do with *Mortal Kombat.* Effectively we had eighteen months apart, but we remianed a strong unit, partly because of our friendship and trust, but also because we have people in our lives who want us to be together and present us as a team.

***Q - And more importantly you're actually being paid to be film-makers, whereas most film-makers in Britain, are not?***

***Jeremy -*** Yes, completely right. However, you must be strong enough to allocate time to make films you want to make and not be completely sold on the money that exists in LA. You must have another life and in fact it makes you more attractive to the Americans. They love it if you say *"I'm sorry I'm not available during that period, I'm producing this film over in Europe"*.

Also, I think it's important for a film producer not to be entirely reliant on one director. I think it takes the strain off that director's talent and it makes the producer feel as though they have value in themselves and that they're not just on the coat tails of this extraordinary blazing talent.

***Q - Is being English a major advantage in America?***

***Jeremy -*** Yes you should be as English as you can. Arrogance is always bad news, but I think it's important to have an English accent, they like that. What you shouldn't do is try and be American, you should try and maintain your Englishness. For many American film makers, the great directors have all been English, Lean and Hitchcock are the names that come up most in Hollywood.

***Q - How did you physically get over to the States to meet agents and managers?***

***Jeremy -*** I had a girlfriend who's mother was very wealthy and at that time Virgin Airlines had just launched - if you flew upper class you got a free economy ticket. So her mother kept coming over and giving me these free economy tickets - Paul and I both went to America on my girlfriend's mother effectively. In fact my girlfriend was very important because her mother had this fabulous house in L.A and that's where we used to stay. So we were very lucky in that respect.

***Q - How expensive is it to relocate over there and how easy is it to do...for instance the Green Card problem?***

***Jeremy -*** When a company employs you to work for them in America, they will give you what's called an O1 visa which is much better than a Green Card. A Green Card means you are taxed in America on your worldwide income, even if you've already been taxed in the UK for any income you've earned there. Whilst trying to raise money, we came in as visitors and could stay for up to six months. If money is really tight, you can get cheap standby plane tickets, then all you need to do is find a friend or even a girlfriend! There's a huge ex-pat community in LA and somebody's bound to know somebody who's got a floor or a couch - it's completely acceptable in LA to get a call from a penniless filmmaker and put them up for a few day. In those few days you then have to lie.

The agents in L.A are constantly trying to find the next Paul Anderson or Danny Boyle - you just call up and lie, *"I've just made this extraordinary film for the BFI, would you like to have a look at it?"* cut off the titles, pass it off as your own and go and show them something. You also try and time it so it's around lunchtime so you can get a free lunch. You do that with CA, William Morris, UTA and ICM and you create a bit of buzz about yourself and get four free lunches. That's how you begin. Then you literally say *"I've got a lot of other films which I've left at home, but this is my latest work"* - you must have a certain amount of charm to get away with it, but it's worth doing.

With Paul, I used to say that he had directed lots of television, *Shopping* was his first feature and that I would send videotapes - but of course you never do, and they never ask for them, they just make a note - *he's done other stuff.*

***Q - Should a new filmmaker go to L.A before they have made a film?***

***Jeremy -*** In the two years that they've been trying to raise money they should go to LA to try and raise money because I think the experience of being exposed to the industry there is very inspiring. It's not as intimidating as it sounds and it also makes you want to achieve it more than ever. If you have something to show, it will be a lot better for you. You will get turned down by a lot of places and that can be quite tough.

***Q - What are the major bonuses of working in the States?***

***Jeremy -*** The major benefit is the coffee! The money to actually have a life and do what you love and not feel that anybody who gives you money is doing you a favour. Everybody here is so grateful to the BBC and Channel Four when they are given money to make a movie. What they fail to realise is that those companies exist to make product for the public. We almost feel like saying, *"well I'm sorry but I have to ask you for money"*, it's that apologetic attitude. In America it's *"Fuck you, I'm going to be the next Tarantino and you should give me money because I'm going to make you money".*

***Q - What are the major drawbacks?***

***Jeremy -*** Unfortunately, people can be insincere in America. It's difficult to identify who in a company has the power to say yes or no. Often you are dealing with people who don't have that power and they're quite frightened for their jobs, therefore they will not commit either way. You tend to get a kind of *yes, maybe*, and you can be strung along. They won't say *No,* because you could be the next *Reservoir Dogs,* and they won't say *Yes,* because you might not be. It's difficult and you have to learn to discriminate between who is really interested and who's not interested. Also, if they think they are doing you a favour, they will screw you to kingdom come. You have to make them think that you could go across town to Warner Brothers, or to Fox or Disney and do the deal there - you have to use leverage.

Fear is the overwhelming atmosphere in LA, you have to make them frightened that they are going to lose the project unless they commit to you. It just doesn't exist here in the UK because there are only one or two companies who do make films, so it's not surprising that you are grateful when one of these companies does give you money.

***Q - What do you think are your biggest mistakes?***

***Jeremy -*** I think we should have had more courage in our convictions when we made *Shopping,* we should have trusted our instincts to make what we believed in and stand by it.

***Q - What do you think were your best decisions?***

***Jeremy -*** To keep the machine running, not to stand still, to keep selling ourselves and keep telling the world that we believed in what we made, even when we had made a film that didn't work. Also, we got two people in our lives who could really help us to keep moving.

***Q - Do you have any final advice or tips?***

***Jeremy -*** At the end of the day, nobody really knows anything, it's all about perception. Even if you have made a film that does not actually work, you must still sell yourself as though you have made the greatest film ever. Don't deny the problems and do learn from the experience, just don't apologise for it. The moment that you are perceived as being apologetic for what you have done, you're weak and you sell yourself short.

# Section 3
# The Toolkit

# READ THIS FIRST!

# LEGAL DISCLAIMER

*The copyright in and to the sample contracts and documents in this book is owned and retained by the originator of the work ("the Owner"). These sample contracts and documents have been created for your general information only. The Owner, the authors of this book and the publishers cannot therefore be held responsible for any losses or claims howsoever arising from any use or reproduction. Nothing in this book should be construed as legal advice. The information provided and the sample contracts and documents are not a substitute for consulting with an experienced entertainment lawyer and receiving counsel based on the facts and circumstances of a particular transaction. Furthermore case law and statutes and European and International law and industry practise are subject to change, and differ from country to country.*

*This legal section has been compiled with the assistance of Helen Tulley of Hammond Suddards Solicitors who wishes to emphasise that the notes and agreements are not a substitute for specific legal advice and are designed for very general guidance only.*

# THE LEGAL TOOLKIT

## notes

### Limited Company or Partnership?

*If you are an independent producer you will need to set up a limited company through which to contract both with financiers and artists in order to give yourself the necessary protection. The limited company can be structured as a joint venture or more usually governed by a shareholder's agreement. You and your fellow producers can effectively act as a partnership in terms of sharing income i.e. profits, if that is what you intend to do. It is a very good idea to enter into an agreement which sets out rules for the conduct of the business of the company as between the directors and/or shareholders. It is particularly important to consider how outside work is to be treated i.e. whether the fees a company director receives for his services on an outside project are to be paid into the company, or to be retained by him personally.*

*A company is treated as a separate legal entity and it is liable for any contractual obligations, warranties and undertakings it enters into. Therefore, if a company is in breach of any of it's obligations, it and not the company's officers (the directors and secretary) will be liable (unless the company's officers have acted fraudulently or wrongfully). If the company has, for example, an obligation to make a payment under the terms of an agreement and it is unable to do so the company may be wound up by it's creditors. This means the assets of the company are gathered in and paid out to those creditors. But the company's directors will not be personally liable for the company's debts (unless the director has acted or traded unlawfully or wrongfully) and the director's personal property is untouched by the winding up.*

*This is an important source of protection to the individual. It is particularly useful in the film industry where even though the expenditure on a film may not be high, the liabilities and damages payable to contracting third parties could be considerable.*

*The downside of having a company is that you must comply with the Companies Acts in relation to how you run and administer the company. In certain circumstances, if you do not comply with the law eg. filing accounts at Companies House, your company can be struck off the register. It can be restored to the register but not without expense and inconvenience.*

*If you trade as a partnership, you are personally responsible for the contractual obligations, warranties and undertakings of the partnership. If you or your partners do not meet those financial obligations and they are over £750 you can be made bankrupt by a creditor. If you are adjudged bankrupt your personal property including your home (but excluding tools of your trade) can be sold off to pay the creditor.*

*As a partner you are jointly and severally liable for the debts of the partnership. Unless you agree otherwise, if your partner binds the partnership to pay money to a third party, the third party can come after you for all of that sum (not just half of it, if for example, there were two partners).*

*A partnership is governed by the Partnership Act 1890 and there are very few legislative rules regarding the conduct of partnerships.*

### Company Directors and the Law

#### *Role of Company Director*

*Directors are agents of the Company and as such occupy a fiduciary position in relation to the Company. All powers entrusted to them are only exercisable in this fiduciary capacity (see Sec. 2)*

*Since directors have control of the Company's business and assets, the law requires them to act honestly in what they consider to be the Company's best interests, not their own.*

*If the directors are also majority shareholders or if they represent the majority shareholders, they must not manage the company so as to unfairly prejudice the minority shareholders.*

*There is also a general duty on the directors to have regard to the interest of employees as well as shareholders.*

*Directors should also have the interest of the creditors particularly when the Company is insolvent (or nearly so) as well as all (sometimes instead) of the interests of the shareholders.*

## Fiduciary Duty

*The directors are under a fiduciary duty which requires them to act in good faith and with loyalty to the Company (akin to a trustees' position)*

*They should not permit a conflict to arise between their personal interests and those of the Company and should disclose any interest of any kind, whether direct or indirect in a contract with the Company (including any loans or guarantees)*

*A director's powers are given to them under the Articles of Association and such powers shall be used for the proper and primary/substantial purposes for which they are given.*

*They should take proper care of the Company's property and should not appropriate such property, failing which they will be accountable to the Company for any personal gains obtained including from knowledge or opportunities of investment which they obtained as directors (unless the Company agrees otherwise).*

*There is a general prohibition on companies making loans, guarantees, etc. available to directors over £5000 (or £20,000 in certain other circumstances).*

## Standards of Performance/Duties of Care Diligence and Skill

*A director is under a duty of care, diligence and skill owed to the Company. He must show an acceptable degree of such care, diligence and skill as would be displayed by a reasonable man.*

*If a director has a certain skill e.g. accountancy, he is required to show proficiency in that skill as would be reasonably expected of a competent member of that profession.*

*A director is not liable for errors in judgement (but is liable for his own negligence and may be held accountable of any loss arising from such negligence).*

*A director may accept (without making investigation) information provided by an apparently reliable source e.g. a co-director or senior employee.*

*He should attend a board and general meetings whenever possible.*

## Directors as Employees

*A director is not necessarily an employee of the Company (although he is liable to Schedule E income tax and national insurance contributions on his fees.)*

*A director who is also an employee should not vote at a board meeting to approve his own contact of employment and (unless the Articles provide otherwise) cannot be counted in the quorum for that purpose of that vote.*

## Accounts and Records

*The directors must prepare a profit and loss account in respect of each financial year of the Company with a balance sheet as at the last day of that financial year reflecting a true and accurate position of the company at the relevant date.*

*The directors must lay a copy of such accounts before the Company in general meeting and file the same with the Register of Companies within certain time limits. The accounts must include directors' and auditors' reports properly signed.*

*The directors must maintain a register of directors and their interests as well as minutes of all board and general meetings.*

# Copyright

*Copyright is in fact a bunch of rights that attaches to the owner of the copyright in certain types of intellectual property (as defined in the CDPA 1988) i.e. literacy, artistic, dramatic and musical works and derivative works including film, sound recordings and published work. The right of copyright rests first in the author or creator of the work (there are some exceptions to this). To qualify*

*for copyright protection the work must be original to the author and not a copy. The bundle of rights given to the creator of the work are set out in the CDPA 1988 and these rights may not be exercised by another without the permission of the author or owner. The restricted acts are:- copying, issuing copies to the public, performing, broadcasting, transmitting by cable or adapting the work.*

*The rights of copyright rest automatically in the author. There is no requirement of notice or registration. In order to provide evidence of creation, an author may send, for example, a screenplay to him/her self in an envelope which is kept sealed so the postmark on the envelope provides evidence of the date of creation.*

*Copyright exists in artistic, musical, literacy and dramatic works for 70 years after the end of the year in which the author dies. For Film it lasts for 70 years after the death of the last to die of the director, scriptwriter, dialogue writer or composer of commissioned music for the film. For soundrecordings, broadcasts, performances, cable transmissions, it lasts 50 years from the end of the year in which the performance etc. was made or made available to the public. The CDPA 1988 has been amended recently to harmonise copyright duration throughout Europe and important changes, including the revival of copyright in certain works, have been made. Any dealings with Copyright works should be checked with your solicitor.*

## Options. Licenses & Assignments

### OPTIONS

*An option over a piece of work is an agreement by the owner of the work not to dispose of the work to a third party for a specified period of time in consideration of the purchaser (i.e. a producer) paying a fixed amount of money. This may be a nominal amount of £1 or a commercial sum negotiated between two parties. If the purchaser exercises the option the owner agrees to assign or licence some or all of the rights in the work to the purchaser. An option is necessary for a purchaser so they can develop a project based on a piece of work without the fear that some other party is doing likewise. An option grants the producer the right to develop a project based on the work to see if it is worth acquiring the work or certain rights in the work, or obtaining permission to exploit all or some of the rights in the work.*

*An option may be taken over a screenplay or more usually over an underlying piece of work such as a novel or a stageplay. The owner of a novel is only likely to grant an option over the work for the specific rights necessary to make and exploit a film or films.*

*It is advisable to annex the licence or assignment to the option agreement with the terms set out and agreed. If you enter into an option and do not agree the terms upon which you will acquire the rights in the work, this is an agreement to agree and may not be enforceable. It also leaves you very vulnerable when it comes to negotiating the terms for any licence or assignment.*

### LICENCES AND ASSIGNMENTS

*A licence is a permission given by the owner allowing you to do certain acts without infringing copyright in their work. Frequently, when you are dealing with published literary works the owner or their agent will only wish to grant you a licence to those specific rights in the work that you need to make and distribute the film. You usually need to acquire ancillary rights (i.e. the video, CD-Rom, book of the film) to make the film commercially attractive and viable, but the owner may insist that they participate in income from this source.*

*A licence fee is payable, usually upon first day of principal photography. This fee can be calculated by reference to a percentage to the budget with a minimum and maximum fee cited. The advantage to the owner of this is that if the film is taken up by a Hollywood studio, for example, and the studio pumps in huge sums for the film, the owner is a direct beneficiary of this. A licence can be for a specific period of time or in perpetuity subject to negotiation. A licence can be exclusive or non-exclusive. If it is exclusive, the owner cannot sell the rights (or otherwise dispose of them) to any one else. If you are making a film you must insist upon an exclusive licence as obviously you (and certainly not your financiers and distributors) do not want a competing product out on the market.*

*An Assignment is a transfer of ownership from the owner to you. Copyright in a work can be broken down into specific rights and those rights can be sold separately. Therefore, you can buy the film rights in the work and the owner can retain the publishing rights or stage rights (as is usually the case). If you are commissioning a script or treatment or engaging creative talent (directors, actors, composers) then you must ensure you own outright all their copyright in their work or performance and this will be affected by an assignment of rights. As with a licence, it is usual for an assignment to set out those rights which are being transferred.*

*In both licences and assignments there is usually a turnaround provision which allows the owner of the work to re-acquire it if the film or programme does not go into production within a specified period of time.*

*Where work is owned jointly by two or more authors/owners you must obtain an assignment from both or all of them, as one joint author/owner acting alone does not have authority to assign rights in the work.*

## Writers Agreement

*If you commission a writer to write a screenplay you must enter into a written agreement with him in which the writer assigns or licences their rights in the screenplay to you (they may assign/licence all their rights or only the specific rights you require i.e. film and ancillary rights. If you do not have this written assignment of rights or an exclusive licence, the writer will remain the owner of the screenplay and could sell the screenplay to another person.*

*A writer may be a member of the Writer's Guild (of the UK or America) and you should clarify with them in the first instance the status of the agreement i.e. whether it is a Guild agreement or not.*

*If it is a Guild agreement then you should refer to the appropriate Guild to confirm the minimum payments have been complied with.*

*A writer's agreement must most importantly contain a waiver of moral rights (see Glossary). Without this it will be very difficult to both raise finance and distribute the film.*

*Usually the writer's fee is broken down into several payments so that they receive part of their fee on commencement, part on delivery of the first draft, part on delivery of the second draft and the final sum on completion. For a film where many re-drafts and polishes may be required, it should be made clear in the agreement that the fee includes payment for such further re-drafts. A Film Producer will usually want a complete buyout to avoid having to make residual, repeat or fees in the future (the Guild agreements provide for minimum payments for repeats etc.).*

*The Producer must have the ability to engage another writer to work on the script if the work produced by the writer is unsatisfactory. If you are the Producer you need to negotiate a right of cut off which allows you to engage another writer to write, for example, the second draft without being obliged to make any further payment to the original writer.*

*You will need the writer to warrant the screenplay is his and he has not assigned or licensed it to any other person and that it is not defamatory, libellous etc. The writer should give an indemnity to you for any breach of warranty or undertaking provided in the agreement.*

*It is unusual for a scriptwriter to retain any rights in the work, but where a writer is also an author they will often wish to retain novelisation rights and occasionally the stage and radio rights. As these rights are of little commercial interest to the film producer (except perhaps any "making of " book), producers usually are happy to allow this, provided they retain a participation in any income derived from such exploitation. A hold back on the exploitation of the rights retained for a number of years is often negotiated so that a stage play or book based on the same treatment does not compete with the film.*

# Contracts & Agreements

## TOP TEN POINTS TO LOOK OUT FOR IN ANY AGREEMENT

*Set out below are some very broad considerations which you should give to any agreement. Of course, each circumstance will require more specific attention. If your liabilities under the agreement could involve you in substantial expense, seek legal advice.*

1. Ask yourself first what interests you need to protect and are they sufficiently protected.

2. Do you have any existing contractual obligations to other people and if you enter into this agreement are you going to be in breach of those existing contractual obligations ?

3. What are your liabilities in this agreement and if things go wrong, what are you liable for? Look out for clauses which make you personally liable even though you may be contracting through a company i.e.. Are you being asked to give a personal guarantee for a loan which is being made to your company?

4. What is the agreement asking you to do and is it reasonable and within your power to deliver or achieve?

5. If you are required under the agreement to do something ask to change any reference to your using your "best endeavours" to "reasonable endeavours".

6. If you are providing your own original work or any intellectual property owned by you under the terms of the agreement what happens if the project does not go ahead. Do you have the chance to regain or repurchase your property?

7. If you are due to receive any royalties or profit share under the agreement make sure that the other party has an obligation to collect in any revenue derived from the film or project, that they must show you their books and you have the right to audit those books. Check also that your share of Net Profits (as defined in the agreement) is as agreed i.e. are you receiving a share of the Producer's net profits or a share of all net profits?

8. What are the possible sources of income to you from the film or project and are all those sources being exploited and if so are you getting a fair share of that income?

9. What sort of controls do you have over the conduct of the other party? Are the promises they are making under the agreement sufficient to cover your interests? What happens if they are in default of their promises?

10. Remember that if the agreement is being provided by the other side, the terms will be very much in their favour. This does not mean that they are necessarily trying to stitch you up, this is just business.

# *Option Agreement (for previous work)*

**This is a guideline only and should not be relied upon without taking legal advice.**

THIS AGREEMENT is made as of the .......... day of 199....

***BETWEEN***

*.............................(hereinafter called "the Owner")*
*of ................................................... of the one part*

***AND***

*...........................(hereinafter called "the Purchaser")*
*of.................................... of the other part.*

***WHEREAS***

*(A) The Owner is the absolute owner free from encumbrances except as hereinafter mentioned of the entire copyright and all other rights throughout the world in an original literary work entitled "..............................." (hereinafter called "the Work" ) written by........................... (hereinafter called "the Author") which expression shall if the Author and the Owner are the same person be construed as a reference to the Owner.*

*(B) The Owner has (as is witnessed by the Owner's execution of these presents) agreed to grant to the Purchaser the sole and exclusive option to acquire by way of partial assignment of copyright, the sole and exclusive film and other rights hereinafter referred to for the consideration and upon and subject to the terms and conditions hereinafter contained*

***NOW THIS AGREEMENT WITNESSETH as follows:-***

*1. In this Agreement the following expressions shall unless the context otherwise requires bear the following meanings:-*

*"First Option Sum" : . ......................Pounds (£..................)*
*"Second Option Sum": ....................Pounds (£..................)*
*"First Option Date" : A date ................from the date hereof*
*"Second Option Date": A date.................following the First Option Date*

*2. (a) In consideration of the immediate payment by the Purchaser to the Owner of the First Option Sum (the receipt of which sum the Owner hereby acknowledges) the Owner hereby grants to the Purchaser the sole and exclusive option (hereinafter called "the First Option") exercisable by notice in writing to the Owner in the manner hereinafter mentioned at any time on or before the First Option Date to purchase from the Owner by way of partial (or full) assignment of copyright the sole and exclusive rights in the Work as more particularly specified in the form of the Deed of Assignment ("the Deed") annexed hereto and by this reference made a part hereof for the sums and upon and subject to the terms and conditions set out in the Deed.*

*(b) The Owner agrees to grant to the Purchaser a further sole and exclusive option (hereinafter called "the Second Option") upon the same terms and conditions as for the First Option provided that the Purchaser pays the Owner the Second Option Sum on or before the First Option Date. Such further Second Option shall be exercisable by notice in writing as aforesaid at any time on or before the Second Option Date*

*(c) Not withstanding anything to the contrary herein contained the First Option Period and (if applicable) the Second Option Period shall be extended until such time as the Owner has provided the Purchaser with evidence of it's title to the rights expressed to be granted in the Deed sufficient to enable the Purchaser if the Purchaser should require to obtain errors and omissions insurance in respect of such title upon customary terms.*

*3. The sums paid to the Owner pursuant to Clause 2 above shall be non returnable in any event and shall be deemed to be paid in advance and on account of the sum payable pursuant to Clause 2 of the Deed.*

*4. (a) The Owner hereby warrants that the Owner is the absolute owner free from encumbrances (save as expressly provided in the Deed) of all such rights in the Work as are referred to in the Deed.*

*(b) The Owner agrees and undertakes during the subsistence of the aforesaid option periods not to dispose of nor deal in any way with any of the rights in the Work which are the subject of the options hereby granted.*

*5 (a) The Purchaser agrees and undertakes not later than ten (10) days after the excercise of the applicable Option to submit an engrossment in the form of the Deed to the Owner for signature and further agrees agrees forthwith upon signature of the same by the Owner to pay to the Owner in exchange for the executed Deed the consideration therein expressed to be immediately payable.*

*(b) In the event that the Purchaser fails to submit an engrossment of the Deed to the Owner for signature within the time limited as aforesaid the consideration in the Deed expressed to be immediately payable shall become due and payable forthwith upon the expiration of the said period of ten (10) days without prejudice to the right of the Purchaser to call upon the Owner at any time thereafter to execute an engrossment of the Deed.*

*6. The Purchaser shall be entitled to write or cause to be written film treatments and /or screenplays and/or adaptations of the Work and undertake so-called pre-production work for the purpose of enabling the Purchaser to decide whether or not the Purchaser wishes to exercise any of the options hereby granted and in connection with the financing production distribtution and exploitation arrangements for the film or films to be based on the Work.*

*7. The notice in writing referred to in Clause 2 hereof shall be deemed to have been duly and properly served if addressed to the Owner and sent by prepaid post or if sent by telex or if sent by facsimile transmission to the above address or any subsequent address duly notified to the Purchaser and the date of service shall be deemed to be the day of delivery in the normal course of posting if posted or the day of sending such telex if telexed or the day of sending such facsimile if sent by facsimile.*

*8. The Purchaser shall be entitled to assign the benefit of this agreement to any third party but shall not thereby be relieved of it's obligations hereunder.*

*9. (a) All sums mentioned herein are exclusive of any Value Added Tax that may be payable thereon*

*(b) All sums payable to the Owner hereunder shall be paid to the irrevocably appointed Agent at it's address above whose receipt thereof shall be a good and valid discharge therefor*

*10. This agreement shall be construed and shall take effect in accordance with the laws of England and subject to the exclusive jurisdiction of the English Courts.*

*AS WITNESS the hands of the parties hereto or their representatives the day and year first above written*

*SIGNED by....................................................................*
*in the presence of:- .......................................................*

*SIGNED by...................................................................*
*For and on behalf of:-...................................................*
*(if a limited company)*

*in the presence of:-.......................................................*

THE TOOLKIT

# *Deed Of Assignment (Original Screenplay)*

**This is a guideline only and should not be relied upon without taking legal advice.**

This Deed is made the .......... day of ............. 19......

***BETWEEN***

*(Name, address) (hereinafter called "the Owner") of the one part*

*and*

*(Name, address) (hereinafter called "the Purchaser") of the other part.*

***WHEREAS***

*A) The Owner is the absolute owner free from encumbrances except as hereinafter mentioned of the copyright and all other rights throughout the world in and to the Treatment and Screenplay entitled.......................... (hereinafter called the "Work") written by.......................... (hereinafter called the "Author", which expression shall if the Author and the Owner are the same person be construed as a reference to the Owner)*

*B) The Owner has agreed to grant and assign the Producer for the consideration hereafter mentioned the* (specify applicable rights) *rights in the Work throughout the world as hereinafter more particularly mentioned.*

***NOW THIS ASSIGNMENT WITNESSETH***

*1.1. In consideration of the payment by the Purchaser to the Owner of the sum of ......................Pounds (£..........) (receipt whereof the Owner hereby acknowledges) the Owner with full title guarantee hereby assigns and grants to the Purchaser (specify applicable rights i.e. all rights) (including but not limited to copyright) of whatever description whether now known or in the future existing in and to the Work TO HOLD the same unto the Purchaser absolutely throughout all parts of the world in which copyright in the Work may now subsist or may be acquired and during all renewals, revivals and extensions thereof and thereafter (in so far as may be or become possible) in perpetuity and except as herein expressly provided to the contrary free from all restrictions and limitations whatsoever including (but not by way of limitation of the generality of the foregoing) free from all so-called "Authors rights" or "droit moral" and any similar right now or hereafter accorded by the laws prevailing in any part of the world (including but not limited to any rights pursuant to sections 77 and 80 of the Copyright Designs and Patents Act 1988) and the Owner hereby expressly waives any so-called "Authors rights", droit moral and any such rights.*

*1.2. Without prejudice to the generality of the assignment of rights in Clause 1.1 above, the Owner hereby confirms and agrees that the assignment of rights hereby made to the Purchaser includes any and all rights of communication to the public by satellite, cable retransmission rights and any and all rental and lending rights, whether now or hereafter known or existing in any country of the world, in and to the products of the Owner's services hereunder and /or the Film (as hereinafter defined) and/or copies thereof and/or any part or version or adaptation of any of the foregoing.*

*2. (a) As further consideration for the rights hereby granted the Purchaser hereby agrees to pay to the Owner*
*(i) upon the first day of principal photography of the first or only film made in exercise of the rights hereby granted and not being part of a television series or serial (hereinafter called "the Film") the sum of (£..............................)*

*(ii) sums from time to time equal to (....................) Percent (....%) of the Net Profits (as defined below) of the Film.*

*For the purposes of this Deed the expression "Net Profits" shall have the same meaning as is accorded thereto in the principal production finance and distribution agreements for the Film.*

*2 (b) The Owner agrees that the consideration payable to the Owner in accordance with the provisions of this Agreement takes into account and includes a payment in respect of all rights of communication to the public by satellite, cable, retransmission rights and any and all rental and lending rights as referred to in Clause 1.2. hereof and that the said payment constitutes equitable and adequate consideration for the assignment of satellite, cable and rental and lending rights, and constitutes and satisfies in full any and all rights which the Owner has or may at any*

*time have to receive equitable, adequate or other remuneration for the exploitation by satellite and cable and the rental or lending of the products of the Owner's services and/or the Film and/or copies thereof and/or any part or version or adaptation of any of the foregoing. Without prejudice to the provisions of this Clause nothing in this Agreement shall prevent the Owner from being entitled to receive income under collection and other agreements negotiated by recognised collection societies under the laws of any jurisdiction PROVIDED THAT this does not imply any obligation or liability on the part of the Purchaser regarding the collection or payment of such monies.*

*3. The Owner hereby represents, warrants and undertakes to and with the Purchaser that:-*

*a) the Owner is the Owner and Author of the Work which was and is wholly original with the Author and nothing therein infringes the copyright or any other rights of any third party*

*b) copyright in the Work subsists or may be acquired in all countries of the world whose laws now provide for copyright protection and that the Owner and the Author have not and will not at any time hereafter do authorise or omit to do anything relating to the Work whereby the subsistence of copyright therein or any part of such copyright may be destroyed or otherwise impaired.*

*c) the rights hereby granted are vested in the Owner absolutely and neither the Owner nor the Author or any other predecessor in title of the Owner heretofore assigned, licensed, granted or in any way dealt with or encumbered the same so as to derogate from the grant hereby made and that the Owner has a good title and full right and authority to make this Deed*

*d) the Work does not constitute a breach of any duty of confidence owed to any party and does not breach any right of privacy and does not contain any libellous or defamatory statement or matter or innuendo of or reference to any person firm company or incident*

*e) the Owner will indemnify and at all times keep the Purchaser fully indemnified from and against all actions, claims, proceedings, costs and damages incurred by or awarded against the Purchaser or any compensation paid or agreed to be paid by the Purchaser on the advice of counsel agreed between the parties hereto (and in default of such agreement within one month from the time such agreement is sought then a counsel decided by the President for the time being of the Law Society) in consequence of any breach, non-performance or non-observance by the Owner of all or any of the covenants, warranties, representations and agreements by the Owner contained in this Deed*

*f) the Owner will and does hereby authorise the Purchaser at the Purchaser's expense to institute prosecute and defend such proceedings and to do such acts and things as the Purchaser in it's sole discretion may deem expedient to protect the rights granted by the Owner to the Purchaser hereunder and to recover damages and penalties for any infringement of the said rights and insofar as may be necessary in the Purchaser's reasonable view to use the name of the Owner for or in connection with any of the purposes aforesaid and the Owner shall in any such proceeding afford the Purchaser all reasonable assistance the Purchaser may require at the expense of the Purchaser in instituting prosecuting or defending such actions unless the said action is occasioned by some breach or non-performance by the Owner of any covenants or warranties herein contained.*

*4. For further securing to the Purchaser the rights hereby granted the Owner hereby undertakes with the Purchaser that the Owner will at the request and expense of the Purchaser do all such further acts and things and execute all such further documents and instruments as the Purchaser may from time to time require for the purpose of confirming the Purchaser's title to the said rights in any part of the world and the Owner hereby appoints the Purchaser it's irrevocable attorney-in-fact with the right but not the obligation to do any and all acts and things necessary for the purpose of confirming the Purchaser's title at the expense of the Purchaser as aforesaid and to execute all such deeds documents and instruments in the name of and on behalf of the Owner which appointment shall be deemed a power coupled with an interest and shall be irrevocable.*

*5. The Owner hereby grants to the Purchaser the right to use and authorise others to use the name, biography and likeness of the Author when exploiting or dealing with the rights hereby granted provided that the Author shall not be represented as personally using or recommending any commercial product other than films or other products of the rights hereby granted based upon the Work.*

*6. The Purchaser shall not be obliged to exercise any of*

*the rights of copyright and other rights in and to the Work or any part thereof granted unto the Purchaser hereunder and if the Purchaser shall not exercise any of these said rights the Purchaser shall not be liable to the Owner in any manner whatsoever.*

*7. The Purchaser shall be fully entitled to negotiate and conclude agreements for the sale performance licensing and other commercial exploitation of the rights hereby granted upon whatever terms the Purchaser considers fair and reasonable and shall not be obliged in any way to seek the approval of the Owner in connection therewith and the Purchaser gives no warranty or representation as to the amount (if any) of any receipts that may arise.*

*8. a) In the event of a film or films being based upon the Work the Purchaser shall give the Author a single card credit on all copies of any such film or films issued under the control of the Purchaser in the form: Screenplay written by ......................... provided however that no casual or inadvertent failure by the Purchaser to accord the Author credit as aforesaid shall be deemed a breach*

*b) The Purchaser will incorporate in it's agreements with the distributors or broadcasters of such films as aforesaid a provision obliging such distributor or broadcaster to accord such credits to the Author but the failure of any distributor or broadcaster to accord such credits shall not constitute a breach by the Purchaser hereof provided however that if the Purchaser shall be notified of such failure the Purchaser shall use all reasonable endeavours but without incurring material expense to ensure that such failure is remedied by such distributor or broadcaster (as the case may be)*

*9. All rights assigned by this Deed shall be irrevocable under all or any circumstances and shall not be subject to reversion rescission termination or injunction in case of breach of the provisions of this Deed by the Purchaser including failure to pay any part of the consideration other than the sum payable under clause 1 hereof. The Owner's remedies shall be limited to an action at law for damages or for an accounting (if applicable). The Purchaser shall not be liable for damages for breach of contract (except for payment of consideration) unless the Purchaser has been given reasonable notice and opportunity to adjust or correct the matter complained of and the same has not been adjusted or corrected within a reasonable time following the notice aforesaid.*

*10. Any notices required to be served hereunder shall be deemed to have been duly and properly served if addressed to the Owner or Purchaser as the case may be and sent in a prepaid envelope or if sent by facsimile transmission to the above address or any subsequent address of the Owner or Purchaser as the case may be duly notified to the Owner or Purchaser respectively and acknowledged and the date of service shall be deemed to be the date of delivery in the normal course of posting if posted or the date of sending if sent by facsimile.*

*11. All sums mentioned herein are exclusive of Value Added Tax that may be payable thereon*

*12. The Purchaser shall be entitled to assign the benefit of this Deed to any third party but shall not thereby be relieved of it's obligations hereunder*

*13. This Deed shall be construed and shall take effect in accordance with the laws of England and subject to the exclusive jurisdiction of the English Courts*

*IN WITNESS WHEREOF the Owner and the Purchaser have executed this Assignment and is hereby delivered as a Deed the day and year first above written*

*SIGNED as a DEED*

*by:....................................................*

*in the presence of:............................................*

*Executed as a DEED by:...................................... (Limited) acting through it's two Directors/Director and Secretary*

# Actors Agreement

**This is a guideline only and should not be relied upon without taking legal advice.**

**(MAIN AGREEMENT)**

Dated:

**PRODUCER: ("the Producer")**
Address:

**ARTIST: ("the Artist")**
Address:

**FILM TITLE: ("the Film")**

**ROLE: ("character")**

1. Services: Producer hereby engages Artist as a performer in the Film portraying in the role described above (as said role may be changed or rewritten at Producer's discretion)

2. Start Date: It is presently contemplated that read through day will commence on....................and rehearsals will commence on.......................and that principal photography shall commence on.................... provided however Artist's services shall commence no later than.....................subject to events of force majeure. Artist agrees to remain available and not accept another engagement which would conflict or interfere with Artist obligations hereunder

3. Guaranteed Period of Engagement: Term: The term of Artist's engagement hereunder shall commence on the start date and continue subject only to the provisions for suspension and termination set out in Exhibit A hereto for a minimum period of ............... (.....) weeks ("Guaranteed Period of Engagement") and thereafter for the period necessary to complete all continuous services required by Producer from Artist in connection with principal photography of the Film. Artist shall perform additional services prior to and after the term in accordance with the provisions of clause 4 hereof

4. Additional Services: The Artist shall on written notice from the Producer perform additional services ("Additional Services") on ..................... or such other or additional day notified to the Artist by the Producer in connection with principal photography of the Film

5. Further Services: If the Producer requires the Artist's services after the Guaranteed Period of Engagement and not for any Additional Services the Artist shall if so requested by the Producer render such further services ("Further Services") which shall include without limitation dubbing and post-synchronisation subject to the Artist's prior professional engagements

6. Basic Compensation: Subject to the provisions of this Agreement and provided that Artist shall keep and perform all covenants and conditions to be kept and performed by Artist hereunder Producer agrees as full compensation for services rendered and for all rights granted to the Producer hereunder to pay Artist as follows:-

(a) Guaranteed Compensation: For the Guaranteed Period of Engagement, Artist shall receive the sum of .................. pounds (£..........) payable as to ........................ pounds (£.........) following the first week of rehearsals inclusive of the read through day and ..................... pounds (£..........) following the .................weeks of rehearsals and as to the balance following the end of the first full week of Artist's services in principal photography of the Film. Such payment shall be made to Artist care of (.......................). If the Artist renders Additional Services, Artist shall receive..........pounds (£.......) for each day after which he attends at the request of the Producer and renders services hereunder. If the Artist renders Further Services, Artist shall receive a further sum (if any) to be negotiated in good faith between the parties for each day or part day (if any) upon which he attends at the request of the Producer and renders services hereunder

7. Credit
(a) If Artist shall keep and perform all covenants and conditions to be kept and performed by the Artist hereunder and if Artist appears readily recognisable in the Film then Artist will be accorded credit in the main titles of the Film on all copies of the Film issued by or under the control of the Producer and in all major paid advertising excluding the customary industry exclusions. The size type and placement of such credit shall be at Producer's sole discretion

8. Transportation and Expenses: From the commencement of principal photography until the expiry of the Term, Producer shall provide Artist with .................. transportation facilities (state what these are if any and whether other expenses will be paid)

9. Conditions: Artist's engagement hereunder is subject to Producer obtaining standard cast insurance for Artist at normal rates

10. References: The term of Artist's engagement hereunder shall be as set forth in this Main Agreement and in Exhibit "A" attached hereto which is incorporated herein by reference. In the event of any express inconsistency between the provisions of this Main Agreement and the provisions of Exhibit / a the provisions of this Main Agreement shall control

IN WITNESS WHEREOF the parties hereto have executed the within Agreement as of the date first set forth hereinabove

(insert name of Producer)

BY:......................................................................

Duly authorised officers:.....................................

Accepted and Agreed to:

........................................................

**EXHIBIT A**

1. The Artist hereby

(a) Warrants that the Artist is not under any obligation or disability which might prevent or restrict the Artist from entering into this agreement or from giving the undertakings or fully observing and performing the terms and conditions of this Agreement or granting the rights and consents referred to herein

(b) Gives all such consents as are or may be required under the Copyright Designs and Patents Act 1988 or any re-enactment consolidation or amendment thereof or any statute of like purpose or effect for the time being in force in any part of the world including but not in limitation of the foregoing all consents under Part II of the said Act in order that the Producer may make the fullest use of the Artist's services provided by the Artist hereunder and furthermore the Artist hereby irrevocably and unconditionally waives all rights relating to the Artist's services in the Film to which the Artist is now or may in the future be entitled pursuant to the provisions of Section 77 80 84 and 85 of the said Act and any other moral rights to which the Artist may be entitled under any legislation now existing or in the future enacted in any part of the world

(c) warrants that the Artist is a "qualifying person" and the performance of the Artist is a "qualifying performance" within the meaning of the Copyright Designs and Patents Act 1988

2. The Artist undertakes that the Artist shall during the subsistence of and subject to the terms and conditions of this Agreement as where and when required by the Producer:-

(a) perform and record the Artist's part

(b) attend for tests conferences fittings rehearsals and the taking of still photographs and other arrangements

(c) dress, make up and wear the Artist's hair (subject to prior consultation with the Artist) as directed by the Director and generally comply with all decisions of the Producer concerning the manner in which the Artist shall render the Artist's services hereunder and be portrayed and presented

(d) render the Artist's services hereunder willingly and to the utmost of the Artist's skill and ability and as directed by the Producer both in connection with the production of the Film and for publicity and other purposes connected therewith Provided Always that nothing in this sub-clause and sub-clause (c) hereof shall be deemed to require the Artist to recommend or endorse any commercial product other than the Film and any commercial gramophone record of the sound track of the Film or to engage in any publicity or other activities for any such purpose (but without prejudice to Clause 5 hereof)

3. The Artist further undertakes:-

(a) that the Artist will comply with all reasonable and notified directions, regulations and rules in force at places where the Artist is required to render services hereunder (including in particular regulations and rules relating to smoking and the taking of photographs) and will comply with the orders given by the Producer of it's representatives from time to time

(b) to keep the Producer informed of the Artist's whereabouts and telephone number from time to time prior to and throughout the engagement

(c) that the Artist will use the Artist's best endeavours to maintain a state of health enabling the Artist fully and efficiently to perform the Artist's services hereunder throughout the engagement and that the Artist will not take part in any activity which might interfere with the due and efficient rendering of such services or which might invalidate any such insurance as is referred to in the preceding sub-clause

(d) that the Artist shall not at any time pledge the credit of the Producer nor incur or purport to incur any liability on it's behalf or in it's name

4. (a) The Artist hereby acknowledges that all rights whatsoever throughout the World in or in any way attaching to the Film and all photographs and sound recordings taken and made hereunder (including all rights of copyright therein and in any written or other material contributed by

the Artist and all such rights therein or in such material as are or may hereafter be conferred or created by international arrangement or convention in or affecting any part of the World whether by way of new or additional arrangement or convention in or affecting any part of the world whether by way of new or additional rights not now comprised in copyright or otherwise) shall belong absolutely to the Producer and the Artist with full title guarantee assigns and grants the same to the Producer throughout the World and throughout all periods for which the said rights or any of them are or may be conferred or created by the law in force in all or any parts of the world and all renewals, revivals and extensions of such periods the Producer may make or authorise any use of the same and may exploit the same in any manner but only in and in connection with the Film
(b) The Artist hereby acknowledges and agrees and confirms that the Producer shall be entitled and it is hereby authorised to adapt change take from add to and use and treat in every way all or any of the products of the Artist's services rendered hereunder and to use reproduce and perform and broadcast and transmit the same with or as part of the work of any other persons and synchronised or not with any music or other sounds or motions as the Producer considers necessary or desirable
(c) For the avoidance of doubt the assignment of rights set out in this Clause includes all satellite cable rental and lending rights ("the Rights") and the Artist agrees that the remuneration payable pursuant to this agreement includes and constitutes equitable and adequate consideration for the assignment and exploitation of the Rights and to the extent permitted by the law the Artist waives the right to receive any further remuneration in relation to the exploitation of the Rights

5. The Producer shall be entitled by written notice to the Artist given at any time to suspend the engagement of the Artist hereunder (whether or not the term of such engagement has commenced) if and so long as:-
(a) the production of the Film or the operation of any studio involved in such production shall be prevented suspended interrupted postponed hampered or interfered with by reason or on account of any event of force majeure fire accident action of the elements war riot civil disturbance sickness epidemic pestilence national calamity act of God or any actual labour disputes (including strikes lockouts or withholding of labour of any kind whether by the direction or with the support of any trade union or other body or otherwise) or illness or incapacity of the Producer of the Director of the Film or any principal artist or principal technician or any cause (apart from those hereinbefore specifically referred to and whether or not similar thereto) not reasonably within the control of the Producer or
(b) the voice of the Artist shall become unsatisfactory in quality or tone
(c) the Artist shall be reason of any illness or physical or mental incapacity or disability be unable in the opinion of the Producer fully to render the Artist's services hereunder or to devote sufficient of the Artist's time ability and attention to such services or
(c) the Artist shall fail refuse or neglect duly to render willingly and to the utmost of the Artist's skill and ability the Artist's full services hereunder or shall fail, refuse or neglect fully to observe or comply with any of the Artist's material obligations under this Agreement or with any of the terms thereof

6. Upon any suspension of the engagement of the Artist hereunder
(a) such suspension shall be effective from the date of the event giving rise to such suspension and shall continue for the duration of such event and for such reasonable period thereafter as may be necessary for the Producer to make arrangements to commence or resume production
(b) the Producer shall during the period of suspension cease to be liable to make any payments of remuneration to the Artist hereunder (or to pay for or provide accommodation or living expenses if the suspension is due to the Artist's default or refusal) save such instalments of remuneration as shall have become due and payable prior to the suspension and the period of engagement hereunder shall be extended by or (if appropriate) the commencement of the Artist's engagement shall be postponed by and the dates for payment of any further instalments of remuneration hereunder shall be postponed (or further postponed as the case may be) by a period equal to that of such suspension
(c) all rights of the Producer in respect of services rendered by the Artist and in all the products thereof previous to such suspension and the benefit of all consents granted hereunder shall not be affected and accordingly shall be or remain vested in the Producer

7. The Producer shall be entitled by written notice to the Artist given at any time to terminate the engagement of the Artist hereunder (without prejudice to any other rights and remedies available to the Producer hereunder)
(a) if any suspension under the provisions of paragraph (a) of clause 6 hereof shall continue for 28 (twenty-eight) consecutive days or 28 (twenty-eight) days in the aggregate or more
(b) if any suspension under the provisions of paragraph (b) or (b) of Clause 5 hereof shall continue for 2 (two) consecutive days or 3 (three) days in the aggregate or more
(c) at any time in the circumstances referred to in

paragraphs (d) or (f) of Clause 5 hereof (whether or not the Producer shall have suspended the Artist's engagement under the provisions of Clause 5 hereof) subject to the Artist being given the opportunity to rectify any default if capable of rectification within 24 (twenty-four) hours of the Producer giving notice of such default

Provided however that if any suspension under the provisions of paragraph (a) of Clause 5 hereof shall continue for six weeks or more then the Artist shall be entitled to terminate this engagement by seven days' written notice to the Producer unless by the expiry of such notice the Producer shall have terminated such suspension but the Producer shall not be entitled to terminate this engagement for the same event subject however to the right of the Producer to suspend or terminate the Artist's engagement for other proper cause including but not limited to the occurrence of a different event (even though of the same nature as a previous one) of force majeure in accordance with the provisions hereof

8. In the case of termination of the engagement of the Artist under the foregoing provisions or by the death of the Artist
(a) such termination shall be effective from the date of the event giving rise to the termination or (if there shall have been a prior suspension) from the date of the event giving rise to the suspension from which such termination arose
(b) any claim which the Producer may have against the Artist in respect of any breach, non-performance or non-observance of any of the material provisions of this Agreement arising prior to such termination or out of which such termination shall arise shall not be affected or prejudiced
(c) the Producer's title to and ownership of all copyrights and all other rights in or in connection with the services rendered by the Artist up to the date of such termination and in all the products of such services shall not be affected and such rights shall accordingly be or remain vested in the Producer
(d) payment to the Artist of the instalments of remuneration due and payable to the Artist up to the effective date of such termination shall operate as payment in full and final discharge and settlement of all claims on the part of the Artist under this Agreement and accordingly the Producer shall not be under any obligation to pay to the Artist any further or other sums on account of salary or otherwise

9. The Artist undertakes at the expenses of the Producer to execute and procure the execution of any document which the Producer may consider necessary for the purpose of carrying into effect the arrangements made by this Agreement or any of them including in particular any documents required to vest in or confirm any rights of copyright or other rights in the Producer

10. The rights and the benefit of all consents granted hereunder to the Producer are irrevocable and without right of rescission by the Artist or reversion to the Artist under any circumstances whatsoever

11. Credit will be given only
(a) if Artist appears recognisably in the Film as released
(b) if this Agreement has not been terminated for the default of the Artist

No casual or inadvertent failure to comply with credit requirements shall be deemed a breach of this Agreement. The sole remedy of Artist for a breach of any of the provisions of this clause or of the Principal Agreement shall be an action at law for damages, it being agreed that in no event shall Artist seek to be entitled to injunctive or other equitable relief by any reason of any of the breach or threatened breach of any credit requirements, nor shall Artist be entitled to seek to enjoin or restrain the exhibition distribution advertising exploitation or marketing of the Film

12. All notices served upon either party by the other hereunder shall be delivered by hand at or sent by pre-paid recorded delivery letter post or by facsimile addressed to the respective addressed hereinbefore contained or any subsequent address duly notified and if delivered by hand shall be deemed to have been served five days after posting and if sent by facsimile shall be deemed served 24 hours after receipt of the facsimile (and facsimile notice shall be confirmed by post). A copy of all notices to the Artist shall be sent to the Agent (if any)

13. The Artist shall treat as confidential and shall not disclose to any third party (save to the Artist's professional advisors whose dissemination of such information they receive shall be limited to use for business purposes i.e. quotes for services or as may be required by law) the provisions of this Agreement or any confidential information concerning the Producer or the Film or it's distributors which may come to the Artist's attention in connection with the Artist's engagement hereunder or otherwise

14. For the avoidance of doubt, it is expressly agreed between the parties that this Agreement and the provision of Artist's services in connection with the Film, is not subject to any collective bargaining agreement or guild or union regulations and the compensation paid to the Artist under clause 6 of the Main Agreement represents full and complete consideration for all of the services of the Artist hereunder and all rights assigned and granted by the Artist

in the products of those services

15. This Agreement shall be governed by and construed in accordance with the laws of England and subject to the exclusive jurisdiction of the Courts of England

## *Accompanying Notes*

*MAIN AGREEMENT*
*Clause 3: The Producer needs to ensure the actor is around for a fixed number of weeks and because the actor agrees to make him/herself available for that period the producer must pay accordingly.*

*Clause 4: Additional services are during principal photography.*

*Clause 6: Further services are post production services where the artist will be available subject to other prior engagements. Sometimes a producer can negotiate a certain number of so called "free" days (3 is the norm) where the artist will render Additional or Further Services free of charge. This gives the Producer more leeway but is only appropriate on big productions. The fee for Further or Additional Services can be agreed in advance and it is customary for the fee to be a daily rate calculated as a pro-rated amount of the weekly sum.*

*EXHIBIT A*
*Clause 4(c): See Glossary of Terms. This may not be legally effective but at present all relevant contracts include such a term.*

*Clause 7: The periods of suspension giving rise to the entitlement of the Producer to terminate the agreement are subject to negotiation.*

*Note 1: It should be made clear whether or not the terms of the agreement are going to be governed by the appropriate Equity agreement or not. Many actors, or more likely their agents, will insist on the application of Equity's terms as Equity has negotiated residual and royalty payments on repeats, video etc. with PACT. However if the project is a film intended for theatrical release you should negotiate a complete buy out of the Artist's performance rights wherever possible. A buy out will be expected by most sales agents, financiers and distributors as they will not want the trouble of having to account to the artists and more importantly, any residual payments will be seen as a drain on the revenue of the film.*

*Note 2: Deferments. If the fee or proportion of the fee is to be deferred, there should be further provisions that should also be mentioned, i.e. that the Deferment will be pro rata and pari passu with all other deferments to persons, providing services to the Film, after which all deferments to companies and firms should be met. All deferred sums are payable in first place from receipts received by the Producer from the exploitation of the Film subject to the recoupment of the production and post production cost of the Film only. It should be emphasised that the Deferment is a contingent amount and is only payable to the extent sufficient receipts are generated. It should also be mentioned that the Producers will use their reasonable endeavours to procure that their auditors or any other firm of Chartered Accountants appointed, will provide an audited detailed statement of all transactions relevant to the production and the income generated which should be made available to the artist and/or representatives by a specified date.*

*Note 3: A Daily Rate is usually calculated at 1/7th of the weekly rate.*

*Note 4: If the artist is a so called star they may insist upon a share of net profits.*

*Note 5: Work exists on bank holidays unless otherwise stated in the contract or accompanying schedule.*

*Note 6: Credit. The size and placement of the credit (billing requirement) is usually negotiated between the parties.*

*Note 7: Material. The artist will sometimes ask for the right to select the photographs of themselves to be used and this is usually granted subject to certain restraints.*

*Note 8: If an actor or their agent is concerned about the ability of a production company to make the payments due to the Artist, they may ask for all the monies due under the agreement to be paid to a third party to be held in an Escrow Account and paid out in accordance with the agreement under the terms of the agreed Escrow arrangement.*

# *Performers Consent*

**This is a guideline only and should not be relied upon without taking legal advice.**

From: *("the Performer")* of *(address)*

To: *(name of company) ("the Company which shall include it's successors assigns and licensees)* of *(address)*

Dated: *(date)*

Dear Sirs

*(Name of film)* (the "Film")

In consideration of the sum of (£ *amount*) paid by the Company to the Performer (the receipt of which the Performer acknowledges). The Performer irrevocably and unconditionally grants to the Company all consents required pursuant to the Copyright, Designs and Patents Act 1988 Part II and all other laws now or in the future in force in any part of the world which may be required for the exploitation of the Performer's performance contained in the Film, whether or not as part of the Film, in any and all media by any manner or means now known or invented in the future throughout the world for the full period of copyright protection pursuant to the laws in force in any part of the world, including all renewals, reversions and extensions.

This letter shall be governed by and construed in accordance with the law of England and Wales the courts of which shall be courts of competent jurisdiction.

Yours faithfully

(signature of Performer)

## *Accompanying Notes*

*Note 1: The Performer's Consent form is specifically for, and only relates to the Performer and their performance. The performers do not own copyright as such in their performance (there is none) but their consent is needed to exploit their performance.*

*Note 2: Consideration must be given in any contract. A contract requires an offer, acceptance and consideration. It is a legal necessity. ("Consideration" does not have to be money, it can be provided by, for example, giving up a legal right).*

# Release Form

**This is a guideline only and should not be relied upon without taking legal advice.**

From: *(name of individual)* of *(address)*

To: *(name of company) ("the Company" which shall include it's successors, assigns and licensees)*

of *(address)*

Dated: *(date)*

Dear Sirs

*(Name of the film)* (the "Film")

1. In consideration of the sum of £1 (*or any other amount*) now paid by the Company to me (the receipt of which I acknowledge) I warrant, confirm and agree with the Company that the Company shall have the right to exploit any films, photographs and sound recordings made by the Company for the Film in which I feature, or any literary, dramatic, musical or artistic work or film or sound recording created by me or any performance by me of any literary, dramatic, musical or artistic work or film or sound recording included by the Company in the Film in any and all media by any and all means now known or invented in future throughout the world for the full period of copyright, including all renewals, revivals, reversions and extensions.

2. I irrevocably and unconditionally grant to you all consents required pursuant to the Copyright, Designs, and Patents Act 1988 Part II * or otherwise under the laws in force in any part of the world to exploit such performances.

3. I irrevocably and unconditionally waive all rights which I may have in respect of the Film pursuant to the Copyright, Designs and Patents Act 1988 Sections 77, 80, 84 and 85**.

4. I consent to the use by the Company of my name, likeness, voice and biography in connection only with the Film.

5. The Company may assign or licence this agreement to any third party.

6. This letter shall be governed by and construed in accordance with the law of England and Wales and subject to the jurisdiction of the English Courts.

Yours faithfully

(signature of the individual)

* *the "Performers Rights"*
** *the Moral Rights of an author*

## *Accompanying Notes*

*Note 1: The release form covers any work created by the individual. This form is more comprehensive than the Performer's Consent which does not contain an assignment of copyright (as there is no copyright as such in a performance) and covers an assignment of any artistic material contributed by the individual to the producer.*

*Note 2: Consideration must be given in any contract. A contract requires an offer, acceptance and consideration. It is a legal necessity. ("Consideration" does not have to be money, it can be provided by, for example, giving up a legal right).*

# *Crew Agreement*

**This is a guideline only and should not be relied upon without taking legal advice.**

Dated:
**PRODUCER: ("the Producer")**
Address:

**CREW MEMBER:("the Crew Member")**
Address:

**FILM TITLE:("the Film")**

1. **Services:** The Producer hereby engages the Crew Member and the Crew Member undertakes and agrees to render to the Producer his/her services (hereinafter called "the Services").

2. **The Period of Engagement** shall commence on or about ...................................... (hereinafter called "the Start Date") and shall continue until the earlier of;
a) completion of the Film in all respects ready for delivery to the principal distributor of the Film
b) termination of the Crew Member's engagement pursuant to the provisions of this agreement

3. **Payment:** Subject to the provisions of this Agreement and the observance and performance by the Crew Member of all his obligations under it the Producer shall pay to the Crew Member the sum of ..................................... per week/ day (or a fixed amount), for all services rendered by the Crew Member in respect of the Film and for all rights in the products of such services
b) all sums payable to the Crew Member under this agreement are exclusive of Value Added Tax ("VAT"). The Producer shall pay such VAT as is properly charged by the Crew Member promptly following receipt of the Crew Member's tax invoice.
c) The Producer is expressly authorised by the Crew Member to deduct and withhold from all sums due to the Crew Member all deductions (if any) in accordance with local laws and regulations from time to time applicable
d) all sums payable under this clause 3 shall be paid directly to the Crew Member, whose receipt shall be a full and sufficient discharge to the Producer.
e) the Crew Member acknowledges that the remuneration provided under this clause 3 shall be inclusive of all guild and union minimum basic fees, overtime and all residual repeat and re-run payments, direct or indirect employment and like taxes and state governmental and / or social security contributions.

4. **Expenses:** All payments of pre-approved expenses to the Crew Member will be issued on a weekly basis by the Producer on provision of relevant invoice therefor.

5. **Duration of Filming:** The filming week shall be a 6 day week where the Producer may nominate such 6 days as in any week but the Crew Member shall not be required to work more than 7 consecutive days without receiving the next consecutive day off. A Filming day will not exceed 14 hours inclusive of meal breaks. Any hours worked in excess of the said 14 hours will at the Producer's sole election either be carried over to the following day or a payment of a pro rata hourly rate shall be paid to the Crew Member on the pay day next falling due.

6. **Rights/consents:** 6.1 The Crew Member with full title guarantee assigns and grants to the Producer the whole of the Crew Member's property right, title, interest in and to the Film and the entire copyright and all other rights in and to all products of the Crew Members services in connection with the Film including all vested future and contingent rights to which the Crew Member is now or may hereafter be entitled under the law in force in any part of the universe for the Producer's use and benefit absolutely for the full period or periods of copyright throughout the universe including all reversions, revivals, renewals and extensions created or provided by the law of any country. The Crew Member undertakes to execute all such documents and takes all such steps as may from time to time be necessary to secure to the Producer the rights in this clause 6.1

6.2 The Producer shall have the right to make, produce, sell, publicly exhibit, lease, license, hire, market, publicise, distribute, exhibit, diffuse, broadcast, adapt and reproduce mechanically graphically electronically or otherwise howsoever by any manner and means (whether now known or hereafter devised) the Film and all products of the Crew Member's services throughout the universe; to permit any third party to exercise any of such rights in the sole discretion of the Producer.

6.3. The Crew Member hereby irrevocably and unconditionally waives all rights relating to the Crew Member's services in the Film to which the Crew Member is now or may in the future be entitled pursuant to the provisions of Section 77 80 84 and 85 of the Copyright, Designs and Patents Act Of 1988 and any other moral

rights to which the Crew Member may be entitled under any legislation now existing or in the future enacted in any part of the world.

7. **Crew Member's warranties**: The crew member hereby warrants, undertakes and agrees that;

7.1 the Crew Member is free to enter into this agreement and has not entered and will not enter into any arrangement which may conflict with it

7.2 the Crew Member will render his/her services in willing co-operation with others in the manner required by the Producer and in accordance with the production schedule established by the Producer.

7.3 The Crew Member shall not without consent in writing of the Producer issue any publicity relating to or otherwise reveal or make public any financial, creative or other confidential information in connection with the Film or the terms of this agreement or the business of the Producer and will not knowingly commit any act which might prejudice or damage the reputation of the Producer or inhibit the successful exploitation of the Film

7.4 The Crew Member is in a good state of health and shall use his/her best endeavours to remain so during the continuance of this agreement

7.5 the Producer shall have the right to make the Crew Member's services available to third parties and the Crew Member will co-operate fully with such third parties and follow all lawful directions and instructions of such third parties

7.6 The Crew Member shall at all times throughout his/her engagement keep the Producer informed of their whereabouts and telephone number

7.7 The Crew Member will not on behalf of the Producer enter into any commitment contract or arrangement with any person or engage any person without the Producer's prior written consent

7.8 The Crew Member shall willingly and promptly co-operate with the Producer and shall carry out such services rendered by the Crew Member as when and where requested by the Producer and follow all reasonable directions and instructions given by the Producer

7.9 the Crew Member shall attend at such locations and times as are reasonably required by the Producer from time to time

7.10 the Crew Member shall comply with and observe all union rules and regulations and all the formal agreements, rules and regulations relating to safety, fire, prevention or general administration in force at any place in which the Crew Member shall be required by the Producer to render any services

7.11 Upon the expiry of earlier termination of the Crew Member's engagement, the Crew Member will deliver up to the Producer all scripts, photographs and other literary or dramatic properties all film materials and all other properties, documents and things, whatsoever which the Crew Member may have in the Crew Member's possession or under the Crew Member's control relating to the Film

7.12 the Crew Member shall indemnify the Producer and keep it fully indemnified against all proceedings, costs, claims, awards, damages, expenses (including without limitation legal expenses) and liabilities arising directly or indirectly from any breach of the Crew Member's undertakings, obligations or warranties hereunder

8. **Credit:** Subject to the Crew Member rendering their services under the terms of this agreement, the Crew Member shall be given credit on the Film. The Producer shall determine in it's discretion the manner and mode of presentation of the Crew Member's credit. The Producer shall not be obliged to accord credit to the Crew Member in any other method of advertising or publicity. No casual or inadvertent failure by the Producer or any third party to comply with providing credit, and no failure by persons other than the Producer to comply with their contracts with the Producer shall constitute a breach of this Agreement by the Producer. The rights and remedies of the Crew Member in the event of a breach of this clause 8, by the Producer shall be limited to the rights (if any) to recover damages in an action at law and in no event shall the Crew Member be entitled by reason of any such breach to enjoin or restrain or otherwise interfere with the distribution, exhibition or exploitation of the Film.

9. **Producer's liability:** The Producer shall not be liable for any loss of or damage to any clothing or other personal property of the Crew Member whether such loss or damage is caused by negligence or otherwise howsoever except to the extent that the Producer receives compensation from

THE TOOLKIT

an insurance company or other third party.

10. **Waiver:** No waiver by the Producer of any failure by the Crew Member to observe any covenant or condition of this agreement shall be deemed to be a waiver of any preceding or succeeding failure or of any other covenant of condition nor shall it be deemed a continuing waiver. The rights and remedies provided for in this agreement are cumulative and no one of them shall be deemed to be exclusive of the others or of any rights or remedies allowed by law. The rights granted to the Producer are irrevocable and shall not revert to the Crew Member under any circumstances whatsoever. In the event that the Producer terminates or cancels (or purports to terminate or cancel) this agreement or any other agreement entered into by and between the Producer and the Crew Member (and even if such cancellation or termination or purported termination or cancellation is ultimately determined by a court to have been without proper or legal cause or ultimately determined by such a court that the Producer committed any material breach of any such agreement) the damage (if any) caused to the Crew Member thereby is not irreparable or sufficient to entitle the Crew Member to injunctive or other equitable relief and the Crew Member shall not have any right to terminate this agreement or any such other agreement or any of the Producer's rights hereunder.



11. **Insurance:** The Producer may secure in it's own name or otherwise at its own expense life accident health cast pre-production and other insurance covering the Crew Member independently or together with others and the Crew Member shall not have any right, title, or interest in or to such insurance. The Crew Member shall assist the Producer to procure such insurance and shall in timely fashion submit to such customary medical and other examinations and sign such applications and other instruments in writing as may be required by the insurance company involved.

12. **Condition precedent:** As a condition precedent to any and all liability of the Producer, the Crew Member shall at the Crew Member's own expense apply for and assist the Producer in applying for and do all such things as may be necessary in support of any application for the Crew Member's membership of any trade union, labour or professional organisation or guild and/or for passports, visas, work permits or other matters necessary to enable the Producer to make use of the Crew Member's services. If as a result of such application being refused, revoked or cancelled the Producer shall be unable to make use of the Crew Member's services this agreement shall be deemed null and void and without effect and without liability whatsoever on the parties save that the Crew Member shall repay to the Producer any sums previously paid to him/her pursuant to clause 3.

13. **Suspension: a) The** Producer shall be entitled by written notice giving reasons for such suspension to the Crew Member at any given time, to suspend the engagement of the Crew Member hereunder (whether or not the term of such engagement has commenced) if and so long as:-
13.a.1 the production of the Film is prevented, suspended, interrupted, postponed, hampered or interfered with by reason or on account of any event of force majeure, fire, accident, action of the elements of war, riot, civil disturbance, sickness, epidemic, pestilence, national calamity, act of God or any actual labour disputes, or illness or incapacity of the Producer or the director of the Film or any principal artist or principal technician or any other cause not reasonably within the control of the Producer,
13.a.2 the Crew Member fails, refuses or neglects duly to render willingly and to the utmost of the Crew Member's skill and ability, the Crew Member's full services or that the Crew Member fails, refuses, or neglects fully to observe or comply with, or perform any of the Crew Member's obligations under this agreement.

13.b.1. suspension shall commence from the date of the event giving rise to such suspension and shall continue for the duration of such event and for such reasonable period thereafter as may be necessary for the Producer to make arrangements to commence or resume production of the Film.
13.b.2 During this period of suspension, the Producer ceases to be liable to make any payments of remuneration or provide accommodation or living expenses if the suspension is due to the Crew Member's neglect, default, disability, incapacity or refusal) save such payment Instalments as shall have become due and payable prior to the suspension and the period of engagement shall be extended or the commencement of engagement shall be postponed by an equal period to the suspension
13.b.3 all rights of the Producer in respect of the services rendered and products of those services thereof by the Crew Member previous to the suspension shall not be affected and shall remain vested in the Producer.
13.b.4 If the Producer pays any remuneration to the Crew Member during any period of suspension arising pursuant to clause 13.a.2, then the Producer may require the Crew

Member's services hereunder without additional payment to the Crew Member for an equal period to the suspension during which the Producer paid remuneration to the Crew Member.

14. **Termination: a.)** The Producer shall be entitled (but not obliged) by written notice giving reasons for the termination to the crew member given at any time, to terminate the engagement of the Crew Member hereunder (without prejudice to any other rights and remedies available to the Producer hereunder) if:-
14.a.1 suspension continues for 3 consecutive weeks or 4 weeks in the aggregate or more, according to clause 13.a.1, or
14.a.2 at any time in the circumstances referred to in clause 13.a.2,
14.a.3 the Crew Member does not fulfil their respective obligations under this Agreement.

14. **b) In the case of termination** of the engagement of the Crew Member under the foregoing provisions or by the death of the Crew Member
14.b.1 such termination shall be effective from the date of the event giving rise to the termination or (if there shall have been a prior suspension) from the date of the event giving rise to the suspension from which such termination arose
14.b.2 any claim which the Producer may have against the Crew Member in respect of any breach, non performance or non observance of any of the material provisions of this Agreement arising prior to such termination or out of which such termination shall arise shall not be affected or prejudiced.
14.b.3 the Producer's title to and ownership of all copyrights and all other rights in or in connection with the services and all other rights in or in connection with the services rendered by the Crew Member up to the date of such termination and in all the products of such services shall not be affected and such rights shall accordingly be or remain vested in the Producer.
14.b.4 payment to the Crew Member of the instalments due and payable to the Crew Member up to the effective date of such termination shall operate as payment in full and final discharge and settlement of all claims on the part of the Crew Member under this agreement and accordingly the Producer shall not be under any obligation to pay to the Crew Member any further or other sums on account of remuneration or otherwise nor shall the producer be under any liability whether by way of damages or otherwise for any inconvenience or loss of publicity or other loss suffered by the Crew Member by reason of the termination of the Crew Member's engagement hereunder (but the provisions of this paragraph shall not affect the Producer's rights referred to in clause 14.b.2.

15. **Conflict:** Nothing contained in this Agreement shall be construed so as to require the commission of any act contrary to law and wherever there is any conflict between any provision of this agreement and any statute law ordinance or regulation contrary to which the parties have no legal right to contract then the latter shall prevail but in such event the provisions of this agreement so affected shall be curtailed and limited only to the extent necessary to bring them within the legal requirements.

16. **Assignment:** The Crew Member expressly agrees that the Producer may transfer and assign this agreement or all or any part of the Producer's rights under it. The Agreement shall inure to the benefit of the Producer's successors, licensees, and assigns but the Producer shall not thereby be relieved of it's obligations.

17. **Self employed status:** The Crew Member warrants to the Producer that the Crew Member is self employed and is not considered to be an employee of the Producer and the Crew Member warrants to the Producer that he/she is personally responsible for all tax, national insurance and/or other taxes levied by the inland revenue (or relevant tax authority if working abroad). The Crew Member shall provide evidence of their self employed status to the Producer. The Crew Member indemnifies and holds harmless the Producer for any liability to pay local or governmental taxes arising from the Crew Member's engagement.

18. Notices: All notices served upon either party by the other hereunder shall be delivered by hand at or sent by prepaid recorded delivery letter post or by facsimile addressed to the respective addressed hereinbefore contained or any subsequent address duly notified and if delivered by hand shall be deemed to have been served five days after posting and if sent by facsimile shall be deemed served 24 hours after receipt of the facsimile (and facsimile notice shall be confirmed by post).

19. This Agreement contains the full and complete understanding between the parties and supersedes all prior agreements and understandings whether written or oral pertaining thereto and cannot be modified except by a written instrument signed by the Crew Member and the

Producer.

20. Nothing contained in this Agreement shall or shall be deemed to constitute a partnership or a contract of employment between the parties.

21. This Agreement shall be construed in accordance with and governed by the laws of England whose courts shall be the courts of the competent jurisdiction.

IN WITNESS WHEREOF the parties hereto have executed the within Agreement as of the date first set forth hereinabove

(insert name of Producer)

By.................................................................................

Duly Authorised Officers...............................................

Accepted and Agreed to:

..........................................................

*VAT number or NI no. if applicable:

## *Accompanying Notes*

*NOTE 1: Deferments. If the fee or proportion of the fee is to be deferred, there should be further provisions that should also be mentioned, i.e. that the Deferment will be pro rata and pari passu with all other deferments to persons, providing services to the Film, after which all deferments to companies and firms should be met. All deferred sums are payable in first place from receipts received by the Producer from the exploitation of the Film subject to the recoupment of the production and post production cost of the Film only. It should be emphasised that the Deferment is a contingent amount and is only payable to the extent sufficient receipts are generated. It should also be mentioned that the Producers will use their reasonable endeavours to procure that their auditors or any other firm of Chartered Accountants appointed, will provide an audited detailed statement of all transactions relevant to the production and the income generated which should be made available to the crew member/ and or representatives by a specified date.*

*NOTE 2: Payment. It should be made clear whether or not this agreement is a non guild or union agreement. Clause 3 (e) refers to a buy out.*

*NOTE 3: Expenses: The travel arrangements to and for the set are usually the responsibility of the crew member. However if on location, the crew member is provided with accommodation and travel expenses depending on the budget of the Film.*

*NOTE 4: Self employment: It is necessary that if the crew member is self employed, the producer receives written confirmation and evidence to prove their status. Otherwise responsibility falls upon the Producer who could be heavily penalised for not paying on time and be subject to the danger of prosecution.*

THE TOOLKIT

# Composers Agreement (Original score)

**This is a guideline only and should not be relied upon without taking legal advice.**

THIS AGREEMENT is made the .......day of ...............199..

BETWEEN:........................................
hereinafter called "the Company" which expression includes it's successors in title licensees and assigns)

AND....................................................
(hereinafter called "the Composer")

WHEREAS:

The Company is currently engaged in the production of a film called "..............." ("the Film") and wishes to engage the services of the Composer to write compose and arrange the Music and record the Recordings (as hereinafter defined) to be included in the Film upon the following terms.

NOW THEREFORE IT IS HEREBY AGREED AS FOLLOWS:-

1. The Company hereby engages the Composer and the Composer undertakes to make available his services as hereinafter provided (hereinafter called "the Services") on the terms and conditions herein contained:

1.1. The Composer shall compose and arrange the music ("the Music")
1.2. The Composer shall perform and record the Music ("the Recordings") and shall record the Music in a first class recording studio to a commercial and technical quality suitable for the synchronisation of the Recordings made therefrom in timed relation with the Film and for the reproduction therefrom of Records for sale to the public. The Composer shall deliver the Recordings to the Company on or before........................199..
1.3. The Composer acknowledges that the soundtrack for the Film shall include certain music and recordings thereof ("the Licensed Music") written and recorded prior to the date hereof and owned or controlled by third parties. The details of the Licensed Music are specified in Schedule A hereof and in rendering the Services hereunder the Composer shall take account of such Licensed Music to be included in the Film and such Licensed Music shall not be deemed to be Recordings or Music hereunder. The Composer shall arrange clearance and pay all necessary fees for all Licensed Music

2. The Composer hereby agrees, warrants and undertakes with the Company that:

2.1 The Composer will render the Services hereunder to the full extent of his creative and artistic skill and technical ability.
2.2. The Music and the Recordings will be wholly original to the Composer and will not infringe the copyright or any other like right of any person firm or company.
2.3. The Composer is free to enter into this Agreement and that he has the unencumbered right to grant to the Company all of the rights and Services hereby granted and that no prior contract or agreement of any kind entered into by the Composer will interfere in any way with the proper performance of this Agreement by the Composer.
2.4. The Composer will execute do and deliver all such acts deeds and instruments as the Company may at it's own expense from time to time require for the purpose of confirming or further assuring it's title to the rights assigned or intended to be assigned hereunder.
2.5 The Composer will indemnify and hold the Company harmless against all claims costs proceedings demands losses damages and expenses arising out of any breach of any of the warranties and representations and agreements on his part contained in this Agreement.
2.6 That no material composed by the Composer recorded on the Recordings will in any way infringe the rights of any third party.
2.7 That the Composer hereby grants to the Company (and it's licensees and assignees) on behalf of the Composer and any person whose performances are embodied on the Recordings the requisite consents pursuant to the provisions of the Copyright Designs and Patents Act 1988 or any similar legislation throughout the world in order that the Company and it's licensees an assignees shall have the fullest use of the Composer's and such persons services hereunder and the products thereof.
2.8 That the Composer and all other persons who have performed on the Recordings hereby irrevocably and unconditionally waive any and all moral rental lending and like rights the composer and such persons may have pursuant to the Copyright Designs and Patents Act 1988 or otherwise in respect of the Recordings the Music and the performances embodied thereon.

3. In consideration of the agreements on the Company's behalf herein contained the Composer with full title guarantee hereby assigns (subject to the rights in the

THE TOOLKIT

Music vested in the Performing Rights Society Limited ("PRS") and it's affiliated societies by virtue of the Composer's membership of PRS) to the Company and it's successors in title (and so far as the same has not been completed at the date hereof by way of immediate assignment of future copyright) and for the full periods of copyright and all renewals and extensions thereof throughout the world ("the Territory") whether now or hereafter existing the entire copyright rental rights and all like rights whether now or hereafter existing in the Recordings and the product of the Services and all Masters thereof and the Composer hereby grants to the Company (it's licensees and assigns) the exclusive right and licence to use the Music in synchronisation with the Film and to use the Music as incorporated in trailers therefor and to record broadcast transmit exhibit and perform for an unlimited number of times and otherwise distribute and exploit by sale hire or otherwise in all and any media (including videos) the Music as part of or in synchronisation with the Film or trailers therefor or upon Records incorporating all or part of the soundtrack of the Film for the full period of copyright and any and all renewals and extensions thereof throughout the universe TO HOLD the same unto the Company absolutely throughout the Territory.



4. The Composer hereby grants to the Company (and warrants and undertakes that it is entitled to make such grant):
4.1. The irrevocable right to issue publicity concerning the Composer's Services and the product of the Services hereunder including the right to use and allow others to use the names professional names likeness, photograph and biography of the Composer and all musicians featured on the Recordings in Connection with the Music, the Recordings and/or the Film and the exercise of the rights granted hereunder.
4.2. The right to decide when and/or whether to commence cease or recommence the production of Records embodying the Recordings on whatsoever label and the right to fix and alter the price at which such Records are sold.
4.3. The right to licence grant transfer or assign without having to obtain any further consent from the Composer all or any of it's rights (including without limitation any or all of it's rights in the Recordings and the Music) hereunder and the benefit of this Agreement to any third party.

5. The Composer hereby further authorises and empowers the Company at the Company's expense to take such steps and proceedings as the Company may from time to time consider or be advised are necessary to protect and reserve to the Company all rights hereby granted or expressed to be granted to the Company and the Composer hereby further authorises and empowers the Company and hereby appoints the Company his Attorney to institute actions and proceedings in the name of the Composer (but in any event at the Company's expense) or otherwise in respect of the infringement or violation of any of the rights hereby assigned or granted or expressed to be assigned or granted.

6. The Composer shall at the Company's request and expense take such steps and proceedings as the Company may require and to execute all or any further documents to vest in the Company and/or to renew and extend any and all rights an/or copyrights assigned or agreed to be assigned hereunder and which are or may hereafter be secured upon the Music and the Recordings or any part thereof and after such renewal or extension to transfer and assign to the Company the rights herein granted for such renewal or extended term. In the event that the Composer shall fail so to do within 7 (seven) business days of receiving a request therefor the Company is hereby authorised and empowered to exercise and perform such acts and to take such proceedings in the name and on behalf of the Composer and as the Attorney-in-fact for the Composer.

7. 7.1. As full and final consideration for the Services hereunder and for the grant of rights in respect of the Music and the Recordings contained herein and for the physical tapes and for all expenses incurred by the Composer in arranging the Recordings the Company shall pay to the Composer the
7.1.1. The sum of £......(.......pounds) payable on signature hereof (receipt of which is hereby acknowledged).
7.1.2. A royalty in respect of Records reproducing only the Recordings sole paid for and not returned and the said royalty shall be calculated upon the Royalty Base Price of each such Record at the rate of 7% (seven percent) ("the Royalty Rate") and subject as hereinafter appears.
7.2. The remuneration payable to the Composer by the Company pursuant to clauses 7.1.1. and 7.1.2. in respect of the Services is and shall represent full and final consideration for the Services and the entire product of such Services and the rights granted to the Company hereunder and shall include any and all residual repeat rerun foreign use exploitation and other fees and payments of whatever nature due to the Composer or the Composer by virtue of any guild or trade union agreement and any and all payments due to the funds of any guild or union or other similar taxes and state and government and social security contributions. No further or additional payment shall be due from the Company to the Composer in respect of any of the foregoing or by reason of the number of hours in a day or days in the week in which the Services shall have been rendered or for any other reason whatever.

7.3. The Company shall ensure that mechanical royalties are payable to the appropriate collection society and/or publisher in respect of the sale of Records embodying the Music.

8.1 . In respect of a Record reproducing the Recordings and also recordings not the subject of this Agreement the royalty payable to the Composer shall be that proportion of the Royalty Rate which the Recordings reproduced on such Record bear to the total number of recordings reproduced thereon.
8.2. No royalties shall be payable upon promotional Records given away free goods Records sold or distributed under any arrangement for the sale of deleted Records promotional Records Records for which the Company is not paid Records sold at a discount at 50% (fifty percent) or more from published price audio-visual Records.
8.3. If in any agreement made between the Company and the Company's licensees or assigns the royalty payable to the Company by the Company's licensees or assigns or the basis upon which such royalty is calculated shall be reduced (including all reduced rate half rate terminal reductions and royalty free provisions) then the royalty and Royalty Rate payable to the Composer shall be reduced by a like proportion.
8.4. The Composer shall have the first option to produce any soundtrack Record of the Film upon terms to be agreed if the Company in it's sole discretion decides to release such a Record. The costs of editing, remixing and converting the Recordings produced for the Film for the purpose of reproducing the Recordings upon Records shall be treated as an advance against the first recoupable from any and all royalties due to the Composer hereunder pursuant to clause 7.1.

9. 9.1. The Company shall supply to the Composer within 90 (ninety) days after the end of June and December in each year a statement showing the latest information received by the Company during such half year period as to the number of Records sold and the amount of royalty due to the Composer. The Company shall be entitled to establish a reserve for potential returns of Records apparently sold in any half year in a reasonable quantity. The Company's liability to pay royalty to the Composer hereunder shall be limited to the amounts thereof actually received by the Company and the Company may deduct and retain from any sum payable to the Composer hereunder any withholding taxes required to be deducted by any government or law.
9.2. The Composer hereby directs the Company to make all payments due to the Composer to (name of agent if any) whose receipt thereof shall be a full and sufficient discharge of the Company's obligations in respect of such payments.

10. 10.1 The Company shall accord the Composer on all positive prints of the Film made by or to the order of the Company a main title credit on a separate card substantially in the form "Original Music by".
10.2. The Company shall instruct the distributors and exhibitors of the Film to accord the Composer credit as hereinabove provided on all prints of the Film issued by such distributors and exhibitors but the Company shall not be liable for the neglect or default of any such distributors or exhibitors so long as it shall have notified the distributors of the credit to which the Composer is entitled hereunder.
10.3. The Company shall use it's best endeavours to afford a credit to the Composer upon all paid advertising for the Film subject to the distributor's usual credit exclusions.
10.4. In respect of soundtrack Records of the Film the Company shall accord the Composer a credit in the form "Original Music by" on the back cover and label of the Record save that such credit shall appear on the front cover and label of the said Records if 50% (fifty percent) or more of the Recordings featured on such Record were performed by the Composer and a credit "Produced by Stephen Warbeck" if 50% (fifty percent) or more of the Recordings featured on such Record were produced by the Composer on the back cover and label thereof but otherwise on the same terms and conditions as set out in this clause.
10.5. No casual or inadvertent failure to accord the Composer or any other party credit hereunder shall constitute a breach of this Agreement by the Company and/or the Composer's remedies in the event of a breach shall be confined to recovery of damages.

11. The Composer acknowledges that it and the Composer has prior to signature hereof received independent expert advice on the contents hereof to enable him to understand fully the terms of this Agreement.

12. In the event of a breach of this Agreement by Company the Composer shall not be entitled to equitable relief or to terminate or rescind this Agreement or any of the rights granted to Company herein or to restrain enjoin or otherwise impair the production distribution advertising or other exploitation of the Film the Composer's sole remedy being an action at law for damages if any.

13. For the purposes hereof the following words shall have the following meanings:

**"Record"** - shall mean vinyl records, compact discs, tapes, cassettes, CDI, CD Roms or any other device or contrivance whether now know or to be invented in the future reproducing sound alone (with or without visual images) but excluding videocassettes, videotapes and/or videodiscs embodying the Film.

**"Recordings"** - shall mean the original sound recordings or combination of recordings recorded hereunder and embodying the Music or any part thereof (whether on recording tape lacquer wax disc or any other material).
**"Master"** - shall mean a 2(two) track stereo Dolby tape recording fully edited equalised and leadered and of a first class standard suitable for synchronisation with the Film and the reproduction of Records therefrom..
**"Royalty Base Price"** - shall mean the retail price upon which royalties payable to the Company are calculated by it's licensees and assigns (net of packaging allowances and sales taxes).
**"Copyright"** - shall mean the entire copyright and design right subsisting under the laws of the United Kingdom and all analogous rights subsisting under the laws of each and every jurisdiction throughout the world.

14. All notices writs legal process or any other documents served under or in respect of this Agreement shall be addressed to the party to be served at the address of that party hereinbefore appearing or at such other address for service as may be notified by each to the other in writing and shall be sent by registered letter or recorded delivery in which event such notice shall be deemed to have been received 3 (three) days after the posting thereof.

15. This Agreement shall be exclusively governed by English law and the High Court of Justice in England shall be the exclusive Court of Jurisdiction. Nothing herein contained shall constitute or create or be deemed to create or constitute a partnership between the parties hereto.

AS WITNESS the hand of the parties the day and year first before written

SIGNED by........................................(...............................)
for and on behalf of...........................(...............................)
in the presence of:.............................(...............................)

SIGNED.............................................(...............................)
in the presence of .............................(...............................)

*Accompanying Notes*

*Clause 1.3: The Composer (or sometimes the Producer) has to arrange for the use of pre existing music that is incorporated in the soundtrack and arrange and pay for licences to use any such music.*

*Clause 3: A Composer cannot assign his/her right to receive payment from PRS and they remain the beneficiaries of any income paid to the PRS, which is a collection society for musicians. The Composer must specifically grant the right to allow the music to be played in sync with the film. This is a specific right. This agreement only allows the Producer to use the music for this purpose and does NOT allow the Producer to publish the music.*

*Clause 5: This gives the Producer the ability to take any legal action to prevent a third party using the music for their film if the Composer does not agree to do so.*

*Clause 6: A "further assurance" clause is used in contracts where a grant or licence of rights is made. This ensures the producer has all the necessary documents to perfect their right or interests in the licence or grant of rights.*

*Clause 7.12: A Composer will often get a royalty from any records made whether the Producer acts as the music publisher or whether they negotiate a deal with a third party. This royalty obligation must be made clear to any publisher as the Producer is primarily liable under this type of agreement to make any such payment to the Composer.*

*Clause 7.3: Mechanical royalties are paid to MCPS and are due when the records are sold.*

*Clause 8.1: The Composer gets a proportion of the royalty rate according to the proportion of his/her music incorporated on the recording i.e. if there were 6 tracks and only 3 were the Composer's music he/she would get half the royalty.*

*Clause 8.3: If the Producer assigns the Composer's agreement to a third party (i.e the distributor/ financier) and under it's deal it gets a lower Royalty Rate then the Composer agrees to accept that lower rate.*

*Clause 8.4: The Composer is given the chance to arrange the music for any record produced.*

# *Location Release Form*

**This is a guideline only and should not be relied upon without taking legal advice.**

From: *(name of company)* of *(address)*

To: *(name of owner of premises)* of *(address)*

Dated: *(date)*

Dear Sirs

*(name of film)* (the "Film)

This letter is to confirm the agreement with us in which you have agreed to make available to us the following premises (the "Premises") *(specify the premises).*

1. The premises shall be made available to us on a sole and exclusive basis in connection with the Film on (dates) (the "Dates").

2.You agree to make available to us the facilities in Schedule A on such days as we require on the Dates.

3. We shall be entitled to use the Premises as we may require on the days on giving you reasonable notice and as are negotiated in good faith between us but subject to the same terms as this agreement and on any additional days. You understand that we may need to return to the Premises at a later date if principal photography and recording is not completed on the Dates.

4. We have notified you of the scenes which are to be shot on or around the Premises and you confirm and agree that you consent to the filming of these scenes and you confirm that you will not make any objection in the future to the Premises being featured in the Film and you waive any and all right, claim and objection of whatever nature relating to the above.

5. We shall be entitled to represent the Premises under it's real name or under a fictional name or place according to the requirements of the Film.

6. We shall be entitled to incorporate all films, photographs and recordings, whether audio or audio-visual, made in or about the Premises in the Film as we may require in our sole discretion.

7. We shall not without your prior consent (not to be unreasonably withheld or delayed) make any structural or decorative alternations which we require to be made to the Premises. We shall at your request properly reinstate any part of the Premises to the condition they were in prior to any alterations.

8. We shall own the entire copyright and all other rights of every kind in and to all film and audio and audio-visual recordings and photographs made in or about the Premises and used in connection with the Film and we shall have the right to exploit the Film by any manner or means now known or in the future invented in any and all media throughout the world for the full period of copyright, including all renewals, reversions and extensions.

9. We shall have the right to assign, licence and/or sub-licence the whole and/or any part of our rights pursuant to this agreement to any company or individual.

10. We agree that we shall indemnify you up to a maximum of £*(amount)* against any liability, loss, claim or proceeding arising under statute or common law relating to the Film in respect of personal injury and/or death of any person and/ or loss or damage to the Premises caused by negligence, omission or default by this company or any person for whom we are legally responsible. You shall notify us immediately in writing of any claim as soon as such claim comes to your attention and we shall assume the sole conduct of any proceedings arising from any such claim.

11.In consideration of the rights herein granted we will pay you the sum of £*(amount)* on *(dates).*

12. You undertake to indemnify us and to keep us fully indemnified from and against all actions, proceedings, costs, claims, damages and demands however arising in respect of any actual or alleged breach or non-performance by you of any or all of your undertakings, warranties and obligations under this agreement.

13.This agreement shall be governed by and construed in accordance with the law of England and Wales and subject to the jurisdiction of the English Courts.

Please signify your acceptance of the above terms by signing and returning to us the enclosed copy.

Signed..........................................

# TOP 21 POINTS TO LOOK FOR IN A SALES AGENT/DISTRIBUTION AGREEMENT

*1. An Advance - Rarely given, usually only if the Film needs completion money, in which case the Sales agent may take a higher commission.*

*2. No. of Years for the rights to be licensed to the Sales Agent/Distributor. From 5 to 35. Standard is 5-10 years.*

*3. Extent of Rights being requested by Sales Agent/ Distributor. i.e. worldwide, worldwide exc. domestic. worldwide exc. America, etc. to be negotiated between the parties.*

*4. Fees/ rate of commission: Usually between 20 - 25%. Sometimes 30% depending on extent of input by sales agent/distributor and this should be limited so that the distributor takes only one commission per country.*

*5. Ownership: Make sure you, the producer, will still own the copyright to the Film - not applicable if you are selling the film to the distributor. If you are licensing the rights to certain territories you will remain the copyright owner.*

*6. CAP on Expenses: Make sure there is a maximum limit on expenses and that you are notified in writing of any large expenses i.e. over a specified amount.*

*7. Direct Expenses: Make sure that overheads of the Distributor are not included in Distribution expenses and will not be added as a further expense.*

*8. Sub Distributor Fees: Make sure that these fees are paid by the Sales agent/distributor out of it's fees and not in addition to the Distribution expenses.*

*9. Consider you position on Net Receipts. i.e. monies after distributor has deducted their commission and fees subject to any sales agreements you enter into with a distributor.*

*10. Errors and Omissions Policy. See if this is to be included in the delivery requirements as this could be an added unexpected expense.*

*11. Cross Collaterisation - where the distributor will offset expenses and losses on their other films against yours. You don't want this.*

*12. P & A (Prints and Advertising) commitment from the Distributor. Negotiate total expenses that will be used on P & A in the contract i.e. a fixed sum.*

*13. Domestic Theatrical Release - negotiate what print run is expected, and in what locations*

*14. Distribution Editing Rights - limit for only censorship requirements although if you are dealing with a major distributor this will not be acceptable.*

*15. Producer's input in the marketing campaign.*

*16. Trailer commitment. Will this be another hidden additional cost ? Make sure theatres have this in plenty time.*

*17. Release window. Get Distributor to commit to release the film within a time frame after delivery of film to distributor.*

*18. Audit Rights. The Producer has the rights to inspect the books re: the distribution of the film.*

*19. If the Sales Agent intends to group your film with other titles to produce an attractive package for buyers, ensure that your film is not unfairly supporting the other films or that you are receiving a disproportionate or unfair percentage.*

*20. Make sure that the rights revert back to the Producer in case of any type of insolvency or if the agent is in material breach of the agreement.*

*21. Check the Delivery requirements very carefully.*

# Glossary Of Contract Terminology

***ABOVE THE LINE*** *- the portion of a film budget that covers creative elements and personnel i.e. story, screenplay rights, producers, directors and principle members of the cast.*

***ACCRUALS*** *- the accumulation of payments due*

***ANCILLARY RIGHTS*** *- other subsidiary rights i.e. the right to make a sequel, soundtrack, computer game etc., merchandising, video, novelisation.*

***ACQUISITIONS*** *- purchases*

***ARBITRATION*** *- an informal method for resolving disputes (by finding the middle ground) which is usually quicker and less expensive than litigation. Usually an arbitrator is agreed in advance by the parties or chosen by the head of an appropriate professional body i.e. Institute of Chartered Accountants etc.*

***BELOW THE LINE*** *- accounting term relating to the technical expenses and labour involved in producing a film.*

***BREACH OF CONTRACT*** *- Failure of one party to fulfil the agreement*

***BREAKEVEN*** *- the point when sales equal costs, where a film is neither in profit nor loss*

***BUY OUT*** *- this term is used in relation to the engagement of artists where no repeat, residual or other fees are required to be paid to the artist in relation to any form of exploitation of the film or programme.*

***BEST ENDEAVOURS*** *- means you have to do all you can including incurring expense in order to carry out your relevant obligation under the agreement.*

***CAP*** *- a ceiling, upper limit. Try to cap expenses in sales agents agreements.*

***COLLATERAL*** *- assets pledged to a lender until the loan is repaid. i.e. with a bank loan a house can be put up for collateral.*

***COMMISSION*** *- a percentage of specified amount received for services performed*

***CONTINGENCY*** *- money set aside for unanticipated costs*

***CREDITOR*** *- one to whom monies are owed*

***CHAIN OF TITLE*** *- contracts and documents that hand down the copyright to the present owner*

***CROSS COLLATERALISE*** *- this is where a party, usually a distributor, will offset losses in one area against gains in other areas. If you are a producer you will want to resist this.*

***DEAL MEMO*** *- a short version of the contract, giving the principal terms of the agreement which can be legally binding - check carefully if this is the intention.*

***DEFERRAL*** *- delay of payment of a fixed sum which is all or part of payments for cast and crew and other services, usually paid out of receipts from the film after the distributor or financier has taken their commission/fee/expenses or been repaid their initial investment (plus a %).*

***DISTRIBUTION EXPENSES*** *- there is no set definition for this term but things to watch for are that the expenses are reasonable and relate directly to the film. It should not include the distributor's overheads and any expenses payable by the distributor to third parties should be negotiated on the best commercial terms available.*

***DISTRIBUTION FEE*** *- This is usually between 30-50% of income received. You should try and negotiate a sliding scale for the fee which reduces as the income from the film increases.*

***ERRORS AND OMISSIONS*** *- insurance protection covering against lawsuits alleging unauthorised use of ideas, characters, plots, plagiarism, titles and alleged slander, libel, defamation of character etc.*

***ESCROW*** *- monies or property held by a third party for future delivery or payment to a party on the occurrence of a particular event or services rendered.*

***EQUITY*** *- the interest or value an owner has in a property but where they have no legal ownership in the property.*

***FAVOURED NATIONS*** *- meaning that the contracting party will be given treatment on an equal footing with others that the other party deals with. i.e. could refer to placement of billing requirements, or profit participation.*

***FORCE MAJEURE*** *- this term is usually defined in the agreement. Generally it means any event which is outside the control of the parties to the agreement i.e. act of God, fire, strike, accident, war, illness of key persons involved in the production, effect of elements etc.*

***GROSS DEAL*** *- a profit participation for the producer or others in the distributor's gross receipts (unusual).*

***GROSS RECEIPTS*** *- this term is usually defined in an agreement to mean all income received from the exploitation of the film by the distributor before any deduction of the distributor's fees and expenses but sometimes it is expressed to include the deduction of such fees and expenses.*

***INDEMNIFY*** *- in essence to secure against loss and damage which may occur in the future or to provide compensation against any loss or damage.*

***INDEMNITY*** *- a promise to make good any loss or damage another has incurred or suffered or may incur. It may not always be appropriate to give an indemnity.*

***IN PERPETUITY*** *- to exist forever.*

***INDUCEMENT LETTER*** *- this is required where a party, usually an artist, director or individual producer, contract through their company (for tax reasons) rather than as individuals. A Producer and/or financier will require the individual to provide personal warranties and undertakings in relation to the ability and authority of their company to state the artist/director/producer will render their services. The letter will also confirm that they have granted the relevant rights to the company which the company then grants to the producer under the principal agreement of engagement.*

***INSOLVENT*** *- where one has liabilities that exceed their assets.*

***JOINT VENTURE*** *- A business by two or more parties who share profits, losses and control.*

***LETTER OF INTENT*** *- a written communication expressing the intent of a person or company to perform whatever services that they provide. This may not be legally binding.*

***LIBEL*** *- a false and malicious publication which defames one who is living (it may not be printed for that purpose - you don't have to show malice in UK libel law).*

***LICENSOR*** *- one who grants a license.*

***LIMITED RECOURSE LOAN*** *- a loan which may only be repaid through specified sources of income i.e. income derived from the exploitation of a film.*

***LABORATORY ACCESS LETTER*** *- this is an instruction to the laboratory to release the negative of the film to named distributors and is required where more than one distributor is being used.*

***MORAL RIGHTS*** *- this is a general term used to describe a bunch of rights which belong to the author of a copyright work. These so called "moral rights" derive from the European principle, which was asserted most forcefully in France and Germany, that an artist has the right to protect their work even if it is the property of another. England only recognised authors "moral rights" in 1988 by the incorporation of those rights into the Copyright Designs and Patents Act. See ss77-79 The right of paternity (i.e. to be identified as the author), the right of integrity (i.e. for the work not to be treated in a derogatory way), the right to object to false attribution. These rights may be waived by the author and in nearly every case they are. A distributor would not find it acceptable for an artist to be able to prevent the distribution of a film on the basis that their moral rights had been infringed. In France and Germany an author cannot by law waive these rights.*

***NEGATIVE COSTS*** *- total of various costs incurred in the acquisition and production of a film in all aspects prior to release. Includes pre production, production, post production costs.*

***NET DEAL*** *- a distribution deal where the distributor recoups all it's costs and collects all it's fees before giving the producer the remainder of the film's revenue.*

***NET PROFIT*** *- there is no set definition of this term as in every case there will be much debate about what may or may not be deducted from the gross receipts to arrive at the net profit. The definition of net profit in any agreement should be looked at very carefully to ensure inter alia expenses and commissions are not being deducted twice i.e. once by the distributor and again by the sub distributor etc.*

***OUTPUT DEAL*** *- a contract through which one party delivers it's entire output to another party. i.e. a distribution agreement between a production company and a distribution company in which the distributor commits to distribute the films that have been or will be produced by the producer.*

***PARRI PASSU*** *- means on a like footing i.e. everyone is to be treated in an equal fashion. For instance, on distribution of net profits everyone gets an equal amount irrespective of their contribution.*

***PRO RATA*** *- means that, for example, if an artist is entitled to payment on a pro rata basis then if they receive a weekly fee for 6 days work and the artist subsequently works only 3 days the artist would receive half the weekly*

*fee i.e. the weekly fee would be pro rated according to the amount of time the artists services were engaged.*

***PER DIEM** - a daily payment. It is usually used in the context of an artist's daily expenses.*

***PRODUCERS SHARE** - means the net sum remaining to the Producer after deductions of distribution fees, expenses (or other deductions that are agreed) and after other profit participants have received their share. The producers share of net profits may be shared with other third parties.*

***PROFIT PARTICIPATION** -percentage participations on net profits*

***REASONABLE ENDEAVOURS** - this is less onerous than best endeavours and simply means you will make a reasonable effort to carry out your obligations.*

***RECOUPMENT** - when the costs and expenses of a film production are recovered from the film's revenue i.e. when production costs have been recouped.*

***RENTAL AND LENDING RIGHTS** - these rights are contained in Directive no. 92 and 100 EEC and have been brought into effect in the UK by regulations which amend the CDPA 1988. The principle behind the changes is that with the development and expansion of video and other similar forms of distribution, an artist should share in the income derived from this commercially important area. However this is of concern to producers and distributors who do not wish to have a continuing obligation to make payments to artists and so all agreements contain a clause stating that the artist recognises that the payment due to the artist under the agreement is adequate and equitable remuneration for these rights and they assign all such rights to the producer. There is uncertainty as to whether such a clause will be legally binding on an artist as the right to remuneration for rental rights is expressed to be unwaivable and this issue has yet to be considered by an English Court.*

***RESIDUALS** - payments for each re run after initial showing. In the case of guild or union agreements minimum residual payments have been agreed.*

***ROYALTIES** - payments to a party for use of the property calculated as a percentage of a defined amount (i.e. net income from video sales).*

***THEATRICAL RELEASE** - exploitation of the film in the cinema as opposed to on television or video etc.*

***TURNAROUND** - e.g. a screenplay development situation where the purchaser or licensee of the property has decided not to go forward with the production or if the production is not screened or does not begin principal photography within a specified time the owner or licensor can serve notice on the owner/licensee so that the screenplay can be re-acquired by the owner/licensor.*

***VENTURE CAPITAL** - financing for new ventures that involves some investment risk but usually offers a share of any profit - there is usually a high premium paid for such investment reflecting the risk taken by the investor.*

***WAIVER** - a relinquishment or surrender of particular rights*

***WARRANTY** - a promise by one party that the other party will rely upon. i.e. in a distribution agreement a producer may warrant that the filming is of a particular quality and standard.*

# The Crew & What They Do

**Production Manager** - *Needed early on. Makes sure the Director has everything he or she needs at an affordable price, keeps in contact with the accountant. Keeps a close eye on the schedule, makes sure and checks that everything works smoothly. Visits the set daily to be aware of everything that is happening.*

**Production Co-ordinator** - *Works with PM. Makes sure there is a smooth flow of information between departments both verbal and written. Prepares call sheets with 2nd AD, schedules, progress reports, orders equipment, co-ordinates transport.*

**The Accountant** - *Takes care of monies throughout the shoot. Arranges for payments that need to be made, expenses etc. Keeps an eye on how the shoot is going with relevance to the budget.*

**Location Manager** - *Organises the recce's (finding locations) and takes care of everything associated with shooting on location. i.e. various permissions, hotel bookings, toilets, car hire, informing police, authorities, residents; to be the liaison on set between crew and location owners.*

**First Assistant Director (1st AD)** - *The link between the production office and set. Must ensure that everything is available that is needed on the day. Keeps in close contact with the Director and the Production Manager as he must know everything there is to know about the script, locations, actors, sets, schedule and how the director intends to shoot. He must aid the director, keeping up the energy and strength of the crew pushing them within sensible limits to keep the show moving at a good pace.*

**Second Assistant Director (2nd AD)** - *A good backup to the 1st. Writes the call sheet in conjunction with the Prod. Co-ordinator, arranges cast calls, pick ups, extras, stunt calls, deals with payments to extras and is present when cast arrives and is available to sort out production problems if and when they arise on set.*

**Third Assistant Director (3rd AD)** - *Assists the 2nd and acts as a Runner.*

**Continuity** - *Observes and records continuity details such as costume, props, script, makes sure shots match during varied takes and that all shots are completed.*

**Storyboard Artist** - *Prepares detailed panels of shots as requested by the Director. On low-budget shoots this may not be deemed to be unnecessary.*

**Director of Photography (DoP)/ Lighting Cameraman** - *Responsible for visual style of the movie. Familiar with all camera, lighting equipment and film stocks. Vital contact between the lab man and production.*

**Camera Operator** - *Operates the camera. Must have familiarity with equipment, camera movement and an eye for framing.*

**Focus Puller/Camera assistant** - *Loads film, keeps the image sharp by following the focus, changes lenses, sets exposure and fits filters as requested by the DoP. 'Checks the gate' after each take.*

**Camera Assistant/Loader** - *Loads film into magazines, cans exposed film and short ends, fills out camera sheets, keeps records on stocks, lenses, filters and 'f' stops used as well as noting any additional info for the labs and production office. Marks each take with clapperboard.*

***Grip*** *- In charge of operating dollies, cranes, laying track, moving cameras, - all heavy work so needs to be strong. If needed they design or construct special rigs and camera mounts.*

***Gaffer*** *- Chief electrician in charge of equipment and connection to power supply. Works closely with DoP explaining and delegating the lighting design. Chooses his own crew of Best Boy, Generator driver and Sparks. Named after a hook that manipulated overhead hanging lights.*

***Sparks*** *- Moves and maintains the lights. Organises power from generator.*

***Best Boy*** *- Assistant to the Gaffer.*

***Sound Recordist*** *- Records production sound, wild tracks, ambiances. Will either have their own kit or will hire from sound houses.*

***Boom Operator*** *- Works in conjunction with the recordist either holding the boom or arranging the necessary mics for a particular scene. Takes care of sound recording sheets which will be used in the editing.*

***Costume Designer*** *- Designs a particular look in conjunction with the Director. Breaks down the script, working out how many costume changes are needed according to story days, meets actors individually to discuss their requirements. Usually the first people from production to meet the actors therefore they set the whole tone of the production. They must shop, hire, or make the costumes and have good social skills to have a good working relationship with the actor. Can have a Costume Assistant.*

***Dresser*** *- Sets up a working wardrobe. Arrives before actors to set up costumes, supervises their dressing, checks their continuity and watches them film throughout the day for continuity. Stands by with wet weather or warm clothing depending on conditions.*

***Make Up Artist and Hair*** *- Breaks down script for effects, special make up or cosmetic make up i.e. bruises, wounds or shaved heads may be needed. Each artist will have their own basic kit and will take care of hiring wigs, special effects and prosthetics. Keeps continuity notes.*

***Production Designer*** *- Works with the director, DoP on visual style of the movie. Responsible for sets either in the studio or on location. Ensures the 'look' of the set and props are as desired.*

***Art Director*** *- Oversees the ideas of the Production designer, arranging furnishings, liaising with construction manager and the art department.*

***Set Director*** *- Responsible for the selection of props and supervising the dressing of sets. Prepares prop lists and works closes with the prop buyer in organising the dressing and striking of sets. Makes continuity notes. On low-budget shoots, the set director and Art director may be deemed to be as one.*

***Prop Master*** *- Physically puts and removes furniture and props on set. Keeps tabs on all props and looks after them during the shoot.*

***Prop Buyer*** *- Responsible for finding appropriate props from specialist sources. Purchases, hires and maintains a record of art dept. budget. Organises collections and returns of hired props. On low budget shoot, prop buyer and Prop master may be deemed to be as one.*

**Construction manager** - *Responsible for building sets within art department budget. Organises materials and extra crew if necessary. Schedules building and striking of sets in conjunction with the production designer.*

**Painters/Carpenters/Plasterers/Runners etc** - *Work with construction manager with building and striking sets.*

**Stills Photographer** - *Shoots production stills for use in press kits, publicity, advertising.*

**Unit Publicist** - *Works with stills photographer making sure the 'right' shots are taken to publicise the film. Takes care of getting publicity whilst shooting, prepares press kits and makes sure that sufficient material is obtained during the production to publicise the film later on.*

**Editor** - *Once rushes are received from set, the editor will assemble the movie. Works closely with the Director.*

**Assistant Editor** - *Aids editor with preparing picture and sound, synchronising rushes if necessary, numbering and logging, maintaining good files and records and storage of all movie elements.*

**Sound Editor** - *Assembles production tracks, effects, music, recording extra effects if necessary, transferring other effects from libraries, taking control of Foley and ADR (Automatic Dialogue Replacement). Ensures all location atmos' are covered with wild tracks. Takes Film to final mix with Editor and Director. Should hear and approve the final optical soundtrack.*

**Assistant Sound Editor** - *Backs up and assists sound editor.*

**Foley Artist** - *Creates Footsteps, sound effects that match the cut movie filling empty scenes.*

**Musician -** *Composes music in accordance with Directors wishes.*

**Music Supervisor -** *Hires musician, locates and clears all required copyrights on additional music tracks.*

# Budget Template for Low-Budget British Feature Film

This budget summary is designed as a guide only. It is based on a film about five young teenagers finding themselves in the urban jungle. It is to be shot, in and around London, over three weeks. It will be shot on Super 16mm negative and edited on a non linear system before blowing up to 35mm. It will be mixed in Dolby stereo. There are no stunts or special effects, no special locations and minimal night shooting. The cast and crew are paid a basic retainer and enough to cover tube fairs. There are also deferred fees that will only paid should the film break into profit. Remember, some crew members like production design, will start work before and end after principle photography.

It is also assumed that there is a dedicated team behind this project, acting as Producer, Writer, Director and Editor. Check with PACT and BECTU for minimum rates for each crew member.

The budget is totalled to the right. There are twenty separate sections which are all summarised over the following pages. Prices are accurate as of going to press, and often subject to special deals. Producers must always confirm all costings with a quote from a company. Do not take these figures as gospel, use them to build your own budget.

## Budget Summary

|  |  |
|---|---|
| 1. Story & Script | £600 |
| 2. Principal Cast | £1000 |
| 3. Director and Principal Crew | £1000 |
| 4. Producers Fee | £2000 |
| **Total Above the Line Costs** | **£4600** |
| | |
| 5. Cast & Crew | £6735 |
| 6. Labs & Processing | £34,626.8 |
| 7. Stock | £5085 |
| 8. Equipment Hire | £7000 |
| 9. Design | £1800 |
| 10. Stunts & Effects | £100 |
| 11. Location &Transportation | £11,880 |
| 12. Post Production & Editing | £33,400 |
| 13. Music | £2,000 |
| 14. Office & Publicity | £6,950 |
| 15. Overheads | £3,950 |
| 16. Delivery | £14,115 |
| 16. Professional fees | £6,000 |
| | |
| **Total Below the Line Costs** | **£138,241.8** |
| | |
| Basic Film Insurance @ 2% | £2,764.84 |
| Contingency @ 20% | £27,648.36 |
| | |
| **Cash Budget Total** | **£168,655** |
| **Deferred Fees** | **£42,200** |
| **Total Budget** | **£210,855** |

cont...

# Budget Outline:

## Section 1 - Story & Script

Story Rights ............ £0
Research ............ £0
Writer Draft 1 ............ £0
Writer Subsequent Drafts ............ £500
Script duplication and binding ............ £100
US Copyright ............ £0

Story & Script Subtotal ............ £600

## Section 2 - Principal Cast

List Principal Cast ............ £1000
Per Diem ............ £0
Overtime ............ £0

Principal Cast Subtotal ............ £1000

## Section 3 - Director & Principal Crew

Director ............ £1000
Principal Crew ............ £0

Director & Principal Crew Subtotal ............ £1000

## Section 4 - Producer's Fee

Executive Producer ............ £0
Producer ............ £2000

Producer's Fee Subtotal ............ £2000

## Section 5 - Cast

List Cast ............ £500
Stand ins ............ £0
Crowd ............ £0
Extras ............ £0
Overtime ............ £0

Cast Subtotal ............ £500

## Section 6 - Crew

Production Manager ............ £435
Production Co-ordinator ............ £300
Production Assistant ............ £225
Production Accountant ............ £0
Location Manager ............ £0
First Assistant Director ............ £225
Second Assistant Director ............ £225
Third Assistant Director ............ £0
Script Continuity ............ £0
Storyboard Artist ............ £0
Director of Photography (DP) ............ £450
Camera Operator ............ £0
Focus Puller/camera assistant ............ £225
Camera assistant/ loader ............ £0
Gaffer ............ £225
Best Boy ............ £225
Key Grip ............ £225
Dolly Grip ............ £225
Extra Grips ............ £0
Sound Recordist ............ £225
Sound Assistant ............ £225
Costume Designer ............ £450
Costume Assistant/ Dresser ............ £225
Make up Artist & Hair ............ £225
Makeup/Hair assistant ............ £0
Production Designer ............ £450
Art Director/ Set Director ............ £450
Prop Master ............ £0
Prop Buyer ............ £0
Construction Manager ............ £0
Labourers (painters, carpenters, runners) ............ £0
Stills Photographer ............ £1000
Unit Publicist ............ £0
Casting Director ............ £0

cont.....

Crew cont.....

Technical Advisor ............................................£0
Animal Wranglers ............................................£0
Child Minders ............................................£0
Drivers ............................................£0

Crew Subtotal ............................................£6235

## Section 7 - Labs & Processing

Negative Processing ....................................£2340
Rush Print ....................................................£0
Negative Cutting ........................................£3000
Super 16mm 1st Answer Print ......................£1468.8
Interpositive ...............................................£1728
Internegative ..............................................£11,700
First Answer Print 35mm ................................£2421
Show Print ....................................................£810
Slash Dupe ....................................................£0
Low Contrast Telecine Print ...............................£810
Leaders & Misc ..............................................£400
Rushes Sound Transfers (mag) ............................£0
Rushes Sound syncing .......................................£0
Sound Transfers (effects) ...................................£0
Telecine to Broadcast tape ...............................£1500
Dupe of Telecine ..........................................£250
Optical Sound Transfer ....................................£999
Non Linear Stages Only
Negative Telecine .........................................£5000
Sound Transfer and sync ....................................£0

**Trailer**

35mm Optical Dupe of selected scenes ............£1500
Rush Print (may not be needed) .......................£0
Sound Transfers ..........................................£250
Negative Cutting ..........................................£150
First Answer Print ..........................................£75
Optical Sound Transfer ......................................£75
Show Print ....................................................£75
Low Contrast Telecine Print ...............................£75

Labs & Processing Subtotal ......................£34,626.8

## Section 8 - Stock

Film Stock (75 rolls) .........................................£3000
Sound Stock (Nagra or DAT) .............................£375
Master Telecine Stock (VT) .................................£80
Dupe of Telecine Stock (VT) ................................£80
Non linear tapestock (if needed) .........................£900
Post Effects Stock .........................................£50
35mm Stills stock & D/P ....................................£150
Foley Session Stock ..........................................£100
DAT Dupe of final sound mix & M&E .....................£50
Extra stock .....................................................£300

Stock Subtotal ...........................................£5085

## Section 9 - Equipment Hire

Camera Department
Basic Camera Kit (includes body, mags, filters etc.)
Zoom lens, Distagon Set of three or 4 prime lenses, Tripod Legs (short &tall, Tripod Head, Video Assist, Camera Tape, Gaffer Tape, Air canister, Camera 2 basic kit/body (for stunts/2nd unit)
All in Deal .......................................................£3000

Grips Department
Dolly, Bowl for camera head, Straight Track, Curved Track, Wedges, Snake Arm, Jib - Cine Jib or smaller, Large Crane plus operator (if needed)
All in Deal .......................................................£1500

Sound Department
Nagra 4/ DAT Recorder time coded
Microphones - Sennheiser 416
Microphones - Sennheiser 816
Microphones - Tie Clip Radio Mikes (at least two)
Boom pole & wind shield
All in Deal .......................................................£1000

Lighting Department
Lighting equipment, Accss. (trace, gels, spun etc.)
All in Deal........................................................ £1000

Accessories/consumables .................................£500

Equipment Hire Subtotal .................................£7000

## Section 10 - Design

Costume Hire ....................£0
Costume Purchase ....................£500
Set Dressing/ Prop Hire ....................£200
Set Dressing/ Prop Purchase ....................£300
Props damage/loss ....................£100
Set Construction ....................£500
Makeup accessories ....................£100
Hair accessories ....................£0
Continuity Stills ....................£100

Design Subtotal ....................£1800

## Section 11 - Stunts & Effects

Stunt Co-ordinator....................£0
Stunt Men ....................£0
Stunt adjustments ....................£0
Stunt equipment/accessories ....................£0
Armourer ....................£0
Ammunition/consumables ....................£0
Pyrotechnics ....................£0
Smoke Machine ....................£100
Snow/rain/wind etc. ....................£0
Prosthetics ....................£0

Stunts & Effects Subtotal ....................£100

## Section 12 - Location & Transportation

Cast Travel ....................£700
Travel ....................£500
Van Hire (camera, grip,sound trucks etc.) ....................£720
Car Hire ....................£360
Trailer Hire ....................£0
Wagon Hire/ Portable Production facilities ....................£0
Mobile toilets ....................£0
Petrol ....................£1500
Parking ....................£200
Location Fees ....................£500
Permits ....................£0
Location office hire ....................£0

cont...

Location & Transport cont...

Studio hire ....................£0
Studio office hire ....................£0
Location Recce ....................£0
Accommodation ....................£0
On set/ location tea & coffee ....................£200
Catering ....................£5000
Location Contact ....................£0
Gratuities ....................£200
Repairs ....................£500
Vehicle Repairs ....................£300
Radio contacts (walkie-talkies) ....................£0
Location electricity ....................£200
Phones ....................£500
Miscellaneous ....................£500

Location & Transportation Subtotal ....................£11,880

## Section 13 - Post Production & Editing

Editor ....................£1000
Assistant Editor.................... £0
Sound Editor ....................£0
Assistant Editor ....................£0
Cutting Room Hire/ Non linear kit ....................£10000
Cutting Room supplies ....................£50
Effects transfer and fees ....................£1000
Foley Studio Hire ....................£3000
Foley Artist ....................£350
Sound Auto conform ....................£3000
Final Mix (5 days) ....................£7500
M&E Mix ....................£1500
Trailer Mix ....................£750
M&E Trailer Mix ....................£750
Titles ....................£1500
Opticals ....................£0
Computer Graphics (CGI & Compositing) ....................£0
Dolby Fee ....................£3000

Post Production & Editing Subtotal ....................£33400

THE TOOLKIT

## Section 14 - Music

Music Composer ........£0
Musician Fees ........£0
Recording Studio Fees ........£0
Music Rights ........£0
Incidental / Library music ........£0
Musician All in Deal ........£2000
Music Supervisor........£0
Music Purchases ........£0
Royalties ........£0
Music Transfers (mag) ........£0

Music Subtotal ........£2000

## Section 15 - Office & Publicity

Office supplies........£150
Post/ Delivery........ £500
Freight/ Courier ........£0
Publicity promotional material ........£100
Trade subscriptions ........£0
Publicity Stills ........£300
Hire of Stills Studio ........£200
Preview Theatre/ Screenings ........£800
Publicity Post/ Delivery ........£500
Attending Markets for Promotion ........£2000
Reshoot Budget ........£1000
Pre Production Expenses ........£200
Pre Production Tests ........£0
Casting Advertising ........£100
Casting venue/offices ........£0
First Aid ........£100
Petrol (office) ........£500
Miscellaneous ........£500

Office Subtotal ........£6950

## Section 16 - Overheads

Office Rent........ £1600
Secretary/PA ........£0
Maintenance ........£150
Phone/Fax ........£1500
Heat/Light ........£500
Bank Charges ........£200

Overheads Subtotal ........£3950

## Section 17 - Delivery

Video Dupe of Master Movie (inc. M&E)........£250
Video Dupe of Master Trailer (inc. M&E)........£30
Errors & Omissions Insurance ........£7500*
Copies of legal docs. i.e. cert. of nationality........£10
Dupes of Master Stills ........£100
VHS copies ........£75
Electronic Press Kit (video) ........2500
Clips Tape ........£200
35mm Print (release) ........£750
35mm Print (release) of trailer ........£75
DAT Dupe of Music ........£75
Continuities (typed) ........£2500
Misc. Certificates ........£50

Sales Agent Delivery Subtotal ........£14,115

## Section 18 - Professional Fees

Legal Fees........£3000
Accountant ........£3000
Auditor ........£0
Completion Bond ........£0

Professional Fees Subtotal ........£6000

## Section 19 - Film Insurance @ 2%

Cast Insurance
Negative Insurance
Equipment Insurance
Office Insurance
Vehicle Insurance

Insurance Subtotal.................................... £2,764.84

**Contingency @ 20%..............................£27,648.36**

## Section 20 - Deferred Fees

Producer's Fee................................................£5000
Director ..........................................................£2000
Editor ..............................................................£2000
Sound Editor ..................................................£1200
Production Manager .......................................£2000
Production Co ordinator..................................£1200
First Assistant Director....................................£2000
Second Assistant Director................................£1200
Director of Photography...................................£2000
Focus Puller/cam. asst....................................£1800
Gaffer ..............................................................£2000
Best Boy ..........................................................£1600
Key Grip ..........................................................£1600
Dolly Grip ........................................................£1600
Sound Recordist ..............................................£1800
Sound Assistant ...............................................£1400
Costume Designer ...........................................£1800
Costume Assistant ...........................................£1000
Make up ..........................................................£1800
Make up Assistant ............................................£1000
Production Designer ........................................£1800
Art Director/Set Director...................................£1000
Construction Manager ......................................£1800
Unit Publicist....................................................£1600

**Deferred Fees Subtotal..............................£42,200**

# Sales Breakdown

**All sales are negotiated and calculated in US$**

| TERRITORY | Max | Min | Probable | Actual |
|---|---|---|---|---|
| Benelux | $25k | $10k | $20k | $20k |
| Canada | $50k | $20k | $20k | $20k |
| French Canada | $25k | $10k | $10k | $0k |
| France | $60k | $15k | $20k | $0k |
| Germany | $75k | $25k | $50k | $50k |
| Greece | $10k | $5k | $5k | $0k |
| Italy | $60k | $10k | $20k | $20k |
| Iceland | $10k | $2k | $4k | $0k |
| Israel | $10k | $2k | $5k | $0k |
| Portugal | $10k | $2k | $3k | $0k |
| Spain | $60k | $15k | $20k | $20k |
| Scandinavia | $50k | $20k | $20k | $20k |
| Czechoslovakia | $10k | $2k | $4k | $0k |
| Hungary | $10k | $2k | $5k | $0k |
| Poland | $10k | $2k | $2k | $0k |
| Romania | $10k | $2k | $2k | $0k |
| CIS | $15k | $5k | $5k | $0k |
| Former Yugoslavia | $10k | $2k | $3k | $0k |
| Turkey | $10k | $2k | $4k | $0k |
| Egypt | $10k | $2k | $2k | $0k |
| Arg/Chile/Uru/Para | $20k | $2k | $5k | $5k |
| Brazil | $20k | $7k | $10k | $0k |
| Colombia | $10k | $2k | $5k | $0k |
| Mexico | $15k | $5k | $5k | $0k |
| Peru/Equa/Bol | $10k | $2k | $2k | $0k |
| Venezuela | $10k | $2k | $2k | $0k |
| Central America | $10k | $2k | $2k | $2k |
| West Indies | $10k | $2k | $2k | $2k |
| India | $30k | $10k | $10k | $0k |
| Pakistan | $10k | $2k | $4k | $0k |
| Hong Kong | $15k | $5k | $5k | $5k |
| Indonesia | $10k | $2k | $3k | $3k |
| Japan | $100k | $20k | $50k | $0k |
| Korea | $80k | $40k | $50k | $50k |
| Malaysia | $10k | $2k | $2k | $2k |
| Philippines | $15k | $5k | $5k | $0k |
| Singapore | $10k | $2k | $2k | $0k |
| Taiwan | $25k | $5k | $5k | $0k |
| Thailand | $10k | $2k | $5k | $0k |
| Burma | $10k | $2k | $3k | $0k |
| South Africa | $25k | $10k | $10k | $10k |
| Australasia | $50k | $10k | $20k | $20k |
| USA | $200k | $20k | $50k | $20k |
| TOTAL | $1235k | $316k | $481k | $269 |

*These figures are based on the sales of a no-star, low-budget, average British film. The figures quoted in the first three columns represent Max., Min. and Probable sales based on the assumption that film is actually sold in a given territory. The fourth column, Actual, is based on what sales are likely to be achieved in total. This fourth column is drawn from Living Spirit's and other production companies' experience. The UK has been excluded due to possibilities of separate sales or buy outs. Genre films also sell more consistently.*

THE TOOLKIT

# Daily Progress Report Sheet

Production Company: AD:

| | | |
|---|---|---|
| Film: | Director: | Date: |
| Started: | Finishing date: | **SCENE Nos** |
| | | Scenes scheduled: |
| Days to date: | Location: | Scenes shot today: |
| Remaining days: | weather: | Scenes part shot: |
| | | Scenes not shot: |

| **TIME** | **SCRIPT** | | | | | | |
|---|---|---|---|---|---|---|---|
| | total scenes: | | | | | Pages: | |
| | scenes deleted: | | | | | Pages: | |
| Call time: | scenes shot to date: | | | | | Pages: | |
| 1st set up completed: | scenes remaining: | | | | | Pages: | |
| Lunch break: to | | ***No. of*** SETUPS | mins | ***No. of*** PICKUPS | mins | ***No. of*** RETAKES | mins |
| Supper break: to | Prev: | | | | | | |
| Breakfast break: to | Today: | | | | | | |
| Unit wrap: | Total: | | | | | | |
| Total hours: | | | | | | | |

| **ACTORS** *(s-start day, w-days worked, sb-standby, c-call, s-set, f-finish)* | | | | | | | **CROWDS** |
|---|---|---|---|---|---|---|---|
| Name | s | w | sb | c | s | f | rate: |
| | | | | | | | |

| **PICTURE NEGATIVE** | | | | | **SOUND** |
|---|---|---|---|---|---|
| | exposed | N.G | Print | waste | |
| Prev: | | | | | |
| Today: | | | | | |
| Total: | | | | | |

**STILLS - colour/b&w:**

ARRIVALS:
TRANSPORT:
CATERING:
PROPS:
EFFECTS:
XTRA CREW:
ABSENTEES:
REMARKS:

# Call Sheet Number........

| | |
|---|---|
| Production Company | Date: |
| | Unit Call: |
| Film: | Costume: |
| Director: | Makeup: |
| Producer: | Weather Report: |
| Line Producer: | Sunrise/sunset: |
| 1st Assistant Director: | |

| **PRODUCTION OFFICE** | **UNIT OFFICE** |
|---|---|
| | |

| **LOCATION/STUDIO** | **Location contact:** |
|---|---|
| | |

| SETS | Sc.No. | D/N | I/E | Pages | Location | synopsis | Cast No. |
|---|---|---|---|---|---|---|---|
| | | | | | | | |

| No. | CAST | CHARACTER | P/U | W/R M/U | ON SET |
|---|---|---|---|---|---|
| | | | | | |

STAND-INS:
CROWD:

**PRODUCTION REQUIREMENTS**

| | |
|---|---|
| MAKEUP/COSTUME: | TRANSPORT: (inc.list, maps,directions) |
| ART DEPT: | PARKING: |
| CAMERA/RUSHES: | TOILETS: |
| LIGHTING: | FACILITIES: |
| ACTION VEHICLES: | SPECIAL NOTES: |
| SFX/WEAPONS: | ADVANCE SCHEDULE: |
| CONSTRUCTION: | CHANGES: |
| MEDICAL: | |
| CATERING: | **ESTIMATED WRAP:** |

THE TOOLKIT

Titre / Title: SPECIMEN FILM CUE SHEET
Ep Title:
Ep No:
No

Genre / Category: FEATURE

Creation: annee/year 1995
Production: annee/year UNITED KINGDOM

Producteur(firme) / Producer: ANY PRODUCTION COMPANY

Realisateur / Director: A DIRECTOR

Destination / First Presentation: CINEMA

| Droits d'execution Performing Rights | Droits mecaniques Mechanical Rights | Droits mecaniques Videogrammes |
|---|---|---|
| Mandat/Mandate | Mandat/Mandate | Mandat/Mandate |

Interpretes principeux / Principal Actors: PRINCIPAL ACTORS

Duree Totale / Total Duration: 120'
Duree Musicale / Musical duration: 6' 47"
Metrage/Length

Distributeur / Distributor

| CONTRIBUTION OU OEUVRE - CONTRIBUTION OF WORK | | | | | AYANTS DROIT - RIGHT OWNERS | | | | |
|---|---|---|---|---|---|---|---|---|---|
| Participation par categorie per category | Categorie ou titre - Category or title | Caracterist Characteristics | Nombre de passages Number of Uses | Duree Duration | CAE | Noms et prenoms - Surnames and forenames | Societe Society | Part Share | No. CAE CAE Number |
| 1 | OPENING AND CLOSING MUSIC | OI | 2 | 2' 00" | C | A COMPOSER | 052 | 6/12 | |
| | | | | | E | A PUBLISHER | 052 | 6/12 | |
| 2 | INCIDENTAL MUSIC | AI | 16 | 4' 13" | C | A COMPOSER | 052 | 6/12 | |
| | | | | | E | A PUBLISHER | 052 | 6/12 | |
| 3 | PRE-EXISTING SONG | PV | 1 | 0' 34" | C | POPULAR COMPOSER | 052 | 3/12 | |
| | | | | | A | POPULAR AUTHOR | 052 | 3/12 | |
| | | | | | E | POPULAR PUBLISHER | 052 | 6/12 | |

------oOo------

**The Performing Right Society Limited**
**PRS**

**Control by PRS publishers is subject to general catalogue or specific sub-publishing agreements in your territory, if any.**

**Page 1**

*supplied by the PRS*

# Script Continuity Sheet

Production Company: | Film: | No:
Producer: | | Date:
Director:
DoP:

| Camera Roll | Sound Roll | Stock | Camera | Scene | Slate | Time | Lens | F-stop | Filters | S/M | D/N | I/E | Synopsis of action |
|---|---|---|---|---|---|---|---|---|---|---|---|---|---|
| | | | | | | | | | | | | | |
| | | | | | | | | | | | | | |
| | | | | | | | | | | | | | |
| | | | | | | | | | | | | | |
| | | | | | | | | | | | | | |
| | | | | | | | | | | | | | |
| | | | | | | | | | | | | | |
| | | | | | | | | | | | | | |
| | | | | | | | | | | | | | |
| | | | | | | | | | | | | | |
| | | | | | | | | | | | | | |
| | | | | | | | | | | | | | |
| | | | | | | | | | | | | | |
| | | | | | | | | | | | | | |

| Special Props | General Comments/ Lighting diagrams |
|---|---|
| | |

THE TOOLKIT

# Script Breakdown Sheet

Production Company: DATE:
FILM:
Dir:
Producer:
1st AD:

| Scene | Synopsis | Location | I/E | D/N | Pages | CAST Nos. |
|---|---|---|---|---|---|---|
| | | | | | | |

| Scene | No. | CAST / CHARACTER | STAND-INS | CROWD | W/R | M/U |
|---|---|---|---|---|---|---|
| | | | | | | |

| Scene | PROPS/ANIMALS | ART DEPT/CONSTRUCTION | SFX/WEAPONS |
|---|---|---|---|
| | | | |

| CAMERA | GRIPS | LIGHTING | EXTRA EQUIPMENT |
|---|---|---|---|
| | | | |

| ACTION VEHCILES | TRUCKS/TRAILERS | EXTRA CREW | MISC |
|---|---|---|---|
| | | | |

# The Film Producers Toolkit Directory

## ACCOUNTANTS

### 101 Film & TV Production Accountants
26 Goodge Street, London, W1P 1FG
Tel 0171 436 1119
Fax 0171 436 8887

### Baker Tilly
2 Bloomsbury Street, London, WC1B 3ST
Tel 0171 413 5100
Fax 0171 413 5101

### Beecham's Chartered Accountants
3 Bedford Row, London, WC1R 4BU
Tel 0171 242 5624
Fax 0171 405 6287

### Berg Kaprow Lewis
35 Ballards Lane, Finchley,
London, N3 1XW
Tel 0181 349 4453
Fax 0181 343 1012

### Casson Beckman
Hobson House, 155 Gower Street, London,
WC1E 6BJ
Tel 0171 387 2888
Fax 0171 388 0600

### Clayman & Co
189 Bickenhall Mansions, Bickenhall
Street, London, W1H 3DE
Tel 0171 935 0847
Fax 0171 224 2216

### Coopers & Lybrand
1 Embankment Place, London, SE1 7EU
Tel 0171 583 5000
Fax 0171 213 2411

### Denison
The Blue Door, Cheney Road,
London, NW1 2TF
Tel 171 713 5062
Fax 0171 713 1550

### Dover Childs
15 Manchester Square, London, W1M 6LB
Tel 0171 935 7609
Fax 0171 486 6457

### Ernst & Young
Becket House, 1 Lambeth Palace Road,
London, SE1 7EU
Tel 0171 928 2000
Fax 0171 928 1345

### Fraser Russell
Fairview House, 71-73 Woodbridge Road,
Guildford, Surrey, GU1 4YZ
Tel 01483 567252
Fax 01483 300081

### Ivan Sopher
5 Elstree Gate, Elstree Way,
Borehamwood, Hertfordshire,
WD6 1JD
Tel 0181 207 0602
Fax 0181 207 6758

### KPMG Peat Marwick
1 Puddle Dock, London, EC4V 3PD
Tel 0171 236 8000
Fax 0171 329 6097

### Learer Roberts
26-28 Bartholomew Square,
London, EC1V 3QH
Tel 0171 250 0330
Fax 0171 251 1401

### Lindford & Co
1 Duchess Street, London, W1N 3DE
Tel 0171 637 2244
Fax 0171 637 2999

### Lubock Fine
Russell Bedford House, City Forum, 250
City Road, London, EC1V 2QQ
Tel 0171 490 7766
Fax 0171 490 5102

### Lucraft Hodgson & Dawes
2-4 Ash Lane, Rustingham, Littlehampton,
West Sussex,
BN16 3BZ
Tel 01903 772244
Fax 01903 771071

### Price Waterhouse
Southwark Towers, 32 London Bridge,
London, SE1 9SY
Tel 0171 939 3000
Fax 0171 378 0647

### Shipleys
10 Orange Street, Haymarket,
London, WC2H 7DR
Tel 0171 312 0000
Fax 0171 312 0022

### Silver Levene
37 Warren Street, London, W1P 5PD
Tel 0171 383 3200
Fax 0171 383 4165/4168

### Stoy Hayward
8 Baker Street, London, W1M 1DA
Tel 0171 486 5888
Fax 0171 487 3686

### The Philip Hills Partnership
3 Quayside Street, Edinburgh,
Midlothian, EH6 6EJ
Tel 0131 555 1599
Fax 0131 555 1029

### Touche Ross
Hill House, 1 Little New Street, London,
EC4A 3TR
Tel 0171 936 3000
Fax 0171 583 8517

## ASSOCIATIONS, ORGANISATIONS & UNIONS

### BAFTA
195 Piccadilly, London, W1V OLN
Tel 0171 734 0022
Fax 0171 734 1792

### BAFTA Scotland
74 Victoria Crescent, Glasgow, G12 9JN
Tel 0141 357 4317
Fax 0141 337 1432

### BBFC (British Board of Film Classification)
3 Soho Square, London, W1V 6HD
Tel 0171 439 7961
Fax 0171 287 0141

### BECTU
111 Wardour Street, London, W1V 4AY
Tel 0171 437 8506
Fax 0171 437 8268

### British Council
Films Department, 11 Portland Place,
London, W1N 4EJ
Tel 0171 389 3065
Fax 0171 389 3041

### British Film Institute
21 Stephen Street, London, W1P 2LN
Tel 0171 255 1444
Fax 0171 436 7950

### British Guild of Animation
26 Noel Street, London, W1V 3RD
Tel 0171 434 2651
Fax 0171 434 9002

### British Screen Finance Ltd.
14-17 Wells Mews, London, W1P 3FL
Tel 0171 323 9080
Fax 0171 323 0092

### Equity
Guild House, Upper St. Martin's Lane,
London, WC2H 9EG
Tel 0171 379 6000
Fax 0171 379 7001

### The Irish Film Board
Rockfort House, St. Augustine Street,
Galway, Ireland.
Tel: 353 91 651398
Fax: 353 91 561405

### MCPS - Mechanical Copyright Protection Society
Elgar House, 41 Streatham High Road,
London, SW16 1ER
Tel 0181 769 4400/0181 664 4400
Fax 0181 769 8792

### MU - Musicians Union
60-62 Clapham Road, London, SW9 OJJ
Tel 0171 582 5566
Fax 0171 582 9805

### NPA - New Producers Alliance
9 Bourlet Close, London, W1RP 7PJ
Tel 0171 580 2480
Fax 0171 580 2484

### PACT - Producers Alliance for Cinema & Television
Gordon House, Greencoat Place, London,
SW1P 1PH
Tel 0171 233 6000
Fax 0171 233 8935

### PRS - Performing Rights Society
29/33 Berners Street, London, W1P 4AA
Tel 0171 580 5544
Fax 0171 631 4138

### Scottish Film Council
74 Victoria Crescent Road, Dowanhill,
Glasgow, Lanarkshire, G12 9JN
Tel 0141 334 4445
Fax 0141 334 8132

### SFD - Society of Film Distributors
22 Golden Square, London, W1R 3PA
Tel 0171 437 4383
Fax 0171 734 0912

### The British Film Commission
70 Baker Street, London, W1M 1DJ
Tel 0171 224 5000
Fax 0171 224 1013

### Women in Film & Television
Garden Studios, 11/15 Betterton Street,
London, WC2H 9BP
Tel 0171 379 0344
Fax 0171 379 2413

### Writers Guild of Grt. Britain
430 Edgeware Road, London, W2 1EH
Tel 0171 723 8074
Fax 0171 706 2413

### BAFTA
195 Piccadilly, London, W1V OLN
Tel 0171 734 0022/465 0277
Fax 0171 734 1009

## AUDIO POST PRODUCTION

### Air Studios
Lyndhurst Hall, Lyndhurst Road,
Hampstead, London, NW3 5NG
Tel 0171 794 0660
Fax 0171 794 8518

### Anvil Post Production Ltd.
Denham Studios, North Orbital Road,
Denham, Uxbridge, Middx, UB9 5HL
Tel 01895 833522
Fax 01895 835006

### Broadcast Film & Video Ltd.
33 West Park, Clifton, Bristol,
Avon, BS8 2LX
Tel 0117 9237087
Fax 0117 923 7090

### Colour Video Services Sound
20A Brownlow Mews, London, WC1N 2LD
Tel 0171 242 7788
Fax 0171 242 8999

### D B Post Production
1-8 Batemans Buildings, South Soho
Square, London, W1V 5TW
Tel 0171 287 9144
Fax 0171 287 9143

### D B Post Production Ltd. Cinema Sound
27-29 Berwick Street, London, W1V 3RF
Tel 0171 437 0136
Fax 0171 439 2012

### De Lane Lea Ltd.
75 Dean Street, London, W1V 5HA
Tel 0171 439 1721
Fax 0171 437 0913

### Delta Sound Services
Shepperton Studios, Studios Road,
Shepperton, Middx,TW17 OQD
Tel 01932 562045
Fax 01932 572396

### Digital Sound House
14 Livonia Street, London, W1V 3PH
Tel 0171 434 2928
Fax 0171 287 9110

### Dolby Laboratories
Interface, Wootton Bassett,
Wiltshire, SN4 8QJ
Tel 01793 842100
Fax 01793 842101

### Goldcrest Post Production Facilities
36-44 Brewer Street, London, W1R 3HP
Tel 0171 439 4177
Fax 0171 437 6411

### Hart Street Studios
4 Forth Street, Edinburgh,
Midlothian, EH1 3LD
Tel 0131 557 0181
Fax 0131 557 9521

### Howarth & Johnston
14 Chalmers Crescent, Edinburgh,
Midlothian, EH9 1TS
Tel 0131 668 3366
Fax 0131 662 4463

### Interact Sound Ltd.
160 Barlby Road, London, W10 6BS
Tel 0181 960 3115
Fax 0181 964 3022

### John Wood Sound
St. Martin's Studios, Greenbank Road,
Ashton on Mersey, Sale, Cheshire
Tel 0161 905 2077
Fax 0161 905 2383

### London Post
34-35 Dean Street, London, W1V 5AP
Tel 0171 439 9080
Fax 0171 434 0714

### M2 Facilities
The Forum, 74-80 Camden Street,
London, NW1 OEG
Tel 0171 387 5001
Fax 0171 387 5025

### Magmasters
20 St. Annes Court, London, W1V 3AW
Tel 0171 437 8273
Fax 0171 494 1281

### Music House
5 Newburgh Street, London, W1V 1LH
Tel 0171 434 9678
Fax 0171 434 1470

### NATS Post Production
10 Soho Square, London, W1V 6NT
Tel 0171 287 9900
Fax 0171 287 8636

### Pinewood Studios
Pinewood Road, Pinewood Road, Iver,
Buckinghamshire, SL0 0HN
Tel 01753 651700
Fax 01753 656844

### Reel Sound Ltd.
Legend Block, Pinewood Studios, Iver
Heath, Iver, Bucks, SL0 0HN
Tel 01753 656372
Fax 01753 653351

### Snake Ranch
90 Lots Road, London, SW10 0QD
Tel 0171 351 7888
Fax 0171 352 5194

### Snaptrax
Denham Studios, North Orbital Road,
Denham, Uxbridge, Middx, UB9 5HH
Tel 01895 833522
Fax 01895 835006

### Twickenham Film Studios
The Barons, St. Margarets, Twickenham,
Middx, TW1 2AW
Tel 0181 892 4477
Fax 0181 891 0168

### Video London Sound Studios
16-18 Ramillies Street, London, W1V 1DL
Tel 0171 734 4811
Fax 0171 494 2553

### Videosonics
13 Hawley Crescent, London, NW1 8NP
Tel 0171 482 2588
Fax 0171 482 0849

### West 1 Television
10 Bateman Street, London, W1V 5TT
Tel 0171 437 5533
Fax 0171 287 8621

### Yorkshire Television
The Television Centre, Leeds, LS3 1JS
Tel 0113 243 8283
Fax 0113 244 5107

## CASTING SERVICES

### PCR (Professional Casting Report)
PO Box 11, London, SW15 6AY
Tel 0181 789 0408
Fax 0181 780 1977

## CATERING

### Bon Appetit
4 Penlee House, Claremount Avenue,
Woking, Surrey, GU22 7SG
Tel 01932 253253
Fax 01932 254976

### Busters on Location Ltd.
65 Thorney Mill Road, Bucks, SL0 9AL
Tel 0181 961 3525
Fax 01895 678276

### Clarkson Catering
Tavern Quay, Sweden Gate,
London, SE16 1TX
Tel 0171 237 6384
Fax 0171 237 6384

### Colemans Film & TV Caterers
140 Ridgeway Drive, Bromley,
Kent, BR1 5BX
Tel 0181 857 8308
Fax 0181 857 8308

### Film Cuisine
308 Smithdown Rd, Liverpool, LI5 5AJ
Tel 0151 722 7416
Fax 0151 733 6172

## Glenn's Star Catering
94 Cumberland Drive, Chessington, Surrey, KT9 1HH
Tel 0181 397 7921

## Hollywood Catering Services
52 Jeffcutt Road, Chelmer Village, Chelmsford, Essex, CM2 6XN
Tel 01245 451051
Fax 01245 359917

## J & J Preparations
Unit 5, Midas Industrial Park, Longbridge Way, Uxbridge, UB8 2YT
Tel 01895 232 627
Fax 01895 257 033

## J & R Catering
Hey Green Lodge, Waters Road, Marsden, Nr Huddersfield, HD7 6NG
Tel 01484 843 842
Fax 01484 843 842

## Kennedy's Caterers Ltd
Park House, Queen St, Morley, Leeds, LS27 9LY
Tel 0113 2532867
Fax 0113 2526112

## Leading Edge
15 Oxton Drv, Tadcaster, N. Yorkshire, LS24 8AH
Tel 01937 834458
Fax 01937 834458

## Reel Food Catering
Westwinds, Peel Road, Thorntonhall, Glasgow, G74 5AG
Tel 0141 141 644 2622

## Set Breaks
4 Gleneagles Close, Stanwell Village, TW19 7PD
Tel 01784 258372
Fax 01784 420347

## Set Meals
Unit 7, Tower Workshops, Riley Road, London, SE1 3DG
Tel 0171 237 0014
Fax 0171 231 8401

## St. Clements Catering
Unit 25, Argyle Way, Ely, Cardiff, CF5 5NJ
Tel 01222 598 121
Fax 01222 592 846

## Tele-Cater
17 Newlands Drive, Lowton, Nr Warrington, Cheshire, WA3 3RY
Tel 01942 726 995
Fax 01942 271 948

## The Location Caterers
Hill Farm, Pipers Ln, Caddington Common, Nr Markyate, Herts, AL3 8QP
Tel 01582 841 892
Fax 01582 842 256

## Tommy Jones
4 Perceton Mains Farm, Perceton, Irvine, Ayrshire, Scotland, KA11 2AJ
Tel 01294 222240
Fax 01294 222240

## VIP Location Catering
23 Kelvinside Gardens East, Glasgow, G20 6BE
Tel 0141 946 1497

## Wood Hall Catering
Teddington Studios, Broom Road, Teddington Lock, Middx, TW11 9NT
Tel 0181 614 2667
Fax 0181 342 9775

# COMPUTER GRAPHICS

## Bionic
Pinewood Studios, Pinewood Road, Iver, Buckinghamshire, SL0 0NH
Tel 01753 655886/656980
Fax 01753 654507

## Bionic Productions Ltd.
Pinewood Studios, Pinewood Road, Iver, Buckinghamshire, SL0 0NH
Tel 01753 655886
Fax 01753 654507

## Bitsoft Ltd.
Black Screen Projection, 193 Hempstead Road, Watford, Hertfordshire, WC1 3HG
Tel 01923 237575
Fax 01923 237575

## Cell
28-30 Osnaburgh Street, London, NW1
Tel 0171 208 1500
Fax 0171 208 1502

## CFX Associates
16-18 Ramilles Street, London, W1V 1DL
Tel 0171 734 3155
Fax 0171 494 3670

## Cinesite Europe Ltd.
9 Carlisle Street, London, W1V 5RG
Tel 0171 973 4000
Fax 0171 943 4040

## Complete
Slingsby Place, Long Acre, London, WC2E
Tel 0171 379 7739
Fax 0171 497 9305

## Computer Film Company
50-51 Berwick Street, London, W1V 3RA
Tel 0171 494 4673
Fax 0171 437 0490

## Digital Arts
3 Soho Street, London, W1V 5FA
Tel 0171 439 0919
Fax 0171 437 1146

## Drum
Second Floor, Fenton House, 55-57 Great Marlborough Street, London, W1V 2DD
Tel 0171 734 5557
Fax 0171 734 4533

## FrameStore
9 Noel Street, London, W1V 4AL
Tel 0171 208 2600
Fax 0171 208 2626

## Infynity Ltd.
49-50 Marlborough House, London, W1V
Tel 0171 434 1665
Fax 0171 734 4229

### London Post
34-35 Dean Street, London, W1V 5AP
Tel 0171 439 9080
Fax 0171 434 0714

### M2 Facilities Group
74-80 Camden Street, The Forum, London, NW1 OEG
Tel 0171 387 5001
Fax 0171 387 5025

### Moving Picture Company
25 Noel Street, London, W1V 3RD
Tel 0171 434 3100
Fax 0171 734 9150

### NATS Post Production
10 Soho Square, London, W1V 6NT
Tel 0171 287 9900
Fax 0171 287 8636

### Peerless Camera Company
32 Bedfordbury, London, WC2N 4DU
Tel 0171 836 3367
Fax 0171 240 2143

### Rushes
66 Old Compton Street, London, W1V 5PA
Tel 0171 437 8676
Fax 0171 734 2519

### Soho 601
71 Dean Street, London, W1V 5HB
Tel 0171 439 2730
Fax 0171 734 3331

### SVC Television
142 Wardour Street, London, W1V 3AU
Tel 0171 734 1600
Fax 0171 437 1854

### The House
Richmond House, 12 Richmond Buildings, Dean Street, London, W1V 5AF
Tel 0171 439 2901
Fax 0171 753 0345

### The Mill
40-41 Great Marlborough Street, London,
Tel 0171 287 4041
Fax 0171 287 8393

### Touch Animation
44 Earlham Street, London, WC2H 9LA
Tel 0171 379 6247
Fax 0171 240 3419

### TSI Video Ltd.
10 Grape Street, London, WC2H 8DY
Tel 0171 379 3435
Fax 0171 379 4589

### West 1 Television
10 Bateman Street, London, W1V 5TT
Tel 0171 437 5533
Fax 0171 287 8621

## COSTUME

### 20th Century Frox
64A Fulham Road, London, SW6 5RP
Tel 0171 731 3242

### Academy Costumes
50 Rushworth Street, London, SE1 ORE
Tel 0171 620 0771
Fax 0171 713 7269

### Allan Scott Costumes
Off Ley Works, Unit F, Prima Road, London, SW9 ONA
Tel 0171 793 1197

### Angels & Bermans
40 Camden Street, London, NW1 OEN
Tel 0171 387 0999
Fax 0171 240 9527

### Barnums
67 Hammersmith Road, London, W14 8UZ
Tel 0171 602 1211
Fax 0171 603 9945

### Damodes
10a Ellingfort Road, Hackney, London, E8
Tel 0181 986 8550
Fax 0181 986 9923

### Escapade
150 Camden High Street, London, NW1
Tel 0171 485 7384
Fax 0171 485 0950

### Flame Military Costumiers
Old Victorian Police Station, 31 Market Street, Torquay, Devon, TQ1 3AW
Tel 01803 211930
Fax 01803 293554

### Granada Television Costume Hire
Quay Street, Manchester, Lancashire, M60 9EA
Tel 0161 832 7211
Fax 0161 832 8809

### Gwen & Janette
Unit 2, 37 Briscoe Road, London, SW19
Tel 0181 544 1092
Fax 0181 544 1092

### Hairaisers Ltd.
9-11 Sunbeam Road, Park Royal, London, NW10 6JP
Tel 0181 965 2500
Fax 0181 963 1600

### Laurence Corner
62-64 Hampstead Road, London, NW1
Tel 0171 813 1010
Fax 0171 813 1413

### RSC Hire Wardrobe
Timothy's Bridge Road, Stratford-upon-Avon, Warwickshire, CV37 9NQ
Tel 01789 205920

### Skin Two
23 Grand Union Centre, Kensal Road, London, W10 5AX
Tel 0181 968 9692
Fax 0181 960 8404

### The BBC Costume Store
Design Group, Victoria Road, North Acton, London, W3
Tel 0181 576 1761
Fax 0181 993 7040

### The Contemporary Wardrobe Collection
The Horse Hospital, Colonnade, Bloomsbury, London, WC1N 1HX
Tel 0171 713 7370
Fax 0171 713 7269

### The Costume Group
12 Wolverton Gardens, Ealing,
London, W5 3LJ
Tel 0181 752 1247

### The Costume Studio
6 Penton Grove, Off White Lion Street,
Islington, London, N1 9HS
Tel 0171 837 6576/0171 338 4481
Fax 0171 837 6576

## DISTRIBUTORS

### Artificial Eye Film Company
13 Soho Square, London, W1V 5FB
Tel 0171 437 2552
Fax 0171 437 2992

### Buena Vista Home Video
Beaumont House, Kensington Village,
Avonmore Road, London, W14 8TS
Tel 0171 605 2400
Fax 0171 605 2795

### Colombia TriStar Video
Horatio House, 77-85 Fulham Palace
Road, London, W6 8JA
Tel 0181 748 6000
Fax 0181 748 4859

### Entertainment in Video
27 Soho Square, London, W1V 5FL
Tel 0171 439 1979
Fax 0171 734 2483

### Feature Film Company
4th Floor, 68-70 Wardour Street, London
Tel 0171 734 2266
Fax 0171 494 0309

### Film Four International
124 Horseferry Road, London, SW1P 2TX
Tel 0171 396 4444
Fax 0171 306 8361

### First Independent Films
69 New Oxford Street,
London, WC1A 1DG
Tel 0171 528 7768
Fax 0171 528 7771

### Guild Film Distribution
14-17 Market Place, Great Tichfield Street,
London, W1N 8AR
Tel 0171 323 5151
Fax 0171 631 3568

### Mayfair Entertainment UK
110 St Martins Lane, London, WC2N 4AD
Tel 0171 304 7922
Fax 0171 867 1121

### Medusa Communications & Marketing Ltd.
Regal Chambers, 51 Bancroft, Hitchin,
Hertfordshire, SG5 1LL
Tel 01462 421818
Fax 01462 420393

### Metro Tartan
79 Wardour Street, London, W1V 3TH
Tel 0171 734 8508
Fax 0171 287 2112

### Polygram
347/353 Chiswick High Rd,
London, W4 4HS
Tel 0181 994 9199
Fax 0181 742 5577

### Rank Film Distributors
127 Wardour Street, London, W1V 4AD
Tel 0171 437 9020
Fax 0171 434 3689

### Twentieth Century Fox
31-32 Soho Square, London, W1V 6AP
Tel 0171 437 7766
Fax 0171 434 2170

### United International Pictures
Mortimer House,37-41 Mortimer Street,
London, W1A 2JL
Tel 0171 636 1655
Fax 0171 636 4118

### Warner Brothers
135 Wardour Street, London, W1V 4AP
Tel 0171 734 8400
Fax 0171 437 2950

## FILM CAMERA HIRE

### Cine Europe
7 Silver Road, White City Industrial Park,
Wood Lane, London, W12 7SG
Tel 0181 743 6762
Fax 0181 749 3501

### GP Film Services
Unit 20, Wadsworth Business Centre, 21
Wadsworth Rd, Perivale, Greenford,
Middx, UB6
Tel 0181 991 1026
Fax 0181 991 9845

### Joe Dunton & Co
7 Northfield Estate, Beresford Avenue,
Stonebridge Park, Wembley, London, HA0
1NW
Tel 0181 903 7311
Fax 0181 903 6713

### Media Film Service
4 Airlinks, Spitfire Way, Heston, Hounslow,
Middx, TW5 9NR
Tel 0181 573 2255
Fax 0181 756 0592

### Panavision Ireland
Ardmore Studios, Herbert Road, Bray,
County Wicklow, Ireland,
Tel 010 3531 2 860811
Fax 010 3531 2 863425

### Panavision Manchester
Manchester Road, Kearsley, Bolton,
Lancashire, BL4 8RL
Tel 01204 705794
Fax 01204 705780

### Panavision Shepperton
Shepperton Studios, Studios Road,
Shepperton, Middx, TW17 OQD
Tel 019325 72440
Fax 019325 72450

### Panavision UK - London
Wycombe Road, Wembley,
Middx, HA0 1QN
Tel 0181 903 7933
Fax 0181 902 3273

### Panavision West One
Cinema House Business Centre, 93 Wardour Street, London, W1V 3TE
Tel 0171 413 0030
Fax 0171 734 4627

### SAMMYS - Samuelson Film Service London
21 Derby Road, Metropolitan Centre, Greenford, Middx, UB6 8UJ
Tel 0181 578 7887
Fax 0181 578 2733

### Tattooist International
Westgate House, 149 Roman Way, London, N7 8XH
Tel 0171 700 3555
Fax 0171 700 4445

## COMMISSIONS & LOCATION SERVICES

### Australian Film Commission
99/101 Regent Street, 2nd Floor, Victory House, London, W1R 7HB
Tel 0171 734 9383
Fax 0171 434 0170

### Bath Film Office
Abbey Chambers, Abbey Church Yard, Bath, Avon, BA1 1LY
Tel 01225 477711
Fax 01225 477221

### British Film Commission
70 Baker Street, London, W1M 1DJ
Tel 0171 224 5000
Fax 0171 224 1013

### Cardiff Film Commission
The Media Centre, Culverhouse Cross, Cardiff, CF5 6XJ
Tel 01222 590240
Fax 01222 590511

### Central England Film Commission (B'ham)
Waterside House, 46 Gas Street, Birmingham, B1 2JT
Tel 0121 643 9309
Fax 0121 643 9064

### Central England Film Commission (E. Midlands)
E.M.D.C., 2-4 Weekday Cross, Nottingham, NG1 2GB
Tel 01159 527 870
Fax 01159 520 539

### Eastern Screen
Anglia Television, Prince of Wales Road, Norwich, NR1 3JG
Tel 01603 767 077
Fax 01603 767 191

### Edinburgh and Lothian Screen Industries Office
Filmhouse, 88 Lothian Rd, Edinburgh, EH3 9BZ
Tel 0131 228 5960
Fax 0131 228 5967

### Gwynedd Film Office
Planning & Development Department, Gwynedd Council, Council Offices, Shire Hall, Caenarfon, Gwynedd, L55 1SH
Tel 01286 679 685
Fax 01286 673 324

### Isle of Man Film Commission
Department of Industry, Illiam Dhone House, Circular Road, Douglas, Isle of Man, IM1 1PJ
Tel 01624 685 674
Fax 01624 685 683

### Lancashire Film & Television Office
Lancashire Enterprises Plc, Enterprise House, 17 Ribblesdale Place, Preston, PR1 3NA
Tel 01772 203 020
Fax 01772 252 640

### Liverpool Film Office
Central Libraries, William Brown Street, Liverpool, L3 8EW
Tel 0151 225 5446
Fax 0151 207 1342

### London Film Commission
c/o Carnival Films & Television, 12 Raddington Road, Ladbroke Grove, London, W10 5TG
Tel 0181 968 0968
Fax 0181 968 0177

### London Underground Ltd.
Film Facilities Administrator, London Transport, 55 Broadway, London, SW1H
Tel 0171 918 3271-5/3610
Fax 0171 918 3134

### Manchester Film Office
Manchester Town Hall, Manchester, M60 2LA
Tel 0161 234 3677/3678
Fax 0161 234 3679

### Northern Screen Commission
Studio 15, Design Works, William Street, Felling, Tyne & Wear, NE10 0JP
Tel 0191 469 1000
Fax 0191 469 7000

### Scottish Screen Locations
Filmhouse, 88 Lothian Rd, Edinburgh, EH3
Tel 0131 229 1213
Fax 0131 229 1070

### Screen Wales
Canolfan sgrin Centre, Llandaf, Cardiff, CF5 2PU
Tel 01222 578 370
Fax 01222 578 654

### South West Film Commission
18 Belle Vue Road, Saltash, Cornwall, PL12 6TG
Tel 01752 841 199
Fax 01752 841 254

### South West Scotland Screen Commission
Gracefield Arts Centre, 23 Edinburgh Road, Dumfries, DG1 1JQ
Tel 01387 263 666
Fax 01387 263 666

### Southern Screen Com.
Regional Business Centre, 4th Floor, Baltic House, Kingston Crescent, Portsmouth
Tel 01705 650 779
Fax 01705 650 789

### The Highlands of Scotland Screen Commission
Economic Development Service, The Highland Council, Glenurquhart Road, Inverness, IV3 5NX
Tel 01463 702 563
Fax 01463 710 848

### Yorkshire Screen Commission
Unit 416, The Workstation, 15 Paternoster Row, Sheffield, S1 2BX
Tel 01142 799 115
Fax 01142 796 522

## FILM EDITING

### Anvil Post Production
Denham Studios, North Orbital Road, Denham, Uxbridge, Middx, UB9 5HL
Tel 01895 833522
Fax 01895 835006

### Avid Technology
Charlotte, 6-14 Windmill St, London, W1P
Tel 0171 307 8000
Fax 0171 307 8001

### De Lane Lea Ltd.
75 Dean Street, London, W1V 5HA
Tel 0171 439 1721
Fax 0171 437 0913

### Edit Hire
Unit 1B, Shepperton Studios, Studios Road, Shepperton, Middx, TW17 0QD
Tel 01932 572253/572523
Fax 01932 569899

### Goldcrest Post Production Facilities Ltd.
36-44 Brewer Street, Entrance in 1 Lexington Street, London, W1R 3HP
Tel 0171 437 7972
Fax 0171 437 6411

### London Editing Machines
Twickenham Film Studios, St. Margarets, Twickenham, Middlesex, TW1 2AW
Tel 0181 744 9828
Fax 0181



### NATS Post Production
10 Soho Square, London, W1V 6NT
Tel 0171 287 9900
Fax 0171 287 8636

### Pinewood Studios
Pinewood Raod, Pinewood Road, Iver, Bucks.
Tel 01753 651700
Fax 01753 656844

### Prominent Facilities
Prominent Studios, 68A Delaney Street, London, NW1 7RY
Tel 0171 284 0242
Fax 0181 284 1020

### Rushes
66 Old Compton Street, London, W1V 5PA
Tel 0171 437 8676
Fax 0171 734 2519

### Salon Productions Ltd.
10 Livonia Street, London, W1V 3PH
Tel 0171 437 0516
Fax 0171 437 6197

### Sam Sneade Editing Ltd.
34-35 Dean Street, London, W1V 5AP
Tel 0171 734 6901
Fax 0171 734 6765

### Shears Post Production Services
Warwick House, Chapone Place, Dean Street, London, W1V 5AJ
Tel 0171 437 8182
Fax 0171 437 8183

### Solus Enterprises
35 Marshall Street, London, W1V 1LL
Tel 0171 734 0645
Fax 0171 287 2197

### Tattooist International
Westgate House, 149 Roman Way, London, N7 8XH
Tel 0171 700 3555
Fax 0171 700 4445

### The Film Editors
6-10 Lexington Street, London, W1R 3HS
Tel 0171 439 8655
Fax 0171 437 0409

### The Mill
40-41 Great Marlborough Street, London, W1V 1DA
Tel 0171 287 4041
Fax 0171 287 8393

### The SOHO group (Soho Images, Soho 601)
71 Dean Street, London, W1V 5HB
Tel 0171 439 2730
Fax 0171 734 3331

### TSI Video Ltd.
10 Grape Street, London, WC2H 8DY
Tel 0171 379 3435
Fax 0171 379 4589

### Wheelers
5A Hansard Mews, London, W14 8RJ
Tel 0171 603 0217/8
Fax 0171 603 5217

## FILM FUNDING & DEVELOPMENT

### Arts Council of England
14 Great Peter Street, London, SW1P 3NQ
Tel 0171 973 6443
Fax 0171 973 6581

### British Film Institute Productions
29 Rathbone Street, London, W1P 1AG
Tel 0171 636 5587
Fax 0171 580 9456

### British Screen Finance
14-17 Wells Mews, London, W1P 3FL
Tel 0171 323 9080
Fax 0171 323 0092

### European Co-Production Fund
14-17 Wells Mews, London, W1P 3FL
Tel 0171 323 9080
Fax 0171 323 0092

### European Script Fund
39C Highbury Place, London, N5 1QP
Tel 0171 226 9903
Fax 0171 354 2706

### Film Four International
124 Horseferry Road, London, SW1P 2TX
Tel 0171 396 4444
Fax 0171 306 8361

### First Film Foundation
9 Bourlet Close, London, W1P 7PJ
Tel 0171 580 2111
Fax 0171 580 2116

### First Reels Project
74 Victoria Crescent Road, Glasgow, Scotland, G12 9JN
Tel 0141 334 4445
Fax 0141 334 8132

### Glasgow Film Fund
74 Victoria Crescent Road, Glasgow, Lanarkshire, G12 9JN
Tel 0141 337 2526
Fax 0141 337 2562

### Northern Ireland Film Council
21 Ormeau Ave, Belfast, Co. Antrim, BT2 8HD
Tel 01232 232444
Fax 01232 239918

### Scottish Film Production Fund
74 Victoria Crescent Road, Glasgow, Lanarkshire, G12 9JN
Tel 0141 334 4445
Fax 0141 334 8132

### Telefilm Canada
22 Kingly Court, London, W1R 5LE
Tel 0171 437 8308
Fax 0171 734 8586

### The Scottish Film Production Fund
74 Victoria Crescent Road, Glasgow, Lanarkshire, G12 9JN
Tel 0141 337 2526
Fax 0141 337 2562

### Welsh Production Fund
Screen Centre, Ty Oldfield Llantrisant Road, Llandaff, Cardiff, South Glamorgan, CF5 2PU
Tel 01222 578633
Fax 01222 578654

## FILM MARKETS

### AFM- American Film Market
Suite 600, 12424 Wilshire Boulevard, L A, C A 90025, USA
Tel +1 310 447 1555
Fax +1 310 447 1666

### CANNES
99 Boulevard Malesherbes, 75008, Paris, France,
Tel +33 1 45 61 66 00
Fax +33 1 45 61 97 60

### Independent Feature Film Market
12th Floor, 104 West 29th Street, New York, NY 10001, USA
Tel +1 212 465 8200
Fax +1 212 465 8525

### MIFED - Milan
Fiera di Milano, Largo Domodossola 1, 20145 Milan, Italy,
Tel +39 2 4801 2912
Fax +39 2 4997 7020

## FILM SCHOOL

### Bournemouth and Poole College of Art and Design
School of Film, TV and AV Production, Wallisdown, Poole, Dorset, BH12 5HH
Tel 01202 538204
Fax 01202 537729

### Bristol University
Dept. of Drama: Theatre, Film & Television, Cantocks Close, Woodland Road, Bristol, BS8 1UP
Tel 0117 928 7838
Fax 0117 928 8251

### Edinburgh College of Art
Lauriston Place, Edinburgh, Midlothian, EH3 9DF
Tel 0131 221 6000
Fax 0131 221 6001

### London College of Printing & Distributive Trades
Media Department, 10 Backhill, Clerkenwell, London, EC1R 5EN
Tel 0171 514 6500
Fax 0171 514 6848

### National Film & Television School
Beaconsfield Studios, Station Road, Beaconsfield, Buckinghamshire, HP9 1LG
Tel 01494 671234
Fax 01494 674042

### National Short Course Training Programme
National Film & Television School, Beaconsfield Studios, Station Road, Beaconsfield, Buckinghamshire, HP9 1LG
Tel 01494 677903
Fax 01494 678708

### Newport School of Art and Design
Field of Film and Photography, PO Box 181, Clarence Place, Newport, Gwent, NP9 0YS
Tel 01633 430088
Fax 01633 432006

### Northern School of Film & TV
Soames Building, 2-8 Merrion Way, Leeds, West Yorkshire, LS2 8BT
Tel 0113 283 3193
Fax 0113 283 3194

### Ravensbourne College of Design & Communication
Walden Road, Chislehurst, Kent, BR7 5SN
Tel 0181 468 7071
Fax 0181 325 8320

### Royal College of Art
School of the Moving Image, Kensington Gore, London, SW7 2EU
Tel 0171 584 5020
Fax 0171 589 0178

### The London International Film School
24 Shelton Street, London, WC2H 9HP
Tel 0171 836 9642/240 0168
Fax 0171 497 3718

### The Surrey Institute of Art & Design
Farnham Campus, Falkner Road, The Hart, Farnham, Surrey, GU9 7DS
Tel 01252 722441
Fax 01252 733869

### University of Westminster
Harrow Campus, Studio M, Northwich Park, Harrow, Middlesex, HA1 3TP
Tel 0171 911 5000
Fax 0171 911 5939

## FINANCIAL - BANKS & GUARANTORS

### Barclays Business Centre
27 Soho Square, London, W1A 4WA
Tel 0171 445 5700
Fax 0171 445 5784

### Berliner Bank (London)
81-82 Gracechurch Street, London, EC3V
Tel 0171 929 4060
Fax 0171 528 8189

### Film Finances Services
111 Hay Hill, London, W1X 7LF
Tel 0171 629 6557
Fax 0171 491 7530

### Guinness Mahon & Co Ltd.
32 St. Mary at Hill, London, EC3P 3AJ
Tel 0171 623 9333
Fax 0171 528 0895

### The First National Bank Of Boston
39 Victoria St, Westminster, London, SW1
Tel 0171 799 3333
Fax 0171 222 5649

## FREIGHT SERVICES

### Aerly Bird Int. courrier & express service.
Room 98G, Southampton House,Cargo Terminal, Heathrow Airport, Middx, TW6
Tel 0181 897 9291
Fax 0181 564 7553

### Air Courier International
Building 214, Exeter Road, Heathrow Airport, Hounslow, TW6 2JQ
Tel 0181 754 0676
Fax 0181 759 4163

### DHL International
Hillbloom House, 1 Dukes Green Avenue, Faggs Road, Feltham, Middx, TW14 OLR
Tel 0345 100 300
Fax 0181 831 5450

### Jet Services Worldwide
Unit 5, Heston Phoenix Distribution Park, North Road, off Phoenix Way, Heston, Middx, TW5 9ND
Tel 0181 759 4991
Fax 0181 759 2403

### Jigsaw Freight
Unit 5, Polygon Business Centre, David Road, Colnbrook, SL3 OQT
Tel 01753 680616
Fax 01753 683016

### Marken International Courier Service
Unit 2, Metrol Centre,St. Johns Road, Isleworth, Middx, TW7 6NJ
Tel 0181 847 5631
Fax 0181 568 6619

### Media Freight Services Ltd.
Unit 9/10 Airlinks, Spitfire Way, Heston, Middx, TW5 9NR
Tel 0181 573 9999
Fax 0181 573 9592

### Midnite Express
Unit 3, The Metro Centre, St. Johns Road, Isleworth, Middx, TW7 6NJ
Tel 0181 568 1568
Fax 0181 847 4418

### Pegasus Group
86-92 Stewarts Road, London, SW8 4UG
Tel 0171 622 1111
Fax 0171 622 1616

### Renown Freight
Unit 4, Central Park Estate,Staines Road, Hounslow, Middx, TW4 5DJ
Tel 0181 570 5151
Fax 0181 572 2102

### SamFreight Ltd.
Technicolour Estate, Bath Road,
Harmondsworth, West Drayton, UB7 ODB
Tel 0181 759 6011
Fax 0181 759 3854

### Team Air Express UK
Crown Way, Horton Road, West Drayton,
Middx, UB7 8HZ
Tel 01895 448 855
Fax 01895 448 851

### XP Express Parcel System
Unit 6, Spitfire Way, Spitfire Industrial
Estate, Middx, TW5 9NW
Tel 0181 813 5000
Fax 0181 813 5232

## GRIPS HIRE

### Cine Europe
7 Silver Road, White City Industrial Park,
Wood Lane, London, W12 7SG
Tel 0181 746 6762
Fax 0181 749 3501

### GP Film Services
Unit 20, Wadsworth Business Centre, 21
Wadsworth Road, Perivale, Greenford,
Middx, UB6 7LQ
Tel 0181 991 1026
Fax 0181 991 9845

### Grip House Ltd.
5-11 Taunton Road, The Metropolitan
Centre, Greenford, Middx, UB6 8UQ
Tel 0181 578 2382
Fax 0181 578 1536

### Grip House North
Unit 5, Orchard Pk Trading Estate,
Maryville, Giffnock,Glasgow, G46 9XX
Tel 0141 638 8786
Fax 0141 638 8786

### Media Film Service Ltd.
4 Airlinks, Spitfire Way, Heston, Hounslow,
Middx, TW5 9NR
Tel 0181 573 2255
Fax 0181 756 0592

### Panavision Grips
Shepperton Studios, Studios Road,
Shepperton, Middx, TW17 0QD
Tel 019325 72609
Fax 019325 70003

### Panavision UK
Wycombe Road, Off Beresford Avenue,
Wembley, Middx, HA0 1QN
Tel 0181 903 7933
Fax 0181 902 3273

### The Grip Firm
Unit 12A, Isleworth Business Complex, St.
Johns Road, Isleworth, Middx, TW7 6NL
Tel 0181 847 1771
Fax 0181 847 1773

## INSURANCE

### Aegis Insurance Brokers
Thrale House, 44/46 Southwark Street,
London, SE1 1UN
Tel 0171 403 7188
Fax 0171 378 6962

### Bain Hogg Ltd.
UK Division, Digby House, Causton Road,
Colchester, Essex, CO1 1YS
Tel 01206 577612
Fax 01206 761202

### Entertainment Brokers International
Sampson & Allen, 1 Kingly Street, London,
W1R 5LF
Tel 0171 287 5054
Fax 0171 287 0679

### Hanover Park Insurance Brokers
Greystoke House, 80-86 Weston Street,
London, SE19 3AF
Tel 0181 771 8844
Fax 0181 771 1697

### Parmead Insurance Brokers
Lion House, 160-166 Borough High Street,
London, SE1 1JR
Tel 0181 467 8656
Fax 0181 295 1659

### Robertson Taylor Insurance Brokers Ltd.
33 Harbour Exchange Square,
London, E14 9GG
Tel 0171 538 9840
Fax 0171 538 9919

### Rollins Hudig Hall Entertainment
Pinewood Studios, Pinewood Road, Iver,
Buckinghamshire, SL0 0NH
Tel 01753 654555
Fax 01753 653152

### Stafford Knight O'Neill
114-116 Charing Cross Road, London,
WC2H OJR
Tel 0171 240 8811
Fax 0171 240 9760

### Stonehouse Conseillers
21 Newman Street, London, W1P 3HB
Tel 0171 636 3788
Fax 0171 636 5980

### White & Wilson Insurance Brokers
3rd Floor, 48 Carnaby Street,
London, W1V 1PF
Tel 0171 734 2858
Fax 0171 734 2860

## LABORATORIES

### Colour Film Services
10 Wadsworth Road, Perivale,
Greenford, Middx, UB6 7JX
Tel 0181 998 2731
Fax 0181 997 8738

### Metrocolor London Ltd.
91-95 Gillespie Road, London, N5 1LS
Tel 0171 226 4422
Fax 0171 359 2353

### Rank Film Laboratories Ltd.
North Orbital Road, Denham, Uxbridge,
Middx, UB9 5HQ
Tel 01895 832323
Fax 01895 832446

### Soho Laboratories
8-14 Meard Street, London, W1V 3HR
Tel 0171 437 0831
Fax 0171 734 9471

### Technicolor Film Services
Bath Road, West Drayton, Middx, UB7
Tel 0181 759 5432
Fax 0181 759 6270

## LIGHTING EQP. HIRE

### AFM Lighting
12 Alliance Road, London, W3 ORA
Tel 0181 752 1888
Fax 0181 752 1432

### Arri Bell Lighting - Birmingham
Unit 73, Standard Ways, Gravelly Ind.Park, Birmingham, West Midlands, B24 8TL
Tel 0121 326 8118
Fax 0121 327 0403

### Arri Bell Lighting - Cardiff
Unit 4, Excelsior Trading Estate, Western Avenue Gabalfa, Cardiff, South Glamorgan, CF4 3AT
Tel 01222 616160
Fax 01222 692383

### Arri Bell Lighting - London
20A Airlinks Industrial Estate, Spitfire Way, Heston, Hounslow, Middx, TW5 9NR
Tel 0181 561 6700
Fax 0181 569 2539

### Arri Bell Lighting - Manchester
Unit 6-8 Orchard Street, Industrial Estate, Salford, Lancashire, M6 6FL
Tel 0161 736 8034
Fax 0161 745 8023

### Cinequip Lighting
Orchard St. Industrial Estate, Salford, Manchester, Lancashire, M6 6FL
Tel 0161 736 8034
Fax 0161 745 8023

### Lee Lighting - Bolton
Manchester Road, Kearsley, Bolton, Lancashire, BL4 8RL
Tel 01204 794000
Fax 01204 571877

### Lee Lighting - Glasgow
110 Lancefield Street, , Glasgow, Lanarkshire, G3 8JD
Tel 0141 221 5175
Fax 0141 248 2751

### Lee Lighting - London
Wycombe Rd , Wembley, Middx, HA0 1QD
Tel 0181 900 2900
Fax 0181 902 5500

### Lee Lighting - Norfolk
Unit 25, Haverscroft Industrial Estate, New Road, Attleborough, Norfolk, NR17 1YE
Tel 01953 452311
Fax 01953 456856

### Lee Lighting Bristol
Unit 4, Avon Riverside Est., Victoria Road, Avonmouth, Bristol, Avon, BS11 9DB
Tel 0117 982 7364
Fax 0117 923 5745

### Michael Samuelson Goleuadau Cymru
Unit K, Llantrisant Bus. Pk., Llantrisant, Pontyclun, Mid Glamorgan, CF7 8LF
Tel 01443 227777
Fax 01443 223656

### Michael Samuelson Lighting Leeds
Unit 9, Maybrook Industrial Park, Armley Road, Leeds, West Yorkshire, LS12 2EL
Tel 0113 2428232
Fax 0113 2454149

### Michael Samuelson Lighting Ltd.
Pinewood Studios, Pinewood Road, Iver, Buckinghamshire, SL0 0NH
Tel 01753 631133
Fax 01753 630485

### Michael Samuelson Lighting Southampton
Meridian TV Centre, Northam, Southampton, Hampshire, SO9 5HZ
Tel 01703 712056
Fax 01703 712056

### Web Lighting Ltd.
Ravenscraig Road, Little Hulton, Manchester, Lancashire, M38 9PU
Tel 01204 862966/ 0181 744 0554
Fax 01204 862977/0181 744 2885

## MUSIC LIBRARIES

### Abaco Music Library
Ridgeway House, Great Brington, Northampton, NN7 4JA
Tel 01604 770 511
Fax 01604 770 022

### Atmosphere Music Ltd.
65 Maltings Pl., Bagleys Lane, Fulham, London, SW6 3AR
Tel 0171 371 5888
Fax 0171 384 2744

### Boosey & Hawkes Music Library
295 Regents Street, London, W1R 8JR
Tel 0171 580 2060
Fax 0171 580 5815/436 5675

### Carlin Production Music
Iron Bridge House, 2 Bridge Approach, Chalk Farm, London, NW1 8BD
Tel 0171 734 3251
Fax 0171 439 2391

### Cavendish Music
295 Regents Street, London, W1R 8JH
Tel 0171 580 2060 ext. 7259
Fax 0171 436 5675

### De Wolfe Music
80-88 Wardour Street, London, W1V 3LF
Tel 0171 439 8481
Fax 0171 437 2744

### Digiffects
5 Newburgh Street, London, W1V 1LH
Tel 0171 434 9678
Fax 0171 434 1470

### KPM Music Ltd.
127 Charing Cross Rd,
London, WC2H OEA
Tel 0171 412 9111
Fax 0171 413 0061

### Magmasters
20 St. Anne's Court, London, W1V 3AW
Tel 0171 437 8273
Fax 0171 494 1281

### Music House International
5 Newburgh Street, London, W1V 1LH
Tel 0171 434 9678
Fax 0171 434 1470

### Omni Music Library
Ridgway House, Great Brington,
Northampton, NN7 4JA
Tel 01604 770 511
Fax 01604 770 022

### The Music Factor
42 Lucerne Road, London, N5 1TZ
Tel 0171 359 2814
Fax 0171 704 8044

## NEGATIVE CUTTING

### Filmoptic
Unit 10, Thames House, Middle Green
Estate, Middle Green Road, Langley,
Slough, Berkshire, SL3 6DF
Tel 01753 554955
Fax 01753 554955

### Mike Fraser Ltd.
6 Silver Road, White City Industrial Park,
London, W12 7SG
Tel 0181 749 6911
Fax 0181 743 3144

### Negative Cutting - Computamatch
71 Dean Street, London, W1V 6DE
Tel 0171 287 1316
Fax 0171 287 0793

### PNC - Pro Negative Cutting
3 Carlisle Street, London, W1V 5RH
Tel 0171 437 2025/2605
Fax 0171 437 7036

### Splice Rite Ltd.
Pinewood Studios, Pinewood Road, Iver
Heath, Buckinghamshire, SL0 0NH
Tel 01753 650006
Fax 01753 650016

### Sylvia Wheeler Film Services Ltd.
1 Woodlands Road, Camberley, Surrey,
G15 3LZ
Tel 01276 63166
Fax 01276 684169

### Triad
Pinewood Studios, Pinewood Road, Iver,
Buckinghamshire, SL0 0NH
Tel 01753 651700 ext. 6256
Fax 01753 656844

### Tru-cut
11 Poland Street, London, W1V 3DE
Tel 0171 437 7257
Fax 0171 734 4772

## PREVIEW THEATRES

### Bloomsbury Theatre
15 Gordon Street, London, WC1H 6AP
Tel 0171 383 5976
Fax 0171 383 4080

### Century Theatre
31-32 Soho Square, London, W1V 6AP
Tel 0171 437 7766
Fax 0171 434 2170

### Columbia TriStar Films UK
St. Margarets House, 19-23 Wells Street,
London, W1P 4DH
Tel 0171 580 2090
Fax 0171 436 0323

### Crown Theatre
86 Wardour Street, London, W1V 3LF
Tel 0171 437 2233
Fax 0171 434 9990

### De Lane Lea Ltd.
75 Dean Street, London, W1V 5HA
Tel 0171 439 1721
Fax 0171 437 0913

### Edinburgh Film & TV Studios
Nine Mile Burn, Penicuik, Midlothian,
Scotland, EH26 9LT
Tel 01968 672 131
Fax 01968 672 685

### Institute of Contemporary Arts
Nash House, The Mall,
London, SW1Y 5AH
Tel 0171 930 0493
Fax 0171 873 0051

### Lumiere Pictures Ltd.
167-169 Wardour St, London, W1V 3TA
Tel 0171 413 0838
Fax 0171 734 1509

### Metro Cinema
11 Rupert Street, London, W1V 7FS
Tel 0171 287 3515
Fax 0171 287 2112

### Mr Youngs Preview Theatre
14/15 D'Arblay Street, London, W1V 3FP
Tel 0171 437 1771
Fax 0171 734 4520

### Odeon Cinema
The Broadway, Wimbledon,
London, SW19 1QG
Tel 0181 540 9978
Fax 0181 543 9125

### Rank Preview
127 Wardour Street, London, W1V 4AD
Tel 0171 437 9020
Fax 0171 434 3689

### The Royal Society of Arts
The Durham Street Auditorium, 8 John
Adam Street, London, WC2N 6EZ
Tel 0171 930 5115
Fax 0171 839 5805

### Warner Brothers Preview Theatre
135 Wardour Street, London, W1V 4AP
Tel 0171 734 8400
Fax 0171 437 5521

### Watermans Arts Centre
40 High Street, Brentford,
Middx, TW8 0DS
Tel 0181 847 5651
Fax 0181 569 8592

## PRODUCTION CONSULTANTS

### The Creative Partnership
13 Bateman Street, London, W1V 5TB
Tel 0171 439 7762
Fax 0171 437 1467

## PRODUCTION & LOCATION SERVICES

### 1st Call Location Vehicles
Bridge House, Three Mills Island Studios.
Three Mill Lane, London, E3 3DZ
Tel 0181 227 1112
Fax 0181 227 1114

### A & D Wheal Location Service Ltd.
Unit 5, 13-15 Sunbeam Road, London,
NW10 6JP
Tel 0171 727 3828
Fax 0181 965 0699

### A & J Exhibition & Film Service
44 Carlton Road, Gidea Park, Romford,
Essex, RM2 5AP
Tel 01708 740341
Fax 01708 740341

### A1 Mobile
2 Back Lane Cottages, Back Lane, Halam,
Nr Newark, Nottinghamshire, NG22 8AG
Tel 01636 814063
Fax 01636 815737

### GP Film Services
Unit 20, Wadsworth Business Centre, 21
Wadsworth Road, Perivale, Ub6 7JD
Tel 0181 991 1026
Fax 0181 991 9845

### Livingstone Dining Services
6 Witherslack Close, Stonehill Rd,
Headleydown, Bordon, Hants, GU35 8HN
Tel 01428 713170
Fax 01428 713170

### Location Facilities Ltd.
St. Albans Farm, Staines Road, Feltham,
Middx, Tw14 0HH
Tel 0181 572 3535
Fax 0181 572 6344

### Luna
Trafalgar House, Compound 2, Brooklands
Industrial Park, Sopwith Drive, Brooklands,
Weybridge, Surrey, KT13 0YU
Tel 01932 342500
Fax 01932 340310

### Marscom
1 Mount Pleasant, Stow on the Wold,
Cheltenham, Gloucestershire, GL54 1AL
Tel 0374 213183
Fax 01608 642031

### Michael Webb
Grasemere, Rosemary Lane, Thorpe
Village, Egham, Surrey, TW20 8PT
Tel 01932 568082
Fax 01932 568082

### Mobile Toilets
Culverden, Crimp Hill Road, Old Windsor,
Windsor, Berkshire, SL4 2RA
Tel 01753 866267
Fax 01753 866267

### On Set Location Services
Clear Farm, Bassingbourn, Royston,
Hertfordshire, SG8 5NL
Tel 0181 840 9723
Fax 0181 840 9723

### Road Runner Film Services
1 Bradford Road, Acton, London, W3 7SP
Tel 0181 742 9292
Fax 0181 749 7347

### Robert/Rennie TV/Film Locations
71 Pine Crescent, Greenhills, East
Kilbride, G75 9HJ
Tel 01355 227 131
Fax 01355 227 131

### S & S Facilities Transport
The Old Cottage, Thomson Walk, Calcot,
Reading, Berkshire, RG3 5SA
Tel 01734 415250/0181 568 2173
Fax 01734 415250

### SAMMYS - Samuelson Film Service London
21 Derby Road, Metropolitan Centre,
Greenford, Middx, UB6 8UJ
Tel 0181 578 7887
Fax 0181 578 2733

### Swan TV & Film Services
233 Eccles New Road, Salford,
Lancashire, M5 2QG
Tel 0161 736 5255
Fax 0161 736 5255

### The Grip House
5-11 Taunton Road, The Metropolitan
Centre, Greenford, Middx, UB6 8UQ
Tel 0181 578 2382
Fax 0181 578 1536

### The Television House
Lenton Lane, Nottingham, Nottingham-
shire, NG7 2NA
Tel 0115 9645104
Fax 0115 9645140

### Traylen Location Services
104 Bedfont Lane, Feltham, Middx, TW14
Tel 0181 890 5029
Fax 0181 751 3581

### Willies Wheels
91 Slough Road, Datchet, Berks, SL3 9AL
Tel 01753 595 110
Fax 01753 594 979

## PROPS HIRE

### A & M Furniture Hire Ltd
The Royals, Victoria Rd, London, NW10
Tel 0181 965 5433
Fax 0181 965 8456

### Animal Ark
The Studio, 29 Somerset Road, Brentford,
Middx, TW8 8BT
Tel 0181 560 3029
Fax 0181 560 5762

### Any Amount of Books
62 Charing Cross Rd, London, WC2H 0BB
Tel 0171 240 8140
Fax 0171 240 1769

### Avant Gardener Ltd.
16 Winders Road, London, SW11 3HE
Tel 0171 978 4253
Fax 0171 978 4253

### Beat About the Bush
Unit 23, Enterprise Way, Triangle Business Centre, Salter Street (off Hythe Rd), London, NW10
Tel 0181 960 2087
Fax 0181 969 2281

### Film Furniture
c/o Raymond Tomlinson Antiques Ltd, Moorside, Tockwith, York, North Yorkshire, YO5 8QG
Tel 01423 358833
Fax 01423 358188

### Floreal
7 Anglers Lane, Kentish Town, London, NW5 3DG
Tel 0171 482 4005
Fax 0171 482 4006

### General Telephone Co.
364 Fulham Road, London, SW10 9UH
Tel 0171 351 7119
Fax 0171 352 6888

### Gimberts (div. of Phoenix Hire)
Phoenix House, Whitworth St, Openshaw, Manchester, Lancashire, M11 2GR
Tel 0161 223 6660
Fax 0161 223 6630

### Granada TV Props General
Quay St, Manchester, Lancashire, M609EA
Tel 0161 832 7211
Fax 0161 832 8809

### Greenery Ltd.
Bridge Farm, Hospital Bridge Road, Whitton, Twickenham, Middx, TW2 6LN
Tel 0181 893 8992
Fax 0181 893 8995

### Jaysigns
10-12 Gaskin Street, London, N1 2RY
Tel 0171 359 9475
Fax 0171 226 3820

### Larsen & Laurens (scientific & medical)
24 Ariel Way, White City, London, W12
Tel 0181 742 9002
Fax 0181 746 2008/0121 382 3132

### Living Props Ltd.
Sevenhills Road, Iver Heath, Iver, Buckinghamshire, SL0 0PA
Tel 01895 835100
Fax 01895 835757

### Neon Effects
Unit 5, Havelock Terrace, Battersea, London, SW8 4AS
Tel 0171 498 1998
Fax 0171 498 0871

### Newman Hire Co Ltd.
16 The Vale, Acton, London, W3 7SB
Tel 0181 743 0741/0181 749 1501
Fax 0181 749 3513

### Palmbrokers
Cenacle Nursery, Taplow Common Road, Burnham, Buckinghamshire, SL1 8NW
Tel 01628 663734
Fax 01628 661047

### Phoenix Hire Ltd.
55 Chase Road, London, NW10 6LU
Tel 0181 961 6161
Fax 0181 961 6162

### Piano Workshop
30a Highgate Road, London, NW5 1NS
Tel 0171 267 7671
Fax 0171 284 0083

### Pictures Prop Company
Seven Stars Corner, Paddenswick Road, London, W6 0UB
Tel 0181 749 2433
Fax 0181 740 5846

### Prop it Up
Basement, Design Building, BBC TV Centre, Wood Lane, London, W12 7RJ
Tel 0181 576 7295
Fax 0181 576 7295

### Props Galore
15-17 Brunel Road, London, W3 7UG
Tel 0181 746 1222
Fax 0181 749 8372

### Relic Antiques & Designs
Brillscote Farm, Lea, Malmesbury, Wiltshire, SN16 9PF
Tel 01666 822332
Fax 01666 825598

### Rent a Sword
180 Frog Lane, Wood Street Village, Guildford, Surrey, GU3 3HD
Tel 01483 234 084

### Rogers & Cowan
43 King Street, Covent Garden, London, WC2E 8RJ
Tel 0171 240 4022
Fax 0171 240 1497

### Scottish Props Enterprise West
24 Craigment Street, Maryhill, Glasgow, Lanarkshire, G20 GBT
Tel 0141 946 0925
Fax 0141 946 0832

### Simon Beardmore
Belmont House, Belmont Road, Leatherhead, Surrey, KT22 7EN
Tel 01372 372701
Fax 01372 361267

### Studio & TV Hire
3 Ariel Way, Wood Lane, White City, London, W12 7SL
Tel 0181 749 3445
Fax 0181 740 9662

### Superhire
1-4 Bethune Road, London, NW10 6NJ
Tel 0181 965 9909
Fax 0181 965 8107

### Swan Music
3 Plymouth Court, 166 Plymouth Grove, Manchester, Lancashire, M13 0AF
Tel 0161 273 3232
Fax 0161 274 4111

### The Neon Circus
3 Hill Road, London, N10 1JE
Tel 0181 964 3381/ 0831 614248
Fax 0181 964 0084

### The Palm Centre
563 Upper Richmond Road West, London, SW14 7ED
Tel 0181 876 3223
Fax 0181 876 6888

### Weird & Wonderful Prop Hire
Elstree Film Studios, Shenley Road, Borehamwood, Hertfordshire, WD6 1JG
Tel 0181 953 2468
Fax 0181 207 6762

## PUBLICISTS

### BMS Barrington Marketing
Suite 5, 20 Molyneux Stt, London, W1H
Tel 0171 262 1976
Fax 0171 262 7899

### Burston Marsteller Ltd.
24/28 Bloomsbury Way, London, WC1A 2P
Tel 0171 831 6262
Fax 0171 430 1033

### Clare Wilford
Unit 31, Waterside, 44-48 Wharf Road, London, N1 7UX
Tel 0171 490 3987
Fax 0171 490 3987

### Corbett & Keene
122 Wardour Street, London, W1V 3TD
Tel 0171 494 3478
Fax 0171 734 2024

### Cowan/Symes
35 Soho Square, London, W1V 5DG
Tel 0171 439 3535
Fax 0171 439 3737

### Creative Publicity
22 Gibsons Hill, London, SW16 3JP
Tel 0181 764 8000
Fax 0171 629 2202

### Dennis Davidson Associates Ltd.
Royalty House, 72/74 Dean Street, London, W1V 3DF
Tel 0171 439 6391
Fax 0171 437 6358

### JAC Publicity & Marketing Consultants Ltd.
36 Great Queen Street, Covent Garden, London, WC2B 5AA
Tel 0171 430 0211
Fax 0171 430 0222

### Mathieu Thomas Ltd.
8 Westminster Palace Gardens, Artillery Row, London, SW1P 1RL
Tel 0171 222 0833
Fax 0171 222 5784

### McDonald and Rutter
100 Ebury Street, London, SW1W 9QD
Tel 0171 734 9009
Fax 0171 730 7492

### Namara Cowan Ltd.
Namara House, 45/46 Poland Street, London, W1V 3DF
Tel 0171 434 3871
Fax 0171 439 6489

### Orlando Kimber Public Relations
56 Dean Street, London, W1V 6HX
Tel 0171 830 8448
Fax 0171 439 1075

### Scope Communications Management
Tower House, 8-14 Southampton Street, London, WC2E 7HA
Tel 0171 379 3234
Fax 0171 240 7729

### Shaw Thing Media
51 Scarborough Road, London, E11 4AL
Tel 0181 518 7346
Fax 0181 518 7347

### Taylor & New
11 Upper Camden Place, Bath, Avon, BA1
Tel 01225 421 804
Fax 01225 424 954

**The Creative Partnership**
13 Bateman Street, London, W1V 5TB
Tel 0171 439 7762
Fax 0171 437 1467

## SALES AGENTS

### Castle Rock International
8 Queen St, Mayfair, London, W1X 7PH
Tel 0171 409 3532
Fax 0171 499 9885

### Ciby Sales
10 Stephen Mews, London, W1P 1PP
Tel 0171 333 8877
Fax 0171 333 8878

### Film Four International
124 Horseferry Road, London, SW1P 2TX
Tel 0171 396 4444
Fax 0171 306 8361

### First Independent Films
69 New Oxford St, London, WC1A 1DG
Tel 0171 528 7767
Fax 0171 528 7770

### Handmade Films
15 Golden Square, London, W1R 3AG
Tel 0171 434 3132
Fax 0171 434 3143

### J & M Entertainment
2 Dorset Square, London, NW1 6PW
Tel 0171 723 6544
Fax 0171 724 7541

### Majestic Films & TV
P O Box 13, Gloucester Mansions, Cambridge Circus, London, WC2H 8HD
Tel 0171 836 8630
Fax 0171 836 5819

### Mayfair Entertainment Int.
110 St. Martin's Lane, London, WC2N 4AD
Tel 0171 304 7911
Fax 0171 867 1184

### Polygram Film International
Academy House, 161-167 Oxford Street, London, W1R 1TA
Tel 0171 439 3000
Fax 0171 437 4370

### Rank Film Distributors
127-133 Wardour St, London, W1V 4AD
Tel 0171 437 9020
Fax 0171 434 3689

### Stranger Than Fiction
68 Upper Richmond Rd, London, SW15
Tel 0181 877 9563
Fax 0181 877 0690

### The Sales Company
62 Shaftesbury Ave, London, W1V 7DE
Tel 0171 434 9061
Fax 0171 494 3293

### Victor Film Company
26 Chandos Street, London, W1M OEH
Tel 0171 636 6620
Fax 0171 636 6511

## SOLICITORS

### Brown Cooper
7 Southampton Place, London, WC1A2DR
Tel 0171 404 0422
Fax 0171 831 9856

### Davenport Lyons & Co
1 Old Burlington Street, London, W1X 1LA
Tel 0171 287 5353
Fax 0171 437 8216

### Denton Hall
5 Chancery Lane, Cliffords Inn, London, EC4A 1BU
Tel 0171 242 1212
Fax 0171 404 0087

### Harbottle & Lewis
Hanover House, 14 Hanover Square, London, W1R 0BE
Tel 0171 629 7633
Fax 0171 493 0451

### Marriot Harrison Solicitors
12 Great James' St, London, WC1N 3DR
Tel 0171 209 2000
Fax 0171 209 2001

### Mishcon De Reya
21 Southampton Row, London, WC1V 5HS
Tel 0171 405 3711
Fax 0171 404 5982

### Olswang
90 Long Acre, London, WC2E 9TT
Tel 0171 208 8888
Fax 0171 208 8800

### Richards Butler
Beaufort House, 15 St. Botolph Street, London, EC3A 7EE
Tel 0171 247 6555
Fax 0171 247 5091

### Schilling & Lom
Royalty House, 72-74 Dean Street, London, W1V 6AE
Tel 0171 453 2500
Fax 0171 453 2600

### The Simkins Partnership
45/51 Whitfield Street, London, W1P 6AA
Tel 0171 631 1050
Fax 0171 436 2744

### Thomas Dillon
1 Fountain Court, Steelhouse Lane, Birmingham, West Midlands, B4 D6DR
Tel 0121 236 5721
Fax 0121 236 3639

## SOUND EQP. HIRE

### Broadcast Film & Video Ltd.
33 West Park, Clifton, Bristol, Avon, BS8
Tel 0117 923 7087
Fax 0117 923 7090

### Dreamhire
18 Chaplin Road, London, NW2 5PN
Tel 0181 451 5544
Fax 0181 451 6464

### Osbourne Sound Eqpt.
9 Meard Street, London, W1V 3HQ
Tel 0171 437 6170
Fax 0171 439 4807

### Richmond Film Services
The Old School, Park Lane, Richmond, Surrey, TW9 2RA
Tel 0181 940 6077
Fax 0181 948 8326

### SAMMYS - Samuelson Film Service London Ltd.
21 Derby Road, Metropolitan Centre, Greenford, Middx, UB6 8UJ
Tel 0181 578 7887
Fax 0181 578 2733

## SPECIAL EFFECTS

### 1st Effects
Shepperton Film Studios, Studios Road, Shepperton, Middx, TW17 0QD
Tel 01932 562611
Fax 01932 572391

### Action Firearms
152 Monega Road, Forest Gate, London
Tel 0181 471 3407
Fax 0181 471 3407

### ALL F/X Ltd.
Little Orchard, Framewood Road, Stoke Poges, Slough, Berkshire, SL3 6PG
Tel 01753 662227
Fax 01753 663269

### Any Effects
64 Weir Road, London, SW19 8UG
Tel 0181 944 0099
Fax 0181 944 6989

### Artem Visual Effects
Perivale Ind. Park, Horsenden Lane, South Perivale, Greenford, Middx, UB6 7RH
Tel 0181 997 7771
Fax 0181 997 1503

### BBC Special Effects
Park Western, 41-44 Kendall Avenue, Acton, London, W3 0RP
Tel 0181 993 9434
Fax 0181 993 8741

### Bickers Action
School Lane, Coddenham, Ipswich, Suffolk, IP6 9PT
Tel 01449 760201
Fax 01449 760614

### Cinesite (Europe) Ltd.
9 Carlisle Street, London, W1V 5RG
Tel 0171 973 4000
Fax 0171 973 4040

### David Jones Fragile Ice & Water
Area No.1, Riverside Works, Railshead Road, Isleworth, Middx, TW7 7BY
Tel 0181 568 7787
Fax 0181 568 7787

### Effects Associates Ltd.
Pinewood Studios, Pinewood Road, Iver, Buckinghamshire, SL0 0NH
Tel 01753 652007
Fax 01753 630127

### Emergency House
Manchester Road, Marsden, Huddersfield, West Yorkshire, HD7 6EY
Tel 01484 846999
Fax 01484 845061

### Especial Effects
86 Woodhurst Avenue, Petts Wood, Orpington, Kent, BR5 1AT
Tel 01689 837251
Fax 01689 837251

### Fantastic Fireworks Ltd.
Rocket Park, Pepperstock, Luton, Bedfordshire, LU1 4LL
Tel 01582 485555
Fax 01582 485545

### Foxtrot Productions Ltd.
Canalot Productions Studios, 222 Kensal Road, Kensington, London, W10 5BN
Tel 0181 964 3555
Fax 0181 960 3811

### FX Projects
Studio House, Rita Road, London, SW8
Tel 0171 582 8750
Fax 0171 793 0467

### Laser Creations International Ltd.
55 Merthyr Terrace, Barnes, London
Tel 0181 741 5747
Fax 0181 748 9879

### Lightforce Special Effects
Shepperton Studios, Studios Road, Shepperton, Middx, TW17 0QD
Tel 01932 572416
Fax 01932 572415

### Peerless Camera Company
32 Bedfordbury, London, WC2N 4DU
Tel 0171 836 3367
Fax 0171 240 2143

### Ray Marston Wig Studio
Unit 24, 44 Earlham Street, London, WC2H 9LA
Tel 0171 379 7953
Fax 0171 379 7953

### Smokebusters
55 Chickerell Road, Swindon, Wiltshire, SN3 2RH
Tel 01793 692636

### Snow Business
56 Northfield Road, Tetbury, Gloucestershire, GL8 8HQ
Tel 01666 502857
Fax 01666 502857

### The Magic Camera Co.
Shepperton Studios, Studios Road, Shepperton, Middx, TW17 0QD
Tel 01932 562611 ext. 2424/5
Fax 01932 568944

### Theatrical Pyrotechnics Ltd.
The Loop, Manston Airport, Ramsgate, Kent, CT12 5DE
Tel 01843 823545
Fax 01843 822655

## STOCK

### 3M
3M House, Bracknell, Berks, RG12 1JU
Tel 01344 858 385
Fax 01344 858 082

### AGFA-GEVAERT Ltd.
Motion Picture Division, 27 Great West Road, Brentford, Middx, TW8 9AX
Tel 0181 231 4310
Fax 0181 231 4315

### Ampex Media Europa
Unit 3, Commerce Park, Theale, Berkshire, RG7 4AB
Tel 01734 302 240
Fax 01734 302 235

### Film Stock Centre BLANX
70 Wardour Street, London, W1V 3HP
Tel 0171 494 2244
Fax 0171 287 2040

### Fuji Photo Film (UK) Ltd.
Fuji Film House, 125 Finchley Road, London, NW3 6JH
Tel 0171 586 5900
Fax 0171 722 4259

### Kodak Ltd.
Motion Picture & TV Imaging, Station Rd, Hemel Hempstead, Herts, HP1 1JU
Tel 01442 61122
Fax 01442 844458

### Orchard Video Ltd.
The Old School House, Barton Manor, Bristol, Avon, BS2 ORL
Tel 0117 941 3898
Fax 0117 941 3797

### PEC Video Ltd.
2-4 Dean Street, London, W1V 5RN
Tel 0171 437 4633
Fax 0171 287 0492

### SAMMYS - Samuelson Film Service London Ltd.
21 Derby Road, Metropolitan Centre, Greenford, Middx, U6 8UJ
Tel 0181 578 7887
Fax 0181 578 2733

### Stanley Productions
147 Wardour Street, London, W1V 3TB
Tel 0171 437 5472
Fax 0171 437 2126

### Zonal
Holmethorpe Ave, Redhill, Surrey, RH1 2N
Tel 01737 767 171
Fax 01737 767 610

## STUDIOS

### Bray Studios
Down Place, Windsor Road, Water Oakley, Windsor, Berkshire, SL4 5UG
Tel 01628 22111
Fax 01628 770 381

### Ealing Studios
(NFTS Ealing Studios Ltd.), Ealing Green, Ealing, London, W5 5EP
Tel 0181 567 6655
Fax 0181 758 8658/8579

### Granada Television
Quay Street, Manchester, M60 9EA
Tel 0161 832 7211/827 2342
Fax 0161 832 8809

### Grip House Studios
Grip House Limited, 5-11 Taunton Rd, Metropolitan Centre, Greenford, Middx, UB6 8UQ
Tel 0181 578 2382
Fax 0181 578 1536

### Jacob Street Studios
9-19 Mill Street, London, SE1 2DA
Tel 0171 232 1066
Fax 0171 252 0118

### Millennium Studios
Elstree Way, Borehamwood, Hertfordshire, WD6 1SF
Tel 0181 236 1400
Fax 0181 236 1444

### Park Royal Studios
1 Barretts Green Rd, London, NW10 7AP
Tel 0181 965 9778
Fax 0181 963 1056

### Pinewood Studios Ltd.
Pinewood Road, Iver, Bucks. SL0 0NH
Tel 01753 651700
Fax 01753 656844

### Shepperton Film Studios
Studios Rd, Shepperton, Midx, TW17 0QD
Tel 01932 562611
Fax 01932 568989

### Teddington Studios Ltd.
Teddington Lock, Middx, TW11 9NT
Tel 0181 977 3252
Fax 0181 943 4050

### Three Mills Island Studios
Three Mill Lane, London, E3 3DU
Tel 0171 363 0033
Fax 0171 363 0034

### Twickenham Film Studios
St. Margarets, Twickenham, Middx, TW1 2AW
Tel 0181 892 4477
Fax 0181 891 0168

### Yorkshire Tyne Tees Television
The Television Centre, Kirkstall Road, Leeds, LS3 1JS
Tel 0113 2438283
Fax 0113 2341293

## STUNTS & WEAPONS

### Action Firearms
152 Monega Rd, Forest Gate, London, E7
Tel 0181 471 3407
Fax 0181 471 3407

### Foxtrot Productions Ltd.
222 Kensal Rd, Kensington, London, W10
Tel 0181 964 3555
Fax 0181 960 3811

### Perdix Firearms Ltd.
P O Box 801, Bath, Avon, BA2 4RL
Tel 01225 444630
Fax 01225 444630

### Prop Farm
Grange Farm, Elmton, Nr Creswell, Worksop, Nottinghamshire, S80 4LX
Tel 01909 723100
Fax 01909 721465

## TELECINE & CONVERSION

### Cell
59-61 Charlotte Street, London, W1P 1LA
Tel 0171 208 1500
Fax 0171 208 1502

### Goldcrest Post Production Facilities
36/44 Brewer Street, London, W1R 3HP
Tel 0171 439 4177
Fax 0171 437 7972

### Metro Video
The Old Bacon Factory, 57-59 Great Suffolk Street, London, SE1 OBS
Tel 0171 928 2088
Fax 0171 261 0685

### Midnight Transfer
15-16 Kingly Court, London, W1R 5LE
Tel 0171 494 1719
Fax 0171 494 2021

### Rushes Post Production
66 Old Compton Street, London, W1V 5PA
Tel 0171 437 8676
Fax 0171 734 2519/3002

### Salon Productions Ltd.
10 Livonia Street, London, W1V 3PH
Tel 0171 437 0516
Fax 0171 437 6197

### Soho Images
71 Dean Street, London, W1V 5BH
Tel 0171 437 0831
Fax 0171 734 9471

### SVC Television
142 Wardour Street, London, W1V 3AU
Tel 0171 734 1600
Fax 0171 437 1854

### Telecine Ltd.
Video House, 48 Charlotte St, London, W1P 1LX
Tel 0171 208 2200
Fax 0171 208 2250/1

### Telefilm Video Services
Twickenham Film Studios, St. Margarets, Twickenham, Middx, TW1 2AW
Tel 0181 744 9828
Fax 0181 744 0357

### The Machine Room
58 Wardour Street, London, W1
Tel 0171 734 3433
Fax 0171 287 3773

### The Mill
40-41 Great Marlborough St, London, W1V
Tel 0171 287 4041
Fax 0171 287 8393

### Twentieth Century Video Ltd.
2nd Floor, (unit 2-5), Wembley Commercial Centre, East Lane, Wembley, Middx, HA9
Tel 0181 904 6271
Fax 0181 904 0172

### Vidfilm Europe
North Orbital Rd, Denham, Uxbridge, Middx,
Tel 01895 583 5555
Fax 01895 835 353

### Yorkshire Tyne Tees Television
Television Centre, Leeds, LS3 1JS
Tel 0113 243 8283
Fax 0113 234 1293

## TITLES & OPTICALS

### FrameStore
9 Noel Street, London, W1V 4AL
Tel 0171 208 2600
Fax 0171 208 2626

### Cine Image Film Opticals
7a Langley Street, Covent Garden, London, WC2H 9JA
Tel 0171 240 6222
Fax 0171 240 6242

### Cinesite (Europe) Ltd.
9 Carlisle Street, London, W1V 5RG
Tel 0171 973 4000
Fax 0171 973 4040

### Filmoptic
Unit 10, Thames House, Middle Green Estate, Middle Green Road, Langley, Slough, Berkshire, SL3 6DF
Tel 01753 554955
Fax 01753 554955

### General Screen Enterprises
Highbridge Estate, Oxford Road, Uxbridge, Middx, UB8 1LX
Tel 01895 231 931
Fax 01895 235 335

### Howell Optical Printers Ltd.
I-Mex House, 6 Wadsworth Road, Perivale, Greenford, Middx, UB6 7JJ
Tel 0181 991 5591
Fax 0181 991 1442

### Optical Film Effects Ltd.
Pinewood Studios, Pinewood Road, Iver, Buckinghamshire, SL0 0NH
Tel 01753 655 486
Fax 01753 656 844

### The Mill
40-41 Great Marlborough Street, London, W1V 1DA
Tel 0171 287 4041
Fax 0171 287 8303

## TRADE PUBLICATIONS

### American Cinematographer Magazine & Manual
Samuelsons Film Services, 21 Derby Road, Metropolitan Centre, Greenford, Middx, UB6 8UJ
Tel 0181 578 7887
Fax 0181 578 2733

### BFI Film & Television Handbook
British Film Institute, 21 Stephen Street, London, W1P 2LN
Tel 0171 957 8922
Fax 0171 436 7950

### KAYS UK Production Manual
Pinewood Studios, Pinewood Road, Iver, Buckinghamshire, SL0 0NH
Tel 0181 749 1214/01753 651171
Fax 0181 964 4604

### KEMPS Directory
Cahners Publishing Company, 34-35 Newman Street, London, W1P 3PD
Tel 0171 637 3663
Fax 0171 580 5559

### Moving Pictures
151-153 Wardour St, London, W1V 3TB
Tel 0171 287 0070
Fax 0171 734 6153

### PCR (Production & Casting Report)
PO Box 11, London, SW15 6AY
Tel 0181 789 0408
Fax 0181 780 1977

### Screen Finance
FT Telecoms and Media, 122 High Street, Chesham, Bucks, HP5 1EB
Tel 01494 771734
Fax 01494 778994

### Screen International
33-39 Bowling Green Lane, London, EC1R
Tel 0171 505 8080
Fax 0171 505 8116

### The Hollywood Reporter
23 Ridgmount Street, London, WC1E 7AH
Tel 0171 323 6686
Fax 0171 323 2314/16

### The Knowledge
Miller Freeman Information Services, Riverbank House, Angel Lane,Tonbridge, Kent, TN9 1BR
Tel 01732 362666
Fax 01732 367301

### The Spotlight
7 Leicester Place, London, WC2H 7BP
Tel 0171 437 7631
Fax 0171 437 5881

**The Stage Newspapers**
47 Bermondsey Street, London, SE1 3XT
Tel 0171 403 1818
Fax 0171 403 1418

**Variety**
34-35 Newman Street, London, W1P
Tel 0171 637 3663
Fax 0171 580 5559

## VIDEO DUBBING & DUPLICATION

**Aztec Video Ltd.**
The Pyramid, 4 Valentine Place, London, SE1 8QH
Tel 0171 401 2477
Fax 0171 401 2351

**Dubbs**
25-26 Poland Stree , London, W1V 3DB
Tel 0171 629 0055
Fax 0171 287 8796

**Holloway Film & Television**
68-70 Wardour Street, London, W1V 3HP
Tel 0171 494 0777
Fax 0171 494 0309

**London Post**
34-35 Dean Street, London, W1V 5AP
Tel 0171 439 9080
Fax 0171 434 0714

**M2 Facilities Group**
74-80 Camden Street, The Forum, London, NW1 OEG
Tel 0171 387 5001
Fax 0171 387 5025

**MetroSoho**
6/7 Great Chapel Street, Soho, London, W1V 3AG
Tel 0171 439 3494
Fax 0171 437 3782

**Metrovideo Ltd.**
The Old Bacon Factory, 57-59 Great Suffolk Street, London, SE1 2BP
Tel 0171 928 2088
Fax 0171 261 0685

**Northern Video Facilities**
4th Floor, Central Buildings, 11 Peter Street, Manchester, M2 5QR
Tel 0161 832 7643
Fax 0161 832 7643

**Rushes**
66 Old Compton Street, London, W1V 5PA
Tel 0171 437 8676
Fax 0171 734 2519

**Satellite Broadcast**
Unit 20, Commerical Way, Abbey Road Industrial Estate, Park Royal, London,
Tel 0181 965 5599
Fax 0181 961 8071

**Soho Images**
8-14 Meard Street, London, W1V 3HR
Tel 0171 437 0831
Fax 0171 734 9471

**The Machine Room Ltd.**
54-58 Wardour Street , London, W1V 3HN
Tel 0171 734 3433
Fax 0171 287 3773

**TSI Video Ltd.**
10 Grape Street, London, WC2H 8DY
Tel 0171 379 3435
Fax 0171 379 4589

**TVi Ltd,**
142 Wardour Street, London, W1V 3AU
Tel 0171 434 2141
Fax 0171 439 3984

**Video Time**
22-24 Greek Street, London, W1V 5LG
Tel 0171 439 1211
Fax 0171 439 7336

**West 1 Television**
10 Bateman Street, London, W1V 5TT
Tel 0171 437 5533
Fax 0171 287 8621

# Index

## Symbols



## A



## B

# C



# D



# E

## F



## G



## H



## I



## J



## K



## L

## T



## U



## V



## W



## X



## Z

# The Film Producers Toolkit Software

runs great on Windows 3.1 or Windows 95

*The computer is the most powerful and versatile tool for producers, bar the telephone of course. With the Producers Toolkit Software you will be able to harness this power, transforming the way you write screenplays, compile budgets and keep on top of contacts on the move.*

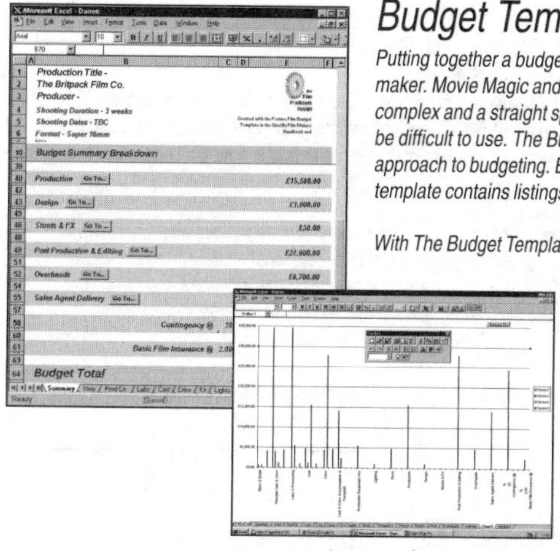


## *Budget Template* *Requires MS Excel*

*Putting together a budget can be a monumental task, especially for a new film-maker. Movie Magic and other software packages are just too expensive and too complex and a straight spreadsheet just doesn't have enough information and can be difficult to use. The Budget Template takes a simple to use, fill in the blanks, approach to budgeting. Especially designed for use with low budget films, the template contains listings of everything you need to make your film.*

*With The Budget Template you can...*

*Easily prepare a budget, all you need to do is fill in the blanks.*

*Quickly establish the cost of your new project as everything is totalled automatically.*

*Impress investors with a comprehensive and professional looking budget.*

## *Databank - FREE*

*The Databank is a Database of film services and product companies based in the UK. It can be installed on any PC running Windows, to give you instant access to addresses and phone numbers. You can also update the information and add new companies as you go. Think of it as a digital address book that's already filled.*

*With the Databank you can...*

*Add details of new companies and contacts.*

*Print out mailshots to any or all of the companies listed.*

*Easily access company details on you PC, ideal if you have a laptop and are on the move.*

*If you have a modem, the Databank is also accessible over the Internet.*

## *Script Formatter* *Requires MS Word*

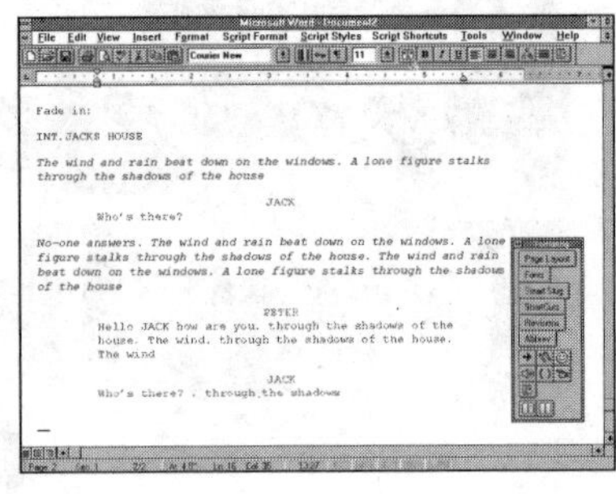

*Writing a screenplay can be a chore, not because of the actual creativity, but because formatting the layout is time consuming and dull. The Screenplay Formatter will conform your screenplay to the standard conventions, doing all the hard work such as scene numbering and page break Cont'd lines automatically.*

*With the Script Formatter you can...*

*Easily insert, edit and format characters, dialogue, action etc.*

*Number scenes and re number after amendments*

*Break pages and insert Cont'd... between broken dialogue or action*

*Assign character names to keys for quick access*

*Customise your scripts appearance, or simply stick to the Hollywood standard*

## *Contracts*

*All the contracts in The Guerrilla Film Makers Handbook and Producers Toolkit are already typed up and laid out. Avoid the headache of typing out pages of text.*

## *Power Tools*

*The computer, bar telephone, is now the most powerful tool any producer can buy. Yet it's only as good as the software that it runs. There are many small programs and utilities that can make film producing a whole heap easier, and we have put together this small package. Some of these programs are shareware and may require separate payment to authors should you decide to continue using them after the free trial period.*

*The Power Tools Kit includes... Footage Calculator (to convert between 35mm and Super 16mm footages and times), Trans Mac (read Macintosh formatted disks on your PC), VAT Calc (automaticaly make VAT calculations), Poster (produce full size, full colour movie posters on your desktop printer), Smart & Sticky (print labels for video tapes, mailing, disks and more...), Video Prompter (always get that speech to camera just right), plus, other utilities being added all the time.*

*The Producers Toolkit Software is available to readers of this book for only £79.95! Registered users will be notified of updates as and when they become available.*

*Cut out this coupon, photocopy or write*

**The Film Producers Toolkit**

*YES! Please send me a copy of the Producers Toolkit Software for the special readers price of only £79.95 plus £3 for P&P, plus VAT (£6 shipping for overseas orders)*

*Name.................................................................*

*Address.................................................................................................................................*

*Postcode.................................................. email....................................................*

| | *Price* |
|---|---|
| *Producers Toolkit Software* | *£79.95* |
| *Shipping* | *£3.00* |
| *VAT @ 17.5%* | *£14.52* |
| *Order Total* | *£97.47* |

*Please enclose a cheque, made payable to Hard Copy, for £97.47 and return to - Hard Copy, PO Box 14323, London, W5 5WJ Allow 28 days for delivery.*